third canadian edition

hrm

Sandra L. Steen
University of Regina

Raymond A. Noe
Ohio State University

John R. Hollenbeck
Michigan State University

Barry Gerhart
University of Wisconsin–Madison

Patrick M. Wright
Cornell University

**McGraw-Hill
Ryerson**
Connect. Learn. Succeed.

About the Authors

Sandra L. Steen teaches in the Paul J. Hill School of Business and the Kenneth Levene Graduate School of Business at the University of Regina. Sandra also leads executive education and professional development sessions with the Centre for Management Development, Faculty of Business Administration. Sandra has an integrated education and background in both Organizational Behaviour and Human Resource Management. She received her MBA from the University of Regina and has more than 25 years of leading, managing, teaching, and consulting across a wide range of organizations in the private, public, and not-for-profit sectors. Sandra teaches in the undergraduate, MBA, and Executive MBA programs at the University of Regina. Along with co-authoring *Human Resource Management*, Third Canadian Edition, Sandra is also co-author with Steven McShane (University of Western Australia) of *Canadian Organizational Behaviour*, Eighth Edition (2012).

Sandra holds the designation of Certified Human Resources Professional (CHRP) and she is a member of the Saskatchewan Association of Human Resource Professionals. She serves as a Commissioner of the Saskatchewan Public Service Commission, the central human resource agency for the provincial government. Sandra has received recognition for her teaching accomplishments including "Inspiring Teacher Award—Business Administration." In her leisure time, Sandra enjoys spending time at the lake with her husband Aaron, and their children, Matt and Jess.

Raymond A. Noe is the Robert and Anne Hoyt Professor of Management at Ohio State University. He was previously a professor in the Department of Management at Michigan State University and the Industrial Relations Center of the Carlson School of Management, University of Minnesota. He received his B.S. in psychology from Ohio State University and his M.A. and Ph.D. in psychology from Michigan State University. Professor Noe conducts research and teaches undergraduate as well as MBA and Ph.D. students in human resource management, managerial skills, quantitative methods, human resource information systems, training, employee development, and organizational behavior. He has published articles in the *Academy of Management Journal, Academy of Management Review, Journal of Applied Psychology, Journal of Vocational Behavior,* and *Personnel Psychology.* Professor Noe is currently on the editorial boards of several journals including *Personnel Psychology, Journal of Applied Psychology,* and *Journal of Organizational Behavior.* Professor Noe has received awards for his teaching and research excellence, including the Herbert G. Heneman Distinguished Teaching Award in 1991 and the Ernest J. McCormick Award for Distinguished Early Career Contribution from the Society for Industrial and Organizational Psychology in 1993. He is also a fellow of the Society for Industrial and Organizational Psychology.

John R. Hollenbeck is currently the Eli Broad Professor of Management at the Eli Broad Graduate School of Business Administration at Michigan State University. He received his Ph.D. in Management from New York University in 1984 and joined the Michigan State faculty that year. Dr. Hollenbeck has published over 60 articles and book chapters, with more than 35 of these appearing in the most highly cited refereed outlets (*Journal of Applied Psychology, Academy of Management Journal, Personnel Psychology,* and *Organizational Behavior and Human Decision Processes*). Dr. Hollenbeck was the acting editor at *Organizational Behavior and Human Decision Processes* in 1995, the associate editor at *Decision Sciences* from 1999 to 2004, and the editor of *Personnel Psychology* between 1996 and 2002. Prior to serving as editor, he served on the editorial board of these journals, as well as the boards of the *Academy of Management Journal, Academy of Management Review, Journal of Applied Psychology,* and *Journal of Management.* Dr. Hollenbeck was the first recipient of the Ernest J. McCormick Award for Early Contributions to the field of Industrial and Organizational Psychology in 1992, and is a Fellow of the American Psychological Association.

Brief Contents

Contents

Welcome to the third Canadian edition of *Human Resource Management*. This book was created to provide you with a focused introduction to HRM in Canada that is rich in content and relevant in its strategic application. The 11 chapters balance theory and application, and present the material in a manner that is intended to be engaging as well as thought-provoking.

Whether you are a prospective or current employee, supervisor, manager, entrepreneur, executive, or HR professional, this third edition is even more focused on supporting your need for the foundational knowledge of Human Resource Management necessary to perform and thrive in organizations today.

New to this edition are additional resources designed to bring real-world relevance to the study of human resource management. New **HR Oops!** features in each part provide real examples of where HR went wrong. New **"Did You Know?"** features in each chapter provide meaningful data on a variety of timely topics. Also look for new perspectives in the well-received resources introduced in the previous edition—the part-opening feature, **Real People and HR** (highlighting insights from human resource professionals and business leaders) and the **Thinking Ethically** exercises (illustrative dilemmas designed to challenge your thinking about topics ranging from the growing use of social media background checks to greenwashing to aggressive recruiting practices).

Engaging, Focused, and Applied

The management of human resources is critical for organizations to provide value to customers, shareholders, employees, and the communities where they are located. Value includes not only profits, but also employee growth and engagement, creation of new jobs, protection of the environment, and contributions to community programs. All aspects of human resource management including acquiring, preparing for, developing, and rewarding employees can help organizations meet their competitive challenges and create value. Also, effective human resource management requires an awareness of broader contextual issues such as economic conditions, legal issues,

and globalization. Both the popular press and academic research show that effective human resource management practices do result in greater value for stakeholders, including employees. For example, in this edition, you will find a broad range of examples featuring organizations throughout Canada that are leading the way in effective human resource management.

An important feature of this book is that it is rich with examples and provides practical applications. Regardless of the direction of your career aspirations, and whether or not you directly manage other employees now or in the future, understanding effective human resource management practices has never been more critical to achieving organizational success as well as personal success and satisfaction. As described in detail in the guided tour of the book, each chapter contains several features that encourage analysis and evaluation of human resource-related situations and applies the chapter concepts.

The author team believes that the focused, engaging, and applied approach distinguishes this book from others that have similar coverage of HR topics. The book has timely coverage of important HR issues, is easy to read, and provides the content, tools, and resources to demonstrate the relevance of HR from the perspective of future and current employees, managers, entrepreneurs, executives, and HR professionals.

Organization

We have made several enhancements to the structure of this edition to organize the key HRM topics more effectively and concisely. The book consists of 11 chapters in five parts as follows:

- **Part 1** discusses several aspects of the human resource environment. To be effective, human resource management must begin with an awareness of the trends and challenges shaping this field, including changes in the workforce, technology, and society as well as the profession of HR itself. Such trends and issues are the topic of *Chapter 1*. On a more detailed level, human resource management must also ensure that the organization's actions comply with and exceed

by offering suggestions and insightful comments that helped us develop and shape this new edition:

Stan Arnold	*Humber College Institute of Technology and Advanced Learning*
Gordon Barnard	*Durham College*
J.J. Collins	*St. Clair College*
Lisa Guglielmi	*Seneca College*
John Hardisty	*Sheridan College*
Nelson Lacroix	*Niagara College*
Carol Ann Samhaber	*Algonquin College*
Don Schepens	*Grant MacEwan University*
Basu Sharma	*University of New Brunswick*
Helen Stavaris	*Dawson College*
Jean Taplin	*Humber College Institute of Technology and Advanced Learning*
Nick Turner	*University of Manitoba, Asper School of Business*
Hua Wang	*University of Toronto*
Chantal Westgate	*McGill University*

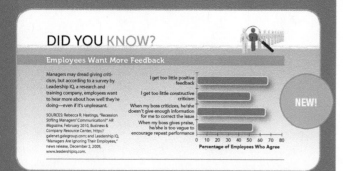
DID YOU KNOW?—*NEW!*

Shares thought-provoking statistics related to chapter topics. Examples include: "Employees Want More Feedback," "Top Seven Dangers for Young Workers (in B.C.)," and "Telecommuters Viewed as More Productive."

REAL PEOPLE AND HR

Each Part opens with a brief profile of a Canadian manager or HR professional. These "in my own words" profiles offer insights into how HRM is practised and reinforce the book's commitment to "real- world" application of the concepts and theories presented in the part.

THINKING ETHICALLY

Focused on ethics. The "Thinking Ethically" feature at the end of each chapter offers challenging ethical issues about human resources that require making and justifying decisions. Examples include: "Talent Poachers" and "Whose Business Is It When You Blog or Tweet?"

CHAPTER OPENING VIGNETTES

Each chapter opens with a look at events and people in real organizations to encourage critical evaluation and application of each situation to the chapter content.

REQUIRED PROFESSIONAL CAPABILITIES (RPC)

For those students pursuing the Certified Human Resources Professional designation, we have identified the **Required Professional Capabilities (RPC)** linked to applicable content areas with the RPC icon in the margin. A full list of the RPCs can be found on the inside front cover of the text

KEY TERMS

Key terms and definitions appear in the margins, so terms are highlighted where they are discussed for easy review and in order to introduce the language of HRM.

HR BEST PRACTICES

Real-world examples of what is working well in HRM. Examples include: "Suncor Energy Receives CAPP Awards for Health and Safety Performance," "'Boomerang Employees' Bring Back Benefits for Employers," and "The YMCA of Greater Toronto: Competency Modelling."

E-HRM

Examples of how technology is used in HR on a daily basis. Each E-HRM feature is highlighted in the chapter and hotlinked within the ebook, with full content appearing in CONNECT. Examples include: "Skype Job Interviews," "The Human Resources Institute of Alberta's (HRIA) Virtual Mentorship Program Eliminates Geographical Boundaries," and "Social HR."

Imaginet Ranks #1 in Queen's School of Business Study

"It's a tremendous honour to be named the Best Small to Medium Employer in Canada," says Rod Giesbrecht, CEO and co-founder of Winnipeg-based software application firm, Imaginet. "Our dynamic culture defines Imaginet and is demonstrated by the team's commitment to providing unsurpassed value to our customers." "We have some of the best people in the world working in Imaginet. They are positive, hard working and results oriented," adds co-founder Joel Semeniuk. "Building a strong company with a great culture is a lot of fun when you have like-minded people who are determined to succeed."

The process to become a "Top Best Small to Medium Employer" is a detailed and competitive process. Rankings are primarily based upon the analyzed results of 21 key engagement drivers detailed in employee opinion surveys, however, the evaluation process also includes assessing organizational practices and perspectives. "We use employee engagement as the standard for determining which organizations are the 'best' employers," said Einar Westerlund, director of project development at the Queen's School of Business Centre for Business Venturing. "In this study, feedback directly from employees about their workplace and their work experience enables us to measure how engaged they are."

Founded in 1997, Imaginet now has offices in the United States and South Africa, in addition to Canada. "As a small-business owner, it's important to build a strong community of high-performing employees who share your passion for the business and its goals," explains Giesbrecht. "We continue to attract new recruits at the top of their game, and as a people. Im going at enjoyed a 360 percent growth over

we introduce ways to measure the effectiveness of human resource management.

What Is a High-Performance Work System?

The challenge facing managers today is how to make their organizations into high-performance work systems with the right combination of people, technology, and organizational structure to make full use of resources and opportunities in achieving their organizations' goals. To function as a high-performance work system, each of these elements must fit well with the others in a smoothly functioning whole. Many manufacturers use the latest in processes including flexible manufacturing technology and just-in-time inventory control (meaning parts and supplies are automatically restocked as needed), but, of course, these processes do not work on their own; they must be run by qualified people. Organizations have to determine what kinds of people fit their needs, and then locate, train, and motivate those special people.[2] According to research, organizations that introduce integrated high-performance work practices usually experience increases in productivity and long-term financial performance.[3]

Creating a high-performance work system contrasts with traditional management practices. In the past, decisions about technology, organizational structure, and human resources were treated as if they were unrelated. An organization might acquire

> **LO1** Define high-performance work systems and identify the elements, outcomes, and conditions associated with such a system.

---

are willing to pay. Stock is the owners' investment in a corporation; when the stock price is rising, the value of that investment is growing. Rather than trying to figure out what performance measures will motivate employees to do the things that generate high profits and a rising stock price, many organizations offer incentive pay tied to those organizational performance measures. The expectation is that employees will focus on what is best for the organization.

These organization-level incentives can motivate employees to align their activities with the organization's goals. Linking incentives to the organization's profits or stock price exposes employees to a high degree of risk. Profits and stock price can soar very high very fast, but they can also fall, as witnessed by many wary investors. The result is a great deal of uncertainty about the amount of incentive pay each employee will receive in each period. Therefore, these kinds of incentive pay are likely to be most effective in organizations that emphasize growth and innovation, which tend to need employees who thrive in a risk-taking environment.[21]

Profit Sharing

Under profit sharing, payments are a percentage of the organization's profits and do not become part of

> **profit sharing**
> Incentive pay in which payments are a percentage of the organization's profits and do not become part of the employees' base salary.

has little or no profit, this incentive pay is small or nonexistent, so employers may not need to rely as much on layoffs to reduce costs.[22]

An organization setting up a profit-sharing plan should consider what to do if profits fall. If the economy slows and profit-sharing payments disappear along with profits, employees may become discouraged or dissatisfied. One way to avoid this kind of problem is to design profit-sharing plans to reward employees for high profits but not penalize them when profits fall. This solution may be more satisfactory to employees but does not offer the advantage of reducing labour costs without layoffs during economic downturns.

Given the limitations of profit-sharing plans, one strategy is to use them as a component of a pay system that includes other kinds of pay more directly linked to individual behaviour. This increases employees' commitment to organizational goals while addressing concerns about fairness.

Stock Ownership

While profit-sharing plans are intended to encourage employees to "think like owners," a stock ownership plan actually makes employees part owners of the organization. Like profit sharing, employee own-

---

HR BEST PRACTICES

The YMCA of Greater Toronto: Competency Modelling

Competency modelling identifies the specific competencies required by employees to support an organization's vision, values, and strategic direction. Melanie Laflamme, vice-president of human resources and organizational development of the YMCA of Greater Toronto was recently recognized for her leadership role in HR including the development of a competency model that serves as a key element of the YMCA's employment brand. "It's very exciting to see the work that's

being done in HR and, in particular, in non-profit is being acknowledged," said Laflamme when she was named the top HR leader for organizations with more than 500 employees at the annual Toronto Business Excellence Rewards. The YMCA of Greater Toronto's competency model consists of seven association-wide competencies and seven leadership competencies that form the foundation for all HR processes including the development of job descriptions, recruitment and selection, training

and development, performance appraisal, and succession planning.

SOURCES: Joan Hill, "Competency Model Helps HR Add Value," *Canadian HR Reporter*, January 30, 2012, pp. 20–21; Rahul Gupta, "Awards Recognize Top CEOs, Human Resource Leaders," *Inside Toronto.com*, November 25, 2010, www.insidetoronto.com/news/business/article/908329--awards-recognize-top-ceos-human-resource-leaders, retrieved March 15, 2012; Shannon Klie, "Awards Honour Top Toronto Leaders," *Canadian HR Reporter*, December 13, 2010, pp. 1 and 13; and www.ymcagta.org.

> **UPDATED!**

---

out geographic limitations. Recruiting and selection can include online job postings, applications, and candidate screening from the company's website or the websites of companies that specialize in online recruiting. The use of social media can expand the reach of staffing efforts to attract employees who are not necessarily looking for jobs. Employees from different geographic locations can all receive the same training over the company's computer network.

to serve as a gateway to the Internet, highlighting links to relevant information).[43] Whether a company uses an intranet or a Web portal, it must ensure that it has sufficient security measures in place to protect employees' privacy.

> The processing and transmission of digitized HR information, especially using computer networking and the Internet.

Sharing of Human Resource Information

Information technology is changing the way HR departments handle record keeping and information sharing. Today, HR employees use technology to automate much of their work in managing employee records and giving employees access to information and enrolment forms for training, benefits, and

E-HRM · connect

See how the HR department of the University of British Columbia is using social media to have a voice in the organization.

> **UPDATED!**

TABLE 1.4 Implications of e-HRM for HRM Practices

HRM PRACTICES	IMPLICATIONS OF E-HRM
Analysis and design of work	Employees in geographically dispersed locations can work together in virtual teams using video-conferencing and other communications technologies.
Recruiting	Employers can post job openings online; use social media to extend the reach of traditional job search efforts; and candidates can apply for jobs online.
Selection	Online simulations, including tests, videos, and email, can measure job candidates' ability to deal with real-life business challenges.
Training	Online learning can bring training to employees anywhere, anytime.
Total rewards	Employees can review salary and incentives information and seek information about and enrol in benefit plans.

Part 1

THE HUMAN
Resource
Environment

Chapter 1

STRATEGIES, TRENDS, AND CHALLENGES
in Human Resource Management

Google has been ranked multiple times as #1 on Fortune Magazine's 100 Best Companies to Work For.

What Do I Need to Know?

After reading this chapter, you should be able to:

LO1 Define human resource management, identify the roles and responsibilities of human resource departments, and explain how human resource management contributes to an organization's performance.

LO2 Summarize areas in which human resource management can support organizational strategies.

LO3 Summarize the types of competencies needed for human resource management.

LO4 Explain the role of supervisors and managers in human resource management.

LO5 Describe typical careers in human resource management.

LO6 Describe trends in the labour force composition and how they affect human resource management.

LO7 Discuss the role of high-performance work systems and how technological developments are affecting human resource management.

LO8 Explain how the nature of the employment relationship is changing and how the need for flexibility affects human resource management.

Earning a Reputation as a Great Employer

What do Molson Coors Canada, the University of Toronto, NB Power, the BC Public Service, and Google have in common? They have all been recently recognized as excellent employers with progressive human resource management practices. The list of employment awards is growing, raising the bar on what it takes to attract, retain, and engage top talent. As labour markets become increasingly competitive, human resource professionals are being called upon to provide people management practices that not only support the organization's priorities but also provide for competitive success in a global marketplace. Organizations strive to create an employment brand that attracts top talent and a reputation as a great place to work.

In addition to Mediacorp Canada's "Top 100 Employers," there are several additional annual competitions, including "Canada's Top 10 Employers for Young People," "Canada's Most Earth-Friendly Employers," "Best Employers for New Canadians," and "Canada's Top 10 Family-Friendly Employers." Organizations are also considered for regional recognition including "Greater Toronto's Top Employers," "Nova Scotia's Top Employers," and "Manitoba's Top 10 Employers."

Perhaps no organization has received more attention or has a stronger employment brand than Google. Google is known for its people practices and employee-first culture that directly contribute to its success. The work environment provides "Googlers" unlimited amounts of free, chef-prepared food at all times of the day, lap pools, onsite massages, car washes, oil changes, drycleaning, laundry service, and haircuts. Google's "20-percent time" gives employees 20 percent of their day to "work on what they're really passionate about"—and tangible organizational outcomes often result. For example, Gmail came about from one Google employee's 20-percent time efforts. Perhaps it is no surprise that Google receives 1,300 résumés every day and is able to attract and retain some of the world's top talent.[1]

Introduction

Organizations of all sizes and in all industries are increasingly recognizing the importance of people.

1,2

"This is a time of rapid change in the market—a time when Canadian organizations are constantly trying to keep pace and remain competitive. In today's knowledge-based economy, we rely on people to generate, develop, and implement ideas"[2] and the "human resource function has an important role in ensuring that organizations have the people capacity to execute strategic objectives."[3]

Human resource management (HRM), centres on the practices, policies, and systems that influence employees' behaviour, attitudes, and performance. Many companies refer to HRM as "people practices." Figure 1.1 emphasizes that there are several important HRM practices that support the organization's business strategy: analyzing work and designing jobs, determining how many employees with specific knowledge and skills are needed (workforce planning), attracting potential employees (recruiting), choosing employees (selection), preparing employees to perform their jobs and for the future (training and development), supporting their performance (performance management), rewarding employees (compensation and rewards), creating a positive work environment (employee and labour relations). In addition, HRM has responsibility for providing safe and healthy work environments and proactively meeting legal requirements. An organization performs best when all of these practices are managed systemically. At companies with effective HRM, employees and customers tend to be more satisfied, and the companies tend to be more innovative, have greater productivity, and develop a more favourable reputation in the community.[4]

In this chapter, we introduce the scope of human resource management, including the ways HRM facilitates and supports organizational strategy. We begin by discussing why human resource management is an essential element of an organization's success. We then turn to the elements of managing human resources: the roles and capabilities needed for effective human resource management. Next, the chapter describes how all managers, not just human resource professionals, participate in the functions and processes of human resource management.

human resource management (HRM)
The practices, policies, and systems that influence employees' behaviour, attitudes, and performance.

L01 ▶ Define human resource management, identify the roles and responsibilities of human resource departments, and explain how human resource management contributes to an organization's performance.

DID YOU KNOW?

Engaged, Enabled Employees Deliver Bottom-Line Benefits

Comparing companies where employees are highly engaged (through communication and leadership) and highly enabled (carefully selected for well-designed jobs with adequate resources and training) with low-engagement, low-enablement companies, the Hay Group found big performance differences.

SOURCE: Hay Group, "Tough Decisions in a Downturn Don't Have to Lead to Disengaged Employees," news release, August 13, 2009, www.haygroup.com.

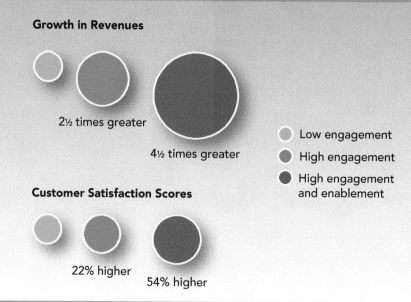

Growth in Revenues

2½ times greater

4½ times greater

Customer Satisfaction Scores

22% higher

54% higher

○ Low engagement

● High engagement

● High engagement and enablement

---

competitive environment. As technology changes the ways organizations manufacture, transport, communicate, and keep track of information, human resource management must ensure that the organization has the right kinds of people to meet the new challenges. Maintaining a high-performance work system might include development of training programs, recruitment of people with new skill sets, and establishment of rewards for such behaviours as teamwork, flexibility, and learning. Chapter 11 examines high-performance work systems in greater detail.

What Are the Responsibilities of HR Departments?

In all but the smallest organizations, a human resource department is responsible for the functions of human resource management. On average, an organization has one HR staff person for every 93 employees served by the department.[9] One way to define the responsibilities of HR departments is to think of HR as a business within the organization with three product lines:[10]

1. *Administrative services and transactions*—Handling administrative tasks (for example, processing tuition reimbursement applications and answering questions about benefits) efficiently and with a commitment to quality. This requires expertise in the particular tasks.

2. *Business partner services*—Developing effective HR systems that help the organization meet its goals for attracting, keeping, and developing people with the skills it needs. For the systems to be effective, HR people must understand the business so it can understand what the business needs.

3. *Strategic partner*—Contributing to the company's strategy through an understanding of its existing and needed human resources and ways HR practices can give the company a competitive advantage. For strategic ideas to be effective, HR people must understand the business, its industry, and its competitors.

Another way to think of HR responsibilities is in terms of specific activities. Table 1.1 details the responsibilities of human resource departments. These responsibilities include the practices introduced in Figure 1.1 plus two areas of responsibility that support those practices: (1) establishing and administering human resource policies and (2) ensuring compliance with legal requirements.

Although the human resource department has responsibility for these areas, many of the requirements are performed by supervisors or others inside

with the necessary knowledge, skills, abilities, and other characteristics that will help the organization achieve its goals. An organization makes selection decisions in order to add employees to its workforce, as well as to transfer existing employees to new positions.

Approaches to recruiting and selection involve a variety of alternatives. Some organizations may actively recruit from many external sources using job postings on their corporate websites, social media, and placing newspaper ads. Other organizations may rely heavily on internal job postings relying upon the availability of current employees with the necessary skills.

At some organizations, the selection process may focus on specific skills, such as experience with a particular programming language or type of equipment. At others, selection may focus on general abilities, such as the ability to work as part of a team or find creative solutions. The focus an organization favours will affect many choices, from the way the organization assesses skills to the questions it asks in interviews. Table 1.2 lists the top five qualities that employers say they are looking for in job candidates.

TRAINING AND DEVELOPING EMPLOYEES

Although organizations base hiring decisions on candidates' existing qualifications, most organizations provide ways for their employees to broaden or deepen their knowledge, skills, and abilities. To

training
A planned effort to enable employees to learn job-related knowledge, skills, and behaviour.

development
The acquisition of knowledge, skills, and behaviours that improve an employee's ability to meet the challenges of a variety of new or existing jobs.

performance management
The process of ensuring that employees' activities and outputs match the organization's goals.

do this, organizations provide for employee training and development. **Training** is a planned effort to enable employees to learn job-related knowledge, skills, and behaviour. For example, many organizations offer safety training to teach employees safe work habits. **Development** involves acquiring knowledge, skills, and behaviour that improve employees' ability to meet the challenges of a variety of new or existing jobs, including preparing employees to work in diverse work teams. Development programs often focus on preparing employees for management responsibility.

MANAGING PERFORMANCE

Managing human resources includes assessing how well employees are performing relative to objectives such as job descriptions and goals for a particular position. The process of ensuring that employees' activities and outputs match the organization's goals is called **performance management**. The activities of performance management include specifying the tasks and outcomes of a job that contribute to the organization's success; providing timely feedback and coaching; and comparing the employee's actual performance and behaviours over some time period with the desired performance and behaviours. Often, rewards—the topic of the next section—are developed to encourage good performance.

COMPENSATION AND REWARDS

The pay and benefits that employees earn play an important role in motivation. This is especially true when rewards such as bonuses are linked to the individual's or team's performance. Decisions about pay and benefits can also support other aspects of an organization's strategy. For example, a company that wants to provide an exceptional level of service or be exceptionally innovative might pay significantly more than competitors in order to attract and keep the best employees. At other companies, a low-cost strategy requires knowledge of industry norms, so that the company does not spend more than market rates of pay for similar positions. Planning pay and benefits involves many decisions, often complex and based on knowledge of a multitude of legal requirements. An important decision is how much to offer in salary or wages, as opposed to bonuses, commissions, and other performance-related pay. Other decisions

TABLE 1.2	Top Qualities Employers Look for in Employees
1. Interpersonal skills
2. Work ethic
3. Initiative/flexibility
4. Honesty/loyalty
5. Strong communication skills (verbal and written)

SOURCES: "Skills Employers Look for in Employees," article by Leigh Goessl, Juan Leer, and Sun Meilan at www.helium.com, accessed May 12, 2010; Dennis Lee, "10 Qualities Interviewers Look For," at www.goldsea.com, accessed May 12, 2010; and www.conferenceboard.ca/education/learning-tools/employability-skills.htm, retrieved February 28, 2012.

involve which benefits to offer, from retirement plans to various kinds of insurance to other more intangible rewards such as opportunities for learning and personal growth. These decisions may also be linked to other decisions and policies aimed at engaging workers as described in the "HR How-To" box. All such decisions have implications for the organization's bottom line, as well as for employee motivation.

Administering pay and benefits is another big responsibility. Organizations need systems for keeping track of each employee's earnings and benefits. Employees need information about their health plans, retirement plan, and other benefits. Keeping track of this involves extensive record keeping and reporting to management, employees, and others, while ensuring compliance with all applicable legislation.

MAINTAINING POSITIVE EMPLOYEE AND LABOUR RELATIONS

Organizations often depend on human resource professionals to help them identify and perform many of the responsibilities related to providing satisfying and engaging work environments and maintaining positive relations with employees. This function often includes providing for communications to employees.

In organizations where employees belong to a union, labour relations entails additional responsibilities. The organization periodically conducts collective bargaining to negotiate an employment contract with union members. The HR department also maintains communication with union representatives to ensure that issues are resolved as they arise.

ESTABLISHING AND ADMINISTERING HUMAN RESOURCE POLICIES

All the human resource activities described so far require fair and consistent decisions, and most require substantial record keeping. Organizations depend on their HR department to help establish policies related to hiring, discipline, promotions, benefits, and the other activities of human resource management. For example, with a policy in place about acceptable use of the Internet, the company can handle inappropriate Internet use more fairly and objectively than if it addressed such incidents on a case-by-case basis. The company depends on HR professionals to help develop and then communicate the policy to every employee, so that everyone knows its importance.

HR HOW-TO

Putting Compensation and Rewards in Perspective

When it comes to attracting, keeping, and motivating workers, a lot of people think first about pay, and certainly getting paid is one important reason we get up and go to work day after day. But to get employees to use all their talents and go the extra mile, companies have to combine decisions about compensation with other efforts at engaging and enabling their people:

- *Link significant differences in pay to high performance*—The best workers should be up for bonuses, promotions, or other measurable rewards. That means compensation budgets should

include money set aside for those rewards.

- *Make sure employees know what is expected of them*—This requires a combination of careful job design and thorough communication. HR staff can work with supervisors to spell out what superior performance looks like for each position in the organization.
- *Give employees plenty of feedback, so performance problems can be identified and corrected early on*—HR can work with supervisors by developing and helping them use systems for performance feedback.

- *Make success possible*—That includes matching qualified people to jobs and participating in efforts to eliminate or improve inefficient work processes. Training should be available to help employees fulfill job requirements, update skills, and advance in their careers.
- *Create a positive climate*—When possible, encourage employees to collaborate and take on authority for decision making in the areas for which they are responsible.

SOURCE: Based on William Werhane and Mark Royal, "Engaging and Enabling Employees," *workspan*, October 2009, pp. 39–43.

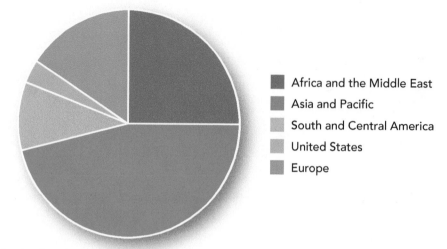

FIGURE 1.3

Where Do Immigrants to Canada Come From (2010)?

- Africa and the Middle East
- Asia and Pacific
- South and Central America
- United States
- Europe

SOURCE: Canada Facts and Figures—Immigration Overview: Permanent and Temporary Residents, http://www.cic.gc.ca/english/pdf/research-stats/facts2010.pdf. Citizenship and Immigration Canada 2011. Reproduced with the permission of the Minister of Public Works and Government Services, 2012.

employees for international assignments and preparing them for those assignments. Employees who take assignments in other countries are called **expatriates**.

Canadian companies must prepare employees to work in other countries. Canadian companies must carefully select employees to work abroad on the basis of their ability to understand and respect the cultural and business norms of the host country. Qualified candidates also need language skills and technical ability. In Chapter 10, we discuss practices for training employees to understand other cultures.

OUTSOURCING

Many organizations are increasingly outsourcing and offshoring business activities. **Outsourcing** refers to the practice of having another company (a vendor, third-party provider, or consultant) provide services. For instance, a manufacturing company might outsource its accounting and transportation functions to businesses that specialize in these activities. Outsourcing gives the company access to in-depth expertise and is often more economical as well. In addition to manufacturing, software development and support, as well as call centre operations are other functions typically considered for outsourcing. **Offshoring**, on the other hand, refers to setting up a business enterprise in another country, for example, setting up a factory in China to manufacture products at less cost than in Canada. Increasingly, organizations are *offshore outsourcing,* that is, the company providing outsourced services is located in another country rather than

expatriates
Employees who take assignments in other countries.

outsourcing
The practice of having another company (a vendor, third-party provider, or consultant) provide services.

offshoring
Setting up a business enterprise in another country (e.g., building a factory in China).

the organization's home country. For example, The Portables, a trade-show display and exhibits maker based in Richmond, B.C., have increased annual sales dramatically since starting its use of offshore outsourcing. Hanif Mulijinai, president and CEO says offshore outsourcing was never the plan for his company. "But we find with some of the newer products, it's a lot easier to get some of the products manufactured in China. It's a lot quicker and less expensive," he says. "Some of the quality of the work they do is very scary, it's so good."[20]

Not only do HR departments help with a transition to outsourcing, but many HR functions are being outsourced. Benefits Canada reports that 59 percent of Canadian employers outsourced some or all HR services and another 10 percent plan to do so within two years.[21] HR functions being outsourced are increasingly expanding from benefits, pension, and payroll administration to including recruiting, relocation, absence management, learning and development, succession planning, and workforce analysis.[22] One of the case studies at the end of the chapter takes a look at Air Canada's $80 million deal with IBM to provide the airline with systems and administrative support for HR operations including payroll, benefits, time management, data management, and employee travel.[23]

MERGERS AND ACQUISITIONS

Increasingly, organizations are joining forces through mergers (two companies becoming one) and acquisitions (one company buying another). These

2. *Cultural steward*—involves understanding the organization's culture and helping to build and strengthen or change that culture by identifying and expressing its values through words and actions.

3. *Talent manager/organizational designer*—knows the ways that people join the organization and move to different positions within it. To do this effectively requires knowledge of how the organization is structured and how that structure might be adjusted to help it meet its goals for developing and using employees' talents.

4. *Strategy architect*—requires awareness of business trends and an understanding of how they might affect the business, as well as opportunities and threats they might present. A person with this capability spots ways effective management of human resources can help the company seize opportunities and confront threats to the business.

5. *Business allies*—know how the business achieves its success, who its customers are, and why customers support what the company sells.

6. *Operational executors*—at the most basic level carry out particular HR functions such as handling the selection, training, or compensation of employees. All of the other HR skills require some ability as operational executor, because this is the level at which policies and transactions deliver results by legally, ethically, and efficiently acquiring, developing, motivating, and deploying human resources.

All of these competencies require interpersonal skills. Successful HR professionals must be able to share information, build relationships, and influence persons inside and outside the organization.

ethics
The fundamental principles of right and wrong.

Ethics in Human Resource Management

Whenever people's actions affect one another, ethical issues arise, and business decisions are no exception. **Ethics** refers to the fundamental principles of right and wrong; ethical behaviour is behaviour that is consistent with those principles. Business decisions, including HRM decisions, should be ethical, but the evidence suggests that is not always what happens. Recent surveys indicate that the general public and managers do not have positive perceptions of the ethical conduct of businesses.

For example, in a Gallup poll on honesty and ethics in 21 professions, only 12 percent of respondents rated business executives high or very high; three times as many rated them low or very low. And from a global perspective, an international poll of Facebook members found that two-thirds believe individuals do not apply values they hold in their personal lives to their professional activities.[24]

The "HR Best Practices" box provides the Code of Ethics for the Canadian Council of Human Resources Associations (CCHRA) that identifies standards for professional and ethical conduct of HR practitioners. For human resource practices to be considered ethical, they must satisfy the three basic standards summarized in Figure 1.5.[25] First, HRM practices must result in the greatest good for the greatest number of people. Second, human resource practices must respect legal requirements including human rights and privacy. Third, managers must treat employees and customers equitably and fairly. To explore how ethical principles apply to a variety of decisions, we will highlight ethical

FIGURE 1.5

Standards for Identifying Ethical Practices

HR BEST PRACTICES

CCHRA's National Code of Ethics

1. *Preamble.* As HR practitioners in the following categories:

   - Certified Human Resources Professionals
   - CHRP Candidates, or
   - CHRP Exam Registrants,

   We commit to abide by all requirements of the Code of Ethics of the Canadian Council of Human Resources Associations (CCHRA), as listed in this document. (Where provincial codes are legislated, those will prevail.)

2. *Competence.* Maintain competence in carrying out professional responsibilities and provide services in an honest and diligent manner. Ensure that activities engaged in are within the limits of one's knowledge, experience, and skill. When providing services outside one's level of competence, or the profession, the necessary assistance must be sought so as not to compromise professional responsibility.

3. *Legal requirements.* Adhere to any statutory acts, regulation, or by-laws which relate to the field of human resources management, as well as all civil and criminal laws, regulations, and statutes that apply in one's jurisdiction. Not knowingly or otherwise engage in or condone any activity or attempt to circumvent the clear intention of the law.

4. *Dignity in the workplace.* Support, promote and apply the principles of human rights, equity, dignity and respect in the workplace, within the profession, and in society as a whole.

5. *Balancing interests.* Strive to balance organizational and employee needs and interests in the practice of the profession.

6. *Confidentiality.* Hold in strict confidence all confidential information acquired in the course of the performance of one's duties, and not divulge confidential information unless required by law and/or where serious harm is imminent.

7. *Conflict of interest.* Either avoid or disclose a potential conflict of interest that might influence or might be perceived to influence personal actions or judgments.

8. *Professional growth and support of other professionals.* Maintain personal and professional growth in human resources management by engaging in activities that enhance the credibility and value of the profession.

9. *Enforcement.* The Canadian Council of Human Resources Associations works collaboratively with its Member Associations to develop and enforce high standards of ethical practice among all its members.

SOURCE: © Reproduced with permission by the Canadian Council of Human Resources Associations. www.chrp.ca/i-am-a-chrp/national-code-of-ethics/code-of-ethics/, retrieved January 24, 2012.

---

dilemmas in human resource management practices throughout the book.

Closely related to the discussion of ethics and ethical practices is HR's role in organizational values and corporate social responsibility. For example, "there is increasing evidence that interest in environmental issues is motivating people's behaviour as consumers, employees and jobseekers."[26] In Chapter 11, we will explore this subject in more depth including a discussion of how eco-friendly firms may have an edge in their ability to attract, retain, and engage top talent.

What Are the HR Responsibilities of Supervisors and Managers?

Although many organizations have human resource departments, HR activities are by no means limited to the specialists who staff those departments. In large organizations, HR departments advise and support the activities of the other departments. In small organizations, there may be an HR specialist, but many HR activities are carried out by supervisors and managers. Either way, non-HR supervisors and managers need to be familiar with the basics of HRM and their role with regard to managing human resources.

L04 ▸ Explain the role of supervisors and managers in human resource management.

As we will see in later chapters, supervisors and managers typically have responsibilities related to all the HR functions. Figure 1.6 shows some HR responsibilities that supervisors and managers are likely to be involved in. Organizations depend on supervisors to help them determine what kinds of work need to be done (job analysis and design) and in what quantities (workforce planning). Supervisors and managers typically interview job candidates and participate in the decisions about which candidates

Adrian Joseph (in photo), a Sri Lankan immigrant with a strong financial and accounting background lacked Canadian work experience but was hired as CFO (chief financial officer) by Toronto's Steam Whistle Brewing only three weeks after his arrival in Canada.

AN AGING WORKFORCE

Canada's population and its labour force are aging. The fastest-growing age group is expected to be workers 55 and older. The 25- to 54-year-old group will decrease its numbers slightly, so its share of the total workforce will fall. And young workers, between the ages of 15 and 24 will actually be fewer in number. This combination of trends will cause the overall workforce to age. Figure 1.8 shows the change in age distribution, as forecast by Statistics Canada between 2011 and 2021. Human resource professionals will therefore spend much of their time on concerns related to creating a work environment that supports the needs of a multigenerational workforce, planning retirement, and reskilling workers. Organizations will struggle with ways to control the rising cost of health-related and other benefits, and many of tomorrow's managers will supervise employees much older than themselves. At the same time, organizations will have to find ways to attract, retain, and prepare the younger generations in the workforce.

Increasingly, older workers say they intend to have a working retirement—*nevertirees*. Despite myths to the contrary, worker performance and learning do not suffer as a result of aging.[30] Older employees are willing and able to learn new technology. More older workers are asking to work part-time or for only a few months at a time as a way to transition to full retirement. Employees and companies are redefining the meaning of retirement to include second careers as well as part-time and temporary work assignments. Although recruiting and retaining older workers may present some challenges related to costs of health care and other benefits, companies are benefiting from these employees' talents and experience.

A DIVERSE WORKFORCE

Another change affecting the Canadian population and labour force is that it is growing more diverse. Over 200 ethnic groups were reported in Canada's most recent census. According to a recent study by the Association for Canadian Studies, 80 percent of Canadians aged 18 to 24 describe their school or workplace as ethnically diverse. Jack Jedwab, the

---

FIGURE 1.8

Age Distribution Projection of the Canadian Population, 2011 and 2021

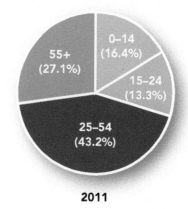

2011

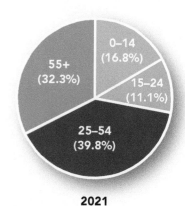

2021

SOURCE: "Age Distribution Projection of the Canadian Population 2011 and 2021," adapted from Statistics Canada website, www40.statcan.gc.ca/l01/cst01/demo23b-eng.htm and www40.statcan.gc.ca/l01/cst01/demo23d-eng.htm, retrieved January 24, 2012.

so have the requirements for creating a high-performance work system. Customers are demanding high quality and customized products, employees are seeking flexible work arrangements, and employers are looking for ways to tap people's creativity and interpersonal skills. Such demands require that organizations make full use of their people's knowledge and skill, and skilled human resource management can help organizations do this.

Among the trends that are occurring in today's high-performance work systems are reliance on knowledge workers, employee engagement, the use of teamwork, and the increasing levels of education of the workforce. The following sections describe these four trends. HR professionals who keep up with change are well positioned to help create high-performance work systems. Chapter 11 will further explore the elements and outcomes of a high-performance work system.

KNOWLEDGE WORKERS

To meet their human capital needs, companies are increasingly trying to attract, develop, and retain knowledge workers. **Knowledge workers** are employees whose main contribution to the organization is specialized knowledge, such as knowledge of customers, a process, or a profession. Knowledge workers are especially needed for jobs in health services, business services, social services, engineering, and management.

> **knowledge workers**
> Employees whose main contribution to the organization is specialized knowledge, such as knowledge of customers, a process, or a profession.

Knowledge workers are in a position of power, because they own the knowledge that the company needs in order to produce its products and services, and they must share their knowledge and collaborate with others in order for their employer to succeed. An employer cannot simply order these employees to perform tasks. Managers depend on the employees' willingness to share information. Furthermore, skilled knowledge workers have many job opportunities, even in a slow economy. If they choose, they can leave a company and take their knowledge to another employer. Replacing them may be difficult and time-consuming.

As more organizations become knowledge-based, they must promote and capture learning at the level of employees, teams, and the overall organization.

The reliance on knowledge workers also affects organizations' decisions about the kinds of people they are recruiting and selecting.[39] They are shifting away from focusing on specific skills, such as how to operate a particular kind of machinery, and toward a greater emphasis on general cognitive skills (thinking and problem solving) and interpersonal skills. Employers are more interested in evidence that job candidates will excel at working in teams or interacting with customers. These skills also support an employee's ability to gather and share knowledge, helping the organization to innovate and meet customer needs. To the extent that technical skills are important, employers often are most interested in the ability to use information technology, including the Internet and statistical software.

Knowledge workers are employees whose value to their employers stems primarily from what they know. Employees such as the ones pictured here have in-depth knowledge of their profession and are hard to replace because of their special knowledge.

EMPLOYEE ENGAGEMENT

To completely benefit from employees' knowledge, organizations need a management style that focuses on developing and engaging employees. Employee engagement refers to the extent that employees are satisfied, committed to, and prepared to support what is important to the organization.

HRM practices such as performance management, training and development, career management, work design, and employee relations are important for creating employee engagement. Jobs must be designed to give employees the necessary latitude for making a variety of decisions. Employees must be properly trained to exert their wider authority and use information resources such as the Internet, as well as tools for communicating information. Employees also need feedback to help them evaluate their success. Pay and other rewards should reflect employees' authority and be related to successful handling of their responsibility. In addition, for engagement to occur, managers must be trained to link employees to resources within and outside the organization, such as customers, co-workers in other departments, and websites with needed information. Managers must also encourage employees to interact with staff throughout the organization, must ensure that employees receive the information they need, and must reward cooperation.

As with the need for knowledge workers, employee engagement shifts the recruiting focus away from technical skills and toward general cognitive and interpersonal skills. Employees who have responsibility for a final product or service must be able to listen to customers, adapt to changing needs, and creatively solve a variety of problems. Chapter 11 will explore employee engagement practices and outcomes in more detail.

TEAMWORK

Modern technology places the information that employees need for improving quality and providing customer service right at the point of sale or production. As a result, the employees engaging in selling and producing must also be able to make decisions about how to do their work. Organizations need to set up work in a way that gives employees the authority and ability to make those decisions. One of the most popular ways to increase employee responsibility and control is to assign work to teams.

employee engagement
The extent that employees are satisfied, committed to, and prepared to support what is important to the organization.

teamwork
The assignment of work to groups of employees with various skills who interact to assemble a product or provide a service.

human resource information system (HRIS)
A computer system used to acquire, store, manipulate, analyze, retrieve, and distribute information related to an organization's human resources.

Teamwork is the assignment of work to groups of employees with various skills who interact to assemble a product or provide a service. In some organizations, technology is enabling teamwork even when workers are at different locations at different times. These organizations use *virtual teams*—teams that rely on communications technologies to keep in touch and coordinate activities.

INCREASING LEVELS OF EDUCATION

The educational attainment of Canada's population is increasing. According to the latest Canadian census data, 17.3 percent of Canada's population 15 years and older had a college certificate or diploma and 11.6 percent a bachelor's degree. These figures are up from 10.4 percent and 6.4 percent respectively, from 1986.[40]

In a survey conducted for a TD Bank Financial Group paper, economists Craig Alexander and Eric Lascalles examined the work of a dozen researchers to discover the rate of return of postsecondary education. The rate of return was calculated using the present value difference between the lifetime earnings of a postsecondary graduate and those of a high-school graduate, factoring in the cost of tuition, academic fees, and lost earnings while students were in school. Annual rates of return for a university degree ranged from 12 percent to 17 percent for men and 16 percent to 20 percent for women; for a college diploma, rates of return were between 15 percent and 28 percent for men, and 18 percent and 28 percent for women.[41]

How Is Technological Change Impacting HRM?

Advances in computer-related technology have had a major impact on the use of information for managing human resources. Large quantities of employee data (including training records, skills, compensation rates, and benefits usage and cost) can easily be stored on personal computers and manipulated with user-friendly spreadsheets or statistical software. Often these features are combined in a human resource information system (HRIS), a computer system used to acquire, store, manipulate, analyze, retrieve, and distribute information related to an

self-service

System in which employees have online access to information about HR issues and go online to enrol themselves in programs and provide feedback through surveys.

other programs. As a result, HR employees play a smaller role in maintaining records, and employees now get information through self-service. This means employees have online access to information about HR issues such as training, benefits, compensation, and contracts; go online to enrol themselves in programs and services; and provide feedback through online surveys. Today, employees routinely look up workplace policies and information about their benefits online, and they may receive electronic notification when deposits are made directly to their bank accounts.

How Is the Employment Relationship Changing?

Trends and developments we have described in this chapter require managers at all levels to make rapid changes in response to new opportunities, competitive challenges, and customer demands. These changes are most likely to succeed in flexible, forward-thinking organizations, and the employees who will thrive in such organizations need to be flexible and open to change as well. In this environment, employers and employees have begun to reshape the employment relationship.[46]

L08 Explain how the nature of the employment relationship is changing and how the need for flexibility affects human resource management.

A NEW PSYCHOLOGICAL CONTRACT

We can think of that relationship in terms of a **psychological contract**, a description of what an employee expects to contribute in an employment relationship

psychological contract

A description of what an employee expects to contribute in an employment relationship and what the employer will provide the employee in exchange for those contributions.

and what the employer will provide the employee in exchange for those contributions.[47] Unlike a written sales contract, the psychological contract is not formally put into words. Instead, it describes unspoken expectations that are widely held by employers and employees. In the traditional version of this psychological contract, organizations expected their employees to contribute time, effort, skills, abilities, and loyalty. In return, the organizations would provide job security and opportunities for promotion.

However, this arrangement is being replaced with a new type of psychological contract.[48] To stay competitive, modern organizations must frequently change the quality, innovation, creativeness, and timeliness of employee contributions and the skills needed to make those contributions. This need has led to organizational restructuring, mergers and acquisitions, layoffs, and longer hours for many employees. Companies demand excellent customer service and high productivity levels. They expect employees to take more responsibility for their own careers, from seeking training to balancing work and family. These expectations result in less job security for employees, who can count on working for several companies over the course of a career. But if four years with a company is typical, that amounts to many employers in the course of one's career.

In exchange for top performance and working longer hours without job security, employees want companies to provide flexible work schedules, effective work environments, more control over how they accomplish work, training and development opportunities, and financial incentives based on how the organization performs. (Figure 1.9 provides a humorous look at an employee who seems to have benefited from this modern psychological contract by obtaining a family-friendly work arrangement.) Employees realize that companies cannot provide

FIGURE 1.9

A Family-Friendly Work Arrangement

SPEED BUMP   Dave Coverly

THINKING ETHICALLY

Whose Business Is It When You Blog or Tweet?

Just as companies have become used to the idea of warning employees that their email messages are not private, along come blogs (Weblogs) and Twitter, with their own set of issues. Although some companies have begun to use blogs and tweets as marketing tools, most are written by individuals who enjoy posting their thoughts online. The dilemma involves the line between what people do as employees and what they do on their own time.

Consider the case of CTV's former Quebec City bureau chief, Kai Nagata who made headlines with his "Why I Quit My Job" blog post. Nagata's very public resignation letter, revealed his "desire for a deeper life purpose at age 24." Another resignation letter also recently went viral. A former Toronto Whole Foods Market employee, emailed a 2,000 word resignation letter to an entire division of the company, denouncing it as a "faux happy [sic] Wal-Mart." The former employee had not intended for his letter to go so public but American blog Gawker.com posted the letter online.

These cases of employees venting online is not new. For example, several years ago, Mark Jen a (now former) Google employee began posting his observations about the company in a blog he named Ninetyninezeros. (Coincidentally or not, this title has one less zero than the number of zeros in a googol, the number that inspired Google's name.) About a week after the entries began, they disappeared temporarily, and they reappeared after some editing. Jen noted that Google was "pretty cool about" his blog, but a few days later, word leaked that he was no longer working for Google.

Other bloggers weighed in. Jeremy Zawodny, who works for Yahoo! and said he spoke to Jen, wrote, "He doesn't believe he was doing anything wrong (neither do I based on what he told me)." Robert Scoble, a Microsoft employee, cautioned, "It's not easy writing in public. All it takes is one paragraph to lose credibility, have people laugh at you, get you sued, create a PR firestorm, or get your boss mad at you."

Alexandra Samuel, director of the Social and Interactive Media Centre at the Emily Carr University for Art & Design in Vancouver suggests that the Internet can encourage some people to be "more outrageous, more extroverted, more disclosing and to kind of try to get their five minutes in the sun."

SOURCES: Sarah Boesveld, "Take This Job and Blog It," *National Post*, July 30, 2011, p. A8; Evan Hansen, "Google Blogger Has Left the Building," *ONetNews.com*, February 8, 2005, www.news.com; Neville Hobson, "Google Blogger Firing Highlights Why Guidelines Are Essential," *WebProNews.com*, February 10, 2005, www.webpronews.com; and Todd Wallack, "Beware If Your Blog Is Related to Work," *San Francisco Chronicle*, January 24, 2005, www.sfgate.com.

QUESTIONS

1. Who might be affected by a blog or tweet written about a company? What kinds of work-related information are public? What information does a company have a right to keep private?
2. Imagine that you work in HR and you learn that an employee of your company has tweeted or blogged about work-related topics. What would you do?

---

an organization that has fluctuating demand for its products and services. And when an organization downsizes by laying off temporary and part-time employees, the damage to morale among permanent full-time workers is likely to be less severe.

Flexible Work Schedules

The globalization of the work economy and the development of e-commerce have made the notion of a 40-hour workweek obsolete. As a result, companies need to be staffed 24 hours a day, seven days a week. Employees in manufacturing environments and call centres are being asked to work 12-hour days or to work afternoon or midnight shifts. Similarly, professional employees face long hours and work demands that spill over into their personal lives.

Many organizations are taking steps to provide more flexible work schedules, to protect employees' free time, and to more productively use employees' work time. Workers consider flexible schedules a valuable way to ease the pressures and conflicts of trying to balance work and nonwork activities. Employers are using flexible schedules to recruit and retain employees and to increase satisfaction and productivity. For example, Best Buy created its Results-Only Work Environment (ROWE) to give employees control over how, when, and where they get the job done, as long as they achieve the desired results.[49] The idea of this initiative is to let employees focus on productivity, rather than whether they are physically present in a meeting or seated behind their desk at a particular time of day. In divisions that have tried ROWE, employees say they are more engaged at work, are more committed to the company, and have improved their family relationships at the same time.

How Is This Book Organized?

This chapter has provided an overview of human resource management as well as a summary of challenges and trends impacting Canadian organizations, employees, and HR professionals. In this book, the topics are organized according to the broad areas of human resource management shown in Table 1.5. The numbers in the table refer to the part and chapter numbers.

Along with examples highlighting how HRM helps a company maintain high performance, the chapters offer various other features to help you connect the principles to real-world situations. "HR Best Practices" boxes tell success stories related to the chapter's topics. "HR Oops!" boxes identify situations gone wrong and invite you to find better alternatives. "HR How-To" boxes provide details about how to carry out a practice in each HR areas. "Did You Know?" boxes are snapshots of interesting statistics related to chapter topics. Many chapters also include an "e-HRM" feature identifying ways that human resource professionals are

applying information technology and the Internet to help their organizations excel in the fast-changing world. Finally, the "Thinking Ethically" box at the end of each chapter demonstrates ethical issues in managing human resources.

TABLE 1.5   Topics Covered in This Book

PART 1: THE HUMAN RESOURCE ENVIRONMENT
1. Strategies, Trends, and Challenges in Human Resource Management
2. The Legal Context for HRM and Creating Safe and Healthy Workplaces
PART 2: PREPARING FOR AND ACQUIRING HUMAN RESOURCES
3. Analyzing Work and Designing Jobs
4. Planning for and Recruiting Human Resources
5. Selecting Employees
PART 3: MANAGING TALENT
6. Training and Developing Employees
7. Managing Employees' Performance
PART 4: COMPENSATING AND REWARDING HUMAN RESOURCES
8. Total Rewards
PART 5: MEETING OTHER HR GOALS
9. Labour Relations
10. Managing Human Resources Globally
11. Creating and Sustaining High-Performance Organizations

SUMMARY

LO1 Define human resource management, identify the roles and responsibilities of human resource departments, and explain how human resource management contributes to an organization's performance.

- Human resource management consists of an organization's "people practices"—the policies, practices, and systems that influence employees' behaviour, attitudes, and performance.

- The HRM process begins with analyzing and designing jobs, then recruiting and selecting employees to fill those jobs. Training and development equip employees to carry out their present jobs and follow a career path in the organization. Performance management ensures employees' activities and outputs match the organization's goals.

- Human resource departments also plan and administer the organization's pay and benefits. They carry out activities in support of employee and labour relations, such as communication programs and collective bargaining. Conducting all these activities involves the establishment and administration of human resource policies.

- Management depends on human resource professionals for help in ensuring compliance with legislation, as well as for support for the organization's strategy—for example, workforce planning and change management.

- HRM contributes to organizational performance by influencing who works for the organization and how these people work. These human resources, if well managed, have the potential to be a source of sustainable competitive advantage, contributing to basic objectives such as productivity, profits, and customer satisfaction.

be automated and handled online. A recent study by Towers Watson revealed that companies are significantly increasing investment in HR technologies. And HR outsourcing is becoming more prevalent in Canada. In 2005, only one-third of Canadian employers outsourced any HR administration, but by 2010, 59 percent outsourced all or some HR services. For example, IBM recently announced an eight-year deal with Air Canada to handle a broad range of Air Canada's HR services. Under the deal, IBM will manage Air Canada's HR contact centre, employee data management, employee travel support, recruiting services, benefits administration, leave management, and payroll.

Questions

1. Why might these senior leaders have such varying views of the role and relevance of HR?
2. Should organizations outsource, perhaps even "fire" their HR departments? Why or why not?

SOURCES: Danielle Harder, "Air Canada Outsources HR to IBM," *Canadian HR Reporter*, November 7, 2011, pp. 2 and 6; Paul McDougall, "IBM Lands $80 Million Air Canada HR Deal," *Information Week*, October 7, 2011; Jean-Francois Potvin, "HR Outsourcing is Gaining Ground," *Benefits Canada*, November 23, 2010, www.benefitscanada.com/news/hr-outsourcing-is-gaining-ground-570?print, retrieved January 21, 2012; Jacqueline Nelson, "Should You Fire Your HR Department?" *Canadian Business*, November 3, 2011, www.canadianbusiness.com/print/54587, retrieved January 18, 2012.

CASE STUDY 1.2: SpiderWeb Inc.

SpiderWeb, a telecommunications company founded in 2008, has posted rapid growth in recent months following the launch of a new smartphone based on leading-edge interactive technology.

SpiderWeb has a total workforce of 150 people, most of whom belong to Generation Y. The organization's head office in Montreal is staffed by 50 employees, while a new plant in the Vancouver suburbs employs 100 people in production and distribution. The company is financially sound and plans to double its workforce over the next two years through developing the American and world markets.

SpiderWeb is strongly influenced by the entrepreneurial management style of its two founders. Still active in the organization, they are responsible in particular for the HR function. To support the firm's anticipated growth, they have decided to create a new position of HR director. After a rigorous selection process, you have been hired to fill this position and are to be in charge of HR at SpiderWeb's two locations.

At your first meetings with the executive committee, composed of the founders and four key managers from Montreal and Vancouver (the finance director, R&D director, operations director, and CEO of the Vancouver plant), you realize that they are fairly apprehensive and uninformed about the new HR function and its strategic dimension, which is of some concern to you.

Findings

A few days after joining the company, you hold a number of meetings with managers and employees from both sites. Your initial findings are striking:

- at first glance, the employees generally seem to be motivated and happy to work for SpiderWeb, particularly since the launch of the new smartphone, which everyone is proud of;

- the company has no HR management policy;
- its senior managers are assigned their duties and the management of major projects on an arbitrary basis;
- this is the first management experience for most of the company's managers;
- up to now supply and demand have served as a guideline for compensation, which is inconsistent and inequitable. This practice is not unanimously approved of and is a source of discontent among employees and executives alike.

The Issues

Many managers confided that they would like to see the company move forward and institute a new and equitable compensation policy. The executive committee also informed you that recruitment is the main HR issue. The scarcity of talent in cutting-edge technology and the low level of awareness of the employer brand, given that the company was established only a few years ago, add to the challenges you face.

You also note several issues that are specific to the Vancouver plant. Its CEO, whose responsibilities include HR management, is the brother of one of the founders. However, he lacks the relevant training and experience to fulfill this function. Many of the plant's employees have spoken to you about his lack of organization and management skills. Nonetheless, the two founders would like to see him continue these duties and want you to assist him in his professional development.

After a brief analysis of the key HR indicators, you realize that there are some serious problems at the Vancouver plant:

- turnover is far too high when compared to the industry average;
- there are numerous disability cases;
- absenteeism is high.

As well, you heard employees at the plant's distribution centre discussing a proposal to apply for union certification. You talked this over with the plant manager, who doesn't seem to be worried or interested in the matter.

Chapter 2

THE LEGAL CONTEXT
for HRM and Creating Safe and Healthy Workplaces

Steven Fletcher, Canada's first quadriplegic MP and Cabinet Minister, is creating a legacy of accomplishments.

What Do I Need to Know?

After reading this chapter, you should be able to:

L01 Discuss the importance of valuing diversity and safety.

L02 Describe the legal framework for human resource management in Canada.

L03 Explain the importance of human rights and the implications for HRM.

L04 Discuss privacy, employment/labour standards, and pay equity and their relevance for HRM.

L05 Explain the context for workplace health and safety.

L06 Identify employers' duties and employees' rights and responsibilities related to workforce health and safety.

L07 Discuss ways employers promote worker health and safety.

Steven Fletcher: Member of Parliament

He's breaking barriers. Steven Fletcher is Canada's first quadriplegic MP and Member of Cabinet. In 1996, Steven, a two-time Manitoba kayaking champion, and recent engineering graduate from the University of Manitoba, was driving to work when he collided with a moose and was paralyzed from the neck down. First elected in a very competitive Winnipeg riding in 2004, Steven was re-elected in three subsequent federal elections, most recently in 2011 when he was appointed to a Cabinet Minister post.

One of Fletcher's first impacts was directly on the House of Commons where aisles were too narrow and elevators too small for his motorized wheelchair. Some of the buildings are more than 150 years old and are not as accessible as one might expect. Because Fletcher needs help to perform the day-to-day aspects of his job—for example, turning the pages of a report—an aide is by his side. But Steven is focused on his ability to contribute, "I made the decision to use what I have. What's important is from the neck up."

A variety of necessary arrangements were needed for him do his job as a parliamentarian. These accommodations included not only building adaptations such as lifts and ramps, but also information technology needs such as wireless voice-activated dialling for his phone system and use of a head mouse for his computer. Although the initial focus was on accommodating Steven Fletcher's needs to allow him to do his job, his legacy already includes a long list of accomplishments achieved for others. "Let's lay the foundation so we'll see people in wheelchairs contributing . . . and it's natural," adds Steven.[1]

Introduction

As we saw in Chapter 1, human resource management takes place in the context of the company's goals and society's expectations for how a company should operate. In Canada, the federal, provincial, and territorial governments have set some limits on how an organization can practise human resource management. Among these limits are requirements intended to foster fairness in hiring and employment practices and to protect the health and safety of workers while they are on the job. Questions about a company's performance in these areas can result in employee turnover, human rights complaints, lawsuits, and negative publicity that often cause serious problems for a company's success and survival. Conversely, a company can gain a competitive advantage over its competitors by going beyond just legal compliance to find ways of linking fair and respectful employment and worker safety to business goals such as building a workforce that is highly motivated and attuned to customers.

One point to make at the outset is that managers often want a list of dos and don'ts that will keep them out of legal trouble. Some managers rely on strict rules such as "Don't ever ask a female applicant if she is married," rather than learning the reasons behind those rules. Clearly, certain practices are illegal or at least inadvisable, and this chapter will discuss these areas. However, managers who merely focus on how to avoid breaking the law are not thinking about how to be ethical or how to acquire and engage people in the best way to carry out the company's mission. This chapter introduces ways to think proactively about fairness in employment and workplace safety.

Valuing Diversity

As we mentioned in Chapter 1, Canada is a diverse nation, and becoming more so. In addition, many Canadian companies have customers and operations in more than one country. Managers differ in how they approach the opportunities and challenges related to this diversity. Some define a diverse workforce as a competitive advantage that brings them a wider pool of talent and greater insight into the needs and behaviours of their diverse

LO1 Discuss the importance of valuing diversity and safety.

customers. These organizations have a policy of *valuing diversity*. Canada's Top 100 Employers includes a specific category to recognize employers that provide the most inclusive workplaces—"Canada's Best Diversity Employers." Employers recently recognized includes Boeing Canada Operations Ltd. (Winnipeg), BC Hydro (Vancouver), Saskatchewan Government Insurance (Regina), University of Toronto (Toronto), and TransCanada Corporation (Calgary).[2]

The practice of valuing diversity has no single form; it is not written into law or business theory. One of the concerns about diversity is that "the majority of Canadian organizations rank diversity as a priority, but 42 percent of them have no strategic plan to foster it" according to a report from the Conference Board of Canada.[3]

Organizations that value diversity may also actively work to meet employment equity goals, which will be discussed later in this chapter. Bell Canada speaks to

Canada's Best Diversity Employers

PRESENTED BY BMO Financial Group

Employers are recognized for being Canada's most inclusive workplaces.

FIGURE 2.1

Prohibited Grounds of Discrimination in Employment

PROHIBITED GROUND	FEDERAL	BC	AB	SK	MB	ON	QC	NB	NS	PE	NL	NT	YT	NU
Age	*	*	*	*	*	*	*	*	*	*	*	*	*	*
National or ethnic origin	*	*	*	*	*	*	*	*	*	*	*	*	*	*
Colour	*	*	*	*	*	*	*	*	*	*	*	*	*	*
Religion or religious creed	*	*	*	*	*	*	*	*	*	*	*	*	*	*
Age	*	*	*	*	*	*	*	*	*	*	*	*	*	*
Sex (including pregnancy and childbearing)	*	*	*	*	*	*	*	*	*	*	*	*	*	*
Sexual orientation	*	*	*	*	*	*	*	*	*	*	*	*	*	*
Marital status	*	*	*	*	*	*	*	*	*	*	*	*	*	*
Family status	*	*	*	*	*	*	*		*	*		*	*	*
Physical or mental disability (includes dependence on drugs or alcohol, with the exception of Quebec, NWT, and Yukon)	*	*	*	*	*	*	*	*	*	*	*	*	*	*
Pardoned conviction	*	*				*	*					*		
Ancestry or place of origin		*	*	*	*	*		*				*	*	*
Political belief		*			*		*		*	*	*	*	*	
Source of income (social condition)		*	*	*			*		*	*		*		

SOURCES: From "Prohibited Grounds of Discrimination in Canada," pp. 1–3, Canadian Human Rights Commission, 1998. Reproduced with the permission of the Minister of Public Works and Government Services Canada, 2004, www.chrc-ccdp.ca/discrimination/grounds-en.asp, retrieved December 6, 2004. *Updates*: From www.chrc-ccdp.ca/publications/prohibited_grounds.en.asp, retrieved April 19, 2008; "Mandatory Retirement in Canada," www.hrsdc.gc.ca/en/lp/spila/clli/eslc/19mandatory_retirement.shtml, retrieved April 13, 2008; and "Retiring Mandatory Retirement," February 21, 2008, www.cbc.ca/newsbackground/retirement/mandatory/retirement.html, retrieved April 19, 2009. *Note*: This chart is for quick reference only; for interpretation or further details, contact the appropriate Human Rights Commission.

sex or race may be a **bona fide occupational requirement (BFOR)**, that is, a necessary (not merely preferred) qualification for performing a job. A typical example is a job that includes handing out towels in a locker room. Requiring that employees who perform this job in the women's locker room be female is a BFOR. However, it is very difficult to think of many jobs where criteria such as sex and race are BFORs. In some cases, a core function of the job may be related to a protected ground. For example, a job may require a specified level of visual capability to be performed effectively and safely, thereby eliminating someone who does not meet this requirement. Employers should seek ways to perform the job so that these restrictions are not needed.

bona fide occupational requirement (BFOR)
A necessary (not merely preferred) requirement for performing a job.

It is the employer's responsibility to prove the existence of a BFOR if any complaint of discrimination should arise. In the widely publicized *Meiorin* case from 1999, Tawny Meiorin, a female forest firefighter, lost her job when she failed to meet a required aerobic fitness standard that had been established by the British Columbia Public Service Employee Relations Commission. This standard had been put in place as a minimum requirement for all firefighters. She lost her job after failing *one* aspect of a minimum fitness standard—taking 49.4 seconds too long to complete a 2.5 kilometre run.[9] She filed a complaint stating that the fitness standard discriminated against women because women usually have less aerobic capability than men. Although the

In the context of religion, this principle recognizes that for some individuals, religious observations and practices may present a conflict with work duties, dress codes, or company practices. For example, some religions require head coverings, or to be able to pray at a particular time, or individuals might need time off to observe the Sabbath or other holy days, when the company might have them scheduled to work. When the employee has a legitimate religious belief requiring accommodation, the employee should communicate this need to the employer. Assuming that it would not present an undue hardship, employers are required to accommodate such religious practices. They may have to adjust schedules so that employees do not have to work on days when their religion forbids it, or they may have to alter dress or grooming requirements.

For employees with disabilities, accommodations also vary according to the individuals'

harassment
Any behaviour that demeans, humiliates, or embarrasses a person, and that a reasonable person should have known would be unwelcome.

needs—increasingly, however, the emphasis is placed on *abilities* and capabilities rather than focusing on disabilities. As shown in Figure 2.3, employers may restructure jobs, make facilities in the workplace more accessible, modify equipment, or reassign an employee to a job that the person can perform. In some situations, an individual may provide his or her own accommodation, which the employer permits, as in the case of a blind worker who brings a service dog to work.

WHAT ABOUT HARASSMENT?

Human rights legislation prohibits all forms of **harassment**. Harassment is "any behaviour that demeans, humiliates, or embarrasses a person, and that a reasonable person should have known would be unwelcome."[14]

For example here is Seneca College's Discrimination/Harassment Policy:

> The right to be free from discrimination and/or harassment on the basis of race, ancestry, place of

---

FIGURE 2.3

Examples of Accommodations

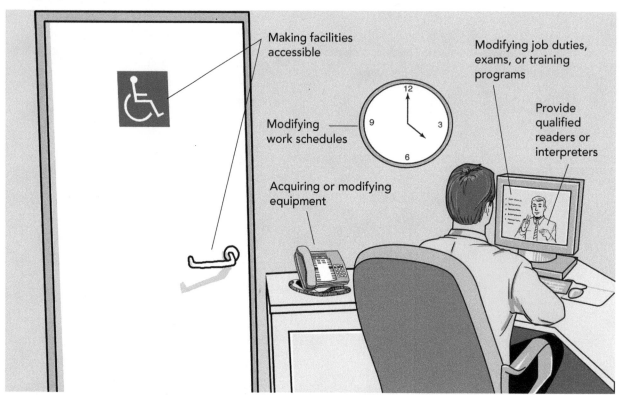

NOTE: Reasonable accommodations do not include hiring an unqualified person, lowering quality standards, or compromising co-workers' safety.

SOURCE: Equal Employment Opportunity Commission, "The ADA: Questions and Answers," www.eeoc.gov/facts/adaqa1.html, retrieved August 28, 2008.

origin, colour, ethnic origin, language or dialect spoken, citizenship, creed, sex, age, marital status, family status, criminal charges or criminal record, mental or physical disability, sexual orientation, political affiliation or union membership. Complaints under this section are dealt with under the College Policy on Discrimination/Harassment.[15]

Sexual harassment refers to unwelcome behaviour that is of a sexual nature or is related to a person's sex. Examples are:

- Question or discussion about a person's sexual life.
- Comments about someone's sexual attractiveness (or unattractiveness).
- Continuing to ask for a date after being refused.
- Writing sexually suggestive notes.
- Telling a woman she should not be performing a particular job.[16]

In general, the most obvious examples of sexual harassment involve *quid pro quo harassment*, meaning that a person makes a benefit (or punishment) contingent on an employee's submitting to (or rejecting) sexual advances. For example, a manager who promises a raise to an employee who will participate in sexual activities is engaging in *quid pro quo* harassment. Likewise, it would be sexual harassment to threaten to reassign someone to a less desirable job if that person refuses sexual favours.

A more subtle, and possibly more pervasive, form of sexual harassment is to create or permit a *hostile work environment*. This occurs when someone's behaviour in the workplace creates an environment in which it is difficult for someone of a particular sex to work. Common complaints in sexual harassment lawsuits include claims that harassers ran their fingers through the plaintiffs' hair, made suggestive remarks, touched intimate body parts, posted pictures with sexual content in the workplace, and used sexually explicit language or told sex-related jokes. In Europe, employers can be liable for creating a hostile work environment if they fail to protect workers from receiving sexually explicit emails such as racy spam messages.[17]

Although a large majority of sexual harassment complaints involve women being harassed by men, sexual harassment can affect anyone. Men have filed complaints that they were harassed by women, and in at least one case a male employee won a lawsuit claiming sexual harassment by his male boss.[18]

To ensure a workplace free from harassment, organizations can follow some important steps. Federally regulated employees are required to develop an anti-harassment policy making it very clear that harassment will not be tolerated in the workplace. Second, all employees need to be made aware of the policy and receive training related to anti-harassment. In addition, the organization can develop a mechanism for reporting harassment in a way that encourages people to speak out. Finally, management can prepare to act promptly to discipline those who engage in harassment, as well as to protect the victims of harassment.

The case of a former British Columbia RCMP officer serves to illustrate the significant consequences of harassment. Ex-Mountie Nancy Sulz was awarded $950,000 by the B.C. Supreme Court for "damages, lost wages, and loss of future earnings" after finding her Staff Sgt. and two subordinate officers caused Sulz "serious psychological harm" related to incidents arising after the birth of a child.[19]

Recently, the definition of harassment has been expanded to include "psychological harassment"—which includes behaviours such as *workplace bullying*. Researchers have recently found that bullying is more destructive than sexual harassment to workers and workplaces. "Bullying is where sexual harassment was 30 years ago," said Janice Rubin, an employment lawyer with Rubin Thomlinson LLP. "Employers are trying to wrap their heads around how to deal with it." Presently only a few provinces have anti-bullying laws that prohibit workplace behaviours such as yelling, rudeness, gossip, or other torments that are forms of psychological harassment.[20] Some new respect-at-work guidelines cite behaviours such as "excessive nitpicking" and "phoning off-duty colleagues at home with work demands" as forms of mistreatment.[21]

Rare is the business owner or manager who wants to wait for the government to identify that his or her organization has failed to meet its legal requirements to treat employees fairly. Instead, out of motives ranging from concern for employee well-being to the desire to avoid costly lawsuits and negative publicity, most companies recognize the importance of complying with these laws and creating respectful workplaces. Often, management depends on the expertise of human resource professionals to help in identifying how to comply. These professionals can help organizations take steps to support these efforts. Figure 2.4 discusses each of the prohibited grounds of discrimination and provides an example of an allegation of discrimination or harassment made in a work-related situation along with the settlement that the complainant received.

sexual harassment
Unwelcome behaviour that is of a sexual nature or is related to a person's sex.

Employment Equity

Canada's employment equity policy was inspired by a report written in 1984 by Justice Rosalie Abella. Employment equity legislation focuses on eliminating employment barriers to the four designated groups who are viewed to have been historically disadvantaged in their employment relationships. The four designated groups are:

- Women
- Members of visible minorities ("persons other than aboriginal peoples, who are non-Caucasian in race or non-white in colour")[22]
- Aboriginal peoples ("persons who are Indians, Inuit, or Metis")[23]
- Persons with disabilities ("persons who have a long-term or recurring physical mental, sensory, psychiatric or learning impairment")[24]

See Table 2.2 for the representation of these four designated workforce groups.

Best practices of exemplary organizations are recognized in the *Employment Equity Act Annual Reports*. Some examples include the Royal Canadian Mint, which accommodates employees with disabilities at its Ottawa and Winnipeg plants by providing portable wireless communications devices to employees with hearing impairments.[25] Operating similarly to a cellphone, this accommodation helps employees with hearing impairments feel safe and comfortable in their workplace. Spectra Energy was also recognized for the partnerships it has developed to increase recruitment of Aboriginal peoples. Northern Opportunities is a partnership of schools and colleges in northeastern British Columbia, Aboriginal communities, and businesses that "attempts to provide a seamless learning pathway from secondary school to postsecondary trades/technology training and careers." Spectra Energy has invested $1.88

Personal Information Protection and Electronic Documents Act (PIPEDA)
Federal law that sets out ground rules for how private sector organizations may collect, use, or disclose personal information.

million into the program, which will bring returns in the ability to attract potential employees that are already trained to the organization's needs.[26]

Protection of Privacy

All of the jurisdictions—provinces, territories, and federal, have privacy laws that regulate how personal information is handled, for example, personal health information and personal financial information. The following section will discuss privacy requirements that connect most directly to the employer–employee relationship.

L04 Discuss privacy, employment/labour standards, and pay equity and their relevance for HRM.

PERSONAL INFORMATION PROTECTION AND ELECTRONIC DOCUMENTS ACT (PIPEDA)

The **Personal Information Protection and Electronic Documents Act (PIPEDA)** is a federal law that "sets out ground rules for how private sector organizations may collect, use, or disclose personal information in the course of commercial activities. This law also gives individuals the right to access and request correction of the personal information these organizations may have collected about them."[27]

The Act's ten principles establish national standards for privacy practices and have implications for human resource departments and their responsibilities to safeguard employee privacy. Decisions made by the federal Privacy Commissioner have confirmed that although employers can collect information on employees about performance, attendance, and potential for advancement there is little an employer can keep from an employee.

For example, an employee of Human Resources and Skills Development Canada demanded to see all the information obtained about her during an assessment review. The employee wanted to see the notes made by the contractor hired to conduct the assessment. These notes contained feedback and comments from other employees. The federal Privacy Commissioner ruled the employee was entitled to this information and that employees cannot be promised confidentiality when they make statements about another person.[28]

Alberta and British Columbia have privacy laws recognized as "substantially similar" to PIPEDA. In these provinces the relevant Personal Information Privacy Act (PIPA), e.g., PIPA Alberta and PIPA BC applies. The "HR How-To" box discusses some of

TABLE 2.2	Representation of Full-time Employees Reporting under the Federal Employment Equity Act

WOMEN	PERSONS WITH DISABILITIES
42.7%	3.2%
VISIBLE MINORITIES	**ABORIGINAL PEOPLES**
16.3%	2.5%

SOURCE: *Annual Report Employment Equity Act*, 2009, www.hrsdc .gc.ca/en, retrieved March 23, 2012. Reproduced with the permission of the Minister of Public Works and Government Services, 2012.

Scotiabank, KPMG, and CN all recently faced class-action lawsuits on behalf of employees over allegations of unpaid overtime. At one point, Canadian Imperial Bank of Commerce faced a potential $600 million lawsuit involving as many as 10,000 current and former CIBC employees from across Canada. The suit alleged that front-line employees such as tellers, account executives, and commercial and personal bankers were given workloads too heavy to be handled in regular working hours. The lead plaintiff in the CIBC case, Dara Fresco, claimed to have been denied approximately $50,000 in unpaid overtime over ten years of employment. "What is unfair is that my colleagues and I are rarely being paid for the overtime that we are working, and that's just not right," said Fresco. The CIBC suit claimed that CIBC failed to pay for overtime work that was required or at least permitted, which is in contravention to the Canada Labour Code. CIBC maintained it has a "clearly defined" overtime policy that "exceeds legislative requirements"—ultimately, the class-action lawsuit bid was dismissed by an Ontario judge.[29]

A variety of important changes to employment/labour standards laws have been made in several jurisdictions. In British Columbia, the Employment Standards Act was amended in order to introduce compassionate care benefits and the federal Employment Insurance Act has expanded the list of persons for whom an employee can claim compassionate care benefits. Minimum wages have increased in several provinces, federal legislation was enacted to provide workers quick payment of unpaid wages in cases of bankruptcy or receivership, and Ontario has amended its Employment Standards Act to provide living organ donors with job-protected leave to help offset financial hardships.[30]

Pay Equity

Pay equity legislation requires that employers are responsible to provide equal pay for work of equal value. **Pay equity** is a principle of nondiscrimination in wages that requires men and women doing work of equal value to the employer to be paid the same. In addition to the federal model, several provinces, as well as Australia, Scandinavian countries, and many U.S. states, have laws to ensure women and men working in female-dominated jobs, for example, nursing, clerical, and retail sales, are paid fairly. The four criteria usually applied are *skill*, *effort*, *responsibility*, and *working conditions*. Chapter 8 includes a discussion of job evaluation, which

pay equity
Equal pay for work of equal value.

applies these criteria to measure the relative value of jobs in the effort to ensure that jobs are paid fairly relative to one another within an organization.

Pay equity legislation is intended to address the *wage gap*—the difference between the earnings of women working full-time versus the earnings of men working full-time. "In Canada, women working full-time still make an average of only 72 cents for every dollar earned by men, and this wage gap has narrowed by just 8 percent since the late 1960s."[31] The irony is that men and women tend to begin their career on an approximately equal footing; however, women fall behind later—often after time away from paid employment to have children. As a result men end up with more experience. Also, men tend to work longer hours, have more education, and are less likely than women to work part-time.[32] Cumulatively, however, these factors do not explain the entire wage gap or earnings gap between men and women. Statistics Canada reported the results of a study of 29 universities related to the salaries of male and female professors. The study revealed that "male university professors earned on average up to $17,300 more than female colleagues."[33] According to the Canadian Association of University Teachers (CAUT), one reason for the wage gap is that women are underrepresented in the highest-paying position of full professor.[34]

The pay equity system has been criticized for the overall lack of progress, and the federal government has completed an extensive pay equity review process expected to result in a more proactive model.[35]

How Are the Laws Enforced?

HUMAN RIGHTS COMMISSIONS

At minimum, employers must comply with the legal requirements of their jurisdictions. To provide oversight and enforce these laws, the federal government, provinces and territories have Human Rights Commissions. For example, the *Canadian Human Rights Commission (CHRC)* provides individuals under federal jurisdiction a means to resolve complaints of discrimination. The CHRC has the power to receive and address allegations of discrimination or harassment complaints based on the 11 prohibited grounds outlined in the Canadian Human Rights Act. The CHRC tries to resolve complaints using mediation and conciliation; however, some complaints only get resolved by using a tribunal. Cases may also be ultimately appealed all the way to the Supreme Court of Canada for final resolution. Recent efforts have also been directed toward early

> *All workers have a right to return home each day safe and sound.*

dispute resolution in order to save time, money, and stress associated with the complaint process.

The Canadian Human Rights Commission is also responsible for auditing federally regulated employers to ensure compliance with the federal Employment Equity Act. In addition, the CHRC enforces pay equity requirements.[36] For example a typical outcome of this enforcement is to provide equal pay increases for jobs that are determined to have similar value to their organizations, e.g., nurses and paramedics or kitchen workers and janitors.

PRIVACY COMMISSIONERS

The Privacy Commissioner of Canada is responsible for ensuring compliance with federal privacy legislation including the Personal Information Protection and Electronic Documents Act. The Privacy Commissioner of Canada has the power to investigate complaints and recommend solutions to employers. To ensure compliance, the Commissioner can publicly identify organizations violating individuals' privacy rights and take the complaint to the Federal Court of Canada. If unable to resolve the complaint, the Court can order the organization to take specific actions and can also award damages.[37] Alberta and British Columbia also have Privacy Commissioners responsible for ensuring compliance with their respective relevant provincial legislation.

One area of interest and concern for both individuals and organizations is the growing use of social media and specifically the growing practice of HR professionals conducting social media background checks on both current and prospective employees. The Office of the Information Privacy Commissioner of Alberta recently published "Guidelines for Social Media Background Checks" (see Table 2.3).

Workplace Health and Safety

7

At the beginning of this chapter we briefly introduced the importance of taking a strategic approach to health and safety. The protection of employee health and safety is regulated by the government. Occupational health and safety legislation is in place for all jurisdictions; however, the effective management of health and safety in the workplace includes more than legal compliance. Increasingly, organizations

L05 Explain the context for workplace health and safety.

are approaching occupational health and safety with a values-based commitment to safe operations as a way to protect people: "All workers have the right to return home each day safe and sound."[38] See the "Did You Know?" box.

TABLE 2.3	Guidelines for Social Media Background Checks

1. Determine what the business purpose is for performing a social media background check. Do you reasonably require personal information that cannot be obtained through traditional means such as interviews or reference checks?

2. Recognize that any information that is collected about an individual is personal information or personal employee information and is subject to privacy laws.

3. Consider the risks of using social media to perform a background check. Conduct a privacy impact assessment to assess the risks.

SOURCE: www.oipc.ab.ca/downloads/documentloader.ashx?id=2933, retrieved March 23, 2012.

versus existing danger. This expanded definition was put into practice in the precedent-setting *Verville v. Canada (Correctional Services)* case where maximum security prison guards at the Kent Penitentiary in British Columbia performed a work refusal when guards were prohibited from carrying handcuffs. Although Correctional Services Canada said availability of handcuffs at control posts was adequate, the judge ruled that employees can refuse work if there is a reasonable possibility of danger.[47]

Employees may file a complaint and request an inspection of the workplace, and their employers cannot retaliate against them for complaining. Employees also have a right to receive information about any hazardous products they handle in the course of their jobs.

The Workplace Hazardous Materials Information System or WHMIS is related to the worker's "right to know." "WHMIS is Canada's national hazard communication program consisting of symbols and warning labels for consumers and material-specific safety data sheets that guide the handling of dangerous substances in the workplace, as well as related worker education and training."[48] WHMIS is implemented through coordinated federal, provincial, and territorial laws to ensure that hazardous products are properly labelled, used, stored, handled, and disposed of safely.

Organizations must have **material safety data sheets (MSDSs)** for hazardous products that employees are exposed to. An MSDS form details the hazards associated with a chemical; the chemical's producer

> **material safety data sheets (MSDSs)**
> Detailed hazard information concerning a controlled (hazardous) product.

or importer is responsible for identifying these hazards and detailing them on the form. Employers must also ensure that all containers of hazardous chemicals are labelled with information about the hazards, and they must train employees in safe handling of the chemicals. Canada is currently working with other countries to harmonize the existing hazard communication systems on chemicals. "It made sense that as international trade in chemical products grows that we should have a standardized system. Canada, the United States, Japan, the European Union (EU), and some other countries had all developed their own systems.[49] Globally Harmonized System of Classification and Labelling of Chemicals System (GHS) is now ready for worldwide implementation.[50]

IMPACT OF OCCUPATIONAL HEALTH AND SAFETY LEGISLATION

Legislation has unquestionably succeeded in raising the level of awareness of occupational safety. However, as depicted in Figure 2.6, the number of Canadians killed on the job has increased in recent years despite a significant reduction in time-loss injuries (Figure 2.7). For example, in Ontario, the number of fatalities has increased from 225 in 1996 to 385 in 2010—an increase of more than 70 percent.[51]

Many workplace accidents are a product of unsafe behaviours, not unsafe working conditions. Because legislation does not directly regulate employee behaviour, little behaviour change can be expected unless employees are convinced of the standards' importance.[52] This principle has been recognized by labour leaders. For example, Lynn Williams, former president of the United Steelworkers, has noted, "We can't count on government. We can't count on employers. We must rely on ourselves to bring about the safety and health of our workers."[53]

Because conforming to the law alone does not necessarily guarantee their employees will be safe, many employers go beyond the letter of the law. In the next section we examine various kinds of employer-initiated safety awareness programs that comply with, and in some cases exceed, legal requirements.

WHMIS Classes and Hazard Symbols

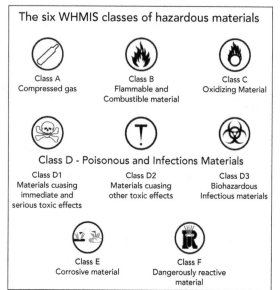

The six WHMIS classes of hazardous materials

Class A
Compressed gas

Class B
Flammable and Combustible material

Class C
Oxidizing Material

Class D - Poisonous and Infections Materials

Class D1
Materials cuasing immediate and serious toxic effects

Class D2
Materials cuasing other toxic effects

Class D3
Biohazardous Infectious materials

Class E
Corrosive material

Class F
Dangerously reactive material

SOURCE: The Hazard Symbols of WHMIS. Health Canada, 2005. Reprinted with the permission of the Minister of Health, 2012.

Employer-Sponsored Health and Safety Programs

Many employers establish safety awareness programs to go beyond mere compliance with occupational health and safety

L07 Discuss ways employers promote worker health and safety.

HR BEST PRACTICES

Suncor Energy Receives CAPP Awards for Health and Safety Performance

Suncor is one of Canada's most integrated energy companies, producing more than 300,000 barrels of oil per day from its oil sands operations; developing and producing natural gas and traditional crude; operating an ethanol plant in Ontario and refineries in Ontario, Alberta, and Colorado; retail operations through its Petro-Canada branded outlets; and wind power projects in Saskatchewan, Alberta, and Ontario.

Suncor's "Journey to Zero" initiative received the President's Award in the Stewards of Excellence Awards of the Canadian Association of Petroleum Producers (CAPP) a few years ago. "Journey to Zero" embeds a safety culture into every aspect of the business. The aim was to achieve a level of safety excellence that results in an injury-free work site. Suncor wants all work processes and systems to be safe, and the company demands employees and contractors

take individual responsibility for safety. "Thanks to tremendous effort by our employees and contractors, safety is becoming integrated into the way we do business," said Steve Williams, Suncor's chief operating officer. "This unwavering commitment to safety is essential for a busy, growing company like Suncor and we remain focused on achieving our vision of a workplace free of occupational injuries and illnesses."

Suncor's "Leading by Metrics" takes this culture of safety a step further by altering the focus to measurement of proactive efforts implemented by front-line employees that prevent injuries from occurring in the first place. Safety metrics like recordable incident frequency, lost-time injury, and severity rates are all *lagging* metrics, revealing "how little they failed" over a particular time period. In 2012, Suncor received the CAPP Health and Safety Performance

Reward for its "Leading by Metrics" initiative. "Leading My Metrics" includes the Leading Indicator Safety Index (LISI), which measures completion of proactive safety efforts in relation to hours worked and the Leadership Safety Contacts Ratio (LSC®), which provides a reference on the support and visibility that Suncor management provided to field operations during the completion of these safety efforts.

SOURCES: CAPP Canadian Association of Petroleum Producers Awards (2012), www.capp.ca/rce/awards/2012/Pages/health-safety-performance-award.aspx, retrieved March 25, 2012; "Suncor Energy Inc. 2011 Annual Report," www.suncor.com/pdf/Suncor_annual_report_2011_en.pdf, retrieved March 26, 2012; "CAPP Stewardship Awards," *BNET*, http://findarticles.com/p/articles/mi_qa5406/is_200705/ai_n21290245, retrieved May 28, 2008; and "Journey to Zero" and "Suncor Energy Safety Initiative Receives CAPP President's Award," www.suncor.com/default.aspx?ID = 2569, retrieved May 28, 2008.

Another means of isolating unsafe job elements is to study past accidents. The **technique of operations review (TOR)** is an analysis method for determining which specific element of a job led to a past accident.[55] The first step in a TOR analysis is to establish the facts surrounding the incident. To accomplish this, all members of the work group involved in the accident give their initial impressions of what happened. The group must then, through discussion, come to an agreement on the single, systematic failure that most likely contributed to the incident, as well as two or three major secondary factors that contributed to it.

An analysis of jobs at Burger King, for example, revealed that certain jobs required employees to walk across wet or slippery surfaces, which led to many falls. Specific corrective action was taken on the basis of analysis of where people were falling

> **technique of operations review (TOR)**
>
> Method of promoting safety by determining which specific element of a job led to a past accident.

and what conditions led to those falls. Now Burger King provides mats at critical locations and has generally upgraded its floor maintenance. The company also makes slip-resistant shoes available to employees in certain job categories.[56]

To communicate with employees about job hazards, managers should talk directly with their employees about safety. Posters, especially if placed near the hazard, serve as a constant reminder, reinforcing other messages.

In communicating risk, managers should recognize that different groups of individuals may constitute different audiences. Research reported by Human Resources and Skills Development Canada indicates that younger workers (15–24 years) have a higher incidence of time-loss injuries than any other age group. In Ontario alone, "almost two young workers are injured every hour of every day and night, seven days a week, and

So you think hearing protection is boring...

think again.

think safety   WORK SAFE BC   HearSafe

WORKING TO MAKE A DIFFERENCE
worksafebc.com

If you have questions about workplace safety, call WorkSafeBC's Call Centre at 604 276-3100, or toll-free in B.C. at 1 888 621-SAFE (7233).

> *WorkSafeBC produces a variety of posters and other resources to communicate job hazards and promote working safely.*

it's often because of what they didn't know."[57] The employer's primary concern with respect to younger workers is to inform them. Training should include specific information about safe procedures, first aid, and any protective equipment related to the job.

A recent study showed a high correlation between shift work in nurses and the risk of developing Type 2 diabetes. Shift workers are also considered at greater risk for obesity. "The relationship now between shift work and Type 2 diabetes is much clearer, the evidence is much stronger and therefore, we need to start looking at ways to intervene and the workplace is an obvious place for that to start," said Jocalyn Clark, a Toronto-based senior editor at PloS Medicine.[58]

Experienced employees sometimes need retraining to jar them from complacency about the real dangers associated with their work.[59] This is especially the case if the hazard in question poses a greater threat to older employees. For example, accidents that involve falling off a ladder are a greater threat to older workers than to younger ones. Over 20 percent of such falls lead to a fatality for workers in the 55-to-65 age group, versus 10 percent for all other workers.[60]

REINFORCING SAFE PRACTICES

To ensure safe behaviours, employers should not only define how to work safely but also reinforce the desired behaviour. One common technique for reinforcing safe practices is implementing a *safety incentive program* to reward workers for their support of and commitment to safety goals. Such programs start by focusing on monthly or quarterly goals or by encouraging suggestions for improving safety. Goals might include good housekeeping practices, adherence to safety rules, and proper use of protective equipment. Later, the program expands to include

more wide-ranging, long-term goals. Typically, the employer distributes awards in highly public forums, such as company or department meetings. Using merchandise for prizes, instead of cash, provides a lasting symbol of achievement. A good deal of evidence suggests that such incentive programs are effective in reducing the number and cost of injuries.[61]

Besides focusing on specific jobs, organizations can target particular types of injuries or disabilities, especially those for which employees may be at risk. For example, the National Society to Prevent Blindness estimates that 1,000 eye injuries occur every day in occupational settings.[62] Organizations can prevent such injuries through a combination of job analysis, written policies, safety training, protective eyewear, rewards and sanctions for safe and unsafe behaviour, and management support for the safety effort. Industries and occupational groups also provide overall organizational safety awards. DRG Resources Corporation, a national resource company, was the recipient of the BC and Yukon Chamber of Mines' Exploration and Safety Award. In a one-year time period DRG had no lost-day accidents in 24,800 hours of copper and gold exploration work.[63]

EMPLOYEE WELLNESS PROGRAMS

Another way to improve the well-being and overall health of employees is to offer an **employee wellness program**, a set of communications, activities, and facilities designed to change health-related behaviours in ways that reduce health risks. Typically, wellness programs aim at specific health risks, such as high blood pressure, high cholesterol levels, smoking, and obesity, by encouraging preventive measures such as exercise and good nutrition. However, many organizations are adopting an integrated strategic approach to wellness that promotes

> **employee wellness program**
> A set of communications, activities, and facilities designed to change health-related behaviours in ways that reduce health risks.

needed to be defined from the bottom of the organization up.[70]

Another challenge in promoting safety internationally is that laws, enforcement practices, and political climates vary from country to country. With the increasing use of offshoring, described in Chapter 1, more companies have operations in countries where safety requirements are far less strict than Canadian standards. Managers and employees in these countries may not think the company is serious about protecting workers' health and safety. In that case, strong communication and oversight will be necessary if the company intends to adhere to the ethical principle of valuing its foreign workers' safety as much as the safety of its Canadian workers.

SUMMARY

L01 Discuss the importance of valuing diversity and safety.

- Although the practice of valuing diversity has no single form, organizations that value diversity are likely to be mindful of the benefits of diversity and work actively to create a work environment in which individuals feel valued and able to perform to their potential.

- Increasingly, organizations are taking a strategic approach to occupational health and safety by adopting a values-based commitment to safe operations.

L02 Describe the legal framework for human resource management in Canada.

- Approximately 90 percent of Canadian employees are covered by provincial and territorial legislation. The remaining 10 percent are covered by federal legislation.

- Although jurisdictional differences exist, laws tend to mirror one another.

L03 Explain the importance of human rights and the implications for HRM.

- Employers can avoid discrimination by avoiding differential treatment of job applicants and employees. Organizations can develop and enforce practices and policies that demonstrate a high value placed on diversity.

- To provide accommodation, companies should recognize individuals' needs. Employers may need to make such accommodations as adjusting schedules or dress codes, making the workplace more accessible, or restructuring jobs.

- Organizations can prevent harassment by developing policies, training employees to recognize and avoid this behaviour, and providing the means for employees to be protected.

- Employment equity initiatives may remove employment barriers to the designated groups.

L04 Discuss privacy, employment/labour standards, and pay equity and their relevance to HRM.

- The Personal Information Protection and Electronic Documents Act (PIPEDA) provides rules about how organizations can collect, use, and disclose information about you.

- Employment/labour standards legislation deals with the minimum standards an employee will receive.

- Pay equity provisions help assure equal pay for work of equal value.

- Human Rights Commissions are responsible for enforcing human rights legislation in their respective jurisdictions. Privacy Commissioners are responsible for enforcing privacy legislation in their jurisdictions.

L05 Explain the context for workplace health and safety

- All jurisdictions in Canada have occupational health and safety legislation. Canada's approach to safety in the workplace is based on the internal responsibility system whereby both employers and employees are responsible for safety.

L06 Identify employers' duties and employees' rights and responsibilities related to workforce health and safety.

- Employers and supervisors have a duty to provide a safe workplace.

- Canada's workers have three fundamental rights that are protected by occupational health and safety legislation.

- Bill C-45, an amendment to the Criminal Code, has created a legal duty on employers to ensure the safety of workers. Employees also have responsibilities including following safety rules and reporting hazardous conditions.

L07 Discuss ways employers promote worker health and safety.

- Besides complying with occupational health and safety regulations, employers often establish safety awareness programs designed to instil an emphasis on safety.

CATSA defended its strict policy regarding uniforms on the grounds that maintaining a professional image in airport security was very important.

Questions

1. By offering Muse a choice of slacks or a knee-length skirt do you feel CATSA provided a reasonable accommodation to this employee? Justify your answer.
2. Because Muse agreed to wear slacks for several years before telling her employer about her concerns should there be any reduced duty on her employer or CATSA to accommodate? Explain.

3. If you had been Muse's supervisor, how would you have handled her request? Is there anything you would have done differently?

SOURCES: Jeffrey R. Smith, "Airport Screener Suspended for Wearing Long Skirt," *Canadian HR Reporter,* December 17, 2007, pp. 1, 11; "Suspended Muslim Airport Screener Offered New Job," *The Globe and Mail,* November 22, 2007, p. A17; and John Goddard, "Guard to Get Back Pay Pending Uniform Review: Airport Screener Will Do Alternative Work During Uniform Assessment," *Toronto Star,* November 21, 2007, p. A14.

CASE STUDY 2.2:   Second Quebec Employer Found Guilty of Criminal Negligence Causing Death

A second employer has been convicted of criminal negligence under the amendments to the Criminal Code brought in by Bill C-45. Pasquale Scrocca, a landscape contractor, admitted that he did not check the brake fluid on a backhoe and had not had the equipment checked by a certified mechanic. Scrocca was operating the backhoe when it failed to brake and pinned one of his employees, Ariello Boccanfuso, to a wall, causing his death. After the incident, a mechanical inspection determined the backhoe had "no braking capacity in the front two wheels, no reservoir, and a total braking capacity of less than 30 percent." Despite Scrocca's argument that he was not aware of the braking issue, the court applied a "conditional sentence of two years imprisonment, less a day" with the sentence to be served in the community.

The first conviction under Bill C-45 was also handed down in Quebec when a Quebec court in 2008 ordered a company convicted of criminal negligence in the death of a worker to pay $110,000. Transpavé, a paving-stone manufacturer in Saint-Eustache, Quebec, pleaded guilty to criminal negligence in the 2005 death of 23-year-old Steve L'Écuyer. L'Écuyer had been crushed by a machine that stacks concrete blocks after pallets with concrete had backed up on the conveyer belt. Inspectors found the machine's safety guard had been disabled for nearly two years.

In his ruling, the judge said the company, managers, and employees weren't aware that the safety guard wasn't working and that there was no intent on the company's part for the system to be down. He also stated the fine reflected the company's willingness to take responsibility for the incident and the $500,000 in safety upgrades the company has made since the accident to bring the plant in line with European standards, which are more stringent than North American standards.

Criminal proceedings are underway and preliminary hearings are scheduled for dates in 2012, against Metron, the company supervisor, and scaffold supplier as a result of a horrific workplace accident resulting in the death of four workers and another sustaining critical injuries when scaffolding collapsed during balcony repairs at a Toronto apartment on December 24, 2009.

Questions

1. How would you rate these employers' commitment to safety? Explain your answer.
2. Do you think company managers should be held accountable for a workplace fatality? Why or why not?
3. Do you think the criminal convictions and pending criminal proceedings described in the case will have any effect on improving the safety of workplaces in Canada? Why or why not?

SOURCES: Norm Keith and Anna Abbott, "Criminal Conviction in Death of Worker," *Canadian HR Reporter,* October 10, 2011, p. 25; "Safety Update: Employer Convicted of Bill C-45 Charge Following Trial," www.ecompliance.com/about-us/safety-updates/2011/10/13/safety-update-employer-convicted-of-bill-c-45-charge-following-trial, retrieved March 24, 2012; Chris Doucette, "4 Workers Killed in Scaffolding Collapse," *The Toronto Sun,* December 25, 2009, www.torontosun.com/news/torontoandgta/2009/12/25/12266386.html, retrieved March 24, 2012; and "Quebec Company Fined $110,000 in Worker's Death," *Canadian HR Reporter,* March 18, 2008.

Practise and learn online with Connect.

ANALYZING WORK
and Designing Jobs

▼ Recent Job Postings

- Lead - Asset Integrity Engineer - Horizon Oil Sands
- Project Manager - Major Projects
- Manager, Nunavut Field Operations - Government of Nunavut
- Director, Petroleum Products - Government of Nunavut
- Bulk Fuel Service Technician

More Jobs

Create an account to keep up to date with job posting notifications.

Job Seeker Login

▼ Featured Employers

- Petroleum Human Resources Council of Canada
- IROC Energy Services
- Canadian Natural
- Hallmark Tubulars Ltd.
- National Oilwell Varco
- Patterson-UTI Drilling Canada Limited
- SAIT Polytechnic
- Cenovus Energy Inc.
- MMR Canada Ltd.
- Tervita Corporation
- SUMMIT LIABILITY SOLUTIONS INC.

Employer Login

Employer Spotlight

Do you remember when you saw possibility in everything?

We still do.

Working in Oil & Gas

Home > Working in Oil & Gas > A Day in the Life

A Day In the Life

Have you ever wondered what it would be like to have a career in oil and gas? Get the whole story from the people in the field, as they tell you about their typical days on the job.

Day in the Life: Craig - Bed Truck Operator

Craig Copeland drives a truck equipped with a winch, loads and unloads equipment and does "spotting" or positioning equipment at the rig site.

Day in the Life: Elaine - Chief Geophysicist

Elaine never imagined working in the oil and gas industry growing up in her home town of Mississauga, Ontario. Upon entering university, she became aware of the exciting world of geophysics, and has never looked back.

Day in the Life: Niclas - Derrickhand

At 25, Nic already has a dream life of travel, good times and a great salary which he credits to hard work in the petroleum industry. Currently, Nic works in the drilling sector as a derrickhand working his way up to become assistant driller for Nabors Drilling International.

Day in the Life: Lance - District Landman

Nine years later and still going strong, Lance worked his way up into his current role as a district landman. The job suits him perfectly, and has close ties to the rural farmers and landowners he frequently works with.

Day in the Life: Rick - District Operations Manager

Rick White worked his way up through the ranks. Now he makes sure that "the crews are at the right place at the right time and that they get the job done."

Day in the Life: Tim - Field Operator

Tim spent 15 years in agricultural retail before applying, and was really surprised at the variety of backgrounds people came from. There is also a lot of responsibility given to individuals who are looking for a challenging career.

Prev Next 1 2 3 4

> *The Petroleum Human Resources Council of Canada's website provides jobseekers with glimpses of a diverse array of jobs in the oil and gas industry.*

{ ## What Do I Need to Know?

After reading this chapter, you should be able to:

LO1 ▶ Summarize the elements of work flow analysis.

LO2 ▶ Describe how work flow is related to an organization's structure.

LO3 ▶ Discuss the significance and outcomes of job analysis.

LO4 ▶ Tell how to obtain information for a job analysis.

LO5 ▶ Summarize recent trends in job analysis.

LO6 ▶ Describe methods for designing a job so that it can be done efficiently.

LO7 ▶ Identify approaches to designing a job to make it motivating.

LO8 ▶ Explain how organizations apply ergonomics to design safe jobs.

LO9 ▶ Discuss how organizations can plan for the mental demands of a job.

What Is Work Flow Analysis?

Before designing its work flow, the organization's planners need to analyze what work needs to be done. Figure 3.1 shows the elements of a work flow analysis. For each type of work, such as producing a product line or providing a support service (accounting, legal support, and so on), the analysis identifies the output of the process, the activities involved, and three categories of inputs: raw inputs (materials and information), equipment, and human resources.

L01 Summarize the elements of work flow analysis.

Outputs are the products of any work unit, whether a department, team, or individual. An output can be as readily identifiable as a completed purchase order, an employment test, or a hot, juicy hamburger. An output can also be a service, such as transportation, cleaning, or answering questions about employee benefits. Even at an organization that produces tangible goods, such as computers, many employees produce other outputs, such as components of the computers, marketing plans, and building security. Work flow analysis identifies the outputs of particular work units. The analysis considers not only the amount of output but also quality standards. This attention to outputs has only recently gained attention among HR professionals. However, it gives a clearer view of how to increase the effectiveness of each work unit.

For the outputs identified, work flow analysis then examines the work processes used to generate those outputs. Work processes are the activities that members of a work unit engage in to produce a given output. Every process consists of operating procedures that specify how things should be done at each stage of developing the output. These procedures include all the tasks that must be performed in producing the output. Usually, the analysis breaks down the tasks into those performed by each person in the work unit. This analysis helps with design of efficient work systems by clarifying which tasks are necessary. Typically, when a unit's work load increases, the unit adds people, and when the work load decreases, some members of the unit may busy themselves with unrelated tasks in an effort to appear busy. Without knowledge of work processes, it is more difficult to identify whether the work unit is properly staffed. Knowledge of work processes also can guide staffing changes when work is automated or outsourced. At Unifi, a textile producer, shop floor data is transmitted in real time to analysts at the company's headquarters. Unifi no longer requires supervisors

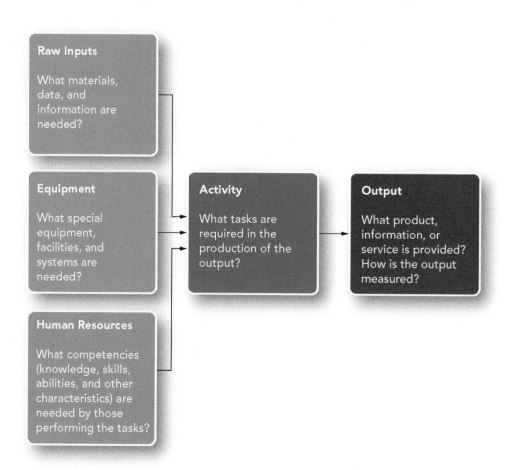

FIGURE 3.1

Developing a Work-Unit Activity Analysis

to carry out the tasks of monitoring and reporting on production.[2] The final stage in work flow analysis is to identify the inputs used in the development of the work unit's product. As shown in Figure 3.1, these inputs can be broken down into the raw inputs (materials and knowledge), equipment, and human skills needed to perform the tasks.

HOW DOES THE WORK FIT WITH THE ORGANIZATION'S STRUCTURE?

Besides looking at the work flow of each process, it is important to see how the work fits within the context of the organization's structure. Within an organization, units and individuals must cooperate to create outputs. Ideally, the organization's structure brings together the people who must collaborate in order to efficiently produce the desired outputs. The structure may do this in a way that is highly centralized (i.e., with authority concentrated in a few people at the top of the organization) or decentralized (with authority spread among many people). The organization may group jobs according to functions (e.g., welding, painting, packaging), or it may set up divisions to focus on products or customer groups.

Although there are an infinite number of ways to combine the elements of an organization's structure,

> **LO2** Describe how work flow is related to an organization's structure.

we can make some general observations about structure and work design. If the structure is strongly based on function, workers tend to have low authority and to work alone at highly specialized jobs. Jobs that involve teamwork or broad responsibility tend to require a structure based on divisions other than functions. When the goal is to empower employees, companies therefore need to set up structures and jobs that enable broad responsibility, such as jobs that involve employees in serving a particular group of customers or producing a particular product, rather than performing a narrowly defined function. The organization's structure also affects managers' jobs. Managing a division responsible for a product or customer group tends to require more experience and cognitive (thinking) ability than managing a department that handles a specific function.[3]

Work design often emphasizes the analysis and design of jobs, as described in the remainder of this chapter. Although all of these approaches can succeed, each focuses on one isolated job at a time. These approaches do not necessarily consider how that single job fits into the overall work flow or structure of the organization. To use these techniques effectively, human resource professionals should also understand their organization as a whole. As the "HR Oops!" emphasizes, without this big-picture appreciation, they might redesign a job in a way that makes sense for the particular job but is out of line with the organization's work flow, structure, or strategy.

HR Oops! { An Undefined Job

One way to see the significance of work design and job analysis is to learn from what happens at companies that fail to define jobs. An anonymous employee of a multimedia company told *Entrepreneur* magazine's Scott Gornall about an editor who was given a new job title, "creative manager of content." Unfortunately, the scope of that job was never specified or explained to others in the company.

The new creative manager appointed himself to teach the others how to be more creative. He placed some magazines in a

cubicle and called a meeting to announce that, henceforth, that space was the Idea Lab, where employees could go to reflect on ideas. He drew up a flow chart to explain the Idea Lab. He called monthly meetings for idea sharing. His colleagues, unimpressed, felt that he was disturbing their work in order to justify his new responsibilities, whatever they were.

Perhaps in principle, a creative manager of content would have met a real need for this publisher, but because the position and its fit with the organization's objectives were

never clearly spelled out, the idea was wasted.

SOURCE: Based on Scott Gornall, "The Superfluous Position," *Entrepreneur*, July 2009, www.entrepreneur.com.

QUESTIONS

1. Why might management be reluctant to prepare a formal job description for a position like "creative manager of content"? What are the pitfalls of not doing so?

2. What advice about the position would you give to this company's managers?

HR HOW-TO

Writing a Job Description

Preparing a job description begins with gathering information from sources who can identify the details of performing a task—for example, persons already performing the job and, the supervisor, or team leader, or, if the job is new, managers who are creating the new position. Other sources of information may include the company's human resource files, such as past job advertisements and job descriptions, as well as general sources of information about similar jobs, such as Human Resources and Skills Development Canada's National Occupational Classification (NOC) system.

Based on the information gathered, the next step is to identify which activities are essential duties of the job. These include mental and physical tasks, as well as any particular methods and equipment to be used in carrying out those tasks. When possible, these should be stated in terms that are broad and goal oriented enough for the person in the position to innovate and improve. For example, "Developing and implementing a system for ordering supplies efficiently" implies a goal (efficiency) as well as a task.

From these sources, the writer of the description obtains the important elements of the description:

- *Title of the job*—The title should be descriptive and, if appropriate, indicate the job's level in the organization.
- *Administrative information about the job*—The job description may identify a division, department, supervisor's title, date of the analysis, name of the analyst, and other information for administering the company's human resource activities.
- *Statement of the job's purpose*—This should be brief and describe the position in broad terms.
- *Essential duties of the job*—These should be listed in order of importance to successful performance and should include details such as physical requirements (e.g., the amount of weight to be lifted), the persons with whom an employee in this job interacts, and the results to be accomplished. This section should include every duty that the job analysis identified as essential.
- *Additional responsibilities*—The job description may state that the position requires additional responsibilities as requested by the supervisor.

SOURCES: Small Business Administration, "Writing Effective Job Descriptions," *Small Business Planner*, www.sba.gov/small businessplanner/, accessed March 10, 2010; and "How to Write a Job Analysis and Description," *Entrepreneur*, www.entrepreneur.com, accessed March 10, 2010.

---

type of job and then modifying it to fit the organization's needs.

Organizations should provide each newly hired employee his or her job description. This helps the employee to understand what is expected, but it shouldn't be presented as limiting the employee's commitment to quality and customer satisfaction. Ideally, employees will want to go above and beyond the listed duties when the situation and their abilities call for that. Many job descriptions include the phrase *and other duties as required* as a way to remind employees not to tell their supervisor, "But that's not part of my job."

OUTCOME OF JOB ANALYSIS: JOB SPECIFICATION

Whereas the job description focuses on the activities involved in carrying out a job, a job specification looks at the qualities or requirements that person performing the job must possess. It is a list of the **competencies**, that is, knowledge, skills, abilities, and other characteristics associated with effective job performance. These competencies may also become part of a *competency model* or *competency framework* that describes competencies the entire organization needs to be successful. The "HR Best Practices" box, found later in this chapter, discusses the use of competency modelling at the YMCA of Greater Toronto.

Knowledge refers to factual or procedural information necessary for successfully performing a task. For example, this course is providing you with knowledge in how to manage human resources. A *skill* is an individual's level of proficiency at performing a particular task—the capability to perform it well. With knowledge and experience, you could acquire skill in the task of preparing job specifications. *Ability*, in contrast to skill, refers to a more general enduring

> **job specification**
> A list of the competencies an individual must have to perform a particular job.

> **competencies**
> Knowledge, skills, abilities, and other characteristics associated with effective job performance.

such as security and health care, may have customers who need services 24/7. Globalization often means that operations take place across many time zones, requiring management at all hours. When a job entails working night shifts, job specifications should reflect this requirement. For most people, working at night disrupts their normal functioning and may cause disorders such as fatigue, depression, and obesity. However, people show wide variability in how well they respond to working at night. Research has found that people who work well at night tend to prefer sleeping late in the morning and staying up late. They also tend to sleep easily at different times of day, like to take naps, and exercise regularly. When job specifications call for night-time work, a person's ability to handle a nocturnal work life may be the most critical competency.[8]

SOURCES OF JOB INFORMATION

Information for analyzing an existing job often comes from incumbents, that is, people who currently hold that position in the organization. They are a logical source of information, because they are most acquainted with the details of the job. Incumbents should be able to provide very accurate information.

> **L04** Tell how to obtain information for a job analysis.

A drawback of relying solely on incumbents' information is that they may have an incentive to exaggerate what they do, to appear more valuable to the organization. Information from incumbents should therefore be supplemented with information from observers, such as supervisors. Supervisors should review the information provided by incumbents, looking for a match between what incumbents are doing and what they are supposed to do. Research suggests that incumbents may provide the most *accurate* estimates of the actual time spent performing job tasks, while supervisors may be more accurate in reporting information about the *importance* of job duties.[9]

The federal government also provides background information for analyzing jobs. Human Resources and Skills Development Canada working with Statistics Canada created the **National Occupational Classification (NOC)** to provide standardized sources of information about jobs in Canada's labour market. The NOC is a tool that uses a four-digit code to classify occupations based on the types and levels of skills required. The NOC classification system (www.hrsdc.gc.ca) supports the needs of employers, individual job seekers, as well as career counsellors, statisticians, and labour market analysts, by providing a consistent way to identify and interpret the nature of work (see Figure 3.5). A recent addition to the site is a publication titled "Job Descriptions: An Employers' Handbook" that may be particularly helpful to managers and human resource professionals.

POSITION ANALYSIS QUESTIONNAIRE

After gathering information, the job analyst uses the information to analyze the job. One of the broadest and best-researched instruments for analyzing jobs is the **Position Analysis Questionnaire (PAQ)**, a standardized tool containing 194 items that represent work behaviours, work conditions, and job characteristics that apply to a wide variety of jobs, and are organized into six sections concerning different aspects of the job:

1. *Information input.* Where and how a worker gets information needed to perform the job.
2. *Mental processes.* The reasoning, decision making, planning, and information processing activities involved in performing the job.
3. *Work output.* The physical activities, tools, and devices used by the worker to perform the job.
4. *Relationships with other persons.* The relationships with other people required in performing the job.
5. *Job context.* The physical and social contexts where the work is performed.
6. *Other characteristics.* The activities, conditions, and characteristics other than those previously described that are relevant to the job.

The person analyzing a job determines whether each item on the questionnaire applies to the job being analyzed. The analyst rates each item on six scales: extent of use, amount of time, importance to the job, possibility of occurrence, applicability, and special code (special rating scales used with a particular item). PAQ headquarters scores the questionnaire and generates a report that describes the scores on the job dimensions.

Using the PAQ provides an organization with information that helps in comparing jobs, even when they are dissimilar. The PAQ also has the advantage that it considers the whole work process, from inputs through outputs. However, the person who fills out the questionnaire must have postsecondary-level

---

National Occupational Classification (NOC)

Tool created by the federal government to provide a standardized source of information about jobs in Canada's labour market.

Position Analysis Questionnaire (PAQ)

A standardized job analysis questionnaire containing 194 questions about work behaviours, work conditions, and job characteristics that apply to a wide variety of jobs.

FIGURE 3.5

Job Description and
Job Specifications for
Specialists in Human
Resources (NOC 1121)

SPECIALISTS IN HUMAN RESOURCES (NOC 1121)

What They Do (Job Description)

Specialists in human resources perform some or all of the following duties:

- Advise managers and employees on the interpretation of personnel policies, compensation and benefit programs and collective agreements.

- Research employee benefit and health and safety practices and recommend changes or modifications to existing policies.

- Plan, develop, implement and evaluate personnel and labour relations strategies including policies, programs and procedures to address an organization's human resource requirements.

- Negotiate collective agreements on behalf of employers or workers, mediate labour disputes and grievances and provide advice on employee and labour relations.

- Research and prepare occupational classifications, job descriptions, salary scales and competency appraisal measures and systems.

- Plan and administer staffing, total compensation, training and career development, employee assistance, employment equity and affirmative action programs.

- Manage programs and maintain human resources information and related records systems.

- Hire and oversee training of staff.

- Coordinate employee performance and appraisal programs.

What You Need (Job Specifications)

- You must complete either a university degree or a professional development program or college diploma in personnel administration or a related field (business administration, industrial relations, commerce, psychology) and five years of experience.

- You may be required to gain experience in a clerical or administrative position related to personnel administration.

- With experience, you may move up the ranks to become a manager.

- One of the factors creating additional complexity in the skills required is the growing and changing body of law applied to human resources. You will be required to interpret and apply these laws and to keep pace with changes.

- Most recent entrants have an undergraduate university degree or a college diploma.

SOURCE: Service Canada website, www.jobfutures.ca/noc/1121.shtml, retrieved March 21, 2008. Reproduced with the permission of the Minister of Public Works and Government Services, 2012.

reading skills, and the PAQ is meant to be completed only by job analysts trained in this method.[10] Also, the descriptions in the PAQ reports are rather abstract, so the reports may not be useful for writing job descriptions or redesigning jobs.

FLEISHMAN JOB ANALYSIS SYSTEM

To gather information about worker requirements, the Fleishman Job Analysis System asks subject-matter experts (typically job incumbents) to evaluate a job in terms of the abilities required to perform the job.[11] The survey is based on 52 categories of abilities, ranging from written comprehension to deductive reasoning, manual dexterity, stamina, and originality. As in the example in Figure 3.6, the survey items are arranged into a scale for each ability. Each begins with a description of the ability and a comparison to related abilities. Below this is a seven-point scale with phrases describing extremely high and low levels of the ability. The person

Fleishman Job Analysis System
Job analysis technique that asks subject-matter experts to evaluate a job in terms of the abilities required to perform the job.

human resource professionals must help plan for new or growing work units. When an organization is trying to improve quality or efficiency, a review of work units and processes may require a fresh look at how jobs are designed.

These situations call for job design, the process of defining the way work will be performed and the tasks that a given job requires, or *job redesign*, a similar process that involves changing an existing job design. To design jobs effectively, a person must thoroughly understand the job itself (through job analysis) and its place in the larger work unit's work flow process (through work flow analysis). Having a detailed knowledge of the tasks performed in the work unit and in the job, a manager then has many alternative ways to design a job. As shown in Figure 3.7, the available approaches emphasize different aspects of the job: the mechanics of doing a job efficiently, the job's impact on motivation, the use of safe work practices, and the mental demands of the job.

> **industrial engineering**
> The study of jobs to find the simplest way to structure work in order to maximize efficiency.

almost anyone can be trained quickly and easily to perform the job. Such jobs tend to be highly specialized and repetitive.

In practice, the scientific method traditionally seeks the "one best way" to perform a job by performing time-and-motion studies to identify the most efficient movements for workers to make. Once the engineers have identified the most efficient sequence of motions, the organization should select workers based on their ability to do the job, then train them in the details of the "one best way" to perform that job. The company also should offer pay structured to motivate workers to do their best. (Chapter 8 discusses pay and pay structures.)

Industrial engineering provides measurable and practical benefits. However, a focus on efficiency alone can create jobs that are so simple and repetitive that workers get bored. Workers performing these jobs may feel their work is meaningless. Hence, most organizations combine industrial engineering with other approaches to job design.

DESIGNING EFFICIENT JOBS

If workers perform tasks as efficiently as possible, not only does the organization benefit from lower costs and greater output per worker, but workers should be less fatigued. This point of view has for years formed the basis of classical **industrial engineering**, which looks for the simplest way to structure work in order to maximize efficiency. Typically, applying industrial engineering to a job reduces the complexity of the work, making it so simple that

> **LO6** Describe methods for designing a job so that it can be done efficiently.

DESIGNING JOBS THAT MOTIVATE

Especially when organizations have to compete for employees, depend on skilled knowledge workers, or need a workforce that cares about customer satisfaction, a pure focus on efficiency will not achieve human resource objectives. These organizations need jobs that employees find interesting and satisfying, and job design should take into account factors that make jobs motivating to employees.

> **LO7** Identify approaches to designing a job to make it motivating.

FIGURE 3.7

Approaches to Job Design

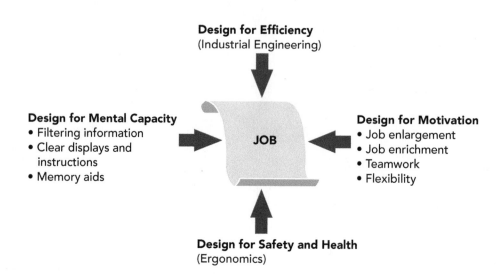

Design for Efficiency
(Industrial Engineering)

Design for Mental Capacity
• Filtering information
• Clear displays and instructions
• Memory aids

JOB

Design for Motivation
• Job enlargement
• Job enrichment
• Teamwork
• Flexibility

Design for Safety and Health
(Ergonomics)

ake jobs less repetitive
ods of job enlargement
o rotation.

, jobs by combining sev-
form a job with a wider
might be combining the
try clerk, and file clerk
ee kinds of work. This
is relatively simple, but
ers will not necessarily
designed job.

tually redesign the jobs
ployees
s. This
nent is
teams.
, a team
n of the
. Team
compo-
roducts
vith job

out,
to which a
ear informati   on about peri   formance
ss from the we   ork itself.

Figure 3.8, th   remember   of each of these
a job has, the r   nore motivating the job
ing to the Job Characteristics Model.
licts that a person with such a job will
ed and will produce more and better
mple, to increase the meaningfulness
ry stents (devices that are surgically
mote blood flow), the maker of these
s its production workers to an annual
hey meet patients whose lives were
oducts they helped to manufacture.[16]
s of the job characteristics approach
include job enlargement, job enrich-
naging work teams, flexible work
telework.

ent

n,   refers to broad-
s of tasks performed. The objective

During the cou
member may (...ally out each
obs handled   by the team.
nembers mig   ht assemble
reactions done   day and pack p
nto cases another day. As v
extension, the enlarged jobs may
still consist of repetitious activities,
but with greater variation among
those activities.

Job Enrichment

The idea of   , or
empowering and engaging workers
by adding more decision-making
authority to their jobs, comes from
the work of Frederick Herzberg.
According to Herzberg's two-fac-
tor theory, individuals are motivated more by the
intrinsic aspects of work (e.g., the meaningfulness
of a job) than by extrinsic rewards such as pay.
Herzberg identified five factors he associated with
motivating jobs: achievement, recognition, growth,

Broadening the types
of tasks performed
in a job.

Enlarging jobs by
combining several
relatively simple jobs
to form a job with a
wider range of tasks.

Enlarging jobs by
moving employees
among several
different jobs.

Engaging workers by
adding more decision-
making authority
to jobs.

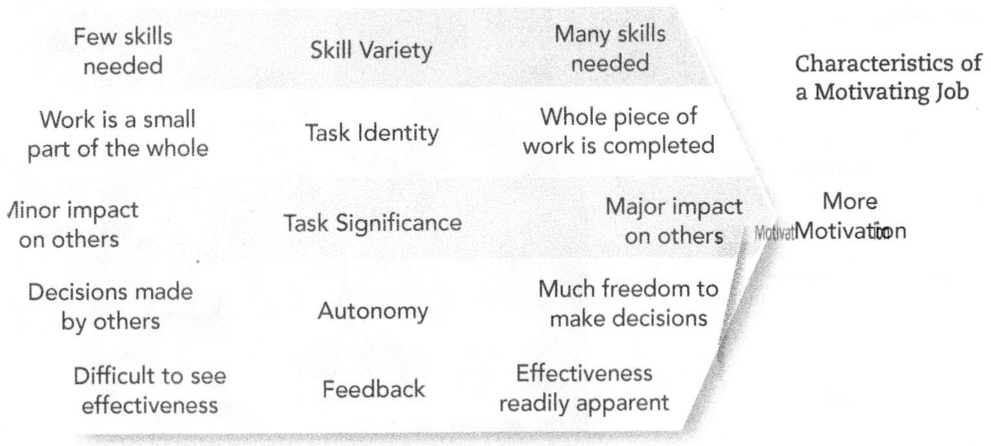

Few skills needed	Skill Variety	Many skills needed	Characteristics of a Motivating Job
Work is a small part of the whole	Task Identity	Whole piece of work is completed	
Minor impact on others	Task Significance	Major impact on others	More Motivation
Decisions made by others	Autonomy	Much freedom to make decisions	
Difficult to see effectiveness	Feedback	Effectiveness readily apparent	

responsibility, and performance of the entire job. Thus, ways to enrich a manufacturing job might include giving employees authority to stop production when quality standards are not being met and having each employee perform several tasks to complete a particular stage of the process, rather than dividing up the tasks among the employees. For a salesperson in a store, job enrichment might involve the authority to resolve customer problems, including the authority to decide whether to issue refunds or replace merchandise.

In practice, however, it is important to note that not every worker responds positively to enriched jobs. These jobs are best suited to employees who are flexible and responsive to others; for these employees, enriched jobs can dramatically improve motivation.[17]

Self-Managing Work Teams

2,3

Instead of merely enriching individual jobs, some organizations empower and engage employees by designing work to be done by self-managing work teams. As described in Chapter 1, these teams have authority for an entire work process or segment. Team members typically have authority to schedule work, hire team members, resolve problems related to the team's performance, and perform other duties traditionally handled by management. Teamwork can give a job such motivating characteristics as autonomy, skill variety, and task identity.

Because team members' responsibilities are great, their jobs usually are defined broadly and include sharing of work assignments. Team members may, at one time or another, perform every duty of the team. The challenge for the organization is to provide enough training so that the team members can learn the necessary skills. Another approach, when teams are responsible for particular work

> **flextime**
> A scheduling policy in which full-time employees may choose starting and ending times within guidelines specified by the organization.

processes or customers, is to assign the team responsibility for the process or customer, then let the team decide which members will carry out which tasks.

A study of work teams at a large financial services company found that the right job design was associated with effective teamwork.[18] In particular, when teams are self-managed and team members are highly involved in decision making, teams are more productive, employees more satisfied, and managers more pleased with performance. Teams also tend to do better when each team member performs a variety of tasks and when team members view their effort as significant.

Flexible Work Schedules

One way an organization can give employees some say in how their work is structured is to offer flexible work schedules. Depending on the requirements of the organization and the individual jobs, organizations may be able to be flexible in terms of when employees work. As introduced in Chapter 1, types of flexibility include flextime and job sharing. Figure 3.9 illustrates alternatives to the traditional 40-hour workweek.

Flextime is a scheduling policy in which full-time employees may choose starting and ending times within guidelines specified by the organization. The flextime policy may require that employees be at work between certain hours, say, 10:00 a.m. and 3:00 p.m. Employees work additional hours before or after this period in order to work the full day. One employee might arrive early in the morning in order to leave at 3:00 p.m. to pick up children after school. Another employee might be a night-owl who prefers to arrive at 10:00 a.m. and work until 6:00, 7:00, or even later in the evening.

Employees who have enriched jobs and/ or work in self-managed teams can be engaged and motivated when they have decision-making authority.

A flextime policy may also enable workers to adjust a specific day's hours in order to make time for outside appointments, children's activities, hobbies, or volunteer work. A work schedule that allows time for community and family interests can be extremely motivating for some employees.

Job sharing is a work option in which two part-time employees carry out the tasks associated with a single job. Such arrangements can enable an organization to attract or retain valued employees who want more time to attend school or to care for family members. The job requirements in such an arrangement include the ability to work cooperatively and coordinate the details of one's job with another person.

> **job sharing**
> A work option in which two part-time employees carry out the tasks associated with a single job.

Although not strictly a form of flexibility on the level of individual employees, another scheduling alternative is the *compressed workweek*. A compressed workweek is a schedule in which full-time workers complete their weekly hours in fewer than five days. For example, instead of working eight hours a day for five days, the employees might complete 40 hours of work in four 10-hour days. This alternative is most common, but some companies use other alternatives, such as scheduling 80 hours over nine days (with a three-day weekend every other week) or reducing the workweek from 40 to 38 or 36 hours. Employees may appreciate the extra days available for leisure, family, or volunteer activities. An organization might even use this schedule to offer a kind of flexibility—for example, letting workers vote on whether they want a compressed workweek during the summer months. This type of schedule has a couple of drawbacks, however. One is that employees may become exhausted on the longer workdays. Another is that if the arrangement involves working more than a specific number of hours during a week, employment/labour standards legislation may require the payment of overtime wages to nonsupervisory employees.

Remote Work Arrangements

Flexibility can extend to work locations as well as work schedules. Before the Industrial Revolution, most people worked either close to or inside their own homes. Mass production technologies changed all this, separating work life from home life, as people began to travel to centrally located factories and offices. Today, however, skyrocketing prices for office space, combined with drastically reduced prices for computers and communication

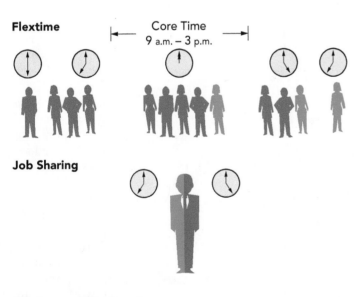

Flextime

Core Time
9 a.m. – 3 p.m.

IBM permits a meal break of up to two hours so employees can do personal tasks.

Job Sharing

Two lawyers, both fathers, share the job of assistant general counsel at Timberland.

FIGURE 3.9

Alternatives to the 8-to-5 Job

Compressed Workweek

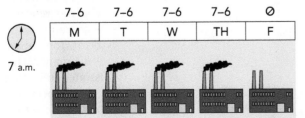

	7–6	7–6	7–6	7–6	Ø
	M	T	W	TH	F

7 a.m.   6 p.m.

All employees of Red Dot Corporation have the option of working ten hours per day, Monday through Thursday.

or people in a
, especially th
icating on a e
generally diff | cult
rs.

i is coming. More
oomers, are inter-
its but, ironically,
id Y. So you have
 now, for differ-
for flexible work
George Horhota,
Vorks, a Barrie,
 of satellite office
distributed work.
ive a choice as to
oday."[20] Approxi-
he workforce are
rs, but there has
mbers as reported
he overall trend to
norm for knowl-
le in managerial,
istrated in Figures
ing performed is
onal office setting

the physical demands of certain jobs so that anyone can perform them. In addition, many interventions focus on redesigning machines and technology—for instance, adjusting the height of a computer keyboard to minimize occupational illnesses, such as carpal tunnel syndrome. The design of chairs and desks to fit posture requirements is very important in many office jobs. One study found that having employees participate in an ergonomic redesign effort significantly reduced the number and severity of repetitive strain injuries (injuries that result from performing the same movement over and over), lost production time, and restricted-duty days.[24]

Often, redesigning work to make it more worker-friendly also leads to increased efficiencies. For example, at International Truck and Engine Corporation, one of the most difficult aspects of truck production was pinning the axles to the truck frame. Traditionally, the frame was lowered onto the axle, and a crew of six people, armed with oversized hammers and crowbars, forced the frame onto the axle. Because the workers could not see the bolts they had to tighten under the frame, the bolts were often fastened improperly, and many workers injured themselves in the process. After a brainstorming session, the workers and engineers concluded it would be better to flip the frame upside down and attach the axles from above. The result was a job that could be done twice as fast by half as many workers, who were much less likely to make mistakes or get injured.[25]

The Canadian Centre for Occupational Health and Safety identifies several workplace conditions that pose ergonomic hazards:[26]

- Repetitive and forceful movements
- Vibration
- Temperature extremes
- Awkward postures that arise from improper work methods
- Improperly designed workstations, tools, and equipment

When jobs have these conditions, employers should be vigilant about opportunities to improve work design, for the benefit of both workers and the organization.

E-HRM	

Check out "Office Work on the Road."

DESIGNING JOBS THAT MEET MENTAL CAPABILITIES AND LIMITATIONS

Just as the human body has capabilities and limitations, addressed by ergonomics, the mind, too, has capabilities and limitations. As more and more work activities become information processing activities, the need to consider *cognitive ergonomics* is likely to be an emerging trend.[27] Besides hiring people with certain mental skills, organizations can design jobs so that they can be accurately and safely performed given the way the brain processes information. Generally, this means reducing the information processing requirements of a job. In these simpler jobs, workers may be less likely to make mistakes or have accidents. Of course, the simpler jobs may also be less motivating. Research has found that challenging jobs tend to fatigue and dissatisfy workers when they feel little control over their situation, lack social support, and feel motivated mainly to avoid errors. In contrast, they may enjoy the challenges of a difficult job where they have some control and social support, especially if they enjoy learning and are

> **LO9** Discuss how organizations can plan for the mental demands of a job.

Ergonomically designed workstations have adjustable components, enabling the employee to modify the workstation to accommodate various job and physical requirements.

KING ETHICALLY

...mmuting Fair to Those at the Office?

...wing number o...mber of ...wo...rkers ...sick of sitting in...tting in ...rush-hour ...e cure is telewo... telework, or ...nuting. Employ Employees who ...tele...co...mmuting cite ...exibility, the chance to ... new job without relocating, ...ork/life flexibility, and ...y to work for stretches ...pted by colleagues check-...eir weekend activities or ...hem to the break room for ...cake.

...ver, not every employee ...ants to) telecommute, ...hose who make the trip to ...ecommuting by others can ...ome difficulties. Greater ... for some employees can ...rk less flexible for others,

...who...re...ire required...to c...over cert...in ...clients, tasks, or ...wo...rk...hours. Superv...som...s...with a last-minute task may f...nd it...easier to hand over the w...ork ...to someone who is on-site. And employees who drive to work each day may feel that telecommuting employees simply have a more comfortable arrangement, which might not seem fair.

SOURCES: Rhymer Rigby, "Employees Feel at Home in the 'Post-Office' World," *Financial Times*, September 8, 2009, Business & Company Resource Center, http://galenet.galegroup.com; Dave Bailey, "How to Gear Up for a Surge in Remote Working," *Computing*, April 2, 2009, Business & Company Resource Center, http://galenet.galegroup.com; and Sam Narisi, "Four Reasons Office Workers Hate Telecommuters," *HR Tech News*, March 6, 2009, www.hrtechnews.com.

QUESTIONS

1. According to this research, telework benefits some employees at the expense of others. Reviewing the ethical principles from Chapter 1, what can a person ethically do when a course of action benefits some people and hurts others?

2. Imagine that you work in HR and your company has decided to adopt telework as a way to retain valued employees. Suggest ways you can help the company proceed with the plan as ethically as possible.

...of making mistakes.[28] Because of this drawback to simplifying jobs, it can be most beneficial to jobs where employees will most appreciate having the mental demands reduced (as in a job that is extremely challenging) or where the costs of errors are severe (as in the job of a surgeon or air-traffic controller).

There are several ways to simplify a job's mental demands. One is to limit the amount of information and memorization the job requires. Organizations can also provide adequate lighting, easy-to-understand gauges and displays, simple-to-operate equipment, and clear instructions. Often, employees try to simplify some of the mental demands of their own jobs by creating checklists, charts, or other aids. Finally, every job requires some degree of thinking, remembering, and paying attention, so for every job, organizations need to evaluate whether their employees can handle the job's mental demands.

Changes in technology sometimes reduce job demands and errors, but in some cases, technology has made the problem worse. Some employees try to juggle information from several sources at once—say, browsing the Internet for information during a team member's business presentation, or repeatedly stopping work on a project to check email or text messages. In these cases, the smartphone or device, and email or text messages are distracting the employees from their primary task. They may convey important information, but they also break the employee's train of thought, reducing performance, and increasing the likelihood of errors. The problem may be aggravated by employees downplaying the significance of these interruptions. For example, in a recent survey of workers, only half said they check their email at work more than once an hour, and more than a third said they check every 15 minutes. However, monitoring software on their computers determined they were actually changing applications to check email up to 30 or 40 times an hour.[29] Canadian Internet users, on average, receive more than 200 emails every week. A study released by Ipsos Reid has found that although 66 percent of Canadians prefer communicating via email over other methods, 44 percent say that can hardly keep up with their email.[30] For highly mobile knowledge workers, the ability to be "always reachable" makes additional mental demands. For example, 92 percent of knowledge workers read, send, make or take work-related messages in nonwork situations.[31]

SUMMARY

LO1 ▸ Summarize the elements of work flow analysis.

- The analysis identifies the amount and quality of a work unit's outputs, which may be products, parts of products, or services.
- Next, the analyst determines the work processes required to produce these outputs, breaking down tasks into those performed by each person in the work unit.
- Finally, the work flow analysis identifies the inputs used to carry out the processes and produce the outputs.

LO2 ▸ Describe how work flow is related to an organization's structure.

- Within an organization, units and individuals must cooperate to create outputs, and the organization's structure brings people together for this purpose. The structure may be centralized or decentralized, and people may be grouped according to function or into divisions focusing on particular products or customer groups.
- A functional structure is most appropriate for people who perform highly specialized jobs and hold relatively little authority. Employee empowerment and teamwork succeed best in a divisional structure. Because of these links between structure and types of jobs, considering such issues improves the success of job design.

LO3 ▸ Define the significance and outcomes of job analysis.

- Job analysis is the process of getting detailed information about jobs. It includes preparation of job descriptions and job specifications.
- Job analysis provides a foundation for carrying out many HRM responsibilities, including work redesign, workforce planning, employee selection and training, performance appraisal, career planning, and job evaluation to determine pay scales.
- Outcomes of job analysis include job descriptions and job specifications. A job description lists the tasks, duties, and responsibilities of a job. Job specifications look at the qualities needed in a person performing the job. They list the competencies, that is, knowledge, skills, abilities, and other characteristics, that are required for successful performance of a job.

LO4 ▸ Tell how to obtain information for a job analysis.

- Information for analyzing an existing job often comes from incumbents and their supervisors. The federal government provides background information about jobs in the National Occupational Classification (NOC).
- Job analysts, employees, and managers may complete a Position Analysis Questionnaire or fill out a survey for the Fleishman Job Analysis System.

LO5 ▸ Summarize recent trends in job analysis.

- Because today's workplace requires a high degree of adaptability, job tasks and requirements are subject to constant change. For example, as some organizations downsize they are defining jobs more broadly, with less supervision of people in those positions.
- Organizations are also adopting project-based structures and teamwork, which also require flexibility and the ability to handle broad responsibilities.

LO6 ▸ Describe methods for designing a job so that it can be done efficiently.

- The basic technique for designing efficient jobs is industrial engineering, which looks for the simplest way to structure work in order to maximize efficiency. Through methods such as time-and-motion studies, the industrial engineer creates jobs that are relatively simple and typically repetitive. These jobs may bore workers because they are so simple.

LO7 ▸ Identify approaches to designing a job to make it motivating.

- According to the Job Characteristics Model, jobs are more motivating if they have greater skill variety, task identity, task significance, autonomy, and feedback about performance effectiveness. Ways to create such jobs include job enlargement (through job extension or job rotation) and job enrichment.
- Self-managing work teams offer greater skill variety and task identity. Flexible work schedules and telework offer greater autonomy.

LO8 ▸ Explain how organizations apply ergonomics to design safe jobs.

- The goal of ergonomics is to minimize physical strain on the worker by structuring the physical work environment around the way the human body works.
- Ergonomic design may involve modifying equipment to reduce the physical demands of performing certain jobs or redesigning the jobs themselves to reduce strain. Ergonomic design may target working conditions associated with ergonomic hazards including repetitive and forceful movements, vibration, temperature extremes, and awkward postures that arise from improper work methods and improperly designed workstations, tools, and equipment.

LO9 Discuss how organizations can plan for the mental demands of a job.

- Employers may seek to reduce mental as well as physical strain. The job design may limit the amount of information and memorization involved. Adequate lighting, easy-to-read gauges and displays, simple-to-operate equipment, and clear instructions can also minimize mental strain.

- Although technology may be used to reduce job demands and errors, technology may also distract employees from primary tasks, e.g., as they retrieve and generate text messages and emails.

Critical Thinking Questions

1. Assume you are the manager/owner of a local coffee house. What are the outputs of your work unit? What are the activities required to produce those outputs? What are the inputs?

2. Based on Question 1, consider the cashier's job of the local coffee house. What are the outputs, activities, and inputs for that job?

3. Consider the "job" of university or college student. Perform a job analysis on this job. What tasks are required in the job? What competencies are necessary to perform those tasks? Prepare a job description based on your analysis.

4. Discuss how the following trends are changing the skill requirements for managerial jobs in Canada:
   a. Increasing use of teamwork
   b. Increasing global competition
   c. Increasing cognitive job demands including the need to be reachable at all times

5. How can a job analysis of each job in the work unit help a supervisor to do his or her job?

6. Consider the job of a customer service representative for a telecommunications provider who handles calls from residential customers for billing inquires and routine service requests. What measures can the employer take to design this job to make it efficient? What might be some drawbacks or challenges of designing this job for efficiency?

7. How might the job in Question 6 be designed to make it more motivating? Would these considerations apply to the cashier's job in Question 2?

8. What ergonomic considerations might apply to each of the following jobs? For each job, what kinds of costs would result from addressing ergonomics? What costs might result from failing to address ergonomics?
   a. A computer programmer
   b. A UPS delivery person
   c. A child care worker

9. What advice do you have for a supervisor who is concerned that employees appear to be distracted during meetings and while performing job tasks due to use of devices such as smartphones to retrieve and create text and email messages?

10. Consider a job you hold now or have held recently. Would you want this job to be redesigned to place more emphasis on efficiency, motivation, ergonomics, or mental processing? What changes would you want, and why? (Or why do you not want the job to be redesigned?)

What's Your HR IQ?

 Connect offers more ways to check what you've learned so far. Find experiential exercises, Test Your Knowledge quizzes, videos, and many other resources to gauge your HR IQ.

CASE STUDY 3.1: Pfizer Outsources Tasks

David Cain loves his job. Well, most of it anyway. As an executive director for global engineering at Pfizer, Cain finds real satisfaction in assessing environmental real estate risks, managing facilities, and overseeing a multi-million-dollar budget for the pharmaceutical giant. What he doesn't love so much: creating PowerPoint slides and riffling through spreadsheets.

Lucky for Cain, Pfizer now lets him punt those tedious and time-consuming tasks to India with the click of a button. PfizerWorks, launched early last year, permits some 4,000 employees to pass off parts of their job to outsiders. You might call it personal outsourcing. With workers in India handling everything from basic market research projects to presentations, professionals such as Cain can focus on higher-value work. "It has really been a godsend," says Cain. "I can send them something in the evening, and the next morning it's waiting for me when I get to the office."

...need is a smart guy ...asks can't easily be ...online form, Cohen ...need an assistant

...rrangement with a ...ork. Pearl employs people with physical disabilities who help with such administrative tasks as organizing a marketing team's research documents on a shared server or scheduling meetings. While the partnership is modest and isn't meant to supplant arrangements in India or administrative jobs, Cohen hopes it will make Pfizer staff even more productive.

Although PfizerWorks hasn't quite reached its first anniversary, Cohen estimates that it has already freed up 66,500 hours for employees. Pfizer finds employees are now spending less money on other providers, such as graphic design shops or market research firms. Employees are asked to rate their satisfaction with the finished product. If the score isn't high enough, a department can refuse to pay, which has happened only a handful of times.

Questions

1. As PfizerWorks is described here, the analysis of work flow and decisions about which tasks to outsource are handled by individual employees, rather than HR teams or outside analysts. What are some advantages and drawbacks of this approach?

2. If you worked in HR for Pfizer, how would you need to adjust job descriptions and requirements to account for employees' ability to outsource tasks?

3. The examples in this case refer to managers and scientists. What positions, if any, at Pfizer should *not* have access to PfizerWorks? Why?

SOURCE: Excerpted from Jena McGregor, "Outsourcing Tasks Instead of Jobs," *Business Week*, March 12, 2009, www.businessweek.com.

/ 3.2: Creative Jobs at W. L. Gore

...-wife team of Bill and Vieve Gore ...& Associates, their aim was not ...products from high-tech materi- ...ved they could create a thriving, ...y giving smart people a chance to ...nd ideas. They believed creativity ...d structure and hierarchy, so they ...ithout managers, assigning teams ...on opportunities.

..., work flow is often about ideas as ...produce good ideas, the company ...ngineers with a profound under- ...of expertise, be it chemistry or the ...prototype. At the same time, the ...success requires that it back only ...al market needs, so expertise must

extend to business knowledge coupled with a willingness to terminate projects that have little chance of success. This pairing of skill sets is especially powerful when an innovation isn't working out because Gore employees are gifted at analyzing the idea to see what aspects can be carried over into new projects, so the company builds on ideas. Also related to business skills, Gore employees must be good at communicating with customers, who can help the company identify needs and assess the value of ideas. This combination of skills is broad because jobs at Gore are broadly defined; in contrast, at many other companies, scientists and engineers communicate mainly with other technical experts, leaving customer communication and market knowledge to the sales force.

The basic principle for organizing work at Gore is the team, established to meet a particular opportunity. Thus,

Chapter 4

PLANNING FOR
and Recruiting Human Resources

Customer preferences and management decisions affect the number and types of employees needed as well as RIM's employment brand.

What Do I Need to Know?

After reading this chapter, you should be able to:

LO1 Discuss how to plan for the human resources needed to carry out the organization's strategy.

LO2 Determine the demand for and supply of workers in various job categories.

LO3 Summarize the advantages and disadvantages of ways to eliminate a labour surplus and avoid a labour shortage.

LO4 Identify the steps in the process of succession planning.

LO5 Discuss the use of employment branding and recruitment policies organizations use to make job vacancies more attractive.

LO6 List and compare sources of job applicants.

LO7 Describe the recruiter's role in the recruitment process, including limits and opportunities.

RIM's Damaged Employment Brand?

Customers have been shunning the once dominant BlackBerry and turning to devices made by Apple, Google, Samsung Electronics, and a host of other rivals. For example, in a recent three-month period, Apple sold 37 million iPhones—that's approximately half the number of BlackBerry subscribers worldwide. Adding to the misery...the flop of RIM's first tablet, profit warnings, and a massive service outage. Does this customer shift and other difficulties affect RIM's employment brand and its reputation as a great place to work?

According to Ziyad Mir, a student in the University of Waterloo's systems design engineering program, known for turning out world-class programmers, times have changed. Although Mir said he admired RIM's success back in 2009 when he was looking for his first work placement, he says times have changed and the brightest students no longer aspire to work at Research In Motion. "It was definitely a really great place to have your first internship," says Mr. Mir, who is now in an internship position at LinkedIn Corp. "But you don't see a lot of the strong students ending up wanting to go to RIM full time, which is sad."[1]

Trends and events that affect the economy and/or organizations create opportunities and problems in obtaining human resources. When customer demand rises (or falls), organizations may need more (or fewer) employees. When the labour market changes—as when more people pursue postsecondary education or when a sizable share of the population retires—the supply of qualified workers may grow, shrink, or change in nature. Organizations recently have had difficulty filling information technology jobs, because the demand for people with these skills outstrips the supply. To prepare for and respond to these challenges, organizations engage in *workforce planning*—defined in Chapter 1 as identifying the numbers and types of employees the organization will require to meet its objectives.

This chapter describes how organizations carry out workforce planning. In the first part of the chapter, we lay out the steps that go into developing and implementing a workforce plan. Throughout each section, we focus especially on recent trends and practices, including downsizing, employing temporary workers, and outsourcing. The remainder of the chapter explores the process of recruiting. We

discuss the importance of employment branding in attracting potential employees, the process by which organizations look for people to fill job openings, and the sources of job candidates. Finally, we discuss the role of recruiters.

What Is Workforce Planning?

Organizations should carry out *workforce planning* so as to meet business objectives and gain an advantage over competitors. To do this, organizations need a clear idea of the strengths and weaknesses of their existing internal labour force. They also must know what they want to be doing in the future—what size they want the organization to be, what products and services it should be producing, and so on. This knowledge helps them define the number and kinds of employees they will need. Workforce planning compares the present state of the organization with its goals for the future, then identifies what changes it must make in its human resources to meet those goals. The changes may include downsizing, training existing employees in new skills, or hiring new employees. The overall goal of workforce planning is to ensure the organization has the right people with the right skills in the right places at the right time.

> Discuss how to plan for the human resources needed to carry out the organization's strategy.

These activities give a general view of workforce planning. They take place in the workforce planning process shown in Figure 4.1. The process consists of three stages: forecasting, goal setting and strategic planning, and program implementation and evaluation.

FORECASTING

The first step in workforce planning is forecasting, as shown in the top portion of Figure 4.1. In forecasting, the HR professional tries to determine the *supply* of and *demand* for various types of human resources. The primary goal is to predict which areas of the organization will experience labour shortages or surpluses.

Forecasting supply and demand can use statistical methods or judgment. Statistical methods capture historic trends in a company's demand for labour. Under the right conditions, these methods predict demand and supply more precisely

forecasting
The attempts to determine the supply of and demand for various types of human resources to predict areas within the organization where there will be labour shortages or surpluses.

FIGURE 4.1

Overview of the
Workforce Planning
Process

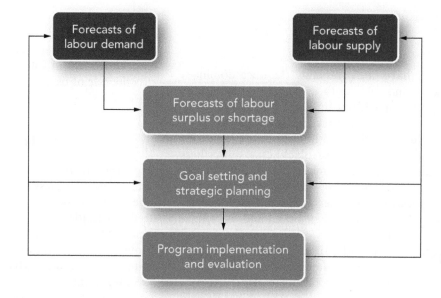

than a human forecaster can using subjective judgment. But many important events in the labour market have no precedent. When such events occur, statistical methods are of little use. To prepare for these situations, the organization must rely on the subjective judgments of experts. Pooling their "best guesses" is an important source of ideas about the future.

Forecasting the Demand for Labour

Usually, an organization forecasts demand for specific job categories or skill areas. After identifying the relevant job categories or skills, the planner investigates the likely demand for each. The planner must forecast whether the need for people with the necessary skills and experience will increase or decrease. There are several ways of making such forecasts.

At the most sophisticated level, an organization might use **trend analysis**, constructing and applying statistical models that predict labour demand for the next year, given relatively objective statistics from the previous year. These statistics are called **leading indicators**— objective measures that accurately predict future labour demand. They might include measures of the economy (such as sales or inventory levels), actions of competitors, changes in technology, and trends in the composition of the workforce. For example, a manufacturer of auto parts that sells its product to automakers would use statistics on the auto

industry, using the numbers from recent time periods to predict the demand for the company's product in a later time period.

Statistical planning models are useful when there is a long, stable history that can be used to reliably detect relationships among variables. However, these models almost always have to be complemented with subjective judgments of experts. There are simply too many "once in a lifetime" changes to consider, and statistical models cannot capture them.

L02 ▸ Determine the demand for and supply of workers in various job categories.

Forecasting the Available Supply of Labour

Once a company has forecast the demand for labour, it needs an indication of the firm's available labour supply. Determining the internal labour supply calls for a detailed analysis of how many people are currently in various job categories or have specific skills within the organization. The planner then modifies this analysis to reflect changes expected in the near future as a result of retirements, promotions, transfers, voluntary turnover, and terminations.

One type of statistical procedure that can be used for this purpose is the analysis of a **transitional matrix**, which is a chart that lists job categories held in one period and shows the proportion of employees in each of those job categories in a future period. It answers two

---

trend analysis
Constructing and applying statistical models that predict labour demand for the next year, given relatively objective statistics from the previous year.

leading indicators
Objective measures that accurately predict future labour demand.

transitional matrix
A chart that lists job categories held in one period and shows the proportion of employees in each of those job categories in a future period.

As the average age of many workers in skilled trades increases, the growing demand for workers in many trades is expected to outstrip supply. There is a potential for employers in some areas to continue to experience a labour shortage because of this. What should HR do to avoid shortages of labour?

questions: "Where did people who were in each job category go?" and "Where did people now in each job category come from?" Table 4.1 is an example of a transitional matrix.

This example lists job categories for an auto parts manufacturer. The jobs listed at the left were held in 2009; the numbers across show what happened to the people in 2012. The numbers represent proportions. For example, 0.95 means 95 percent of the people represented by a row in the matrix. The column headings under 2012 refer to the row numbers. The first row is sales manager, so the numbers under column (1) represent people who became sales managers. Reading across the first row, we see that 95 percent of the people who were sales managers in 2009 are still sales managers in 2012. The other 5 percent correspond to column (8), "Not in organization," meaning that 5 percent of people who are not still sales managers have left the organization. In the second row are sales representatives. Of those who were sales reps in 2009, 5 percent were promoted to sales manager, 60 percent are still sales reps, and 35 percent have left the organization. In row (3) half (50 percent) of sales apprentices are still in that job, but 20 percent are now sales reps, and 30 percent have left the organization. This pattern of jobs shows a career path from sales apprentice to sales representative to sales manager. Of course, not everyone is promoted, and some people leave instead.

Reading down the columns provides another kind of information: the sources of employees holding the positions in 2012. In the first column, we see that most sales managers (95 percent) held that same job three years earlier. The other 5 percent were promoted from sales representative positions. Skipping over to column (3), half the sales apprentices on the payroll in 2012 held the same job three years before, and the other half were hired from outside the organization. This suggests that the organization fills sales manager positions primarily through promotions, so planning for this job would focus on preparing sales representatives. In contrast, planning to meet the organization's needs for sales apprentices

TABLE 4.1   Transitional Matrix: Example for an Auto Parts Manufacturer

2009	2012							
	(1)	(2)	(3)	(4)	(5)	(6)	(7)	(8)
1. Sales manager	0.95							0.05
2. Sales representative	0.05	0.60						0.35
3. Sales apprentice		0.20	0.50					0.30
4. Assistant plant manager				0.90	0.05			0.05
5. Production manager				0.10	0.75			0.15
6. Production assembler					0.10	0.80		0.10
7. Clerical							0.70	0.30
8. Not in organization	0.00	0.20	0.50	0.00	0.10	0.20	0.30	

size recruitment and selection of new

ke this are extremely useful for chart-
trends in the company's supply of
important, if conditions remain some-
, they can also be used to plan for the
:ample, if we believe we are going to
of labour in the production assembler
n the next three years, we can plan to
Still, historical data may not always
te future trends. Planners need to com-
forecasts of labour supply with expert
or example, managers in the organiza-
hat a new training program will likely
umber of employees qualified for new
gs. Forecasts :ecasts of labour supply also should
to account th)unt the organization's pool of skills.
organizations ations include inventories of employ-
lls in an HR d1 HR database. When the organization
forecasts that it will it will need new skills in the future,
planners can consult consult the database to see how many
existing employees have those skills.

Besides looking at the labour supply within the
organization, the planner should examine trends in
the external labour market. The planner should keep
abreast of labour market forecasts, including the
size of the labour market, the unemployment rate,
and the kinds of people who will be in the labour
market. For example, we saw in Chapter 1 that the
labour market is aging and that immigration is an
important source of new workers. Important sources
of data on the external labour market are available
from Statistics Canada. Details and news (releases
from *The Daily*) are available at the Statistics Canada website (www.statcan.ca).

Determining Labour Surplus or Shortage

On the basis of the forecasts for labour demand and
supply, the planner can compare the figures to determine whether there will be a shortage or surplus of
labour for each job category. Determining expected
shortages and surpluses allows the organization to
plan how to address these challenges.

Issues related to a labour surplus or shortage
can pose serious challenges for the organization.
Manufacturers, for example, expect to have difficulty filling skilled-trades positions such as jobs for
ironworkers, machinists, plumbers, and welders.
Demand for these jobs is strong and is likely to continue as important infrastructure such as bridges and
tunnels ages. Although, the average age of trades-
people is rising above 55, and young people have
tended to be less attracted to these jobs, assuming,
often incorrectly, that manufacturing-related jobs
will be difficult to find or will not pay well.[2]

GOAL SETTING AND STRATEGIC PLANNING

The second step in workforce planning
is goal setting and strategic planning, as
shown in the middle of Figure 4.1. The
purpose of setting specific numerical goals
is to focus attention on the issue and provide a basis for measuring the organization's success
in addressing labour short-
ages and surpluses. The
goals should come directly
from the analysis of labour
supply and demand. They
should include a specific
figure indicating what
should happen with the
job category or skill area and a specific timetable for
when the results should be achieved.

> Summarize the advantages and disadvantages of ways to eliminate a labour surplus and avoid a labour shortage.

For each goal, the organization must choose one
or more human resource strategies. A variety of strategies are available for handling expected shortages
and surpluses of labour. The top of Table 4.2 shows
major options for reducing an expected labour surplus, and the bottom of the table lists options for
avoiding an expected labour shortage.

This planning stage is critical. The options differ widely in their expense, speed, and effectiveness.
Options for reducing a labour surplus cause differing
amounts of human suffering. The options for avoiding a labour shortage differ in terms of how easily
the organization can undo the change if it no longer faces a labour shortage. For example, an organization probably would not want to handle every
expected labour shortage by hiring new employees.
The process is relatively slow and involves expenses
to find and train new employees. Also, if the shortage becomes a surplus, the organization will have to
consider laying off some of the employees. Layoffs
involve another set of expenses, such as severance
pay, and they are costly in terms of human suffering.

Another consideration in choosing an HR strategy is whether the employees needed will contribute
directly to the organization's success. Organizations
are most likely to benefit from hiring and retaining
employees who have competencies that are part of
the organization's competency framework as discussed in Chapter 3.

Organizations try to anticipate labour surpluses
far enough ahead that they can freeze hiring and let
natural attrition (people leaving on their own) reduce
the labour force. Unfortunately for many workers,
organizations often stay competitive in a fast-changing environment by responding to a labour surplus
with downsizing, which delivers fast results. The
impact is painful for those who lost jobs, as well as

The Team Tim Hortons Scholarship program is one of the ways Tim Hortons reduces turnover and retains talent in tight labour markets.

its human resources, the more layoffs hurt productivity.[5]

Why do so many downsizing efforts fail to meet expectations? There seem to be several reasons. First, although the initial cost savings give a temporary boost to profits, the long-term effects of an improperly managed downsizing effort can be negative. Downsizing leads to a loss of talent, and it often disrupts the social networks through which people are creative and flexible.[6]

Also, many companies wind up rehiring. Downsizing campaigns often eliminate people who turn out to be irreplaceable. In one survey, 80 percent of the firms that had downsized wound up replacing some of the very people they had laid off. In one firm, a bookkeeper making $9 an hour was let go. Later, the company realized she knew many things about the company that no one else knew, so she was hired back as a consultant—for $42 an hour.[7] However, recent trends in employment suggests that companies will not rehire employees for many of the jobs eliminated when they restructured, introduced automation, or moved work to lower-cost regions.[8]

Finally, downsizing efforts often fail, because employees who survive the purge become self-absorbed and afraid to take risks. Motivation drops, because any hope of future promotions—or any future—with the company dies. Many employees start looking for other employment opportunities. The negative publicity associated with a downsizing campaign can also hurt the company's image in the labour market, so it is harder to recruit employees later.

Many problems with downsizing can be reduced with better planning. Instead of slashing jobs across the board, successful downsizing makes strategic cuts that improve the company's competitive position, and management addresses the problem of employees becoming demoralized. Boeing learned this lesson the hard way in the 1990s, when it reduced its workforce by letting workers choose whether they wanted to accept a buyout package in exchange for leaving. Workers with the most experience (and best prospects elsewhere) were most likely to leave, so when Boeing's orders increased and it needed to rehire later, it was competing in the labour market for the best people. To avoid that situation when it needed to cut 10,000 jobs in 2009, Boeing avoided voluntary reductions and instead required managers to pick which employees' positions would be eliminated.[9]

Reducing Hours

Given the limitations of downsizing, many organizations are more carefully considering other avenues for eliminating a labour surplus (shown in Table 4.2). One alternative seen as a way to spread the burden more fairly is cutting work hours, generally with a corresponding reduction in pay. Besides the thought that this is a more equitable way to weather a slump in demand, companies choose a reduction in work hours because it is less costly than layoffs requiring severance pay, and it is easier to restore the work hours than to hire new employees after a downsizing effort. Window maker Pella, for example, put its employees on a four-day workweek, and Dell Computer offered its employees a chance to take extra (unpaid) days off at the end of the year.[10]

Early-Retirement Programs

Another popular way to reduce a labour surplus is with an early-retirement program. As we discussed in Chapter 1, the average age of the Canadian workforce is increasing. But even though many baby boomers are approaching traditional retirement age, early indications are that this group has no intention of retiring soon.[11] Several forces fuel the drawing out of older workers' careers. First, the improved health of older people in general, combined with the decreased physical labour required by many jobs, has made working longer a viable option. Also, many workers fear their retirement savings and pension plans supplemented by the Canada Pension Plan will still not be enough to cover their expenses. Finally, protection from discrimination and eliminating mandatory retirement have limited organizations' ability to force older workers to retire. However, under the pressures associated with an aging labour force, many employers try to encourage older workers to leave voluntarily by offering a variety of early-retirement incentives. The more lucrative of these programs succeed by some measures. Research suggests that these programs encourage lower-performing older workers to retire.[12] Sometimes they work so well that too many workers retire.

Many organizations are moving from early-retirement programs to *phased-retirement programs*. In a phased-retirement program, the organization can continue to enjoy the experience of older workers while reducing the number of hours these employees work, as well as the cost of those employees. This option also can give older employees the psychological benefit of easing into retirement, rather than being thrust entirely into a new way of life.[13]

Employing Temporary and Contract Workers

While downsizing has been a popular way to reduce a labour surplus, the most widespread methods for eliminating a labour shortage are hiring temporary and contract workers and outsourcing work. Employers may arrange to hire a temporary worker through an agency that specializes in linking employers with people who have the necessary skills. The employer pays the agency, whom in turn pays the temporary worker. Employers may also contract directly with individuals, often professionals, to provide a particular service. Temporary and contract employment is popular with employers, because it gives them the flexibility they need to operate efficiently when demand for their products changes rapidly. Refer to the nearby "HR How-To" box.

In addition to flexibility, temporary employment often offers lower costs. Using temporary workers frees the employer from many administrative tasks and financial burdens associated with being the "employer of record." The cost of employee benefits, including vacations, pension, life insurance, workers' compensation, and employment insurance, may account for 40 percent of payroll expenses for permanent employees. Assuming the agency pays for these benefits, a company using temporary workers may save money even if it pays the agency a higher rate for that worker than the usual wage paid to a permanent employee.

Agencies that provide temporary employees also may handle some of the tasks associated with hiring. Small companies that cannot afford their own testing programs often get employees who have been tested by the staffing agency. Many staffing agencies also train employees before sending them to employers. This reduces employers' training costs and eases the transition for the temporary worker and employer.

Finally, temporary workers may offer benefits not available from permanent employees. Because the temporary worker has little experience at the employer's organization, this person brings an objective point of view to the organization's problems and procedures. Also, a temporary worker may have a great deal of experience in other organizations that can be applied to the current assignment.

Besides using a staffing agency, a company can obtain workers for limited assignments by entering into contracts with them. If the person providing the services is an independent contractor, rather than an employee, the company does not pay employee benefits, such as health insurance and vacations. As with using temporary employees, the savings can be significant, even if the contractor works at a higher rate of pay.

As discussed in Chapter 1, this strategy carries risks, however. If the person providing the service is a contractor and not an employee, the company is not supposed to directly supervise the worker. The company can tell the contractor what criteria the finished assignment should meet, but not, for example, where or what hours to work. This distinction is significant, because if the company treats the contractor as an employee, the company has certain legal obligations, related to overtime pay and withholding income taxes.

When an organization wants to consider using independent contractors as a way to expand its labour force temporarily, human resource professionals can help by alerting the company to the need to verify that the arrangement will meet legal requirements. A good place to start is with the advice provided at the Canada Revenue Agency website (www.cra.gc.ca). In addition, the organization may need to obtain legal or financial services advice.

Outsourcing

Instead of using a temporary employee to fill a single job, an organization might want a broader set of services. As discussed in Chapter 1, contracting with another organization to perform a broad

HR HOW-TO

Using Temporary Employees and Contractors

Many full-time employees perceive temporary workers as a threat to their own job security. Such an attitude can interfere with cooperation and, in some cases, lead to outright sabotage if the situation is not well managed.

One way organizations should manage this situation is to complete any downsizing efforts before bringing in temporary or contract workers. Surviving a downsizing is almost like experiencing a death in the family. A decent time interval needs to occur before new temporary workers are introduced. Without the delay, the surviving employees will associate the downsizing effort (which was a threat) with the new temporary employees (who could be perceived as outsiders brought in to replace old friends). If an upswing in demand follows a downsizing effort, the organization should probably begin meeting its expanded demand for labour by granting overtime to core employees. If the demand persists, the organization will be more certain that the upswing will last and future layoffs will be unnecessary. The extended stretches of overtime will eventually tax the full-time employees, so they will accept using temporary workers to help lessen their load.

The organization may also try to select "nonthreatening' temporary workers, especially those who enjoy temporary assignments for their variety or flexibility. Many temporary-staffing firms attract people with this outlook.

Organizations that use temporary or contract workers must avoid treating them as second-class citizens. One way to do this is to ensure that the agency provides temporary employees with benefits comparable to those enjoyed by the organization's permanent workers. For example, one temporary agency, MacTemps, gives its workers long-term health coverage, full disability insurance, and complete dental coverage. This not only reduces the benefit gap between the temporary and permanent workers but also helps attract the best temporary workers in the first place.

---

set of services is called *outsourcing*. Organizations use outsourcing as a way to operate more efficiently and save money. They choose outsourcing firms that promise to deliver the same or better quality at a lower cost. One reason they can do this is that the outside company specializes in the services and can benefit from economies of scale (the economic principle that producing something in large volume tends to cost less for each additional unit than producing in small volume). This efficiency is often the attraction for outsourcing human resource functions such as payroll. Costs also are lower when the outsourcing firm is located in a part of the world where wages are relatively low.

The first uses of outsourcing emphasized manufacturing and routine tasks. However, technological advances in computer networks and transmission have speeded up the outsourcing process and have helped it spread beyond manufacturing areas and low-skilled jobs. For example, DuPont moved legal services associated with its $100 million asbestos case litigation to a team of lawyers working in the Philippines. The work is a combination of routine document handling and legal judgments such as determining the relevance of a document to the case. Salaries for legal professionals in the Philippines are about one-fifth the cost of their North-American counterparts.[14]

Outsourcing may be a necessary way to operate as efficiently as competitors, but it does pose challenges. Quality-control problems, security violations, and poor customer service have sometimes wiped out the cost savings attributed to lower wages. To ensure success with an outsourcing strategy; companies should follow these guidelines:

- Learn about what the provider can do for the company, not just the costs. Make sure the company has the necessary skills, including an environment that can meet standards for clear communication, on-time shipping, contract enforcement, fair labour practices, and environmental protection.[15] Some companies are keeping outsourcing inside Canada in order to meet this full set of requirements.
- Do not offshore any work that is proprietary or requires tight security.[16]
- Start small and monitor the work closely, especially in the beginning, when problems are most likely.[17]
- Look for opportunities to outsource work in areas that promote growth, for example, by partnering

with experts who can help the organization tap new markets.[18]

Overtime and Expanded Hours

Organizations facing a labour shortage may be reluctant to hire employees, even temporary workers, or to commit to an outsourcing arrangement. Especially if the organization expects the shortage to be temporary, it may prefer an arrangement that is simpler and less costly. Under some conditions, these organizations may try to garner more hours from the existing labour force, asking them to go from part-time to full-time or to work overtime.

A major downside of overtime is that the employer must pay nonmanagement employees additional pay above and beyond their normal wages for work done overtime. Even so, employers see overtime pay as preferable to the costs of hiring and training new employees. The preference is especially strong if the organization doubts that the current higher level of demand for its products will last long.

For a short time at least, many workers appreciate the added compensation for working overtime. Over extended periods, however, employees feel stress and frustration from working long hours. Overtime therefore is best suited for short-term labour shortages.

IMPLEMENTING AND EVALUATING THE WORKFORCE PLAN

For whatever HR strategies are selected, the final stage of workforce planning involves implementing the strategies and evaluating the outcomes. This stage is represented by the bottom part of Figure 4.1. When implementing the HR strategy, the organization must hold some individual accountable for achieving the goals. That person also must have the authority and resources needed to accomplish those goals. It is also important that this person issue regular progress reports, so the organization can be sure that all activities occur on schedule and that the early results are as expected.

In evaluating the results, the most obvious step is checking whether the organization has succeeded in avoiding labour shortages or surpluses. Along with measuring these numbers, the evaluation should identify which parts of the planning process contributed to success or failure. For example, consider a company where meeting human resource needs requires that employees continually learn new skills. If there is a gap between needed skills and current skill levels, the evaluation should consider whether the problem lies with failure to forecast the needed skills or with implementation. Are employees signing up for training, and is the right kind of training available?

APPLYING WORKFORCE PLANNING TO EMPLOYMENT EQUITY

As we discussed in Chapter 2, many organizations have a human resource strategy that includes employment equity to manage diversity or meet government requirements. Meeting employment equity goals requires that employers carry out an additional level of workforce planning aimed at those goals. In other words, besides looking at its overall workforce and needs, the organization looks at the representation of subgroups in its labour force—for example, the proportion of women and visible minorities.

Employment equity plans forecast and monitor the proportion of employees who are members of various protected groups (women, Aboriginal peoples, people with disabilities, and visible minorities). The planning looks at the representation of these employees in the organization's job categories and career tracks. The planner can compare the proportion of employees who are in each group with the proportion each group represents in the labour market. For example, the organization might note that in a labour market that consists of 20 percent visible minorities, 60 percent of its customer service employees are members of a visible minority. This type of comparison is called a **workforce utilization review**. The organization can use this process to determine whether there is any subgroup whose proportion in the relevant labour market differs substantially from the proportion in the job category.

workforce utilization review
A comparison of the proportion of employees in protected groups with the proportion that each group represents in the relevant labour market.

If the workforce utilization review indicates that some group—for example, Aboriginal peoples—makes up 10 percent of the relevant labour market for a job category but that this same group constitutes only 5 percent of the employees actually in the job category at the organization, this is evidence of *underutilization*. That situation could result from problems in selection or from problems in internal movement (promotions or other movement along a career path). One way to diagnose the situation would be to use transitional matrices, such as that shown in Table 4.1 earlier in this chapter. The federal public service is the largest employer in Canada with more than 176,000 employees.[19] Figure 4.2 compares participation of its employment equity groups with workforce availability.

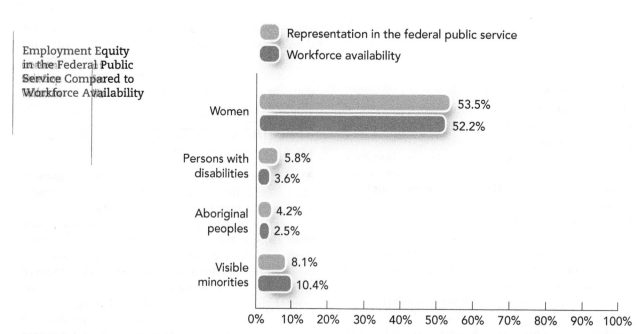

Employment Equity in the Federal Public Service Compared to Workforce Availability

Representation in the federal public service
Workforce availability

Women — 53.5% / 52.2%
Persons with disabilities — 5.8% / 3.6%
Aboriginal peoples — 4.2% / 2.5%
Visible minorities — 8.1% / 10.4%

SOURCE: "Employment Equity in the Federal Public Service—Not There Yet: Preliminary Findings of the Standing Senate Committee on Human Rights," February 2007, pp. 11–12, www.parl.gc.ca/39/1/parlbus/commbus/senate/com-e/huma-e/rep-e/rep07feb07-e.pdf, retrieved May 23, 2008.

The steps in a workforce utilization review are identical to the steps in the workforce planning process shown in Figure 4.1. The organization must assess current utilization patterns, then forecast how these are likely to change in the near future. If these analyses suggest the organization is underutilizing certain groups and if forecasts suggest this pattern is likely to continue, the organization may need to set goals and timetables for changing. The planning process may identify new strategies for recruitment or selection. The organization carries out these HR strategies and evaluates their success.

What Is Succession Planning?

Organizations have always had to prepare for the retirement of their leaders, but the need is more intense than ever. The aging of the workforce means that a greater share of employees are reaching retirement age. Many organizations are fuelling the trend by downsizing through early-retirement programs. As positions at the top of organizations become vacant, many organizations have determined that their middle managers are fewer and often unprepared for top-level responsibility. This situation has raised awareness of the need for a particular type of workforce planning, succession planning—the process of identifying and tracking high-potential employees who will be able to fill top management positions or other key positions when they become vacant. Figure 4.3 breaks the succession planning process into seven steps. It begins with identifying the positions to be planned for and the employees to be included in the plan. Planning should also include establishing position requirements and deciding how to measure employees' potential for being able to fill those requirements. The organization needs to develop a process for reviewing the existing talent. The next step is to link succession planning with other human resource systems. Finally, the organization needs a way to provide employees with feedback about career paths available to them and how they are progressing toward their goals.

Succession planning offers several benefits.[20] It forces senior management to regularly and thoughtfully review the company's leadership talent. It assures that top-level management talent is available. It provides a set of development experiences that managers must complete to be considered for top management positions, so the organization does not promote managers before they are ready. Succession planning systems also help attract and retain ambitious employees by providing development opportunities.

Succession planning focuses on *high-potential employees*, that is, employees the organization believes can succeed in higher-level business

The process of identifying and tracking high-potential employees who will be able to fill top management positions or other key positions when they become vacant.

Identify the steps in the process of succession planning.

n Plan

anning," in J. Hedge
ational Interventions
09.

of a business unit,
rketing or finance),

sion planning sys-
gers for each posi-
s the organization
the most talented
re enough manag-
otential employees
r managerial jobs
avoid this problem
ed leaders, wders, which builds
y.

sources

pter shows, it is difficult
how many (if any) new
n will have to hire in a

given year in a given job category. The role of recruitment is to build a supply of potential new hires that the organization can draw on as the need arises. In some regions and industries in Canada, labour shortages have become the norm, and employers are becoming increasingly creative in their efforts to identify and attract job seekers. In human resource management, consists of any practice or activity carried on by the organization with the primary purpose of identifying and attracting potential employees.[22] It thus creates a connection between workforce planning and the actual selection of new employees (the topic of the next chapter).

Because of differences in companies' strategies, they may assign different degrees of importance to recruiting.[23] According to a survey of more than 400 human resource professionals conducted by Workopolis, 55 percent of respondents said, "recruiting/staff retention is as important to their business as profitability."[24] In general, however, all companies have to make decisions in three areas of recruiting: human resource policies, recruitment sources, and the characteristics and behaviour of the recruiter. As shown in Figure 4.4, these aspects of recruiting have different effects on whom the organization ultimately hires. Human resource policies influence the characteristics of the positions to be filled. Recruitment sources influence the kinds of job applicants an organization reaches. And the nature and behaviour of the recruiter affect the characteristics of both the vacancies and the applicants. Ultimately, an applicant's decision to accept a job offer—and the organization's decision to make the offer—depend on the *fit* between vacancy characteristics and applicant characteristics.

The remainder of this chapter explores these three aspects of recruiting: human resource policies, recruitment sources, and recruiter traits and behaviours.

Any activity carried on by the organization with the primary purpose of identifying and attracting potential employees.

Human Resource Policies

An organization's *human resource policies* are its decisions about how it will carry out human resource management, including how it will fill job openings. These policies influence the nature of the positions that are vacant. (The nearby "HR Best Practices" box describes

Discuss the use of employment branding and recruitment policies organizations use to make job vacancies more attractive.

FIGURE 4.4

Three Aspects of Recruiting

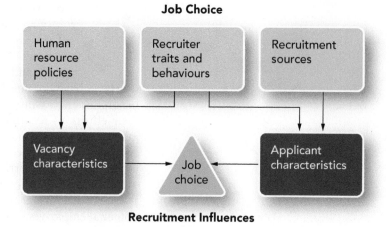

Job Choice

Human resource policies

Recruiter traits and behaviours

Recruitment sources

Vacancy characteristics

Job choice

Applicant characteristics

Recruitment Influences

how firms actively cultivate a continuing connection to former employees.) According to the research on recruitment, it is clear that characteristics of the vacancy are more important than recruiters or recruiting sources for predicting job choice.[25] Several policies are especially relevant to recruitment:

- *Internal versus external recruiting*—Organizations with policies to "promote from within" try to fill vacancies by recruiting candidates internally—that is finding candidates who already work for the organization. Opportunities for advancement make a job more attractive to applicants and employees. Decisions about internal versus external recruiting affect the nature of jobs, recruitment sources, and the nature of applicants, as we will describe later in the chapter.

- *Lead-the-market pay strategies*—Pay is an important job characteristic for almost all applicants. Organizations have a recruiting advantage if their policy is to take a "lead the market" approach to pay—that is, pay more than the current market wages for a job. Higher pay can also make up for a job's less desirable features, such as working on a night shift or outdoors in extreme weather conditions. Organizations that compete for applicants based on pay may use bonuses, stock options, and other forms of pay besides wages and salaries. Chapter 8 will take a closer look at these and other decisions about pay.

- *Employer branding*—Besides advertising specific job openings, as discussed in the next section, organizations may promote themselves as a good place to work in general. **Employer branding,** or *employment branding,* or *recruitment branding* is a strategic approach of attaching a visual, emotional, or cultural brand to an organization.

employer branding
A strategic approach of attaching a visual, emotional, or cultural brand to an organization.

Employer branding uses marketing techniques to attract, engage, and retain employees in the effort to become an *employer of choice.* For example, when an organization is recognized as one of "Canada's 50 Best Managed Companies" (www.canadas50best.com), the organization acquires the ability to use this well-known designation in various mediums—for example, print or a company website—to support and enhance their recruitment efforts.

An *employment brand* is the impression the company makes on employees and job seekers. Marketing it successfully is the same as marketing any other brand.[26] "The secret to an effective employment brand is differentiating an organization from the competition, targeting key benefits of the job to the right labour segments, and using multiple platforms to reach the right audiences."[27] This employment brand, the image an employer projects to potential hires, should be honest and paint a realistic picture of the company.[28] Just as marketers talk about the unique features of their products, employers need to first understand their own strengths and weaknesses and what they can offer top talent that their rivals cannot.[29] For example employers strive to be recognized not only as one of Canada's Top 100 Employers (www.canadastop100.com) but also to earn a spot in one of the other targeted categories, e.g., "Canada's Top Family-Friendly Employers" or "Canada's Top Employers for Young People."

When an organization is recognized as a top employer, they are likely to experience a dramatic increase in the number of résumés they receive. Employer branding is not the

HR BEST PRACTICES

"Boomerang Employees" Bring Back Benefits for Employers

An employee who leaves a company to pursue other ventures and is later rehired is what has become known as a "boomerang employee." Many career experts say, that as competition for top talent intensifies, companies will open the door even wider to its "alumni," placing particular focus on former high-performing employees. "It'll be a growing trend because there's such a skills shortage, one that's only going to get worse," predicts Larry Gibbons, vice-president of human resources at Kinectrics Inc., an engineering and technical services company in Toronto that has rehired former employees.

Few companies go as far as Ernst and Young to stay on good terms with former employees. Through its alumni relations program, the Toronto-based accounting firm actively cultivates a continuing connection with those who have moved on.

"We want to have a life-long relationship with our people, no matter where they are," says E&Y's director of national marketing. About five years ago, the company decided to substantially beef up the alumni program. Former employees were asked what they would like provided by the company. Continuing education was a top request. Now former staffers have access to webcasts sponsored by E&Y that discuss developments in the accounting profession, such as regulatory changes. A newsletter is sent out a couple of times a year and several social events are held for former staff. When people leave the firm, they're given a password to the alumni website, which includes a directory of current and former employees, updates on what former E&Y staff are doing, a place to post résumés, and a list of job vacancies at the company.

Encouraging former employees to consider E&Y again is definitely one of the aims of the program. At E&Y, 13 percent of new hires last year were boomerangs, the previous year the figure was 15 percent.

One of the benefits of rehiring former staff is the positive message it sends about the firm to those starting out. Toronto-based partner, Luana Comin-Sartor, rejoined Ernst & Young after a lengthy sojourn at a telecom firm. Many of her younger colleagues seek out her advice about their own career prospects. "People see me as having a more objective view, because I did leave." She also gets calls from former employees thinking about returning.

The chance to recapture some of its talent isn't the only reason E&Y puts so much effort into staying in touch. There are obvious business benefits for the consulting firm in maintaining a strong relationship with those who move on to other companies, which might need its services. "These are people we've trained, worked with, invested "Wherever they go, we'd like them to be an ambassador for the firm."

SOURCE: Ann Kerr, "Many Happy Returns" and "Accounting Firm Makes Sure to Stay in Touch with Past Staff," *The Globe and Mail*, June 30, 2004, p. C1.

exclusive domain of the private sector. "Savvy governments across the country are beginning to build and market a solid employment brand, creating catchy tag lines to grab the attention of jobseekers. The tag line for B.C.'s public service is 'Where Ideas Work' while in Nova Scotia it is 'Make a Difference.' "[30]

Recruitment Sources

Another critical element of an organization's recruitment strategy is its decisions about where to look for applicants. The total labour market is enormous and spread over the entire globe. As a practical matter, an organization will draw from a small fraction

L06 List and compare sources of job applicants.

of that total market. The methods the organization chooses for communicating its labour needs and the audiences it targets will determine the size and nature of the labour market the organization taps to fill its vacant positions.[31] A person who responds to a job advertisement on the Internet is likely to be different from a person responding to a sign hanging outside a factory. The "Did You Know?" box presents some data on sources of recruitment. Each of the major sources from which organization draw recruits has advantages and disadvantages.

INTERNAL SOURCES

As we discussed with regard to human resource policies, an organization may emphasize internal or external sources of job applicants. Internal sources are employees who currently hold other positions

DID YOU KNOW?

Four in Ten Positions Are Filled with Insiders

In a survey of large, well-known businesses, respondents said over one-third of positions are filled with people who already work for the company and accepted a promotion or transfer.

SOURCE: Gerry Crispin and Mark Mehler, "CareerXroads 9th Annual Source of Hire Study," February 2010, www.careerxroads .com . (This report includes 2008 data for sources of hire because the authors believe 2009 is not representative.)

Sources of Hire

All External Sources, 61%

Internal Movement, 39%

Note: "Internal movement" refers to jobs filled from employees currently in the company who are referred by managers or receive promotions or transfers; "all external sources" refers to employees found using sources outside the company such as electronic recruiting from company or job websites, employment agencies, colleges and universities, walk-in applicants, newspaper ads, and referrals.

---

in the organization. Organizations recruit existing employees through **job posting**, or communicating information about the vacancy on company bulletin boards, in employee publications, on corporate intranets, and anywhere else the organization communicates with employees. Managers also may identify candidates to recommend for vacancies. Policies that emphasize promotions and even lateral moves to achieve broader career experience can give applicants a favourable impression of the organization's jobs. The use of internal sources also affects what kinds of people the organization recruits.

For the employer, relying on internal sources offers several advantages.[32] First, it generates applicants who are well known to the organization. In addition, these applicants are relatively knowledgeable about the organization's vacancies, which minimizes the possibility they will have unrealistic expectations about the job. Finally, filling vacancies through internal recruiting is generally cheaper and faster than looking outside the organization.

CCL Industries, a Toronto-based specialty packaging company, has provided leadership training to about 1,000 employees since the 1990s to grow talent within the organization. This "leadership pool" is used to staff projects and assignments as well as prepare employees for additional responsibilities and challenges. In addition, CCL attributes this initiative to enhanced employee morale—employees feel valued

job posting
The process of communicating information about a job vacancy on company bulletin boards, in employee publications, on corporate intranets, and anywhere else the organization communicates with employees.

direct applicants
People who apply for a vacancy without prompting from the organization.

referrals
People who apply for a vacancy because someone in the organization prompted them to do so.

because of the investment the company is making in them.[33]

EXTERNAL SOURCES

Despite the advantages of internal recruitment, organizations often have good reasons to recruit externally.[34] For entry-level positions and perhaps for specialized upper-level positions, the organization has no internal recruits from which to draw. Also, bringing in outsiders may expose the organization to new ideas or new ways of doing business. An organization that uses only internal recruitment can wind up with a workforce whose members all think alike and therefore may be poorly suited to innovation.[35] And finally, companies that are able to grow during a slow economy can gain a competitive edge when other organizations are forced to avoid hiring, freeze pay increases, or even lay off talented people.[36] So organizations often recruit through direct applicants and referrals, advertisements, employment agencies, schools, and websites.

Direct Applicants and Referrals

Even without a formal effort to reach job applicants, an organization may hear from candidates through direct applicants and referrals. **Direct applicants** are people who apply for a vacancy without prompting from the organization. **Referrals** are people who apply because someone in the organization prompted them to do so. According to the survey results shown in Figure 4.5, the largest share (over one-fourth) of new employees hired by large companies came from referrals, and the next largest share (over 22 percent) came from direct applications made at the employer's website.[37] The target of an organization's recruitment efforts may also involve direct sourcing including identifying and contacting **passive job seekers**—individuals who are not actively seeking a job, but represent a significant source of top talent. These sources of recruits share characteristics that make them excellent pools from which to draw.

One advantage is that many direct applicants are to some extent already "sold" on the organization. Most have done some research and concluded there is enough fit between themselves and the vacant position to warrant submitting an application, a process called *self-selection*, which, when it works, eases the pressure on the organization's recruiting and selection

passive job seekers
Individuals who are not actively seeking a job.

systems. A form of aided self-selection occurs with referrals. Many job seekers look to friends, relatives, and acquaintances to help find employment. Using these social networks not only helps the job seeker, but also simplifies recruitment for employers. Current employees (who are familiar with the vacancy as well as the person they are referring) decide that there is a fit between the person and the vacancy, so they convince the person to apply for the job.

An additional benefit of using such sources is that it costs much less than formal recruiting efforts. Considering these combined benefits, referrals and direct applications are among the best sources of new hires. Some employers offer current employees financial incentives for referring applicants who are hired and perform acceptably on the job (e.g., if they stay 180 days). Other companies play off their good reputations in the labour market to generate direct applications.

The major downside of referrals is that they limit the likelihood of exposing the organization to fresh

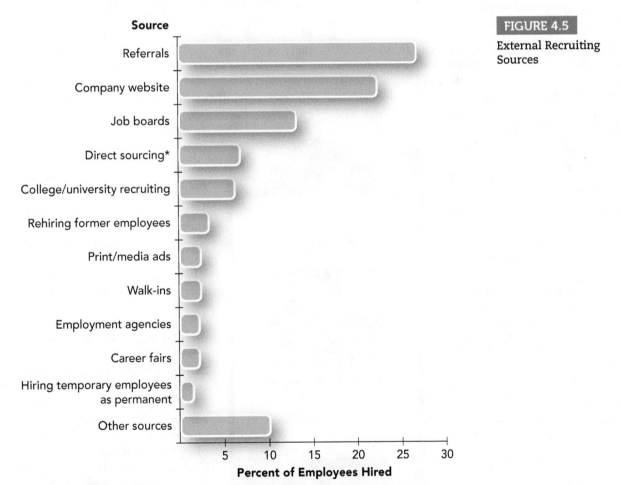

Source

- Referrals
- Company website
- Job boards
- Direct sourcing*
- College/university recruiting
- Rehiring former employees
- Print/media ads
- Walk-ins
- Employment agencies
- Career fairs
- Hiring temporary employees as permanent
- Other sources

5   10   15   20   25   30
Percent of Employees Hired

FIGURE 4.5

External Recruiting Sources

*Direct sourcing includes research by the employer, such as searching internal databases of résumés and social-networking websites to identify and contact people who seem to be well-qualified but did not apply.

SOURCE: Gerry Crispin and Mark Mehler, "CareerXroads 9th Annual Source of Hire Study," February 2010, www.careerxroads.com (data for 2009).

viewpoints. People tend to refer others who are like themselves. Furthermore, sometimes referrals contribute to hiring practices that are or that appear unfair, an example being **nepotism**, or the hiring of relatives. Employees may resent the hiring and rapid promotion of "the boss's son" or "the boss's daughter," or even the boss's friend.

nepotism
The practice of hiring relatives.

Ads in Newspapers and Magazines

Open almost any newspaper or magazine and you can find ads for job openings. These ads typically generate a less desirable group of applicants than direct applications or referrals, and do so at greater expense. However, few employers can fill all their vacancies purely through direct applications and referrals, so they usually need to advertise. Also, an employer can take many steps to increase the effectiveness of recruitment through advertising.

The person designing a job advertisement needs to answer two questions:

- What do we need to say?
- To whom do we need to say it?

With respect to the first question, an ad should give readers enough information to evaluate the job and its requirements, so they can make a well-informed judgment about their qualifications. Providing enough information may require long ads, which cost more. The employer should evaluate the additional costs against the costs of providing too little information: vague ads generate a huge number of applicants, including many who are not reasonably qualified or would not accept the job if they learned more about it. Reviewing all these applications to eliminate unsuitable applicants is expensive. In practice, the people who write job ads tend to overstate the skills and experience required, perhaps generating too few qualified candidates. For example, some have blamed the shortage of qualified engineers on job advertising that requires experience with particular processes or software programs, rather than looking for broader abilities that can be transferred to new applications.[38]

Specifying whom to reach with the message helps the advertiser decide where to place the ad. The most common medium for advertising jobs is the classified section of local newspapers. These ads are relatively inexpensive, yet they reach many people in a specific geographic area who are currently looking for work (or at least interested enough to be reading the classifieds). On the downside, this medium offers little ability to target skill levels. Typically, many of the people reading classified ads are either over- or underqualified for the position. Also, people not looking for work rarely read the classifieds; these people may include candidates the organization might lure from their current employers. For reaching a specific part of the labour market, including certain skill levels and more people who are employed, the organization may get better results from advertising in professional or industry journals.

QR (Quick Response) codes are becoming powerful recruitment tools because they can take applicants directly to customized information such as a website, video, or to the company's social media such as Facebook, Twitter, and LinkedIn without the need to type in a Web address.

Electronic Recruiting

In recent years, employers have shifted using their spending on job ads away from print media to online job advertising or a combination of the two. A recent survey by the Conference Board found that the number of online job ads rose by 24 percent over the previous year.[39] Online recruiting generally involves posting career information at company websites to address people who are interested in the particular company and posting paid advertisements at career services to attract people who are searching for jobs. Companies are also turning to the use of social media including Facebook, Twitter, and LinkedIn to seek out job candidates. For

, manager of recruitment unsuccessful attracting the account manager opening, and online job boards. So Moulday turned to candidates who matched the qualification and ultimately hired one passive candidate who wasn't aware of the job or looking.[40] Most large companies and many smaller ones make career information available at their websites. To make that information easier to find, they may register a link, e.g., www.bellcareers.ca to access information about careers at Bell. To be an effective recruiting tool, corporate career information should move beyond generalities, offering descriptions of open positions and an easy way to submit a résumé. One of the best features of this kind of electronic recruiting is the ability to target and attract job candidates whose values match the organization's values and whose skills match the job requirements.[41] Candidates also appreciate an email response that the company has received the résumé—especially a response that gives a timetable about further communications from the company.

connect

See how recruiting for **talent is done in the virtual world.**

Accepting applications at the company website is not so successful for smaller and less well-known organizations, because fewer people are likely to visit the website. These organizations might get better results by going to the national job board websites, such as working.com, Monster.ca, and Workopolis.com, which attract a vast array of applicants. At these sites, job seekers submit standardized résumés. Employers can search the site's database for résumés that include specified key terms, and they can also submit information about their job opportunities, so that job seekers can search that information by key term. With both employers and job seekers submitting information to and conducting searches on them, these sites offer an efficient way to find matches between job seekers and job vacancies. However, a drawback is that the big job websites can provide too many leads of inferior quality, because they are so huge and serve all job seekers and employers, not a select segment.

Because of this limitation of the large websites, smaller, more tailored websites called "niche boards" focus on certain industries, occupations, or geographic areas. For example, Atlantic Canada's Career Beacon is a regional-based job board popular with applicants who live in Atlantic Canada and have no intention of relocating. In addition, companies can improve the effectiveness of online advertising by employing more interactive tools, such as social networking. For example, Ernst & Young's Facebook page contains information and discussion boards aimed at students. Riding the popularity of websites such as YouTube, some employers and recruitment websites have started offering video workplace "tours" to give potential employees a new way to get a glimpse of the organization's employment brand.[42]

Public Employment Agencies

Employers can register job vacancies at the federal government's Service Canada website, "Job Bank" (www.jobbank.gc.ca). In addition to posting job openings, employers can access information and links to government forms, services, and programs. Prospective employees can narrow their job search by province and are also provided access to a variety of resources and career navigation tools.

Vancouver Police Department (VPD) recruiters created online personas on Second Life. Organizations like the VPD and the Ontario Public Service are using virtual world recruiting to attract real-life employees.

Staffing Services Companies

In addition to providing temporary employees, staffing services companies, such as Randstad and Adecco, provide assistance to employers in attracting permanent applicants. Job seekers apply to the staffing services company and are usually screened for suitability. These agencies differ significantly in the types of services provided. It is important for both job seekers and employers to research and thoroughly assess private agencies so as to work with the firm that will best meet their needs and expectations.

Staffing companies provide their services for a fee. Usually these fees are paid by the employer for the service of receiving employee referrals.

For managers or professionals, an employer may use the services of a type of private agency called an *executive search firm* (ESF). People often call these agencies "headhunters" because, unlike other employment agencies, they find new jobs for people almost exclusively already employed. For job candidates, dealing with executive search firms can be sensitive. Typically, executives do not want to advertise their availability, because it might trigger a negative reaction from their current employer. ESFs serve as a buffer, providing confidentiality between the employer and the recruit. That benefit may give an employer access to candidates it cannot recruit in other, more direct ways.

yield ratio · A ratio that expresses the percentage of applicants who successfully move from one stage of the recruitment and selection process to the next.

Universities and Colleges

Most universities and colleges have placement services that seek to help their graduates obtain employment. On-campus interviewing is the most important source of recruits for entry-level professional and managerial vacancies.[43] Organizations tend to focus especially on universities and colleges that have strong reputations in areas for which they have critical needs—say petroleum engineering or accounting.[44]

Many employers have found that successfully competing for the best students requires more than just signing up prospective graduates for interview slots. One of the best ways to establish a stronger presence on a campus is with a cooperative education or internship program. These programs give an organization early access to potential applicants and let the organization assess their capabilities directly.

Another way of increasing the employer's presence on campus is to participate in university and college job fairs. In general, a job fair is an event where many employers gather for a short time to meet large numbers of potential job applicants. Although job fairs can be held anywhere (such as at a hotel or convention centre), campuses are ideal because of the many well-educated, not-yet-employed individuals there. Job fairs are an inexpensive means of generating an on-campus presence. They can provide one-on-one dialogue with potential recruits or by displaying a QR code allow students to instantly access detailed company information.

EVALUATING THE QUALITY OF A SOURCE

In general, there are few rules that say what recruitment source is best for a given job vacancy. Therefore, it is wise for employers to monitor the quality of all their recruitment sources. One way to do this is to develop and compare **yield ratios** for each source.[45] A yield ratio expresses the percentage of applicants who successfully move from one stage of the recruitment and selection process to the next. For example,

Capt. Jen Causey, an artillery officer with the 2nd Regiment, Royal Canadian Horse Artillery, based in Petawawa, Ontario, was staffing the booth at a Women in Leadership Career Fair at the University of Toronto. She is chatting with Cora Cheng, a second-year mechanical engineering student at U of T. How do career fairs benefit employers and the students at the same time?

the organization might find the number of candidates interviewed as a percentage of the total number of résumés generated by a given source (i.e., number of interviews divided by number of résumés). A high yield ratio (large percentage) means the source is an effective way to find candidates to interview. By comparing the yield ratios of different recruitment sources, HR professionals can determine which is the best or most efficient for the type of vacancy.

Another measure of recruitment success is the *cost per hire*. To compute this amount, find the cost of using a particular recruitment source for a particular type of vacancy. Then divide that cost by the number of people hired to fill that type of vacancy. A low cost per hire means that the recruitment source is efficient; it delivers qualified candidates at minimal cost.

To see how HR professionals use these measures, look at the examples in Table 4.3. This table shows the results for a hypothetical organization that used six kinds of recruitment sources to fill a number of vacancies. For each recruitment source, the table shows four yield ratios and the cost per hire. To fill these jobs, the best two sources of recruits were local universities and employee referral programs. Company websites generated the largest number of recruits (1,000 résumés). However, only 20 were judged acceptable, of which only half accepted employment offers, for a cumulative yield ratio of 20/1,000, or 2 percent. Recruiting at renowned universities generated highly qualified applicants, but relatively few of them ultimately accepted positions with the organization. Executive search firms produced the highest cumulative yield ratio. These generated only 20 applicants, but all of them accepted interview offers, most were judged acceptable, and 79 percent of these acceptable candidates took jobs with the organization. However, notice the cost per hire. The executive search firms charged $90,000 for finding these 15 employees, resulting in the largest cost per hire. In contrast, local colleges and universities and company websites provided modest yield ratios at one of the lowest costs per hire. Employee referrals provided excellent yield ratios at a slightly higher cost.

Recruiter Traits and Behaviours

As we showed in Figure 4.4, the third influence on recruitment outcomes is the recruiter, including this person's characteristics and the way he or she behaves. The ideal recruiter is a *talent magnet*—top recruiters are able to attract talent. The recruiter affects the nature of both the job vacancy

L07 Describe the recruiter's role in the recruitment process, including limits and opportunities.

TABLE 4.3 **Results of a Hypothetical Recruiting Effort**

	RECRUITING SOURCE					
	LOCAL COLLEGE/ UNIVERSITY	RENOWNED COLLEGE/ UNIVERSITY	EMPLOYEE REFERRALS	NEWSPAPER AD	EXECUTIVE SEARCH FIRMS	COMPANY WEBSITE
Résumés generated	200	400	50	500	20	1,000
Interview offers accepted	175	100	45	400	20	80
Yield ratio	**87%**	**25%**	**90%**	**80%**	**100%**	**8%**
Applicants judged acceptable	100	95	40	50	19	40
Yield ratio	**57%**	**95%**	**89%**	**12%**	**95%**	**50%**
Accept employment offers	90	10	35	25	15	20
Yield ratio	**90%**	**11%**	**88%**	**50%**	**79%**	**50%**
Cumulative yield ratio	90/200 **45%**	10/400 **3%**	35/50 **70%**	25/500 **5%**	15/20 **75%**	20/1,000 **2%**
Cost	$30,000	$50,000	$15,000	$20,000	$90,000	$500
Cost per hire	**$333**	**$5,000**	**$428**	**$800**	**$6,000**	**$25**

and the applicants generated. However, the recruiter often gets involved late in the recruitment process. In many cases, by the time a recruiter meets some applicants, they have already made up their minds about what they desire in a job, what the vacant job has to offer, and their likelihood of receiving a job offer.[46]

Many applicants approach the recruiter with some skepticism. Knowing it is the recruiter's job to sell them on a vacancy, some applicants discount what the recruiter says, in light of what they have heard from other sources, such as friends, published sources, and professors. When candidates are already familiar with the company through knowing about its products, the recruiter's impact is especially weak.[47] For these and other reasons, recruiters' characteristics and behaviours seem to have limited impact on applicants' job choices.

> **realistic job preview**
> Background information about a job's positive and negative qualities.

CHARACTERISTICS OF THE RECRUITER

Most organizations have to choose whether their recruiters are specialists in human resources or experts at particular jobs (i.e., those who currently hold the same kinds of jobs or supervise people who hold the jobs). According to some studies, applicants perceive HR specialists as less credible and are less attracted to jobs when recruiters are HR specialists.[48] The evidence does not completely discount a positive role for HR specialists in recruiting. It does indicate, however, that these specialists need to take extra steps to ensure that applicants perceive them as knowledgeable and credible.

In general, applicants respond positively to recruiters whom they perceive as warm and informative. "Warm" means the recruiter seems to care about the applicant and to be enthusiastic about the applicant's potential to contribute to the organization. "Informative" means the recruiter provides the kind of information the applicant is seeking. The evidence of impact of other characteristics of recruiters—including their age, sex, and race—is complex and inconsistent.[49]

BEHAVIOUR OF THE RECRUITER

Recruiters affect results not only by providing plenty of information, but by providing the right kind of information. Perhaps the most-researched aspect of recruiting is the level of realism in the recruiter's message. Because the recruiter's job is to attract candidates, recruiters may feel pressure to exaggerate the positive qualities of the vacancy and to downplay its negative qualities. Applicants are highly sensitive

to negative information. The highest-quality applicants may be less willing to pursue jobs when this type of information comes out.[50] But if the recruiter goes too far in a positive direction, the candidate can be misled and lured into taking a job that has been misrepresented. Then unmet expectations can contribute to a high turnover rate. When recruiters describe jobs unrealistically, people who take those jobs may come to believe that the employer is deceitful.[51]

Many studies have looked at how well **realistic job previews**—background information about jobs' positive and negative qualities—can get around this problem and help organizations minimize turnover among new employees. On the whole, the research suggests that realistic job previews have a weak and inconsistent effect on turnover.[52] Although recruiters can go overboard in selling applicants on the desirability of a job vacancy, there is little support for the belief that informing people about the negative characteristics of a job will "inoculate" them so that the negative features don't cause them to quit.[53]

Finally, for affecting whether people choose to take a job, but even more so, whether they stick with a job, the recruiter seems less important than an organization's human resource policies that directly affect the job's features (pay, security, advancement opportunities, and so on).

ENHANCING THE RECRUITER'S IMPACT

Nevertheless, although recruiters are probably not the most important influence on people's job choices, this does not mean recruiters cannot have an impact. Most recruiters receive little training.[54] If we were to determine what does matter to job candidates, perhaps recruiters could be trained in those areas.

Researchers have tried to find the conditions in which recruiters do make a difference. Such research suggests that an organization can take several steps to increase the positive impact that recruiters have on job candidates:

- *Recruiters should provide timely feedback.* Applicants dislike delays in feedback. They may draw negative conclusions about the organization (for starters, that the organization doesn't care about their application).
- *Recruiters should avoid offensive behaviour.* They should avoid behaving in ways that might convey the wrong impression about the organization.[55] Figure 4.6 quotes applicants who felt they had extremely bad experiences with recruiters.

Their statements provide examples of behaviours to avoid.

- *The organization can recruit with teams rather than individual recruiters.* Applicants view job experts as more credible than HR specialists, and a team can include both kinds of recruiters. HR specialists on the team provide knowledge about company policies and procedures and ensure the integrity of the process, consistency, and compliance with human rights legislation.

Through such positive behaviour, recruiters can give organizations a better chance of competing for talented human resources. In the next chapter, we will describe how an organization selects the candidates that best meet its needs.

FIGURE 4.6

Recruits Who Were Offended by Recruiters

_____ has a management training program which the recruiter had gone through. She was talking about the great presentation skills that _____ teaches you, and the woman was barely literate. She was embarrassing. If that was the best they could do, I did not want any part of them. Also, _____ and _____ 's recruiters appeared to have real attitude problems. I also thought they were chauvinistic. (Arts undergraduate)

I had a very bad campus interview experience . . . the person who came was a last-minute fill-in. . . . I think he had a couple of "issues" and was very discourteous during the interview. He was one step away from yawning in my face. . . . The other thing he did was that he kept making these—nothing illegal, mind you—but he kept making these references to the fact that I had been out of my undergraduate and first graduate programs for more than ten years now. (MBA with ten years of experience)

One firm I didn't think of talking to initially, but they called me and asked me to talk with them. So I did, and then the recruiter was very, very rude. Yes, very rude, and I've run into that a couple of times. (Engineering graduate)

_____ had set a schedule for me which they deviated from regularly. Times overlapped, and one person kept me too long, which pushed the whole day back. They almost seemed to be saying that it was my fault that I was late for the next one! I guess a lot of what they did just wasn't very professional. Even at the point when I was done, where most companies would have a cab pick you up, I was in the middle of a snowstorm and they said, "You can get a cab downstairs." There weren't any cabs. I literally had to walk 12 or 14 blocks with my luggage, trying to find some way to get to the airport. They didn't book me a hotel for the night of the snowstorm so I had to sit in the airport for eight hours trying to get another flight. . . . They wouldn't even reimburse me for the additional plane fare. (Industrial relations graduate student)

The guy at the interview made a joke about how nice my nails were and how they were going to ruin them there due to all the tough work. (Engineering undergraduate)

THINKING ETHICALLY

Talent Poachers

In the escalating war for top talent, the fine line between aggressive recruiting and the unethical solicitation of talent is getting fuzzy. The object of "talent poachers" is to provide their organizations with top talent. But not unlike an endangered species, this top talent is in scarce supply. As a result, talent poachers pursue employees who have not even expressed any interest in leaving their current organizations.

Shantal Feltham, president and CEO of Stiris Research Inc. a London, Ontario-based clinical research firm, didn't look far when she needed a director of business development, seven years ago. "I turned to our competitor," says Feltham. "I hired away one of their star employees." Four years ago, she also hired away a vice-president from her former employer. "I knew she would be a perfect fit for the company," Ms. Feltham says. "I pursued her for three years."

Businesses of all sizes are likely to resent having their workforce pilfered, and often these "poached" employees are top performers. Accounting firm Mintz & Partners LLP creates "cones of silence" around their staff by installing spam filters on all of its computers to block incoming emails from all known recruiters. Receptionists flag incoming calls from potential recruiters and screen callers indicating "the person they seek is unavailable," says Lyle Strachan, Mintz's chief operating officer in Toronto. "Recruiting is rampant. We know our people are constantly getting tempting offers laid at their feet," Mr. Strachan says. "We're making it known that we value their contributions, and that we will do everything we possibly can to listen to their concerns, and meet their needs."

Talent poachers are well aware of these types of employer tactics and use some strategies of their own. Poachers will call potential "poachees" at home or create new email accounts to get around spam filters that block their names. Executives and professionals also respond favourably to poachers who remind them they are known to be well-respected, top performers in their field. It is expected that the war for talent is just starting to heat up and recruiting will continue to get more aggressive for professional and executive talent. "In some industries, there used to be kind of a club, an unwritten agreement that they wouldn't try to go into each other's organizations," says Tom Long, a Toronto-based partner with Egon Zehnder International, a global executive recruiting firm with offices worldwide. "Frankly, I think that's a thing of the past."

SOURCES: Bryan Borzykowski, "How to Keep Employee Poachers at Bay," *Special to Globe and Mail Update,* August 24, 2011, www.theglobeandmail.com/report-on-business/small-business/sb-managing/human-resources/how-to-keep-employee-poachers-at-bay/article1909725/, retrieved March 18, 2012; Lisa Orndorff, Regan Halvorsen, and Anne St. Martin, "Taxing Expats, Poaching Talent, E-Newsletters," *HR Magazine,* May 2007, p. 33; Wallace Immen, "Warning: Poachers Will Be Fought on Site," *The Globe and Mail,* October 18, 2006, p. C1; and Erin Pooley, "The Perils of Poaching," *Canadian Business,* January 31–February 13, 2005, p. 63.

QUESTIONS

1. Where is the line between aggressive recruiting and unethical solicitation of talent?
2. What obligations, if any, does an employee have to its current employer?
3. Is there any way for an organization to protect itself from talent poachers?

SUMMARY

L01 Discuss how to plan for the human resources needed to carry out the organization's strategy.

- The first step in workforce planning is forecasting. Through trend analysis and good judgment, the planner tries to determine the supply of and demand for various human resources.
- On the basis of whether a surplus or a shortage is expected, the planner sets goals and creates a strategy for achieving those goals. The organization then implements its HR strategy and evaluates the results.

L02 Determine the demand for and supply of workers in various job categories.

- The planner can look at leading indicators, assuming historical patterns will continue in the future. Trend analysis can convert several leading indicators into a single prediction of labour needs and supply.

- Analysis of a transitional matrix can help the planner identify which job categories can be filled internally and where high turnover is likely.

Summarize the advantages and disadvantages of ways to eliminate a labour surplus and avoid a labour shortage.

- To reduce a surplus, downsizing, pay reductions, and demotions deliver fast results but at a high cost in human suffering that may hurt surviving employees' motivation and future recruiting. Transferring employees, requiring them to share work, a hiring freeze, early-retirement packages, and retraining also have various advantages and disadvantages.

- To avoid a labour shortage, requiring overtime is the easiest and fastest strategy, which can easily be changed if conditions change. However, overtime may exhaust workers and can hurt morale. Similarly, using temporary employees, outsourcing, transferring, retraining, hiring new employees, and using technology offer advantages and disadvantages requiring careful consideration.

Discuss the steps in the succession planning process.

- Succession planning ensures that the organization identifies qualified employees to fill organizational roles that are anticipated to become available in the future.

- Succession planning focuses on high-potential employees.

Discuss the use of employment branding and recruitment policies organizations use to make job vacancies more attractive.

- Internal recruiting (hiring from within) generally makes job vacancies more attractive, because candidates see opportunities for growth and advancement. Lead-the-market pay strategies make jobs economically desirable.

- Employer branding projects an image of the organization, including its culture and key benefits.

List and compare sources of job applicants.

- Internal sources, promoted through job postings, generate applicants who are familiar to the organization and motivate other employees by demonstrating opportunities for advancement. However, internal sources are usually insufficient for all of an organization's labour needs. Direct applicants and referrals, newspaper and magazine advertising, staffing agencies, and universities and colleges offer advantages and issues to be assessed.

- Electronic recruiting gives organizations access to a global labour market, tends to be inexpensive, and allows convenient searching of databases; however, organizations may receive many applications from unqualified applicants. E-cruiting has become increasingly targeted and sophisticated and has expanded to applications such as social networking and virtual world recruiting.

Describe the recruiter's role in the recruitment process, including limits and opportunities.

- Through their behaviour and other characteristics, recruiters influence the nature of the job vacancy and the kinds of applicants generated. Applicants tend to perceive job experts as more credible than recruiters who are HR specialists.

- Recruiters can improve their impact by providing timely feedback, avoiding behaviour that contributes to a negative impression of the organization, and teaming up with job experts.

Critical Thinking Questions

1. Suppose an organization expects a labour shortage to develop in key job areas over the next few years. Recommend general responses the organization could make in each of the following areas:
   a. Recruitment
   b. Training and development
   c. Rewards (pay, employee benefits, and work environment)
2. Review the sample transitional matrix shown in Table 4.1. What jobs experience the greatest turnover (employees leaving the organization)? How might an organization with this combination of jobs reduce the turnover?
3. In the same transitional matrix, which jobs seem to rely the most on internal recruitment? Which seem to rely most on external recruitment? Why?
4. Why do organizations combine statistical and judgmental forecasts of labour demand, rather than relying on statistics or judgment alone? Give an example of a situation in which each type of forecast could be inaccurate.
5. Some organizations have detailed employment equity plans, complete with goals and timetables, for women, Aboriginal employees, people with disabilities, and visible minorities, yet have no formal workforce plan for the organization as a whole. Why might this be the case? What does this practice suggest about the role of human resource management in these organizations?
6. Is succession planning becoming more or less important? Explain your answer.
7. Give an example of a human resource policy that would help attract a larger pool of job candidates.

Give an example of a human resource policy that would likely reduce the pool of candidates. Would you expect these policies to influence the quality as well as the number of applicants? Why or why not?

8. Discuss the relative merits of internal versus external recruitment. Give an example of a situation in which each of these approaches might be particularly effective.

9. List the jobs you have held. How were you recruited for each of these? From the organization's perspective, what were some pros and cons of recruiting you through these methods?

10. Recruiting people for jobs that require international assignments is increasingly important for many organizations. Where might an organization go to recruit people interested in such assignments?

11. A large share of HR professionals have rated electronic recruiting as their best source of new talent. What qualities of electronic recruiting do you think contribute to this opinion? What is your reaction to the use of social networks, e.g., Facebook, Twitter, and LinkedIn for recruiting purposes? How are job fairs changing due to the use of QR codes and virtual recruiting, e.g., Second Life?

12. How can organizations improve the effectiveness of their recruiters?

What's Your HR IQ?

Connect offers more ways to check what you've learned so far. Find experiential exercises, Test Your Knowledge quizzes, videos, and many other resources to gauge your HR IQ.

CASE STUDY 4.1:   Apple's Make-vs.-Buy Decision

In a turnaround from a trend in which high-tech (and other) manufacturers have outsourced the making of important components in order to increase efficiency and focus on what they do best, Apple has recently made moves that seem aimed at bringing the design of microchips back in-house. Apple is known for innovative design, and along with that, it tends to keep details of what it makes highly secret. Making chip design a company process, rather than a product to buy, gives Apple more control over the process—and over the secrecy.

Of course, the decision to handle its own development has huge implications for human resource management. The company needs all-new labour forecasts, a larger labour force, and an intense push to bring in technical talent. Recently, Apple has been hiring many new engineers. Products they could be assigned include microchips that require less power to operate devices including iPhones and iPads, as well as circuitry to improve the graphics displayed in games and videos played on its devices. A top-notch team could, at least in theory, come up with unique improvements that will take rivals by surprise.

One way to acquire a lot of talent fast is to acquire entire companies and make them part of Apple. And that's one move Apple has been making. The company recently acquired P.A. Semi, a startup company that designs microchips. Its products could be used to run iPhones and iPods. Observers are guessing that chips developed by P.A. Semi could take the place of chips Apple has been buying from Samsung for its iPhone.

Samsung had customized the chips to Apple's specifications. Apple could be worried that a company such as Samsung might intentionally or unintentionally start applying some of Apple's ideas to chips made for competitors' products.

Another bit of evidence about Apple's hunt for talent is visible online at the LinkedIn networking site, where members list their job histories. According to the *Wall Street Journal*, more than 100 people on the site have current job titles at Apple plus past jobs involving microchips. Their prior companies include Intel, Samsung, and Qualcomm. One recent hire was the chief technology officer from Advanced Micro Devices' graphic products group. Furthermore, it's possible to evaluate job openings that Apple has been posting. These have included positions that involve expertise in handwriting recognition technology and microchips used in managing displays.

Apple has been seen at job fairs, too. Its recruiters participated in a job fair for employees who were being laid off at Spanison, a company that makes memory chips and recently declared bankruptcy.

Questions

1. Given the ideas presented about Apple's strategy, what HR actions would be most suitable for supporting that strategy? (Consider especially the options in Table 4.2.)

2. What challenges would you expect to be most significant for Apple's HR staff in meeting these human resource requirements?

3. What sources of job applicants would you recommend that Apple use to meet the needs described above?

SOURCES: Yukari Iwatani Kane and Don Clark, "In Major Shift, Apple Builds Its Own Team to Design Chips," *Wall Street Journal*, April 30, 2009, http://online.wsj.com; "Apple Turning to Chip Design for Its Innovation," *Information Week*, April 30, 2009, Business & Company Resource Center, http://galenet.galegroup.com; and "Apple Increases Investment in British Chip Designer," *Information Week*, June 26, 2009, Business & Company Resource Center, http://galenet.galegroup.com.

CASE STUDY 4.2: Recruiters Slip-Up Using Technology

Aileen Siu, an acting team leader in the Ontario cabinet office, learned a powerful lesson when she intended to forward an email to a colleague but actually sent the message back to the job applicant with one sentence: "This is the ghetto dude that I spoke to before." Evon Reid, an honours student at the University of Toronto had applied for a media analyst position at the cabinet office. "Ghetto dude? It means I'm black. It's very insulting. It's still pretty shocking to me." Reached on vacation, Craig Sumi, manager of the department, said Sui is "an unclassified, part-time employee....low level." Reid told the Toronto Star: "She may be very low level to them but she was given a lot of responsibility. She was my only link into the cabinet office so she was very important to me."

Reid received apologies from both Craig Sumi and Premier Dalton McGuinty who contacted Reid by phone. The premier told him, "he deserved an apology and there was no one better to deliver it than him," according to Reid. Sui said she was "multi-tasking" when she hit the wrong button and copied Reid. She also insisted the email didn't refer to anyone "outside my circle of friends." "It wasn't directed at Evon at all. That was internal....it didn't have anything to do with any of the applicants," said Siu, 26, a recent University of Toronto political science graduate.

Other recruiting blunders using technology may not result in media firestorms like the previous example but are still worthy of further reflection. As recruiters mine LinkedIn profiles in their industry or area, they spend a lot of time on the site, however, they sometimes neglect their own profiles. For example, recruiters that post "CONNECT WITH ME" in the name field of their own LinkedIn profile come across as desperate and unappealing to candidates. As organizations also turn to Twitter to announce job openings, some recruiters fail to interact with their followers. By focusing on pushing information out to followers rather than also engaging in two-way communication, they appear to lack sincerity and follow-through with prospective candidates.

Questions

1. In your opinion, what is the cause(s) of these inappropriate recruiter behaviours?
2. What important lessons can recruiters learn from these blunders?

SOURCES: Lesley Young, "Careless Click Lands HR Staffer in Hot Water," *Canadian HR Reporter*, August 13, 2007, pp. 1–2, Linda Diebel, "'Ghetto Dude' Email Sent by Mistake: Province," July 21, 2007, p. A3; Linda Diebel, "McGuinty Apologies for 'Ghetto Dude' Email," *Toronto Star*, July 23, 2007, p. A2; "Mistakes Recruiters Make on LinkedIn," www.recruiter.com/recruiting-news/mistakes-recruiters-linkedin/, retrieved March 18, 2012; and "What are Common Mistakes that Employers Make When Using Twitter as a Recruiting Tool?" www.focus.com/questions/what-are-common-mistakes-employers-make-when-using-twitter/, retrieved March 18, 2012.

 | Practise and learn online with Connect.

Chapter 5

SELECTING EMPLOYEES

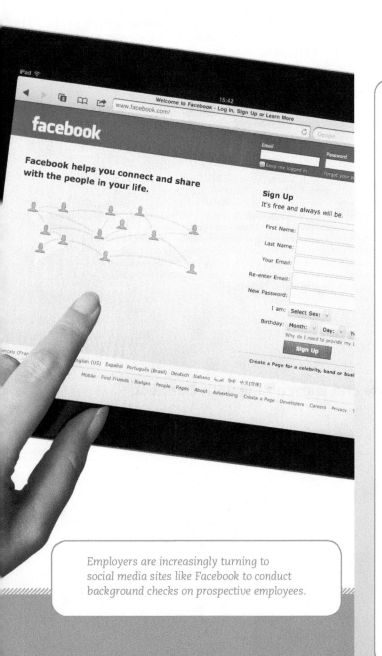

Employers are increasingly turning to
social media sites like Facebook to conduct
background checks on prospective employees.

What Do I Need to Know?

After reading this chapter, you should be able to:

LO1 ▸ Identify the elements of the selection process.

LO2 ▸ Define ways to measure the success of a selection method.

LO3 ▸ Summarize the legal requirements for employee selection.

LO4 ▸ Compare the common methods used for selecting human resources.

LO5 ▸ Describe major types of employment tests.

LO6 ▸ Discuss how to conduct effective interviews.

LO7 ▸ Explain how employers carry out the process of making a selection decision.

Should You Google Yourself?

Hiring the right person is perhaps the most important decision a manager can make. The inherent risks and potential costs of a bad hire are causing organizations of all sizes to look for creative ways to conduct background checks of potential employees.

"Who types a potential candidate's name into Google or looks them up on Facebook?" Ryan Berger, a Vancouver-based lawyer asks at social media seminars he conducts for employers. Invariably, almost everyone raises their hand, he says. "Oftentimes, people's first reaction when they meet someone or they're dealing with someone new, they'll punch them into Google and see what comes up," Berger adds.

This growing trend prompted Offices of the Privacy Commissioners of both Alberta and British Columbia to recently release "Guidelines for Social Media Background Checks" to help protect individual privacy. Employers are cautioned to follow the guidelines when using social media or search engines like Google to seek out information about potential employees. Even so, job seekers need to be aware that sites such as Twitter and Facebook may still be making them look good or bad to potential employers. According to Louise Fox, director of Toronto's Protocol Solutions: "Don't put anything online that you wouldn't want your mom to read or have published in the newspaper."[1]

Introduction

Hiring decisions are about finding the people who will be a good fit with the job and the organization. Any organization that appreciates the competitive edge provided by good people must take the utmost care in choosing its members. The organization's decisions about selecting people are central to its ability to survive, adapt, and grow. Selection decisions become especially critical when organizations face tight labour markets or must compete for talent with other organizations in the same industry. If a competitor keeps getting the best applicants, the remaining companies have to make do with who is left.

This chapter will familiarize you with ways to increase the effectiveness of employee selection. The chapter starts by describing the selection process and how to evaluate possible methods for carrying out that process. It then takes an in-depth look at the most widely used methods: applications and résumés, employment tests, and interviews. The chapter ends by describing the process by which organizations arrive at a final selection decision.

What Are the Steps in the Selection Process?

Through the process of selection, organizations make decisions about who will be chosen to fill job openings. Selection begins with the candidates identified through recruitment and attempts to reduce their number to the individuals best qualified to perform the available jobs and fit with the culture of the organization. At the end of the process, the selected individuals are placed in jobs with the organization.

LO1 ▸ Identify the elements of the selection process.

The process of selecting employees varies considerably from organization to organization and from job to job. At most organizations however, selection includes the steps illustrated in Figure 5.1. First, a human resource professional reviews the applications received to see which meet the requirements of the job. For candidates who meet the requirements, the organization administers tests and reviews work samples to assess the candidates' competencies. Those with the best capabilities are invited to

FIGURE 5.1

Steps in the Selection Process

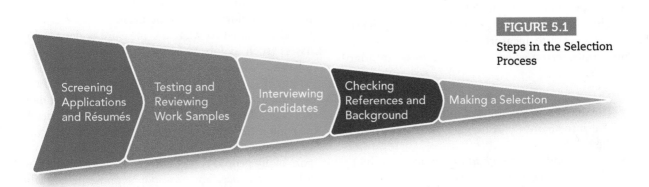

Screening Applications and Résumés | Testing and Reviewing Work Samples | Interviewing Candidates | Checking References and Background | Making a Selection

the organization for one or more interviews. Often, supervisors and team members are involved in this stage of the process. By this point, the decision makers are beginning to form conclusions about which candidates are most desirable. For the top few candidates, the organization should check references and conduct background checks to verify that the organization's information is correct. Then supervisors, teams, and other decision makers select a person to receive a job offer. In some cases, the candidate may negotiate with the organization regarding salary, benefits, and the like. If the candidate accepts the job, the organization places him or her in that job.

How does an organization decide which of these elements to use, and in what order? Some organizations simply repeat a selection process that is familiar. If members of the organization underwent job interviews, they conduct job interviews, asking familiar questions. However, what organizations *should* do is to create a selection process in support of its job descriptions and specifications. In Chapter 3, we explained that a job specification identifies the competencies required for successfully performing a job. The selection process should be set up in such a way that it lets the organization identify people who have the necessary competencies. When the Canadian Security and Intelligence Service (CSIS) hires Intelligence Officers, it looks for people who have specific education, experience, characteristics, and personal attributes. For example, CSIS wants people with a bachelor's degree, "have strong interpersonal skills, be motivated, be adaptable, and be empathetic and sensitive to the culture mores of a changing Canadian society." The selection process for Intelligence Officers assesses these attributes during the suitability interview, an in-depth panel interview, and a psychological assessment. Candidates who survive the entire range of interviews and tests, not to mention the intensive security screening process, also spend time in an interview with CSIS executives.[2]

This kind of strategic approach to selection requires ways to measure the effectiveness of selection tools. From science, we have basic standards for this:

- The selection method provides *reliable* information.
- The method provides *valid* information.
- The information can be *generalized* to apply to the candidates.
- The method offers *high utility* (practical value).
- The selection criteria are *legal*.

> **reliability**
> The extent to which a measurement generates consistent results, i.e., is free from random error.
>
> **validity**
> The extent to which performance on a measure (such as a test score) is related to what the measure is designed to assess (such as job performance).

What Are the Criteria for Evaluating Selection Methods?

RELIABILITY

The **reliability** of a type of measurement indicates how free that measurement is from random error.[3] A reliable measurement therefore generates consistent results.

Assuming that a person's intelligence is fairly stable over time, a reliable test of intelligence should generate consistent results if the same person takes the test several times. Organizations that construct intelligence tests therefore should be able to provide (and explain) information about the reliability of their tests.

> **L02** Define ways to measure the success of a selection method.

Usually, this information involves statistics such as *correlation coefficients*. These statistics measure the degree to which two sets of numbers are related. A higher correlation coefficient signifies a stronger relationship. At one extreme, a correlation coefficient of 1.0 means a perfect positive relationship—as one set of numbers goes up, so does the other. If you took the same vision test three days in a row, those scores would probably have nearly a perfect correlation. At the other extreme, a correlation of –1.0 means a perfect negative correlation—when one set of numbers goes up, the other goes down. In the middle, a correlation of 0 means there is no correlation at all. For example, the correlation between weather and intelligence would be at or near 0. A reliable test would be one for which scores by the same person (or people with similar attributes) have a correlation close to 1.0.

VALIDITY

For a selection measure, **validity** describes the extent to which performance on the measure (such as a test score) is related to what the measure is designed to assess (such as job performance). Although we can reliably measure such characteristics as weight and height, these measurements do not provide much information about how a person will perform most kinds of jobs. Thus, for most jobs, height and weight provide little validity as selection criteria. One way to determine whether a measure is valid is to compare many people's scores on that measure with their job performance. For example, suppose people who score above 60 words per minute on a keyboarding test consistently get high marks for their performance in data-entry jobs. This observation suggests the keyboarding test is valid for predicting success in that job.

As with reliability, information about the validity of selection methods often uses correlation coefficients. A strong positive (or negative) correlation between a measure and job performance means the measure should be a valid basis for selecting (or rejecting) a candidate. This information is important, not only because it helps organizations identify the best employees, but also because organizations can ensure that their selection process is fair and objective. Three ways of measuring validity are criterion-related, content, and construct validity.

Criterion-Related Validity

The first category, criterion-related validity, is a measure of validity based on showing a substantial correlation between test scores and job performance scores. In the example in Figure 5.2, a company compares two measures—an intelligence test and a university or college grade point average—with performance as sales representative. In the left graph, which shows the relationship between the intelligence test scores and job performance, the points for the 20 sales representatives fall near the 45-degree line. The correlation coefficient is near 0.90 (for a perfect 1.0, all the points would be on the 45-degree line). In the graph at the right, the points are scattered more widely. The correlation between university or college GPA and sales representatives'

performance is much lower. In this hypothetical example, the intelligence test is more valid than GPA for predicting success at this job.

Two kinds of research are possible for arriving at criterion-related validity:

1. **Predictive validation.** This research uses the test scores of all applicants and looks for a relationship between the scores and future performance. The researcher administers the tests, waits a set period of time, and then measures the performance of the applicants who were hired.

2. **Concurrent validation.** This type of research administers a test to people who currently hold a job, then compares their scores to existing measures of job performance. If the people who score highest on the test also do better on the job, the test is assumed to be valid.

Predictive validation is more time-consuming and difficult, but it is the best measure of validity. Job applicants tend to be more motivated to do well on the tests, and their performance on the tests is not influenced by their firsthand experience with the job. Also, the group studied is more likely to include people who perform poorly on the test—a necessary ingredient to accurately validate a test.[4]

criterion-related validity
A measure of validity based on showing a substantial correlation between test scores and job performance scores.

predictive validation
Research that uses the test scores of all applicants and looks for a relationship between the scores and future performance of the applicants who were hired.

concurrent validation
Research that consists of administering a test to people who currently hold a job, then comparing their scores to existing measures of job performance.

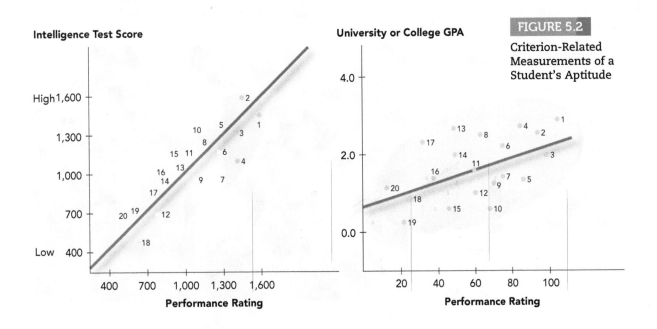

FIGURE 5.2

Criterion-Related Measurements of a Student's Aptitude

Content and Construct Validity

Another way to show validity is to establish **content validity**—that is, consistency between the test items or problems and the kinds of situations or problems that occur on the job.[5] A test that is "content-valid" exposes the job applicant to situations that are likely to occur on the job. It tests whether the applicant has the knowledge, skills, or ability, that is, competencies to handle such situations.

In the case of a company using tests for selecting a construction superintendent, tests with content validity included organizing a random list of subcontractors into the order they would appear at a construction site and entering a shed to identify construction errors that had intentionally been made for testing purposes.[6] More commonly today, employers use computer-role-playing games in which software is created to include situations that occur on the job. The game measures how the candidate reacts to the situations, and then it computes a score based on how closely the candidate's responses match those of an ideal employee.[7]

The usual basis for deciding that a test has content validity is through expert judgment. Experts can rate the test items according to whether they mirror essential functions of the job. Because establishing validity is based on the experts' subjective judgments, content validity is most suitable for measuring behaviour that is concrete and observable.

For tests that measure abstract qualities such as intelligence or leadership ability, establishment of validity may have to rely on **construct validity**. This involves establishing that tests really do measure intelligence, leadership ability, or other such "constructs," as well as showing that mastery of this construct is associated with successful performance of the job. For example, if you could show that a test measures something called "mechanical ability," and that people with superior mechanical ability perform well as assemblers, then the test has construct validity for the assembler job. Tests that measure a construct usually measure a combination of behaviours thought to be associated with the construct.

ABILITY TO GENERALIZE

Along with validity in general, we need to know whether a selection method is valid in the context in which the organization wants to use it. A **generalizable** method applies not only to the conditions in which the method was originally developed—job, organization, people, time period, and so on. It also applies to other organizations, jobs, applicants, and so on. In other words, is a selection method that was valid in one context also valid in other contexts?

Researchers have studied whether tests of intelligence and thinking skills (called *cognitive ability*) can be generalized. The research has supported the idea that these tests are generalizable across many jobs. However, as jobs become more complex, the validity of many of these tests increases. In other words, they are most valid for complex jobs.[8]

PRACTICAL VALUE

Not only should selection methods such as tests and interview responses accurately predict how well individuals will perform, they should produce information

content validity
Consistency between the test items or problems and the kinds of situations or problems that occur on the job.

construct validity
Consistency between a high score on a test and a high level of a construct such as intelligence or leadership ability, as well as between mastery of this construct and successful performance on the job.

generalizable
Valid in other contexts beyond the context in which the selection method was developed.

Football teams have been using cognitive tests to select players assuming that intelligence can be generalized to the job requirements, especially on teams that compete using complex offensive and defensive schemes. What other things, in addition to intelligence, would teams need to look for?

that actually benefits the organization. Being valid, reliable, and generalizable adds value to a method. Another consideration is the cost of using the selection method. Selection procedures such as testing and interviewing cost money. They should cost significantly less than the benefits of hiring the new employees. Methods that provide economic value greater than the cost of using them are said to have **utility**.

The choice of a selection method may differ according to the job being filled. If the job involves providing a product or service of high value to the organization, it is worthwhile to spend more to find a top performer. At a company where salespeople are responsible for closing million-dollar deals, the company will be willing to invest more in selection decisions. At a fast-food restaurant, such an investment will not be worthwhile; the employer will prefer faster, simpler ways to select workers who enter orders, prepare food, and keep the facility clean.

utility
The extent to which the selection method provides economic value greater than its cost.

Because background and reference checks may unearth information about protected grounds such as age or religious affiliation, or other personal information, human rights commissions recommend that the applicant should first receive a conditional job offer. The employer's conditional job offer is offered subject to a successful background and reference check.

An important principle of selection is to combine several sources of information about candidates, rather than relying solely on interviews or a single type of testing. The sources should be chosen carefully to relate to the characteristics identified in the job description. When organizations do this, they are increasing the validity of the decision criteria. They are more likely to make hiring decisions that are fair and unbiased. They also are more likely to choose the best candidates.

What Are the Legal Standards for Selection?

Whether selecting a new employee or promoting an employee from within the organization, the selection process needs to be conducted in a way that avoids human rights and privacy complaints. Human rights legislation and privacy legislation described in Chapter 2 have implications for the selection process.

L03 Summarize the legal requirements for employee selection.

- The interview needs to be conducted in a way that candidates can be assessed without drawing out information that is not relevant to the job being filled. As summarized in Table 5.1, the organization may not ask questions on an application form or in an interview that gathers information about prohibited grounds of discrimation, even indirectly. For example, asking candidates for the dates they attended high school might indirectly gather information about applicants' age.
- Interview notes are made by interviewers to help distinguish among candidates. Even if these notes are only used by the interviewers, they cannot include references to prohibited grounds of discrimination (e.g., "black woman, 45-ish" would be inappropriate to include in interview notes).[9]
- Candidates must provide their consent before a background or reference check can be conducted.

Job Applications and Résumés

Nearly all employers gather background information on applicants at the beginning of the selection process. The usual ways of gathering background information are by asking applicants to fill out application forms and provide résumés. Organizations also verify the information by checking references and conducting background checks.

Asking job candidates to provide background information is inexpensive.

L04 Compare the common methods used for selecting human resources.

The organization can get reasonably accurate information by combining applications and résumés with background checks and well-designed interviews.[10] A major challenge with applications and résumés is the sheer volume of work they generate for the organization. Especially considering how easy it is for candidates to submit applications or résumés online, human resource departments need to take steps to ensure they are not swamped with more than they can handle.

APPLICATIONS

Asking each applicant to fill out an employment application is a low-cost way to gather basic data from many applicants. It also ensures that the organization has certain standard categories of information, such as mailing address and employment history, from each.

TABLE 5.1   Guidelines for Applications and Interviews

SUBJECT	AVOID ASKING	PREFERRED	COMMENTS
Name	about name change: whether it was changed by court order, marriage, or other reason. for maiden name.		Ask after selection if needed to check on previously held jobs or educational credentials.
Address	for addresses outside Canada.	Ask place and duration of current or recent address.	
Age	for birth certificates, baptismal records, or about age in general.	Ask applicants whether they are eligible to work under Canadian laws regarding age restrictions.	If precise age is required for benefit plans or other legitimate purposes, it can be determined after selection.
Sex	about pregnancy, childbearing plans, or child care arrangements.	Ask applicant if the attendance requirements can be met.	During the interview or after selection, the applicant, for purposes of courtesy, may be asked which of Dr., Mr., Mrs., Miss, or Ms. is preferred.
Marital status	whether the applicant is single, married, divorced, engaged, separated, widowed, or living common-law. whether the applicant's spouse may be transferred. about the spouse's employment.	If transfer or travel is part of the job, the applicant can be asked whether he or she can meet these requirements. Ask whether there are any circumstances that might prevent completion of a minimum service commitment.	Information on dependants can be determined after selection if necessary.
Family status	about number of children or dependants. about child care arrangements.	Ask if the applicant would be able to work the required hours and, where applicable, overtime.	Contacts for emergencies and/or details on dependants can be determined after selection.
National or ethnic origin	about birthplace, nationality of ancestors, spouse, or other relatives. whether born in Canada. for proof of citizenship.	Ask if the applicant is legally entitled to work in Canada.	Documentation of eligibility to work (papers, visas, etc.) can be requested after selection.
Photographs	for photo to be attached to applications or sent to interviewer before interview.		Photos for security passes or company files can be taken after selection.
Religion	about religious affiliation. for references from clergy or religious leader. whether the applicant will work a specific religious holiday.	Explain the required work shift, and ask whether such a schedule poses problems for the applicant.	Reasonable accommodation of an employee's religious beliefs is the employer's duty.
Disability	for a list of all disabilities, limitations, or health problems. whether the applicant drinks or uses drugs. whether the application has ever received psychiatric care or been hospitalized for emotional problems. whether the applicant has received workers' compensation.	Disclose any information on requirements or standards early in the process. Then ask whether the applicant has any condition that might affect ability to do the job.	A disability is only relevant to job ability if it: • threatens the safety or property of others. • prevents the applicant from safe and adequate job performance even when reasonable efforts are made to accommodate the disability.

(continued on next page)

TABLE 5.1 Guidelines for Applications and Interviews (*continued*)

SUBJECT	AVOID ASKING	PREFERRED	COMMENTS
Pardoned conviction	whether an applicant has ever been convicted. whether the applicant has ever been arrested. whether the applicant has a criminal record.	If bonding is a job requirement, ask whether the applicant is eligible.	
Sexual orientation	About the applicant's sexual orientation.		Contacts for emergencies and/or details on dependants can be determined after selection.

NOTE: This table provides examples and is not intended as a complete listing of all guidelines. The examples are based on federal human rights legislation; some provincial laws vary and may affect these examples.

SOURCE: "A Guide to Screening and Selection in Employment," Canadian Human Rights Commission, February 2001, pp. 3–5, www.chrc-ccdp.ca/publications/screening_employment-en.asp. Retrieved April 3, 2004. Reproduced with the permission of the Minister of Public Works and Government Services, 2012.

Employment applications include areas for applicants to provide several types of information:

- *Contact information.* The employee's name, address, phone number, and email address.
- *Work experience.* Companies the applicant worked for, job titles, and dates of employment.
- *Educational background.* High school, college, or university attended and diploma(s) or degree(s) awarded.
- *Applicant's signature.* Signature or verification following a statement that the applicant has provided true and complete information.

The application form may include other areas for the applicant to provide additional information, such as specific work experiences, technical skills, certifications, or memberships in professional or trade associations. Also, including the date on an application is useful for keeping up-to-date records of job applicants. The application form should not request information that might violate human rights legislation. For example, questions about an applicant's birthplace, marital status, or number of children would be inappropriate.

By reviewing application forms, HR staff can identify which candidates meet minimum requirements for education and experience. They may be able to rank applicants—for example, giving applicants with five years' experience a higher ranking than applicants with two years' experience. In this way, the applications enable the organization to narrow the pool of candidates to a number it is prepared to test and interview.

RÉSUMÉS

The usual way applicants introduce themselves to a potential employer is by submitting a résumé. An obvious drawback of this information source is that applicants control the content of the information, as well as the way it is presented. This type of information is therefore biased in favour of the applicant and (although this is unethical) may not even be accurate. However, this inexpensive way to gather information does provide employers with a starting point. Organizations typically use résumés as a basis for deciding which candidates to investigate further.

As with employment applications, an HR staff member reviews the résumés to identify candidates meeting such requirements including competencies, educational background, related work performed, and types of equipment the person has used. Because résumés are created by the job applicants (or the applicants have at least approved résumés created by someone they hire), they also may provide some insight into how candidates communicate and present themselves. Employers tend to decide against applicants whose résumés are unclear, messy, or contain mistakes. On the positive side, résumés may enable applicants to highlight accomplishments that might not show up in the format of an employment application. Review of résumés is most valid when the content of the résumés is assessed in terms of the criteria associated with successful job performance.

Organizations are increasingly turning to Web-based applicant tracking systems to centralize the handling of résumés and job applications from both internal and external applicants. Typically this involves completing an online application form on the employer's website and uploading a résumé. In many cases, information is electronically extracted from the résumé and inserted into the application form. Before submitting the application, the applicant verifies the information and performs any necessary edits.

An **applicant tracking system (ATS)** is a software application that streamlines the flow of information between job seekers, HR staff, and hiring managers. As organizations expand their corporate websites into interactive career centres, applicant tracking systems provide capabilities including multilingual support for global locations, generating applicant confirmation letters, pre-screening applications and résumés for education, specific competencies, and experience. Applicant tracking systems also support various data handling and report generation requirements associated with hiring employees, for example, storing résumés, tracking candidate sources, and connecting applications to specific hiring managers or job openings. By automating the process to match available talent with current job opportunities, the efficiency and speed of the overall hiring process is improved. Organizations can streamline the process, build relationships with candidates, cut hiring cycle-time, and increase the probability of hiring an available and interested candidate.[11]

applicant tracking system (ATS)

A software application that streamlines the flow of information between job seekers, HR staff, and hiring managers.

negligent hiring

A situation where an employer may be found liable for harm an employee causes to others if references and background checks were not performed adequately at the time of hiring.

REFERENCES

Application forms often ask that applicants provide the names of several references. Applicants provide the names and contact information of former employers or others who can vouch for their abilities and past job performance. In some situations, the applicant may provide letters of reference written by those people. It is then up to the organization to have someone contact the references to gather information or verify the accuracy of the information provided by the applicant.

As you might expect, references are not an unbiased source of information. Most applicants are careful to choose references who will say something positive. In addition, former employers and others may be afraid that if they express negative opinions, they will be sued. Their fear is understandable. In a former case, an employee sued his former supervisor for comments about how the employee had succeeded in overcoming attendance problems related to a struggle with multiple sclerosis. The employee felt that the disclosure of his prior attendance problems was defamatory.[12] (Disclosing his medical condition also would have posed problems for the potential future employer's ability to comply with human rights legislation.) This case shows that even well-intentioned remarks can cause problems.

Usually the organization checks references after it has determined that the applicant is a finalist for the job. Questions asked in reference checks need to adhere to the same requirements as applications and interviews (see Table 5.1).[13] Employers also have a duty to protect workers and the public from harassment or violence arising from placing an unfit or dangerous person in the workplace. **Negligent hiring** refers to a situation where an employer may be found liable for harm an employee causes to others if references and background checks were not performed adequately at the time of hiring. In these cases, the employer may be found to "have known or should have known" that an employee might cause harm to others in the workplace.

Contacting references for all applicants would be time-consuming, and it does put a burden on the people contacted. Part of that burden is the risk of giving information seen as too negative or too positive. If the person who is a reference gives negative information, there is a chance the candidate will claim *defamation*, meaning the person damaged the applicant's reputation by making statements that cannot be proved truthful.[14] At the other extreme, if the person gives a glowing statement about a candidate, and the new employer later learns of misdeeds such as sexual misconduct or workplace violence, the new employer might sue the former employer for *misrepresentation*.[15]

Because such situations occasionally arise, often with much publicity, people who give references tend to give as little information as possible. Most organizations have policies that the human resource department will handle all requests for references and that they will only verify employment dates and sometimes the employee's final salary. In organizations without such a policy, HR professionals should be careful—and train managers to be careful—to stick to observable, job-related behaviours and to avoid broad opinions that may be misinterpreted. In spite of these drawbacks of references, the risks of not learning about significant problems in a candidate's past outweigh the possibility of getting only a little information. "An HR manager may be in the interesting position of declining to give an elaborate reference for any employee who intends to leave her organization, yet demand one for a person she wishes to hire. And applicants may find themselves to be essentially unemployable, as they discover they can't be hired without a satisfactory reference from their former employer."[16]

BACKGROUND CHECKS

A background check is a way to verify that applicants are as they represent themselves to be. Unfortunately, not all candidates are open and honest. About eight out of ten large companies and over two-thirds of smaller organizations say they conduct criminal record background checks.[17]

Companies like BackCheck™ specialize in pre-employment background checks such as criminal record checks, credit inquiries, education verifications, employment verifications, driving records, identity cross-checks, and reference checks. For example, Scotiabank has recently expanded their range of pre-employment screening with BackCheck to include criminal reference checks and identity verifications in addition to reference checking, employment and educational verifications, explains Stephen White, senior manager, global employment strategies, Scotiabank Group.[18]

Angus Stewart, vice-president of forensics and leader of corporate intelligence at KPMG LLP in Toronto, says that knowing what to look for is key to a successful search. "Education fraud is the most common," he says, adding that people lie about the degree they received or the institutions they attend. There is also the "diploma mill issue": people state degrees they ordered online from phoney institutions. "There's quite a bit of that."[19]

Also fuelling this growing use of background checks are applicants using complex and high-tech means to fraudulently impress employers. For example, a counterfeiting ring operating out of a house in Markham, Ontario may have supplied thousands of people with forged university degrees and transcripts as well as forged immigration documents, according to York Regional Police. The police confiscated forged degrees from the University of Toronto, the University of Western Ontario, Cape Breton University, and many others. Even university officials were hard pressed to detect the fakes. "These were of such high quality that our university people had to do a double take," said Detective Fred Kerr. "From an employer point of view, you're not going to catch what's wrong with them."[20]

Before performing a background check, employers need to keep in mind they need to get consent from the candidate. As discussed earlier in the chapter, conducting a background check after extending a contingent job offer can help to protect the potential employer from a discrimination claim if the applicant is not hired. Consent is also needed to comply with privacy legislation. As discussed in the opening feature of this chapter and in Chapter 2, employers also need to "tread carefully" when it comes to social media checks or random background checks using search engines like Google.

Employment Tests and Work Samples

When the organization has identified candidates whose applications or résumés indicate they meet basic requirements, the organization continues the selection process with this narrower pool of candidates. Often, the next step is to gather objective data through one or more

L05 Describe major types of employment tests.

Checking out employees is a growth industry as more organizations such as BackCheck™ conduct background checks on potential employees. Technology has helped reduce costs and streamline the process.

employment tests. These tests fall into two broad categories:[21]

1. **Aptitude tests** assess how well a person can learn or acquire skills and abilities. In the realm of employment testing, the best-known aptitude test is the General Aptitude Test Battery (GATB). The Public Service Commission of Canada also provides other employment-related tests such as the Administrative Support: The Office Skills Test (OST), which assesses the individual's aptitude for following directions, filing, arithmetic, checking, and vocabulary.[21]

2. **Achievement tests** measure a person's existing knowledge and skills. For example, some organizations use interactive tests to assess applicants' skills using software such as Outlook, Excel, and PowerPoint.

> **aptitude tests**
> Tests that assess how well a person can learn or acquire skills and abilities.
>
> **achievement tests**
> Tests that measure a person's existing knowledge and skills.
>
> **cognitive ability tests**
> Tests designed to measure such mental abilities as verbal skills, quantitative skills, and reasoning ability.

Before using any test, organizations should investigate the test's validity and reliability. Besides asking the testing service to provide this information, it is wise to consult more impartial sources of information, such as the ones described in Table 5.2. The nearby "HR How-To" box discusses some types of employment tests used to screen job applicants.

PHYSICAL ABILITY TESTS

Physical strength and endurance play less of a role in the modern workplace than in the past, thanks to the use of automation and current technology. Even so, many jobs still require certain physical abilities or psychomotor abilities (those connecting brain and body, as in the case of eye–hand coordination). When these abilities are essential to job performance or avoidance of injury, the organization may use physical ability tests. These evaluate one or more of the following areas of physical ability: muscular tension, muscular power, muscular endurance, cardiovascular endurance, flexibility, balance, and coordination.[22] Although these tests can accurately predict success at certain kinds of jobs, they also tend to exclude women and people with disabilities. As a result, use of physical ability tests can make the organization vulnerable to human rights complaints. It is therefore important to be certain that the abilities tested for really are essential to job performance or that the absence of these abilities really does create a safety hazard.

The RCMP have invested significant effort to develop an effective test to assess candidates' physical abilities—Physical Abilities Requirement Evaluation (PARE). The PARE is a job-related physical ability test developed as a result of extensive research and simulates a critical incident in which a police officer chases, controls, and apprehends a suspect.[23]

COGNITIVE ABILITY TESTS

Although fewer jobs require muscle power today, brainpower is essential for most jobs. Organizations therefore benefit from people who have strong mental abilities. **Cognitive ability tests**—sometimes called "intelligence tests"—are designed to measure such mental abilities as verbal skills (skill in using written and spoken language), quantitative skills (skill in working with numbers), and reasoning ability (skill in thinking through the answer to a problem). Many jobs require all of these cognitive skills, so employers often get valid information from general tests. The Public Service Commission of Canada uses the General Competency Test Level 1 (GCT1) to measure thinking skills (understanding written material, solving numerical problems, and drawing

TABLE 5.2 Sources of Information About Employment Tests	
Mental Measurements Yearbook	Descriptions and reviews of tests that are commercially available
Principles for the Validation and Use of Personnel Selection Procedures (Society for Industrial and Organizational Psychology)	Guide to help organizations evaluate tests
Standards for Educational and Psychological Tests (American Psychological Association)	Description of standards for testing programs
Tests: A Comprehensive Reference for Assessments in Psychology, Education, and Business	Descriptions of thousands of tests
Test Critiques	Reviews of tests, written by professionals in the field

HR HOW-TO

Testing 101

Cognitive Ability

The Wonderlic Class Cognitive Ability Test (formerly the Wonderlic Personnel Test) is one of the most widely used employment tests to measure specific cognitive abilities. It is a 12-minute timed test with 50 questions.

Sample question: Three individuals form a partnership and agree to divide the profits equally. X invests $9,000, Y invests $7,000, and Z invests $4,000. If the profits are $4,800, how much less does X receive than if the profits were divided in proportion to the amount invested. [Answer: $560]

What it demonstrates: Cognitive ability tests measure an individual's ability to learn, adapt, solve problems, and understand instructions and are considered an important predictor of job success.

Emotional Intelligence

Based on research by psychologist Dr. Daniel Goleman, who claims a combination of self-awareness, empathy, and social skills is as important as factual knowledge in achieving success.

Sample question: You are a college student who had hoped to get an A in a course that was important for your future career aspirations. You have just found out you got a C– on the midterm. What do you do?

a) Sketch out a specific plan for ways to improve your grade and resolve to follow through.
b) Decide you do not have what it takes to make it in that career.
c) Tell yourself it really doesn't matter how much you do in the course, concentrate instead on other classes where your grades are higher.
d) Go see the professor and try to talk her into giving you a better grade.

[Answer: The most emotionally intelligent answer is 'a'—10 points; 'b'—0 points; 'c'—5 points; 'd'—0 points.]

What it shows: Proponents claim the combination of self-awareness, empathy, and social skills these tests measure are essential to success and effective leadership.

Personality

Many tests are available that ask questions about behavioural traits and tendencies. The usual approach is for the applicant to select their level of agreement or disagreement to each of a series of statements that assesses his/her approach to life and relationships.

Sample questions: Rate yourself on a five-point scale from strongly disagree to strongly agree: "I enjoy meeting new people," "I sometimes make mistakes," "I'm easily disappointed."

What it measures: Traits—for example, extroversion; agreeableness, and conscientiousness.

SOURCES: "Wonderlic Cognitive Ability Test Family," Wonderlic website, www.wonderlic.com/assessments/ability/cognitive-ability-tests, retrieved June 18, 2012; "EI quiz," HayGroup website: www.haygroup.com/leadershipandtalentondemand/demos/ei_quiz.aspx, retrieved June 18, 2012; Personality questionnaire examples," www.shldirect.com/personality_questionnaire_examples.html; retrieved June 18, 2012; and Wallace Immen, "Testing 101," *The Globe and Mail,* January 26, 2005, p. C2.

logical conclusions) for administrative support position selection decisions. See Figure 5.3 for a sample question and answer from the General Competency Test Level 1 (GCT1). The GCT2 is used to assess general cognitive abilities required for officer-level positions.[24] Many reliable tests are commercially available. The tests are especially valid for complex jobs and for those requiring adaptability in changing circumstances.[25]

JOB PERFORMANCE TESTS AND WORK SAMPLES

Many kinds of jobs require candidates who excel at performing specialized tasks, such as operating a certain machine, handling calls from customers, or designing advertising materials. To evaluate candidates for such jobs, the organization may administer tests of the necessary skills. Sometimes the candidates take tests that involve a sample of work, or they may show existing samples of their work. Testing may involve a simulated work setting, perhaps in a testing centre or in a computerized "virtual environment."[26] Examples of job performance tests include tests of keyboarding speed and *in-basket tests.* An in-basket test measures the ability to juggle a variety of demands, as in a manager's job. The candidate is presented with simulated emails and messages describing the kinds of problems that confront a person in the job. The candidate has to decide how

FIGURE 5.3

Sample Question from the Public Service Commission of Canada's General Competency Test: Level 1 (GCT1)

Government   Gouvernement
of Canada   du Canada
MEMORANDUM   NOTE DE SERVICE

TO: All employees
FROM: Manager

We are pleased to announce that our Ministry's budget has been increased and consequently we will experience an increase in staff size. Because new positions will become available, we will be holding interviews within the next few weeks.

The main focus of this memo is to indicate a change concerning:

1. better ministerial policy.
2. better budget publicity.
3. more human resources.
4. more office space.

SOURCE: General Competency Test Level (GCT 1)—Instructions and Sample Questions, http://www.psc-cfp.gc.ca/ppc-cpp/test-examen/gct1-ecg1/index-eng.htm. Public Service Commission 2011. Reproduced with the permission of the Minister of Public Works and Government Services, 2012.

to respond to these messages, and in what order. Examples of jobs for which candidates provide work samples include graphic designers and writers.

Tests for selecting managers may take the form of an **assessment centre**—a wide variety of specific selection programs that use multiple selection methods to rate applicants or job incumbents on their management potential. An assessment centre typically includes in-basket tests, tests of more general abilities, and personality tests. Combining several assessment methods increases the validity of this approach. For example, the Public Service Commission of Canada uses the *Human Resources Consultant Simulation Exercise*, which "simulates important aspects of a human resource consultant's job." The candidate receives exercise items including memoranda, letters, and reports and is given three hours to review the items and complete a written action plan, and prepare for an oral presentation. The next step is to make an oral presentation (30 minutes maximum) to the selection panel followed by questions from the panel. The final phase requires the candidate to provide assistance and advice to a manager as part of an interactive exercise.[27]

Job performance tests have the advantage of giving applicants a chance to show what they can do,

> **assessment centre**
> A wide variety of specific selection programs that use multiple selection methods to rate applicants or job incumbents on their management potential.

which leads them to feel that the evaluation was fair.[28] The tests also are job-specific—that is, tailored to the kind of work done in a specific job. So they have a high level of validity, especially when combined with cognitive ability tests and a highly structured interview.[29] This advantage can become a disadvantage, however, if the organization wants to generalize the results of a test for one job to candidates for other jobs. The tests are more appropriate for identifying candidates who are generally able to solve the problems associated with a job, rather than for identifying which specific skills or traits the individual possesses.[30] Developing different tests for different jobs can become expensive. One way to save money is to prepare computerized tests that can be delivered online to various locations.

PERSONALITY INVENTORIES

In some situations, employers may also want to know about candidates' personalities. For example, one way psychologists think of personality is in terms of the "Big Five" traits: extroversion, adjustment, agreeableness, conscientiousness, and inquisitiveness (explained in Table 5.3). There is evidence that people who score high on conscientiousness tend to excel at work, especially when they also have high cognitive ability.[31] For people-related jobs like sales and management, extroversion and agreeableness also seem to be associated with success.[32]

Strong social skills help conscientious people ensure that they get positive recognition for their hard work.[33]

The usual way to identify a candidate's personality traits is to administer one of the personality tests that are commercially available. The employer pays for the use of the test, and the organization that owns the test then scores the responses and provides a report about the test taker's personality. An organization that provides such tests should be able to discuss the test's validity and reliability. Assuming the tests are valid for the organization's jobs, they have advantages. Administering commercially available personality tests is simple, and these tests should be able to demonstrate they do not violate human rights requirements. On the downside, compared with intelligence tests, people are better at "faking" their answers to a personality test to score higher on desirable traits.[34] For example, people tend to score higher on conscientiousness when filling out job-related personality tests than when participating in research projects.[35] Ways to address this problem include using trained interviewers rather than surveys, collecting information about the applicant from several sources, and letting applicants know that several sources will be used.[36]

A recent study found that 35 percent of organizations use personality tests when selecting personnel.[37] One reason is organizations' greater use of teamwork, where personality conflicts can be a significant problem. Traits such as agreeableness and conscientiousness have been associated with effective teamwork.[38] In addition, an organization might try to select team members with similar traits and values in order to promote a strong culture where people work together harmoniously, or they instead might look for a diversity of personalities and values as a way to promote debate and creativity.[39]

TABLE 5.3	Five Major Personality Dimensions Measured by Personality Inventories
1. Extroversion	Sociable, gregarious, assertive, talkative, expressive
2. Adjustment	Emotionally stable, non-depressed, secure, content
3. Agreeableness	Courteous, trusting, good-natured, tolerant, cooperative, forgiving
4. Conscientiousness	Dependable, organized, persevering, thorough, achievement-oriented
5. Inquisitiveness	Curious, imaginative, artistically sensitive, broadminded, playful

HONESTY, ALCOHOL, AND DRUG TESTS

No matter what employees' personalities may be like, organizations want employees to be honest and to behave safely. Some organizations are satisfied to assess these qualities on the basis of judgments from reference checks and interviews. Others investigate these characteristics more directly through the use of tests.

The most famous kind of honesty test is the polygraph, the so-called "lie detector" test. As a result of controversies associated with the use of polygraph tests, testing services have developed paper-and-pencil honesty (or integrity) tests. Generally these tests ask applicants directly about their attitudes toward honesty and integrity and their own experiences in situations inside and outside work. Most of the research into the validity of these tests has been conducted by the testing companies, but evidence suggests they do have some ability to predict such behaviour as theft of the employer's property.[40]

As concerns about substance abuse and the harmful impacts of alcohol and drugs on employee safety and

People who participate in Google's annual Code Jam—a global programming competition—typically exhibit one of the "Big Five" personality traits

performance have grown, so has the use of alcohol and drug testing. As a measure of a person's past exposure to drugs, chemical testing has high reliability and validity. However, these tests are controversial for several reasons. Some people are concerned that they invade individuals' privacy. Others object from a legal perspective. Taking urine, saliva, and/or blood samples involves invasive procedures, and accusing someone of drug use is a serious matter. And, although breathalyzer tests can measure how much alcohol has been consumed and the person's level of impairment, current drug tests cannot measure impairment or assess if an employee is capable of performing the job.[41]

Employers considering the use of drug or alcohol tests should ensure that their testing programs conform to the drug and alcohol testing policy outlined in their relevant human rights legislation. As discussed in Chapter 2, the Canadian Human Rights Act prohibits discrimination related to a disability, and dependence on drugs or alcohol is considered a disability that must be accommodated to the point of undue hardship. For example, "The Canadian Human Rights Commission Policy on Alcohol and Drug Testing" prohibits the following types of testing:

- Pre-employment drug testing
- Pre-employment alcohol testing
- Random drug testing
- Random alcohol testing of employees in non-safety-sensitive positions.[42]

The approach to drug testing in Western Canada has tended to emphasize safety and has directly conflicted with Ontario Court of Appeal decisions. For example, the Alberta Court of Appeal recently upheld the employer's right to immediately terminate a new employee who failed a pre-employment drug screening test that was part of the hiring process for Kellogg Brown & Root (KBR), a subsidiary of Houston-based oil-and-gas giant, Haliburton. The employee had started work and been on the job for nine days when his marijuana-positive test results came back. The Alberta Court of Appeal ruled that the terminated employee was not an addict, but rather a recreational drug user, therefore he was not disabled and did not require accommodation. The Court ruled that there was no discrimination because the employer's drug testing policy was connected to workplace safety.[43]

MEDICAL EXAMINATIONS

Especially for physically demanding jobs, organizations may wish to conduct medical examinations to see that the applicant can meet the job's requirements. Employers may also wish to establish an employee's physical condition at the beginning of employment, so that there is a basis for measuring whether the employee has suffered a work-related disability later on. At the same time, as described in Chapter 2, organizations may not discriminate against individuals with disabilities who could perform a job with reasonable accommodations. Likewise, they may not use a measure of physical ability that discriminates against women, older workers, etc., unless those requirements are valid in predicting the ability to perform a job. Medical exams must be related to job requirements and may not be given until the candidate has received a conditional job offer. Therefore, organizations must be careful in how they use medical examinations. Many organizations make selection decisions first, then conduct the exams to confirm that the employee can handle the job, with any reasonable accommodations required. Limiting the use of medical exams in this way also holds down the cost of what tends to be an expensive process.

Interviews

Supervisors and team members most often get involved in the selection process at the stage of employment interviews. These interviews bring together job applicants and representatives of the employer to obtain information and evaluate the applicant's qualifications and organizational fit. While the applicant is providing information, he or she is also forming opinions about what it is like to work for the organization. Most organizations use interviewing as part of the selection process. In fact, this method is used more than any other.

L06 Discuss how to conduct effective interviews.

nondirective interview
A selection interview in which the interviewer has great discretion in choosing questions to ask each candidate.

INTERVIEWING TECHNIQUES

Interview techniques include choices about the type of questions to ask and the number of people who conduct the interview. Several question types are possible:

- In a **nondirective interview**, the interviewer has great discretion in choosing questions. The candidate's reply to one question may suggest other questions to ask. Non-directive interviews typically include open-ended questions about the candidate's strengths, weaknesses, career goals, and work experience. Because these interviews give

DID YOU KNOW?

What Turns Off an Interviewer

Interviewers gather information from what job applicants tell them and also from how they behave. Frankly, some behaviours are a turnoff. In a recent survey, HR professionals identified ways that job applicants can kill their prospects.

SOURCE: Based on Diana Middleton, "Avoid These Interview Killers," *Wall Streeet Journal*, November 14, 2009, http://online.wsj.com.

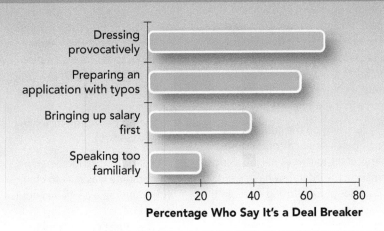

the interviewer wide latitude, their reliability is not great and some interviewers ask questions that are not valid or even legal.

- A **structured interview** establishes a set of questions for the interviewer to ask. Ideally, the questions are related to job requirements and cover relevant knowledge, skills, and experiences. The interviewer is supposed to avoid asking questions that are not on the list. Although interviewers may object to being restricted, the results may be more valid and reliable than with a nondirective interview.
- A **situational interview** is a structured interview in which the interviewer describes a situation likely to arise on the job and asks the candidate what he or she would do in that situation. This type of interview may have high validity in predicting job performance.[44]
- A **behavioural interview** is a situational interview in which the interviewer asks the candidate to describe how he or she handled a type of situation in the past. Questions about the candidates' actual experiences tend to have the highest validity.[45]

The "HR Best Practices" box examines some specific questions that may be part of an effective behavioural interview.

BMO Financial Group has been using behavioural interviews since the early 1990s for almost every position it fills. BMO even offers prospective employees advice about what a good answer includes—see Table 5.4. BMO Financial Group views behavioural interviews as most effective for external candidates because internal candidates have existing performance reviews and have been through the process at some point.[46]

The common setup for either a nondirective or structured interview is for an individual (an HR professional or the supervisor for the vacant position) to interview each candidate face to face. However, variations on this approach are possible. In a **panel interview**, several members of the organization meet to interview each candidate. A panel interview gives the candidate a chance to meet more people and see how people interact in that organization. It provides the organization with the judgments of more than one person, to reduce the effect of personal biases in selection decisions. Panel interviews can be especially appropriate in organizations that use teamwork. At the other extreme, some organizations conduct interviews without any interviewers; they use a computerized interviewing process. The candidate enters replies to the questions interactively and results are submitted electronically. Such a format eliminates a lot of personal bias—along with the opportunity to see how people interact. Therefore, electronic interviews are useful for gathering objective data, rather than assessing people skills.

structured interview
A selection interview that consists of a predetermined set of questions for the interviewer to ask.

situational interview
A structured interview in which the interviewer describes a situation likely to arise on the job, then asks the candidate what he or she would do in that situation.

behavioural interview
A structured interview in which the interviewer asks the candidate to describe how he or she handled a type of situation in the past.

panel interview
Selection interview in which several members of the organization meet to interview each candidate.

HR BEST PRACTICES

Interview Questions that Can Get Boffo Results

Behavioural interviewing is based on the premise that past behaviour is the best predictor of future behaviour. Behavioural interviewing offers at least a couple of key advantages relative to traditional methods:

- By focusing on the critical competencies or attributes most important to successful job performance, the interview has a valid basis for person-to-job matching.
- Because candidates are asked similar questions, the interviewer can make objective comparisons between candidates.

Here are five behavioural interview questions that are somewhat unexpected and are likely to produce revealing results:

1. "Tell us about a best-in-class standard or practice that you've introduced."

This question can uncover results-orientation and may be adapted for less senior positions, for example, "Tell us about a recent example of something you have done to improve your efficiency at work."

2. "Describe a situation when a subordinate was able to change your mind on a particular course of action."
    - This question is useful to uncover team leadership capabilities.

3. "Tell us about the most unpopular decision you have made."
    - This question can tell you a lot about a candidate's leadership and negotiation skills.

4. "Describe a time when you were faced with a challenging situation that involved balancing competing interests in your personal life with issues in the workplace."
    - This question can uncover how employees effectively balance their work/life by using creative and innovative solutions.

5. "Describe a crisis situation and how you handled it."
    - This question can provide key insights into the candidate's ability to assess and respond quickly.

Behavioural description interviews are flexible and can be applied and adapted to any situation or organization.

SOURCE: Sarah B. Hood, "Hire Echelon," *Canadian Business*, June 7–20, 2004, pp. 71–73.

ADVANTAGES AND DISADVANTAGES OF INTERVIEWING

The wide use of interviewing is not surprising. People naturally want to see prospective employees firsthand. As we noted in Chapter 1, the top qualities that employers seek in new hires include communication skills and interpersonal skills. Talking face to face can provide evidence of these skills. Interviews can give insights into candidates' personalities and interpersonal styles. They are more valid, however, when they focus on job knowledge and

TABLE 5.4   BMO's Advice to Job Seekers about Behavioural Interviews
YOUR BMO INTERVIEW
Behavioural-focused questions are used to understand and draw on your past work experience as being the best predictor of how in a similar situation you would behave in the future. When answering these types of questions a good answer includes: • A description of the situation where the behaviour took place. • An account of the actions you took to handle the situation or resolve the problem. Be specific and concise. • An explanation of the results. Demonstrate to the interviewer that you understand how your actions impacted the results, what the outcomes were, and what you learned.
Don't ignore failures. An interviewer will want to hear about situations that didn't turn out as hoped. We all have experiences we wish we could "do over." What an interviewer will want to know is how would you do it over?
Spend some time anticipating questions you may encounter and think of ways you might answer them. This way you will feel more confident and prepared. Good luck!

SOURCE: "Interviewing at BMO: Your BMO Interview," www.bmo.com/home/about/banking/careers/tools-and-resources/interviewing-at-bmo, retrieved April 2, 2012.

When interviewing candidates, it's valid to ask about willingness to travel if that is a requirement of the job. Interviewers might ask questions about previous business travel experiences and/or how interviewees handled situations requiring flexibility and self-motivation (qualities that would be an asset in someone who is travelling alone and solving business problems on the road).

skill. Interviews also provide a means to check the accuracy of information on the applicant's résumé or job application. Asking applicants to elaborate about their experiences and offer details reduces the likelihood of a candidate being able to invent a work history.[47]

Despite these benefits, interviewing is not necessarily the most accurate basis for making a selection decision. Research has shown that interviews can be unreliable, low in validity,[48] and biased against a number of different groups.[49] Interviews are also costly. They require that at least one person devote time to interviewing each candidate, and the applicants typically have to be brought to one geographic location. Interviews are also subjective, so they place the organization at greater risk of discrimination complaints by applicants who were not hired, especially if those individuals were asked questions not entirely related to the job.

Organizations can avoid some of these pitfalls.[50] Human resource staff should keep the interviews focused, structured, and standardized. The interview should focus on accomplishing a few goals, so that at the end of the interview, the organization has ratings on several observable measures, such as ability to express ideas. The interview should not try to measure abilities and skills—for example, intelligence—that tests can measure better. As noted earlier, situational and behavioural interviews are especially effective for doing this. Organizations can prevent problems related to subjectivity by training interviewers and using more than one person to conduct interviews. Training typically includes focusing on the recording of observable facts, rather than on making subjective judgments, as well as developing interviewers' awareness of their biases.[51] Finally, to address costs of interviewing, some organizations

videotape interviews or use video calling technology, e.g., Skype.

E-HRM

Find out about Skype job interviews.

PREPARING TO INTERVIEW

Organizations can reap the greatest benefits from interviewing if they prepare carefully. A well-planned interview should be standardized, comfortable for the participants, and focused on the job and the organization. The interviewer should have a quiet place in which to conduct interviews without interruption. This person should be trained in how to ask objective questions, what subject matter to avoid, and how to detect and handle his or her own personal biases or other distractions in order to fairly evaluate candidates.

The interviewer should have enough documents to conduct a complete interview. These should include a list of the questions to be asked, with plenty of space for recording the responses. When the questions are prepared, it is also helpful to determine how the answers will be assessed. For example, if questions are asked about how interviewees have handled certain situations, consider what responses are best in terms of meeting job requirements. If the job requires someone who develops new and creative solutions to problems, then a response that shows innovative behaviour would receive a higher score. The interviewer also should have a copy of the interviewee's employment application and résumé, to review before the interview and refer to during the interview. If possible, the interviewer should also have printed information about the organization and the job. Near the beginning of the interview, it is a good idea to go over the job specifications, organizational policies, and so on, so that the interviewee has a clearer understanding of the organization's needs and expectations.

The interviewer should schedule enough time to review the job requirements, discuss the interview questions, and give the interviewee a chance to ask questions. To close, the interviewer should thank the candidate for coming and provide information about what to expect—for example, that the organization will contact a few finalists within the next two weeks or that a decision will be made by the end of the week.

multiple-hurdle model
Process of arriving at a selection decision by eliminating some candidates at each stage of the selection process.

Selection Decisions

1,3

After reviewing applications, scoring tests, conducting interviews, and checking references, the organization needs to make decisions about which candidates to place in which jobs. In practice, most organizations find more than one qualified candidate to fill an open position. The selection decision typically combines ranking based on objective criteria along with subjective judgments about which candidate will make the greatest contribution.

L07 Explain how employers carry out the process of making a selection decision.

HOW ORGANIZATIONS SELECT EMPLOYEES

The selection decision should not be a simple matter of whom the supervisor likes best or which candidate will take the lowest offer. Also, as the "HR Oops!" box emphasizes, job candidates' confidence does not necessarily mean they are competent. Rather, the people making the selection decision should look for the best fit between candidate and position. In general, the person's performance will result from a combination of ability and motivation. Often, the selection is a choice among a few people who possess the basic qualifications. The decision makers therefore have to decide which of those people have the best combination of ability and motivation to fit in the position and in the organization as a whole.

The usual process for arriving at a selection decision is to gradually narrow the pool of candidates for each job. This approach, called the **multiple-hurdle model**, is based on a process such as the one shown earlier in Figure 5.1. Each stage of the process is a hurdle, and candidates who overcome a

HR Oops!

Style Over Substance

Employers intend to pick the candidates who will perform the best on the job, but often they may be picking the candidates who perform best in the job interview. According to a recent experiment, people assume candidates are competent when they behave with confidence, whether or not they actually demonstrate competence.

In the experiment, people were assigned to teams of four to solve math problems. The team members gave leadership roles to the member who dominated the group by speaking with confidence, declaring opinions more often, and

using body language that signalled certainty. Whether or not that team member had the best math skills, the team members rated that person as highly competent.

Applying that experiment to employee selection, it's important for an interviewer to sort out whether a candidate is simply speaking with confidence or actually providing evidence of competent behaviour. Unless the job requirements focus on an ability to inspire confidence, the candidate's assertive behaviour may not be the most important trait to measure. Instead, the employer probably needs to

base the selection decision on more objective criteria.

SOURCE: Based on Caitlin McDevitt, "The Competence-Confidence Disconnect," *Inc.* April 24, 2009, www.inc.com.

QUESTIONS
1. For what kinds of jobs would it be relevant to look for a candidate who behaves confidently in a job interview?
2. When conducting job interviews, how can you increase the likelihood that you are evaluating relevant job skills, not just deciding who is most persuasive?

THINKING ETHICALLY

Checking Out a Candidate's Facebook Profile

The Internet has become the first stop for many recruiters and hiring managers to determine if a potential candidate is a good fit. Many job seekers are not aware of these instant background checks. In a recent Adecco Workplace Insights survey, 66 percent of Generation Y respondents were unaware that seemingly private photos, comments, and statements were audited by potential employers.

"It's a lot more common than I think the prospective employees realize," says Lynne Perry-Reid, a Calgary recruiter and co-founder of Corporate Connections. "Especially now that a lot of recruiters tend to be younger, maybe in their 30s, everyone is really involved in things [like] Facebook," she says, "so you can easily just type in someone's name to find out about them because you're already hooked into that network."

In a formal job interview, employers are not legally permitted to ask questions about a candidate's age, marital status, sexual orientation, or ethnicity but the individual's profile can reveal all of these things to a prospective employer. Amber MacArthur, social media author and strategist cautions that all it takes is one click from a rogue contact to make details posted to a relatively secure profile—public information.

Controversy has also recently surrounded the practice of some companies to ask candidates to turn over Facebook login information as part of the hiring process. Facebook's chief privacy officer, Erin Egan offered this advice: "If you are a Facebook user, you should never have to share your password." Facebook has also warned employers not to demand the passwords of job applicants.

SOURCES: Michelle McQuigge, "Company Wants Your Facebook Password? Just Say No," *Globe and Mail*, March 28, 2012, B19; "Your Profile on Social Sites Can Make or Break Your Job Opportunities," *Financial Post*, September 19, 2007, www.canada.com/nationalpost/news/working/story, retrieved September 21, 2007; Derek Sankey, "Facebook Background Checks," *Calgary Herald*, 2007, http://working.canada.com/calgary/resources/story, retrieved April 4, 2008; Kristin Gissaro, "The Invasion of Recruiters on Social Networking Sites," www.ere.net.blogs/generational_recruiting, retrieved April 4, 2008.

QUESTIONS
1. Are employers crossing the line when they look up job candidates on a social networking site such as Facebook?
2. What do you do to ensure your own online profile presents a positive image to potential employers? What would you do if you were asked by a prospective employer to provide your Facebook password?
3. Suppose you are a recruiter and have identified an applicant who possesses excellent knowledge, skills, ability, and experience required for a position in your organization. Then you discover an awkward image of the prospective employee on a social media site. What would you do? What if you found that the applicant had recently tweeted: "omg i hate my job and my boss is a jerk."

---

hurdle continue to the next stage of the process. For example, the organization reviews applications and/or résumés of all candidates, conducts some tests on those who meet minimum requirements, conducts initial interviews with those who had the highest test scores, follows up with additional interviews or testing, and then selects a candidate from the few who survived this process. Another, more expensive alternative is to take most applicants through all steps of the process and then to review all the scores to find the most desirable candidates. With this alternative, decision makers may use a **compensatory model**, in which a very high score on one type of assessment can make up for a low score on another.

compensatory model
Process of arriving at a selection decision in which a very high score on one type of assessment can make up for a low score on another.

Whether the organization uses a multiple-hurdle model or conducts the same assessments on all candidates, the decision maker(s) needs criteria for choosing among qualified candidates. An obvious strategy is to select the candidates who score highest on tests and interviews. However, employee performance depends on motivation as well as ability. It is possible that a candidate who scores very high on an ability test might be "overqualified," that is, the employee might be bored by the job the organization needs to fill, and a less-able employee might actually be a better fit. Similarly, a highly motivated person might learn some kinds of jobs very quickly, potentially outperforming someone who has the necessary skills. Furthermore, some organizations have policies of developing employees for career paths in the organization. Such organizations might put less emphasis on the skills needed for a particular job and more emphasis on hiring candidates who share the organization's values, show that they have the people skills to work with others in the organization, and are able to learn the skills needed for advancement.

Finally, organizations have choices about who will make the decision. Sometimes the immediate supervisor or manager makes the final decision, often alone. This person may couple knowledge of the job with a judgment about who will fit in best with others in the department. The decision could also be made by a human resource professional using standardized, objective criteria. Especially in organizations that value teamwork, selection decisions may be made by a work team or other panel of decision makers.

COMMUNICATING THE DECISION

The human resource department is often responsible for notifying applicants about the results of the selection process. When a candidate has been selected, the organization should communicate the offer to the candidate. The offer should include the job responsibilities, work schedule, rate of pay, starting date, and other relevant details. If placement in a job requires that the applicant complete a medical examination, the offer should state that contingency. The person communicating the offer should also indicate a date by which the candidate should reply with an acceptance or rejection of the offer. For some jobs, such as management and professional positions, the candidate and organization may negotiate pay, benefits, and work arrangements before they arrive at a final employment agreement.

The person who communicates this decision should keep accurate records of who was contacted, when, and for which position, as well as of the candidate's reply. The HR department and the immediate supervisor also should be in close communication about the job offer. When an applicant accepts a job offer, the HR department must notify the supervisor, so that he or she can be prepared for the new employee's arrival.

SUMMARY

L01 Identify the elements of the selection process.

- Selection typically begins with a review of candidates' employment applications and résumés. The organization administers tests to candidates who meet requirements, and qualified candidates undergo one or more interviews.

- Organizations check references and conduct background checks to verify the accuracy of information provided by candidates. A candidate is selected to fill each vacant position. Candidates who accept offers are placed in the positions for which they were selected.

L02 Define ways to measure the success of a selection method.

- One criterion is reliability, which indicates the method is free from random error, so that measurements are consistent. A selection method should also be valid, meaning that performance on the measure (such as a test score) is related to what the measure is designed to assess (such as job performance).

- A selection method also should be generalizable, so that it applies to more than one specific situation. Each selection method should have utility, meaning it provides economic value greater than its cost. Finally, selection methods should meet the legal requirements for employment decisions.

L03 Summarize the legal requirements for employee selection.

- The selection process must comply with human rights and privacy legislation and be conducted in a fair and consistent manner. Selection methods must be valid for job performance. Questions may not gather information about prohibited grounds.

L04 Compare the common methods used for selecting human resources.

- Nearly all organizations gather information through employment applications and résumés. These methods are inexpensive, and job applications standardize basic information received from all applicants. The information is not necessarily reliable, because each applicant provides the information.

- References and background checks help to verify the accuracy of the information. Employment tests and work samples are more objective. To be legal, any test must measure abilities that actually are associated with successful job performance. Tests should be selected to be related to successful job performance and avoid human rights violations.

- Interviews are widely used to obtain information about a candidate's interpersonal and communication skills and to gather more detailed information about a candidate's background. Structured interviews are more valid than unstructured ones. Situational and behavioural interviews provide greater validity than general questions. Interviews are costly and may introduce bias into the selection process. Organizations can minimize the drawbacks through preparation and training.

L05 Describe major types of employment tests.

- Physical ability tests measure strength, endurance, psychomotor abilities, and other physical abilities. They can be accurate but can discriminate and are not always job-related.
- Cognitive ability tests, or intelligence tests, tend to be valid, especially for complex jobs and those requiring adaptability. Job performance tests tend to be valid but are not always generalizable.
- Personality tests measure personality traits such as extroversion and adjustment. Organizations may use honesty tests as well as pre-employment drug tests in some circumstances, e.g., for safety-sensitive jobs. A medical examination may be a condition of employment, but to avoid discrimination against persons with disabilities, organizations usually administer a medical exam only after making a conditional job offer.

L06 Discuss how to conduct effective interviews.

- Interviews should be focused, structured, and standardized. Interviewers should identify job requirements and create a list of questions related to the requirements. Interviewers should be trained to recognize their own personal biases and conduct objective interviews. Panel interviews can reduce problems related to interviewer bias. Interviewers also should be prepared to provide information about the job and the organization.

L07 Explain how employers carry out the process of making a selection decision.

- The organization should focus on the objective of finding the person who will be the best fit with the job and organization.
- Decision makers may use a multiple-hurdle model, in which each stage of the selection process eliminates some of the candidates from consideration at the following stages. An alternative is a compensatory model, in which all candidates are evaluated with all methods. A candidate who scores poorly with one method may be selected if he or she scores very high on another measure.

Critical Thinking Questions

1. What activities are involved in the selection process? Think of the last time you were hired for a job. Which of those activities were used in selecting you? Should the organization that hired you have used other methods as well?
2. Why should the selection process be adapted to fit the organization's job specifications?
3. Choose two of the selection methods identified in this chapter. Describe how you can compare them in terms of reliability, validity, ability to generalize, utility, and compliance with human rights legislation.
4. Why does predictive validation provide better information than concurrent validation? Why is this type of validation more difficult?
5. Do you think recent privacy guidelines will affect organizations' use of social media background checks? Explain.
6. Suppose your organization needs to hire several computer programmers, and you are reviewing résumés you obtained from an online service. What kinds of information will you want to gather from the "work experience" portion of these résumés? What kinds of information will you want to gather from the "education" portion of these résumés? What methods would you use for verifying or exploring this information? Why would you use those methods?

7. For each of the following jobs, select two kinds of tests you think would be most important to include in the selection process. Explain why you chose those tests.
   a. City bus driver
   b. Pharmaceutical sales representative
   c. Member of a team that sells complex high-tech equipment to manufacturers
   d. Member of a team that makes a component of the equipment in (c)
8. Suppose you are a human resource professional at a large retail chain. You want to improve the company's hiring process by standardizing interviews, so that every time someone is interviewed for a particular job category, that person answers the same questions. You also want to make sure the questions asked are relevant to the job and comply with human rights legislation. Think of three questions to include in interviews for each of the following jobs. For each question, state why you think it should be included.
   a. Cashier at one of the company's stores
   b. Store manager
   c. Accounts payable clerk at company headquarters
9. How can organizations improve the quality of their interviewing so that interviews provide valid information?

10. The following questions are favourites of three seasoned hiring managers. For each of the following questions provide your opinion of:
    i. What you think the interviewer is after
    ii. The best answer
    iii. The worst answer
    a. Del Rollo, director of hospitality, Jackson-Triggs Niagara Estate, Niagara-on-the-Lake asks: "*What is the greatest service experience you've had?*"
    b. Gary Hellard, manager of recruiting, WestJet Airlines, Calgary asks: "*Tell us what began as your most frustrating or tough day, and what you did so that it ended up being your most productive day.*"
    c. Nancy Blair, office leader, Egon Zehnder International Inc., Calgary asks: "*What do you hope this job is not?*"

SOURCE: Tony Martin, "Why Are They Asking Me This?" Report on Business, *The Globe and Mail,* September 26, 2007, www.theglobeandmail.com, retrieved September 27, 2007.

11. Some organizations set up a selection process that is long and complex. In some people's opinion, this kind of selection process not only is more valid but also has symbolic value. What can the use of a long, complex selection process symbolize to job seekers? How do you think this would affect the organization's ability to attract the best employees?

What's Your HR IQ?

Connect offers more ways to check what you've learned so far. Find experiential exercises, Test Your Knowledge quizzes, videos, and many other resources to gauge your HR IQ.

CASE STUDY 5.1: How Google Searches for Talent

Since 2003, Goggle's has been hosting an annual international programming competition that attracts around 10,000 participants who "race to solve a series of complex algorithms within a limited amount of time." Participants compete for cash prizes ranging from $250 for 76th–100th place to $10,000 for first place and possibly a job offer with Google. Google has also hosted country-specific Code Jams—Code Jam Africa and Code Jam India.

Here is a glimpse into Code Jam India:

It is the first day of spring in India, a day celebrated with riotous colour and revelry. But in one corner of Bangalore, India's info tech hub, the sunny Saturday is heavy with tension. At an Internet café, a group of engineers and math majors, all in their 20s, hunch over terminals, ready to write some killer code—and with luck, launch careers with one of the world's premier tech companies, Google Inc.

It's the Google India Code Jam, a contest to find the most brilliant coder in South and Southeast Asia. The fastest will win $6,900—and more importantly, the offer of a coveted job at one of Google's research and development centres. At the stroke of 10:30 a.m., the contestants begin, emerging exhausted three hours later. "It's been incredibly difficult and awesome," says Nirin Gupta, a computer science undergrad at the Indian Institute of Technology at Bombay.

Some 14,000 aspirants registered from all over South and Southeast Asia for the first round in February. The top 50 were selected for the finals in Bangalore: 39 from India, 8 from Singapore, and 3 from Indonesia. "It's a dog-eat-dog world," says Robert Hughes, president of TopCoder Inc., the testing company that runs the Code Jams. "Wherever the best talent is, Google wants them."

And the winner is . . . one of these clever IIT grads from India, right? Surprisingly, no. Ardian Poernomo, a third-year undergrad computer engineering student at Singapore's Nanyang Technological University, lands in first place. The number two finisher, Pascal Alfadian, a second-year student at the Universitas Katolik Parahyangan in West Java, is Indonesian, too. Poernomo didn't commit to taking a job with Google, however. He may go for a doctorate degree in computer science in the United States.

Still, Google now has a new pool of Asian talent to choose from. According to Krishna Bharat, head of Google's India research and development centre, all the finalists will be offered jobs. And Google needs them. The search company has been frustrated by its inability to find top-notch engineers for its centre in India, according to industry insiders.

Google's frustrations in India stem from two factors. One is the red-hot job market in Indian tech. Engineering students are assured of a job a year before they graduate. And Google makes things hard for itself by having some of the most exacting hiring standards going. The contest is an example. Participants are tested on aptitude in problem solving, on designing and writing code, and on testing peer-written work. Finalists are asked to create and test software for unique Web searches and to get from point A to B in a city with a minimum number of turns. The final challenge is programming a war-based board game, a task so complex that only winner Poernomo completed it.

For Google, the Code Jam will serve as a shortcut through its hiring regime. Candidates normally go through a seven-stage process that can last months—and at the end of it, they're more likely to be rejected than hired. Much of that screening can be set aside for Code Jam winners.

Questions

1. Why do you think Google uses a competition (Code Jam) as one of its selection methods? What are some benefits of this method?

2. What knowledge, skills, abilities, or other characteristics of computer programmers would the Code Jam *not* evaluate?

3. Would you predict that the Code Jam is a valid and reliable selection method for Google programmers? Would you advise Google to use similar methods for other positions in the company? Explain.

SOURCES: "Google Code Jam 2012," http://code.google.com/code-jam, retrieved April 4, 2012; Allie Townsend, "Google Code Jam," *TimeSpecials:* Top 10 Nerdy Competitions," October 4, 2010, www.time.com/time/specials/packages/article/0,28804,2023019_2023018_2023034,00.html, retrieved April 4, 2012; and Josey Puliyenthuruthel, "How Google Searches—for Talent," *BusinessWeek,* April 11, 2005, http://web6.infotrac.galegroup.com.

CASE STUDY 5.2: Speed Interviewing

Metzti Bryan stood along with about 100 other graphic communications management students in the school cafeteria at Toronto's Ryerson University waiting for the sound of a gong. When the gong sounded, the students charged into the cafeteria in frantic search of their first interview. After ten minutes, the gong sounded again to signal the next interview at this "speed-interviewing" event. Over a total of 120 minutes each student would speak with 12 potential employers. "It's like a race," said Ms. Bryan, describing the experience as both nerve-wracking and energizing. Ms. Bryan got the job she wanted and now conducts speed interviews for her employer.

Employers who recently took part in "CGA Speed Interview Nights" shared some insights about what they were looking for. Neil Focht, accounting manager at Enterprise Holdings Inc. says that little things, like a good handshake count. Neil adds: "It's good to give specific examples of past situations without giving too much detail."

McMaster University, Canada's third-largest medical school has been using a similar type of screening method—applicants rotate through 12 mini-interviews that are exactly eight minutes long. They are given the chance to discuss one scenario or answer one question before having to move quickly to the next interview when a bell sounds. The mini-interviews focus on both ethical issues and realistic medical scenarios.

Questions

1. In your opinion, does "speed interviewing" increase the validity of a selection process? Why or why not?

2. What additional selection methods might be appropriate for the initial screening of job applicants (i.e., prior to the speed interviewing process)?

3. Would you prefer this interview process to a traditional panel interview? Why or why not?

SOURCES: Zosia Bielski, "On Your Marks, Get Set....Hire!" *Globe and Mail,* December 1, 2009, L.1; "Speed Interviewing: What Employers Want," *CGA CareerView,* January 3, 2012, http://cgacareerview .wordpress.com/2012/01/03/speed-interviewing-what-employers-want/, retrieved March 28, 2012; and Anne Marie Owens, "Medical School's Novel Entrance Test—12 Eight Minute Interviews," *National Post,* April 5, 2004, pp. A1, A5.

 Practise and learn online with Connect.

Part 3

MANAGING TALENT

Real People and HR

...Joy Serne, Senior Director, Culture, Learning, and Employee Experience, Farm Credit Canada

Joy Serne is the senior director, Culture, Learning, and Employee Experience, with Farm Credit Canada (FCC). Joy previously held positions throughout FCC in the areas of operations, re-engineering, and IT. She holds a bachelor of science in agriculture and agricultural economics from the University of Saskatchewan.

Name...
Joy Serne.

Job...
Senior director, culture, learning, and employee experience—Farm Credit Canada (FCC).

Adjective people would use to describe you...
Focused.

First job...
Working at Kentucky Fried Chicken as a cashier.

First HR job...
Compensation and classification advisor.

Biggest challenges or issues facing FCC from a talent management perspective...
We're currently in a great position as an employer of choice in Canada. We know the competition is going to get a lot tougher as the talent pool shrinks. Our big challenge is to keep striving to improve our employee experience so we can attract and keep the best of the best.

Most challenging aspect of your job...
Finding the time to do everything that can be done.

Most rewarding aspect of your job...
Seeing new HR strategies come to life and hearing others in the business say we really add value to FCC.

How FCC decides what training, learning, and development methods to use...
FCC bases its methods on *The Six Disciplines of Breakthrough Learning: How to Turn Training and Development into Business Results*. This is the essential guidebook for developing training that helps employees transfer what they learn into day-to-day actions that drive business results.

FCC's approach to management and leadership development...
We believe that the primary job of leaders is to inspire others to achieve outstanding results. We are currently building a new leadership strategy to ensure we support our leaders and equip them to effectively communicate, coach, and model our culture.

Four essential attributes that make someone a great HR professional...
1. Integrity displayed through both words and actions.
2. Passion for people and the business.
3. Vision for how HR can help move the business forward.
4. Willingness to continually listen and learn.

If you had to pick an alternative career...
Finance.

Best career advice that you ever received...
Find work you are passionate about and you will always be happy.

Advice for someone beginning a career...
Work hard and don't be scared to take on new challenges and ask questions. If you want to be respected by others in your organization, apply yourself to understanding whatever business you are in and look for ways to add value for that business.

SOURCE: Reprinted with the kind permission of Joy Serne.

Chapter 6

TRAINING AND
Developing Employees

{

What Do I Need to Know?

After reading this chapter, you should be able to:

LO1 Discuss how to link training and development to organizational needs and strategy.

LO2 Explain how to assess training needs and determine employees' readiness.

LO3 Describe how to plan and design an effective training program.

LO4 Summarize how to implement and evaluate a successful training program.

LO5 Describe training methods for employee orientation and diversity management.

LO6 Discuss the approaches organizations use for employee development.

LO7 Explain how managers and peers develop employees through mentoring and coaching.

LO8 Identify the steps in the career management process and how managers are dealing with some critical development-related challenges.

TELUS intends to get new grads' careers off to a kick-start with its Learning 2.0 initiative that includes a flexible rotation program.

What's In It for New Grads at TELUS?

TELUS, a telecommunications provider with more than 35,000 employees globally, has restructured its approach to corporate learning with an organization-wide vision called "Learning 2.0." One of the changes in TELUS's transformed approach is the shift to include more opportunities for social, team member-driven and developed learning. For example, business, finance, technology, and engineering grads are provided flexible rotation programs. These 24–36 month rotation programs are intended to provide opportunities to obtain mentorship and real project experience—"explore your interests and passions, take on challenging roles and assignments, and take ownership of a variety of projects." According to Adrian Bourassa, IT project manager: "the program vastly exceeded my expectations because it provided the opportunity to build relationships with leaders from all over the company and establish a strong network of alumni from the program. Program sponsors are committed to making a significant investment in training, learning and development for all members."[1]

Introduction

Training consists of an organization's planned efforts to help employees acquire job-related knowledge, skills, abilities, and behaviours, with the goal of applying these on the job. A training program may range from formal classes to one-on-one mentoring, and it may take place on the job or at remote locations. No matter what its form, training can benefit the organization when it is linked to organizational needs and when it motivates employees.

As we noted in Chapter 1, employees' commitment to their organization depends on how their managers treat them. To "win the war for talent" managers must be able to identify high-potential employees, make sure the organization uses the talents of these people, and reassure them of their value, so that they remain satisfied and stay with the organization. Managers also must be able to listen. Although new employees need direction, they expect to be able to think independently and be treated with respect. In all these ways, managers provide for **employee development**—the combination of formal education, job experiences, relationships, and assessment of personality and abilities to help employees prepare for the future of their careers. Human resource management establishes a process for employee development that prepares employees to help the organization meet its goals.

Table 6.1 summarizes the traditional differences between training and development.

This chapter describes how to plan and carry out an effective training program and explores the purpose and activities of employee development. We begin by discussing how to develop effective training in the context of the organization's strategy. Next, we discuss how organizations assess employees' training needs. We then review training methods and the process of evaluating a training program, and discuss some special applications of training: orientation of new employees and the management of diversity. We also examine the relationships among development, training, and career management and look at development approaches, including formal education, assessment, job experiences, and interpersonal relationships. The chapter emphasizes the types of competencies that are strengthened by each development method, so employees and their managers can choose appropriate methods when planning for development. The steps of the career management process, emphasizing the responsibilities of employee and employer at each step of the process are discussed. The chapter concludes with a discussion of special challenges related to employee development, e.g., the so-called glass ceiling and dysfunctional managers.

> **employee development**
>
> The combination of formal education, job experiences, relationships, and assessment of personality and abilities to help employees prepare for the future of their careers.

TABLE 6.1   Training versus Development

	TRAINING	DEVELOPMENT
Focus	Current	Future
Use of work experiences	Low	High
Goal	Preparation for current job	Preparation for changes
Participation	Required	Voluntary

Training, Learning, and Development Linked to Organizational Needs and Strategy

2,6

Workplace training and employee development are key ingredients in the competitiveness of firms and ultimately of national competitiveness.[2] Rapid change, especially in the area of technology, requires that employees continually learn new skills. The new psychological contract, described in Chapter 1, has created the expectation that employees invest in their own career development, which requires learning opportunities. Growing reliance on teamwork creates a demand for the ability to solve problems in teams, an ability that often requires formal training. Finally, the diversity of the Canadian population,

> **LO1** Discuss how to link training and development to organizational needs and strategy.

coupled with the globalization of business, requires that employees be able to work well with people who are different from them. Successful organizations often take the lead in developing this ability.

Some organizations are developing their employer brand and reputation as a talent developer. These organizations emphasize training, career, and developmental opportunities as a means of gaining competitive advantage in the war for talent.[3] How are Canadian firms investing in and supporting learning? How does Canada compare with other countries? The Conference Board of Canada explores these and other questions in its *Learning and Development Outlook 2011*. The report reveals that Canadian firms continue to under-invest in learning and that Canada lags the United States and other countries in employee training, This could have serious adverse effects on long-term productivity, performance, innovation, and competitiveness.[4]

This survey of employers revealed that spending on learning and development continued to decline in 2010—dropping 13 percent since 2008 and almost 40 percent since the early 1990s—the average per employee direct expenditure on training and development across all industries in Canada was $688 and the average Canadian employee received 25 hours of training in 2010 (this is down 10 percent from 2008, when the average employee received 28 hours of training and development).

One way for organizations to remain competitive, even in the face of challenging economic conditions is to ensure they have a strong learning culture. However, the International Institute for Management Development (IMD) reports that Canada has slipped by various measures of importance placed on workforce training. The IMD recently ranked Canada as 25th place (out of 59 countries ranked)—slipping from 12th place in 2002 and 21st place in 2006. That leaves Canada just behind China; slightly ahead of India, but well below Japan, Switzerland, and Demmark.[5]

With training so essential in modern organizations, it is important to provide training that is effective. An effective training program actually teaches what it is designed to teach, and participants learn skills and behaviours that will help the organization achieve its goals. Training programs may prepare employees for future positions in the organization, enable the organization to respond to change, reduce turnover, enhance worker safety, improve customer service and product design, and meet many other goals. To achieve those goals, HR professionals approach training through **instructional design**—a process of systematically developing training to meet specified needs.[6]

A complete instructional design process includes the steps shown in Figure 6.1. It begins with an assessment of the needs for training—what the organization requires that its people learn. Next, the organization ensures that employees are ready for training in terms of their attitudes, motivation, basic skills, and work environment. The third step is to plan the training program, including the program's objectives, instructors, and methods. The organization then implements the program. Finally, evaluating the results of the training provides feedback for planning future training programs.

To carry out this process more efficiently and effectively, a growing number of organizations are using a **learning management system (LMS)**, a computer application that automates the administration, development, and delivery of a company's training programs.[7] Managers and employees can use the LMS to identify training and development needs and enrol in courses. LMSs can make learning programs more widely available and help companies reduce travel and other costs by providing online training. Administrative tools let managers track course enrolments and program completion. The system can be linked to the organization's performance management system to plan

> **instructional design**
> A process of systematically developing training to meet specified needs.
>
> **learning management system (LMS)**
> A computer application that automates the administration, development, and delivery of training and development programs.

FIGURE 6.1

Stages of Instructional Design

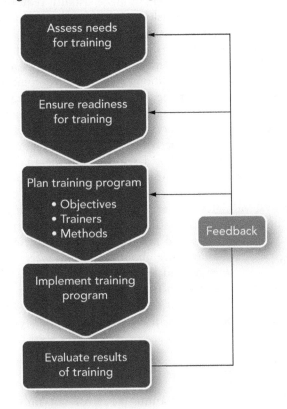

FIGURE 6.1

Stages of Instructional Design

for and manage training needs, training outcomes, and associated rewards together.

What Is Needs Assessment?

Instructional design logically should begin with a **needs assessment**, the process of evaluating the organization, individual employees, and employees' tasks to determine what kinds of training, if any, are necessary. As this definition indicates, the needs assessment answers questions in the three broad areas:[8]

> **LO2** Explain how to assess training needs and determine employees' readiness.

1. *Organization*—What is the context in which training will occur?
2. *Person*—Who needs training?
3. *Task*—What topics should the training cover?

The answers to these questions provide the basis for planning an effective training program.

A variety of conditions may prompt an organization to conduct a needs assessment. Management may observe that some employees lack basic skills or are performing below expectations. Decisions to produce new products, apply new technology, or design new jobs should prompt a needs assessment because these changes tend to require new skills. The decision to conduct a needs assessment also may be prompted by outside forces, such as customer requests or legal requirements.

The outcome of the needs assessment is a set of decisions about how to address the issues that prompted the needs assessment. These decisions do not necessarily include a training program, because some issues should be resolved through methods other than training—for example, plans for better rewards to improve motivation, better hiring decisions, and better safety precautions.

ORGANIZATION ANALYSIS

Usually, the needs assessment begins with the **organization analysis**. This is a process for determining the appropriateness of training by evaluating the characteristics of the organization. The organization analysis looks at training needs in light of the organization's strategy, resources available for training, and management's support for training activities.

Training needs will vary depending on whether the organization's strategy is based on growing or shrinking its workforce, whether it is seeking to serve a broad customer base or focusing on the specific needs of a narrow market segment, and various other strategic scenarios. A company cutting costs with a downsizing strategy may need to train employees in job search skills. The employees who remain following a downsizing may need cross-training so they can handle a wider variety of responsibilities.

Anyone planning a training program must consider whether the organization has the budget, time, and expertise for training. Even if training fits the organization's strategy, it can be viable only if the organization is willing to support the investment. Managers increase the success of training when they support it through such actions as helping trainees see how they can use their newly learned knowledge, skills, and behaviours on the job.[9] Conversely, the managers will be most likely to support training if the people planning it can show that it will solve a significant problem or result in a significant improvement, relative to its cost.

needs assessment
The process of evaluating the organization, individual employees, and employees' tasks to determine what kinds of training, if any, are necessary.

organization analysis
A process for determining the appropriateness of training by evaluating the characteristics of the organization.

PERSON ANALYSIS

Following the organizational assessment, needs assessment turns to the remaining areas of analysis: person and task. The **person analysis** is a process for determining individuals' needs and readiness for training. It involves answering several questions:

- Do performance deficiencies result from a competency gap—that is, a lack of knowledge, skill, or ability? (If so, training is appropriate; if not, other solutions are more relevant.)
- Who needs training?
- Are these employees ready for training?

The answers to these questions help the manager identify whether training is appropriate and which employees need training. In certain situations, such as the introduction of a new technology or service, all employees may need training. However, when needs assessment is conducted in response to a performance issue, training is not always the best solution.

The person analysis is therefore critical when training is considered in response to a performance issue. In assessing the need for training, the manager should identify all the variables that can influence performance. The primary variables are the person's ability and skills, his or her mindset and motivation, the organization's input (including clear directions, necessary resources, and freedom from interference and distractions), performance feedback, and positive consequences to motivate good performance. Of these variables, only ability and skills can be affected by training. Therefore, before planning a training program, it is important to be sure that any performance issue results from a deficiency in knowledge and skills. Otherwise, training dollars will be wasted, because the training is unlikely to have much effect on performance.

The person analysis also should determine whether employees are ready to undergo training. In other words, the employees to receive training not only should require additional knowledge and skill, but must be willing and able to learn. We will explore this aspect a little later in this chapter.

TASK ANALYSIS

The third area of needs assessment is **task analysis**, the process of identifying the tasks and competencies (knowledge, skills, and behaviour) that

person analysis
A process for determining individuals' needs and readiness for training.

task analysis
The process of identifying the tasks and competencies that training should emphasize.

readiness for training
A combination of employee characteristics and positive work environment that permit training.

training should emphasize. Usually, task analysis is conducted along with person analysis. Understanding shortcomings in performance usually requires knowledge about the tasks and work environment as well as the employee.

To carry out the task analysis, the HR professional looks at the conditions in which tasks are performed. These conditions include the equipment and environment of the job, time constraints (e.g., deadlines), safety considerations, and performance standards. These observations form the basis for a description of work activities, or the tasks required by the person's job. For a selected job, the analyst interviews employees and their supervisors to prepare a list of tasks performed in that job. Then the analyst validates the list by showing it to employees, supervisors, and other subject-matter experts and asking them to complete a questionnaire about the *importance, frequency,* and *difficulty* of the tasks. The information from these questionnaires is the basis for determining which tasks will be the focus of the training.

Readiness for Training

Effective training requires not only a program that addresses real needs, but also a condition of employee readiness. **Readiness for training** is a combination of employee characteristics and positive work environment that permit training. The necessary employee characteristics include ability to learn the subject matter, favourable attitudes toward the training, and motivation to learn. A positive work environment is one that encourages learning and avoids interfering with the training program.

EMPLOYEE READINESS CHARACTERISTICS

To be ready to learn, employees need basic learning skills, especially *cognitive ability,* which includes being able to use written and spoken language, solve math problems, and use logic to solve problems. However, recent forecasts of the skill levels of the workforce indicate that many companies will have to work with employees who lack basic skills.[10] For example, they may need to provide literacy training before some employees will be ready to participate in job-related training.

Employees learn more from training programs when they are highly motivated to learn—that is, when they really want to learn the content of the training program.[11] Employees tend to feel this way if they believe they are able to learn, see potential benefits from the training program, are aware of their need to learn, see a fit between the training and their career goals, and have the basic skills needed for participating in the program. Managers can influence a ready attitude in a variety of ways. For example, they can provide feedback that encourages employees, establish rewards for learning, and communicate with employees about the organization's career paths and future needs.

WORK ENVIRONMENT

Readiness for training also depends on two broad characteristics of the work environment: situational constraints and social support.[12] *Situational constraints* are the limits on training's effectiveness that arise from the situation or the conditions within the organization. Constraints can include a lack of money for training, lack of time for training or practising, and failure to provide proper tools and materials for learning or applying the lessons of training.

Social support refers to the ways the organization's people encourage training, including giving trainees positive feedback and encouragement, sharing information about participating in training programs, and expressing positive attitudes toward the organization's training programs. Support can come from employees' peers as well as from supervisors and managers. The organization can formally provide peer support by establishing groups of employees who meet regularly to discuss their progress. For example, group members can share how they coped with challenges related to what they learned. Schlumberger, which provides oil field services, sets

up online "communities of practice," where geologists, physicists, managers, engineers, and other employees around the world can trade knowledge to solve problems.[13] Organizations can also assign experienced employees as mentors to trainees, providing advice and support.

How to Plan and Design the Training Program

Planning begins with establishing objectives for the training program. Based on those objectives, the planner (usually a specialist in the training or HR department) decides who will provide the training, what topics the training will cover, what training methods to use, and how to evaluate the training.

LO3 ▶ Describe how to plan and design an effective training program.

OBJECTIVES OF THE PROGRAM

Formally establishing objectives for the training program has several benefits. First, a training program based on clear objectives will be more focused and more likely to succeed. Employees learn best when they know what the training is supposed to accomplish. Finally, down the road, establishing objectives provides a basis for measuring whether the program succeeded, as we will discuss later in this chapter.

Effective training objectives have three components:

- They include a statement of what the employee is expected to do, the quality or level of performance that is acceptable, and the conditions under which the employee is to apply what he or she learned (for instance, physical conditions, mental stresses, or equipment failure).[14]

Extreme Hockey and Sport, located in Regina, Saskatchewan, has developed a reputation for satisfied customers served by knowledgeable and dedicated employees. Management of this retail sports specialty store supports employee training through intensive product knowledge sessions.

- They include performance standards that are measurable.
- They identify the resources needed to carry out the desired performance or outcome. Successful training requires employees to learn and also employers to provide the necessary resources.

A related issue at the outset is who will participate in the training program. Some training programs are developed for all employees of the organization or all members of a team. Other training programs identify individuals who lack desirable skills or have potential to be promoted, then provide training in the areas of need that are identified for the particular employees. When deciding whom to include in training, the organization has to avoid illegal discrimination. The organization must not—intentionally or unintentionally—exclude anyone due to a prohibited ground of discrimination, for example, sex, race, or age. During the training, all participants should receive equal treatment, such as equal opportunities for practise. In addition, the training program should provide accommodation for trainees with disabilities.

IN-HOUSE OR CONTRACTED OUT?

An organization can provide an effective training program, even if it lacks expertise in training. Many companies and consultants provide training services to organizations. Colleges and technical institutes often work with employers to train employees in a variety of skills.

To select a training service, an organization can send several vendors a *request for proposal (RFP)*, a document outlining the type of service needed, the type and number of references needed, the number of employees to be trained, the date by which the training is to be completed, and the date by which proposals should be received. A complete RFP also indicates funding for the project and the process by which the organization will determine its level of satisfaction. Putting together a request for proposal is time-consuming, but worthwhile because it helps the organization clarify its objectives, compare vendors, and measure results.

Vendors that believe they are able to provide the services outlined in the RFP submit proposals that provide the types of information requested. The organization reviews the proposals to eliminate any vendors that do not meet requirements and to compare the vendors that do qualify. They check references and select a candidate, based on the proposal and the vendor's answers to questions about its experience, work samples, and evidence that its training programs meet objectives.

The cost of purchasing training from a contractor can vary substantially. In general, it is much costlier to purchase specialized training tailored to the organization's requirements than to participate in a seminar or training course that teaches general skills or knowledge. Even in organizations that send employees to outside training programs, someone in the organization may be responsible for coordinating the overall training program. Called *training administration*, this is typically the responsibility of a human resources professional. Training administration includes activities before, during, and after training sessions.

What Training Methods Are Available?

Whether the organization prepares its own training programs or buys training from other organizations, it is important to verify that the content of the training relates directly to the training objectives. Relevance to the organization's needs and objectives ensures that training money is well spent. Tying training content closely to objectives also improves trainees' learning, because it increases the likelihood that the training will be meaningful and helpful.

After deciding on the goals and content of the training program, planners must decide how the training will be conducted. Figure 6.2 shows the percentages of companies using various broad categories of training methods. Although instructor-led classroom training continues to be the most dominantly used delivery method, it has gradually lost ground to other methods during the last decade. In 2000, 80 percent of all learning delivery was done in the classroom, but by 2010, classroom learning represented just 58 percent of learning delivery.[15]

CLASSROOM INSTRUCTION

At school, we tend to associate learning with classroom instruction, and that type of training is most widely used in the workplace, too. Classroom instruction typically involves an instructor leading a group. Instructors often use slides, discussions, case studies, question-and-answer sessions, and role playing. Actively involving trainees enhances learning.

When the course objectives call for presenting information on a specific topic to many trainees, classroom instruction is one of the least expensive and least time-consuming ways to accomplish that goal. Learning will be more effective if trainers enhance lectures with job-related examples and opportunities for hands-on learning.

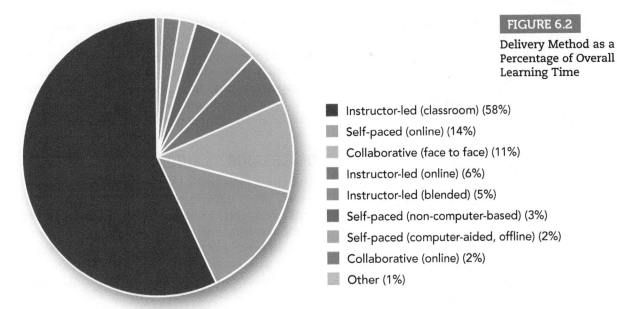

FIGURE 6.2

Delivery Method as a
Percentage of Overall
Learning Time

■ Instructor-led (classroom) (58%)

■ Self-paced (online) (14%)

■ Collaborative (face to face) (11%)

■ Instructor-led (online) (6%)

■ Instructor-led (blended) (5%)

■ Self-paced (non-computer-based) (3%)

■ Self-paced (computer-aided, offline) (2%)

■ Collaborative (online) (2%)

■ Other (1%)

Note: Total does not add to 100 due to rounding.

SOURCE: Carrie Lavis, "Learning and Development Outlook 2011" (Ottawa: The Conference Board of Canada, October 2011), p. 22. Reprinted with the permission of the Conference Board of Canada.

Technology has expanded the notion of the classroom to classes of trainees scattered in various locations. With *distance learning*, trainees at different locations attend programs online, using their computers to view lectures, participate in discussions, and share documents. Technology applications in distance learning may include videoconferencing, email, instant messaging, document-sharing software, and Web cameras.

AUDIOVISUAL TRAINING

Training need not require that trainees necessarily attend a class. Trainees can also work independently, using course material prepared in presentations, podcasts, videos, or workbooks. These methods can also supplement classroom instruction. Users of audiovisual training often have some control over the presentation. They can review material and may be able to slow down or speed up the lesson. Videos can show situations and equipment that cannot be easily demonstrated in a classroom. Another advantage of audiovisual presentations is that they give trainees a consistent presentation, not affected by an individual trainer's goals and skills. Challenges include ensuring that employees know when and how to use the relevant learning tools e.g., podcasts; encouraging collaboration and interaction among trainees, and ensuring that employees can obtain necessary downloads from their particular location with their mobile device. The problems associated with these methods may include trying to present

Mobile technology is useful not only for entertainment, but can also be used for employees who travel and need to be in touch with the office. iPods, smartphones, and tablets, also give employees the ability to listen to and participate in training programs at their own leisure.

too much material, poorly written dialogue, overuse of features such as humour or music, and drama that distracts from the key points.[16]

COMPUTER-BASED TRAINING

Although almost all organizations use classroom training, new technologies are gaining in popularity as technology improves and becomes less expensive. With computer-based training, participants receive course materials and instruction distributed over the Internet or on a storage device such as a USB memory stick or CD-ROM. Often, these materials are interactive, so participants can answer questions and try out techniques, with course materials adjusted according to participants' responses. Online training programs may allow trainees to submit questions and to participate in online discussions. Multimedia capabilities enable computers to provide sounds, images, and video presentations, along with text. Computer-based training is generally less expensive than putting an instructor in a classroom of trainees.[17]

Current applications of computer-based training can extend its benefits:

- **E-learning** involves receiving training via the Internet or the organization's intranet, typically through some combination of Web-based training modules, distance learning, and virtual classrooms. E-learning uses electronic networks for delivering and sharing information, and it offers tools and information for helping trainees improve performance. Training programs may include links to other online information resources and to trainees and experts for collaboration on problem solving. The e-learning system may also process enrolments, test and evaluate participants, and monitor progress.
- *Electronic performance support systems (EPSS)* provide access to skills training, information, and expert advice when a problem occurs on the job.[18] As employees need to learn new skills, they can use the EPSS, which gives them access to the particular information they need, such as detailed instructions on how to perform an unfamiliar task. Using an EPSS is faster and more relevant than attending classes, even classes offered online.

e-learning
Receiving training via the Internet or the organization's intranet.

on-the-job training (OJT)
Training methods in which a person with job experience and skill guides trainees in practising job skills at the workplace.

apprenticeship
A work-study training method that teaches job skills through a combination of on-the-job training and technical training.

internship
On-the-job learning sponsored by an educational institution as a component of an academic program.

The best e-learning combines the advantages of the Internet with the principles of a good learning environment. It takes advantage of the Web's dynamic nature and ability to use many positive learning features, including hyperlinks to other training sites and content, control by the trainee, and ability for trainees to collaborate.

ON-THE-JOB TRAINING

Although people often associate training with classrooms, much learning occurs while employees are performing their jobs. **On-the-job training (OJT)** refers to training methods in which a person with job experience and skill guides trainees in practising job skills at the workplace. This type of training takes various forms, including apprenticeships and internships.

An **apprenticeship** is a work-study training method that teaches job skills through a combination of on-the-job training and technical training. The OJT component of an apprenticeship involves the apprentice assisting a certified journeyperson in the work place. Typically, the technical training is provided by local trade schools, high schools, community colleges, and technical institutes. On average, 85 percent of the apprentice's two-to-five-year training is spent in the workplace, the rest is spent at a training institution.[19] Some apprenticeship programs are sponsored by individual companies, others by employee unions. Apprenticeship programs are usually administered by provincial and territorial government departments with support from advisory bodies such as apprenticeship and certification boards. To provide greater mobility across Canada for skilled workers, apprentices who have completed their training and certified journeypersons are able to obtain a "Red Seal" endorsement after completing an interprovincial standards exam that allows them to practise their trade anywhere in Canada.[20] For trainees, a major advantage of apprenticeship is the ability to earn an income while learning a trade, that is, "earning while learning." In addition, training through an apprenticeship is usually effective because it involves hands-on learning and extensive practice.

An **internship** is on-the-job learning sponsored by an educational institution as a component of an academic program. The sponsoring school works with local employers to place students in positions where they can gain experience related to their area of study. For example, summer internships are an integral component of the University of British Columbia's MBA program.[21]

Cooperative education is a plan of higher education that incorporates paid work experience as an important component of academic studies. Cooperative education is being readily accepted by government, business, and industry in Canada and throughout the world. Universities, colleges, technical schools, and high schools are offering co-op programs to thousands of students in a growing number of disciplines.[22]

To be effective, OJT programs should include several characteristics:

- The organization should issue a policy statement describing the purpose of OJT and emphasizing the organization's support for it.
- The organization should specify who is accountable for conducting OJT. This accountability should be included in the relevant job descriptions.
- The organization should review OJT practices at companies in similar industries.
- Managers and peers should be trained in OJT principles.
- Employees who conduct OJT should have access to lesson plans, checklists, procedure manuals, training manuals, learning contracts, and progress report forms.
- Before conducting OJT with an employee, the organization should assess the employees' level of basic skills.[23]

The OJT program at Canadian Air Transport Security Authority (CATSA) has many of these characteristics. After completing extensive classroom training including role-plays, and hands-on practice in a training lab, screening officers participate in "live-line-on-the-job training." Point leaders pay careful attention to the screening officers while they conduct various searches and investigations of passengers and their belongings. One class of trainees intercepted an item that looked like a rocket propelled grenade on the X-ray machine. After the police responded and searched the bag, it turned out to be cologne. Ten minutes later, on the same screening line, the search of a passenger's carry-on bag yielded over $30,000 in U.S. currency. Local police and Canadian Border Services Agency officers attended the checkpoint and conducted their investigations. Through this live-line OJT, trainees received invaluable first-hand experience of how to deal with the discovery of contraband at the screening checkpoint and work with stakeholders such as police, airport security, air carriers, and airport authorities.[24]

SIMULATIONS

A simulation is a training method that represents a real-life situation, with trainees making decisions resulting in outcomes that mirror what would happen on the job. Simulations enable trainees to see the impact of their decisions in a staged, risk-free environment. They are used to teach production and process skills as well as management and interpersonal skills.

Simulators must have elements identical to those found in the work environment. The simulator needs to respond exactly as equipment would under the conditions and response given by the trainee. For this reason, simulators are expensive to develop and need constant updating as new information about the work environment becomes available. Still, they are an excellent training method when the risks of a mistake on the job are great. Trainees do not have to be afraid of the impact of wrong decisions when using the simulator, as they would be with on-the-job training. Also, trainees tend to be enthusiastic about this type of learning and to learn quickly, the lessons are generally related very closely to job performance.

When simulations are conducted online, trainees often participate by creating avatars, or computer depictions of themselves, which they manipulate onscreen to play roles as workers or other participants in a job-related situation. One example is British Petroleum's use of Second Life to train new gas station employees in the safety features of gasoline storage tanks and piping systems. In Second Life, BP built three-dimensional renderings of the tank and pipe systems at a typical gas station. Trainees can "see" underground and observe the effect of using safety devices to control the flow of gasoline in a way they could never have done in real life.[25]

Virtual reality is a computer-based technology that provides an interactive, three-dimensional learning experience. Using specialized equipment or viewing the virtual model on a computer screen, trainees

cooperative education
A plan of higher education that incorporates paid work experience as an integral part of academic studies.

simulation
A training method that represents a real-life situation, with trainees making decisions resulting in outcomes that mirror what would happen on the job.

avatars
Computer depictions of trainees, which the trainees manipulate in an online role-play.

virtual reality
A computer-based technology that provides an interactive, three-dimensional learning experience.

move through the simulated environment and interact with its components. Devices relay information from the environment to the trainees' senses. For example, audio interfaces, gloves that provide a sense of touch, treadmills, or motion platforms create a realistic but artificial environment. Devices also communicate information about the trainee's movements to a computer. Virtual reality applications are as diverse as surgery and welding.[26]

BUSINESS GAMES AND CASE STUDIES

Training programs use business games and case studies to develop employees' management skills. A case study is a detailed description of a situation that trainees study and discuss. Cases are designed to develop higher-order thinking skills, such as the ability to analyze and evaluate information. They also can be a safe way to encourage trainees to take appropriate risks, by giving them practice in weighing and acting on uncertain outcomes. There are many sources of case studies, including the Richard Ivey School of Business, Wilfrid Laurier University, Harvard Business School, and McGraw-Hill publishing company.

With business games, trainees gather information, analyze it, and make decisions that influence the outcome of the game. For instance, Markstrat integrated into a marketing course, requires participants to use strategic thinking (such as analyzing competitors) to increase their share of the market.[27] Games stimulate learning because they actively involve participants and mirror the competitive nature of business. A realistic game may be more meaningful to trainees than techniques such as classroom instruction.

Training with case studies and games requires that participants come together to discuss the cases or the progress of the game. This requires face-to-face or virtual meetings. Also, participants must be willing to be actively involved in analyzing the situation and defending their decisions.

BEHAVIOUR MODELLING

Research suggests that one of the most effective ways to teach interpersonal skills is through behaviour modelling.[28] This involves training sessions in which participants observe other people demonstrating the desired behaviour, then have opportunities to practise the behaviour themselves. For example, a training program could involve several days of four-hour

experiential programs
Training programs in which participants learn concepts and apply them by simulating behaviours involved and analyzing the activity, connecting it with real-life situations.

adventure learning
A teamwork and leadership training program based on the use of challenging, structured outdoor activities.

sessions, each focusing on one interpersonal skill, such as communicating or coaching. At the beginning of each session, participants hear the reasons for using the key behaviours, then they watch a video of an expert performing the key behaviours. They practise through role-playing and receive feedback about their performance. In addition, they evaluate the performance of the expert in the video and discuss how they can apply the behaviour on the job.

EXPERIENTIAL PROGRAMS

To develop teamwork and leadership skills, some organizations enrol their employees in a form of training called **experiential programs**. In experiential programs, participants learn concepts and then apply them by simulating the behaviours involved and analyzing the activity, connecting it with real-life situations.[29]

Experiential training programs should follow several guidelines. A program should be related to a specific business problem. Participants should feel challenged and move outside their comfort zones but within limits that keep their motivation strong and help them understand the purpose of the program.

One form of experiential program, called **adventure learning**, uses challenging, structured outdoor activities, which may include difficult sports such as dog-sledding or mountain-climbing. Other activities may be structured tasks like climbing walls, completing rope courses, climbing ladders, or making "trust falls" (in which each trainee falls backward into the arms of other group members).

The impact of adventure learning programs has not been rigorously tested, but participants report they gained a greater understanding of themselves and the ways that the organization insist that entire work groups participate together. This encourages people to see, discuss, and correct the kinds of behaviour that keep the group from performing well. The "HR Oops!" box shows one potential limitation of adventure learning.

Before requiring employees to participate in experiential programs, the organization should consider the possible drawbacks. Because these programs are usually physically demanding and often require participants to touch each other, companies face certain risks. Some employees may be injured or may feel that they were sexually harassed or that their privacy was invaded. Also, human rights and employment equity legislation (discussed in Chapter 2) raises

HR Oops!

When Training Crashes

Edy Greenblatt conducts adventure training in which participants experience how a team of four people must work together to put on a performance on the flying trapeze. Everyone learns firsthand how hard it is to listen while swinging high above the ground and wondering if they'll fall.

While Greenblatt has seen her clients learn a lot about teamwork under pressure, she also has seen and heard about the limits of adventure training. She recalls that one team of trainees told her about an earlier outing with a boss whose leadership they doubted. The training exercise only reinforced their doubts. The boss became terrified and started crying, and the team concluded, "He's the loser we thought he was."

Trainer Linda Henman doesn't even bother recommending adventure learning anymore. She says when groups would spend the morning learning teamwork skills with her, then move to an afternoon of practising teamwork through wilderness navigation, they would return complaining that the time outside had been wasted. They preferred to focus on work-related issues.

SOURCE: Based on Holly Dolezalek, "Extreme Training," *Training*, January 20, 2010, Business & Company Resource Center, http://galenet.galegroup.com.

QUESTIONS

1. Given the criticisms of adventure learning, why do you think it remains an attractive option to some? Would you want to participate in one of these training programs? Why or why not?
2. Imagine that you are an HR manager in a company where an executive wants to sign the sales team up for adventure learning. What steps could you take to increase the likelihood that the effort will benefit the organization?

questions about requiring employees with disabilities to participate in physically demanding training experiences.

TEAM TRAINING

A possible alternative to experiential programs is team training, which coordinates the performance of individuals who work together to achieve a common goal. An organization may benefit from providing such training to groups when group members must share information and group performance depends on the performance of the individual group members. Success depends on individuals coordinating their activities to make decisions, perhaps in dangerous situations—for example in the airline industry or in the military.

Ways to conduct team training include cross-training and coordination training.[30] In **cross-training**, team members understand and practise each other's skills so they are prepared to step in and take another member's place.

For example, Toronto Hydro cross-trains supervisors so they can work across specializations. Jodi Engle, manager of organizational development and performance at Toronto Hydro says, "This enhances their skills. It's a great retention strategy, it gives them more variety and makes their job more meaningful."[31]

Coordination training trains the team in how to share information and decisions to obtain the best team performance. This type of training is especially important for commercial aviation and surgical teams. Both of these kinds of teams must monitor different aspects of equipment and the environment at the same time sharing information to make the most effective decisions regarding patient care or aircraft safety and performance.

ACTION LEARNING

Another form of group building is **action learning**. In this type of training, teams or work groups get an actual problem, work on solving it, commit to an action plan, and are accountable for carrying out the plan.[32] Ideally, the project is one for which the efforts and results will be visible not only to participants but also to others in the organization. The visibility and impact of the task are intended to make participation exciting, relevant, and engaging. To heighten the learning,

cross-training
Team training in which team members understand and practise each other's skills so that they are prepared to step in and take another member's place.

coordination training
Team training that teaches the team how to share information and make decisions to obtain the best team performance.

action learning
Training in which teams get an actual problem, work on solving it, commit to an action plan, and are accountable for carrying it out.

One of the most important features of organizations today is teamwork. Experiential programs, including team-building exercises like wall-climbing and rafting, help build trust and cooperation among employees.

organizations can get their best leaders involved as mentors and coaches to the participants.

The effectiveness of action learning has not been formally evaluated. This type of training seems to result in a great deal of learning, however; and employees are able to apply what they learn, because it involves actual problems the organization is facing. The group approach also helps teams identify behaviours that interfere with problem solving.

Implementing and Evaluating the Training Program

1,6

Learning permanently changes behaviour. For employees to acquire knowledge and skills in the training program and apply what they have learned in their jobs, the training program must be implemented in a way that applies what we know about how people learn.

L04 Summarize how to implement and evaluate a successful training program.

PRINCIPLES OF LEARNING

Researchers have identified a number of ways employees learn best.[33] Table 6.2 summarizes ways training can best encourage learning. In general, effective training communicates learning objectives clearly, presents information in distinctive and memorable ways, and helps trainees link the subject matter to their jobs.

Employees are most likely to learn when training is linked to their current job experiences and tasks.[34] There are a number of ways trainers can make this link. Training sessions should present material using familiar concepts, terms, and examples. As far as possible, the training context—such as the

physical setting or the images presented on a computer—should mirror the work environment. Along with physical elements, the context should include emotional elements. For example, in training store employees to handle upset customers, the physical context is more relevant if it includes trainees acting out scenarios of employees dealing with unhappy customers. The role-play interaction between trainees adds emotional realism and further enhances learning.

To fully understand and remember the content of the training, employees need a chance to demonstrate and practise what they have learned. Trainers should provide ways to actively involve the trainees, have them practise repeatedly, and have them complete tasks within a time that is appropriate in light of the learning objectives. Practise requires physically carrying out the desired behaviours, not just describing them. People tend to benefit most from practise that occurs over several sessions, rather than one long practise session.[35]

Training sessions should offer feedback so that trainees understand whether or not they are succeeding. Effective feedback focuses on specific behaviours and is delivered as soon as possible after the trainees practise or demonstrate what they have learned.[36]

Well-designed training helps people remember the content. Training programs need to break information into chunks that people can remember. Research suggests that people can attend to no more than four to five items at a time. If a concept or procedure involves more than five items, the training program should deliver information in shorter sessions or chunks.[37] Other ways to make information more memorable include presenting it with visual images and practising some tasks enough that they become automatic.

TABLE 6.2 Ways that Training Helps Employees Learn

TRAINING ACTIVITY	WAYS TO PROVIDE TRAINING ACTIVITY
Communicate the learning objective.	• Demonstrate the performance to be expected. • Give examples of questions to be answered.
Use distinctive, attention-getting messages.	• Emphasize key points. • Use pictures, not just words.
Limit the content of training.	• Group lengthy material into chunks. • Provide a visual image of the course material. • Provide opportunities to repeat and practise material.
Guide trainees as they learn.	• Use words as reminders about sequence of activities. • Use words and pictures to relate concepts to one another and to their context.
Elaborate on the subject.	• Present the material in different contexts and settings. • Relate new ideas to previously learned concepts. • Practise in a variety of contexts and settings.
Provide memory cues.	• Suggest memory aids. • Use familiar sounds or rhymes as memory cues.
Transfer course content to the workplace.	• Design the learning environment so that it has elements in common with the workplace. • Require learners to develop action plans that apply training content to their jobs. • Use words that link the course to the workplace.
Provide feedback about performance.	• Tell trainees how accurately and quickly they are performing their new skill. • Show how trainees have met the objectives of the training.

SOURCE: Adapted from R. M. Gagne, "Learning Processes and Instruction," *Training Research Journal* 1 (1995/96), pp. 17–28.

Written materials should have an appropriate reading level. A simple way to assess **readability**—the difficulty level of written materials—is to look at the words being used and at the length of sentences. If training materials are too difficult to understand, several adjustments can help. The basic approach is to re-write the material looking for ways to simplify it—e.g., add checklists and illustrations and substitute simple, concrete words for abstract or unfamiliar words.

MEASURING RESULTS OF TRAINING

After a training program ends, or at intervals during an ongoing training program, organizations should ensure that the training is meeting objectives. The "HR How-To" box discusses steps to increase the value obtained form training. The stage to prepare for evaluating a training program is when the program is being developed. Along with designing course objectives and content, the planner should identify how to measure achievement of objectives. Depending on the objectives, the evaluation can use one or more of the measures shown in Figure 6.3:[38]

- *Reaction.* Satisfaction with the program.
- *Learning.* Knowledge and skills gained.
- *Behaviour.* Behaviour changes.
- *Results.* Improvements in individual and organizational performance.

The Conference Board of Canada reports that over 89 percent of organizations administer reaction-level training evaluations, and that an increasing number of organizations are conducting learning, behaviour, and results-level training evaluations.[39]

The usual way to measure whether participants have acquired information is to administer tests on paper or electronically. Trainers or supervisors can observe whether participants demonstrate the desired competencies. Changes in company performance have a variety of measures, many of which organizations keep track of for preparing performance appraisals, annual reports, and other routine

readability
The difficulty level of written materials.

HR HOW-TO

8 Steps to Effective Training Feedback

Imagine spending one-half of a year's salary on a new car and just leaving it parked in front of the house forever. The car never roars down the highway, so there's no way to gauge performance. It's never taken grocery shopping, so it's impossible to assess the trunk space. And the sound system is never cranked up. So nobody has any idea how good it is. Few people would do that with a new car. But a remarkable number of organizations do the equivalent with employee training. They invest a substantial amount of money without ever doing preparatory work beforehand or seeking an accurate picture afterward on what they gained for their money.

There are eight key steps to getting the most value from training budgets and obtaining the best information about training outcomes:

1. *Identify training needs.* Before training even starts, identify the kind of training the organization needs and wants to do, whether for new regulations, new technology, or differentiation in the market. Regardless of whether it is offered in-house or by an outside supplier, run pilot projects and learn from them before deploying programs more widely throughout the organization.

2. *Create employee competency profiles.* Before training actually starts, prepare a core competency

profile for all employees. This helps determine which employees need what training and, as an added bonus, provides the organization with a system-wide inventory of the skills that already exist in-house.

3. *Ask the basics.* As soon as an individual has completed training, it is a good idea to ask the basic question: "Did you find the training satisfactory?" This helps send a signal to the employee that the organization cares about training quality.

4. *Find out what was learned.* Organizations need to go beyond the basics and ask the employee: "Have you learned anything?" Follow up by asking for elaboration. Not enough organizations take this step, even though it is useful to gauge relevance and determine where training programs need tweaking.

5. *Gauge the mid-term impact on the job.* Few companies actually get to the heart of the impact of training on an individual's job. But new tools can make this step easy. Web-based tools, including 360-degree feedback, can help a trainer prepare detailed questionnaires for the employee and his/her peers, subordinates, clients, suppliers and supervisor, asking for observations about changed or improved behaviour. This should

be done about three months after the training.

6. *Determine the effect on business.* To gain a precise measurement of the impact training has had on business results, ask: "Did the trainee's division log improved sales or operating efficiencies since the training?" "Has there been a dollars-and-cents improvement to the bottom-line that can be traced back to the training?" "Has customer satisfaction improved against specific objectives?"

7. *Measure the return on investment.* Measuring the return on investment of training and reporting back to executives helps mould the shape of future training programs. Ask: "How much did sales or earnings rise for every dollar spent on training?"

8. *Gauge the long-term job impact.* Prepare detailed questionnaires for the employee and those around him/her about six to 12 months after training completion. The questions should be tied to what the employee does and is supposed to do. This kind of long-term follow-up is rarely done but can provide invaluable data about the long-term value of different kinds of training.

SOURCE: Jacques Gaumond, "8 Steps to Effective Training Feedback," *Canadian HR Reporter*, November 5, 2007, pp. 24–25.

---

documents, in order to demonstrate the final measure of success shown in Figure 6.3—results, including return on investment (ROI).

Evaluation Methods

Evaluation of training should look for **transfer of training**, or on-the-job use of

transfer of training
On-the-job use of knowledge, skills, and behaviours learned in training.

knowledge, skills, and behaviours learned in training. Transfer of training requires that employees actually learn the content of the training program and that the necessary conditions are in place for employees to apply what they learned. Thus, the assessment can look at whether employees have an opportunity to perform the

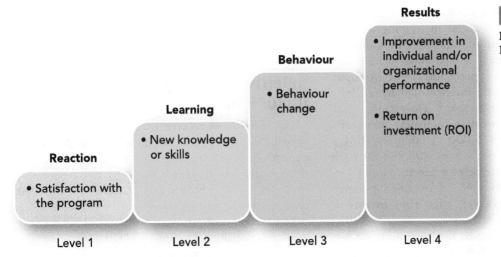

FIGURE 6.3

Measures of Training
Evaluation

skills related to the training. The organization can measure this by asking employees three questions about specific training-related tasks:

1. Do you perform the task?
2. How many times do you perform the task?
3. To what extent do you perform difficult and challenging learned tasks?

Assessment of training also should evaluate training *outcomes*, that is, what (if anything) has changed as a result of the training. The relevant training outcomes are the ones related to the organization's goals for the training and its overall performance. Possible outcomes include the following:

- Trainee and supervisor satisfaction with the training program (reaction)
- Information such as facts, techniques, and procedures that trainees can recall after the training (learning)
- Skills that trainees can demonstrate in tests or on the job (behaviour)
- Changes in behaviour related to the content of the training, for example, concern for safety or support of diversity (behaviour)
- Improvements in individual, group, or company performance, for example, greater customer satisfaction, more sales, fewer defects (results)

DID YOU KNOW?

Use of Learning Evaluation Methods

Most learning activities are still evaluated at a Level 1.

SOURCE: Carrie Lavis, "Learning and Development Outlook 2011" (Ottawa: The Conference Board of Canada, October 2011), p. 35. Reprinted with the permission of the Conference Board of Canada.

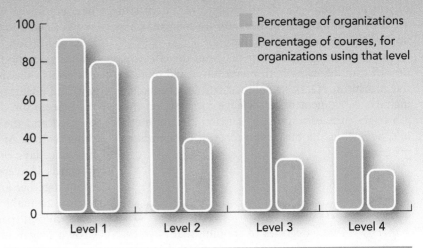

Training is a significant part of many organizations' budgets. Businesses that invest in training want to achieve a high return on investment—the monetary benefits of the investment compared to the amount invested, expressed as a percentage. For example, IBM's e-learning program for new managers, Basic Blue, costs $8,708 per manager.[40] The company has measured an improvement in each new manager's performance worth $415,000. That gives IBM a benefit of $415,000 − $8,708 = $406,292 for each manager. This is an extremely large return on investment: $406,292/$8,708 = 46.65, or 4,665 percent! In other words, for every $1 that IBM invests in Basic Blue, it receives almost $47.

For any of these methods, the most accurate but most costly way to evaluate the training program is to assess performance, knowledge, or behaviours among all employees before the training, then to train only some of the employees. After the training is complete, the performance, knowledge, or behaviour are again assessed, and the trained group is compared to the untrained group. A simpler but less accurate way to assess the training is to conduct a *pre-test* and *post-test* on all trainees, comparing their performance, knowledge, or behaviours before and after the training. This form of measurement does not rule out the possibility that change resulted from something other than training (e.g., a change in the rewards system). The simplest approach is to use only a post-test. Of course, this type of measurement does not enable accurate comparisons, but it may be sufficient, depending on the cost and purpose of the training.

The purpose of evaluating training is to help with future decisions about the organization's training programs. Using the evaluation, the organization may identify a need to modify the training and gain information about the kinds of changes needed. The organization may decide to expand on successful areas of training and cut back on training that has not delivered significant benefits.

TD Bank Financial Group evaluates the effectiveness of training using both quantitative and qualitative measures. TD uses a comprehensive process that includes assessment of knowledge increase, on-the-job confidence, effectiveness of materials and methods, as well as the business impact of their training programs.[41]

orientation
Training designed to prepare employees to perform their jobs effectively, learn about their organization, and establish work relationships.

Applications of Training

1,2,3,6

Two categories of training that have become widespread among North American companies are orientation of new employees and training in how to manage workforce diversity.

ORIENTATION OF NEW EMPLOYEES— ONBOARDING

Many employees receive their first training during their first days on the job. This training is the organization's orientation program—its training designed to prepare employees to perform their jobs effectively, learn about the organization, and establish work relationships. Organizations provide for orientation because, no matter how realistic the information provided during employment interviews and site visits, people feel shock and surprise when they start a new job.[42] Also, employees need to become familiar with job tasks and learn the details of the organization's practices, policies, and procedures. Many

L05 ▸ Describe training methods for employee orientation and diversity management.

HR professionals are rethinking traditional approaches to orientation due to pressures to maximize early productivity and engagement by creating a positive first impression. According to the Human Capital Institute, 90 percent of newly hired employees decide whether they'll remain with the company during the first six months.[43] Increasingly, employee orientation is referred to as *onboarding*, reflecting the critical role these programs play. The "HR Best Practices" box describes the Canadian Cancer Society's onboarding program.

The objectives of orientation programs include making new employees familiar with the organization's rules, policies, and procedures. Such a program provides information about the overall company and about the department in which the new employee will be working. The topics include social as well as technical aspects of the job.

Orientation processes may combine various training methods such as printed and audiovisual materials, classroom instruction, on-the-job training, and e-learning. Decisions about how to conduct the orientation depend on the type of material to be covered and the number of new employees, among other factors. At Toronto-based I Love Rewards, the first five days on the job are spent in the "I Love Rewards University," where new recruits "sit in a room together and learn everything from dress code to how to make the organization's drink of choice, the RedPoint (part Sour Puss raspberry liqueur, part Crown Royal, and part Red Bull)."[44] At Bayer Inc. new employee orientation starts with making the

HR BEST PRACTICES

Canadian Cancer Society's Onboarding Program

The Canadian Cancer Society, Ontario Division, decided to take a more strategic approach to onboarding. The division has hundreds of employees and thousands of volunteers across Ontario who carry out the society's mission to eradicate cancer and enhance the quality of life of those living with the disease.

One objective was to reduce voluntary turnover by equipping new hires with a greater understanding of, and connection to, the work of the society as a whole. In an organization that is geographically diverse (46 locations across the province), multifaceted (portfolios include prevention, advocacy, research, and education) and has many external alliances, it is important to get people up to speed quickly so they can make a strong, sustainable start.

Foundation Knowledge

The onboarding plan contained many elements. One part focused on "foundation knowledge." The objective was to give every new hire, regardless of his/her position or level, a consistent macro understanding of the Society—including things such as key people, portfolios, and programs. Thought was given to the timing of different onboarding activities so the process would unfold in a logical and integrated way throughout the first year of employment. These activities

are incorporated into detailed checklists to promote a consistent experience and ensure all elements are covered.

People Remember Stories

New employees can become overwhelmed by having to absorb too much too soon. They don't yet have the organization-specific navigational skills to discern what's important in the mountain of binders, reports, intranet resources, and other information provided. The HR team's solution was to develop an approach that reinforces the Society's brand and ensures a consistent and reliable method of providing information.

A typical volunteer, Ray, was selected to help guide the new employee through the organization's massive intranet and essential links. Through his story as both a volunteer and cancer survivor, Ray helps the new hire absorb static information—mission, cancer research, and statistics, organization structure, and fundraising activities—in a more logical, dynamic, and memorable way. For example, Ray talks about his community work and his family's participation in the Canadian Cancer Society Relay for Life, a national fundraising event. He then invites the new hire to click on appropriate links to drill deeper into fundraising information.

Experience: Managers Can't Do It All

Recognizing the importance of developing quality relationships early in a new employee's tenure, the society developed a series of discussion guides to help new employees, their managers, and their internal and external clients talk about mutual expectations. In one guide, a new hire and her manager ask each other a set of questions to help define the "soft" side of the working relationship. For example: "What type of recognition is important to you?" and "How do you prefer to collaborate?" Another guide helps a new employee interview key clients to understand their priorities and expectations. This helps the employee take action and establish credibility early on.

Future Plans Include Measurement, Enhancements

Future program enhancements include the development of specific departmental orientation modules and a survey that solicits confidential feedback about program usage and impact from both new hires and hiring managers. This will provide quantitative and qualitative information that can be translated into design enhancements.

SOURCE: Deborah Kyrzakos and Sue Nador, "Canadian Cancer Society Launches New Onboarding Program," *Canadian HR Reporter*, March 10, 2008, p. 12.

new hires feel like they're already part of the company before their first day on the job. Bayer Inc.'s Toronto office uses an approach to onboarding new employees called "Hello Bayer," in which new hires log on to the internal onboarding website and take a virtual tour of the facility—"great for locating their cubicle's nearest washroom—or read up on workplace minutiae like parking spaces, security passes, and even company acronyms." Philip Blake,

president and CEO of Bayer says, "It's all about feeling comfortable, fitting in and feeling wanted and welcome. This onboarding gives people the opportunity to see everything that they're coming to."[45]

DIVERSITY TRAINING

In response to human rights and employment equity legislation and market forces, many organizations today are concerned about managing diversity—creating an inclusive environment that allows all employees to contribute to organizational goals and experience personal growth. This environment includes access to jobs as well as fair and positive treatment of all employees. Chapter 2 described how organizations manage diversity by anticipating employee needs and complying with legal requirements. Many organizations also provide training designed to teach employees attitudes and behaviours that support the management of diversity, such as appreciation of cultural differences and demonstrating behaviours that are respectful of employees with diverse values and backgrounds. Training designed to change employee attitudes about diversity and/or develop skills needed to work with a diverse workforce is called **diversity training**. These programs generally emphasize either attitude awareness and change or behaviour change.

Programs that focus on attitudes have objectives to increase participants' awareness of cultural and ethnic differences, as well as differences in personal characteristics and physical characteristics (such as disabilities). For example, at Air Canada, employees receive training about the nuances of different cultures. "Cultures are very different and little gestures that you may experience from a customer, you may experience them differently than they're meant to be," says Louise McEvoy, general manager of languages and diversity for Air Canada.[46]

Programs that focus on behaviour aim at changing the organizational policies and individual behaviours that inhibit employees' personal growth and productivity. Sometimes these programs identify incidents that discourage employees from achieving their potential. The existing evidence regarding diversity training suggests that some characteristics make diversity training more effective.[47] Most importantly, the training should be tied to business objectives, such as understanding customers. The support and involvement of top management, and the involvement of stakeholders at all levels, also are important. For example, Gayle Johnson, former human resources head of Regina-based Conexus Credit Union went to the nearby Piapot Reserve to meet with its chief, band councillors, and community members to learn the best way to hire and retain Aboriginal employees. She decided to hire groups of ten Aboriginal employees at a time to reduce their sense of isolation in the workplace and tailored a ten-week training program for these new hires. She also prepared her staff for the arrival of the new employees by discussing cultural differences and

why the diversity initiative was key to the business.[48] Diversity training should emphasize learning behaviours and skills, not blaming employees. Finally, the program should be well structured, connected to the organization's rewards for performance, and include a way to measure the success of the training.

Approaches to Employee Development

6

The definition of employee development provided near the beginning of this chapter indicates that it is future-oriented. Development implies learning that is not necessarily related to the employee's current job.[49] Instead, it prepares employees for other positions in the organization and increases their ability to move into jobs that may not yet exist.[50] Development also may help employees prepare for changes in responsibilities and requirements in their current jobs, such as changes resulting from new technology, work designs, or customers.

LO6 Discuss the approaches organizations use for employee development.

DEVELOPMENT FOR CAREERS

The concept of a career has changed in recent years. In the traditional view, a career consists of a sequence of positions within an occupation or organization.[51] For example, an engineer might start as a staff engineer, then with greater experience earn promotions to the positions of advisory engineer, senior engineer, and vice-president of engineering. In these examples, the career resembles a set of stairs from the entry to a profession or organization to the senior levels.

Recently, however, changes such as downsizing and restructuring have become the norm, so the concept of a career has become more fluid. Today's employees are more likely to have a **protean career**, one that frequently changes based on changes in the person's interests, abilities, and values and in the work environment. For example, an engineer might decide to take a sabbatical from her position to become a manager with Engineers without Borders, so she can develop managerial skills and decide whether she likes being a manager. As in this example, employees in protean careers

diversity training
Training designed to change employee attitudes about diversity and/or develop skills needed to work with a diverse workforce.

protean career
A career that frequently changes based on changes in the person's interests, abilities, and values, and in the work environment.

take responsibility for managing their careers. This concept is consistent with the modern *psychological contract* described in Chapter 1. Employees look for organizations to provide, not job security and a career ladder to climb, but instead development opportunities and flexible work arrangements.

To remain marketable, employees must continually develop new skills. Beyond knowing job requirements, employees need to understand the business in which they are working and be able to cultivate valuable relationships with co-workers, managers, suppliers, and customers. They also need to follow trends in their field and industry, so they can apply technology and knowledge that will match emerging priorities and needs. Learning such skills requires useful job experiences as well as effective training programs. More employees will follow a spiral career path in which they cross the boundaries between specialties and organizations. As organizations provide for employee development (and as employees take control of their own careers), they well need to (1) determine their interests, skills, and areas of needed development and (2) seek development experiences involving jobs, relationships, and formal courses. As discussed later in the chapter, organizations can meet these needs through a system for *career management* or *development planning*. Career management helps employees select development activities that prepare them to meet their career goals. It helps employers select development activities in line with their human resource needs.

The many approaches to employee development fall into four broad categories: formal education, assessment, job experiences, and interpersonal relationships.[52] Figure 6.4 summarizes these four methods. Many organizations combine these approaches.

FORMAL EDUCATION

Organizations may support employee development through a variety of formal educational programs, either at the workplace or off-site. These may include workshops designed specifically for the organization's employees, short courses offered by consultants, colleges, or universities, and MBA and executive MBA programs. As discussed earlier in this chapter, these programs may involve methods including lectures by business experts, business games and simulations, and experiential programs.

Many companies, including SaskTel, IBM, PCL, and KPMG LLP, operate training and development centres that offer in-house training. Universities including Queen's, the University of Western Ontario, the University of Alberta, and UBC as well as colleges including Humber, Conestoga, Durham, Seneca, and Grant MacEwan offer management and professional development programs to organizations. A growing number of companies and educational institutions are also using distance learning and other e-learning options to reach their audiences.

assessment
Collecting information and providing feedback to employees about their behaviour, communication style, or skills.

ASSESSMENT

Another way to provide for employee development is **assessment**—collecting information and providing

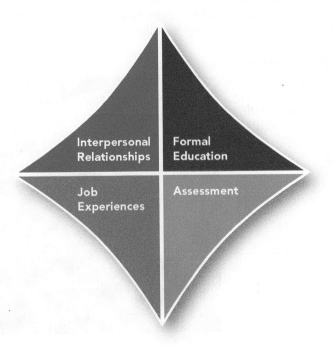

FIGURE 6.4

The Four Approaches to Employee Development

Interpersonal Relationships

Formal Education

Job Experiences

Assessment

feedback to employees about their behaviour, communication style, or skills.[53] Information for assessment may come from the employees, their peers, managers, and customers. The most frequent uses of assessment are to identify employees with managerial potential to measure current managers' strengths and weaknesses. Organizations also use assessment to identify managers with potential to move into higher-level executive positions. Organizations that assign work to teams may use assessment to identify the strengths and weaknesses of individual team members and the effects of the team members' decision-making and communication styles on the team's productivity.

For assessment to support development, the information must be shared with the employee being assessed. Along with that assessment information, the employee needs suggestions for correcting skill weaknesses and for using skills already learned. The suggestions might be to participate in training courses or develop skills through new job experiences. On the basis of the assessment information and available development opportunities, employees should develop action plans to guide their efforts at self-improvement.

It is increasingly recognized that excellent technical skills are not enough for individuals or organizations to be successful. "Strong people skills are equally important to attracting clients, building lasting relationships with both clients and colleagues, and expanding business."[54] As a result, organizations vary in the methods and sources of information they use in developmental assessment. Many organizations appraise performance. Organizations with sophisticated development systems may use psychological tests to measure employees' skills, personality types, and communication styles. They may collect self, peer, and manager ratings of employees' behaviour and style of working with others. Assessment of emotional intelligence (EQ) increase employees' self-awareness and facilitates their development with respect to intrapersonal and interpersonal skills,

> **benchmarks**
> A measurement tool that gathers ratings of a manager's use of skills associated with success in managing.

adaptability, and handling of stress.[55] Applying this kind of information about employees' preferences or tendencies helps organizations understand the communication, motivation, teamwork, work styles, and leadership of the people in their groups.

A development method that focuses on measuring management skills is an instrument called **benchmarks**. This measurement tool gathers ratings of a manager's use of skills associated with success in managing. The items measured by benchmarks are based on research into the lessons that executives learn in critical events of their careers.[56] Items measure the 16 skills and perspectives listed in Table 6.3. Research has found that managers who have these skills are more likely to receive positive performance evaluations, be considered promotable, and be promoted.[57]

360-Degree Feedback

As we will discuss in more detail in Chapter 7, a recent trend in performance appraisals, is *360-degree feedback*—performance measurement by the employee's supervisor, peers, direct reports, and customers. Often the feedback involves rating the individual in terms of skills, competencies, and work-related behaviours. For development purposes, the rater would identify an area of behaviour as a strength of that employee or an area requiring further development. The results presented to the employee show how he or she was rated on each item and how self-evaluations differ from other raters' evaluations. The individual reviews the results, seeks clarification from the raters, and sets specific development goals based on the strengths and weaknesses identified.[58]

One way to develop employees is to begin with an assessment, which may consist of assigning an activity to a team and seeing who brings what skills and strengths to the team. How can this assessment help employees?

TABLE 6.3   Skills Related to Success as a Manager

Resourcefulness	Can think strategically, engage in flexible problem solving, and work effectively with higher management.
Doing whatever it takes	Has perseverance and focus in the face of obstacles.
Being a quick study	Quickly masters new technical and business knowledge.
Building and mending relationships	Knows how to build and maintain working relationships with co-workers and external parties.
Leading subordinates	Delegates to employees effectively, broadens their opportunities, and acts with fairness toward them.
Compassion and sensitivity	Shows genuine interest in others and sensitivity to employees' needs.
Straightforwardness and composure	Is honourable and steadfast.
Setting a developmental climate	Provides a challenging climate to encourage employees' development.
Confronting difficult employee situations	Acts decisively and fairly when dealing with difficult employee situations.
Team orientation	Accomplishes tasks through managing others.
Balance between personal life and work	Balances work priorities with personal life so that neither is neglected.
Decisiveness	Prefers quick and approximate actions to slow and precise ones in many management situations.
Self-awareness	Has an accurate picture of strengths and weaknesses and is willing to improve.
Hiring talented staff	Hires talented people for the team.
Putting people at ease	Displays warmth and a good sense of humour.
Acting with flexibility	Can behave in ways that are often seen as opposites.

SOURCE: Adapted with permission from C. D. McCauley, M. M. Lombardo, and C. J. Usher, "Diagnosing Management Development Needs: An Instrument Based on How Managers Develop," *Journal of Management* 15 (1989), pp. 389–403.

There are several benefits of 360-degree feedback. Organizations collect multiple perspectives of performance, allowing employees to compare their own personal evaluations with the views of others. This method also establishes formal communications about behaviours and skill ratings between employees and their internal and external customers. Several studies have shown that performance improves and behaviour changes as a result of participating in upward feedback and 360-degree feedback systems.[59] Potential limitations of 360-degree feedback include the significant amount of time for raters to complete the evaluations. If raters, especially peers or direct reports, provide negative feedback, some managers might try to identify and punish them. A facilitator is needed to help interpret results. Finally, simply delivering ratings to a manager does not provide ways to act on the feedback (for example, development planning, meeting with raters, or taking courses). As noted earlier,

any form of assessment should be accompanied by suggestions for improvement and development of an action plan.

JOB EXPERIENCES

Most employee development occurs through **job experiences**[60] the combination of relationships, problems, demands, tasks, and other features of an employee's job. Using job experiences for employee development assumes that development is most likely to occur when the employee's skills and experiences do not entirely match the skills required for the employee's current job. To succeed, employees must stretch their skills. In other words, they must learn new skills, apply their skills and knowledge in new ways, and master new experiences.[61] For example, companies that want to prepare employees to expand overseas markets are assigning them to a variety of international jobs.

job experiences
The combination of relationships, problems, demands, tasks, and other features of an employee's job.

The usefulness of job experiences for employee development varies depending on whether the employee views the experiences as positive or negative sources of stress. When employees view job experiences as positive stressors, the experiences challenge them and stimulate learning. When they view job experiences as negative stressors, employees may suffer from high levels of harmful stress. Of the job demands studied, managers were most likely to experience negative stress from creating change and overcoming obstacles (adverse business conditions, lack of management support, lack of personal support, or a difficult boss). Research suggests that all of the job demands except obstacles are related to learning.[62] Organizations should offer job experiences that are most likely to increase learning, and they should consider the consequences of situations that involve negative stress.

Various job assignments can provide for employee development. The organization may enlarge the employee's current job or move the employee to different jobs. Lateral moves include job rotation, transfer, or temporary assignment to another organization. The organization may also use downward moves or promotions as a source of job experience. Figure 6.5 summarizes these alternatives.

Job Enlargement

As Chapter 3 stated in the context of job design, *job enlargement* involves adding challenges or new responsibilities to employees' current jobs. Examples include completing a special project, switching roles within a work team, or researching new ways to serve customers. An accountant might join a task force developing new career paths for professional employees. The work on the project could give the accountant a leadership role through which he or she learns about the company's career development system while also practising leadership skills to help the task force reach its goals. In this way, job enlargement not only makes a job more interesting, but also creates an opportunity for employees to develop new skills.

Job Rotation

Another job design technique that can be applied to employee development is *job rotation*, moving employees through a series of job assignments in one or more functional areas. At Purdy's Chocolates in British Columbia, employees are provided development opportunities. Plant workers are given the chance to run a shift to see if they have the potential to replace a lead hand or become a warehouse manager in the future.[63]

Job rotation helps employees gain an appreciation for the company's goals, increases their understanding of different company functions, develops a network of contacts, and improves problem-solving and decision-making skills.[64] However, the rotation of employees through a department may hurt productivity and increase the workload of those who remain after employees are rotated out. Job rotation is most likely to succeed when it meets certain conditions:[65]

- The organization establishes and communicates clear policies about which positions are eligible

FIGURE 6.5

How Job Experiences Are Used for Employee Development

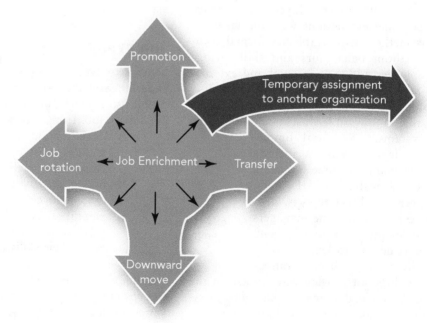

for job rotation. Job rotation for nonmanagement employees as well as managers can be beneficial, depending on the program's objectives.

- Employees and their managers understand and agree on the expectations for the job rotation, including which skills are to be developed.
- Goals for the program support business goals. These might including exposing high-potential employees to a variety of business units, customers, or geographic areas in preparation for management positions or rotating experienced, talented employees through several business units to mentor or coach them.
- The rotation schedule is realistic, taking into account how long employees will need to become familiar with their new position, as well as how much time is needed for employees to complete the assignments.
- Top management is committed to the program's success.
- Someone is responsible for measuring whether the program is meeting it goals.

Transfers, Promotions, and Downward Moves

Most companies use upward, downward, and lateral moves as an option for employee development. In a transfer, the organization assigns an employee to a position in a different area of the company. Transfers do not necessarily increase job responsibilities or compensation. They are usually lateral moves, that is, moves to a job with a similar level of responsibility. They may involve relocation to another part of the country or even to another country.

Because transfers can provoke anxiety, many companies have difficulty getting employees to accept them. Employees most willing to accept transfers tend to be those with high career ambitions, a belief that the organization offers a promising future, and a belief that accepting the transfer will help the company succeed.[66]

A downward move occurs when an employee is given less responsibility and authority. The organization may demote an employee because of poor performance or move the employee to a lower-level position in another function so that the employee can develop different skills. The temporary cross-functional move is the most common way to use downward moves for employee development. For example, engineers who want to move into management often take lower-level positions, such as shift supervisor, to develop their management skills.

Many employees have difficulty associating transfers and downward moves with development; these changes may feel more like forms of punishment. Employees will be more likely to accept transfers and downward moves as development opportunities if the organization provides information about the change and its possible benefits and involves the employee in planning the change. Employees are also more likely to be positive about such a recommendation if the organization provides clear performance objectives and frequent feedback.

A promotion involves moving an employee into a position with greater challenges, more responsibility, and more authority than in the previous job. Usually promotions include pay increases. Because promotions improve the person's pay, status, and feelings of accomplishment, employees are more willing to accept promotions than lateral or downward moves.

transfer
Assignment of an employee to a position in a different area of the company, usually in a lateral move.

downward move
Assignment of an employee to a position with less responsibility and authority.

promotion
Assignment of an employee to a position with greater challenges, more responsibility, and more authority than in the previous job, usually accompanied by a pay increase.

Working outside one's home country is the most important job experience that can develop an employee for a career in the global economy.

Even so, employers can increase the likelihood that employees will accept promotions by providing the same kind of information and assistance that are used to support transfers and downward moves. Organizations can more easily offer promotions if they are profitable and growing. In other conditions, opportunities for promoting employees may be limited.

Temporary Assignments with Other Organizations

In some cases, an employer may benefit from the skills an employee can learn at another organization. The employer may encourage the employee to participate in an externship—a full-time temporary position at another organization.

Temporary assignments can include a sabbatical—a leave of absence from an organization to renew or develop skills. Employees on sabbatical often receive full pay and benefits. Sabbaticals let employees get away from the day-to-day stresses of their jobs and acquire new skills and perspectives. Sabbaticals also allow employees more time for personal pursuits such as writing a book or spending more time with family members.

INTERPERSONAL RELATIONSHIPS

Employees can also develop skills and increase their knowledge about the organization and its customers by interacting with a more experienced organization member. Two types of relationships used for employee development are *mentoring* and *coaching*.

externship
Employee development through a full-time temporary position at another organization.

sabbatical
A leave of absence from an organization to renew or develop skills.

mentor
An experienced, productive senior employee who helps develop a less experienced employee (a protégé or mentee).

L07 Explain how managers and peers develop employees through mentoring and coaching.

Mentors

A mentor is an experienced, productive senior employee who helps develop a less experienced employee, called the *protégé* or *mentee*. Most mentoring relationships develop informally as a result of interests or values shared by the mentor and protégé. According to research, the employees most likely to seek and attract a mentor have certain personality characteristics: emotional stability, ability to adapt their behaviour to the situation, and high needs for power and achievement.[67] Mentoring relationships also can develop as part of the organization's planned effort to bring together successful senior employees with less experienced employees.

One major advantage of formal mentoring programs is that they ensure access to mentors for all employees. A mentoring program also can ensure that high-potential employees are matched with wise, experienced mentors in key areas—and that mentors in positions of authority are hearing about the real-life challenges of the organization's employees.[68] However, in an artificially created relationship, mentors may have difficulty providing counselling and coaching.[69] Mentoring programs tend to be most successful when they are *voluntary* and participants understand the details of the program. Rewarding managers for employee development is also important, because it signals that mentoring and other development activities are worthwhile. In addition, the organization should carefully select mentors on the basis of their interpersonal and technical competencies, train them for the role, and evaluate whether the program has met its objectives.[70] Information technology can help organizations meet some of these guidelines.

Bell Canada's mentoring program, "Mentor Match," has been recognized as one of the best. Mentor Match is open to employees at all levels and uses an online cross-functional mentoring program. Protégés/mentees browse a pool of possible mentors using a search tool. A list of suitable mentors is generated according to the profile of the protégé/mentee. From a strategic perspective, Mentor Match is expected to improve employee retention, enhance performance and productivity, and accelerate the development of employees. Because it is fully automated, Mentor Match can track data and generate results such as signup statistics. All the necessary mentoring tools such as mentoring agreements, suggestions, and templates are available online.[71]

Mentors and protégés can both benefit from a mentoring relationship. Table 6.4 summarizes the advantages of mentoring programs to both protégés and mentors. Protégés receive career support, including coaching, protection, sponsorship, challenging assignments, and visibility among the organization's managers. They also receive benefits of a positive relationship—a friend and role model who accepts them, has a positive opinion toward them, and gives them a chance to talk about their concerns. Employees with mentors are also more likely to be promoted, earn higher salaries, and have more influence within their organization.[72] Acting as a mentor gives managers a chance to develop their interpersonal skills and increase their feeling they are contributing something important. Working with the protégé on technical matters such as new research in the field may also increase the mentor's technical knowledge.

So that more employees can benefit from mentoring, some organizations use *group mentoring programs*, which assign four to six protégés to a successful senior employee. A potential advantage of group mentoring is that protégés can learn from each other as well as from the mentor.

Coaching

A **coach** is a peer or manager who works with an employee to provide a source of motivation, help him or her develop skills, and provide reinforcement and feedback. Coaches may play one or more of three roles:[73.]

1. Working one-on-one with an employee, as when giving feedback.
2. Helping employees learn for themselves—for example, helping them find experts and teaching them to obtain feedback from others.
3. Providing resources such as mentors, courses, or job experiences.

William Gray, president of Corporate Mentoring Solutions Inc. and former

UBC professor, draws a distinction between mentoring and coaching. Gray describes mentoring as developing the "whole person" and coaching involves developing a specific skill set.[74]

Research suggests that coaching helps managers improve by identifying areas for improvement and setting goals.[75] Coaching is most likely to succeed if coaches are empathetic, supportive, practical, and self-confident but don't act infallible or try to tell others what to do.[76]

Career Management Systems

6

Employee development is most likely to meet the organization's needs if it is part of a human resource system of career management. In practice, organizations' career management systems vary. Some rely heavily on informal relationships, while others are sophisticated programs. As shown in Figure 6.6, a basic career management system involves four steps: data gathering, feedback, goal setting, and action planning and follow-up.

LO8 Identify the steps in the career management process and how managers are dealing with some critical development-related challenges.

Ways to make this system more effective including gathering data in areas associated with success, keeping feedback confidential and specific, involving higher level management in planning and follow-up, and crafting action plans that are realistic and targeted to building expertise needed for the person's career path.[77] Human resource professionals can also contribute to the system's success by

coach
A peer or manager who works with an employee to provide a source of motivation, help him or her develop skills, and provide reinforcement and feedback.

TABLE 6.4 Advantages of Mentoring Programs	
FOR PROTÉGÉS/MENTEES	**FOR MENTORS**
• Breaks down "silos" throughout the organization	• Maintains a pulse on the organization by keeping regular contact and communication with employees
• Increases communication	• Enhances interpersonal and leadership competencies
• Supports continuous learning throughout all levels of the organization	
• Enhances career development and growth	
• Improves employee satisfaction and engagement	
• Fosters a culture where employees support and help one another	

SOURCE: Adapted from Conference Board of Canada, "Mentoring—Low Cost, Big Benefits," www.conferenceboard.ca/humanresource/mentoring-inside.htm, retrieved February 24, 2005.

FIGURE 6.6

Steps in the Career Management Process

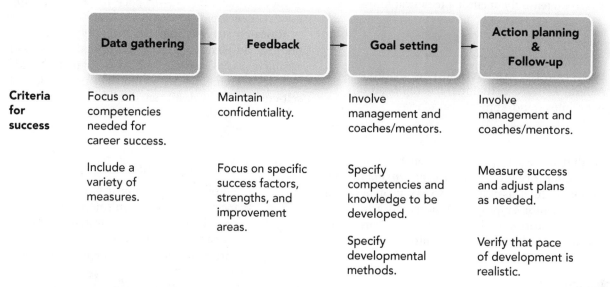

Criteria for success	Data gathering	Feedback	Goal setting	Action planning & Follow-up
	Focus on competencies needed for career success.	Maintain confidentiality.	Involve management and coaches/mentors.	Involve management and coaches/mentors.
	Include a variety of measures.	Focus on specific success factors, strengths, and improvement areas.	Specify competencies and knowledge to be developed.	Measure success and adjust plans as needed.
			Specify developmental methods.	Verify that pace of development is realistic.

ensuring it is linked to other HR practices such as performance management, training, and recruiting.

DATA GATHERING

In discussing the methods of employee development, we highlighted several assessment tools. Such tools may be applied to the first stage of career development. **Self-assessment** refers to the use of information by employees to determine their career interests, values, aptitudes, behavioural tendencies, and development needs. The employee's responsibility is to identify opportunities and development needs. The organization's responsibility is to provide assessment information for identifying strengths, weaknesses, interests, and values.

Self-assessment tools often include psychological tests such as the Myers-Briggs Type Inventory (MBTI), the Strong-Campbell Interest Inventory, and the Self-Directed Search. The MBTI identifies individuals' preferences for source of energy, means of information gathering, way of decision making and lifestyle. The Strong-Campbell Inventory helps employees identify their occupational and job interests. The Self-Directed Search identifies employees' preferences for working in different kinds of environments—sales, counselling, and so on. Tests may also help employees identify the relative value they place

on work and leisure activities. Self-assessment tools can help an employee consider his or her current career status, future plans, and the fit between the career and current situation and resources. Some organizations provide counsellors to help employees in the self-assessment process and to interpret the results of psychological tests.

Completing a self-assessment can help employees identify a development need. This need can result from gaps between current skills or interests and the type of work or position the employee has or wants.

FEEDBACK

In the next step of career management, **feedback**, employees receive information about their competencies and where these assets fit into the organization's plans. The employee's responsibility is to identify what skills she or he could realistically develop in light of the opportunities available. The organization's responsibility is to communicate the performance evaluation and the opportunities available to the employee, given the organization's long-range plans. Opportunities might include promotions and transfers. Some organizations develop and communicate **career paths**—the identified pattern or progression of jobs or roles within an organization to provide clarity about how an employee may progress into more senior

self-assessment
The use of information by employees to determine their career interests, values, aptitudes, behavioural tendencies, and development needs.

feedback
Information employers give employees about their skills and knowledge and where these assets fit into the organization's plans.

career paths
The identified pattern or progression of jobs or roles within an organization.

positions. Career paths may include a wide variety of jobs or may provide specific information related to cumulative responsibilities for a managerial, technical, or professional career. Career-path information can also enhance the discussion of opportunities between employees and their managers by providing consistent language related to how jobs and roles are defined in the organization.[78]

Another form of feedback or reality check encouraged by career coaches involves "checking your Google score" to see how many pages on the Web have your name on them. This awareness will help detect misconceptions about your "personal brand." Whether you took part in a 10-kilometre run and your time made it to the sponsor's site, your bio appears on your company's website, or your Facebook profile has been indexed, you have an online identity that can be viewed by anyone with access to a search engine.[79]

GOAL SETTING

On the basis of the information from the self-assessment and feedback, the employee sets short- and long-term career objectives. These goals usually involve one or more of the following categories:

- Desired roles, such as becoming a team leader within three years.
- Level of competency—for example, to apply one's budgeting skills to improve the unit's cash flow problems.
- Work setting—for example, to move to corporate marketing within two years.
- Skill acquisition, such as learning how to use the company's human resource information system.

As in these examples, the goals should be specific, and they should include a date by which the goal is to be achieved. It is the employee's responsibility to identify the goal and the method of determining her or his progress toward each goal. Usually the employee discusses the goals with his or her manager. The organization's responsibilities are to ensure that the goal is specific, challenging, and achievable, and to help the employee reach the goal.

ACTION PLANNING AND FOLLOW-UP

In the final step, employees prepare an action plan for *how* they will achieve their short- and long-term career goals. The employee is responsible for identifying the steps and timetable to reach the goals. The employer should identify resources needed, including courses, work experiences, and relationships.

Action plans may involve any one or a combination of the development methods discussed earlier in the chapter—training, assessment, job experiences, or the help of a mentor or coach. The approach used depends on the particular developmental needs and career objectives. For example, suppose the program manager in an information systems department uses feedback from clients to determine that greater knowledge of project management software is needed. The manager plans to increase that knowledge by reading articles (formal education), meeting with software vendors, and contacting the vendors' customers to ask them about the software they have used (job experiences). The manager and his supervisor agree that six months will be the target date for achieving the higher level of knowledge through these activities.

The outcome of action planning often takes the form of a *development plan*. Figure 6.7 is an example of a development plan for a project manager. Development plans usually include descriptions of strengths and weaknesses, career goals, and development activities for reaching each goal.

Development-Related Challenges

A well-designed system for employee development can help organizations face widespread challenges: the glass ceiling and dysfunctional behaviour by managers.

THE GLASS CEILING

As we mentioned in Chapter 1, women and other members of the employment equity target groups are rare in the top level of Canadian corporations. Observers of this situation have noted that it looks as if an invisible barrier is keeping these individuals from reaching the top jobs, a barrier that has come to be known as the **glass ceiling**. For example, according to the most recent data from Catalyst, only 14.5 percent of board seats in Canada's Financial Post 500 companies are held by women.[80]

The glass ceiling is likely caused by a lack of access to training programs, appropriate developmental job experiences, and developmental relationships such as mentoring.[81] With regard to developmental relationships, women and other members of the employment equity groups often have trouble finding mentors. They may not

glass ceiling
Circumstances resembling an invisible barrier that keep most women and other members of the employment equity groups from attaining the top jobs in organizations.

FIGURE 6.7

Development Plan

Name: _____   **Title:** Project Manager   **Immediate Manager:** _____

Competencies
Please identify your three greatest strengths and areas for improvement.
Strengths
- Strategic thinking and execution (confidence, command skills, action orientation).
- Results orientation (creating a motivating work environment, perseverance).
- Spirit for winning (building team spirit, customer focus, respect colleagues).

Areas for Improvement
- Patience (tolerance of people or processes and sensitivity to pacing).
- Written communications (ability to write clearly and succinctly).
- Overly ambitious (too much focus on successful completion of projects rather than developing relationships with individuals involved in the projects).

Career Goals
Please describe your overall career goals.
- *Long-term.* Accept positions of increased responsibility to a level of general manager (or beyond). The areas of specific interest include but are not limited to product and brand management, technology and development, strategic planning, and marketing.
- *Short-term.* Continue to improve my skills in marketing and brand management while utilizing my skills in product management, strategic planning, and global relations.

Next Assignments
Identify potential next assignments (including timing) that would help you develop toward your career goals.
- Manager or director level in planning, development, product, or brand management. Timing estimated to be Spring 2013.

Training and Development Needs
List both training and development activities that will either help you develop in your current assignment or provide overall career development.
- Master's degree classes will allow me to practise and improve my written communications skills. The dynamics of my current position, teamwork, and reliance on other individuals allow me to practise patience and to focus on individual team members' needs along with the success of the project.

Employee _____   **Date** _____
Immediate Manager _____   **Date** _____
Mentor _____   **Date** _____

---

participate in the organization's, profession's, or community's "old boys' network." Also, managers in the organization may prefer to interact with people who have similar status, or may avoid interacting with certain people because of discomfort or negative stereotypes.[82] However, the glass ceiling metaphor has been criticized because it describes an absolute barrier at a specific high level in organizations and fails to incorporate the complex and varied challenges women and other members of the employment equity target groups face in their careers. A better

metaphor may be a *labyrinth*, connoting a complex journey with many twists and turns and puzzles to solve along the way to the top jobs.[83]

Organizations can use development systems to help break through the glass ceiling or "navigate the labyrinth." Managers making developmental assignments need to carefully consider whether stereotypes are influencing the types of assignments men and women receive. A formal process for regularly identifying development needs and creating action plans can make these decisions more objective.

THINKING ETHICALLY

Can You Teach People to Be Ethical?

Ethical leadership is critical for employees in many settings. For example, in an industrial environment, ethical leadership of safety programs puts employees' well-being ahead of short-term cost savings. And in the accounting profession, high ethical standards are essential for preserving a firm's reputation. Therefore, organizations have an interest in developing ethical leaders who in turn foster ethical behaviour among all employees.

Jim Spigener, a safety consultant, recalls working with a chief executive whose son had recently become a civil engineer for a construction company. Spigener asked his client whether he hoped that the construction company's CEO placed the same value on his employees' safety that the client placed on his own employees' safety. The startled client replied that he hoped his son's CEO had higher standards. In this way, Spigener was coaching his CEO client to think about safety in a new, personal way—hoping that the client, in his role as a leader, would begin to express this new understanding to others at the company.

Many accounting firms use mentoring relationships to foster commitment to integrity and ethical decision making. Ernst & Young, for example, matches newly hired staff members with mentors and has set up a system where the staff can post comments about the mentoring and coaching behaviours they observe. One of the most important ways mentors can develop ethical behaviour is by modelling that behaviour themselves. Mentors also try to help employees sort out the nuances of how to behave ethically amidst the real-world challenges of time pressures and office politics.

SOURCES: Jim Spigener, "Leaders Who 'Get' Safety: Values and Personality Shape Personal Ethics," *Industrial Safety & Hygiene News*, October 2009, Business & Company Resource Center, http://galenet.gale

group.com; and Robert Giagnon, "More than a Legacy," *CA Magazine*, September 2009, Business & Company Resource Center, http://galenet.galegroup.com.

QUESTIONS

1. Compare the example of the safety consultant coaching a CEO with the example of Ernst & Young mentoring accountants. How are these development approaches similar and different?
2. Besides coaches or mentors, what other resources could an organization provide to develop ethical employees? Which of these do you think would be most effective, and why?
3. Can an organization "develop" ethical employees, or is it just a matter of hiring people who are already ethical? How much effort should an organization put into developing strengths in the area of ethics?

Indra Nooyl became the first woman CEO of PepsiCo back in 2006. Her success at the company gives her the distinction of being one of the women to break through the glass ceiling.

DYSFUNCTIONAL MANAGERS

A manager who is otherwise competent may engage in some behaviours that make him or her ineffective or even "toxic"—someone who stifles good ideas and drives away employees. These dysfunctional behaviours include insensitivity to others, inability to be a team player, arrogance, poor conflict-management skills, inability to meet business objectives, and inability to adapt to change.[84] For example, a manager who has strong technical knowledge but is abrasive and discourages employees from contributing their ideas is likely to have difficulty motivating employees and may alienate people inside and outside the organization.

When a manager is an otherwise valuable employee and is willing to improve, the organization may try to help him or her change the dysfunctional behaviour. The usual ways to provide this type of development include assessment, training, and counselling. Development programs for managers with dysfunctional behaviour may also include specialized programs such as one called Individual Coaching for Effectiveness (ICE). The ICE program includes diagnosis, coaching, and support activities tailored to each manager's needs.[85] Psychologists conduct the diagnosis, coach and counsel the manager, and develop action plans for implementing new skills on the job. Research suggests that managers who participate in programs like ICE improve their skills and are less likely to be terminated.[86] One possible conclusion is that organizations can benefit from offering development opportunities to valuable employees with performance problems, not just to star performers.

SUMMARY

L01 Discuss how to link training and development to organizational needs and strategy.

- Organizations need to establish training programs that are effective.
- Organizations create such programs through instructional design. This process begins with a needs assessment, then ensures readiness for training, plans a training program, implements the program, and evaluates the results.

L02 Explain how to assess training needs and determine employees' readiness.

- Needs assessment consists of an organization analysis, person analysis, and task analysis.
- The organization analysis determines the appropriateness of training by evaluating the characteristics of the organization, including its strategy, resources, and management support. The person analysis determines individuals' needs and readiness for training. The task analysis identifies the tasks, knowledge, skills, and behaviours that training should emphasize.
- Readiness for training is a combination of employee characteristics and positive work environment that permit training.

L03 Describe how to plan and design an effective training program.

- Planning begins with establishing objectives for the training program. These should define an expected performance or outcome, the desired level of performance, and the conditions under which the performance should occur.
- On the basis of the objectives, the planner decides who will provide the training, what topics the training will cover, what training methods to use, and how to evaluate the training.
- Even when organizations purchase outside training, someone in the organization, usually a member of the HR department, is responsible for training administration.
- The training methods selected should be related to the objectives and content of the training program. Methods include classroom instruction; audiovisual instruction; computer-based training; on-the-job training methods such as apprenticeships, internships, and cooperative education; business games and cases; experiential programs; and team training.

L04 Summarize how to implement and evaluate a successful training program.

- Implementation should apply principles of learning. In general, effective training communicates learning objectives, presents information in distinctive and memorable ways, and helps trainees link the subject matter to their jobs. Consideration should also be given to ensuring employees have the required workplace literacy skills to succeed and perform well in their jobs.
- Training can be evaluated at four levels—reaction, learning, behaviour, and results. Evaluation of training should look for transfer of training by measuring whether employees are performing the tasks taught

in the training program. Assessment of training also should evaluate training outcomes.

L05 ► Describe training methods for employee orientation and diversity management.

- Employee orientation (onboarding) is training designed to prepare new employees to perform their job effectively, learn about the organization, and establish work relationships. A typical orientation program includes information about the overall company and the department in which the new employee will be working, covering social as well as technical aspects of the job.
- Orientation programs may combine several training methods, from printed materials to on-the-job training to e-learning.
- Diversity training is designed to change employee attitudes about diversity and/or develop skills needed to work with a diverse workforce.

L06 ► Discuss the approaches organizations use for employee development.

- Organizations may use formal educational programs at the workplace or offsite such as in workshops, college and university programs, company-sponsored training, or programs offered by independent institutions.
- Organizations may use the assessment process to help employees identify strengths and areas requiring further development.
- Job experiences help employees develop by stretching competencies as they meet new challenges.
- Interpersonal relationships with a more experienced member of the organization—often in the role of mentor or coach can help employees develop their understanding of the organization and its customers.

L07 ► Explain how managers and peers develop employees through mentoring and coaching.

- A mentor is an experienced, productive senior employee who helps develop a less experienced employee. Although most mentoring relationships develop informally, organizations can link mentoring to development goals by establishing a formal mentoring program.
- A coach is a peer or manager who works with an employee to motivate the employee, help him or her develop skills, and provide reinforcement and feedback.

L08 ► Identify the steps in the career management process and how managers are dealing with some critical development-related challenges.

- In the first step, data gathering, employees determine their career interests, values, aptitudes, and behavioural tendencies, looking for opportunities and areas needing development.
- The second step is feedback, during which the organization communicates information about the employee's skills and knowledge and how these fit into the organization's plan.
- The employee then sets goals and discusses them with his or her manager, who ensures that the goals are specific, challenging, and attainable.
- Finally, the employee works with his or her manager to create an action plan for development activities that will help the employee achieve the goals.
- The "glass ceiling" is a barrier that has been observed preventing women and other members of the employment equity target groups from achieving top jobs in an organization. Development programs can ensure that these employees receive access to development resources.
- For dysfunctional managers who have the potential to contribute to the organization, the organization may offer development targeted at correcting the areas of dysfunction.

Critical Thinking Questions

1. "Melinda!," bellowed Toran to the company's HR specialist, "I've got a problem, and you've got to solve it. I can't get people in this plant to work together as a team. As if I don't have enough trouble with our competitors and our past-due accounts, now I have to put up with running a zoo. You're responsible for seeing that the staff gets along. I want a training proposal on my desk by Monday." Assume you are Melinda.
   a. Is training the solution to this problem? How can you determine the need for training?
   b. Summarize how you would conduct a needs assessment.

2. How should an organization assess readiness for learning? In Question 1, how do Toran's comments suggest readiness (or lack of readiness) for learning?
3. Many organizations turn to e-learning as a less expensive alternative to classroom training. What are some other advantages of substituting e-learning for classroom training? What are some disadvantages?
4. Consider your current job, or one you have held recently.
   a. How was orientation (onboarding) handled?
   b. What types of training did you receive for the job?
   c. How did orientation (onboarding) and training affect your performance on the job? Your commitment to the organization?

d. Would it be appropriate to provide employee orientation (onboarding) purely online? Why or why not?

e. Is there anything the organization could have done to make the orientation (onboarding) and/or training processes more effective?

5. Why do organizations provide diversity training? What kinds of goals are most suitable for such training?

6. What are the four broad categories of development methods? Why might it be beneficial to combine all of these methods into a formal development program?

7. Recommend a development method for each of the following situations, and explain why you chose that method.

a. An employee recently promoted to the job of plant supervisor is having difficulty motivating employees to meet quality standards.

b. A sales manager annoys salespeople by directing every detail of their work.

c. An employee has excellent leadership skills but lacks knowledge of the financial side of business.

d. An organization is planning to organize its production workers into teams for the first time.

8. Many people feel that mentoring relationships should occur naturally, in situations where senior managers feel inclined to play that role. What are some advantages of setting up a formal mentoring program, rather than letting senior managers decide how and whom to help?

9. How is a coach different than a mentor? What are some advantages of using someone outside the organization as a coach? Some disadvantages?

10. Why should organizations be interested in helping employees plan their careers? What benefits can companies gain? What are the risks?

11. What metaphors were used to describe the barriers that women and other employment equity group members still face to advancement into senior executive positions? Can you think of any other relevant metaphors? Which metaphor do you feel is most relevant? Why?

12. Why might an organization benefit from giving employee development opportunities to a dysfunctional manager, rather than simply dismissing the manager? Do these reasons apply to nonmanagement employees as well?

What's Your HR IQ?

 Connect offers more ways to check what you've learned so far. Find experiential exercises, Test Your Knowledge quizzes, videos, and many other resources to gauge your HR IQ.

CASE STUDY 6.1: Building Foundation Skills at Loewen Windows

Loewen Windows is one of Canada's largest premium wood window and door manufacturers. Based in Steinbach, Manitoba, Loewen employs almost 1,700 people, however it comes from humble roots—starting as a small family-owned sawmill in the early 1900s.

As Loewen needed more employees for their expanding production needs in Manitoba, one of the workers in the plant approached the HR manager to let her know that there were several new families that had just arrived from Germany and needed work. In total, 15 people were extended job offers, however, Loewen faced several challenges associated with having a diverse workforce with varying English language skills. Due to communication issues, employees took longer than necessary to complete work tasks. Communication and cultural differences among employees impeded cross-training efforts and led to misunderstandings and internal conflict. Workers' safety was also affected because company safety training and work instructions were geared for an audience who spoke English as their first language and managers found it difficult to assess whether employees fully understood shop floor safety procedures.

Loewen's Foundation Skills program was introduced initially as a pilot project to allow employees to upgrade their "English as an additional language" and improve their literacy skills. Specific objectives for the program were created including being able to read and discuss safe work procedure documents; being able to communicate orally with their co-workers and supervisors; and being able to fully participate in Loewen Windows production, using English when following and giving instructions.

Most of the employees taking part in the program work on the shop floor—93 percent are plant labourers, however administrative staff and leaders have also participated in the program. Loewen partnered with community group, Southeast English Language and Literacy Services for Adults, an organization that focuses on working with local immigrants. Employees enrolled in the program attend four hours of class per week for 20 weeks. Loewen picks up 50 percent of the fees and the full cost of the books, and the other 50 percent is covered by government funding. Participants in the program attend class half on company time and half on their own time.

As a result of this program, Loewen has benefited through high employee retention rates—which has reduced hiring costs and improved efficiencies. Participants in the program also learn new jobs faster and operational flexibility has improved because workers are able to provide vacation and illness coverage for others in busy departments. Managers see employees' time away from their job tasks for training as an investment in safety, the community, and their employees.

Questions

1. Loewen's commitment to continuous learning emphasizes a belief that the organization benefits when employees learn and enhance their abilities. How should Loewen evaluate the effectiveness of its Foundation Skills program?
2. How do employees benefit from this investment in learning?
3. Do you think Loewen's Foundation Skills program is a good model for other organizations? Why or why not?

SOURCES: Alison Campbell, "A Clear View of Safety at Loewen Windows," Case Study: April 2010, The Conference Board of Canada; /www.loewen.com/hr/CareerToolbox.html, retrieved April 9, 2012; and "Section 4.9 Loewen Windows Pilot Project: New Employees English Language Training Program," *Centre for Canadian Language Benchmarks*, www.language.ca/display_page.asp?page_id=850, retrieved April 9, 2012.

CASE STUDY 6.2: The World is IBM's Classroom

When ten IBM management trainees piled into a minibus in the Philippines for a weekend tour last October, the last thing they expected was to wind up local heroes. Yet that's what happened in the tiny village of Carmen. After passing a water well project, they learned the effort had stalled because of engineering mistakes and a lack of money. The IBMers decided to do something about it. They organized a meeting of the key people involved in the project and volunteered to pay $250 out of their own pockets for additional building materials. Two weeks later the well was completed. Locals would no longer have to walk four miles for drinkable water. And the trainees learned a lesson in collaborative problem-solving. "You motivate people to take the extra step, you create a shared vision, you divide the labour, and the impact can be big," says Erwin van Overbeek, 40, who runs environmental sustainability projects for IBM clients. While saving a village well wasn't part of the group agenda for that trip, it's the kind of experience the architects of IBM's Corporate Service Corps (CSC) had in mind when they launched the initiative. Modelled on the U.S. Peace Corps, the program aims to turn IBM employees into global citizens. Last year, IBM selected 300 top management prospects out of 5,400 applicants. It then trained and dispatched them to emerging markets for a month in groups of eight to ten to help solve economic and social problems. The goals, says IBM's human resources chief, J. Randall MacDonald, is to help future leaders "understand how the world works, show them how to network, and show them how to work collaboratively with people who are far away."

Like most corporations, IBM trains managers in classrooms, so this represents a dramatic departure. And while other companies encourage employees to volunteer for social service, IBM is the first to use such programs for management training, says Rosabeth Moss Kanter, a professor at Harvard Business School.

The program is growing rapidly. This year some 500 people will participate, and the list of countries will expand from five to nine, including Brazil, India, Malaysia, and South Africa. The teams spend three months before going overseas reading about their host countries, studying the problems they're assigned to work on, and getting to know their teammates via teleconferences and social networking websites. On location, they work with local governments, universities, and business groups to do anything from upgrading technology for a government agency to improving public water quality.

Participating in the program is not without its risks. Charlie Ung, a new-media producer from IBM Canada, got malaria while working in Ghana and spent a week in the hospital. Other participants report encounters with wild dogs in Romania. IBM planners deliberately choose out-of-the-way places and bunk the teams in guest houses that lack such amenities as Western food and CNN. "We want them to have a transformative experience, so they're shaken up and walk away feeling they're better equipped to confront the challenges of the 21st century," says Kevin Thompson, the IBMer who conceived of the CSC program and now manages it.

IBM concedes that one month overseas is a short stint, but it believes participants can pick up valuable lessons. Debbie Maconnel, a 45-year old IT project manager, says the trip prompted her to change her management style. She coordinates the activities of 13 people in the United States and 12 in India, Mexico, and China. She used to give assignments to the overseas employees and then leave them on their own. Now she spends more time trying to build a global team.

Questions

1. Based on the information given but in your own words, what are the training objectives for IBM's Corporate Service Corps? Based on the information given, how well would you say the program is meeting those objectives? What additional measures would help you evaluate the program's success?

2. Which of the training methods described in this chapter are incorporated into the Corporate Service Corps?

How well suited are these methods to achieving IBM's objectives.

3. Suggest some ways that IBM can help participants apply on the job what they have learned from their one-month service project?

SOURCE: Excerpted from Steve Hamm, "The World IS IBM's Classroom," *BusinessWeek*, March 12, 2009, www.businessweek.com.

 **Practise and learn online with Connect.**

Chapter 7

MANAGING EMPLOYEES'
Performance

{
What Do I Need to Know?

After reading this chapter, you should be able to:

LO1 ▸ Identify the activities involved in performance management.

LO2 ▸ Discuss the purposes of performance management systems.

LO3 ▸ Define five criteria for measuring the effectiveness of a performance management system.

LO4 ▸ Compare the major methods for measuring performance.

LO5 ▸ Describe major sources of performance information in terms of their advantages and disadvantages.

LO6 ▸ Define types of rating errors and explain how to minimize them.

LO7 ▸ Explain how to effectively provide performance feedback.

LO8 ▸ Summarize ways to achieve performance improvement.

LO9 ▸ Discuss legal and ethical issues that affect performance management.

Michael McCain is the president and CEO of Maple Leaf Foods. Maple Leaf Foods' performance management process supports a culture of high-performance focusing on both results and behaviours aligned with organizational values.

Performance Management at Maple Leaf Foods

At Maple Leaf Foods, employee performance is based on not only achieving specific outcomes, but also demonstrating behaviours that are consistent with the 21 corporate values developed by president and CEO Michael McCain. This focus on *how* results are achieved includes things like "Do What's Right" (act with integrity, behave responsibly, and treat people with respect) and "Dare to be Transparent" (have the courage to be candid and direct, and communicate openly). McCain describes Maple Leaf Foods' high-performance culture as "innovative, action-oriented, and non-political" and is key to driving the company's success. At Maple Leaf Foods every employee's performance is ranked based on two key performance dimensions—results achieved and values consistency.[1]

Introduction

Performance management is the process through which managers ensure that employees' activities and outputs contribute to the organization's goals. This process requires knowing what activities and outputs are desired, observing whether they occur, and providing feedback to help employees meet expectations. In the course of providing feedback, managers and employees may identify performance issues and establish ways to resolve those issues.

In this chapter we examine a variety of approaches to performance management. We begin by describing the activities involved in managing performance, then discuss the purpose of carrying out this process. Next, we discuss specific approaches to performance appraisal, including the strengths and weaknesses of each approach. We also look at various sources of performance information. The next section explores the kinds of errors that commonly occur during the assessment of performance, as well as ways to reduce those errors. Then we describe ways of giving performance feedback effectively and intervening when performance must improve. Finally, we summarize legal and ethical issues affecting performance management.

The Process of Performance Management

Although many employees have come to dread the annual "performance appraisal" meeting, at which a boss picks apart the employee's behaviours and

apparent attitudes from the past year, performance management can potentially deliver many benefits. Effective performance management can tell top performers that they are valued, encourage communication between managers and their employees, establish uniform standards for evaluating employees, and help the organization identify its strongest performers. Consultant Dick Grote asserts that performance appraisals, properly done, meet an

> **LO1** Identify the activities involved in performance management.

"ethical obligation of leadership" by providing information that all members of an organization want to know so they can succeed: "What is it you expect of me? How am I doing at meeting your expectations?"[2]

To meet these objectives, performance management includes several activities. As shown in Figure 7.1, these are defining performance, measuring performance, and providing performance feedback. First, the organization specifies which aspects of performance are relevant to the organization. These decisions are based on job analysis, described in Chapter 3. Next, the organization measures the relevant aspects of performance by conducting performance appraisals. Finally, through performance feedback sessions, managers give employees information about their performance so they can maintain and adjust their behaviour to meet the organization's goals. When there are performance gaps, the feedback session should include efforts to identify and resolve the underlying problems. In addition, performance feedback can come through the organization's rewards, as described in Chapter 8. Using this performance management process helps managers and employees focus on the organization's goals.

Computer software and Internet-based performance management systems are available to help managers at various stages of the performance management process. Software can help managers customize performance measurement forms. The manager uses the software to establish a set of performance standards for each job. The manager rates each employee according to the predetermined standards, and the software provides a report that compares the employee's performance to the standards and identifies the employee's strengths and weaknesses. Other software offers help with diagnosing performance gaps. This type of software asks questions—for example, "Does the employee work under time pressure?" The answers suggest reasons for performance issues and ways the manager can help the employee enhance his or her performance. One of the chapter-ending case studies discusses how Canadian startup Rypple's Web-based performance

FIGURE 7.1

Stages of the Performance Management Process

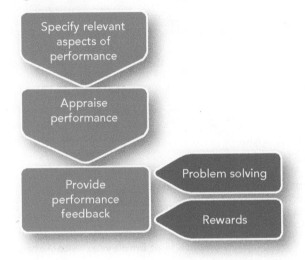

management platform has been adopted by companies including Facebook Inc.

According to the Hay Group, companies on its Global Most Admired list, which it prepares for *Fortune* magazine, have chief executive officers who understand that performance measurement helps the organization motivate people and link performance to rewards.[3] Many of these executives report that performance measurement encourages employees to cooperate and helps the company focus on smooth operations, customer loyalty, and employee development. And in a survey of 164 chief financial officers (CFOs), performance management emerged as a top priority—73 percent said that, within their first 100 days on the job, "they were expected to come up with a new plan for performance management."[4] However, despite the importance placed on performance management, less than half of responding organizations (46 percent) to a recent Conference Board of Canada survey say their performance management system is "effective" or "very effective."[5] See Figure 7.2.

Perhaps surprisingly, employees also appear to appreciate the importance of performance management including performance reviews. Results of a recent Ceridian Canada and Harris Decima survey stated that 71 percent of employees said their review made them feel valued and 91 percent said their performance reviews either met (79 percent) or exceeded (12 percent) their expectations.[6]

What Are the Purposes of Performance Management?

2,3,5,6

Organizations establish performance management systems to meet three broad purposes: strategic, administrative, and developmental. *Strategic purpose* means effective performance management helps the organization achieve its business objectives. It does this by helping to link employees' behaviour with the organization's goals. Performance management starts with defining what the organization expects from each employee. It measures each employee's performance to identify where those expectations are and are not being met. This enables the organization to take

> **L02** Discuss the purposes of performance management systems.

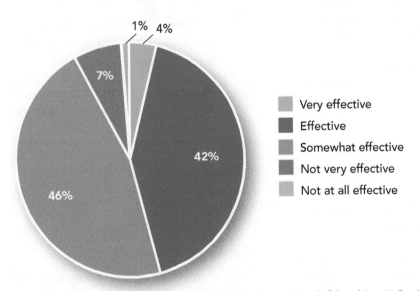

FIGURE 7.2

Effectiveness of Performance Management System

1% 4%

7%

42%

46%

- Very effective
- Effective
- Somewhat effective
- Not very effective
- Not at all effective

SOURCE: "Compensation Planning Outlook 2012" (Ottawa: Conference Board of Canada), p. 17. Reprinted with the permission of the Conference Board of Canada.

DID YOU KNOW?

Employees Want More Feedback

Managers may dread giving criticism, but according to a survey by Leadership IQ, a research and training company, employees want to hear more about how well they're doing—even if it's unpleasant.

SOURCES: Rebecca R. Hastings, "Recession Stifling Managers' Communication?" *HR Magazine*, February 2010, Business & Company Resource Center, http://galenet.galegroup.com; and Leadership IQ, "Managers Are Ignoring Their Employees," news release, December 2, 2009, www.leadershipiq.com.

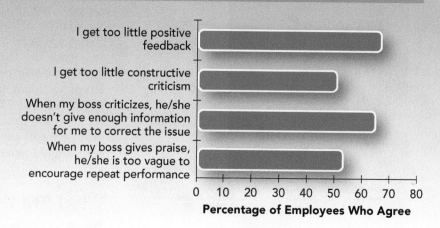

corrective action, such as training, incentives, or discipline. Performance management can achieve its strategic purpose only when measurements are truly aligned with the organization's goals and when the goals and feedback about performance are communicated to employees. Just Born, the company that makes Peeps and Mike and Ike candy, meets the strategic purpose of performance management. Its system has employees and managers meet to agree on several personal objectives through which each employee will help meet the objectives of his or her department. Together, they identify whatever training the employee needs and meet regularly to discuss the employee's progress in meeting the objectives.[7]

The *administrative purpose* of a performance management system refers to how organizations use the system to provide information for day-to-day decisions about salary, benefits, and recognition programs. Performance management can also support decision making related to employee retention, termination for poor performance, and hiring or layoffs. Because performance management supports these administrative decisions, the information in a performance appraisal can have a great impact on the future of individual employees. Managers recognize this, which is the reason they may feel uncomfortable conducting performance appraisals when the appraisal information is negative and, therefore, likely to lead to a layoff, disappointing pay increase, or other negative outcome.

Finally, performance management has a *developmental purpose*, meaning that it serves as a basis for developing employees' knowledge and skills. Even

employees who are meeting expectations can become more valuable when they receive and discuss performance feedback. Effective performance feedback makes employees aware of their strengths and of the areas in which they can improve. Discussing areas in which employees fall short can help the employees and their manager uncover the source of problems and identify steps for improvement. Although discussing shortcomings may feel uncomfortable, it is necessary when performance management has a developmental purpose.

What Are the Criteria for Effective Performance Management?

In Chapter 5, we saw that there are many ways to predict performance of a job candidate. Similarly, there are many ways to measure the performance of an employee. For performance management to achieve its goals, its methods for measuring performance must be effective. Selecting these measures is a critical part of planning a performance management system. As summarized in Figure 7.3, several criteria determine the effectiveness of performance measures.

L03 Define five criteria for measuring the effectiveness of a performance management system.

- *Fit with strategy*—A performance management system should aim at achieving employee behaviour

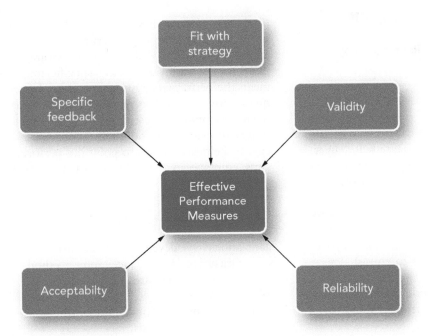

FIGURE 7.3

Criteria for Effective Performance Measures

and attitudes that support the organization's strategy, goals, and culture. If a company emphasizes customer service, then its performance management system should define the kinds of behaviour that contribute to good customer service. Performance appraisals should measure whether employees are engaging in those behaviours. Feedback should help employees improve in those areas. When an organization's strategy changes, human resource professionals should help managers assess how the performance management system should change to serve the new strategy.

- *Validity*—As we discussed in Chapter 5, *validity* is the extent to which a measurement tool actually measures what it is intended to measure. In the case of performance appraisal, validity refers to whether the appraisal measures all the relevant aspects of performance and omits irrelevant aspects of performance. Figure 7.4 shows two sets of information. The circle on the left represents

all the information in a performance appraisal; the circle on the right represents all relevant measures of job performance. The overlap of the circles contains the valid information. Information that is gathered but irrelevant is "contamination." Comparing salespeople on the basis of how many calls they make to customers could be a contaminated measure. Making a lot of calls does not necessarily improve sales or customer satisfaction, unless every salesperson makes only well-planned calls. Information that is not gathered but is relevant represents a deficiency of the performance measure. For example, suppose a company measures whether employees have good attendance records but not whether they work efficiently. This limited performance appraisal is unlikely to provide a full picture of employees' contribution to the company. Performance measures should minimize both contamination and deficiency.

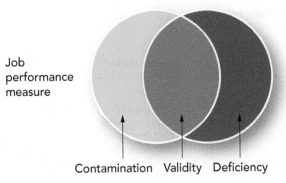

Job performance measure

Actual, or "true," job performance

Contamination   Validity   Deficiency

FIGURE 7.4

Contamination and Deficiency of a Job Performance Measure

- *Reliability*—With regard to a performance measure, reliability describes the consistency of the results that the performance measure will deliver. *Interrater reliability* is consistency of results when more than one person measures performance. Simply asking a supervisor to rate an employee's performance on a scale of 1 to 5 would likely have low interrater reliability; the rating will differ depending on who is scoring the employees. *Test-retest reliability* refers to consistency of results over time. If a performance measure lacks test-retest reliability, determining whether an employee's performance has truly changed over time will be impossible.

- *Acceptability*—Whether or not a measure is valid and reliable, it must meet the practical standard of being acceptable to the people who use it. For example, the people who use a performance measure must believe that it is not too time-consuming. Likewise, if employees believe the measure is unfair, they will not use the feedback as a basis for improving their performance.

- *Specific feedback*—A performance measure should specifically tell employees what is expected of them and how they can meet those expectations. Being specific helps performance management meet the goals of supporting strategy and developing employees. Being specific may also mean the performance measure can be defined in quantitative terms. If a measure does not specify what an employee must do to help the organization achieve its goals, it does not support the strategy. If the measure fails to point out performance gaps, employees will not know how to improve.

How Is Performance Measured?

Organizations have developed a wide variety of methods for measuring performance. Some methods rank each employee to compare employees' performance. Other methods break down the evaluation into ratings of individual attributes, behaviours, or results. Many organizations use a measurement system that includes a variety of these measures. Table 7.1 compares these methods in terms of our criteria for effective performance management.

LO4 Compare the major methods for measuring performance.

MAKING COMPARISONS

The performance appraisal method may require the rater to compare one individual's performance with

TABLE 7.1   Basic Approaches to Performance Management

| APPROACH | CRITERIA | | | | |
	FIT WITH STRATEGY	VALIDITY	RELIABILITY	ACCEPTABILITY	SPECIFICITY
Comparative	Poor, unless manager takes time to make link	Can be high if ratings are done carefully	Depends on rater, but usually no measure of agreement used	Moderate; easy to develop and use but resistant to normative standard	Very low
Attribute	Usually low; requires manager to make link	Usually low; can be fine if developed carefully	Usually low; can be improved by specific definitions of attributes	High; easy to develop and use	Very low
Behavioural	Can be quite high	Usually high; minimizes contamination and deficiency	Usually high	Moderate; difficult to develop, but accepted well for use	Very high
Results	Very high	Usually high; can be both contaminated and deficient	High; main problem can be test-retest—depends on timing of measure	High; usually developed with input from those to be evaluated	High regarding results, but low regarding behaviours necessary to achieve them

that of others. This method involves some form of ranking, in which some employees are the highest performers, some are average, and others are not meeting expectations. The usual techniques for making comparisons are simple ranking, forced distribution, and paired comparison.

Simple ranking requires managers to rank employees in their group from the highest performer to the lowest performer. In a variation on this approach, *alternation ranking*, the manager works from a list of employees. First, the manager decides which employee is the highest performer and crosses that person's name off the list. From the remaining names, the manager selects the lowest performing employee and crosses off that name. The process continues with the manager selecting the second-highest, second-lowest, third-highest, and so on until all the employees have been ranked. The major downside of ranking involves validity. To state a performance measure as broadly as "highest" or "lowest" doesn't define what exactly is effective or ineffective about the person's contribution to the organization. Ranking therefore raises questions about fairness.

Another way to compare employees' performance is with the **forced-distribution method**. This type of performance measurement assigns a certain percentage of employees to each category in a set of categories. For example, the organization might establish the following percentages and categories:

- Exceptional—5 percent
- Exceeds expectations—25 percent
- Meets expectations—55 percent
- Below expectations—10 percent
- Significantly below expectations—5 percent

The manager completing the performance appraisal would rate 5 percent of his or her employees as exceptional, 25 percent as exceeding expectations, and so on. A forced-distribution approach works best if the members of a group really do vary this much in terms of their performance. It overcomes the temptation to rate everyone high in order to avoid conflict. Research simulating some features of forced rankings found that they improved performance when combined with goals and rewards, especially in the first few years, when the system eliminated the lowest performers.[8] However, a manager who does very well at selecting, motivating, and training employees will have a group of high performers. This manager would have difficulty assigning employees to the lower categories. In that situation, saying that some employees are "below expectations" or "significantly below expectations" not only will be inaccurate, but will hurt morale.

The Conference Board of Canada reports that although only 15 percent of surveyed organizations use a forced-distribution performance management system, an additional 3 percent of organizations are considering its use in the coming year and a further 44 percent of surveyed organizations have guidelines or recommendations to ensure a normal distribution of performance ratings.[9] Figure 7.5 provides an illustration of these findings.

Another variation on rankings is the **paired-comparison method**. This approach involves comparing each employee with each other employee

---

simple ranking
Method of performance measurement that requires managers to rank employees in their group from the highest to the lowest performer.

forced-distribution method
Method of performance measurement that assigns a certain percentage of employees to each category in a set of categories.

paired-comparison method
Method of performance measurement that compares each employee with each other employee to establish rankings.

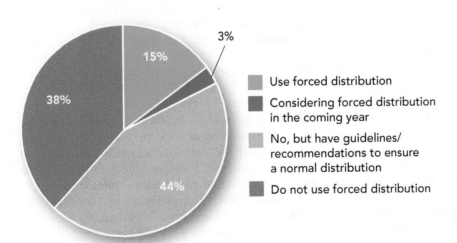

SOURCE: "Compensation Planning Outlook 2012" (Ottawa: Conference Board of Canada), p. 19. Reprinted with the permission of the Conference Board of Canada.

FIGURE 7.5

Forced Performance Distribution and Guidelines

- Use forced distribution
- Considering forced distribution in the coming year
- No, but have guidelines/recommendations to ensure a normal distribution
- Do not use forced distribution

3%
15%
38%
44%

to establish rankings. Suppose a manager has five employees, Jaida, Ramat, Caitlin, Ming, and David. The manager compares Jaida's performance to Ramat's and assigns one point to whichever employer is the higher performer. Then the manager compares Jaida's performance to Caitlin's, then to Ming's, and finally to David's. The manager repeats this process with Ramat, comparing his performance to Caitlin's, Ming's, and David's. When the manager has compared every pair of employees, the manager counts the number of points for each employee. The employee with the most points is considered the top-ranked employee. Clearly, this method is time-consuming if a group has more than a handful of employees. For a group of 15, the manager must make 105 comparisons.

In spite of the drawbacks, ranking employees offers some benefits. It counteracts the tendency to avoid controversy by rating everyone favourably or near the centre of the scale. Also, if some managers tend to evaluate behaviour more strictly (or more leniently) than others, a ranking system can erase that tendency from performance scores. Therefore, ranking systems can be useful for supporting decisions about how to distribute pay raises or layoffs. Some ranking systems are easy to use, which makes them acceptable to the managers who use them. A major drawback of rankings is that often they are not linked to the organization's goals. Also, a simple ranking system leaves the basis for ranking open to interpretation. In that case, the rankings are not helpful for employee development and may hurt morale or result in legal challenges.

RATING INDIVIDUALS

Instead of focusing on arranging a group of employees from best to worst, performance measurement can look at each employee's performance relative to a uniform set of standards. The measurement may evaluate employees in terms of attributes (characteristics, traits, or competencies) believed necessary for success in the job or in the organization. Or the measurements may identify whether employees have *behaved* in desirable ways, such as helping co-workers or working safely. The performance management system must identify the desired attributes or behaviours, then provide a form on which the manager can rate the employee in terms of those attributes or behaviours. Typically, the form includes a rating

graphic rating scale
Method of performance measurement that lists attributes and provides a rating scale for each attribute; the employer uses the scale to indicate the extent to which an employee displays each attribute.

mixed-standard scales
Method of performance measurement that uses several statements describing each attribute to produce a final score for that attribute.

scale, such as a scale from 1 to 5, where 1 is the lowest level of performance and 5 is the highest.

Rating Attributes

The most widely used method for rating attributes is the **graphic rating scale**. This method lists attributes and provides a rating scale for each. The employer uses the scale to indicate the extent to which the employee being rated displays the attributes. The rating scale may provide points to circle (as on a scale going from 1 for poor to 5 for distinguished), or it may provide a line representing a range of scores, with the manager marking a place along the line. Figure 7.6 shows an example of a graphic rating scale that uses a set of ratings from 1 to 5. A drawback of this approach is that it leaves to the particular manager the decisions about what is "excellent initiative" or "commendable teamwork" or "poor interpersonal skills." The result is low reliability, because managers are likely to arrive at different judgments.

To get around this problem, some organizations use **mixed-standard scales**, which use several statements describing each attribute to produce a final score for that attribute. The manager scores the employee in terms of how the employee compares to each statement. Consider the sample mixed-standard scale in Figure 7.7. To create this scale, the organization determined that the relevant attributes are initiative, client orientation, and relations with others. For each attribute, statements were written to describe a person having a high level of that attribute, a medium level, and a low level. The sentences for the attributes were rearranged so that the nine statements about the three attributes are mixed together. The manager who uses this scale reads each statement, then indicates whether the employee performs above (+), at (0), or below (−) the level described. The key in the middle section of Figure 7.7 tells how to use the pluses, zeros, and minuses to score performance. Someone who excels at every level of performance (pluses for high, medium, and low performance) receives a score of 7 for that attribute. Someone who fails to live up to every description of performance (minuses for high, medium, and low) receives a score of 1 for that attribute. The bottom of Figure 7.7 calculates the scores for the ratings used in this example.

Rating attributes is the most popular way to measure performance in organizations. In general,

FIGURE 7.6

Example of a Graphic Rating Scale

The following areas of performance are significant to most positions. Indicate your assessment of performance on each dimension by circling the appropriate rating.

PERFORMANCE DIMENSIONS	RATING				
	OUTSTANDING	EXCEEDS EXPECTATIONS	MEETS EXPECTATIONS	DEVELOPMENTAL	BELOW EXPECTATIONS
Client service	5	4	3	2	1
Communication	5	4	3	2	1
Leadership	5	4	3	2	1
Professionalism	5	4	3	2	1
Teamwork	5	4	3	2	1
Interpersonal skills	5	4	3	2	1
Initiative	5	4	3	2	1
Creativity	5	4	3	2	1
Problem solving	5	4	3	2	1

attribute-based performance methods are easy to develop and can be applied to a wide variety of jobs and organizations. If the organization is careful to identify which attributes are associated with high performance, and to define them carefully on the appraisal form, these methods can be reliable and valid. However, appraisal forms often fail to meet this standard. In addition, measurement of attributes may not be clearly linked to the organization's strategy. Furthermore, employees tend perhaps rightly to be defensive about receiving a mere numerical rating on some attribute. How would you feel if you were told you scored 2 on a 5-point scale of initiative or communication skill? The number might seem arbitrary, and it doesn't tell you how to improve.

Rating Behaviours

One way to overcome the drawbacks of rating attributes is to assess employees' behaviour. To rate behaviours, the organization begins by defining which behaviours are associated with success on the job. Which kinds of employee behaviour help the organization achieve its goals? The appraisal form asks the manager to rate an employee in terms of each of the identified behaviours.

One way to rate behaviours is with the **critical-incident method**. This approach requires managers to keep a record of specific examples of the employee behaving in ways that are either effective or ineffective. Here's an example of a critical incident in the performance evaluation of an appliance repairperson:

A customer called in about a refrigerator that was not cooling and was making a clicking noise every few minutes. The technician prediagnosed the cause of the problem and checked his truck for the necessary parts. When he found he did not have them, he checked the parts out from inventory so that the customer's refrigerator would be repaired on his first visit and the customer would be satisfied promptly.

This incident provides evidence of the employee's knowledge of refrigerator repair and concern for efficiency and customer satisfaction. Evaluating performance in this specific way gives employees feedback about what they do well and what requires improvement. The manager can also relate the incidents to how the employee is helping the company achieve its goals. Keeping a daily or weekly log of critical incidents requires significant effort, however, and managers may resist this requirement. Also, critical incidents may be unique, so they may not support comparisons among employees.

critical-incident method

Method of performance measurement based on managers' records of specific examples of the employee behaving in ways that are either effective or ineffective.

FIGURE 7.7

Example of a Mixed-Standard Scale

Three competencies being assessed:

Initiative (INTV)

Client orientation (CLO)

Relations with others (RWO)

Levels of performance in statements:

High (H)

Medium (M)

Low (L)

Instructions. Please indicate next to each statement whether the employee's performance is above (+), equal to (0), or below (−) the statement.

INTV	H	1.	This employee is a real self-starter. The employee always takes the initiative and his/her supervisor never has to prod this individual.	+
CLO	M	2.	Although this employee has some difficulty anticipating client needs, s/he is usually friendly and approachable.	+
RWO	L	3.	This employee has a tendency to get into unnecessary conflicts with other people.	0
INTV	M	4.	While generally this employee shows initiative, occasionally his/her supervisor must prod him/her to complete work.	+
CLO	L	5.	This employee frequently needs assistance in handling customer requests.	+
RWO	H	6.	This employee is on good terms with everyone. S/he can get along with people even when s/he does not agree with them.	−
INTV	L	7.	This employee has a bit of a tendency to sit around and wait for directions.	+
CLO	H	8.	This employee creates and maintains long-term client relationships.	−
RWO	M	9.	This employee gets along with most people. Only very occasionally does s/he have conflicts with others on the job, and these are likely to be minor.	−

Scoring Key:

	STATEMENTS		SCORE
HIGH	MEDIUM	LOW	
+	+	+	7
0	+	+	6
−	+	+	5
−	0	+	4
−	−	+	3
−	−	0	2
−	−	−	1

Example score from preceding ratings:

	STATEMENTS		SCORE
	HIGH	MEDIUM	LOW	
Initiative	+	+	+	7
Client orientation	0	+	+	6
Relations with others	−	−	0	2

An employee's performance measurement differs from job to job. For example, a car dealer's performance is measured by the dollar amount of sales, the number of new customers, and customer satisfaction surveys. How would the performance measurement of a car dealer differ from those of a company CEO?

behaviourally anchored rating scale (BARS)

Method of performance measurement that rates behaviour in terms of a scale showing specific statements of behaviour that describe different levels of performance.

A **behaviourally anchored rating scale (BARS)** builds on the critical incident approach. The BARS method is intended to define performance dimensions specifically, using statements of behaviour that describe different levels of performance.[10] (The statements are "anchors" of the performance levels.) The scale in Figure 7.8 shows various performance levels for "listening, understanding, and responding." The statement at the top (rating 5) describes the highest level of listening, understanding, and responding. The statement at the bottom describes behaviour associated with ineffective or

---

Competency: Listening, Understanding, and Responding to Customers

5 — Understands the underlying reasons for the customer's behaviour; anticipates and plans for future interactions.

Understands and responds to the customer's underlying issues; responds using knowledge of the customer's perspectives and concerns.
4

3 — Listens and responds to customer's unexpressed emotions; solicits input, paraphrases the customer's words, mirrors body language and tone of voice.

Listens and responds to customer's expressed emotions; asks questions and responds to customer's feelings or concerns.
2

1 — Provides inappropriate information or service; demonstrates ineffective or counterproductive behaviours in working with the customer, e.g., displayed boredom or interrupted the client.

FIGURE 7.8

BARS Rating Dimension: Customer Service Representative

SOURCE: Adapted from "Manager's HR Toolkit," BC Public Service Agency, www.hrtoolkit.gov.bc.ca/staffing, retrieved February 16, 2005.

counterproductive performance. These statements are based on data about past performance. The organization gathers many critical incidents representing effective and ineffective performance, then classifies them from most to least effective. When experts about the job agree the statements clearly represent levels of performance, they are used as anchors to guide the rater. Although BARS can improve interrater reliability, this method can bias the manager's memory. The statements used as anchors can help managers remember similar behaviours, but at the expense of other critical incidents.[11]

A **behavioural observation scale** (BOS) is a variation of a BARS. Like a BARS, a BOS is developed from critical incidents.[12] However, while a BARS discards many examples in creating the rating scale, a BOS uses many of them to

> **behavioural observation scale (BOS)**
> A variation of BARS, which uses all behaviours necessary for effective performance to rate performance at a task.

define all behaviours necessary for effective performance (or behaviours that signal ineffective performance). As a result, a BOS may use 15 behaviours to define levels of performance. Also, a BOS asks the manager to rate the frequency with which the employee has exhibited the behaviour during the rating period. These ratings are averaged to compute an overall performance rating. Figure 7.9 provides a simplified example of a BOS for measuring the behaviour "overcoming resistance to change."

A major drawback of this method is the amount of information required. A BOS can have 80 or more behaviours, and the manager must remember how often the employee exhibited each behaviour in a 6-to-12-month rating period. This is taxing enough for one employee, but managers often must assess

FIGURE 7.9

Example of a Behavioural Observation Scale

Overcoming Resistance to Change

Directions. Rate the frequency of each behaviour from 1 (Almost Never) to 5 (Almost Always).

1. Describes the details of the change to employees.
   Almost Never   1   2   3   4   5   Almost Always

2. Explains why the change is necessary.
   Almost Never   1   2   3   4   5   Almost Always

3. Discusses how the change will affect the employee.
   Almost Never   1   2   3   4   5   Almost Always

4. Listens to the employee's concerns.
   Almost Never   1   2   3   4   5   Almost Always

5. Asks the employee for help in making the change work.
   Almost Never   1   2   3   4   5   Almost Always

6. If necessary, specifies the date for a follow-up meeting to respond to the employee's concerns.
   Almost Never   1   2   3   4   5   Almost Always

Score. Total number of points = _____

Performance

Points	Performance Rating
6–10	Below expectations
11–15	Developmental
16–20	Meets expectations
21–25	Exceeds expectations
26–30	Outstanding

Scores are set by management.

ten or more employees. Even so, compared to BARS and graphic rating scales, managers and employees have said they prefer BOS for ease of use, providing feedback, maintaining objectivity, and suggesting training needs.[13]

Another approach to assessment builds directly on a branch of psychology called *behaviourism*, which holds that individuals' future behaviour is determined by their past experiences—specifically, the ways in which past behaviours have been reinforced. People tend to repeat behaviours that have been rewarded in the past. Providing feedback and reinforcement can therefore modify individuals' future behaviour. Applied to behaviour in organizations, organizational behaviour modification (OBM) is a plan for managing the behaviour of employees through a formal system of feedback and reinforcement. Specific OBM techniques vary, but most have four components:[14]

1. Define a set of key behaviours necessary for job performance.
2. Use a measurement system to assess whether the employee exhibits the key behaviours.
3. Inform employees of the key behaviours, perhaps in terms of goals for how often to exhibit the behaviours.
4. Provide feedback and reinforcement based on employees' behaviour.

OBM techniques have been used in a variety of settings. For example, a community health agency used OBM to increase the rates and timeliness of critical job behaviours by showing employees the connection between job behaviours and the agency's accomplishments.[15] This process identified job behaviours related to administration, record keeping, and service provided to clients. Feedback and reinforcement improved staff performance. OBM also increased the frequency of safety behaviours in a processing plant.[16]

Behavioural approaches such as organizational behaviour modification and rating scales can be very effective. These methods can link the company's goals to the specific behaviour required to achieve those goals. Behavioural methods also can generate specific feedback, along with guidance in areas requiring improvements. As a result, these methods tend to be valid. The people to be measured often help in developing the measures, so acceptance tends to be high as well. When raters are well trained, reliability also tends to be high. However, behavioural methods do not work as well for complex jobs in which it is difficult to see a link between behaviour and results or there is more than one good way to achieve success.[17]

Measuring Results

Performance measurement can focus on managing the objective, measurable results of a job or work group. Results might include sales, costs, or productivity (output per worker or per dollar spent on production), among many possible measures. Two of the most popular methods for measuring results are measurement of productivity and management by objectives.

Productivity is an important measure of success, because getting more done with a smaller amount of resources (money or people) increases the company's profits. Productivity usually refers to the output of production workers, but it can be used more generally as a performance measure. To do this, the organization identifies the products—set of activities or objectives—it expects a group or individual to accomplish. At a repair shop, for instance, a product might be something like "quality of repair." The next step is to define how to measure production of these products. For quality of repair, the repair shop could track the percentage of items returned because they still do not work after a repair and the percentage of quality-control inspections passed. For each measure, the organization decides what level of performance is desired. Finally, the organization sets up a system for tracking these measures and giving employees feedback about their performance in terms of these measures. This type of performance measurement can be time-consuming to set up, but research suggests it can improve productivity.[18]

Management by objectives (MBO) is a system in which people at each level of the organization set goals in a process that flows from top to bottom, so employees at all levels are contributing to the organization's overall goals. These goals become the standards for evaluating each employee's performance. An MBO system has three components:[19]

1. Goals are specific, difficult, and objective. The goals listed in the second column of Table 7.2 provide two examples for a bank.
2. Managers and their employees work together to set the goals.
3. The manager gives objective feedback through the rating period to monitor progress toward the goals. The two right-hand columns in Table 7.2 are examples of feedback given after one year.

organizational behaviour modification (OBM)

A plan for managing the behaviour of employees through a formal system of feedback and reinforcement.

management by objectives (MBO)

A system in which people at each level of the organization set goals in a process that flows from top to bottom, so employees at all levels are contributing to the organization's overall goals; these goals become the standards for evaluating each employee's performance.

TABLE 7.2 Management by Objectives: Two Objectives for a Bank

KEY RESULT AREA	OBJECTIVE	% COMPLETE	ACTUAL PERFORMANCE
Loan portfolio management	Increase portfolio value by 10% over the next 12 months	90	Increased portfolio value by 9% over the past 12 months
Sales	Generate fee income of $30,000 over the next 12 months	150	Generated fee income of $45,000 over the past 12 months

MBO can have a very positive effect on an organization's performance. In 70 studies of MBO's performance, 68 showed that productivity improved.[20] The productivity gains tended to be greatest when top management was highly committed to MBO. Also, because staff members are involved in setting goals, it is likely that MBO systems effectively link individual employees' performance with the organization's overall goals. The "HR Best Practices" box, found later in this chapter, discusses methods to ensure employees' performance ratings are assessed consistently.

In general, evaluation of results can be less subjective than other kinds of performance measurement. This makes measuring results highly acceptable to employees and managers alike. Results-oriented performance measurement is also relatively easy to link to the organization's goals. However, measuring results has problems with validity, because results may be affected by circumstances beyond each employee's performance. Also, if the organization measures only final results, it may fail to measure significant aspects of performance that are not directly related to those results. If individuals focus only on aspects of performance that are measured, they may neglect significant skills

balanced scorecard
An organizational approach to performance management that integrates strategic perspectives including financial, customer, internal business processes, and learning and growth.

or behaviours. For example, if the organization measures only productivity, employees may not be concerned enough with customer service. The outcome may be high efficiency (costs are low) but low effectiveness (sales are low, too).[21] Finally, focusing strictly on results does not provide guidance on how to improve.

Balanced Scorecard

The **balanced scorecard** is an organizational approach to performance management that integrates strategic perspectives including financial, customer, internal business processes, and learning and growth. Robert S. Kaplan and David P. Norton developed this widely adopted approach, illustrated in Figure 7.10. The basic idea is that managers are encouraged to go beyond meeting just traditional financial targets, and recognize and simultaneously monitor the progress of other important goals such as customer and employee satisfaction.[22] Use of a balanced scorecard provides the means to align strategy at all levels of the organization and serves as "an excellent guide to measure and manage

Coaches provide feedback to their team just as managers provide feedback to their employees. Feedback is important so that individuals know what they are doing well and what areas they may need to work on.

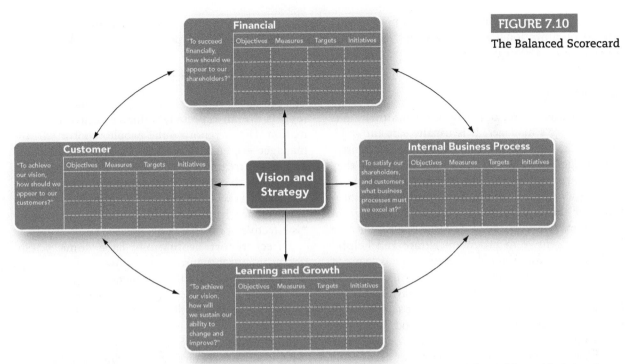

FIGURE 7.10

The Balanced Scorecard

SOURCE: Robert S. Kaplan and David P. Norton, "Using the Balanced Scorecard as a Strategic Management System," *Harvard Business Review*, July/August 2007, p. 153. Reprinted by permission of *Harvard Business Review*. © 2007 by the Harvard Business School Publishing Corporation. All rights reserved.

the performance of all employees."[23] Balanced scorecards are widely used in both the public and private sector. A sampling of the organizations that use balanced scorecards as part of their strategic management and performance management systems include: J. D. Irving Ltd., Canadian Cancer Society, Carleton University, Nova Scotia Power Inc., The Cooperators, and Great-West Life Assurance Company.

What Are the Sources of Performance Information?

All the methods of performance measurement require decisions about who will collect and analyze the performance information. To qualify for this task, a person should have an understanding of the job requirements and the opportunity to see the employee doing the job. The traditional approach is for managers to gather information about their employees' performance and arrive at performance ratings. However, many sources are possible. Possibilities of information sources include managers, peers, direct reports, self, and customers.

L05 ▸ Describe major sources of performance information in terms of their advantages and disadvantages.

Using just one person as a source of information poses certain problems. People tend to like some people more than others, and those feelings can bias how an employee's efforts are perceived. Also, one person is likely to see an employee in a limited number of situations. A supervisor, for example, cannot see how an employee behaves when the supervisor is not there—for example, when a service technician is at the customer's facility. To get as complete an assessment as possible, some organizations combine information from most or all of the possible sources, in what is called a *multi-rater* or *360-degree performance appraisal*.

The John Molson School of Business at Montreal's Concordia University conducted a study to learn about the experiences of 101 large Canadian organizations with 360-degree programs. The study found that 43 percent of the organizations surveyed used 360-degree, that is, multi-rater approaches. Companies are using 360-degree performance appraisal because of advantages including increased measurement accuracy and perceived fairness. Respondents also identified challenges such as resistance from individuals because of concerns about the process being time-, cost-, and energy-consuming, trust issues including anonymity of

360-degree performance appraisal
Performance measurement that combines information from the employee's managers, peers, direct reports, self, and customers.

feedback, and the need to ensure a clear purpose and link to organizational strategy are in place before implementing 360-degree appraisal.[24]

MANAGERS

The most-used source of performance information is the employee's manager. It is usually safe for organizations to assume that supervisors have extensive knowledge of the job requirements and that they have enough opportunity to observe their employees. In other words, managers possess the basic qualifications for this responsibility. Another advantage of using managers to evaluate performance is that they have an incentive to provide accurate and helpful feedback, because their own success depends so much on their employees' performance.[25] Finally, when managers try to observe employee behaviour or discuss performance issues in the feedback session, their feedback can improve performance, and employees tend to perceive the appraisal as accurate.[26]

Still, in some situations, problems can occur with using supervisors as the source of performance information. For employees in some jobs, the supervisor does not have enough opportunity to observe the employee performing job duties. A sales manager with many outside salespeople cannot be with the salespeople on many visits to customers. Even if the sales manager does make a point of travelling with salespeople for a few days, they are likely to be on their best behaviour while the manager is there. The manager cannot observe how they perform at other times.

PEERS

Another source of performance information is the employee's peers or coworkers. Peers are an excellent source of information about performance in a job where the supervisor does not often observe the employee. Examples include law enforcement and sales. For these and other jobs, peers may have the most opportunity to observe the employee in day-to-day activities. Peers have expert knowledge of job requirements. They also bring a different perspective to the evaluation and can provide extremely valid assessments of performance.[27]

Peer evaluations obviously have some potential disadvantages. Friendships (or rivalries) have the potential to bias ratings. Research, however, has provided little evidence that this is a problem.[28] Another disadvantage is that when the evaluations are done to support administrative decisions, peers are uncomfortable with rating employees for decisions that may affect themselves. Generally, peers

are more willing to participate in reviews to be used for employee development.[29]

DIRECT REPORTS

For evaluating the performance of managers, direct reports are an especially valuable source of information. Direct reports—the people reporting to the manager—often have the best chance to see how well a manager treats employees. Dell, for example, asks employees to rate their manager in terms of measures such as whether the employee receives ongoing performance feedback and whether the supervisor "is effective at managing people."[30]

Direct report evaluations have some potential problems because of the power relationships involved. Direct reports are reluctant to say negative things about the person to whom they report; they prefer to provide feedback anonymously. Managers, however, have a more positive reaction to this type of feedback when the employees are identified. When feedback requires that the direct reports identify themselves, they tend to give the manager higher ratings.[31] Another problem is that when managers receive ratings from direct reports, the employees have more power, so managers tend to emphasize employee satisfaction, even at the expense of productivity. This issue arises primarily when the evaluations are used for administrative decisions. Therefore, as with peer evaluations, direct report evaluations are most appropriate for developmental purposes. To protect employees, the process should be anonymous and use at least three employees to rate each manager.

SELF

No one has a greater chance to observe the employee's behaviour on the job than does the employee himself or herself. Self-ratings are rarely used alone, but they can contribute valuable information. A common approach is to have employees evaluate their own performance before the feedback session. This activity gets employees thinking about their performance. Areas of disagreement between the self-appraisal and other evaluations can be fruitful topics for the feedback session. Employee self-assessment offers a way to balance power in a process that tends to be manager-dominated. Areas of disagreement between the self-rating and the manager's rating should be used to create dialogue and reach mutual agreement during the feedback session.[32]

The obvious problem with self-ratings is that individuals have a tendency to inflate assessments of their performance. Especially if the ratings will be used for administrative decisions, exaggerating one's contributions has practical benefits. Also, social psychologists have found that, in general, people tend to blame outside circumstances for their failures while taking a large part of the credit for their successes. Supervisors can reduce this tendency by providing frequent feedback, but, because people tend to perceive situations this way, self-appraisals are not appropriate as the basis for administrative decisions.[33]

CUSTOMERS

Services are often produced and consumed on the spot, so the customer is often the only person who directly observes the service performance and may be the best source of performance information. Many companies in service industries have introduced customer evaluations of employee performance. Marriott Corporation provides a customer satisfaction card in every room and emails surveys to a random sample of its hotel customers. Whirlpool's Consumer Services Division conducts both mail and telephone surveys of customers after factory technicians have serviced their appliances. These surveys allow the company to evaluate an individual technician's customer-service behaviours while in the customer's home.

Using customer evaluations of employee performance is appropriate in two situations.[34] The first is when an employee's job requires direct service to the customer or linking the customer to other services within the organization. Second, customer evaluations are appropriate when the organization is interested in gathering information to determine what products and services the customer wants. That is, customer evaluations contribute to the organization's goals by enabling HRM to support the organization's marketing activities. In this regard, customer evaluations are useful both for evaluating an employee's performance and for helping to determine whether the organization can improve customer service by making changes in HRM activities such as training or compensation.

The weakness of using customer feedback for performance measurement is their expense. The expenses of a traditional survey can add up to hundreds of dollars to evaluate one individual. Many organizations therefore limit the information gathering to short periods once a year.

Errors in Performance Measurement

As we noted in the previous section, one reason for gathering information from several sources is that

performance measurements are not completely objective, and errors can occur. People observe behaviour, and they have no practical way of knowing all the circumstances, intentions, and outcomes related to that behaviour, so they interpret what they see. In doing so, observers make a number of judgment calls, and in some situations may even distort information on purpose. Therefore, fairness in rating performance and interpreting performance appraisals requires that managers understand the kinds of distortions that commonly occur.

L06 Define types of rating errors and explain how to minimize them.

TYPES OF RATING ERRORS

Several kinds of errors and biases commonly influence performance measurements. Usually people make these errors unintentionally, especially when the criteria for measuring performance are not very specific.

Similar to Me

A common human tendency is to give a higher evaluation to people we consider similar to ourselves. Most of us tend to think of ourselves as effective. If others seem to be like us in some way—physical characteristics, family or economic background, attitudes, or beliefs—we expect them to be effective as well. Research has demonstrated that this effect, called the **similar-to-me error**, is strong. One unfortunate result (besides inaccuracy) is that when similarity is based on characteristics such as race or sex, the decisions may be discriminatory.[35]

> **similar-to-me error**
> Rating error of giving a higher evaluation to people who seem similar to oneself.

> **contrast error**
> Rating error caused by comparing employee's performance to co-workers rather than to an objective standard.

Contrast

Sometimes, instead of comparing an individual's performance against an objective standard, the rater compares that individual with other employees. Suppose an employee is completely competent and does exactly what the job requires. But that employee has several co-workers who are outstanding; they keep breaking sales records or thinking up innovative ways to shave time off production processes. If the person rating the employee is contrasting the employee's performance with the exceptional co-workers and gives lower performance ratings than the employee deserves, this is **contrast error**. The reduced rating does not accurately reflect what the employee is accomplishing.

Errors in Distribution

Raters often tend to use only one part of a rating scale—the low scores, the high scores, or the middle of the range. Sometimes a group of employees really do perform equally well (or poorly). In many cases, however, similar ratings for all members of a group are not an accurate description of performance, but an error in distribution. When a rater inaccurately assigns high ratings to all employees, this is called a leniency error. When a rater incorrectly gives low ratings to all employees, holding them to unreasonably high standards, the resulting error is called a strictness error. Rating all employees as somehow "average" or in the middle of the scale is called the central tendency. These errors pose two problems. First, they make it difficult to distinguish among employees rated by the same person. Decisions about promotions, job assignments, and so on are more difficult if employees all seem to be performing at the same level. Second, these errors create problems in comparing the performance of individuals rated by different raters. If one rater is lenient and the other is strict, employees of the strict rater will receive significantly fewer rewards than employees of the lenient rater. The rewards are not tied to actual performance but are to some degree erroneous.

Recency Emphasis

Raters sometimes base an annual rating only on the employee's most recent work. Raters may have difficulty remembering things that happened several months to a year ago versus work from a few weeks before the performance review. This recency emphasis error can also occur when the supervisor is rushing the evaluation process because of heavy workload or lack of time.[36]

Focus on Activities

Rushing due to insufficient time or heavy workload may also contribute to a focus on activities, which happens when employees are assessed on how busy they appear rather than how effective they are in achieving results.[37]

leniency error
Rating error of assigning inaccurately high ratings to all employees.

strictness error
Rating error of giving low ratings to all employees, holding them to unreasonably high standards.

central tendency
Incorrectly rating all employees at or near the middle of a rating scale.

recency emphasis
Rating error that occurs when an annual rating is based only on most recent work performed.

focus on activities
Rating error when employees are assessed on how busy they appear rather than how effective they are in achieving results.

halo error
Rating error that occurs when the rater reacts to one positive performance aspect by rating the employee positively in all areas of performance.

horns error
Rating error that occurs when the rater responds to one negative aspect by rating an employee low in other aspects.

Halo and Horns

Another common problem is that raters often fail to distinguish among different aspects of performance. Consider a research lab that hires chemists. A chemist who expresses herself very well may appear to have greater knowledge of chemistry than a chemist with poor communication skills. In this example, a rater could easily fail to distinguish between communication skills and scientific skills.

This type of error can make a person look better, or worse, overall. When the rater reacts to one positive performance aspect by rating the employee positively in all areas of performance, the bias is called the halo error. As in the example of the chemist who communicates well, giving the impression of overall intelligence. In contrast, when the rater responds to one negative aspect by rating an employee low in other aspects, the bias is called the horns error. Suppose an employee sometimes arrives to work late. The rater takes this as a sign of lack of motivation, lack of ambition, and inability to follow through with responsibility—an example of the horns error.

When raters make halo and horns errors, the performance measurements cannot provide the specific information needed for useful feedback. Halo error signals that no aspects of an employee's performance need improvement, possibly missing opportunities for employee development. Horns error tells the employee that the rater has a low opinion of the employee. The employee is likely to feel defensive and frustrated, rather than motivated to improve.

WHAT CAN BE DONE TO REDUCE ERRORS?

Usually people make these errors unintentionally, especially when the criteria for measuring performance are not very specific. Raters can be trained how to avoid rating errors.[38] Prospective raters watch video segments with story lines designed to lead them to make specific rating errors. After rating the fictional employees in the videos, raters discuss their rating decisions and how such errors affected their rating decisions.

HR BEST PRACTICES

Calibrating Talent

Effective performance management systems rate performance consistently. This foundation is the basis for reliability of performance management systems, and it is critical to creating fairness in how employees' performance is assessed. By definition, performance management systems assess how well an employee meets the expectations associated with the job and the organization's goals; but according to a study of 5,970 employees who each report to two managers, the majority of the employees received inconsistent performance ratings. "The study found that employees rated outstanding by one manager were rated lower by their other manager 62 percent of the time."

Many companies use a calibration process to make sure that performance appraisals are consistent across managers. This process is ideally led by an experienced facilitator such as a senior human resource professional, who brings together supervisors and managers to discuss each employee's rating and its rationale. Some organizations are taking this a step further, using these meetings not only to calibrate performance but also to have meaningful discussions about the organization's talent. These types of discussions reinforce succession planning.

A Toronto-based utility, Direct Energy, also enhances the calibration process with technology that provides real-time access to performance ratings as they happen. Terry Fox, director of HR operations, describes how calibration works at Direct Energy: "The focus is on the high-value discussion about who the high-performers are and why, and finding ways to share the pool of high-performing employees with peers to help those people develop."

SOURCES: Joanne Sammer, "Calibrating Consistency," *HR Magazine*, January 2008, pp. 73–75; Christee Gabour Atwood, "Implementing Your Succession Plan," *T+D*, November 2007, p. 54; and David Brown, "Performance Management Systems Need Fixing," *Canadian HR Reporter*, April 11, 2005, p. 1.

Training programs offer tips for avoiding the errors in the future.

Another training method for raters focuses not on errors in rating, but on the complex nature of employee performance.[39] Raters learn to look at many aspects of performance that deserve their attention. Actual examples of performance are studied to bring out various performance dimensions and the standards for those dimensions. The objective of this training is to help raters evaluate employees' performance more thoroughly and accurately.

POLITICAL BEHAVIOUR IN PERFORMANCE APPRAISALS

Unintentional errors are not the only cause of inaccurate performance measurement. Sometimes the people rating performance distort an evaluation on purpose, to advance their personal goals. This kind of appraisal politics is unhealthy, especially because the resulting feedback does not focus on helping employees contribute to the organization's goals. High-performing employees who are rated unfairly will become frustrated, and low-performing employees who are overrated will be rewarded rather than encouraged to improve. Therefore, organizations try to identify and discourage appraisal politics.

Several characteristics of appraisal systems and company culture tend to encourage appraisal politics. Appraisal politics are most likely to occur when raters are accountable to the employee being rated, the goals of rating are not compatible with one another, performance appraisal is directly linked to highly desirable rewards, top executives tolerate or ignore distorted ratings, and senior employees tell newcomers company "folklore" that includes stories about distorted ratings.

Political behaviour occurs in every organization. Organizations can minimize appraisal politics by establishing an appraisal system that is fair. One technique is to hold a **calibration session**, a meeting at which managers discuss employee performance ratings and provide evidence supporting their ratings with the goal of eliminating the influence of rating errors. According to a recent poll conducted by the Society for Human Resource Management (SHRM), more than half of organizations conduct

calibration session
Meeting at which managers discuss employee performance ratings and provide evidence supporting their ratings with the goal of eliminating the influence of rating errors.

formal calibration sessions and 35 percent of organizations report "regularly" changing ratings as a result of these sessions.[40] As they discuss ratings and the ways they arrive at ratings, managers may identify undervalued employees, notice whether they are much harsher or more lenient than other managers, and help each other focus on how well ratings are associated with relevant performance outcomes. For example, when consultant Dick Grote leads calibration meetings for his clients, he often displays flip charts, one for each rating on a scale, and gives each manager a different coloured Post-it Note pad. On their Post-it Notes, the managers write the names of each employee they assess, and they attach a note for the rating they would give that employee. The distribution of colours on the flip charts provide visually strong information about how the different managers think about their employees, A cluster of green notes on "outstanding" and yellow notes on "meets expectations" would suggest that one manager is a much tougher rater than others, and they could then discuss how they arrive at these different conclusions.[41] Calibrating talent is also discussed in the nearby "HR Best Practices" box. The organization can also help managers give accurate and fair appraisals by training them to use the appraisal process, encouraging them to recognize accomplishments that the employees themselves have not identified, and fostering a climate of openness in which employees feel they can be honest about their weaknesses.[42]

Performance Feedback

1,2,3

Once the manager and others have measured an employee's performance, this information needs to be shared with the employee. Although the feedback stage of performance management is essential, it may be uncomfortable to managers and employees and may even undermine employee engagement

> When giving performance feedback, do it in an appropriate meeting place. Meet in a setting that is neutral and free of distractions. What other factors are important for a feedback session?

and commitment if not handled effectively. In a productive and meaningful performance feedback session both parties need to feel heard, understood, and respected even if they don't necessarily agree on all of the points discussed.[43]

L07 Explain how to effectively provide performance feedback.

SCHEDULING PERFORMANCE FEEDBACK

Performance feedback should be a regular, expected management activity. The practice or policy at many organizations is to give formal performance feedback once a year. But annual feedback is not enough. One reason is that managers are responsible for dealing with performance gaps as soon as they occur. If the manager notices a problem with an employee's behaviour in June, but the annual appraisal is scheduled for November, the employee will miss months of opportunities for improvement.

Another reason for frequent performance feedback is that feedback is most effective when the information does not surprise the employee. If an employee has to wait for up to a year to learn what the manager thinks of his work, the employee will wonder whether he is meeting expectations. Employees should instead receive feedback so often that they know what the manager will say during their annual performance review. Generational differences in the workplace also contribute to different perspectives about what is timely feedback. Gen-Y employees may expect immediate feedback because their reference points are often built around short-time frames and accomplishments.[44] For example, Ernst and Young created an online "Feedback

Zone," where employees can request or submit performance feedback at any time beyond the formal evaluations required twice a year.

PREPARING FOR A FEEDBACK SESSION

Managers should be well prepared for each formal feedback session. The manager should create the right context for the meeting. The location should be neutral. If the manager's office is the site of unpleasant conversations, a conference room may be more appropriate. In announcing the meeting to an employee, the manager should describe it as a chance to discuss the role of the employee, the role of the manager, and the relationship between them. Managers should also say (and believe) that they would like the meeting to be an open dialogue. As

discussed in the "HR How-To" box, the content of the feedback session and the type of language used can determine the success of this meeting.

Managers should also enable the employee to be well prepared. The manager should ask the employee to complete a self-assessment ahead of time. The self-assessment requires employees to think about their performance over the past rating period and to be aware of their strengths and weaknesses, so they can participate more fully in the discussion. Even though employees may tend to overstate their accomplishments, the self-assessment can help the manager and employee identify areas for discussion. When the purpose of the assessment is to define areas for development, employees may actually understate their performance. Also, differences between the manager's and the employee's rating may be fruitful areas

HR HOW-TO

Discussing Employee Performance

Employees and managers often dread feedback sessions, because they expect some level of criticism, and criticism feels uncomfortable. However, there are ways to structure communication about employee performance so that it feels more constructive.

More important, ensure that communication flows in both directions. It should begin with clear expectations laid out—sometimes in detail—well before the feedback session, so that employees have a fair chance to succeed. Employees should know what "meets" and "outstanding" performance look like, if those are the terms used in rating their performance. Employees should be so clear about what is desired that during the time leading up to the meeting, they can be gathering examples of situations in which they met or exceeded expectations. Managers also should be gathering these examples. The meeting should allow enough time for both participants to present, discuss, and learn

from the examples they have identified. Based on what this discussion reveals, the employee or manager should discuss revising goals, setting new goals, or figuring out how to meet unfulfilled goals.

Discussions should consider how the employee's actions have (or have not) been contributing to the employee's, team's, and company's business objectives. This helps the conversation move away from vague discussion of personality toward goal-oriented, objective performance measures.

When an employee's performance falls below expectations, the manager should prepare ahead of time to be sure the facts of the situation are clear and complete. The employee and manager should discuss the issue before the manager writes conclusions on the appraisal form, to ensure that the report will be fair. Whether performance is disappointing or delightful, the manager should be direct and clear in discussing it, focusing on observable behaviours.

The discussions should include plans for the future. The manager should hear the employee's ideas about what he or she needs to continue improving his or her contributions to the organization. The manager should consider a variety of possible needs, including further training or coaching, removing obstacles to high performance, and adopting employee suggestions to improve work processes. Ending with an action plan takes some of the sting out of criticism—and helps employees apply praise in a way that makes them more valuable.

SOURCES: Christine V. Bonavita, "The Importance of Performance Evaluations," *Employment Law Strategist*, March 1, 2009, Business and Company Resource Centre, http://galenet.galegroup.com; "Boost the Value of Performance Reviews," *HR Focus*, December 2009, Business and Company Resource Centre, http://galenet.galegroup .com; and Carolyn Heinze, "Fair Appraisals," *Systems Contractor News*, July 2009, Business and Company Resource Centre, http://galenet.galegroup.com.

for discussion. This approach to performance feedback is consistent with creating a coaching culture to manage, assess, and develop employees and requires managers to have well-developed coaching skills.[45]

CONDUCTING THE FEEDBACK SESSION

During the feedback session, managers can take any of three approaches. In the "tell-and-sell" approach, managers tell the employees their ratings and then justify those ratings. In the "tell-and-listen" approach, managers tell employees their ratings and then let the employees explain their side of the story. In the "problem-solving" approach, managers and employees work together to solve performance problems in an atmosphere of respect and encouragement. Not surprisingly, research demonstrates that the problem-solving approach is superior. Perhaps surprisingly, most managers rely on the tell-and-sell approach.[46] Managers can improve employee satisfaction with the feedback process and improve performance by creating two-way communication, by letting employees voice their opinions and discuss performance goals.[47]

Applying some additional principles will also make performance feedback more effective. Feedback should include a balanced and accurate assessment of how the employee is doing. The discussion should include a specific discussion of areas in which the employee's performance met, exceeded, and fell short of expectations. Any areas of required improvement should lead to problem solving.

The content of the feedback should emphasize behaviour, not personalities. For example, "You did not meet the deadline" can open a conversation about what needs to change, but "You're not motivated" may make the employee feel defensive and angry. As the nearby "HR Oops!" box shows, even employees who are told they are meeting performance goals may not see this as a compliment. The feedback session should end with goal setting and a decision about when to follow up.

Performance Improvement

When performance evaluation indicates that an employee's performance is below expectations, the feedback process should launch an effort to address the performance gap. Even when the employee is meeting current standards, the

> **L08** Summarize ways to achieve performance improvement.

HR Oops!

We're All Above Average

For all the worries about delivery criticism, it turns out that poor performance isn't the only problem: employees don't want to hear they're doing their jobs, if it means they sound "average." Although the very idea of average would imply that many employees rate near the middle, and the very idea of goal setting would be that you want employees to meet a challenge, managers and HR experts report that most employees think they're *above* average and *exceed* expectations.

Penny Wilson, director of corporate learning and development at Talecris Biotherapeutics suggests that HR departments "could do a better job of explaining that 'meets' is a good rating, and that we need those solid performers." But John Lewison, director of human resources at MDRC, says that over his career at six different companies, "I've seen every word used for every category. And no matter what you do, people figure out pretty quickly what 'average' is and don't want to be in that category."

Part of the problem may be that the use of forced-distribution methods and links between appraisals and compensation have created a climate in which employees are afraid they won't be rewarded (or will be let go) if they get anything but a stellar review.

SOURCE: Based on Adrienne Fox, "Curing What Ails Performance Reviews," *HR Magazine*, January 2009, pp. 52–56.

QUESTIONS

1. If an employee receives performance feedback that implies the employee is "average" or has met (but not exceeded expectations), how would you expect the employee to react to the feedback during an appraisal interview? How well would this feedback affect the strategic and developmental purposes of performance management?

2. How could performance appraisals or feedback sessions be modified to address employees' resistance to being considered average?

feedback session may identify areas in which the employee can improve in order to contribute more to the organization in a current or future job. In sum, the final feedback stage of performance management involves identifying areas for improvement and ways to improve performance in those areas.

As is shown in Figure 7.11, the most effective way to improve performance varies according to the employee's ability and motivation. In general, when employees have high levels of ability and motivation, they perform at or above expectations. But when they lack ability, motivation, or both, corrective action is needed. The type of action called for depends on what is missing:

- *Lack of ability*—When a motivated employee lacks knowledge, skills, or abilities in some area, the manager may offer training, and more detailed feedback. Sometimes it is appropriate to restructure the job so the employee can meet the job demands.
- *Lack of motivation*—Managers with an unmotivated employee can explore ways to demonstrate that the employee is being treated fairly and rewarded adequately. The solution may be as simple as delivering more positive feedback.

Employees may also benefit from a referral for counselling or help with stress management.

- *Lack of both*— Employees whose performance is below expectations because they have neither the motivation nor the ability to perform the job may not be a good fit for the position. Performance may improve if the manager directs their attention to the significance of the problem by withholding rewards or by providing specific feedback.

A documented performance improvement plan may be introduced by the supervisor as a means to discuss and reach agreement on next steps. A **performance improvement plan** is a summary of performance gaps and includes an action plan mutually agreed to by the employee and supervisor with specific dates to review progress. If employees do not respond by improving their performance, the organization may have to discipline or terminate these underperformers.

As a rule, employees who combine high ability with high motivation are solid performers. As Figure 7.11 indicates, managers should

performance improvement plan
Summary of performance gaps and includes an action plan mutually agreed to by the employee and supervisor with specific dates to review progress.

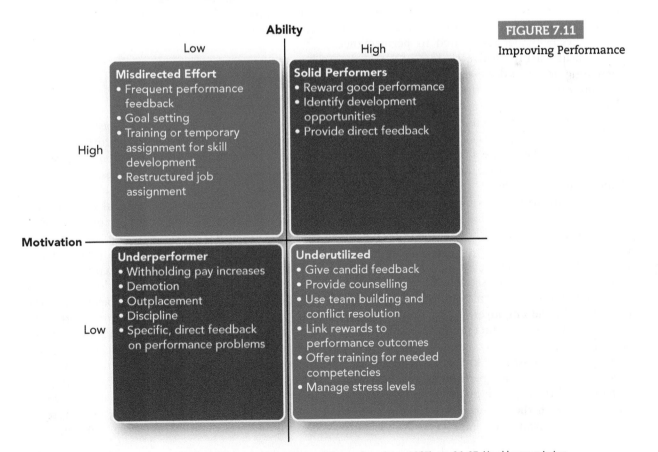

Ability

	Low	High
High	**Misdirected Effort** • Frequent performance feedback • Goal setting • Training or temporary assignment for skill development • Restructured job assignment	**Solid Performers** • Reward good performance • Identify development opportunities • Provide direct feedback
Low	**Underperformer** • Withholding pay increases • Demotion • Outplacement • Discipline • Specific, direct feedback on performance problems	**Underutilized** • Give candid feedback • Provide counselling • Use team building and conflict resolution • Link rewards to performance outcomes • Offer training for needed competencies • Manage stress levels

Motivation

FIGURE 7.11

Improving Performance

SOURCE: Based on M. London, *Job Feedback* (Mahwah, NJ: Lawrence Erlbaum Associates, 1997), pp. 96, 97. Used by permission.

by no means ignore these employees on the grounds of leaving well enough alone. Rather, such employees are likely to appreciate opportunities for further development. Rewards and direct feedback help to maintain these employees' high motivation levels.

What Are the Legal and Ethical Issues?

2,3,4

In developing and using performance management systems, human resource professionals need to ensure that these systems meet legal requirements, such as the avoidance of discrimination related to any of the prohibited grounds, avoiding psychological harassment, and protecting employees' privacy.

> **LO9** Discuss legal and ethical issues that affect performance management.

LEGAL REQUIREMENTS FOR PERFORMANCE MANAGEMENT

Because performance measures play a central role in decisions about pay, promotions, and discipline, employment-related legal challenges may be directed at an organization's performance management system. Legal challenges related to performance management usually involve charges of illegal discrimination or unjust dismissal.

Claims often allege that the performance management system discriminated against employees on the basis of one of the protected grounds identified in human rights legislation such as age or sex. Many performance measures are subjective, and measurement errors, such as those described earlier in the chapter, can easily occur.

With regard to lawsuits filed on the grounds of unjust dismissal, the usual claim is that the person was dismissed for reasons besides the ones that the employer states. In this type of situation, courts generally focus on the employer's performance management system, looking to see whether the dismissal could have been based on poor performance. To defend itself, the employer would need a performance management system that provides evidence to support its employment decisions.

To protect against both kinds of legal challenges, it is important to have a performance management system based on valid job analyses, as described in Chapter 3, with the requirements for job success clearly communicated to employees. Performance measurement should evaluate behaviours or results, on the basis of objective criteria. The organization should use multiple raters (including self-appraisals) and train raters in how to use the system. The organization should provide for a review of all performance ratings by upper-level managers and set up a system for employees to appeal when they believe they were evaluated unfairly. Along with feedback, the system should include a process for coaching or training employees to help them improve, rather than simply dismissing poor performers. Supervisors must also be careful to ensure performance feedback does not go beyond "reasonable criticism." The Ontario Court of Appeal provided guidance to what a supervisor can and cannot do in the context of performance appraisal and performance improvement in the case of Viren Shah, a 12-year employee at Xerox Canada Ltd. The court determined that Shah's manager passed beyond the "bounds of reasonableness" when Shah received critical performance reviews that were not based on any substantiated concerns and the manager's behaviour was described as "authoritarian, impatient, and intolerant."[48] As discussed in Chapter 2, provinces including Ontario, Saskatchewan, and Quebec have passed legislation that expands the definition of harassment, but employees in other provinces also have protection from employers who go too far in their criticism of employees.[49]

EMPLOYEE MONITORING AND EMPLOYEE PRIVACY

Computer technology and other types of employee monitoring now support many performance management systems. Organizations often store records of employees' performance ratings, disciplinary actions, and work-rule violations in electronic databases. Many companies use personal computers to monitor productivity and other performance measures electronically.

Although electronic monitoring can improve productivity, it also generates privacy concerns. Critics point out that an employer should not monitor employees when it has no reason to believe that anything is wrong. They complain that monitoring systems threaten to make the workplace an electronic sweatshop in which employees are treated as robots, robbing them of dignity. Some note that employees' performance should be measured by accomplishments, not just time spent at a desk or workbench. Electronic systems should not be a substitute for careful management. Monitoring may be used

THINKING ETHICALLY

Do Financial Goals Get Managers in Trouble?

The owners of a corporation naturally expect the company's managers and employees to work to increase the company's value (often expressed in terms of its stock price). Other basic financial goals for a business are to increase profits through greater sales or lower costs. But can a company's people focus on those goals too much?

Susan Annunzio of the Hudson Highland Center for High Performance conducted a study in which she concluded that the main cause of employees' difficulties in improving profits and innovating was an excessive focus on short-term financial results. When she talked to employees about their group's performance, 10 percent said they worked in high-performing groups, and 38 percent said they working in "nonperforming" groups. Of those in the nonperforming groups, one-third said their groups used to be high-performing, but they began to fail when managers started raising their standards at the same time they were reducing budgets and staff.

Why does that happen? One opinion is that managers feel pressured to keep cutting costs to deliver greater profits in each quarterly financial statement. They can eliminate valuable employees, and the remainder feel their jobs are becoming impossible. Organizational psychologist Richard Hagberg worked with a sales vice-president who was urged to meet daily sales targets yet at the same time to cut staff to meet profit goals. The vice-president wanted to plan improvements to the product line and develop a new competitive strategy, but his time was spent figuring out how to squeeze more work from a shrinking staff.

Other employees fear that the only way to meet targets is through unethical practices such as faking their performance data. Annunzio interviewed a factory manager who was given the goal of reducing operating costs. The manager thought of ways to meet the target within a month, but he spread the improvements over a year so that his boss wouldn't immediately come back with a stiffer goal for him to meet.

SOURCES: Jim Spigener, "Leaders Who 'Get' Safety: Values and Personality Shape Personal Ethics," *Industrial Safety & Hygiene News*, October 2009, Business & Company Resource Center, http://galenet.galegroup.com; and Robert Giagnon, "More than a Legacy," *CA Magazine*, September 2009, Business & Company Resource Center, http://galenet.galegroup.com.

QUESTIONS

1. Who benefits when a company's employees are focused on making the company more profitable?
2. Do goals related to short-term profits—for this month or this quarter ever conflict with longer-term goals? Explain. Do these goals conflict with ethical standards? Explain.
3. Imagine that you are one of the managers described in this story or another manager who believes you cannot meet financial targets without deception or harm to the company. What should you do?

---

more positively to gather information for coaching employees and helping them develop their skills.

When monitoring is necessary, managers should communicate the reasons for using it. For example, companies argue that global positioning systems (GPS) are used to improve the efficiency of locating, dispatching, and routing employees to job sites. However, GPS systems may be used to create a *geofence*—an invisible boundary based on GPS tracking software that alerts the boss by email or instant messaging if any employee strays outside his or her designated work area.[50] Canada's Privacy Commissioner, Jennifer Stoddard cautions employers to consider the privacy rights of workers before they install GPS in their vehicle fleets and to clearly explain to employees how GPS will be used.[51] As discussed in Chapter 2, the federal Personal Information Protection and Electronic Documents Act (PIPEDA) has additional implications for performance management. For example, organizations are required to ensure that personal information including an employee's performance review is securely protected, retained only for a specified time, and accessible to the employee.

SUMMARY

L01 ► **Identify the activities involved in performance management.**

- Performance management is the process through which managers ensure that employees' activities and outputs contribute to the organization's goals.
- The organization begins by specifying which aspects of performance are relevant; the relevant aspects of performance are measured through performance appraisal; and finally, in performance feedback sessions, managers provide employees with information about their performance so they can modify their behaviour to meet the organization's goals.

L02 ► **Discuss the purposes of performance management systems.**

- Organizations establish performance management systems to meet three broad purposes:
  - *Strategic purpose.* Meeting business objectives by helping to link employees' behaviour with the organization's goals.
  - *Administrative purpose.* Providing information for day-to-day decisions about salary, benefits, recognition, and retention or termination.
  - *Developmental purpose.* Using the system as a basis for developing employees' knowledge and skills.

L03 ► **Define five criteria for measuring the effectiveness of a performance management system.**

- Performance measures should fit with the organization's strategy by supporting its goals and culture.
- Performance measures should be valid, that is, measure all the relevant aspects of performance and not measure irrelevant aspects of performance.
- Measures should provide interrater and test-retest reliability, that is, appraisals are consistent among raters and over time.
- Measures should be acceptable to the people who use them or receive feedback from them.
- Finally, a performance measure should specifically tell employees what is expected of them and how they can meet those expectations.

L04 ► **Compare the major methods for measuring performance.**

- Performance measurement may use ranking systems such as simple ranking, forced distribution, or paired comparisons to compare one individual's performance with that of other employees.

- Although time-consuming, and may be seen as unfair under some circumstances, ranking counteracts some forms of rater bias and helps distinguish employees for administrative decisions.
- Other approaches involve rating employees' attributes, behaviours, or outcomes. Rating attributes is relatively simple but not always valid and requires a great deal of information, but these methods can be very effective.
- Rating results, such as productivity or achievement of objectives, tends to be less subjective than other kinds of rating; however, validity may be a problem because of factors outside the employee's control.
- A balanced scorecard is a widely used strategic approach.

L05 ► **Describe major sources of performance information in terms of their advantages and disadvantages.**

- Performance information may come from an employee's self-appraisal and from appraisals by the employee's manager, employees, peers, and customers.
- Organizations may combine many sources into a 360-degree performance appraisal.
- Employees' supervisors may produce accurate information, and peers are an excellent source of information about performance in a job where the supervisor does not often observe the employee. Disadvantages are that friendships (or rivalries) may bias ratings and peers may be uncomfortable with the role of rating a friend. Direct reports often have the best chance to see how a manager treats employees; however, employees may be reluctant to contribute candid opinions about a supervisor unless they can provide information anonymously.
- Self-appraisals may be biased, but they do come from the person with the most knowledge of the employee's behaviour on the job, and they provide a basis for discussion in feedback sessions, opening up fruitful comparisons and areas of disagreement between the self-appraisal and other appraisals.
- Customers may be an excellent source of performance information, although obtaining customer feedback tends to be expensive.

L06 ► **Define types of rating errors and explain how to minimize them.**

- A common tendency is to give higher evaluations to people we consider similar to ourselves.

- Other errors involve using only part of the rating scale or contrasting an employee unfavourably with very high performers.

- Giving all employees ratings at the high end of the scale is called leniency error. Rating everyone at the low end of the scale is called strictness error. Rating at or near the middle is called central tendency.

- Basing an employee's rating only on the most recent work performed is called recency emphasis; and focusing on activities—for example, how busy the employee looks, rather than results—is also problematic. Halo/horns error refers to rating employees positively/negatively in all areas because of strong/weak performance observed in one area.

- Ways to reduce rater error are training raters to be aware of their tendencies to make rating errors and training them to be sensitive to the complex nature of employee performance so they will consider many aspects of performance in greater depth.

- Politics also may influence ratings. Organizations can minimize appraisal politics by establishing a fair appraisal system, and bringing managers together to discuss ratings in calibration meetings.

L07 ▸ Explain how to effectively provide performance feedback.

- Performance feedback should be a regular, scheduled management activity, carried out in a way that both parties feel heard, understood, and respected.

- Managers should prepare by establishing a neutral location, emphasizing that the feedback session will be a chance for discussion and asking the employee to prepare a self-assessment.

- During the feedback session, managers should strive for a problem-solving approach and encourage employees to voice their opinions and discuss performance goals. The manager should look for opportunities to reinforce desired behaviour and should limit criticism. The discussion should focus on behaviour and results rather than on personalities.

L08 ▸ Summarize ways to achieve performance improvement.

- If an employee is motivated but lacks ability, provide training, give detailed feedback about performance, and consider restructuring the job.

- For an employee with ability but lacking motivation, investigate whether outside problems are a distraction, and if so refer the employee for help.

- If the problem has to do with the employee not feeling appreciated or rewarded, try to meet the employee's needs and evaluate whether additional rewards are appropriate.

- For an employee lacking both ability and motivation, consider whether the employee is a good fit for the position. Specific feedback or withholding rewards may spur improvement, or the employee may have to be demoted or terminated.

- Solid employees who are high in ability and motivation will continue so and may be able to contribute even more if the manager provides appropriate direct feedback, rewards, and opportunities for development.

L09 ▸ Discuss legal and ethical issues that affect performance management.

- Lawsuits related to performance management usually involve charges of discrimination, psychological harassment, or unjust dismissal.

- Managers must make sure that performance management systems and decisions treat employees equally, without regard to their age, sex, or other protected grounds.

- A system is more likely to be legally defensible if it is based on behaviours and results, and if multiple raters evaluate each person's performance. The system should also include a process for coaching and training employees.

- An ethical issue of performance management is the use of employee monitoring. This type of performance measurement provides detailed, accurate information, but employees may find it unwelcome.

Critical Thinking Questions

1. How does a complete performance management system differ from the use of annual performance appraisals only?
2. Give two examples of an administrative decision that would be based on performance management information. Give two examples of developmental decisions based on this type of information.
3. How can involving employees in the creation of performance standards improve the effectiveness of a performance management system? Consider the criteria for effectiveness listed in the chapter.
4. Consider how you might rate the performance of three instructors from whom you are currently taking a course. (If you are currently taking only one or two courses, consider this course and two you recently completed.)
   a. Would it be harder to *rate* the instructors' performance or to *rank* their performance? Why?
   b. Write three items to use in rating the instructors—one each to rate them in terms of a competency, a behaviour, and an outcome.

c. Which of the three items do you think is most valid? Most reliable? Why?

d. Many educational institutions use surveys or questionnaires to gather data from students about their instructors' performance. Would it be appropriate to use the data for administrative decisions? Developmental decisions? Other decisions? Why or why not?

5. Imagine that a pet supply store is establishing a new performance management system to help employees provide better customer service. Management needs to decide who should participate in measuring the performance of each of the store's salespeople. From what sources should the store gather information? Why?

6. Would the same sources be appropriate if the store in Question 5 will use the performance appraisals to support decisions about which employees to promote? Explain.

7. Suppose you were recently promoted to a supervisory job in a company where you have worked for two years. You genuinely like almost all your co-workers, who now report to you. The only exception is one employee, who dresses more formally than the others and frequently tells jokes that embarrass you and the other workers. Given your preexisting feelings for the employees, how can you measure their performance fairly and effectively?

8. Continuing the example in Question 7, imagine that you are preparing for your first performance feedback session. You want the feedback to be effective—that is, you want the feedback to result in improved performance. List five or six steps you can take to achieve your goal.

9. Besides giving employees feedback, what steps can a manager take to improve employees' performance?

10. Suppose you are a human resource professional helping to improve the performance management system of a company that sells and services office equipment. The company operates a call centre that takes calls from customers having problems with their equipment. Call centre employees are supposed to verify that the problem is not one the customer can easily handle (e.g., equipment that will not operate because it has come unplugged). Then, if the problem is not resolved over the phone, the employees arrange for service technicians to visit the customer. The company can charge the customer only if a service technician visits, so performance management of the call centre employees focuses on productivity—how quickly they can complete a call and move on to the next caller. To measure this performance efficiently and accurately, the company uses employee monitoring.

a. How would you expect the employees to react to the monitoring? How might the organization address the employees' concerns?

b. Besides productivity in terms of number of calls, what other performance measures should the performance management system include?

c. How should the organization gather information about the other performance measures?

What's Your HR IQ?

 Connect offers more ways to check what you've learned so far. Find experiential exercises, Test Your Knowledge quizzes, videos, and many other resources to gauge your HR IQ.

CASE STUDY 7.1:   Performance Management Takes a Page from Facebook

In the world of Facebook and Twitter, people love to hear feedback about what they're up to. But sit them down for a performance review, and suddenly the experience becomes traumatic.

New companies are taking a page from social networking sites to make the performance management process more fun and useful. Accenture has developed a Facebook-style program called Performance Multiplier in which among other things employees post status updates, photos, and two or three weekly goals that can be viewed by fellow staffers. Even more immediate: software from Toronto startup, Rypple, lets people post Twitter-length questions about their performance in exchange for anonymous feedback. Companies ranging from sandwich chain Great Harvest Bread Company to Mozilla have signed on as clients. When Facebook recently decided to update its performance review process it also chose Rypple, which offered significant appeal to both Facebook employees and managers.

Such initiatives end the dreaded rite of annual reviews by making performance feedback a much more real-time and ongoing process. Stanford University management professor Robert Sutton argues that performance reviews "mostly suck" because they're conceived from the top rather than designed with employees' needs in mind. "If you have regular conversations with people, and they know where they stand, then the performance evaluation is maybe unnecessary," says Sutton.

What Rypple's and Accenture's tools do is create a process in which evaluations become dynamic—and more democratic. Rypple, for example, gives employees the chance to post brief, 140-character questions, such as "What did you think of my presentation?" or "How can I run meetings better?" The queries are emailed to managers, peers, or anyone else the user selects. Short anonymous responses are then aggregated and sent back, providing a quick-and-dirty 360-degree review. The basic service is free. But corporate clients can pay for a premium version that includes tech support, extra security, and analysis of which topics figure highest in employee posts. Rypple's co-founders have also launched software called TouchBase that's meant to replace the standard annual review with quick monthly surveys and discussions.

Accenture's software, which it's using internally and hoping to sell to outside clients, is more about motivating employees than it is about measuring them. With help from management guru Marcus Buckingham, the consultancy's product has a similar look and feel to other corporate social networks. The major difference is that users are expected to post brief goals for the week on their profile page, as well as a couple for each quarter. If they don't, the lack of goals is visible to their managers, who are also alerted to the omission by email. By prompting people to document and adjust their goals constantly, Accenture hopes the formal discussion will improve. You don't have to desperately re-create examples of what you've done," says Buckingham. Typically,

"managers and employees are scrambling to fill [evaluation forms] out in the 24 hours before HR calls saying 'where's yours?'"

If having your performance goals posted for the world to see sounds a bit Orwellian, consider this: Rypple reports that two-thirds of the questions posted on its service come from managers wanting feedback about business questions or their own performance. The biggest payoff of these social network-style tools may prove to be better performance by the boss.

Questions

1. Based on the information given, discuss how well Performance Multiplier and Rypple meet the criteria for effective performance management: fit with strategy, validity, reliability, acceptability, and specific feedback.

2. How suitable would these tools be for fulfilling the strategic, administrative, and developmental purposes of performance management?

3. Think of a job you currently hold, used to have, or would like to have. Imagine that this employer introduced Performance Multiplier or Rypple to your workplace. Describe one aspect of performance you would like to seek feedback about, and identify which people you would ask to provide that feedback. What concerns, if any, would you have about using one of these programs to seek feedback about your performance?

SOURCES: Jena McGregor, "Performance Review Takes a Page from Facebook," *Business Week*, March 2, 2009, www.businessweek.com; and Iain Marlow, "Fixing the Dreaded Performance Review," *Globe and Mail*, July 15, 2011, B13.

CASE STUDY 7.2:   When Good Reviews Go Bad

Based on her performance reviews at Merrill Lynch, Kathleen Bostjancic was amazing, at least for a few years. In one appraisal report, her boss said Bostjancic "continues to deliver top-caliber product," and he wrote, "Her judgment is impeccable." After three years, her pay more than doubled to reflect her apparent value to the company.

Then something changed; Bostjanic noticed the difference around the time she took a maternity leave. Her economist boss phoned and asked her to take on a newly created position, Washington policy analyst. But when she returned to work with a plan for the position, her plan was rejected, and tension grew. A year later, Bostjancic's boss issued a memo advising her that her work must "improve dramatically." Seven months later, she was told that she was being laid off in a downsizing effort; the company hired a replacement two months afterward.

A former Citigroup employee also recalls that good reviews before maternity leave didn't do much to help her situation when she returned to work. Wan Li says one performance appraisal after another reported she

was exceeding expectations. Then as she neared maternity leave, she was transferred from a key job in the Structured Trade Finance Group to a support position that would (Li recalls being told) be "more manageable" for her. Upon her return from maternity leave, Li tried to transfer from her temporary support post to a revenue-generating job, but she was instead transferred to another support role. Three years later, following a second maternity leave, Li received a call announcing that her job had been eliminated in a "restructuring."

At Bank of Tokyo-Mitsubishi, Paula Best was progressing well in her career. She was responsible for securities lending and apparently handled the responsibility well enough that the bank added management of international lending to the scope of her job. Best thought she should be made a vice-president, like the other employees who reported to the department manager of securities lending. What was holding back her promotion? It wasn't her performance according to the appraisals; she was rated at the level of "Achieves +", and Best recalls that her vice-president promised her a promotion. After two more years and still no promotion, Best complained to the bank's HR department that she believed she was a victim of sex and race discrimination. Soon thereafter, Best and four other employees in her department were laid off.

How could these three employees with glowing performance appraisals be laid off by the institutions that once seemed to value them? Of course, one possibility is that the recent financial crisis required all of these institutions to make hard choices among many valued employees. It's also possible that the three women's performance deteriorated in the time after their last favourable review. Two of the three employers have publicly claimed that their decisions were justified. Merrill Lynch has said that Bostjancic's manager treated her appropriately after maternity leave; Bank of Tokyo says it fully investigated Best's complaints and found that management had made appropriate decisions given her level of responsibility.

Whether or not these decisions were justified, they have proved costly in terms of negative publicity and legal actions. Bostjancic filed a discrimination lawsuit, which is ongoing as of this writing. Li filed a discrimination lawsuit against Citigroup, which was settled to avoid further expense. Best is part of a class-action lawsuit filed against Bank of Tokyo. Meanwhile, among the hundreds of thousands of financial-industry jobs lost in the financial crisis, almost three-quarters of the layoffs have involved women. Notable examples include Zoe Cruz, who had been co-president at Morgan Stanley, and Erin Callan, formerly chief financial officer at Lehman Brothers. The impact is especially dramatic in top-level jobs, where women were already scarce. In one recent survey of executives across industries, 19 percent of women said they'd been laid off in the past two years, compared with 6 percent of male executives.

Questions

1. Which purposes of performance management did the appraisals described in this case fulfill? Which purposes did they *not* fulfill?

2. How can managers and HR departments minimize the likelihood of disputes arising over whether employees are continuing to perform at the same level?

3. If you had been in the HR departments of the companies described in this case, and the employees had come to you with their concerns, what would you have done in each situation?

SOURCES: Anita Raghavan, "Terminated: Why the Women of Wall Street Are Disappearing," *Forbes,* March 16, 2009, Business & Company Resource Center, http://galenet.co; Alan Kline and Rebecca Sausner, "Taking Charge in Turbulent Times," *US Banker,* October 1, 2009, Business & Company Resource Center, http://galenet.galegroup.com; and Geraldine Fabrikant, "Bank of America Hires Former Top Citigroup Executive," *The New York Times,* August 4, 2009, Business & Company Resource Center, http://galenet.galegroup.com.

Part 4

COMPENSATING
and Rewarding Human Resources

{ Chapter 8
Total Rewards

Real People and HR

...Deborah Samagalski, Director, Total Rewards—EPCOR Utilities Inc.

Deborah leads the Total Rewards team in EPCOR's human resources department, which encompasses all compensation, pension, benefits, wellness, Human Resource Information Service (HRIS), strategic management, and administration. She has also worked on various corporate acquisitions, including EPCOR's most recent transition of American Water (Arizona and New Mexico) into the newly created EPCOR Water (USA) Inc.

Prior to working at EPCOR, Deborah worked in Total Rewards departments ranging from a world headquarters to an individual country perspective. Her extensive experience across several industries (computing, financial, engineering, and utilities) was developed through positions based in the U.S., South Pacific, and Canada.

Deborah has a bachelor of commerce degree from the University of Alberta and her list of memberships includes the WorldatWork Association, Canadian Pension and Benefits Institute (CPBI), Conference Board Compensation Research Centre (CRC), and Employer Committee on Health Care (ECHC). Deborah is an active sponsor and volunteer for Autism Speaks Canada as well as a strong proponent of Health and Wellness within EPCOR and in her personal life.

Name...
Deborah Samagalski

Job...
Director, Total Rewards—EPCOR Utilities Ltd.

Adjective people would use to describe you...
Dedicated. Always a person first and position second—the foundation to a great team.

First job...
Shampoo girl at a hair salon (at 12 years old)—learned to take initiative and developed various interpersonal skills.

First HR job...
AIESEC intern in HR at NCR World Headquarters (Dayton, Ohio)—worked on Asia/South Pacific headcount reporting, roll up of country submissions for compensation sales incentives, and managed expatriate employees within the Pacific group.

Most challenging aspect of your job...
Encouraging 'big-picture' thinking and facilitating HR program integration with organizational short- and long-term business strategies. Advocating and supporting all HR professionals as true business partners.

Most rewarding aspect of your job...
Making a difference and having an impact on the work experience of my team as well as others in the organization. Getting positive feedback from internal and external stakeholders' with regard to understanding and valuing our contributions along with the programs and strategies we communicate and implement.

EPCOR's approach to Total Rewards...
EPCOR's Total Rewards programs are designed to attract, retain, and motivate employees through market competitive programs; create a performance culture that rewards superior performance; link with the business strategy; and support the corporation's vision of: *People*, *Operational Excellence*, *Environment and Safety*, and *Growth*.

Four essential attributes that make someone a great HR professional...
- Being approachable and considerate—you will be invited into conversations and learning situations that wouldn't otherwise be open to you.
- Being open-minded and thinking big picture—think beyond what you (think you) know and consider all factors from both a short- and longer-term perspective. Always contemplate what and who may be affected.
- Continuous learning—the world is changing at a rapid pace and others are relying on us to know what's going on and to offer innovative ideas for staying ahead of the game.
- Focus on the "how" as much as the "what"—how we interact and perform has as much or more impact as what we do (similar to the 'two ears and one mouth' concept—use them proportionately).

If you had to pick an alternative career...
Communications or public speaking comes to mind first. Leading or being an advocate for an organization or cause and taking tremendous effort to ensure others understood and ultimately supported the same objectives would be my goal. I get very energized by speaking to audiences (small and large) and connecting with them.

Best career advice that you ever received...
Don't limit yourself to what is in your comfort zone. Seek new opportunities, ask loads of questions, and jump in when the time is right.

Advice for someone beginning his/her career...
Don't be in a hurry (unless the opportunity arises, then go for it!). It is *so* important to learn the little things first (build your foundation) and to understand everything from the grass roots level—there is no job that is too menial to start with—you'll be amazed at what you can learn and what people will get you involved in if you just ask questions, offer to get involved, and continuously learn and apply your knowledge.

SOURCE: Reprinted courtesy of Deborah Samagalski.

Chapter **8**

TOTAL REWARDS

Grocery chain Longo's has implemented a total rewards approach to compensating and rewarding employees.

{
What Do I Need to Know?
After reading this chapter, you should be able to:

L01 Discuss how organizations implement a "total rewards" approach to compensating and rewarding employees.

L02 Identify the kinds of decisions and influences involved in providing base pay to employees.

L03 Describe alternatives to job-based pay.

L04 Describe how organizations recognize individual, team, and organizational performance through the use of incentives.

L05 Discuss the role of benefits as part of employee total rewards.

L06 Summarize the types of employee benefits offered by employers.

L07 Discuss the importance of effectively communicating the organization's approach to total rewards.

L08 Discuss issues related to compensating and rewarding executives.

Total Rewards at Longo's

Family-run grocery chain Longo's, in business since 1956 and based in Vaughan, Ontario, has more than doubled its number of employees during the past six years—from 1,800 to 4,400. "When we did our engagement surveys, we weren't getting credit for some of the great things we had in place and there were some clearly identified gaps that needed to be addressed within our total rewards offering," says Liz Volk, vice-president of HR.

Longo's enhanced total rewards approach consists of five parts:

- *Compensation*, e.g., bonus program;
- *Benefits*, e.g., flexible health and dental plan;
- *Growth and Opportunity*, e.g., tuition reimbursement;
- *Recognition and Performance*, e.g., service awards; and
- *Work/Life Balance*, e.g., team sponsorship program.

Longo's is focusing on increasing "visibility and transparency around total rewards." For example, each Longo's employee recently received an individualized rewards statement, which outlines compensation, benefits, and a retirement savings plan, and also includes information about wellness programs, corporate social responsibility, training and development, and other opportunities, says Volk. Longo's also put up total rewards communication boards in each of its 25 stores and managers are encouraged to discuss total rewards in daily team member huddles and direct employees to the total rewards boards to see what's new.[1]

total rewards
A comprehensive approach to compensating and rewarding employees.

Introduction

1,2,5

Many organizations are recognizing the strategic value of adopting a comprehensive approach to compensating and rewarding employees, frequently referred to as **total rewards**. Figure 8.1 shows how a total rewards strategy reflecting the organization's culture, business and HR strategy is a powerful tool to attract, motivate, and retain satisfied employees while achieving desired business results.

Organizations such as Longo's and RBC define their approach to employee compensation and benefits to take into account the "overall work experience provided to employees."[2] Organizations with this total rewards approach create a *value proposition* for current and prospective employees that considers the total value they receive for contributing their time and energy to the company. Because compensation, benefits, and the work experience have a major impact on employee attitudes and behaviours, total rewards influence what kinds of employees are attracted to (and remain with) the organization. A Watson Wyatt survey on strategic rewards and pay practices reported that Canadian companies cited the primary reason for developing a total rewards strategy was to align rewards with the business strategy.[3] As shown in Figure 8.2, the Conference Board of Canada's Compensation Planning Outlook 2012 identified the top rewards activities and priorities for the next 12 to 18

L01 Discuss how organizations implement a "total rewards" approach to compensating and rewarding employees.

Total Rewards Model
Strategies to Attract, Motivate, and Retain Employees

FIGURE 8.1

Total Rewards Model

SOURCE: Courtesy of WorldatWork Canada.

Top Rewards Activities and Priorities

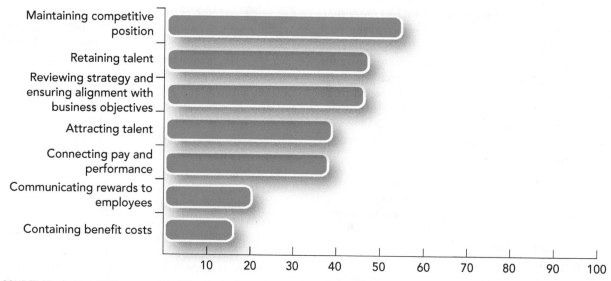

SOURCE: Nicole Stewart, "Compensation Planning Outlook 2012" (Ottawa: Conference Board of Canada, October 2007), p. 12. Reprinted with the permission of the Conference Board of Canada.

months include: maintaining competitive position; retaining talent; reviewing strategy and ensuring alignment with business objectives; attracting talent; and connecting pay and performance.[4]

Employees care about policies affecting their compensation, benefits, and the work experience itself because the policies affect the employee's income, well-being, and security. Also, employees consider these elements a sign of status and success. They attach great importance to compensation and rewards when they evaluate their relationship and satisfaction with their employers. As the workforce becomes increasingly diverse, the definition of what employees expect in exchange for their work will become increasingly complex. For example, Table 8.1 provides some

total compensation
All types of financial rewards and tangible benefits and services employees receive as part of their employment.

generational total rewards preferences for consideration. This chapter addresses total rewards, however, the primary emphasis will be on forms of **total compensation**, that is, direct and indirect compensation including base pay, incentives, and benefits received in exchange for the employee's contribution of time, talent, effort, and results.[5] In addition, Chapter 1 discussed attributes of work environments where employees are more likely to experience satisfaction and engagement, Chapter 6 explored learning and development opportunities provided employees, and Chapter 7 examined performance processes. A comprehensive "Total Rewards Inventory" checklist outlining elements that could be included in an organization's value proposition is provided in Figure 8.3.

TABLE 8.1   Generational Emphasis Within Total Rewards

Traditionalist (1922–1945)	Incentives and stocks, promotions, health benefits (life/disability), pensions, stability, formal recogntion, community involvement
Baby Boomers (1946–1964)	High-visibility projects, promotions, support around work/life issues, personal learning and development, onsite facilities, industry recognition
Gen-X (1965–1980)	Training and development, challenging tasks/stretch assignments, independent work environment, project variety, work/life balance, flexible work arrangements, variable pay
Gen-Y (1981–2000)	Meaningfulness of work/projects, manager feedback, casual work environment, daily work/life balance, access to senior leaders, mentoring, social activities, community involvement, flextime

SOURCE: Adapted from Adwoa K. Buahene and Giselle Kovary, "The Great Divide," *HR Professional*, October/November 2007, p. 27.

FIGURE 8.3

Total Rewards Inventory

To get a comprehensive view of your organization's value proposition, simply check off the rewards your organization currently provides.

Compensation	Benefits	Work/Life		Performance & Recognition	Development & Career Opportunities
Base Wages ☐ Salary Pay ☐ Hourly Pay ☐ Piece Rate Pay **Premium Pay** ☐ Shift Differential Pay ☐ Weekend/Holiday Pay ☐ On-Call Pay ☐ Call-In Pay ☐ Hazard Pay ☐ Bilingual Pay ☐ Skill-Based Pay **Variable Pay** ☐ Commissions ☐ Team-Based Pay ☐ Bonus Programs 　☐ Referral Bonus 　☐ Hiring Bonus 　☐ Retention Bonus 　☐ Project Completion Bonus ☐ Incentive Pay 　Short-Term: 　☐ Profit Sharing 　☐ Individual Performance–Based Incentives 　☐ Performance-Sharing Incentives 　Long-Term: 　☐ Restricted Stock 　☐ Performance Shares 　☐ Performance Units 　☐ Stock Options/Grants	**Legally Required/Mandated** ☐ Employment Insurance ☐ Workers' Compensation Insurance ☐ Canada Pension Plan/Quebec Pension Plan **Health & Welfare** ☐ Medical Plan ☐ Dental Plan ☐ Vision Plan ☐ Prescription Drug Plan ☐ Flexible Spending Accounts (FSAs) ☐ Health Reimbursement Accounts (HRAs) ☐ Health Savings Accounts (HSAs) ☐ Life Insurance ☐ Spouse/Dependent Life Insurance ☐ AD&D Insurance ☐ Short-Term/Long-Term Disability Insurance **Retirement** ☐ Defined Benefit Plan ☐ Defined Contribution Plan ☐ Profit-Sharing Plan ☐ Hybrid Plan **Pay for Time Not Worked** ☐ Vacation ☐ Holiday ☐ Sick Leave ☐ Bereavement Leave ☐ Leaves of Absence (personal, medical, family)	**Workplace Flexibility/ Alternative Work Arrangements** ☐ Flextime ☐ Flexible Schedules ☐ Telecommuting ☐ Alternative Work Sites ☐ Compressed Workweek ☐ Job Sharing ☐ Part-Time Employment ☐ Seasonal Schedules **Paid and Unpaid Time Off** ☐ Maternity/Family Leave ☐ Sabbaticals **Health and Wellness** ☐ Employee Assistance Programs ☐ On-Site Fitness Facilities ☐ Discounted Fitness Club Rates ☐ Preventive Care Programs ☐ Weight Management Programs ☐ Smoking Cessation Assistance ☐ On-Site Massages ☐ Stress Management Programs ☐ Voluntary Immunization Clinics ☐ Wellness Initiatives ☐ Health Screenings ☐ Nutritional Counselling ☐ On-Site Nurse ☐ Business Travel Health Services ☐ Occupational Health Programs ☐ Disability Management ☐ Return-to-Work Programs ☐ Reproductive Health/Pregnancy Programs **Community Involvement** ☐ Community Volunteer Programs ☐ Matching Gift Programs ☐ Shared Leave Programs ☐ Disaster Relief Funds ☐ Sponsorships/Grants ☐ In-Kind Donations	**Caring for Dependants** ☐ Dependant Care Reimbursement Accounts ☐ Dependant Care Travel-Related Expense Reimbursement ☐ Dependant Care Referral and Resource Services ☐ Dependant Care Discount Programs or Vouchers ☐ Emergency Dependant Care Services ☐ Childcare Subsidies ☐ On-Site Caregiver Support Groups ☐ On-Site Dependant Care ☐ Adoption Assistance Services ☐ After-School Care Programs ☐ University and college/Scholarship Information ☐ Scholarships ☐ Mother's Privacy Rooms ☐ Summer Camps and Activities **Financial Support** ☐ Financial Planning Services and Education ☐ Adoption Reimbursement ☐ Transit Subsidies ☐ Savings Bonds **Voluntary Benefits** ☐ Long-Term Care ☐ Auto/Home Insurance ☐ Pet Insurance ☐ Legal Insurance ☐ Identity Theft Insurance ☐ Employee Discounts ☐ Concierge Services ☐ Transit Passes ☐ Parking **Culture Change Initiatives** ☐ Work Redesign ☐ Team Effectiveness ☐ Diversity/Inclusion Initiatives ☐ Work Environment Initiatives	**Performance** ☐ Manager/Employee 1:1 Meetings ☐ Performance Reviews ☐ Project Completion/Team Evaluations ☐ Performance Planning/Goal-Setting Sessions **Recognition** ☐ Service Awards ☐ Retirement Awards ☐ Peer Recognition Awards ☐ Spot Awards ☐ Managerial Recognition Programs ☐ Organization-Wide Recognition Programs ☐ Exceeding Performance Awards ☐ Employee of the Month/Year Awards ☐ Appreciation Luncheons, Outings, Formal Events ☐ Goal-Specific Awards (quality, efficiency, cost savings, productivity, safety) ☐ Employee Suggestion Programs	**Learning Opportunities** ☐ Tuition Reimbursement ☐ Tuition Discounts ☐ Corporate Universities ☐ New Technology Training ☐ On-the-Job Learning ☐ Attendance at Outside Seminars and Conferences ☐ Access to Virtual Learning, Podcasts, Webinars ☐ Self-Development Tools **Coaching/Mentoring** ☐ Leadership Training ☐ Exposure to Resident Experts ☐ Access to Information Networks ☐ Formal or Informal Mentoring Programs **Advancement Opportunities** ☐ Internships ☐ Apprenticeships ☐ Overseas Assignments ☐ Internal Job Postings ☐ Job Advancement/Promotion ☐ Career Ladders and Pathways ☐ Succession Planning ☐ On/Off Ramps Through Career Lifecycle ☐ Job Rotations

SOURCE: Based on WorldatWork "Your Total Rewards Inventory," p. 4, retrieved May 5, 2008.

This chapter opens by describing the role of **direct compensation**, all types of financial rewards employees receive as part of their employment, and defines the kinds of influences on managers making pay level decisions. We describe methods of evaluating jobs and market data to develop effective pay structures. Next, we look at the elements of incentive pay systems. The many kinds of incentive pay fall into three broad categories: incentives linked to individual, team, or organizational performance. Choices from these categories should consider not only their strengths and weaknesses, but also their fit with the organization's goals. This chapter also looks at **indirect compensation**, the benefits and services employees receive in exchange for their work, including the important role benefits play. The chapter also covers why and how organizations should effectively communicate with employees about their total rewards. Finally, this chapter looks at an issue also linked to organizational performance—executive compensation.

Decisions About Base Pay

5

Because pay is important both in its effect on employees and on account of its cost, organizations need to plan what they will pay employees in each job. An unplanned approach, in which each employee's pay is independently negotiated, will likely result in unfairness, dissatisfaction, and rates that are either overly expensive or so low that positions are hard to fill. Organizations therefore make decisions about two aspects of pay structure: job structure and pay level. **Job structure** consists of the relative pay for different jobs within the organization. It establishes relative pay among different functions and different levels of responsibility. For example, job structure defines the difference in pay between an entry-level accountant and an entry-level assembler, as well as the difference between an entry-level accountant, the accounting department manager, and the organization's comptroller. **Pay level** is the average amount (including wages, salaries, and incentives) the organization pays for a particular job. Together, job structure and pay levels establish a **pay structure** that helps the organization achieve goals related to employee motivation, cost control, and the ability to attract and retain talented human resources.

The organization's job structure and pay levels are policies of the organization. Establishing a pay structure simplifies the process of making decisions about individual employees' pay by grouping together employees with similar jobs. As shown, in Figure 8.4, human resource

---

direct compensation
Financial rewards employees receive in exchange for their work.

indirect compensation
The benefits and services employees receive in exchange for their work.

job structure
The relative pay for different jobs within the organization.

pay level
The average amount (including wages, salaries, and bonuses) the organization pays for a particular job.

pay structure
The pay policy resulting from job structure and pay-level decisions.

LO2 Identify the kinds of decisions and influences involved in providing base pay to employees.

FIGURE 8.4

Issues in Developing a Pay Structure

Legal Requirements
- Human rights
- Employment/ labour standards
- Pay equity

Market Forces
- Product markets
- Labour markets

Organization's Goals
- High-quality workforce
- Cost control
- Equity and fairness
- Legal compliance

Pay Level Decision
Job Structure Decision
Pay Structure Decision
- Pay rates
- Pay grades
- Pay ranges
- Pay differentials

professionals develop this pay structure based on legal requirements, market forces, and the organization's goals, such as attracting a high-quality workforce and meeting principles of fairness.

What Are the Legal Requirements?

All of an organization's decisions about compensation and rewards, need to at least comply with the applicable laws. As discussed in Chapter 2, although these laws differ across federal, provincial, and territorial jurisdictions, a common core of legal requirements exists.

1,5

- *Human rights legislation*—Employers may not base differences in rewards on an employee's age, sex, race, or other prohibited grounds of discrimination. Any differences in pay must instead be tied to such business-related considerations as job responsibilities or performance.
- *Employment/labour standards acts*—The Canada Labour Code and the relevant provincial and territorial laws include minimum requirements for wages, hours of work, overtime pay, vacation, statutory holidays, as well as other specific provisions. Executives, professionals, administrative, and outside sales employees are usually considered "exempt" employees and are not eligible for certain provisions such as overtime pay that "non-exempt" employees receive.
- *Pay equity legislation*—Pay equity legislation is in place federally and in several provincial jurisdictions, and attempts to address the wage gap between female and male-dominated jobs to

ensure that jobs of equal value within the organization receive similar rates of pay. Organizations use job evaluation (described later in the chapter) to establish the worth of an organization's jobs in terms of such criteria as their difficulty and their importance to the organization. The employer then compares the evaluation points awarded to each job with the pay for each job. If jobs have the same number of evaluation points, they should be paid equally.

Economic Influences on Pay

An organization cannot make spending decisions independently of the economy. Organizations must keep costs low enough that they can sell their products profitably, yet they must be able to attract workers in a competitive labour market. Decisions about how to respond to the economic forces of product markets and labour markets limit an organization's choices about pay structure.

2,3,4,5

PRODUCT AND LABOUR MARKETS

The organization's *product market* includes organizations that offer competing goods and services—competing to serve the same customers. Organizations under pressure to cut labour costs may respond by reducing staff levels, freezing pay levels, postponing hiring decisions, or requiring employees to bear more of the cost of benefits such as insurance premiums. However, organizations also compete to obtain human resources in *labour markets*—competing with other firms to hire the same skilled employees.

Two employees who do the same job cannot be paid different wages because of gender, race, age or other prohibited grounds of discrimination. It would be illegal to pay these two employees differently because one is male and the other is female. Only if there are differences in their experience, skills, seniority, or job performance are there legal reasons why their pay might be different.

PAY LEVEL: DECIDING WHAT TO PAY

Although legal requirements and economic influences limit organizations' choices about pay levels, there is a range within which organizations can make decisions.[6] The size of this range depends on the details of the organization's competitive environment. If many workers are competing for a few jobs, employers will have more choice, however, in tight labour markets workers will have more choice.

When organizations have a broad range in which to make decisions about pay, they can choose to pay at, above, or below the rate set by market forces. Economic theory holds that the most profitable level, all things being equal, would be at the market rate. Often, however, all things are *not* equal from one employer to another. For instance, an organization may gain an advantage by paying above the market rate if it uses the higher pay as one means to attract top talent and then uses these excellent employees' knowledge to be more innovative, produce higher quality, or work more efficiently.

This approach is based on the view of employees as resources. Higher pay may be an investment in superior human resources. Having higher labour costs than your competitors is not necessarily bad if you also have the best and most effective workforce, which produces more products of better quality. Pay policies are one of the most important human resource tools for encouraging desired employee behaviours and discouraging undesired behaviours. Therefore, organizations must evaluate pay as more than a cost, but also as an investment that can generate returns in attracting, retaining, and motivating a high-quality workforce. Of course, employers do not always have this much flexibility. Some companies are under intense pressure to charge low prices for their products, and some companies are trying to draw workers from a pool that is too small to satisfy all employers' needs.

> **benchmarking**
> A procedure in which an organization compares its own practices against those of successful competitors.

GATHERING INFORMATION ABOUT MARKET PAY

To compete for talent, organizations use **benchmarking**, a procedure in which an organization compares its own practices against those of successful competitors. In terms of compensation, benchmarking involves the use of pay surveys. These provide information about the going rates of pay at competitors in the organization's product and labour markets. An organization can conduct its own surveys, but the federal government and other organizations make a great deal of data available already.

For example, the federal government's Job Futures website (www.jobfutures.org) provides earnings data by province, territory, and nationally, for occupations listed in the National Occupational Classification (NOC). Many industry, trade, and professional groups also collect wage and salary data. Employers should check with the relevant groups to see what surveys are available. Consulting firms also will provide data, including the results of international surveys, and can tailor data to the organization's particular needs. Human resource professionals need to determine whether to gather data focusing on particular industries, regions, or on job categories.

HOW DO EMPLOYEES JUDGE PAY FAIRNESS?

4,5

In developing a pay structure, it is important to keep in mind employees' perceptions about fairness. If employees perceive their pay as unfair they may experience pay dissatisfaction and be less motivated to achieve organizational goals. Employees evaluate their pay relative to the pay of other employees. Social scientists have studied this kind of comparison and developed *equity theory* to describe how people make judgments about fairness.[7] According to equity theory, people measure outcomes such as pay in terms of their inputs. For example, an employee might think of her pay in terms of her degree, her three years of experience, and her 45+ hour workweeks.

To decide whether a certain level of pay is equitable, the person compares her ratio of outcomes and inputs with other people's outcome/input ratios. The person in the previous example might notice that an employee with less education or experience is earning more than she is (unfair) or that an employee who works 55 hours a week is earning more (fair). In general, employees compare their pay and contributions using several considerations:

- What they think employees in other organizations earn for doing the same job.
- What they think other employees holding different jobs within the organization earn for doing work at the same or different levels.
- What they think other employees in the organization earn for doing the same job as theirs.

How employees respond to their impressions about equity can have a great impact on the organization. Typically, if employees see their pay as equitable, their attitudes and behaviour continue unchanged. If employees see themselves as receiving an advantage, they usually rethink the situation to see it as merely equitable. But if employees conclude that they are underrewarded, they are likely to make up the difference in one of three ways. They might put forth less effort (reducing their inputs), find a way to increase their outcomes (e.g., asking for a raise), or withdraw by leaving the organization or refusing to cooperate.

Job Structure: Relative Value of Jobs

Along with market forces and principles of fairness, organizations consider the relative contribution each job should make to the organization's overall performance. One typical way of doing this is with a **job evaluation**, an administrative procedure for measuring the relative internal worth of the organization's jobs. Usually, the organization does this by assembling and training a job evaluation committee, consisting of people familiar with the jobs to be evaluated. The committee often includes a human resource specialist and, if its budget permits, may hire an outside consultant.

To conduct a job evaluation, the committee identifies each job's *compensable factors*, meaning the characteristics of a job that the organization values and chooses to pay for. As shown in Table 8.2, an organization might consider the effort required and skill requirements of people performing information technology-related jobs. Other compensable factors might include working conditions and responsibility. Based on the job attributes defined by job analysis (discussed in Chapter 3), the jobs are rated for each factor. The rater assigns each factor a certain number of points, giving more points to factors when they are considered more important and when the job requires a high level of that factor. Often the number of points comes from one of the *point manuals* published by trade groups and management consultants. If necessary, the organization can adapt the scores in

the point manual to the organization's situation or even develop its own point manual. As in the example in Table 8.2, the scores for each factor are totalled to arrive at an overall evaluation for each job.

Job evaluations provide the basis for decisions about *relative internal worth*—value of the job within the organization, necessary to meet pay equity requirements as discussed in Chapter 2. According to the sample assessments in Table 8.2, the job of systems analyst is worth more to this organization than the job of data entry clerk. Therefore, the organization would be willing to pay significantly more for the work of a systems analyst than it would for the work of a data entry clerk.

The organization may limit its pay survey to jobs evaluated as *key jobs*. These are jobs that have relatively stable content and are common among many organizations, so it is possible to obtain survey data about what people earn in these jobs. Organizations can make the process of creating a pay structure more practical by defining key jobs. Research for creating the pay structure is limited to the key jobs that play a significant role in the organization. Pay for the key jobs can be based on survey data, and pay for the organization's other jobs can be based on the organization's job structure. A job with a higher evaluation score than a particular key job would receive higher pay than that key job.

> **job evaluation**
> An administrative procedure for measuring the relative internal worth of the organization's jobs.

Pay Structure: Putting It All Together

The pay structure reflects decisions about how much to pay (pay level) and the relative value of each job (job structure). The organization's pay structure should reflect what the organization knows about market forces, as well as its own unique goals and the relative contribution of each job to

TABLE 8.2   Job Evaluation of Three Jobs

| | COMPENSABLE FACTORS | | | | |
JOB TITLE	SKILL	EFFORT	RESPONSIBILITY	WORKING CONDITIONS	TOTAL
Data entry clerk	20	40	20	30	**110**
Computer programmer	80	60	50	20	**210**
Systems analyst	110	70	70	20	**270**

achieving the goals. By balancing this external and internal information, the organization's goal is to set levels of pay that employees will consider equitable and motivating. Organizations typically apply the information by establishing some combination of pay rates, pay grades, and pay ranges. Within this structure, they may state the pay in terms of a rate per hour, commonly called an **hourly wage**, a rate of pay for each unit produced, known as a **piecework rate**, or a rate of pay per week, month or year worked, called a **salary**.

PAY RATES

If the organization's main concern is to match what people are earning in comparable jobs, the organization can base pay directly on market research into as many of its key jobs as possible. To do this, the organization looks for survey data for each job title. If it finds data from more than one survey, it must weight the results according to their quality and relevance. In light of that knowledge, the organization decides what it will pay for the job.

The next step is to determine salaries for the non-key jobs, for which the organization has no survey data. Instead, the person developing the pay structure creates a graph like the one in Figure 8.5. The vertical axis shows a range of possible pay rates, and the horizontal axis measures the points from the job evaluation. The analyst plots points according to the job evaluation and pay rate for each key job. Finally, the analyst fits a line, called a **pay policy line**, to the

hourly wage
Rate of pay for each hour worked.

piecework rate
Rate of pay for each unit produced.

salary
Rate of pay for each week, month or year worked.

pay policy line
A graphed line showing the mathematical relationship between job evaluation points and pay rate.

points plotted. (This can be done statistically, using a procedure called regression analysis.) Mathematically, this line shows the relationship between job evaluation and rate of pay. Using this line, the analyst can estimate the market pay level for a given job evaluation. Looking at the graph gives approximate numbers, or the regression analysis will provide an equation for calculating the rate of pay.

The pay policy line reflects the pay structure in the market, which does not always match rates in the organization (see key job F in Figure 8.5). Survey data may show that people in certain jobs are actually earning significantly more or less than the amount shown on the pay policy line. For example, some kinds of expertise are in short supply. People with that expertise can command higher pay, because they can easily leave one employer to get higher pay somewhere else. Suppose, in contrast, that local businesses have laid off many warehouse employees. Because so many of these workers are looking for jobs, organizations may be able to pay them less than the rate that job evaluation points would suggest.

When job structure and market data conflict in these ways, organizations have to decide on a way to resolve the two. One approach is to stick to the job evaluations and pay according to the employees' worth to the organization. Organizations that do so will be paying more or less than they have to, so they will likely have more difficulty competing for customers or employees. A way to moderate this approach is to consider the importance of each

FIGURE 8.5

Pay Policy Lines

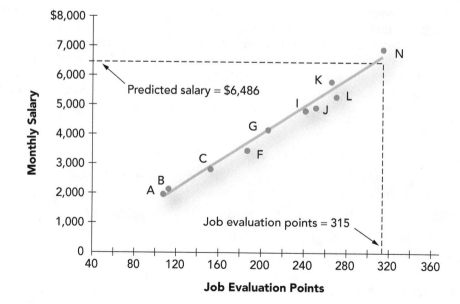

position to the organization's goals.[8] If a position is critical for meeting the organization's goals, paying more than competitors pay may be worthwhile.

At the other extreme, the organization could base pay entirely on market forces. However, this approach also has some practical drawbacks. One is that employees may conclude that pay rates are unfair. Two vice-presidents or two supervisors will expect to receive similar pay because their responsibilities are similar. If the differences between their pay are large, because of different market rates, the lower-paid employee will likely be dissatisfied. Also, if the organization's development plans include rotating managers through different assignments, the managers will be reluctant to participate if managers in some departments receive lower pay. Organizations therefore must weigh all the objectives of their pay structure to arrive at suitable rates.

PAY GRADES

A large organization could have hundreds or even thousands of different jobs. Setting a pay rate for each job would be extremely complex. Therefore, many organizations group jobs into **pay grades**—sets of jobs having similar worth or content, grouped together to establish rates of pay. For example, the organization could establish five pay grades, with the same pay available to employees holding any job within the same grade.

A drawback of pay grades is that grouping jobs will result in rates of pay for individual jobs that do not precisely match the levels specified by the market and the organization's job structure. Suppose, for example, that the organization groups together its senior accountants (with a job evaluation of 255 points) and its senior systems analysts (with a job evaluation of 270 points). Surveys might show that the market rate of pay for systems analysts is higher than that for accountants. In addition, the job evaluations give more points to systems analysts. Even so, for simplicity's sake, the organization pays the same rate for the two jobs, because they are in the same pay grade. The organization would have to pay more than the market requires for accountants or pay less than the market rate for systems analysts (so it would probably have difficulty recruiting and retaining them).

PAY RANGES

Usually, organizations want some flexibility in setting pay for individual jobs. They want to be able

pay grades
Sets of jobs having similar worth or content, grouped together to establish rates of pay.

pay ranges
A set of possible pay rates defined by a minimum, maximum, and midpoint of pay for employees holding a particular job or a job within a particular pay grade or band.

to pay the most valuable employees the highest amounts and to give rewards for performance. Flexibility also helps the organization balance conflicting information from market surveys and job evaluations. Therefore, pay structure usually includes a **pay range** for each job or pay grade. In other words, the organization establishes a minimum, maximum, and midpoint of pay for employees holding a particular job or a job within a particular pay grade or band. Employees holding the same job may receive somewhat different pay, depending on where their pay falls within the range.

A typical approach is to use the market rate or the pay policy line as the midpoint of a range for the job or pay grade. The minimum and maximum values for the range may also be based on market surveys of those amounts. Figure 8.6 shows an example of pay ranges based on the pay policy line in Figure 8.5. Notice that the jobs are grouped into five pay grades, each with its own pay range. In this example, the range is widest for employees who are at higher levels in terms of their job evaluation points. That is because the performance of these higher-level employees will likely have more effect on the organization's performance, so the organization needs more latitude to reward them. For instance, as discussed earlier, the organization may want to select a higher point in the range to attract an employee who is more critical to achieving the organization's goals.

Usually pay ranges overlap somewhat, so that the highest pay in one grade is somewhat higher than the lowest pay in the next grade. Overlapping ranges gives the organization more flexibility in transferring employees among jobs, because transfers need not always involve a change in pay. On the other hand, the less overlap, the more important it is to earn promotions in order to keep getting raises. Assuming the organization wants to motivate employees through promotions (and assuming enough opportunities for promotion are available), the organization will want to limit the overlap from one level to the next.

Alternatives to Job-Based Pay

The traditional and most widely used approach to developing a pay structure focuses on setting pay for jobs or groups of jobs.[9] This emphasis on jobs has some limitations. The

L03 Describe alternatives to job-based pay.

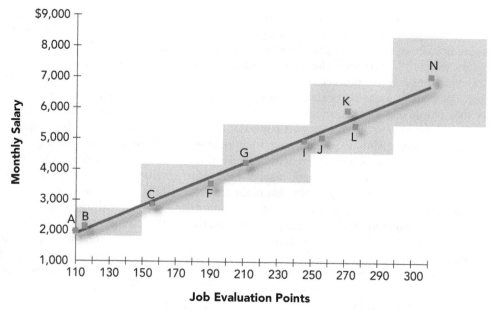

FIGURE 8.6

Sample Pay Grade Structure

- Current pay for job
- Pay policy line

precise definition of a job's responsibilities can contribute to an attitude that some activities "are not in my job description," at the expense of flexibility, innovation, quality, and customer service. Organizations may avoid change because it requires repeating the time-consuming process of creating job descriptions and related paperwork. Another change-related problem is that when the organization needs a new set of competencies, the existing pay structure may be rewarding the wrong behaviours. Finally, a pay structure that rewards employees for winning promotions may discourage them from gaining valuable experience through lateral career moves.

Organizations have responded to these problems with a number of alternatives to job-based pay structures. Some organizations have found greater flexibility by **broadbanding**—reducing the number of pay ranges in the organization's pay structure. For example, in the 1990s IBM changed from a pay structure with 5,000 job titles and 24 salary grades to one with 1,200 jobs and 10 bands. Broadbanding reduces the opportunities for promoting employees, so organizations that eliminate layers in their job descriptions must find other ways to reward employees.

Another way organizations have responded to the limitations of job-based pay has been to move away from the link to jobs and toward pay structures that

broadbanding

Reducing the number of pay ranges in the organization's pay structure.

competency-based pay systems

Pay structures that set pay according to the employees' levels of skill or knowledge and what they are capable of doing.

reward employees based on their knowledge and skills (competencies).[10] **Competency-based pay systems** (also known as *skill-based pay systems)* are pay structures that set pay according to the employees' level of skill or knowledge and what they are capable of doing. Paying for competencies makes sense at organizations where changing technology requires employees to continually widen and deepen their knowledge. Competency-based pay also supports efforts to involve employees and enrich jobs because it encourages employees to add to their knowledge so they can make decisions in many areas. In this way, competency-based pay helps organizations become more flexible and innovative. More generally, competency-based pay can encourage a climate of learning and adaptability and give employees a broader view of how the organization functions.

A disadvantage associated with this type of pay system is that it rewards employees for acquiring skills but does not provide a way to ensure that employees actually use their new skills.[11] The result may be that the organization is paying employees more for learning skills that the employer is not benefiting from. The challenge for HRM is to design work so that the work design and pay structure support one another.

PAY STRUCTURE AND ACTUAL PAY

Usually, the human resource department is responsible for establishing the organization's pay structure. But building the structure is not the end of the organization's decisions about pay structure. The structure represents the organization's policy, but what the organization actually does may be different. As part of its management responsibility, the HR department therefore should compare actual pay to the pay structure, making sure that policies and practices match.

A common way to do this is to measure a *compa-ratio,* the ratio of average pay to the midpoint of the pay range. Figure 8.7 shows an example. Assuming the organization has pay grades, the organization would find a compa-ratio for each pay grade: the average paid to all employees in the pay grade divided by the midpoint for the pay grade. If the average equals the midpoint, the compa-ratio is 1. More often the compa-ratio is somewhat above 1 (meaning the average pay is above the midpoint for the pay grade) or below 1 (meaning the average pay is below the midpoint).

Assuming that the pay structure is well planned to support the organization's goals, the compa-ratios should be close to 1. A compa-ratio greater than 1 suggests that the organization is paying employees more than planned and may have difficulty keeping costs under control. A compa-ratio less than 1 suggests that the organization may be underpaying employees and may have difficulty attracting and retaining qualified employees.

> **incentive pay**
> Forms of pay linked to an employee's performance as an individual, group member, or organization member.

Incentive (Variable) Pay

2,5

The first part of this chapter discussed the framework for total rewards and setting pay for jobs. Now we focus on using pay to recognize and reward employees' contributions to the organization's success.

In contrast to decisions about pay structure, organizations have wide discretion in setting performance-related pay, called **incentive pay** or *pay for performance.* Organizations can tie incentive pay to individual performance, profits, or many other measures of success.

> **L04** Describe how organizations recognize individual, team, and organizational performance through the use of incentives.

They select incentives based on their costs, expected influence on performance, and fit with the organization's broader HR and company policies and goals. These decisions are significant. A study of 150 organizations found that the way organizations paid employees was strongly associated with their level of profitability.[12]

Many organizations offer incentive pay in the effort to energize, direct, or influence employees' behaviour. According to the Conference Board of Canada, 86 percent of Canadian organizations have at least one incentive pay plan. These plans are particularly popular in the private sector—94 percent of companies reported having one or more plans while 60 percent of public sector organizations also have one or more incentive plans.[13] Incentive pay is influential because the amount paid is linked to certain predefined behaviours or outcomes. For example, an organization can pay a salesperson a *commission* for closing a sale, or the members of a production department can earn a *bonus* for meeting a monthly production goal. Knowing they can earn extra money for closing sales or meeting departmental goals, the employees often try harder or get more creative than they might without the incentive pay. In addition, the policy of offering higher pay for higher performance may make an organization attractive to high performers when it is trying to recruit and retain these valuable employees.[14]

For incentive pay to motivate employees to contribute to the organization's success, the plans must

Finding a Compa-Ratio

Pay Grade: 1
Midpoint of Range: $4,675 per month

Salaries of Employees in Pay Grade
Employee 1 $5,306
Employee 2 $4,426
Employee 3 $5,223
Employee 4 $5,114

Compa-Ratio

$$\frac{\text{Average}}{\text{Midpoint}} = \frac{\$5,017.25}{\$4,675.00} = 1.07$$

Average Salary of Employees
$5,306 + $4,426 + $5,523 + $5,114 = $20,069
$20,069 ÷ 4 = $5,017.25

be well designed. In particular, effective plans meet the following requirements:

- Performance measures are linked to the organization's goals.
- Employees believe they can meet performance standards.
- The organization gives employees the resources they need to meet their goals.
- Employees value the rewards given.
- Employees believe the reward system is fair.
- The plan takes into account that employees may ignore any goals that are not rewarded.

The "HR How-To" box provides some additional ideas for creating and implementing an effective incentive-pay plan even when resources are limited. Since incentive pay is linked to particular outcomes or behaviours, the organization is encouraging them to demonstrate those desired outcomes and behaviours. As obvious as that may sound, the implications are more complicated. If incentive pay is extremely rewarding, employees may focus on only the performance measures rewarded under the plan and ignore measures that are not rewarded. Many call centres pay employees based on how many calls they handle, as an incentive to work quickly and efficiently. However, speedy call handling does not necessarily foster good customer relationships. Organizations may combine a number of incentives so employees do not focus on one measure to the exclusion of others.

Another criticism is the concern that individual pay for performance can "foster an individualistic culture or a culture of entitlement."[15] Employees must also believe they have the ability and resources to meet the performance standards and that the performance standards are under their control. As we will discuss in the section on rewards for organizational performance, this is a challenge in the case of incentives based on an organization's profits or stock price. Employees at lower levels of the organization may doubt that they have much influence

HR HOW-TO

Stretching Incentive Pay Dollars

One advantage of incentive pay is that, because it is targeted to reinforcing desired behaviours and outcomes, there are ways to get a lot of value from it even when budgets are tight. Here are some ideas for getting the most out of an incentive-pay plan:

- Be very clear about what behaviours or outcomes you want to encourage. Many options are available, from delighting customers to reducing costs to selling the products that have the biggest profit margins. Direct most or all of the incentive pay to rewarding performance on the measurements that will have the most impact on the organization's success.
- Set up objective ways to measure whether the individual or group earns the incentive, so

that rewards don't become a popularity contest or lottery. The measurement should include a minimum level of performance required for receiving part or all of the reward.

- Communicate with employees. Especially if money is tight, be candid about the company's resources. Invite ideas about what employees would appreciate receiving, so that you'll be spending on what matters most.
- Combine the forms of incentive pay with nonmonetary rewards such as thank-you notes and public recognition for group and individual accomplishments. In some cases, employees may be wowed by a chance to have breakfast with the boss or attend a meeting with a company expert.
- When delivering the reward, communicate what accomplishment

led to the award, so employees see the connection—and that the company also notices what they have contributed.

- Consider giving managers a pool of money to use for granting bonuses when individuals or groups exhibit the desired performance or exceed objectives.
- Grant bonuses or other incentives frequently. Smaller payouts delivered more frequently can keep excitement higher for the same amount of money as the organization would have spent on an annual bonus.

SOURCES: "How to Reward Employees on a Budget," *Inc.* April 19, 2010, www.inc.com; and "Try Two Bonus Tactics Suited for Tough Times," *HR Specialist: Compensation & Benefits,* March 2010, Business & Company Resource Center, http://galenet.galegroup.com.

over these performance measures. Therefore, these incentives likely will not have much effect on these employees' behaviour, at least in large companies.

Other attitudes that influence the success of incentive pay include whether employees value the rewards and think the pay plan is fair. Most, if not all, employees value pay, but it is important to remember that earning money is not the only reason people try to do a good job. As discussed in other chapters (see Chapters 1, 6, and 11), people also want interesting work, appreciation for their efforts, flexibility, and a sense of belonging to the work group—not to mention the inner satisfaction of work well done. Therefore, a complete plan for compensating and rewarding employees has many components, from pay to work design to developing managers so they can exercise positive leadership.

We will now identify elements of incentive pay systems. We consider each option's strengths and limitations with regard to these principles. The many kinds of incentive pay fall into three broad categories: incentives linked to individual, team, or organizational performance. Choices from these categories should consider not only their strengths and weaknesses, but also their fit with the organization's goals. The choice of incentive pay may affect not only the level of motivation, but also the kinds of employees who are attracted to and stay with the organization. For example, there is some evidence that organizations with team-based rewards will tend to attract employees who are more team-oriented.[16]

Given the potential impact, organizations not only should weight the strengths and weaknesses in selecting types of incentive pay but also should measure the results of these programs (see "Did You Know?").

PAY FOR INDIVIDUAL PERFORMANCE

Organizations may reward individual performance with a variety of incentives.

- *Piecework rate*—As an incentive to work efficiently, some organizations pay production workers a piecework rate, a wage based on the amount workers produce. This rate is often paid in addition to employees' base pay. The amount paid per unit is set at a level that rewards employees for above-average production volume. An obvious advantage of piece rates is the direct link between how much work the employee does and the amount the employee earns. However, for complex jobs or jobs with hard-to-measure outputs, piecework plans do not apply very well. Also, unless a plan is well-designed to include performance standards, it may not reward employees for focusing on quality or customer satisfaction if it interferes with the day's output. In Figure 8.8,

DID YOU KNOW?

Investing in Human Resources

In a recent survey of more than 750 organizations in 66 countries, only one out of five said they measure the return on investment (ROI) of incentive programs, but more want to move in that direction. Companies that measure the ROI of rewards tend to think of pay as an investment in human resources aimed at bringing out top performance. Companies that don't measure ROI typically think of pay as simply a cost of doing business.

SOURCE: Tom McMullen, *Reward Next Practices* (Hay Group, August 2009), www.haygroup.com.

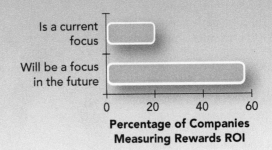

FIGURE 8.8

How Incentives Sometimes "Work"

SOURCE: DILBERT, reprinted by permission of United Features Syndicate, Inc.

the employees quickly realize they can earn huge bonuses by writing software "bugs" and then fixing them, while writing bug-free software affords no chance to earn bonuses.

- *Standard hour plans*—Another quantity-oriented incentive for production workers is the **standard hour plan**, an incentive plan that pays workers extra for work done in less than a preset "standard time." The organization determines a standard time to complete a task, such as tuning up a car engine. If the mechanic completes the work in less than the standard time, the mechanic receives an amount of pay equal to the wage for the full standard time. Working that fast over the course of a week could add significantly to the mechanic's pay. In terms of their pros and cons, standard hour plans are much like piecework plans. They encourage employees to work as fast as they can, but not necessarily to care about quality or customer service.
- *Merit pay*—Almost all organizations have established some program of **merit pay**—a system of linking pay increases to ratings on performance appraisals.

> **standard hour plan**
> An incentive plan that pays workers extra for work done in less than a preset "standard time."

> **merit pay**
> A system of linking pay increases to ratings on performance appraisals.

An advantage of merit pay is that it provides a method for rewarding performance in all of the dimensions measured in the organization's performance management system. If that system is appropriately designed to measure all the important job behaviours, then the merit pay is linked to the behaviours the organization desires. This link seems logical, although so far there is little research showing the effectiveness of merit pay.[17] A drawback of merit pay, from the employer's standpoint, is that it can quickly become expensive. Managers at a majority of organizations rate most employees' performance in the top two categories (out of four or five).[18] Therefore, the majority of employees are eligible for the biggest merit increases, and their pay rises rapidly. Another drawback of merit pay is that it assumes that performance is based on employees' ability and motivation, however, performance may be enhanced or reduced by factors beyond the employees' control, e.g., economic conditions.

Many salespeople in the auto industry earn a straight commission, meaning that 100 percent of their pay comes from commission instead of a salary. What type of individual might enjoy a job like this?

- *Performance bonuses*—Like merit pay, performance bonuses reward individual performance, but bonuses are not rolled into base pay. The employee must re-earn them during each performance period. In some cases, the bonus is a one-time reward. Bonuses may also be linked to objective performance measures rather than potentially subjective ratings. Bonuses for individual performance can be extremely effective and give the organization great flexibility in deciding what kinds of behaviour to reward.
- *Commissions*—A variation on piece rates and bonuses is the payment of commissions, or pay calculated as a percentage of sales. For instance, a furniture salesperson might earn commissions equalling 6 percent of the price of the furniture the person sells during the period. In a growth-oriented organization, sales commissions need not be limited to salespeople.

PAY FOR TEAM PERFORMANCE

Employers may address the drawbacks of individual incentives by including team incentives in the organization's compensation plan. To earn team incentives, employees must cooperate and share knowledge so that the entire team can meet its performance targets. Widely used team incentives include gainsharing, bonuses, and team awards.

Gainsharing

Organizations that want employees to focus on efficiency may adopt a gainsharing program, which measures increases in productivity and effectiveness and distributes a portion of each gain to employees. For example, if a factory enjoys a productivity gain worth $30,000, half the gain might be the company's share. The other $15,000 would be distributed among the employees in the factory. Knowing that they can enjoy a financial benefit from helping the company be more productive, employees supposedly will look for ways to work more efficiently and improve the way the factory operates.

Gainsharing addresses the challenge of identifying appropriate performance measures for complex jobs. Even for simpler jobs, setting acceptable standards and measuring performance can be complicated. Gainsharing frees employees to determine how to improve their own and their team's performance. It also broadens employees' focus beyond their individual interests. But in

contrast to profit sharing, discussed later, it keeps the performance measures within a range of activity that most employees believe they can influence. Organizations can enhance the likelihood of a gain by providing a means for employees to share knowledge and make suggestions, as we will discuss later in this chapter.

Gainsharing is most likely to succeed when organizations provide the right conditions. Among the conditions identified, the following are among the most common:[19]

- Management commitment.
- Need for change or strong commitment to continuous improvement.
- Management acceptance and encouragement of employee input.
- High levels of cooperation and interaction.
- Employment security.
- Information sharing on productivity and costs.
- Goal setting.
- Commitment of all involved parties to the process of change and improvement.
- Performance standards and calculations that employees understand and consider fair and that is closely related to managerial objectives.
- Employees who value working in teams.

Team Bonuses and Awards

In contrast to gainsharing plans, which typically reward the performance of all employees at a facility, bonuses for team performance tend to be for smaller work groups.[20] These bonuses reward the members of a group for attaining a specific goal, usually measured in terms of physical output. Team awards are similar to team bonuses, but they are more likely to use a broad range of performance measures, such as cost savings, successful completion of a project, or even meeting deadlines.

Both types of incentives have the advantage that they encourage group or team members to cooperate so that they can achieve their goal. However, depending on the reward system, competition among individuals may be replaced by competition among teams. Competition may be healthy in some situations, as when teams try to outdo one another in satisfying customers. On the downside, competition may also prevent necessary cooperation among teams. To avoid this, the organization should carefully set the performance goals for these incentives so that concern for costs or sales

commissions
Incentive pay calculated as a percentage of sales.

gainsharing
Team incentive program that measures improvements in productivity and effectiveness and distributes a portion of each gain to employees.

Team members that meet a sales goal or a product development team that meets a deadline or successfully launches a product may be rewarded with a bonus for team performance. What are some advantages and disadvantages of team bonuses?

does not obscure other objectives, such as quality, customer service, and ethical behaviour.

PAY FOR ORGANIZATIONAL PERFORMANCE

2,5

Two important ways organizations measure their performance are in terms of their profits and their stock price. In a competitive marketplace, profits result when an organization is efficiently providing products that customers want at a price they are willing to pay. Stock is the owners' investment in a corporation; when the stock price is rising, the value of that investment is growing. Rather than trying to figure out what performance measures will motivate employees to do the things that generate high profits and a rising stock price, many organizations offer incentive pay tied to those organizational performance measures. The expectation is that employees will focus on what is best for the organization.

These organization-level incentives can motivate employees to align their activities with the organization's goals. Linking incentives to the organization's profits or stock price exposes employees to a high degree of risk. Profits and stock price can soar very high very fast, but they can also fall, as witnessed by many wary investors. The result is a great deal of uncertainty about the amount of incentive pay each employee will receive in each period. Therefore, these kinds of incentive pay are likely to be most effective in organizations that emphasize growth and innovation, which tend to need employees who thrive in a risk-taking environment.[21]

Profit Sharing

Under **profit sharing**, payments are a percentage of the organization's profits and do not become part of the employees' base salary. Organizations use profit sharing for a number of reasons. It may encourage

> **profit sharing**
> Incentive pay in which payments are a percentage of the organization's profits and do not become part of the employees' base salary.

employees to think more like owners, taking a broad view of what they need to do in order to make the organization more effective. They are more likely to cooperate and less likely to focus on narrow self-interest. Also, profit sharing has the practical advantage of costing less when the organization is experiencing financial difficulties. If the organization has little or no profit, this incentive pay is small or nonexistent, so employers may not need to rely as much on layoffs to reduce costs.[22]

An organization setting up a profit-sharing plan should consider what to do if profits fall. If the economy slows and profit-sharing payments disappear along with profits, employees may become discouraged or dissatisfied. One way to avoid this kind of problem is to design profit-sharing plans to reward employees for high profits but not penalize them when profits fall. This solution may be more satisfactory to employees but does not offer the advantage of reducing labour costs without layoffs during economic downturns.

Given the limitations of profit-sharing plans, one strategy is to use them as a component of a pay system that includes other kinds of pay more directly linked to individual behaviour. This increases employees' commitment to organizational goals while addressing concerns about fairness.

Stock Ownership

While profit-sharing plans are intended to encourage employees to "think like owners," a stock ownership plan actually makes employees part owners of the organization. Like profit sharing, employee ownership is intended as a way to encourage employees to focus on the success of the organization as a whole. The drawbacks of stock ownership as a form of incentive pay are similar to those of profit sharing. Specifically, it may not have a strong effect on individuals' motivation. Employees may not see a strong link between their actions and the company's stock price, especially in larger organizations. The link between pay and performance is even harder to appreciate because the financial benefits mostly come when the stock is sold—typically when the employee leaves the organization. Ownership programs usually take the form of *stock options* or *employee stock ownership plans*. These are illustrated in Figure 8.9.

Stock Options

One way to distribute stock to employees is to grant **stock options**—the right to buy a certain number of shares of stock at a specified price. (Purchasing the stock is called *exercising* the option.) Suppose that in 2010 a company's employees received options to purchase the company's stock at $10 per share. The employees will benefit if the stock price rises above $10 per share, because they can pay $10 for something (a share of stock) that is worth more than $10. If in 2013 the stock is worth $18, they can exercise their options and buy stock for $10 a share. If they want to, they can sell their stock for the market price of $18, receiving a gain of $8 for each share of stock. Of course, stock prices can also fall. If the 2013 stock price is only $8, the employees would not exercise the options.

Traditionally, organizations have granted stock options to their executives. In recent years, many organizations pushed eligibility for options further down in the organization's structure. The share of companies granting stock options to at least half of their employees has grown from less than one-quarter to more than half. Some studies suggest that organizations perform better when a large percentage of top and middle managers are eligible for long-term

stock options
Rights to buy a certain number of shares of stock at a specified price.

employee stock ownership plan (ESOP)
An arrangement in which the organization distributes shares of stock to all its employees by placing it in a trust.

incentives such as stock options. This evidence is consistent with the idea of encouraging employees to think like owners.[23]

Corporate scandals have drawn attention to another challenge of using stock options as incentive pay. As with other performance measures, employees may focus so much on stock price that they lose sight of other goals, including ethical behaviour. Ideally, managers would bring about an increase in stock price by adding value in terms of efficiency, innovation, and customer satisfaction. But there are other, unethical ways to increase stock price by tricking investors into thinking the organization is more valuable and more profitable than it actually is. Hiding losses and inflating the recorded value of revenues are just two ways some companies have boosted stock prices, enriching managers until these misdeeds come to light.

Employee Stock Ownership Plans

While stock options are most often used with top management, a broader arrangement is the **employee stock ownership plan (ESOP)**. In an ESOP, the organization distributes shares of stock to its employees by placing the stock into a trust managed on the employees' behalf. Employees receive regular reports on the value of their stock, and when they leave the organization, they may sell the stock to the organization or (if it is a publicly traded company) on the open market.

WestJet's Share Purchase Program enables WestJetters to receive up to 20 percent of their salaries in WestJet shares. Shares can be purchased as common shares or can be directed into RRSPs with WestJet matching the employee's contributions.[24] And, it is estimated there are around 1,000 Facebook employees who became instant millionaires when their restricted stock units were converted to actual shares during Facebook's recent stock market launch.[25]

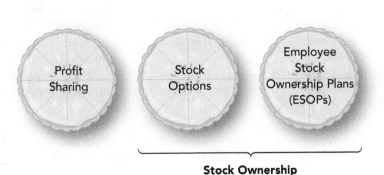

FIGURE 8.9

Types of Pay for Organizational Performance

Profit Sharing   Stock Options   Employee Stock Ownership Plans (ESOPs)

Stock Ownership

Although ESOPs are the most common form of employee ownership they raise a number of issues. On the negative side, they carry a significant risk for employees. Problems with the company's performance therefore can take away significant value from the ESOP. Many companies set up ESOPs to hold retirement funds, so these risks directly affect employees' retirement income.

Still, ESOPs can be attractive to employers. Along with tax and financing advantages, ESOPs give employers a way to build pride in and commitment to the organization. Employees have a right to participate in votes by shareholders (if the stock is registered on a national exchange, such as the TSX).[26] This means employees participate somewhat in corporate-level decision making. Refer to Table 8.3 for a summary of the advantages and disadvantages of individual, team, and organizational incentives.

What Is the Role of Employee Benefits?

Employees at almost every organization receive more than dollars and cents in exchange for their efforts. They also receive a package of employee benefits—compensation in forms other than cash (indirect compensation). Examples include paid vacation time, employer-paid health insurance, and pension plans, among a wide range of possibilities.

As part of the total compensation provided to employees, benefits serve functions similar to pay. Benefits contribute to attracting, retaining, and motivating employees. The variety of possible benefits also helps employers tailor their offerings to the

> **employee benefits**
> Compensation in forms other than cash.

kinds of employees they need. Employers need to examine their benefits package regularly to see whether they still meet employees' needs and expectations. Even if employers spend large sums on benefits and services, if employees do not understand how to use them or why they are valuable, the cost of the benefits will be largely wasted.[27] Employers need to communicate effectively so that the benefits succeed in motivating employees.

Employees have come to expect that benefits will help them maintain economic security. Canada Pension Plan/Quebec Pension Plan, company pension plans, and retirement savings plans help employees prepare for their retirement. Insurance plans help to protect employees from unexpected costs such as prescription drugs. This important role of benefits is one reason that some benefits are subject to government regulation. Benefits, such as Employment Insurance, are required by law.

Even though many kinds of benefits are not required by law, they have become so common that today's employees expect them. Many employers find that attracting qualified workers requires them to provide health and retirement benefits of some sort. A large employer without such benefits would be highly unusual and would have difficulty competing in the labour market. A national survey conducted by Ipsos-Reid found that Canadian employees value their health benefits. As reported by Benefits Canada, 91 percent of survey respondents said that other than salary, a "good job" was defined as having a good benefits package—"benefits are serving as a proxy or a marker for a good workplace."[28]

Like other forms of compensation and rewards, benefits impose significant costs.

> **L05** Discuss the role of benefits as part of employee total rewards.

TABLE 8.3 An Overview of Incentive Pay

CRITERION	INCENTIVES	ADVANTAGES	DISADVANTAGES
Individual performance	Piecework rates, sales commissions	Exert most powerful impact on productivity.	Do not promote teamwork or ensure a corresponding increase in product quality. May be difficult to measure.
Team performance	Gainsharing, team-based incentive plans	Encourage teamwork.	Yield a moderate impact on productivity.
Organizational performance	Profit sharing and stock sharing, including stock ownership, stock options, and employee stock ownership plan	Increase shareholder returns and company profit.	Generate only a small increase in productivity.

SOURCE: "Implementing Total Rewards Strategies," *SHRM Foundation*, p. 12, www.shrm.org/FOUNDATION/07RewardsStratReport.pdf, retrieved May 6, 2008.

On average, out of every dollar spent on compensation, 30 cents or more go to benefits and this share has grown over the past decades.[29] An organization managing its labour costs must pay careful attention to the cost of its employee benefits.

Overall, employers are concerned about balancing various issues related to benefits provided to employees. Several forces have made benefits and services a significant part of compensation packages. One is that laws require employers to provide certain benefits, such as contributions to Canada Pension Plan and Employment Insurance. Also, tax laws can make benefits favourable. For example, employees do not pay income taxes on most benefits they receive, but they pay income taxes on cash compensation. Therefore, an employee who receives a $1,000 raise "takes home" less than the full $1,000, but an employee who receives an additional $1,000 worth of benefits receives the full benefits. Another cost advantage of paying benefits is that employers, especially large ones, often can get a better deal on insurance or other programs than employees can obtain on their own. Finally, some employers assemble creative benefits packages to set them apart in the competition for talent.

What Benefits Are Required by Law?

1,5

Governments require various forms of security to protect workers from financial hardships of being out of work. Because these benefits are required by law, employers cannot gain an advantage in the labour market by offering them, nor can they design the nature of these benefits.

- **Canada Pension Plan (CPP)/Quebec Pension Plan (QPP).** These plans, established in 1966, cover all workers in Canada who are age 18 and older and have annual income exceeding $3,500. CPP/ QPP is a mandatory contributory plan that provides retirement pensions, disability benefits, and survivor benefits. Workers who meet eligibility requirements receive retirement benefits according to their age and earnings history.

> **LO6** Summarize the types of employee benefits offered by employers.

- **Employment Insurance (EI).** This federally mandated program provides temporary financial assistance to unemployed workers who have lost their jobs through no fault of their own, while they look for another job or upgrade their skills.

Coverage is also extended to eligible workers who are sick, are pregnant, or are caring for a newborn or adopted child. In addition, EI can assist employees when they are caring for a gravely ill family member.

- **Workers' Compensation Acts.** Provincial programs that provide benefits to workers who suffer work-related injuries or illnesses. Workers' compensation operates under a principle of *no-fault liability*, meaning that an employee does not need to show that the employer was grossly negligent in order to receive compensation, and the employer is protected from lawsuits. The benefits fall into three major categories: wage-loss benefits, medical services, and rehabilitative services. Workers' compensation is entirely funded by employers—neither workers nor the government contribute. The amount employers pay depends on the industry and kinds of occupations involved as well as the size of the employer's payroll. Organizations can minimize the cost of this benefit by keeping workplaces safe and making employees and their managers conscious of safety issues, as discussed in Chapter 2.

What Optional Benefits Do Some Employers Provide?

Other types of benefits are optional. These include various kinds of insurance, retirement plans, and paid leave. Part-time workers often receive fewer benefits than full-time employees. The most widely offered benefits are paid leave for vacations and holidays (that exceed the legally required minimums specified in employment/labour standards legislation), life and medical insurance, and retirement plans. The extent to which the employer pays for the benefit varies widely among organizations. Some organizations require employees to pay a significant percentage of the premiums for insurance plans such as dental coverage. Other organizations pick up 100 percent of the premiums.

Benefits such as health insurance usually extend to employees' dependants. To ensure an employer does not face a charge of discrimination where the relevant jurisdiction includes sexual orientation

---

Canada Pension Plan (CPP)/Quebec Pension Plan (QPP)

A contributory, mandatory plan that provides retirement pensions, disability benefits, and survivor benefits.

contributory plan

All costs of the plan are funded by employees, employers, and the plan's own investments.

Employment Insurance (EI)

A federally mandated program to provide temporary financial assistance to unemployed workers.

Workers' Compensation Acts

Provincial programs that provide benefits to workers who suffer work-related injuries or illnesses.

and/or marital status as a protected ground of discrimination, employers cover different-sex as well as same-sex partners.

PAID LEAVE

Employment/labour standards legislation outlines minimum vacation entitlements and paid holidays. Many employers provide vacation and holidays in addition to the minimum legislated requirements. Some organizations also offer additional days off for personal reasons or to contribute their time to a charitable organization.

Sick leave programs pay employees for days not worked because of illness. The amount of sick leave is often based on length of service, so that it accumulates over time—for example, one day added to sick leave for each month of service. Employers have to decide how many sick days to grant and whether to let them continue accumulating year after year.

An organization's policies for time off may include other forms of paid and unpaid leave. For a workforce that values flexibility, the organization may offer paid *personal days*, days off that employees may schedule according to their personal needs, with the supervisor's approval. Typically, organizations offer a few personal days in addition to sick leave. *Floating holidays* are paid holidays that vary from year to year. The organization may schedule floating holidays so that they extend a Tuesday or Thursday holiday into a long weekend. Organizations may also give employees discretion over the scheduling of floating holidays. Employers should establish policies for leaves without pay—for example, leaves of absence to pursue nonwork goals or to meet family needs. Unpaid leave is also considered an employee benefit because the employee usually retains seniority and benefits during the leave.

GROUP INSURANCE AND BENEFITS

As we noted earlier, rates for group insurance are typically lower than for individual policies. Also, insurance benefits are not subject to income tax, as wages and salaries are. When employees receive insurance as a benefit, rather than higher pay so they can buy their own insurance, employees can get more for their money. Because of this, most employees value group insurance. The most common types of insurance and benefits offered as employee benefits are medical, life insurance, and disability insurance.

- *Medical insurance.* The policies typically cover medical expenses that are incurred over and above provincially funded medical coverage. Some employers offer additional coverage, such as dental care, vision care, and prescription drug programs. As is discussed in this chapter's "Thinking Ethically" feature, employers must also make choices about coverage of so-called "lifestyle drugs," that is, drugs considered "cosmetic" or "discretionary." Examples are medical treatments for obesity, infertility, erectile dysfunction, male pattern baldness, and smoking cessation.[30] An alternative to traditional employer-provided medical insurance is a **health spending account**, in which an employer puts aside a specific amount of money per employee to cover health-related costs. Employees decide what health care services they will purchase with their allocation. Major insurers, such as Great-West Life, administer the health spending account, usually for a fixed percentage fee. Health spending accounts are particularly attractive to small companies because the cost to the employer for employee benefits and administration is capped.[31]

> **health spending account**
> A specific amount of money set aside per employee by the employer to cover health-related costs.

- *Employee wellness program.* One way to lower the cost of health insurance is to reduce employees' need for health care services. Employers may try to do this by offering an employee wellness program, a set of communications, activities, and facilities designed to change health-related behaviours in ways that reduce health risks discussed in Chapter 2. Typically, wellness programs aim at specific health risks, such as high blood pressure, high cholesterol levels, smoking, and obesity, by encouraging preventive measures such as exercise and good nutrition. However, many organizations are adopting an integrated strategic approach to wellness that promotes a corporate culture to support employees in taking responsibility for their health and overall wellness. According to recent research by the International Foundation of Employee Benefit Plans, the prevalence of wellness programs has grown significantly over the last ten years, with more than 40 percent of Canadian employers implementing new programs since 2008. And 60 percent of the Canadian organizations surveyed said they provide program incentives such as fitness discounts (29 percent), gift cards and gift certificates (27 percent), and non-cash incentives such as prizes and raffles (27 percent) to boost employee participation.[32] "Incentives create more interest in the program and inspire people who aren't usually active to get involved," explains Kathleen Jones, business solutions manager at Fraser & Hoyt Incentives in Halifax.[33]

- *Employee assistance program (EAP).* As discussed in Chapter 2 an employee assistance program (EAP) provides confidential counselling services to employees experiencing personal problems. Many organizations also extend these services to family members. Left untreated, personal problems may cause an employee to lose their ability to cope and work performance will suffer. Employees must be able to feel confident the program respects their confidentiality. Other considerations include the range of offerings provided (some EAP providers offer a very broad range of services that may overlap with health, wellness and lifestyle-related services), proximity to counsellors, client references, and availability of effectiveness reporting measures.[34]

- *Life insurance.* Employers may provide life insurance to employees or offer the opportunity to buy coverage at low group rates. With a *term life insurance* policy, if the employee dies during the term of the policy, the employee's beneficiaries receive a payment called a *death benefit*. In policies purchased as an employee benefit, the usual death benefit is a multiple of the employee's yearly pay. The policies may provide additional benefits for accidental death. Along with a basic policy, the employer may give employees the option of purchasing additional coverage, usually at a nominal cost.

- *Disability insurance.* Employees risk losing their incomes if a disability makes them unable to work. Disability insurance provides protection against this loss of income. Typically, **short-term disability insurance** provides benefits for six months or less. **Long-term disability insurance** provides benefits after that initial period, potentially for the rest of the disabled employee's life. Disability payments are a percentage of the employee's salary—typically 50 to 70 percent. Payments under short-term plans may be higher. Often the policy sets a maximum amount that may be paid each month. Because its limits make it more affordable, short-term disability coverage is offered by more employers.

E-HRM	connect™

Check out "Health Benefits: The Growing Use of eClaims."

RETIREMENT PLANS

Employers have no obligation to offer retirement plans beyond the protection of CPP/QPP security, but many offer some form of pension or retirement savings plan. More than 6 million employees in Canada are members of registered pension plans (RPPs).[35] Figure 8.10 provides a breakdown of registered pension plans and members by type of plan.

An additional issue facing employers' approaches to retirement plans is a growing interest in **phased retirement**, a gradual transition into full retirement by reducing hours or job responsibility.[36] Employers are facing an increasing demand for phased retirement programs from employees who are healthier, living longer, and have personal or financial reasons to continue working in some capacity. Employers also benefit from retaining older workers with valued skills and experience who wish to

short-term disability insurance
Insurance that pays a percentage of a disabled employee's salary as benefits to the employee for six months or less.

long-term disability insurance
Insurance that pays a percentage of a disabled employee's salary after an initial period and potentially for the rest of the employee's life.

phased retirement
A gradual transition into full retirement by reducing hours or job responsibility.

Dofasco Inc. operates a 100-acre recreational facility park in Hamilton, Ontario, for employees, retirees, and their families. These facilities include double NHL-size ice surfaces, a twin gymnasium complex, track, golf driving range, miniputt, tennis courts, kids' playground, and baseball diamonds. Can you think of other organizations that offer unique benefits and services?

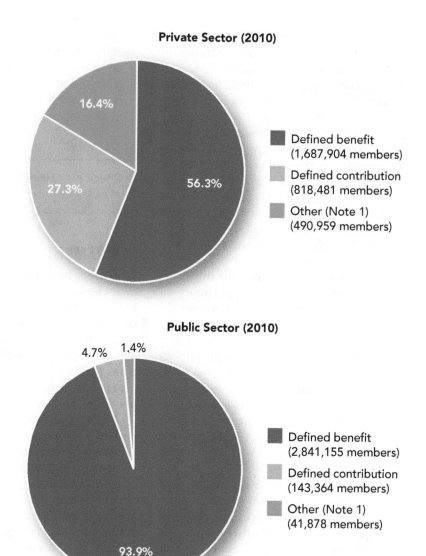

FIGURE 8.10

Membership in
Registered Pension
Plans by Type of Plan
and Sector

NOTE 1: Includes members of plans that have characteristics of both DB and DC plans; plans with benefits that are better than provided by DB or DC plans; or plans that have difference classes of employees.

SOURCES: Statistics Canada, "Registered Pension Plans (RPPs) and Members, by Type of Plan and Sector," May 9, 2011, www.statcan.gc.ca/tables-tableaux/sum-som/l01/cst01/famil120c-eng.htm; and www.statcan.gc.ca/tables-tableaux/sum-som/l01/cst01/famil120b-eng.htm, retrieved May 17, 2012.

retire gradually. Phased retirement also provides the employer with more time to transfer knowledge and skills to younger employees[37]; however, many employers are worried about the implications and costs of providing benefits coverage to older employees.

Employers have a choice of using defined benefit plans or defined contribution plans. Both are described below:

- *Defined benefit plans.* Employers have a choice of using registered retirement plans (RPPs) that define the amount to be paid out after retirement or plans that define the amount the employer will

defined benefit plan
A pension plan that guarantees a specified level of retirement income.

invest each year. A **defined benefit plan** guarantees a specified level of retirement income. Usually the amount of this defined benefit is calculated for each employee based on the employee's years of service, age, and earnings level (e.g., a percentage of the average of the employee's five highest-earnings years). These calculations typically result in pension payments that may provide 70 percent of pre-retirement income for a long-service employee. Using years of service as part of the basis for calculating benefits gives employees an incentive to stay with the organization as long as they can, so it can help to reduce voluntary turnover. Overall, 75 percent of employees in Canada with an RPP, were in a defined benefit pension plan, however, participation in this type of plan has declined from more than 85 percent a decade earlier,[38] largely due to the migration of new and existing employees to defined contribution plans in the private sector. For example, effective January 1, 2012, RBC stopped offering new Canadian hires access to its defined benefit plan. Existing employees can remain in RBC's defined benefits plan or switch to the defined contribution plan, which was made attractive through features such as higher employer contributions.[39]

- *Defined contribution plans.* An alternative to defined benefits is a **defined contribution plan,** which sets up an individual account for each employee and specifies the size of the investment into that account, rather than the amount to be paid out upon retirement. The amount the retiree receives will depend on the account's performance. These plans free employers from the risks that investments will not perform as well as expected. They put the responsibility for wise investing squarely on the shoulders of each employee. A defined contribution plan is also easier to administer. Considering the advantages to employers, it is not surprising that a growing share of retirement plans in the private sector are defined contribution

defined contribution plan

A retirement plan in which the employer sets up an individual account for each employee and specifies the size of the investment into that account.

plans. Defined contribution plans also offer an advantage to employees in today's highly mobile workforce. They do not penalize employees for changing jobs. With these plans, retirement earnings are less related to the number of years an employee stays with any particular company.

FAMILY-FRIENDLY BENEFITS AND SERVICES

As employers have recognized the importance of employees' need to balance their work and outside commitments including the care of family members, pursuit of education, personal development, and volunteer activities, many have implemented "family-friendly" HR practices. Options such as flextime and telework were discussed in Chapter 1. In addition, some organizations provide benefits and services including child and/or elder care, parental leave top-up, and adoption assistance. For example, the Ontario Public Service supports employees who are new mothers with maternity and paternity leave top-up payments (up to 93 percent of salary for 32 weeks) as well as parental top-up for new fathers and adoptive parents (up to 93 percent of salary for 17 weeks). Georgian College also offers maternity and parental top-ups as well as a variety of alternative working options from telecommuting to reduced hours in the summer.[40]

According to Statistics Canada, approximately 2.7 million Canadians provided unpaid care to people 65 years and older in 2007 (last year statistics were available). Many of these people are referred to as the "sandwich generation"—with dual responsibility of raising children and providing care for aging parents or relatives. Due to the aging of the baby boomers and their delay in having children the sandwich generation is expected to grow, resulting in

Many organizations provide an extensive range of family-friendly benefits. What types of benefits would help to alleviate stress at the workplace?

increased stress and demands on employees.[41] Some employers have responded by providing benefits and services including access to counselling, flexible schedules, referral services, and access to information and other resources available in the community or region.

The value of these family-friendly benefits accrue to not only employees but to employers as well in the form of increased productivity, enhanced commitment, and reduced stress.[42]

OTHER BENEFITS

2,3,5

The scope of possible employee benefits is limited only by the imagination of the organization's decision makers. Figure 8.11 outlines emerging benefits expected to be the most popular over the next few years. Organizations have developed a wide variety of benefits to meet the needs of employees and to attract and keep the kinds of workers who will be of value to the organization. Traditional extras include

subsidized cafeterias, onsite health care for minor injuries or illnesses, and moving expenses for newly hired or relocating employees. Stores and manufacturers may offer employee discounts on their products. See the "HR Oops!" box.

To encourage learning and attract the kinds of employees who wish to develop their knowledge and skills, many organizations offer *tuition reimbursement* programs. A typical program covers tuition and related expenses for courses that are relevant to the employee's current job or future career at the organization. Employees are reimbursed for these expenses after they demonstrate they have completed an approved course. The nearby "HR Best Practices" box discusses tuition reimbursement as an important perk at many organizations on top employer lists.

Especially for demanding, high-stress jobs, organizations may look for benefits that help employees put in the necessary long hours and alleviate stress. Recreational activities such as onsite basketball courts or company-sponsored softball teams provide for social interaction as well as physical activity.

FIGURE 8.11

Emerging Benefits

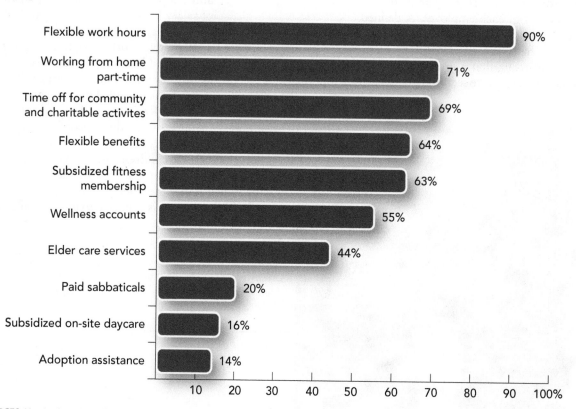

SOURCES: Hewitt Associates, "Emerging Benefits Focus on Flexibility," *Canadian HR Reporter*, December 17, 2007, pp. 20, 27; and Kira Vermond, "Sabbaticals: Time Out for the Burned Out," *Globe and Mail Update*, November 2, 2007, www.theglobeandmail.com, retrieved November 8, 2007.

HR Oops!

Underestimating the Importance of Employee Discounts

Part of knowing what employees value is knowing what they don't want to lose. Brian Dunn learned that the hard way as an executive of Best Buy.

Dunn hoped to improve profitability by cutting costs, and he thought employees would accept a smaller employee discount. To be certain, the company monitored comments on its employee social-networking site, the Watercooler.

The results were soon in: employees flooded the site with 54 pages of comments, most of them furious.

Just five days later, Dunn reviewed the reaction with senior management. The decision was easy: Best Buy backed down and restored the employee discount to its original level.

QUESTIONS

1. Are you surprised that employee discounts are a highly valued benefit at Best Buy? Why or why not? What kinds of employees would this benefit attract?

2. Suggest a way that Best Buy could have reduced the costs of benefits without sparking employee anger.

SOURCE: Based on Matthew Boyle, "Look Before You Chop Employee Perks," *BusinessWeek*, February 20, 2009, www.businessweek.com.

Selecting Employee Benefits

2,3,4,5

Although the government requires certain benefits, employers have wide latitude in creating the total benefits package they offer employees.[43] Decisions about which benefits to include should take into account the organization's goals, its budget, and the expectations of the organization's current employees and those it wishes to recruit in the future. Employees have come to expect certain things from employers. An organization that does not offer the expected benefits will have more difficulty attracting and keeping talented workers. Also, if employees believe their employer feels no commitment to their welfare, they are less likely to feel committed to their employer.

AN ORGANIZATION'S OBJECTIVES

A logical place to begin selecting employee benefits is to establish objectives for the benefits package. This helps an organization select the most effective benefits and monitor whether the benefits are doing what they should. Unfortunately, research suggests that most organizations do not have written objectives for benefits.

Among companies that do set goals, the most common objectives include controlling the cost of health care benefits and retaining employees.[44] The first goal explains the growing use of wellness programs and employee-directed health plans. For the second goal, employers need to learn what employees care about. In some cases, the approach may be indirect, helping the company distinguish itself as an employer that certain kinds of employees will be attracted and committed to. For example, a

Hill and Knowlton has received recognition as a great place to work and for its travelling refreshment cart to celebrate the end of the week.

HR BEST PRACTICES

Tuition Reimbursement Can Put Employees at the Top

Mandy Webster arrived at the Vancouver Fraser Port Authority (VFPA) as a temporary employee in a low skill job. Personal issues had forced her to leave university a few years before, with only a handful of credits and few career opportunities. Today, she is the document support analyst at VFPA and on her way to completing a bachelor of arts degree. The VFPA is picking up the tab for her $15,000 tuition fees, plus her books and supplies. On top of that, Webster has been given "education days" to cover some of the time she needs for classes.

"It's almost too good to be true," she says. "To me it was a no-brainer. I can take care of my unfinished business and do it without missing a mortgage payment." She applied for a tuition reimbursement last year reasoning, "it was time to make a move or I would get too comfortable." Webster uses words such as "invigorating" and "rejuvenating" to describe the return to education—even though a BA will have little value in her current role. "There was a time when I was sinking a bit," she says. "I feel a new sense of ambition and excitement and I feel like I'm accomplishing something."

Canadian studies on how much firms spend on tuition reimbursement for courses unrelated to an employee's current role—or the return on investment—are hard to come by. However, this is an important perk at many organizations on top employer lists.

Christine Dioszeghy, director of human resources with the VFPA and the person who approved Webster's application, doesn't need numbers to tell her the story. "We want to hire continuous learners," she says. "Even if these skills are not related, they're still somebody broadening their business acumen."

Some organizations are willing to pay for courses not directly related to a specific job as long as they will contribute to the organization in some way. At VFPA, the employee has to make a formal application that makes a case for the course and a reason for the company to foot the bill.

Christie Digital, a Waterloo, Ontario–based video projection design and manufacturing firm, offers a similar program. Kimberley Hogan, vice-president of HR, says most employees apply to upgrade

their education—such as a technologist with a college diploma who wants to earn a university degree—but there are those who simply want to try something new. "At the end of the day, anybody going out and learning and taking that initiative to learn new things, to learn new technologies—all of that is going to benefit Christie," she says. "Somebody who is working as a young technician on the floor and wants to get his engineering degree, it's not pertinent today but, in the future, he'll be somebody we can move into our engineering organization."

In the long term, Hogan says investing in training now, even if it's unrelated, offsets future recruitment costs. "To hire one engineer, if we go outside and we use a recruiting firm, on average we're going to spend $30,000 a year," she says. "If I can keep them and upgrade their skills and I can grow the future managers of the company, that's good."

SOURCE: Danielle Harder, "Tuition Reimbursement Can Put Employees at the Top," *Canadian HR Reporter*, March 24, 2008. pp. 17, 21.

company that establishes itself as committed to the environment could offer benefits in line with that goal—say bicycle storage for commuters and vouchers for taking the bus to work.[45] Employees with a passion for the environment would be especially engaged by such offerings.

EMPLOYEES' EXPECTATIONS AND VALUES

Employees expect to receive benefits that are legally required and widely available, and they value benefits they are likely to use. For example, the "HR Oops!" box illustrates the value employees place on

product discounts. To meet employee expectations about benefits, it can be helpful to see what other organizations offer. Employers should also consider that the value employees place on various benefits is likely to differ from one employee to another. As outlined earlier in the chapter, a basic demographic factor such as age can influence the kinds of benefits employees want. However, these were only general observations; organizations should check which considerations apply to their own employees and identify more specific needs and differences.

The choice of benefits may influence current employees' satisfaction and may also affect the organization's recruiting, in terms of both the ease of recruiting and the kinds of employees attracted to the organization.

FLEXIBLE BENEFITS

Organizations can address differences in employees' needs and engage their employees by offering **flexible benefits plans** in place of a single benefits package for all employees. These plans, often called flexible benefits or *flex benefits*, offer employees a set of alternatives from which they can choose the types and amounts of benefits they want. The plans vary. Some impose minimum levels for certain benefits, such as health care coverage; some allow employees to receive money in exchange for choosing a "light" package; and some let employees pay extra for the privilege of receiving more benefits. For example, some plans let employees give up vacation days for more pay or to purchase extra vacation days in exchange for a reduction in pay.

Flexible benefits plans have a number of advantages.[46] The selection process can make employees more aware of the value of the benefits, particularly when the plan assigns each employee a sum of money to allocate to benefits. Also, the individual choice in a flexible benefits plan enables each employee to match his or her needs to the company's benefits, increasing the plan's actual value to the employee. Superior Propane, a Calgary-based Canadian marketer of propane and appliances, switched to a flex benefits plan for its 1,800 employees. Terry Gill, vice-president of human resources, says that Superior Propane changed to flex benefits to "attract a more diverse group of employees to fit in with our new performance-based culture. We realized that most employees wanted opportunity and choice—a 'one-size-fits-all' plan wouldn't work."[47]

A drawback of flexible benefits plans is that they have a higher administrative cost, especially in the design and startup stages. Organizations can avoid some of the higher cost, however, by using software packages and standardized plans that have been developed for employers wishing to offer flexible benefits. Another possible drawback is that employee selection of benefits will increase rather than decrease costs, because employees will select the kinds of benefits they expect to need the most. For example, an employee expecting to need a lot of dental work is more likely to sign up for a dental plan. The heavy use of the dental coverage would then drive up the employer's premiums for that coverage. Costs can also be difficult to estimate when employees select their benefits. Organizations frequently respond by requiring employees to share in the costs of benefits.

Communicating Total Rewards to Employees

"Communication is often a weak link. An average program well-communicated will do better than an outstanding program poorly communicated."[48] A comprehensive communications strategy is required to help employees understand the total value the organization is investing in its approach to compensating and rewarding employees. This is essential so that total rewards can achieve their objectives including focusing employees on organizational goals, attracting and retaining employees, and creating a motivating environment.

L07 Discuss the importance of effectively communicating the organization's approach to total rewards.

Because they interact with their employees each day, managers play a significant role in communication. The HR department should prepare them to explain to their employees why the organization's approach to compensating and rewarding employees is designed as it is, and to determine whether employee concerns indicate a need for change. Employees are interested in their compensation and rewards and they need a great deal of detailed information. It follows that technology such as the Internet and supporting databases can play a significant role. More employers are using technology to provide employees with tools and information related to both communication and administration of employee compensation and rewards.

Employees and job applicants often lack a clear sense of the market value of total rewards that an organization offers. For example, research asking employees about their benefits has shown that employees significantly underestimate the cost and value of their benefits.[49] Probably a major reason for their lack of knowledge is a lack of communication from employers. When New Brunswick Power teamed up with its union to communicate the benefits of the move to a flexible benefits plan, the objective was to "get the message out to workers that this was their plan, they owned it, and they needed to get an understanding of how it worked." The company provided training sessions, and gave every employee a video to take home and watch and discuss with their families.[50]

flexible benefits plan
A benefits plan that offers employees a set of alternatives from which they can choose the types and amounts of benefits they want.

Employers have many options for communicating information about benefits. Recent research from SunLife showed that different generational groups have different preferences for receiving information from their employers about rewards—baby-boomers are most likely to prefer paper-based communications, Gen-X appreciates online communication, and Gen-Y prefers online communication to anything else.[51] To increase the likelihood that employees will receive and understand the messages, employers can combine several media, such as videos, brochures, question-and-answer meetings, online total rewards statements, intranet pages, memos, presentations, and email.

Communication efforts are also moving beyond ensuring employees receive and understand the messages to "driving action, enabling employees to make the best possible use of the programs available to them," according to Diane McElroy, a senior vice-president with Aon Hewitt in Toronto. McElroy adds that some employers are even developing total rewards statements for *prospective* employees as part of the job offer. "Some organizations are providing these statements when they make offers to job candidates. That way, if the potential new hire receives another offer—especially one with a higher base salary—he or she can make an informed comparison and determine whether a bigger paycheque really does mean great compensation. This can be a smart approach in a tight labour market."[52] In summary, an investment of creativity in employee communication can reap great returns in the form of committed, satisfied employees, and the achievement of organizational objectives including employee attraction and retention.

Executive Compensation and Rewards

2, 4, 5

The media have drawn public attention to the issue of executive compensation and rewards. The issue attracts notice because of the very high pay that the top executives of major North American companies have received in recent years. A significant part of executive compensation comes in the form of company stock. For example, in 2010 Frank Stronach of Magna International received a $205,988 base salary but also received $17,006,353 in stock options, a bonus of $41,908,220, and "other" compensation

L08 Discuss issues related to compensating and rewarding executives.

of $2,690,726 for a total rewards package of $61,811,287. Richard Waugh of the Bank of Nova Scotia received a base salary of $1,208,333, bonus of $1,600,000, $3,925,000 in company shares and an additional $3,925,000 in stock options.[53]

Although high amounts like this apply to only a small proportion of the total workforce, the issue of executive pay is relevant to pay structure in terms of equity theory. As we discussed earlier in the chapter, employees draw conclusions about the fairness of pay by making comparisons among employees' inputs and outcomes. By many comparisons, CEO pay is high. In 2010, Canada's 100 highest paid CEOs of companies listed on the TSX received $8.38 million in total compensation, a 27 percent increase from 2009.[54] The Conference Board Task Force on Executive Compensation and Pay Governance endorses ensuring strong links between an organization's financial performance and executive compensation, referred to as *value leverage* i.e., "pay percentile equals performance percentile"—a percentage change in executive compensation should directly relate to a percentage change in their organization's performance.[55] To help make sense of all the numbers, the Financial Post publishes its CEO Scorecard, which provides *Bang for Buck* ratings for Canadian executives. For example, an executive scoring "around $1 is getting what they should be getting, according to a proprietary algorithm which takes into account a CEO's comparative compensation and company revenue as well as their performance" in their industry-related TSX index. The CEO Scorecard provides a helpful snapshot to see what companies likely overspent on executive compensation and what companies are likely getting a bargain.[56]

Overall, executive compensation and rewards are complicated due to the increased number of items included, for example, direct pay, short- and long-term incentives, stock options, and benefits. Top executives help to set the tone or culture of the organization, and employees at all levels are affected by behaviour at the top. As a result, the equity of executive compensation and rewards can affect more employees than, say, the compensation and rewards received by warehouse workers or sales clerks. Another way to think about the equity of CEO pay is to compare it with the pay of other employees in the organization. Again, equity theory would consider not only the size of the executive pay relative to pay for other employees but also the amount the CEOs contribute. In 2010, Canada's 100 highest paid CEOs received 189 times the average Canadian worker's wage, up from 105 times the average Canadian worker's wage in 1998. For example, Canadian workers earned an average wage

Frank Stronach of Magna International is one of Canada's highest paid executives.

of $44,366 in 2010. By 12:00 noon on January 3, 2011, the "average" CEO on the top 100-best paid list had already earned that amount.[57]

EXECUTIVE INCENTIVES AND BENEFITS

Because executives have a much stronger influence over the organization's performance than other employees do, incentive pay for executives warrants special attention. Assuming that incentives influence performance, decisions about incentives for executives should have a great impact on how well the executives and the organization perform. Along with overall pay levels for executives, organizations need to create incentive plans for this small but important group of employees.

To encourage executives to develop a commitment to the organization's long-term success, executive compensation often combines short-term and long-term incentives. *Short-term incentives* include bonuses based on the year's profits, return on investment, or other measures related to the organization's goals. Sometimes, to gain tax advantages, the actual payment of the bonus is deferred (e.g., by making it part of a retirement plan). *Long-term incentives* include stock options and stock purchase plans. The rationale for these long-term incentives is that executives will want to do what is best for the organization because that will cause the value of their stock to grow. Renowned investor, Warren Buffett is credited with coining "have skin in the game" in reference to the importance of a firm's executive sharing a stake in the organization's success.

As well as legally required benefits and the benefits extended to other employees in the organization, executives often receive extra benefits and services. These executive benefits and services may include such far-reaching benefits as use of corporate aircraft, company-provided or -subsidized homes, memberships and tickets to sporting and cultural events, in addition to benefits such as company cars, electronic devices, sabbaticals, and extended vacations.

PERFORMANCE MEASURES FOR EXECUTIVES

The balanced-scorecard approach discussed in Chapter 7 is useful in designing executive pay. Whirlpool, for example, has used a balanced scorecard that combines measures of whether the organization is delivering value to shareholders, customers, and employees. These measures are listed in Table 8.4. Rewarding achievement of a variety of goals in a balanced scorecard reduces the temptation to win bonuses by manipulating financial data.

TABLE 8.4   Balanced Scorecard for Whirlpool Executives

TYPE OF MEASURES	VALUE CREATION
Shareholder value	Economic value added Earnings per share Cash flow Total cost productivity
Customer value	Quality Market share Customer satisfaction
Employee value	High-performance culture index High-performance culture deployment Training and development diversity

SOURCE: E. L. Gubman, *The Talent Solution* (New York: McGraw-Hill, 1998).

THINKING ETHICALLY

Should "Lifestyle" Be Covered?

In recent years a variety of widely publicized "lifestyle" drugs to treat conditions such as obesity, male erectile dysfunction, infertility, and male pattern baldness have become available. As a result, the line between the medical and social dimensions of health is blurring. Although some employers consider these drugs "cosmetic" or "discretionary" and refuse to include them in their health care plans, other employers are willing to share or fund the coverage. According to a Hewitt Associates' survey, more than one-half of employers provide coverage for infertility treatments, and smoking cessation medication. However, only one-third of employers covered drugs to treat obesity and only 5 percent of employers were willing to pay for drugs to treat male pattern baldness. Employers that provide coverage for "lifestyle" drugs often put in cost-control measures—for example, annual or lifetime dollar maximums, or capping coverage for smoking cessation medications at $825 (lifetime) and for obesity drugs at $1,325 (annually).

SOURCES: Sarah Beech, "Lifestyle Choices," *Benefits Canada*, March 2008, p. 45; Sarah Beech, "Rethinking Coverage for 'Lifestyle' Drugs," *Benefits Canada*, October 10, 2007, www.benefitscanada.com, retrieved October 18, 2008; and Joel Lexchin, "Lifestyle Drugs: Issues for Debate," *CMAJ*, May 15, 2001, p. 164, www .cmaj.ca/cgi/content/full/164/10/1449, retrieved May 8, 2008.

QUESTIONS

1. Should "lifestyle drugs" be included in an organization's benefits coverage? Why or why not?

2. Should an employer be able to intervene in the physician–patient relationship to assess whether a treatment is "medically necessary"?

3. Would your answer to Question 1 be different if the treatment in question were for easing the suffering of a cancer patient rather than treating male pattern baldness or obesity?

ETHICAL ISSUES

Incentive pay for executives lays the groundwork for significant ethical issues. When an organization links pay to its stock performance, executives need the ethical backbone to be honest about their company's performance even when dishonesty or clever shading of the truth offers the tempting potential for large earnings. As recent scandals involving WorldCom, Enron, Nortel Networks, and other companies have shown, the results can be disastrous when unethical behaviour is implicated.

Among these issues is one we have already touched on in this chapter: the difficulty of setting performance measures that encourage precisely the behaviour desired. In the case of incentives tied to stock performance, executives may be tempted to inflate the stock price in order to enjoy bonuses and valuable stock options. The intent is for the executive to boost stock value through efficient operations, technological innovation, effective leadership, and so on. Unfortunately, individuals at some companies determined that they could obtain faster results through accounting practices that stretched the norms in order to present the company's performance in the best light. When such practices are discovered to be misleading, stock prices plunge and the company's reputation is damaged, sometimes beyond repair.

A related issue when executive pay includes stock or stock options is insider trading. When executives are stockholders, they have a dual role as owners and managers. This places them at an advantage over others who want to invest in the company. An individual, a pension fund, or other investors have less information about the company than its managers do—for example, whether product development is proceeding on schedule, whether a financing deal is in the works, and so on. An executive who knows about these activities could therefore reap a windfall in the stock market by buying or selling stock based on his or her knowledge about the company's future. Although regulators place strict limits on this "insider trading," some executives have violated these limits. In the worst cases, executives have sold stock, secretly knowing their company was failing, before the stock price collapsed. The losers are the employees, retirees, and other investors who hold the now-worthless stock.

As recent news stories have reminded us, linking pay to stock price can reward unethical behaviour, at least in the short term and at least in the minds of a handful of executives. Yet, given the motivational power of incentive pay, organizations cannot afford to abandon incentives for their executives. These temptations are among the reasons that executive positions demand individuals who maintain the highest ethical standards.

SUMMARY

L01 ▸ Discuss how organizations implement a "total rewards" approach to compensating and rewarding employees.

- Many organizations are recognizing the strategic value of taking a comprehensive approach to compensating and rewarding employees. This "total rewards" approach frequently involves creating a value proposition for current and prospective employees that clearly identifies all of the aspects that are valued by employees in exchange for their time and expertise.
- Canadian companies take a total rewards approach to attract and retain valued employees and improve capacity to meet organizational goals.

L02 ▸ Identify the kinds of decisions and influences involved in providing base pay to employees.

- Organizations make decisions to define a job structure, or relative pay for different jobs within the organization. They establish relative pay for different functions and different levels of responsibility for each function.
- Organizations must also establish pay levels, or the average paid for the different jobs. These decisions are based on the organization's goals, market data, legal requirements, and principles of fairness. Together job structure and pay level establish a pay structure policy.
- Organizations typically begin with a job evaluation to measure the relative worth of their jobs. The organization then creates a pay structure that includes pay grades or pay ranges for each job in the organization.

L03 ▸ Describe alternatives to job-based pay.

- To obtain more flexibility, organizations may reduce the levels in the organization's job structure. This process of delayering or broadbanding involves creating broad bands of jobs within pay ranges.
- Other organizations reward employees according to their competencies. They establish competency-based pay systems, or structures that set pay according to the employees' level of knowledge and what they are capable of doing.

L04 ▸ Describe how organizations recognize individual, team, and organizational performance through the use of incentives.

- Organizations may recognize individual performance through such incentives as piecework rates, merit pay,

sales commissions, and bonuses for meeting individual performance objectives.
- Common team incentives include gainsharing, bonuses, and team awards.
- Incentives for meeting organizational objectives include profit sharing and stock ownership.

L05 ▸ Discuss the role of benefits as part of employee total rewards.

- Like pay, benefits and services help employers attract, retain, and provide a source of motivation for employees. Employees expect at least a minimum level of benefits, and providing more than the minimum helps an organization compete in the labour market.
- Benefits and services are also a significant expense, but employers provide benefits and services because employees value them and many are required by law.

L06 ▸ Summarize the types of employee benefits offered by employers.

- Employers must contribute to the Canada Pension Plan/Quebec Pension Plan, Employment Insurance, and Workers' Compensation. In addition, employers offer various kinds of insurance, retirement plans, and paid leave.
- Due to the increasing costs of providing employee benefits, many Canadian organizations are seeking ways to hold back the costs. Many employers have responded to work/life role conflicts by offering family-friendly benefits.
- Organizations need to establish objectives and select benefits that support those objectives. Flexible benefits are a means to give employees control over the benefits they receive.

L07 ▸ Discuss the importance of effectively communicating the organization's approach to total rewards.

- A comprehensive communications strategy is needed to help employees understand and value all the components in an organization's approach to total rewards. Managers and the human resource department share responsibility for this important requirement.
- Technology can provide employees access to information and other tools associated with administration of compensation and rewards.

- Employers have many options for communicating information about total rewards. Using a combination of media increases employees' understanding.

L08 ▶ Discuss issues related to compensating and rewarding executives.

- Executive compensation has drawn public scrutiny because top executive compensation is much higher than the average worker's pay.

- Chief executive officers have an extremely large impact on the organization's performance, but critics complain that when performance falters, executive pay does not decline as fast as the organization's profits or stock price.

- Performance measures should encourage behaviour that is in the organization's best interests, including ethical behaviour.

Critical Thinking Questions

1. Some individuals evaluate prospective employers' job offers based only on direct pay considerations. What additional factors should be considered when evaluating job offers from employers?

2. Why might an organization choose to pay employees more than the market rate? Why might it choose to pay less? What are the consequences of paying more or less than the market rate?

3. What are the advantages of establishing pay ranges, rather than specific pay levels, for each job? What are the drawbacks of this approach?

4. Suppose a small startup business wants to establish a competency-based pay structure. What would be some advantages of this approach? List the issues the company should be prepared to address in setting up this system. Consider the kinds of information you will need and the ways employees may react to the new pay structure.

5. With some organizations and jobs, pay is primarily wages or salaries, and with others, incentive pay is more important. For each of the following jobs, state whether you think the pay should emphasize base pay (wages and salaries) or incentive pay (bonuses, profit sharing, and so on). Give a reason for each.
   a. An accountant at a manufacturing company
   b. A salesperson for a software company
   c. A mechanic for a major airline
   d. A marketing manager for a consumer packaged-goods firm
   e. A recruitment specialist for the federal government

6. Why do some organizations link incentive pay to the organization's overall performance? Is it appropriate to use stock performance as an incentive for employees at all levels? Why or why not?

7. Why do employers provide employee benefits, rather than providing all compensation in the form of pay and letting employees buy the benefits and services they want?

8. Of the benefits discussed in this chapter, list the ones you consider essential—those benefits you would require in any job offer. Why are these benefits important to you?

9. Why is it important to communicate information about total rewards? Suppose you work in the HR department of a company that has decided to add new elements to its total rewards—onsite massage plus an increased budget to support learning and development opportunities for all employees. How would you recommend communicating this change? What information should your messages include? How would you know if your communication strategy was successful?

10. Do you think executive total compensation is too high? Why or why not?

What's Your HR IQ?

 Connect offers more ways to check what you've learned so far. Find experiential exercises, Test Your Knowledge quizzes, videos, and many other resources to gauge your HR IQ.

CASE STUDY 8.1:   How Fog Creek Software Pays Developers

When Joel Spolsky and Michael Pryor founded Fog Creek Software, their vision was of a company run by people whose technical backgrounds meant they understood what really motivates programmers. The company would hire the best, make them comfortable, pay them well, and then get out of the way so they could create great products.

Early on, Spolsky and Pryor set out to develop a pay structure that would be consistent with the company's mission. They decided that the system should be so objective that there would be no questioning or judgment calls about which employee earns how much. And the results would be so objective and fair that there would be no incentive to be secretive about what any employee earns.

Like any computer pro, Spolsky went online for ideas. He discovered that Construx, a software consulting firm, had posted online an outline for measuring levels of the software profession. Using this as a starting point, Spolsky created a job structure for Fog Creek. The structure is straightforward: every employee is assigned to a level between 8 (summer interns) and 16 (chief executive officer). Assignment to a level is not a judgment call but is based on a formula incorporating the employee's experience, skills, and scope of responsibility.

- Experience is measured as the number of years of full-time experience in the field of the employee's job at Fog Creek, counting only years after the employee finished school. At any given level, every employee earns the same salary.
- Skills are defined with descriptive statements along a continuum. For example, at the lowest level is a programmer "learning the basic principles of software engineering" who needs close supervision. At the other extreme would be someone who makes a unique contribution—a programmer who "has consistently had major success during participation in all aspects of small and large projects."
- Scope of responsibility ranges from primarily supporting another employee to running multiple projects.

Based on this job structure, Spolsky created a chart that is used for assigning each employee to a level.

Spolsky also created a chart that indicates the base salary for each level, based on market salaries obtained from sources such as Salary.com and Glassdoor.com. Each employee earns the amount specified by the chart. Every year, the company's managers review each employee's work to see if the employee should be assigned to a new level. Every employee who is reassigned then earns the amount associated with the new level. Employees also earn a bonus based on the company's profits for the year.

Fog Creek's system has been challenged by the stiff competition for programmer talent. If the company paid extra to lure in new employees at a higher rate, the existing employees would demand a raise or see their treatment as unfair. Rather than expect employees to accept the "salary inversion" of newer employees earning more than their more-experienced colleagues, Fog Creek has responded to talent crunches by raising the salaries of all employees at a given level to make them as high as the going market rate for that level. Spolsky believes that the solution is expensive but essential for maintaining equity and keeping talent.

Questions

1. How well does Fog Creek Software's pay structure meet (a) legal requirements; (b) the conditions of product markets; and (c) the conditions of labour markets?
2. Joel Spolsky set out to create a pay structure that's objective. Based on the information given, how objective would you say Fog Creek's system is? What other qualities besides objectivity do you think Fog Creek employees might care about?
3. Fog Creek is a small company with a few dozen technical employees. How might its pay structure need to change (if at all), if the company grows to hundreds of employees? Would these changes likely appeal to the employees?

SOURCES: Joel Spolsky, "Why I Never Let Employees Negotiate a Raise," *Inc.*, April 2009, www.inc.com; and Fog Creek Software, "Careers" and "About the Company," corporate website, www.fogcreek.com, accessed April 21, 2010.

CASE STUDY 8.2:   Incentive Pay Part of the Strategy at Nucor

Nucor is not your average steel company. Compared with its traditionally managed competitors, Nucor is aggressively pushing decision making down to the lowest levels of the hierarchy, and it links two-thirds of pay to performance, specifically production levels. That strategy has opened the company up to employee-driven changes that have made the company efficient, flexible, and innovative. Its use of new technology in the form of electric arc furnaces lets the company shut down and start up operations faster to meet demand for its process

of melting down scrap metal and shaping it to meet customers' needs.

Nucor's practices may be different, but the company resembles its competitors in one way: when building construction crashed to a halt and manufacturing orders dried up, Nucor joined other steel companies in facing a shocking drop-off in demand. As orders fell, so did output: in the last quarter of 2008, production went from 95 percent of capacity to 50 percent, and it continued to fall to 45 percent in 2009.

At that point, Nucor's reliance on incentive pay went from an advantage in motivating workers to a serious problem of how to keep morale up. As bonuses shrank, total compensation fell by up to 40 percent. The company looked at its overall performance in 2008, which included a modest profit despite the end-of-the-year downturn, and paid all its employees profit sharing totalling $270 million. In addition, the company awarded a special one-time bonus of up to $2,000. More recently, it began offering financial counselling and the option to withdraw funds from employees' profit-sharing accounts.

Of course the pain is felt at the top as well. Incentive pay is the norm for executives at most companies, and Nucor is no exception. Chief Executive Officer Dan DiMicco saw a 23 percent drop in his total compensation in 2008, for example. Much of the drop was caused by a 46 percent decline in the value of stock awarded to DiMicco.

One advantage of tying part of employee's pay to profits is that Nucor can afford to keep more workers on board during lean times. The company has avoided layoffs and assigned otherwise-idle workers to review safety programs, find ways to cut costs, carry out preventive maintenance, and even mow the lawns. If Nucor can't motivate workers with money, it can at least show them the company is trying to save their jobs.

Employees seem to appreciate the effort. CEO DiMicco told a reporter, "[Our employees] go further than we would ever think to ask. It makes you feel really good about being a leader in this company when you have that kind of support."

That positive attitude has helped management lead the company to prepare for growth even as employees endured hard times. It's a commitment that is likely to reap dividends as demand picks up and profits begin to roll in again. With production rising about 70 percent of capacity and expected to hit 90 percent in some mills, the future is again looking bright for Nucor and its employees.

Questions

1. Nucor gives its employees a relatively great say in decision making along with compensation tied to performance. Discuss how incentive pay could be more effective when it is linked to greater authority and room to innovate?

2. When times are tough, incentive pay falls even if employees are trying hard. In that case, should companies find other ways to reward employees? Why or why not? Evaluate Nucor's use of a "special bonus" in this situation.

3. Cutting compensation by paying smaller production bonuses and no profit sharing when orders dried up might have helped Nucor avoid layoffs. Evaluate the fairness of this approach. Does the fact that the chief executive also earned less make the situation fairer? Would you rather work for a company that lays off employees in lean times or one that offers no incentive pay in lean times? Why?

SOURCES: Nanette Byrnes, "Pain, but No Layoffs at Nucor," *Business Week,* March 26, 2009, www.businessweek.com; Adam Bell, "Nucor CEO DiMicco Sees Total Pay Drop 23 Percent in 2008," *Charlotte (N.C.) Observer,* March 26, 2009, Business & Company Resource Center, http://galenet.galegroup.com; Stella M. Hopkins, "Special Bonus, Profit-Sharing Options Aid Nucor Workers," *Charlotte (N.C.) Observer,* August 16, 2009, Business & Company Resource Center, http://galenet.galegroup.com; and Edmond Lococo, "Nucor Posts Second Straight Profit as Shipments Rise," *Business Week,* April 26, 2010, www.businessweek.com.

 **Practise and learn online with Connect.**

Real People and HR

...Kelly Parascandalo, Director, Customer Provisioning and Assurance Operations—Bell Canada

Kelly Parascandalo joined Bell Canada in 1992, after completing her bachelor's degree from York University. At Bell Canada she progressed from clerk through the management ranks in various departments within Bell Canada. Kelly has been a director within Bell Canada since 2001 and is currently the director of customer provisioning and assurance operations within the field services team.

Kelly is responsible for leading teams across the world, ensuring that service assurance and provision orders are processed or resolved prior to being dispatched to outside field technicians.

Name...
Kelly Parascandalo

Job...
Director, customer provisioning and assurance operations at Bell Canada

Adjective people would use to describe you...
Confident

First job...
Counter help at Country Style Donuts when I was 13. My first real job was a counsellor at a halfway house for people with mental health issues. We were responsible for helping them with day to day tasks required to function within a group home setting. I was accountable for coaching the residents on hygiene, peer relationships, household chores and other issues that may arise with their well-being on a daily basis.

First job with international responsibilities...
My first job with international responsibilities was at Bell Canada, director of our Home Phone Help Desk. The work had been outsourced to India three months earlier and had not been as successful as Bell was expecting from a customer satisfaction perspective. I came into the role to develop a strategy to improve processes, training, and cultural issues that could be implemented to enable us to offer an improved customer experience.

Biggest human resource management challenge you've faced as a manager accountable for global operations...
Finding ways to bridge the cultural differences between an international workforce and our local customers' needs. It's important to understand the cultural variations offshore that could be impacting your customer's needs. This enables you to modify programs, processes, and training in unique ways that honours and respects the international culture while still meeting your corporate expectations.

Most rewarding aspect of your job...
It allows for constant learning. Working with various global operations you have the opportunity to learn about different businesses models, cultures, and operations. You work within a larger expanded network than you would normally be exposed to, enabling you to learn from a broader range of experiences and perspectives.

Four essential attributes that make someone more likely to be successful in a global assignment...
- Open-minded—must be willing to learn/understand/accept different cultures and experiences.
- Enterprising—must be able to drive change and develop new processes/programs that can be adapted globally.
- Intuitive—many of the cultural norms are not explicitly stated but must be intuited through observation and discussion.
- Disciplined—managing resources globally requires discipline in terms of practices and processes implemented in order to ensure that your business and people are being managed effectively when you are not on-site to oversee the day to day operations.

What a company can do to prepare an employee for a global work assignment...
By ensuring that clear expectations and priorities are established. It's also important that they provide the employee with sufficient time to enable them to understand the operation and the culture that they are entering into. Lastly, the company needs to be prepared to be flexible in changing some of their processes and programs while never compromising on what they need to deliver for their customers.

Best career advice that you ever received...
Not to waste time talking about how capable you are and show people you are capable. Your accomplishments will always speak louder than your words.

Advice for someone beginning a career in a global organization...
Invest a lot of time in building relationships especially with employees and colleagues located in different countries. They will provide insights and perspectives that you may not otherwise have access to that can help shape how and what you deliver.

SOURCE: Reprinted with the kind permission of Kelly Parascandalo.

Chapter 9

LABOUR RELATIONS

Air Canada's labour dispute with its pilots resulted in an arbitration process imposed by the federal government.

{ ## What Do I Need to Know?

After reading this chapter, you should be able to:

L01 Define unions and labour relations and their role in organizations.

L02 Identify the labour relations goals of management, labour unions, and society.

L03 Summarize laws and regulations that affect labour relations.

L04 Describe the union organizing process.

L05 Explain how management and unions negotiate collective agreements.

L06 Summarize the practice of collective agreement administration.

L07 Describe more cooperative approaches to labour–management relations.

Air Canada's Union Troubles

The surge in pilot sick calls began just one day after Air Canada management tabled its final offer during lengthy and difficult contract talks. More than a dozen pilots in Montreal claimed their absence on the busy March break weekend was due to either fatigue or stress. However, Air Canada asserted the pilot sick calls were sanctioned by their union and should be considered an illegal strike. According to Air Canada, pilot absences inconvenienced many Air Canada customers and contributed to cancellations and delays for 60 out of 660 flights during the busy March break weekend. Earlier in the same month, Air Canada had threatened to lock out its pilots while the union that represents ground crew and mechanics had served strike notice. At the request of the federal Labour Minister, the Canada Industrial Relations Board quickly intervened and ordered the pilots back to work. The Air Canada Pilots Association representing its 3,000 pilots was ordered to take all reasonable steps to bring an end to the "strike." In a letter to union members, union chairman, Captain Jean-Marc Belanger said that he was "frustrated by the airline's refusal to negotiate and by the federal government's decision to force workers into a collective agreement."[1]

Introduction

This chapter explores human resource activities in organizations where employees belong to unions or where employees are seeking to organize unions. We begin by formally defining unions and labour relations, then describe the history, scope, and impact of union activity. We next summarize government laws and regulations affecting unions and labour relations. The following three sections detail types of activities involving unions: union organizing, collective agreement negotiation, and collective agreement administration. Finally, we identify ways in which unions and management are working together in arrangements that are more cooperative than the traditional labour–management relationship.

Role of Unions and Labour Relations

1,2,4

In Canada today, most workers act as individuals to select jobs that are acceptable to them and to negotiate pay, benefits, flexible hours, and other work conditions. Especially when there is stiff competition for labour and employees have hard-to-replace skills, this arrangement produces satisfactory results for most employees. At times, however, workers have believed their needs and interests do not receive enough consideration from management. One response by workers is to act collectively by forming and joining labour **unions**, organizations formed for the purpose of representing their members' interests and resolving conflicts with employers.

L01 ▸ Define unions and labour relations and their role in organizations.

Unions have a role because some degree of conflict is inevitable between workers and management.[2] For example, managers can increase profits by lowering workers' pay, but workers benefit in the short term if lower profits result because their pay is higher. Still, this type of conflict is more complex than a simple tradeoff, such as wages versus profits. Rising profits can help employees by driving up profit sharing or other benefits, and falling profits can result in layoffs and a lack of investment. Although employers can use programs like profit sharing to help align employee interests with their own, some remaining divergence of interests is inevitable. Labour unions represent worker interests and the collective bargaining process provides a way to manage the conflict. In other words, through systems for hearing complaints and negotiating agreements, unions and managers resolve conflicts between employers and employees.

As unionization of workers became more common, universities and colleges developed training in how to manage union–management interactions. This specialty, called **labour relations**, emphasizes skills that managers and union leaders can use to foster effective labour–management cooperation, minimize costly forms of conflict (such as strikes), and seek win-win solutions to disagreements. Labour relations involves three levels of decisions:[3]

unions
Organizations formed for the purpose of representing their members' interests in dealing with employers.

labour relations
A field that emphasizes skills managers and union leaders can use to minimize costly forms of conflict (such as strikes) and seek win-win solutions to disagreements.

1. *Labour relations strategy.* For management, the decision involves whether the organization will work with unions or develop (or maintain) nonunion operations. This decision is influenced by outside forces such as public opinion and competition. For unions, the decision involves whether to resist changes in how unions relate to the organization or accept new kinds of labour–management relationships.

2. *Negotiating contracts.* As we will describe later in the chapter, collective agreement negotiations

in a union setting involve decisions about pay structure, job security, work rules, workplace safety, and many other issues. These decisions affect workers' and the employer's situation for the term of the contract.

3. *Administering collective agreements.* These decisions involve day-to-day activities in which union members and the organization's managers may have disagreements. Issues include complaints of work rules being violated or workers being treated unfairly in particular situations. A formal grievance procedure is typically used to resolve these issues.

Later sections in this chapter describe how managers and unions carry out the activities connected with these levels of decisions, as well as the goals and legal constraints affecting these activities.

craft union

Labour union whose members all have a particular skill or occupation.

industrial union

A labour union whose members are linked by their work in a particular industry.

Canadian Labour Congress (CLC)

A union federation that serves as an umbrella organization for dozens of affiliated Canadian and international unions, as well as provincial federations of labour and regional labour councils.

NATIONAL AND INTERNATIONAL UNIONS

Most union members belong to a national or international union. Figure 9.1 shows the number of workers covered by Canada's top-ten labour organizations.

These unions may be either craft or industrial unions. The members of a **craft union** all have a particular skill or occupation. Examples include the International Brotherhood of Electrical Workers for electricians and the United Brotherhood of Painters and Allied Trades for painters. Craft unions are often responsible for training their members through apprenticeships and for supplying craft workers to employers. For example, an employer would send requests for electricians to the union,

which would decide which electricians to send out. In this way, craft workers may work for many employers over time but have a constant link to the union. A craft union's bargaining power depends greatly on its control over the supply of its workers.

In contrast, **industrial unions** consist of members who are linked by their work in a particular industry. Examples include the Canadian Union of Public Employees and the Communications, Energy and Paperworkers Union of Canada. Typically, an industrial union represents many different occupations. Membership in the union is the result of working for a particular employer in the industry. Changing employers is less common than it is among craft workers, and employees who change employers remain members of the same union only if they happen to move to other employers covered by that union. Another difference is that whereas a craft union may restrict the number of skilled craftspeople—say, carpenters—to maintain higher wages, industrial unions try to organize as many employees in as wide a range of skills as possible.

With respect to union federations, the **Canadian Labour Congress (CLC)** has the largest coverage affiliation, with more than 3 million covered workers. The Canadian Labour Congress (CLC) is a union federation that serves as an umbrella organization for dozens of affiliated Canadian and international unions, as well as provincial federations of labour and regional labour councils. An important responsibility of the CLC is to represent labour's interests in issues such as wages and benefits, ensuring safe and healthy workplaces, environmental issues,

Kenneth Georgetti, president of the Canadian Labour Congress (CLC).

FIGURE 9.1

Top-Ten Labour Organizations (2010)

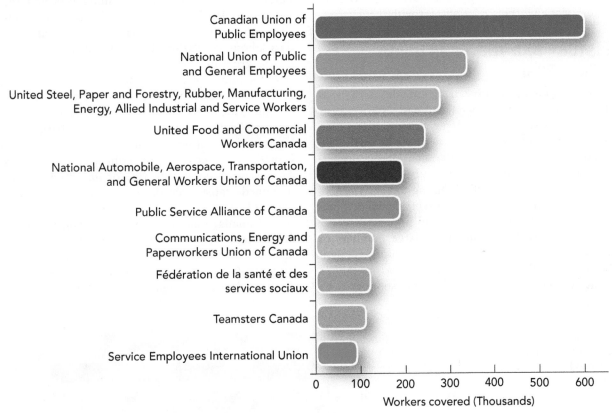

SOURCE: Human Resources and Skills Development Canada, "Top-Ten Labour Organizations, 2010," Table 3, www.hrsdc.gc.ca/eng/labour/labour_relations/info_analysis/overview/2010/section_6.shtml, retrieved May 16, 2012. Reprinted with the permission of the Minister of Public Works and Government Services, 2012.

and even international issues such as humanitarian efforts.[4] The organization also provides information, support, and analysis that member unions can use in their activities.

LOCAL UNIONS

Most national unions consist of multiple local units. Even when a national union plays the most critical role in negotiating the terms of a collective bargaining agreement, negotiation occurs at the local level for work rules and other issues that are locally determined. In addition, administration of the agreement largely takes place at the local union level. As a result, most day-to-day interaction between labour and management involves the local union.

Membership in the local union depends on the type of union. For an industrial union, the local may correspond to a single large facility or to a number of small facilities. In a craft union, the local may cover a city or a region.

> **union steward**
> An employee elected by union members to represent them in ensuring that the terms of the collective agreement are enforced.

Typically, the local union elects officers, such as president, vice-president, and treasurer. The officers may be responsible for contract negotiation, or the local may form a bargaining committee for that purpose. When the union is engaged in bargaining, the national union provides help, including background data about other settlements, technical advice, and the leadership of a representative from the national office.

Individual members participate in local unions in various ways. At meetings of the local union, they elect officials and vote on resolutions to strike. Most of workers' contact is with the **union steward**, an employee elected by union members to represent them in ensuring that the terms of the agreement are enforced. The union steward helps to investigate complaints and represents employees to supervisors and other managers when employees file grievances alleging contract violations.[5] When the union deals with several employers, as in the case of a craft union, a *business representative* performs some of the same functions as a union steward. Because of union stewards' and business representatives' close involvement with employees, it is to management's advantage to cultivate positive working relationships with them.

HISTORY AND TRENDS IN UNION MEMBERSHIP

Labour unions have existed in Canada as early as 1812. Unionism in Canada had early ties to Britain, as tradesmen active in the British trade union movement immigrated to Canada and settled in Atlantic Canada. The first national labour organization, a forerunner of the Canadian Labour Congress, was formed in 1873. During the early 1900s labour activities escalated as workers demanded better wages, shorter workdays, and improved working conditions. Strikes involving large numbers of workers were frequent, with the Winnipeg General Strike in 1919 being one of the largest. As labour politics developed, unionization was supported by the Co-operative Commonwealth Federation (CCF Party), which later became the New Democratic Party (NDP). Collective bargaining was first recognized in 1937. Post–World War II, U.S. unions began to spread into Canada and influenced Canada's labour legislation. Unionization levels continued to grow in both the private and public sectors until the mid-1990s despite pressures on unions that labour costs had not kept pace with productivity.[6]

Union membership in Canada peaked in 1994, reaching 36.1 percent of employees.[7] In 2010, labour organizations reported that 4,645,095 workers in Canada were covered by collective agreements. The overall unionization rate or *union density* has remained stable over the past four years at 31.5 percent.[8]

In Canada, unionization is much higher in the public sector than the private sector—in 2011 unionization rates were 74.7 percent in the public sector, in contrast to 17.5 percent in the private sector.[9] As is illustrated in Figure 9.2, union membership

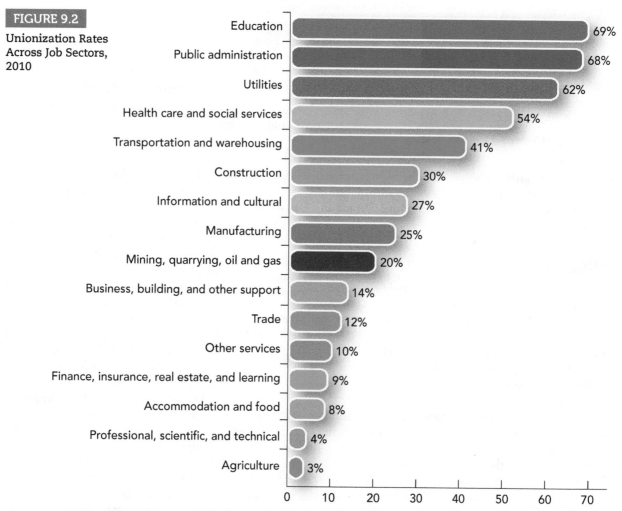

FIGURE 9.2

Unionization Rates Across Job Sectors, 2010

Sector	Rate
Education	69%
Public administration	68%
Utilities	62%
Health care and social services	54%
Transportation and warehousing	41%
Construction	30%
Information and cultural	27%
Manufacturing	25%
Mining, quarrying, oil and gas	20%
Business, building, and other support	14%
Trade	12%
Other services	10%
Finance, insurance, real estate, and learning	9%
Accommodation and food	8%
Professional, scientific, and technical	4%
Agriculture	3%

SOURCE: Sharanjit Uppal, "Unionization 2011: Unionization Rates in the First Half of 2010 and 2011 Chart B," Statistics Canada, www.statcan.gc.ca/pub/75-001-x/2011004/article/11579-eng.htm#a5, retrieved May 21, 2012.

FIGURE 9.3

Union Coverage by Province, 2010

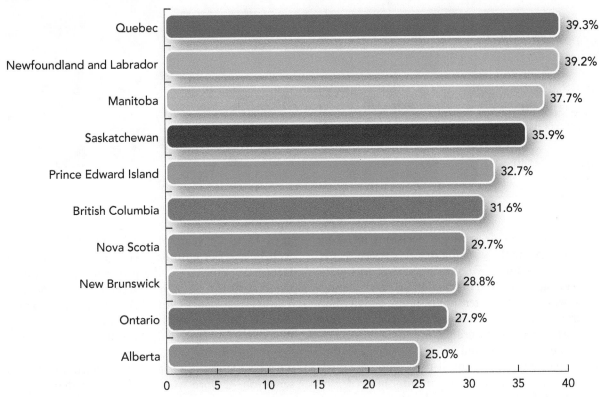

Province	Percentage
Quebec	39.3%
Newfoundland and Labrador	39.2%
Manitoba	37.7%
Saskatchewan	35.9%
Prince Edward Island	32.7%
British Columbia	31.6%
Nova Scotia	29.7%
New Brunswick	28.8%
Ontario	27.9%
Alberta	25.0%

SOURCE: Human Resources and Skills Development Canada, "Union Coverage by Province, 2010," Table 2, www.hrsdc.gc.ca/eng/labour/labour_relations/info_analysis/overview/2010/section_6.shtml, retrieved May 16, 2012. Reprinted with the permission of the Minister of Public Works and Government Services.

is concentrated in public administration; education; utilities; and health care and social services. Among the least unionized sectors are agriculture, professional, scientific, and technical; and accommodation and food.

Figure 9.3 illustrates the significant variation in rates of union membership among the provinces. Quebec (39.3 percent) and Newfoundland and Labrador (39.2 percent) have the highest rates of unionization. Alberta (25.0 percent) and Ontario (27.9 percent) have the lowest rates of union density. Unionization also varies by firm size. Unionization is most common in large organizations.

The overall decline in union membership has been attributed to several factors.[10] The factor cited most often seems to be change in the structure of the economy. Much recent job growth has occurred among women and youth in the service sector of the economy, while union strength has traditionally been among urban blue-collar workers, especially middle-aged workers.

Another force working against union membership is management efforts against union organizing. In a survey, almost half of large employers said their most important labour goal was to be union-free. Efforts to control costs have contributed to employer resistance to unions.[11] On average, unionized workers receive higher pay than their nonunionized counterparts, and the pressure is greater because of international competition. In the past, union membership across an industry such as automobiles or steel resulted in similar wages and work requirements for all competitors. Today, North American producers have to compete with companies that have entirely different pay scales and work rules, often putting the North American companies at a disadvantage. Another way management may be contributing to the decline in union membership is by adopting human resource practices that increase employees' commitment to their job and employer. Competition for scarce human resources can lead employers to offer much of what employees traditionally sought through union membership. Government regulations, too, can make unions seem less important. Stricter regulation in such areas as workplace safety and human rights leaves fewer areas in which unions can show an advantage over what employers already have to offer.

DID YOU KNOW?

Differences Among the Sexes—Unionization Rate (2011)

For the seventh year in a row the unionization rate for women surpassed that of men.

SOURCE: Sharanjit Uppal, "Unionization 2011: Differences Between the Sexes," Statistics Canada, www.statcan.gc.ca/pub/75-001-x/2011004/article/11579-eng.htm#a5, retrieved May 21, 2012.

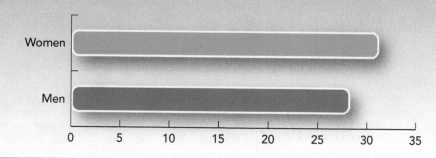

Unions have made strategic decisions in recent years to organize the growing private-service sector. This sector includes workers employed in hotels, home care agencies, and offices. Often, these employees are women. This extension of union activity into the service sector has been one reason for the most significant transformation in union membership, that is, the mix of men and women. In 1977, women represented only 12 percent of total union membership, however, in 2011, women outnumbered men in the workforce and as members of unions. As reported by Statistics Canada, in 2011, 31.1 percent of women were members of unions in contrast to 28.2 percent of men.[12] Reasons for the increase in women membership in unions can be attributed to the increasing:

- Number of women in the paid workforce
- Number of women in the highly unionized public sector
- Unionization of part-time employees (many of whom are women)
- Number of women employed in nontraditional male-dominated occupations and industries[13]

The mindset with respect to collective action and unionization is also an important consideration of union leaders. Union density among employees aged 15 to 24 years of age is only 16.4 percent—well below the national average.[14] CLC president Georgetti emphasized the group-minded nature of Generation Y: "We have noted that Generation Y travels in packs" and "this bodes well for selling this group of workers on the notion of collective action."[15] However, Prem Benimadhu with the Conference Board of Canada, suggests that younger workers are less likely to want or need union representation—"Once workers figure out that they can negotiate successfully on their own behalf, it will be hard for unions to convince them to join up and pay dues for the same service," he concludes.[16] An example of an initiative likely to appeal to younger workers is CUPE's workplace environmental guide "Healthy, Clean & Green: A Workers' Action Guide to a Greener Workplace," which shows workers ways to tackle environmental problems such as climate change.[17]

As Figure 9.4 indicates, the percentage of Canadian workers who belong to unions, although much higher than in the United States, is lower than in many countries. More dramatic is the difference in "coverage"—the percentage of employees whose

CUPE's "A Workers' Action Guide to a Greener Workplace" provides advice to members about what they can do to influence their employers to become more environmentally friendly.

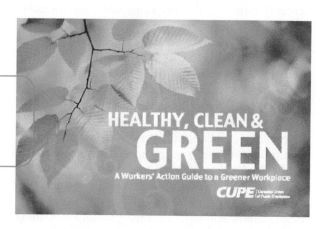

Harley-Davidson and the International Association of Machinists and Aerospace Workers have cooperated to produce good results. In general though, companies wishing to become more competitive need to continually monitor their labour relations strategies.

terms and conditions of employment are governed by a union contract, whether or not the employees are technically union members. In western Europe, it is common to have coverage rates of 80 to 90 percent, so the influence of labour unions far outstrips what membership levels would imply.[18] Also, employees in western Europe tend to have a larger formal role in decision making than in Canada. This role, including worker representatives on boards of directors, is often mandated by the government. But as markets become more and more global, pressure to cut labour costs and increase productivity is likely to be stronger in every country. Unless unions can help companies improve productivity or organize new production facilities opened in lower-wage

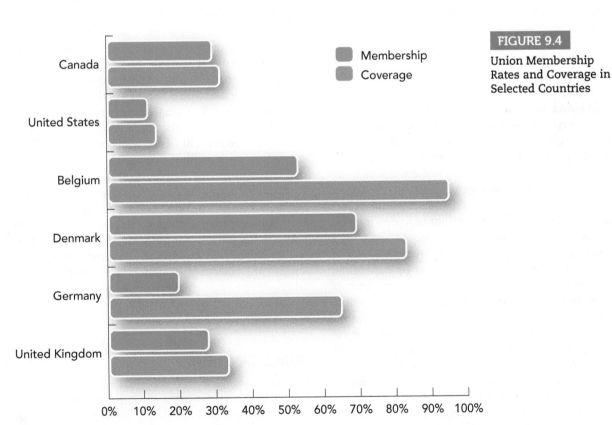

FIGURE 9.4

Union Membership Rates and Coverage in Selected Countries

NOTE: Data for 2007, except U.S. coverage rate for 2005.

SOURCES: Eurofund, "Industrial Relations Context," European Industrial Relations Dictionary, updated July 24, 2009, www.eurofund.europa.eu; Organization for Economic Cooperation and Development, "Trade Union Density (%) in OECD Countries 1960–2007," February 25, 2009, www.oecd.org; Statistics Canada, "Union Coverage Rates," modified November 25, 2008, www.statcan.gc.ca; and Lawrence Mishel, Jared Bernstein, and Sylvia Allegretto, *The State of Working America 2006/2007* (Ithaca, NY: ILR Press, 2007), Figure 3W, accessed at Economic Policy Institute's State of Working America website, www.stateofworkingamerica.org.

countries, union influence may decline in countries where it is now strong.

WHAT IS THE IMPACT OF UNIONS ON COMPANY PERFORMANCE?

2,4

Organizations are concerned about whether union organizing and bargaining will hurt their performance, in particular unions' impact on productivity, profits, and stock performance. Researchers have studied the general relationship between unionization and these performance measures. Through skillful labour relations, organizations can positively influence outcomes.

There has been much debate regarding the effects of unions on productivity.[19] The view that unions decrease productivity is based on work rules and limits on workloads set by union contracts and production lost to such union actions as strikes and work slowdowns. At the same time, unions can have positive effects on productivity.[20] They can reduce turnover by giving employees a route for resolving problems.[21] Unions emphasize pay systems based on seniority, which remove incentives for employees to compete rather than cooperate. The introduction of a union also may force an employer to improve its management practices and pay greater attention to employee ideas.

Although there is evidence that unions have both positive and negative effects on productivity, most studies have found that union workers are more productive than nonunion workers. Still questions remain. Are highly productive workers more likely to form unions, or does a union make workers more productive? The answer is unclear. In theory, if unions caused greater productivity, we would expect union membership to be rising, not falling as it has.[22]

Even if unions do raise productivity, a company's profits and stock performance may still suffer if unions raise wage and benefits costs by more than the productivity gain. On average, union members receive higher wages and more generous benefits than nonunion workers, and evidence shows that unions have a large negative effect on profits. Also, union coverage tends to decline faster in companies with a lower return to shareholders.[23] In summary, companies wishing to become more competitive need to continually monitor their labour relations strategy.

These studies look at the average effects of unions, not at individual companies or innovative labour relations. Some organizations excel at labour relations, and some have worked with unions to meet business needs. The "HR Best Practices" box, found later in this chapter, features an agreement between

auto parts giant Magna International and the Canadian Auto Workers that although not without controversy, may signal a new model for effective and flexible labour relations.

What Are the Goals of Each Group?

4

Resolving conflicts in a positive way is usually easiest when the parties involved understand each other's goals. Although individual cases vary, we can draw some general conclusions about the goals of labour unions and management. Table 9.1 provides a summary of current negotiation issues from the perspective of management and unions. Society, too, has goals for labour and business, given form in the laws regulating labour relations.

LO2 Identify the labour relations goals of management, labour unions, and society.

GOALS OF MANAGEMENT

Management goals are to increase the organization's profits and/or increase productivity. Managers tend to prefer options that lower costs and raise output. When deciding whether to discourage employees from forming a union, a concern is that a union will create higher costs in wages and benefits, as well as raise the risk of work stoppages. Managers may also fear that a union will make managers and workers into adversaries or limit management's discretion in making business and employment decisions.

When an employer has recognized a union, management's goals continue to emphasize restraining costs and improving output. Managers continue to prefer to keep the organization's operations flexible, so they can adjust activities to meet competitive challenges and customer demands. Therefore, in their labour relations, managers prefer to limit increases in wages and benefits and to retain as much control as they can over work rules and schedules.

GOALS OF UNIONS

In general, unions have the goals of obtaining pay, job security, and working conditions that satisfy their members and of giving members a voice in decisions that affect them. Traditionally, they obtain these goals by gaining power in numbers. The more workers who belong to a union, the greater the union's power. More members translates into greater ability to halt or disrupt operations. Larger unions also have greater financial resources for continuing a strike; the union can help to make up for the wages the workers lose during a strike. The threat of a long strike—stated or implied—can make an employer more willing to meet the union's demands.

As we noted earlier, union membership is indeed linked to better compensation. Statistics Canada reported that full-time unionized workers received on average, hourly earnings 21 percent higher than the non-unionized workers in 2010. Union membership has an even greater impact on part-time workers. Unionized part-timers averaged 61.5 percent higher earnings than non-unionized part-timers.[24]

Unions typically want to influence the *way* pay and promotions are determined. Unlike management, which tries to consider employees as individuals so that pay and promotion decisions relate to performance differences, unions try to build group solidarity and avoid possible arbitrary treatment of employees. To do so, unions try to have any pay differences based on seniority, on the grounds that this measure is more objective than performance evaluations. As a result, where workers are represented by a union, it is common for all employees in a particular job classification to be paid at the same rate. As well as

working to advance the interests of members, unions often engage in social unionism, that is, activities intended to influence social and economic policies of government. For example, CAW, Canada's largest private-sector union, is actively supporting far-ranging issues including retirement security for everyone, "Buy Canadian" policies, saving the national gun registry, helping make Canada a leader in ending AIDS, and clean wind energy.[25]

However, the survival and security of a union ultimately depends on its ability to ensure a regular flow of new members and member dues to support the services it provides. In 1946, Supreme Court of Canada Justice Ivan Rand brought down a significant decision that affected union financial security in Canada. The case came about as part of an arbitrated settlement of the labour dispute between the Ford Motor Company and the United Auto Workers. The Rand Formula is a union security provision that makes the payment of labour union dues mandatory even if the worker is not a member of the union. The rationale for the principle was that every employee benefits from union representation.[26] Unions typically place high priority on negotiating two types of contract provisions with an employer that are critical to a union's security and

> **social unionism**
> A type of unionism that attempts to influence social and economic policies of government.

> **Rand Formula**
> A union security provision that makes payment of labour union dues mandatory even if the worker is not a member of the union.

TABLE 9.1 Current Issues

MANAGEMENT ISSUES	UNION ISSUES
1. Wages	1. Wages
2. Productivity	2. Employment security
3. Business competitiveness	3. Health benefits
4. Flexible work practices	4. Pensions
5. Organizational change	5. Outsourcing and contracting out
6. Health benefits	6. Organizational change
7. Pensions	7. Employment and pay equity
8. Outsourcing and contracting out	8. Training and skills development
9. Employment and pay equity	9. Flexible work practices
10. Technological change	10. Variable pay
11. Training and skills development	11. Productivity
12. Employment security	12. Technological change
13. Variable pay	13. Business competitiveness

NOTE: Respondents were given a list of 13 possible choices and asked to indicate the top three negotiation issues for both management and union.

SOURCE: David K. Shepherdson, "Industrial Relations Outlook 2012 Going Sideways, With a Twist," November 2011, *The Conference Board of Canada*, p. 15. Reprinted with permission by the Conference Board of Canada.

viability: checkoff provisions and provisions relating to union membership or contribution.

Under a **checkoff provision**, the employer, on behalf of the union, automatically deducts union dues from employees' paycheques.

The strongest union security arrangement is a **closed shop**, under which a person must be a union member before being hired or the **union shop**, an arrangement that requires an employee to join the union within a certain time after beginning employment.

These provisions are ways to address unions' concern about "free riders"—employees who benefit from union activities without belonging to a union. By law, all members of a bargaining unit, whether union members or not, must be represented by the union. If the union is required to offer services to all bargaining unit members even though some of them do not pay dues, it may not have enough financial resources to operate successfully.

GOALS OF SOCIETY

The activities of unions and management take place within the context of society, with society's values driving the laws and regulations that affect labour relations. As long ago as the late 1800s and early 1900s, industrial relations scholars saw unions as a way to make up for individual employees' limited bargaining power.[27] At that time, clashes between workers and management could be violent, and many people hoped that unions would replace the violence with negotiation. Since then, observers have expressed concern that unions in certain industries have become too strong, achieving their goals at the expense of employers' ability to compete or meet other objectives. Overall, however, societal goals for government include ensuring that neutral rules exist to ensure balance is maintained between the powers of unions and employers.

Rather than being left to the activities of unions and management, many societal goals are also enforced through laws and regulations. As discussed in Chapter 2, human rights, pay equity, employment equity, privacy and other types of legislation determine how workers are treated by their employers. In addition, as we will see in the next section, a set of laws and regulations also exists to give workers the right to choose to join unions.

checkoff provision
A requirement that the employer, on behalf of the union, automatically deducts union dues from employees' paycheques.

closed shop
A union security arrangement under which a person must be a union member before being hired.

union shop
A union security arrangement that requires employees to join the union within a certain amount of time after beginning employment.

Laws and Regulations Affecting Labour Relations

The laws and regulations pertaining to labour relations affect unions' size and bargaining power, so they significantly affect the degree to which unions, management, and society achieve their varied goals. These laws and regulations set limits on union structure and administration and the ways in which unions and management interact.

LO3 ▸ Summarize laws and regulations that affect labour relations.

Canada's overall labour relations legal framework is decentralized and relatively complex. Since a ruling of the Supreme Court of Canada in 1925, responsibility for labour relations is primarily a provincial/territorial responsibility. Which organizations fall under federal versus provincial/territorial legislation was discussed in Chapter 2. Federally regulated private-sector employees are regulated by the Canada Labour Code (Part 1—Industrial Relations). In addition, private-sector employees in Nunavut, the Yukon, and the Northwest Territories are also regulated by the Canada Labour Code. Each province and territory has its own distinct labour laws. Each jurisdiction—federal, provincial, and territorial—also has laws governing public-sector employees. There are additional labour statutes that apply to specific occupations determined to be essential services, for example, teachers, law enforcement officers, firefighters, and health care employees. For example, in Alberta, health care workers are not allowed to take job action.

Although access to collective bargaining is a protected right under Canada's Charter of Rights and Freedoms, the right to strike is not a protected right and governments have recently been uncharacteristically active in intervening to end labour disputes. The Conference Board of Canada, in its "Industrial Relations Outlook 2012," reported that during the first seven months of 2011 (latest data available), the federal government had intervened in more than 80 work stoppages involving more than 500 workers—including striking Canada Post workers. This represented more federal government interventions than the cumulative total for the previous 30 years (1980–2010). This trend appears to be continuing. For example the federal government recently passed back-to-work legislation that

HR HOW-TO

Avoiding Unfair Labour Practices

A common core of labour legislation prohibits employers, unions, and individuals from engaging in unfair labour practices. Each jurisdiction in Canada has specific provisions dealing with unfair labour practices by management and unions.

Some of the most common examples of unfair labour practices that management must not engage in:

1. Interfering in the formation of a union or contributing to it financially (although, there have been allowances for the providing of an office for the union to conduct business and for paid leave for union officials conducting union business)

2. Discriminating against an employee because the individual is or is not a member of a union

3. Discriminating against an employee because the individual chooses to exercise rights granted by labour relations law

4. Intimidating or coercing an employee to become or not become a member of a union

Activities that a union is not permitted to engage in include:

1. Seeking to compel an employer to bargain collectively with the union if the union is not the certified bargaining agent

2. Attempting at the workplace and during working hours to persuade an employee to become or not become a union member

3. Intimidating, coercing, or penalizing an individual because he or she has filed a complaint or testified in any proceeding pursuant to the relevant labour law

4. Engaging in, encouraging, or threatening illegal strikes

5. Failing to represent employees fairly

SOURCE: Hermann Schwind, Hari Das, and Terry Wagar, *Canadian Human Resource Management*, 9th ed. (Toronto: McGraw-Hill Ryerson, 2010), p. 507.

---

sent labour disputes at Air Canada involving pilots, mechanics, baggage handlers, and other ground crew to binding arbitration, and within hours of a recent strike by engineers, conductors, and freight traffic controllers shutting down CP freight rail service, federal Labour Minister, Lisa Rait said she is prepared to table legislation to end the strike. "We want to make sure that they're doing the best that they can, but they understand as well that if they cannot conclude their deal, we will have the ability to intervene," Raitt told reporters in Ottawa.[28]

Although some differences exist among jurisdictions, the main features of labour legislation in Canada can be summarized as follows:

- Methods to certify a union that will represent a group of employees
- Requirement of the employer to recognize the union chosen by the majority of its employees and to accept the union as the employees' exclusive representative for bargaining purposes
- Responsibility to bargain in good faith with the intention to reach an agreement
- Requirement of the employer to deduct union dues from employees
- Minimum length of a collective agreement (at least one year)

- Regulation of strike and lockout activities
- Creation of a labour relations board (or specialized tribunal) to interpret and enforce the labour laws in their jurisdiction
- Prohibition of identified **unfair labour practices** by management and labour (see the "HR How-To" box)

There is a **Labour Relations Board (LRB)** (or similar structure) in each jurisdiction that serves as a specialized quasi-judicial tribunal with authority to interpret and enforce the labour laws in their jurisdiction.

PREVENTION OF UNFAIR LABOUR PRACTICES

When someone believes that an unfair labour practice has taken place, he or she may file a complaint with the appropriate Labour Relations Board for the jurisdiction. All parties are provided a copy of the complaint and the process usually involves the Labour Relations Board conducting a preliminary investigation to determine if the complaint has merit and if it may be possible for the parties to resolve the

unfair labour practice

A prohibited conduct of an employer, union, or individual under the relevant labour legislation.

Labour Relations Board (LRB)

A specialized tribunal with authority to interpret and enforce the labour laws in their jurisdiction.

complaint themselves. If the Labour Relations Board finds the complaint has merit and determines the complaint cannot be resolved through the parties, the Labour Relations Board will conduct a formal hearing with the parties present. Either the case can be dismissed at this point or the Labour Relations Board has the authority to issue orders to halt unfair labour practices. If the union or employer does not comply with the Labour Relations Board order, the order can be referred to the courts for enforcement.[29]

What Is the Union Organizing Process?

1,4

Unions begin their involvement with an organization's employees by conducting an organizing campaign. To meet its objectives, a union needs to convince a majority of workers that they should receive better pay or other employment conditions and that the union will help them do so. The employer's objectives will depend on its strategy—whether it seeks to work with a union or convince employees that they are better off without union representation.

L04 Describe the union organizing process.

THE PROCESS OF ORGANIZING

The organization process begins with a membership application such as the one shown in Figure 9.5. Union representatives contact employees, present their message about the union, and invite them to sign an application for membership. By signing the application and paying a nominal fee in some jurisdictions, the employee indicates they want the union to represent them.

When the necessary number of employees have signed membership applications, the union will apply to the appropriate Labour Relations Board for certification. Requirements differ among jurisdictions. For example, if the employer is in the private sector and falls under federal jurisdiction, the local

FIGURE 9.5

Example of an Application for Membership

APPLICATION FOR MEMBERSHIP

Ontario Public Service Employees Union, 100 Lesmill Road, Toronto, ON M3B 3P8

I hereby apply for and accept membership in, and authorize OPSEU, its agents or representatives, to act for me as my exclusive representative in collective bar-gaining, in respect to all the terms and conditions of my employment and to negotiate contracts with my employer covering all such matters.

X_____ Date_____
(Signature of applicant)

On behalf of the above organization, I hereby accept this application.

X_____ Date_____
(Signature of recruiter)

Last name (please print)_____

First name (please print)_____

Address_____ Apt. #_____

City_____ Prov. _____ Postal code_____

Phone (home)_____ Phone (work)_____

Employed by (name of college)_____

Campus_____ Department_____

First name (please print)_____

☐ Faculty: ☐ Faculty: ☐ Support: ☐ Support:
   Part-time   Sessional   Part-time   Non-recurring project

Home or secure e-mail address_____

SOURCE: Ontario Public Service Employees Union.

can be certified without a vote if more than 50 percent of employees sign applications. If fewer than 50 percent of employees signed, the Canada Industrial Relations Board will conduct an election among the employees. For the union to be certified, at least 35 percent of employees in the work group must vote and more than 50 percent of these voting employees must vote in favour of unionizing.[30]

| E-HRM | connect |

Check out "Unions and Flash Mobs."

MANAGEMENT STRATEGIES

Sometimes an employer will recognize a union after a majority of employees have signed membership applications. More often, there is a hotly contested election campaign. During the campaign, unions try to persuade employees that their wages, benefits, treatment by employers, and chances to influence workplace decisions are too poor or small and that the union will be able to obtain improvements in these areas. Management typically responds with its own messages providing an opposite point of view. Management messages say the organization has provided a valuable package of wages and benefits and has treated employees well. Management also argues that the union will not be able to keep its promises but will instead create costs for employees, such as union dues and lost income during strikes. For example, when the CAW organized about 140 Starbucks workers at ten stores in Vancouver,

Susan Spratt, lead union negotiator with Starbucks, "alleges the company has fought off further organizing in part by removing managers and promising better conditions at stores where the union has tried to sign up members."[31]

Employers use a variety of methods to avoid unionization in organizing campaigns.[32] Their efforts range from hiring consultants to distributing leaflets and letters to presenting the company's viewpoint at meetings of employees. Some management efforts go beyond what the law permits, especially in the eyes of union organizers. This impression is supported by an increase in charges of employer unfair labour practices and awards of back pay since the late 1960s.[33] Why would employers break the law? One explanation is that the consequences, such as reinstating workers with back pay, are small compared to the benefits.[34] If coercing workers away from joining a union saves the company the higher wages, benefits, and other costs of a unionized workforce, management may feel an incentive to accept costs like back pay.

Supervisors have the most direct contact with employees. Thus, as Table 9.2 indicates, it is critical that they establish good relationships with employees even before there is any attempt at union organizing. Supervisors also must know what *not* to do if a union drive takes place. They should be trained in the legal principles discussed earlier in this chapter.

CAN A UNION BE DERCERTIFIED?

Union members' right to be represented by unions of their own choosing also includes the right to vote out an existing union. The action is called *decertifying* the union. Decertification follows the same process as a representation election. An application to decertify a union may not be acted upon during a legal strike or lockout. In some jurisdictions when a collective agreement is in place, decertification applications may

Wal-Mart Canada closed its store in Jonquière, Quebec, six months after workers obtained union certification.

TABLE 9.2 What Supervisors Should and Should Not Do to Reduce the Likelihood of Unionization

WHAT TO DO
Report any direct or indirect signs of union activity to a core management group.
Deal with employees by carefully stating the company's response to pro-union arguments. These responses should be coordinated by the company to maintain consistency and to avoid threats or promises. Take away union issues by following effective management practices all the time:

- Deliver recognition and appreciation.
- Solve employee problems.
- Protect employees from harassment or humiliation.
- Provide business-related information.
- Be consistent in treatment of employees.
- Accommodate special circumstances where appropriate.
- Ensure due process in performance management.
- Treat all employees with dignity and respect.

WHAT TO AVOID
Threatening employees with harsher terms and conditions of employment or employment loss if they engage in union activity.
Interrogating employees about pro-union or anti-union sentiments that they or others may have or reviewing union authorization cards or pro-union petitions.
Promising employees that they will receive favourable terms or conditions of employment if they forgo union activity.
Spying on employees known to be, or suspected of being, engaged in pro-union activities.

SOURCE: Excerpted from "Unshackle Your Supervisors to Stay Union Free," by J. A. Segal in *HR Magazine*, June 1998. Copyright 1998 by Society for Human Resource Management, Alexandria, VA. Used with permission. All rights reserved.

only be filed during specified "open periods." Laws in some jurisdictions require the employer to post and annually circulate information related to union decertification.

Collective Bargaining

When a union has been certified, that union represents employees during contract negotiations. In **collective bargaining**, a union negotiates on behalf of its members with management representatives to arrive at a contract defining conditions of employment for the term of the contract and to resolve differences in the way they interpret the contract. Typical collective agreements include provisions for pay, benefits, work rules, and resolution of workers' grievances. Table 9.3 shows typical provisions negotiated in collective agreements.

Collective bargaining differs from one situation to another in terms of *bargaining structure*—that is, the range of employees and employers covered by the contract. An agreement may involve a narrow group of employees in a craft union or a broad group in an industrial union. Agreements may cover one or several facilities of the same employer, or the bargaining structure may involve several employers. Many more interests must be considered in collective bargaining for an industrial union with a bargaining structure that includes several employers than in collective bargaining for a craft union in a single facility.

LO5 Explain how management and unions negotiate collective agreements.

collective bargaining
Negotiation between union representatives and management representatives to arrive at an agreement defining conditions of employment for the term of the agreement and to administer that agreement.

The majority of collective agreement negotiations take place between unions and employers that have been through the process before. In the typical situation, management has come to accept the union as an organization it must work with. The situation can be very different when a union has just been certified and is negotiating its first collective agreement.

As part of its programming, the Labour Relations Board British Columbia makes available a free-of-charge information session that is offered to an employer or union either

TABLE 9.3 Typical Provisions in Collective Agreements

Rights of Parties	*Recognition of Union Security*
	• Union membership
	• Union security
	• Leave for union business
	• Restrictions on contracting out
	Management Rights to Test
	• Drug and alcohol testing
	• Intelligence and aptitude testing
	• Electronic surveillance
	• Internet/telephone monitoring
	• Medical examinations
	• Other tests
	Employee Rights/Security
	• Harassment
	• Employment Equity Program
	• Assistance programs, e.g., substance abuse
Organization of Work	*Technological Change*
	• Advance notice
	• Obligation to provide training, instruction, or retraining
	• Layoff protection
	• Wage protection
	• Special leaves, severance pay, and/or retirement offers
	Distribution of Work
	• Flexibility in work assignment
	• Job rotation
	• Semi-autonomous work groups or teams
	• Job sharing
Labour Relations	*Labour Relations*
	• Grievance procedures
	• Bargaining method or approach
	• Application of the agreement
	• Job evaluation (position evaluation)
	• Joint committees
	• Participation (other than committees)
Education, Training, and Development	*Education, Training, and Employee Development*
	• Leave
	• Reimbursement for tuition fees and books
	• Multiskilling, i.e., flexibility for the employee
	• Contribution to a training fund
	• Apprenticeship programs
Conditions of Work	*Work Schedule*
	• Normal hours of work
	• Type of work schedules
	• Special provisions
	Overtime
	• Clause limiting the use of overtime
	• Compensatory days in lieu of pay (banking)
	• Overtime pay
	• Meal allowance (overtime)

(continued on next page)

TABLE 9.3　Typical Provisions in Collective Agreements (*continued*)

Conditions of Work (*continued*)	*Job Security and Termination* • No layoffs while the agreement is in effect • Layoffs by seniority • Bumping rights • Retention of seniority • Work sharing (reduction in hours to avoid layoffs) • Education/training with pay • Supplementary employment insurance benefit *Pay* • Cost-of-living allowance • Wage guarantees *Leaves and Vacations* • Paid holidays • Annual vacation • Family leave • Paid sick leave plan *Benefits* • Private group insurance plans • Pension plans (funding, administration) *Provisions Relating to Part-Time Workers* • Maximum hours of work normally allowed • Ratio of part-time to full-time workers • Holidays, vacations, sick leave, benefits, pension plan, seniority

SOURCE: "Collective Agreement Provisions," Human Resources and Skills Development website, www.hrsdc.gc.ca, retrieved November 2, 2004. Reproduced with the permission of the Minister of Public Works and Government Services, 2012.

jointly or separately as requested to help reach a first collective agreement.[35] Due to the recognized difficulties associated in reaching a first agreement, the legislation in some jurisdictions provides a process to ensure a first agreement can be reached. Under the Canada Labour Code, the federal Minister of Labour can direct the Canada Industrial Relations Board to establish the terms and conditions of a first collective agreement for the parties. This process would require the use of arbitration,[36] a process discussed later in this chapter.

BARGAINING OVER NEW COLLECTIVE AGREEMENTS

Clearly, the outcome of collective agreement negotiations can have important consequences for labour costs, productivity, and the organization's ability to compete. Therefore, unions and management need to prepare carefully for collective bargaining. Preparation includes establishing objectives for the agreement, reviewing the old agreement, gathering data (such as compensation paid by competitors and the company's ability to survive a strike), predicting the likely demands to be made, and establishing the cost of meeting the demands.[37] This preparation

can help negotiators develop a plan for how to negotiate. Different situations and goals call for different approaches to bargaining, such as the following alternatives proposed by Richard Walton and Robert McKersie:[38]

- *Distributive bargaining* divides an economic "pie" between two sides—for example, a wage increase means giving the union a larger share of the pie.
- *Integrative (mutual-gains) bargaining* looks for win-win solutions, or outcomes in which both sides benefit. If the organization's labour costs hurt its performance, integrative bargaining might seek to avoid layoffs in exchange for work rules that improve productivity.
- *Attitudinal structuring* focuses on establishing a relationship of trust. The parties are concerned about ensuring that the other side will keep its part of any bargain.
- *Intraorganizational bargaining* addresses conflicts within union or management groups or objectives, such as between new employees and workers with high seniority or between cost control and reduction of turnover.

The collective bargaining process may involve any combination of these alternatives.

Negotiations go through various stages.[39] In the earliest stages, many more people are often present than in later stages. On the union side, this may give all the various internal interest groups a chance to participate and voice their goals. Their input helps communicate to management what will satisfy union members and may help the union achieve greater solidarity. At this stage, union negotiators often present a long list of proposals, partly to satisfy members and partly to introduce enough issues that they will have flexibility later in the process. Management may or may not present proposals of its own. Sometimes management prefers to react to the union's proposals.

During the middle stages of the process, each side must make a series of decisions, even though the outcome is uncertain. How important is each issue to the other side? How likely is it that disagreement on particular issues will result in a strike? When and to what extent should one side signal its willingness to compromise?

In the final stage of negotiations, pressure for an agreement increases. Public negotiations may be only part of the process. Negotiators from each side may hold one-on-one meetings or small-group meetings where they escape some public relations pressures. A neutral third party may act as a go-between or facilitator. In some cases, bargaining breaks down as the two sides find they cannot reach a mutually acceptable agreement. The outcome depends partly on the relative bargaining power of each party. That power, in turn, depends on each party's ability to withstand a strike, which costs the workers their pay during the strike and costs the employer lost production and possibly lost customers.

WHAT HAPPENS WHEN BARGAINING BREAKS DOWN?

The intended outcome of collective bargaining is an agreement with terms acceptable to both parties. If one or both sides determine that negotiation alone will not produce such an agreement, bargaining breaks down. To bring this impasse to an end, the union may strike, or the parties may bring in outside help to resolve their differences.

Strikes and Lockouts

A strike is a collective decision of the union members not to work or to slow down until certain demands or conditions are met. The union members vote, and if the majority favours a strike, they all go on strike at that time or when union leaders believe the time is right. Strikes are typically accompanied

by *picketing*—the union stations members near the work site with signs indicating the union is on strike. During the strike, the union members do not receive pay from their employer, but the union may be able to make up for some of the lost pay. The employer loses production unless it can hire replacement workers, and even then, productivity may be reduced. Often, other unions support striking workers by refusing to cross their picket line—for example, refusing to make deliveries to a company during a strike. A lockout on the other hand, is initiated by the employer. A lockout is a closure of a place of employment or refusal of the employer to provide work as a way to compel employees to agree to certain demands or conditions.

The vast majority of labour–management negotiations do not result in a strike or lockout. Figure 9.6 shows a chronological perspective of work stoppages in Canada for 1980–2010. As shown in Figure 9.7, Canada lost only 0.03 percent of total working time to strikes and lockouts in 2010 in contrast to 0.11 percent in 2005. The estimated number of person-days lost through strikes and lockouts has fluctuated significantly in recent years ranging from more than 4.1 million in 2005 to 0.9 million in 2008, 2.2 million in 2009, and 1.2 million in 2010.[40] Not only do workers lose wages and employers lose production, but the negative experience of a strike or lockout can make future interactions more difficult. When strikes or lockouts do occur, the conduct of each party during the strike can do lasting harm to labour–management relations. Violence by either side or threats of job loss or actual job loss because jobs went to replacement workers can make future relations difficult.

What Are the Alternatives to Strikes and Lockouts?

Because strikes and lockouts are so costly and risky, unions and employers generally prefer other methods for resolving conflicts. Three of the most common alternatives are mediation, conciliation, and arbitration. All of these rely on a neutral third party, who usually is appointed by the federal or provincial Minister of Labour.

The least formal and most widely used of these procedures is mediation, in which a third party or

strike
A collective decision by union members not to work or to slow down until certain demands or conditions are met.

lockout
A closure of a place of employment or refusal of the employer to provide work as a way to compel employees to agree to certain demands or conditions.

mediation
Conflict resolution procedure in which a mediator hears the views of both sides and facilitates the negotiation process but has no formal authority to dictate a resolution.

FIGURE 9.6

Number of Strikes and Lockouts; Workers Involved (000s), 1980–2010

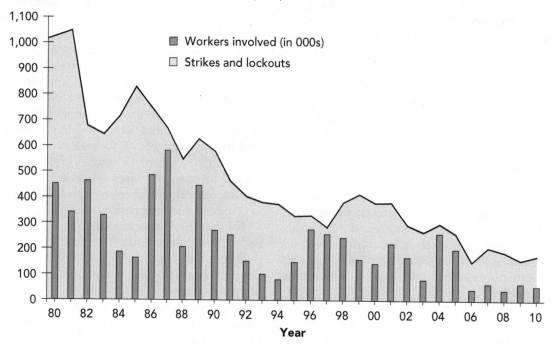

SOURCE: Sharanjit Uppal, "Unionization 2011," Statistics Canada, Table 4, "Major Wage Settlements, Inflation and Labour Disputes," www.statcan.gc.ca/pub/75-001-x/2011004/tables-tableaux/11579/tbl04-eng.htm, retrieved May 21, 2012.

FIGURE 9.7

Proportion of Estimated Working Time Lost to Strikes and Lockouts, 1980–2010 (percentage)

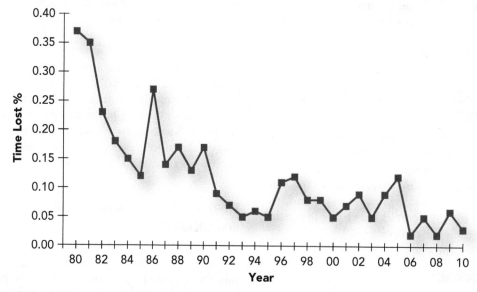

SOURCE: Sharanjit Uppal, "Unionization 2011," Statistics Canada, Table 4, "Major Wage Settlements, Inflation and Labour Disputes," www.statcan.gc.ca/pub/75-001-x/2011004/tables-tableaux/11579/tbl04-eng.htm, retrieved May 21, 2012.

mediator hears the views of both sides and facilitates the negotiation process. He or she has no formal authority to impose a resolution, so a strike remains a possibility. In a survey studying negotiations between unions and large businesses, mediation was used in almost four out of ten negotiation efforts.[41]

Conciliation, most often used for negotiations with governmental bodies, typically reports on the reasons for the dispute, the views and arguments of both sides, and (sometimes) a recommended settlement, which the parties may decline. The public nature of these recommendations may pressure the parties to reach a settlement. Even if they do not accept the conciliator's recommended settlement, the hope of this process is that the conciliator will identify or frame issues in a way that makes agreement easier. Sometimes merely devoting time to this process gives the parties a chance to reach an agreement. In most jurisdictions in Canada, conciliation is mandatory before a strike or lockout can be called. Again, however, there is no guarantee that a strike or lockout will be avoided.

The most formal type of outside intervention is arbitration, under which an arbitrator or arbitration board determines a settlement that is *binding*, meaning the parties have to accept it. There is wide acceptance of "rights arbitration," which focuses on enforcing or interpreting agreement terms, but arbitration in the writing of collective agreements or setting of agreement terms has traditionally been reserved for special circumstances such as negotiations between unions and government agencies, where strikes may be illegal or especially costly. Occasionally, arbitration has

conciliation
Conflict resolution procedure in which a third party to collective bargaining reports the reasons for a dispute, the views and arguments of both sides, and possibly a recommended settlement, which the parties may decline.

arbitration
Conflict resolution procedure in which an arbitrator or arbitration board determines a binding settlement.

also been used with businesses in situations where strikes have been extremely damaging. For example, in the case of the Air Canada labour disputes discussed at the chapter opening, the back-to-work legislation included a provision to impose a settlement if the two sides couldn't reach an agreement.

It may be suggested that the general opinion that union and management representatives are in the best position to resolve conflicts themselves because they are closer to the situation than an arbitrator is being tested by the significant number of recent government interventions in labour disputes.

Administration of the Collective Agreement

4

Although the process of negotiating a collective agreement (including the occasional strike) receives the most publicity, other union–management activities occur far more often. Bargaining over a new contract typically occurs only about every three years, but administering labour agreements goes on day after day, year after year. The two activities are linked, of course. Vague or inconsistent language in the agreement can make administering the agreement more difficult. The difficulties can create conflict that spills over into the next round of negotiations.[42] Events during negotiations—strikes, the use of replacement workers, or violence by either side—also can lead to difficulties in working successfully under a conflict.

LO6 Summarize the practice of collective agreement administration.

Collective agreement administration includes carrying out the terms of the agreement and resolving conflicts over

Canada Post locked out workers following a series of rotating strikes.

interpretation or violation of the agreement. Under a collective agreement, the process for resolving these conflicts is called a **grievance procedure**. This procedure has a key influence on success in collective agreement administration. A grievance procedure may be started by an employee or discharged employee who believes the employer violated the agreement or by a union representative on behalf of a group of workers or union representatives.

For grievances launched by an employee, a typical grievance procedure follows the steps shown in Figure 9.8. The grievance may be settled during any of the four steps. In *Step 1*, the employee talks to his or her supervisor about the problem. If this conversation is unsatisfactory, the employee may involve the union steward in further discussion. The union steward and employee decide whether the problem has been resolved and, if not, whether it is a violation of the collective agreement. If the problem was not resolved and does seem to be an agreement violation, the union moves to *Step 2*, putting the grievance in writing and submitting it to a

> **grievance procedure**
> The process for resolving union–management conflicts over interpretation or violation of a collective agreement.

manager. The union steward meets with a management representative to try to resolve the problem. Management consults with the labour relations staff and puts its response in writing too at this second stage. If Step 2 fails to resolve the problem, the union appeals the grievance to top management and representatives of the labour relations staff. The union may involve more local or national officers in discussions at this stage (see *Step 3* in Figure 9.8). The decision resulting from the appeal is put into writing. If the grievance is still not resolved, the union may decide (*Step 4*) to appeal the grievance to an arbitrator. If the grievance involves a discharged employee, the process may begin at Step 2 or 3 however, and the time limits between steps may be shorter. Grievances filed by the union on behalf of a group may begin at Step 1 or Step 2.

The majority of grievances are settled during the earlier steps of the process. This reduces delays and avoids the costs of arbitration. If a grievance does reach arbitration, the arbitrator makes the final ruling in the matter.

FIGURE 9.8

Steps in an Employee-Initiated Grievance Procedure

Step 1
- Employee (and union steward) discusses problem with supervisor.
- Union steward and employee decide whether problem was resolved.
- Union steward and employee decide whether contract was violated.

Step 2
- Written grievance is submitted to production superintendent, another manager, or labour relations representative.
- Steward and manager discuss grievance.
- Management puts response in writing.

Step 3
- Union appeals grievance to top management and senior labour relations staff.
- Additional local or national union officers may be involved.
- Decision resulting from appeal is put into writing.

Step 4
- Union decides whether to refer unresolved grievance to arbitration.
- Union appeals grievance to arbitration for binding decision.

SOURCES: Adapted from T. A. Kochan, *Collective Bargaining and Industrial Relations* (Homewood, IL: Richard D. Irwin, 1980), p. 395; and J. A. Fossum, *Labour Relations* (Boston: McGraw-Hill/Irwin, 2002), pp. 448–52.

Employers can assess the grievance procedure in terms of various criteria.[43] One consideration is effectiveness: how well the procedure resolves day-to-day questions about the collective agreement. A second basic consideration is efficiency: whether it resolves issues at a reasonable cost and without major delays. The company also should consider how well the grievance procedure adapts to changing circumstances. For example, if sales drop off and the company needs to cut costs, how clear are the provisions related to layoffs and subcontracting of work? In the case of contracts covering multiple business units, the procedure should allow for resolving local contract issues, such as work rules at a particular facility. Companies should also consider whether the grievance procedure is fair—whether it treats employees equitably and gives them a voice in the process.

From the point of view of employees, the grievance procedure is an important means of getting fair treatment in the workplace. Its success depends on whether it provides for all the kinds of issues that are likely to arise (such as how to handle a business slowdown), whether employees feel they can file a grievance without being punished for it, and whether employees believe their union representatives will follow through. Too many grievances may indicate a problem—for example, the union members or managers do not understand how to uphold the collective agreement or have no desire to do so. At the same time, a very small number of grievances may also signal a problem. A very low grievance rate may suggest a fear of filing a grievance, a belief that the system does not work, or a belief that employees are poorly represented by their union.

Labour–Management Cooperation

2,4

The traditional understanding of union–management relations is that the two parties are adversaries, meaning each side is competing to win at the expense of the other. There have always been exceptions to this approach. And since at least the 1980s, there seems to be wider acceptance of the view that greater cooperation can increase employee commitment and motivation while making the workplace

L07 Describe more cooperative approaches to labour–management relations.

more flexible.[44] Also, evidence suggests that employees who worked under traditional labour relations systems and then under the new, more cooperative systems prefer the cooperative approach.[45]

Cooperation between labour and management may feature employee involvement in decision making, self-managing employee teams, joint labour–management committees, broadly defined jobs, and sharing of financial gains and business information with employees.[46] The search for a win-win solution requires that unions and their members understand the limits on what an employer can afford in a competitive marketplace.

Without the union's support, efforts at employee involvement are less likely to survive and less likely to be effective if they do survive.[47] Unions have often resisted employee involvement programs, precisely because the programs try to change workplace relations and the role that unions play. Union leaders have often feared that such programs will weaken unions' role as independent representatives of employee interests.

An effective day-to-day relationship between labour and management is critical to achieving cooperation. In an adversarial type of environment, union–management communication consists of dealing with grievances; however, a cooperative model requires effective communication, trust, and mutual respect as the foundation for the day-to-day relationship. Many management and union leaders recognize that new approaches are needed to handle mutual concerns—"A sense of shared purpose is required to increase the effectiveness of the organization."[48]

Labour–management committees provide a relatively flexible approach to labour–management cooperation in the workplace. Over the past two decades, the use of *joint labour–management committees* has been growing. More than 80 percent of labour and management respondents to a Conference Board of Canada study reported that they have experience in using joint labour–management committees. The most common issues that such committees deal with are summarized in Table 9.4.

TABLE 9.4	Most Common Joint Labour–Management Committees

1. Pay, benefits, pensions
2. Business issues/updates
3. General labour relations
4. Training/apprenticeships
5. Job evaluation/classifications/postings
6. Operations/technology
7. Hours of work/scheduling

SOURCE: Judith Lendvay-Zwicki, "The Canadian Industrial Relations System: Current Challenges and Future Options," Conference Board Document, April 2004, p. 17, www.conferenceboard.ca, retrieved April 19, 2004.

HR BEST PRACTICES

Magna International and the CAW's Framework for Fairness Agreement

After maintaining a mostly union-free workplace for more than 50 years, Aurora, Ontario–based automotive parts giant Magna International announced a peace agreement with the Canadian Auto Workers (CAW) that could bring about wide-scale unionization of 18,000 employees at 45 Magna plants in Ontario. By adopting the agreement, known as the "Framework of Fairness Agreement" (FFA), the CAW gave up the ability to strike in exchange for an immediate $3-per-hour wage increase for production workers (with annual improvements), layoff and job security protections, paid educational leave, and a skilled trades program.

In a press release, Magna founder Frank Stronach said the "traditional, confrontational model of labour relations is unproductive and wastes energy that would be better focused on creating the conditions [that] would be fair to employees and would ensure that Magna remains competitive in the global automotive industry." Stronach calls the FFA a "new, innovative, flexible, and efficient model of labour relations." Although the deal has generated criticism from some within the Canadian labour movement, former CAW national president Buzz Hargrove says "that having Magna onside will boost the union's lobbying power when it goes to governments with concerns about trade deals and the Canadian auto industry."

SOURCES: Chris Vander Doelen, "Windsor Modules Makes Most of Magna Deal," *The Windsor Star,* November 13, 2007, p. B1; Sonja Puzic, "Magna Workers Back New Deal: Windsor Modules Employees First to Adopt Groundbreaking Pact," *The Windsor Star,* November 8, 2007, p. A1; Lesley Young, "Unlikely Allies Team Up," *Canadian HR Reporter,* November 5, 2007, p. 1; and Todd Humber, "Frank and Buzz: The New Felix and Oscar," *Canadian HR Reporter,* November 5, 2007, p. 30.

THINKING ETHICALLY

Is the Seniority System Fair?

Traditionally, union contracts have called for pay and promotion systems that reward employees with higher pay and advancement as they achieve greater seniority, that is, more years on the job. In a company, with a unionized workforce, employees with comparable amounts of experience would have comparable earnings. Employees with greater seniority would earn more than newer employees and employees with the most seniority would be promoted if they met the minimum requirements of the job opportunity.

Some people have questioned whether tying pay and advancement to seniority is effective or even fair. For example, a top-performing, recently hired employee with educational qualifications that exceed the requirements of a desired job may become frustrated when he/she is not even selected for an interview because many employees with greater seniority applied. However, union leaders view the seniority clause as the means to ensure fairness in how employees are rewarded in an organization.

In a survey of Canadian organizations, consulting firm Watson Wyatt found that one of the top five reasons that employees quit their jobs is dissatisfaction with promotional opportunities.

SOURCE: Virginia Galt, "Stress, Not Money, Main Cause of Turnover," *The Globe and Mail,* December 15, 2007, p. B10.

QUESTIONS

1. Why do you think unions have traditionally favoured a system of linking pay and advancement to seniority? Who benefits? Why do you think management might favour a system of linking pay and advancement to performance? Who benefits?
2. What employee rights does seniority-based pay fulfill? What standards for ethical behaviour does it meet? (See Chapter 1 to review a description of employee rights and ethical standards.)
3. What employee rights does a performance-based pay and promotion system fulfill? What standards for ethical behaviour does it meet?

Employers build cooperative relationships by the way they treat employees—with respect and fairness, in the knowledge that attracting talent and minimizing turnover are in the employer's best interests. "In the end we must look for opportunities to create a more collaborative culture in Canadian workplaces to ensure the long-term sustainability of our businesses."[49]

SUMMARY

LO1 Define unions and labour relations and their role in organizations.

- A union is an organization formed for the purpose of representing its members in resolving conflicts with employers.

- Labour relations is the management specialty emphasizing skills that managers and union leaders can use to minimize costly forms of conflict and to seek win-win solutions to disagreements.

- In Canada, union membership has declined marginally from a peak in 1994. Unionization is associated with more generous compensation and higher productivity but lower profits. Unions may reduce a business's flexibility and economic performance.

LO2 Identify the labour relations goals of management, labour unions, and society.

- Management goals are to increase the organization's profits and/or productivity. Managers generally expect that unions will make these goals harder to achieve.

- Unions have the goal of obtaining pay and working conditions that satisfy their members.

- Society's values have included the hope that the existence of unions will replace conflict or violence between workers and employers with fruitful negotiation.

LO3 Summarize laws and regulations that affect labour relations.

- Laws and regulations affect the degree to which management, unions, and society achieve their varied goals.

- Canada's overall labour relations legal framework is decentralized with responsibility for labour relations shared among the federal, provincial, and territorial governments.

- A common core of labour legislation exists that includes prohibiting unfair labour practices by management and labour. Labour Relations Boards or similar quasi-judicial tribunals exist within each jurisdiction to administer and enforce labour laws.

LO4 Describe the union organizing process.

- Organizing begins when union representatives contact employees and invite them to sign a membership application. When the required numbers of employees have signed membership applications, the union will apply to their appropriate Labour Relations Board for certification.

- Requirements for certification differ among federal, provincial, and territorial jurisdictions.

LO5 Explain how management and unions negotiate collective agreements.

- Negotiations take place between representatives of the union and the management bargaining unit.

- The process begins with preparation, including research into the other side's strengths and demands. The union presents its demands, and management sometimes presents demands as well. Then the sides evaluate the demands and the likelihood of a strike.

- In the final stages, pressure for an agreement increases, and a neutral third party may be called on to help reach a resolution. If bargaining breaks down, the impasse may be broken with a strike, lockout, mediation, conciliation, or arbitration.

LO6 Summarize the practice of collective agreement administration.

- Collective agreement administration is a daily activity under the collective agreement. It includes carrying out the terms of the agreement and resolving conflicts over interpretation or violation of the agreement.

- Conflicts are resolved through a grievance procedure that begins with an employee talking to his or her supervisor about the problem and possibly involving the union steward. If this does not resolve the conflict, the union files a written grievance and union and management representatives meet to discuss the problem. If this effort fails, the union appeals the grievance to top management and ultimately the use of an arbitrator may be required for final resolution.

LO7 Describe more cooperative approaches to labour–management relations.

- In contrast to the traditional view that labour and management are adversaries, some organizations and unions work more cooperatively.

- Cooperation may feature employee involvement in decision making, self-managing employee teams, joint labour–management committees, broadly defined jobs, and sharing of financial gains and business information with employees. Cooperative labour relations seem to contribute to an organization's success.

Critical Thinking Questions

1. Why do employees join unions? Did you ever belong to a union? If you did, do you think union membership benefited you? If you did not, do you think a union would have benefited you? Why or why not?
2. Why do managers at most companies prefer that unions not represent their employees? Can unions provide benefits to an employer? Explain.
3. How has union membership in Canada changed over the past few decades? How does union membership in Canada compare with union membership in other countries? How might these patterns in union membership affect the HR decisions of an international company?
4. What legal responsibilities do employers have regarding unions? What are the legal requirements affecting unions?
5. Suppose you are the HR manager for a chain of restaurants. You learn that union representatives have been encouraging the stores' employees to sign applications for membership. What events can follow in this process of organizing? Suggest some ways that you might respond in your role as HR manager.
6. If the parties negotiating a collective agreement are unable to reach a settlement, what actions can resolve the situation?
7. Why are most negotiations settled without a strike or lockout? Under what conditions might management choose to accept a strike?
8. What are the usual steps in a grievance procedure? What are the advantages of resolving a grievance in the first step? What skills would a supervisor need so grievances can be resolved in the first step?
9. The "HR Best Practices" box in this chapter gives an example of union–management cooperation between Magna International and the CAW. What does the employer gain from this effort? What do workers gain? Do you think the cooperative effort eliminates the union's role? Explain.

What's Your HR IQ?

 Connect offers more ways to check what you've learned so far. Find experiential exercises, Test Your Knowledge quizzes, videos, and many other resources to gauge your HR IQ.

CASE STUDY 9.1:   Wal-Mart Reacts to Unionization

Wal-Mart Canada Corp. dealt a decisive blow to union forces, announcing it will shut down the first Wal-Mart store to successfully certify in North America in almost a decade. "We honestly were hoping we could avoid this—it's a sad day for us," Wal-Mart spokesperson Andrew Pelletier said of the decision to shutter the four-year-old outlet in Jonquière, Quebec, which the retailer says was losing money. "Despite nine days of meeting with the union over more than a three-month period, we have been unsuccessful in reaching an agreement that would allow the store to operate efficiently and, ultimately, profitably."

"We're all in shock," said one employee reached the next day at the Jonquière store. Michael Fraser, the United Food and Commercial Workers Union president, was not available for comment. The store's 190 workers will be offered "generous" severance packages and career counselling," Mr. Pelletier said.

While the big-box giant has never before closed a store in this country for economic reasons, the news does not come as a surprise. The announcement of the closure of the Jonquière store was the latest event in a long-standing fight between the world's biggest retailer and unions determined to organize the corporation's workers throughout North America. Wal-Mart insists it does not promote an anti-union agenda. "We bargained in good faith," Mr. Pelletier said.

However, union organizers and some industry analysts say otherwise. "Wal-Mart, like a lot of other companies with a nonunionized workforce, is scared to death of unions," said David Abella, an analyst at New-York based Rochdale Investment Management. Even if they could manage that store with the union, it could lead to a domino effect across Canada and the United States. The UFCW scored a minor victory recently when a Saskatchewan appeal overturned a decision barring the province's labour board from accessing internal Wal-Mart documents, among them one titled "Wal-Mart: A Manager's Tool Box to Remaining Union-Free." Jonquière's certification was viewed as a big win for the UFCW, one that has not been realized since 1996, when the Ontario Labour Relations Board unionized a Wal-Mart in Windsor, Ontario. The store was later decertified after a high-profile campaign by anti-union employees, which included allegations of union misconduct.

"Shutting down the Jonquière store for any reason is completely legal," said Anil Verna, a professor of industrial relations at the University of Toronto. "Any business can open or close as they see fit. Most of the time it is about whether the operations are profitable or not. In this case, the timing kind of looks suspicious, but not knowing the numbers for the store, it's difficult to make a conclusive inference that [unionization] had anything to do with it."

SOURCE: Hollie Shaw, "Wal-Mart Closes First Union Store in Quebec," *Financial Post*, February 10, 2005, pp. A1, A9. Material reprinted with permission of The National Post Company, a Can West Partnership.

What's Happened Since?

In 2008, Wal-Mart closed a tire-and-lube garage in Gatineau, Quebec (just across the river from Ottawa) after an arbitrator imposed the first-ever collective agreement on a Wal-Mart operation in North America. The five mechanics and manager were offered jobs at other (non-unionized) Wal-Mart locations. The approximately 150 workers at the Gatineau Wal-Mart were also certified in 2008, however were unable to negotiate a collective agreement. In the summer of 2010, a collective agreement was also arbitrator-imposed, but just over one year later, employees at the Wal-Mart Gatineau voted to decertify the union. "This follows an application made by our Hull associates earlier this year to decertify the union at their store," said Andrew Pelletier, Wal-Mart's vice president of corporate affairs and sustainability. "Wal-Mart respects the decision of our Hull associates. They have made their views clear in this matter." The United Food and Commercial Workers Canada union declined to comment.

In the meantime, Wal-Mart unionization efforts in western Canada were also being undertaken. In December 2008, the Wal-Mart store in Weyburn, Saskatchewan was granted union certification by the Saskatchewan Labour Relations Board. The certification came almost five years after the UFCW applied to represent workers at the store—delays including two Wal-Mart applications to the Supreme Court of Canada to suspend the process prolonged the certification process. However, the saga has not ended there—the certification order was overturned, then restored on appeal, and a variety of allegations and challenges have been exchanged. As of March 2012, a collective agreement is still not in place at North America's only unionized Wal-Mart.

Questions

1. Do you believe that Wal-Mart is "anti-union"? Explain your response.
2. What impact could a unionized Wal-Mart have on other unionized workers in Canada?
3. Would you be willing to pay more for products from a unionized Wal-Mart? Explain.

SOURCES: "Wal-Mart Closes Shop Where Union Contract Imposed," *CBC News*, October 16, 2008, www.cbc.ca/news/canada/ottawa/story/2008/10/16/walmart-garage.html, retrieved May 24, 2012; "Wal-Mart in Weyburn Certified as UFCW Canada Unionized Store," December 8, 2008, www.ufcw.ca/index.php?option=com_content&view=article&id=615&catid=5&Itemid=99&lang=en, retrieved May 24, 2012; Sabrina Kraft, "Wal-Mart Saga: Union Appeals Ruling," *Weyburn Review*, July 13, 2011, www.weyburnreview.com/article/20110713/WEYBURN0101/110719953/-1/weyburn/wal-mart-saga-union-appeals-ruling, retrieved May 24, 2012; "Quebec Wal-Mart Workers Leave Union," *CBC News*, October 31, 2011, www.cbc.ca/news/canada/ottawa/story/2011/10/31/ottawa-gatineau-walmart-workers.html, retrieved May 24, 2012; and www.sasklabourrelationsboard.com/pdfdoc/166-10%20UFCW%20v%20%20Walmart, retrieved May 24, 2012.

CASE STUDY 9.2:   Labour Peace in the City of Toronto?

Toronto Mayor, Rob Ford was elected on the platform of reducing the City's budget shortfall and "he has taken direct aim at civic employees." The City's approach to collective bargaining includes seeking major concessions from its outside workers with changes to job security and benefit reductions. Ford has promised to "stop the gravy train" and cut waste at City Hall.

Doug Holyday, deputy-mayor and chairman of the city's employee and labour relations committee singled out a series of specific provisions the City would like to "quash" in its contract talks with its two biggest unions. "Over the years, a lot of things have crept into the contract that prevent us from operating in the most effective manner." Holyday adds, "A lot of these things in the contract are certainly not in contracts in other municipalities, and the private sector certainly would never consider them." For example, the City has a complex and lengthy "bumping" process to displace employees with less seniority; management needs to obtain

union consent to change scheduled shifts; and "running lunches," which allow workers to go home early when they eat their lunch on the job. However, Local 416 president, Mark Ferguson countered some of Mr. Holyday's statements on CBC Radio: "I take issue with him saying that things have 'crept in' to the collective agreement, that's completely false. There's a free collective-bargaining process where the two sides have negotiated a contract over the years."

Mayor Ford appears to be achieving his mandate and without a major work stoppage that had been viewed as inevitable by those observing the negotiations. The City recently negotiated a settlement during an all-night marathon bargaining session with its outside workers that has been described as a "big win" for Mayor Rob Ford. Mr. Ford called the settlement "fantastic" for taxpayers, however, Local 416 president, Mark Ferguson called the City a "bully" for threatening to impose new working conditions unless a deal was struck. Some of the specific negotiated terms included agreement to streamline layoff and redeployment rules—for example, only workers with at least 15 years of seniority will retain the former protection from layoffs if their jobs are contracted out.

Toronto's apparent labour peace has continued to expand—subsequent settlements have been reached with most of the City's inside workers, recreation workers have a deal, part-time long-term care workers are heading into arbitration, and a brief strike by library workers is over. Mayor Ford and his team including deputy-mayor Holyday, Bruce Anderson—HR director, and veteran negotiator Bob Reynolds, are credited with developing and implementing a successful negotiating strategy that had four key points: start negotiations early; keep the pressure on; focus on a single goal—changing job security protections; and take the case for reform (to deliver better service to residents) public by engaging the media.

Questions

1. What is your analysis of the situation that was faced by The City of Toronto and its stakeholders—for example, City of Toronto taxpayers and residents, employees, managers, and unions?

2. Do you think public sector unions should make sacrifices in difficult economic times when governments are facing deficits? Why or why not?

3. What effect might the actions of Mayor Rob Ford have on labour-management relations at the City of Toronto in the future? On other public sector collective bargaining processes and outcomes? Is this apparent labour peace at the City of Toronto likely to be sustainable?

SOURCES: David K. Shepherdson, "Industrial Relations Outlook 2012 Going Sideways, With a Twist," November 2011, *The Conference Board of Canada,* p. 2; Gee Marcus, "Kudos to Ford's Team for Labour Peace," *The Globe and Mail,* March 31, 2012, p. A19; Gee Marcus, "Mayor Scores a Big Win Just When It Counts," *The Globe and Mail,* February 6, 2012, p. A6; and Patrick White, "City Reveals Bargaining Objectives in Feud with Unions," *The Globe and Mail,* January 4, 2012, p. A7.

Practise and learn online with Connect.

Chapter 10

MANAGING
Human Resources Globally

{

What Do I Need to Know?

After reading this chapter, you should be able to:

LO1 ▶ Summarize how the growth in international business activity affects human resource management.

LO2 ▶ Identify the factors that most strongly influence HRM in international markets.

LO3 ▶ Discuss how differences among countries affect workforce planning at organizations with international operations.

LO4 ▶ Describe how companies select and train human resources in a global labour market.

LO5 ▶ Discuss challenges related to compensating and rewarding employees globally.

LO6 ▶ Explain how employers prepare employees for international assignments and for their return home.

Lululemon continues to build its business through new product categories and global expansion.

Lululemon Focuses on Global Growth

Vancouver-based Lululemon Athletica Inc. is a designer and retailer of yoga-inspired sportswear. Founded in 1998 by Chip Wilson, a University of Calgary economics graduate, Lululemon has profitably grown into a well-respected international retailer. Global growth is an important part of Lululemon's strategy—expanding to 174 stores compared with 130 just a year ago. Annual sales recently hit $1 billion for the first time and Wilson has left the company in the hands of Christine Day, *Report on Business* magazine's CEO of the Year. "Chip has created a legacy that has inspired the world and the mantle of leadership and care for the culture, values and mission of Lululemon is now in our hands," said Day. "I am proud to be leading Lululemon and excited about our future." Lululemon's global brand is recognized not only as a clothing brand but a lifestyle choice. Lululemon's "laidback, community-oriented and self-motivational culture" has made it a household name in Canada, and a growing retail presence in the United States, Australia, and Hong Kong. Global expansion also includes Europe—a showroom recently opened in London. Lululemon's showroom strategy has already been proving successful in other promising markets such as Malibu and Boca Raton—creating a cozy retail space with limited inventory and part-time store hours—enabling staff to go into the community to teach yoga classes and participate in local events.[1]

Introduction

This chapter discusses the HR issues that organizations must address in a world of global competition. We begin by describing how the global nature of business is affecting human resource management in contemporary organizations. Next, we identify how global differences among countries affect the organization's decisions about human resources. In the following sections we explore workforce planning, selection, training, and compensation practices in international settings. Finally, we examine guidelines for managing employees on international assignments.

HRM in a Global Environment

1,2

The environment in which organizations operate is rapidly becoming a global one. More and more companies are entering international markets by exporting their products, building facilities in other countries, and entering into alliances with foreign companies. At the same time, companies based in other countries are investing in setting up operations in Canada. Indeed, most organizations now function in the global economy. The HRM function needs to continuously reexamine its role in supporting this expanding pace of business globalization. This requires HRM to:

L01 Summarize how the growth in international business activity affects human resource management.

- Align HRM processes and functions with global requirements.
- Adopt a *global mindset* including a thorough understanding of the global environment and the impact on managing people worldwide.
- Enhance its own capabilities and competencies to become a business partner in acting on global business opportunities.[2]

What is behind the trend toward expansion into global markets? Foreign countries can provide a business with new markets in which there are millions or billions of new customers; developing countries often provide such markets, but developed countries do so as well. In addition, companies set up operations overseas because they can operate with lower labour costs. As discussed in Chapter 1, outsourcing jobs to lower-cost nations will continue to increase. For example, countries such as the "BRICs" (Brazil, Russia, India, and China) are particularly attractive, because they offer both low-cost labour and fast-growing economies. Finally, thanks to advances in telecommunications and information technology, companies can more easily spread work around the globe, wherever they find the right mix of labour costs and abilities. Teams with members in different time zones can keep projects moving around the clock, or projects can be assigned according to regions with particular areas of expertise. Many high-tech companies have set up 20 percent or more of their research and development work in India and China, where engineers are not only well trained and affordable, but also are familiar with the needs of their fast-growing marketplace. In India, for example, Microsoft is developing software that translates text in ten Indian languages, and Hewlett-Packard has been developing a Gesture Keyboard, which allows users to enter phonetic scripts used in the region. IBM has set up 86 software development centres around the world, many of them specializing in particular applications.[3]

Global activities are simplified and encouraged by trade agreements among nations; for example, most

As companies in Canada and the United States cut software jobs and outsource to other countries in order to drive down costs, countries such as India continue to see employment rates rise.

countries in Western Europe belong to the European Union (EU) and share a common currency, the euro. Canada, Mexico, and the United States have encouraged trade among themselves with the North American Free Trade Agreement (NAFTA). The World Trade Organization (WTO) resolves trade disputes among more than 100 participating nations.

As these trends and arrangements encourage international trade, they increase and change the demands on human resource management. Organizations with customers or suppliers in other countries need employees who understand those customers or suppliers. Organizations that operate facilities in foreign countries need to understand the laws and customs that apply to employees in those countries. They may have to prepare managers and other employees to take international assignments. They have to adapt their human resource plans and policies to different settings. Even if some practices are the same worldwide, the company now has to communicate them to its international workforce. A variety of international activities require managers to understand HRM principles and practices prevalent in global markets.

home country
The country in which an organization's headquarters is located.

host country
A country (other than the home country) in which an organization operates a facility.

third country
A country that is neither the home country nor the host country of an employer.

EMPLOYEES IN AN INTERNATIONAL WORKFORCE

When organizations operate globally, their employees are very likely to be citizens of more than one country. Employees may come from the employer's home country, a host country, or a third country. The **home country** is the country in which the organization's headquarters is located. For example, Canada is the home country of Fairmont Hotels and Resorts, because Fairmont's headquarters are in Toronto. A Fairmont employee who is a Canadian citizen and works at Fairmont's headquarters or one of its Canadian properties is therefore a *home-country national*.

A **host country** is a country (other than the home country) in which an organization operates a facility. Barbados is a host country of Fairmont because Fairmont has operations there. Any Barbadian workers hired to work at Fairmont's Barbados property would be *host-country nationals*, that is, employees who are citizens of the host country.

A **third country** refers to a country that is neither the home country nor the host country. (The organization may or may not have a facility in the third country.) In the example of Fairmont's operations in Barbados, the company could hire an Australian manager to work there. The Australian manager would be a *third-country national*, because the manager is neither from the home country (Canada) nor from the host country (Barbados).

When organizations operate globally, they need to decide whether to hire home-country nationals, host-country nationals, or third-country nationals for the overseas operations. Usually, they hire a combination of these. In general, employees who take assignments in other countries are called expatriates. In the Fairmont example, the Canadian and Australian managers working in Barbados would be expatriates during those assignments.

The extent to which organizations use home-country, host-country, or third-country nationals varies. In Venezuela, Pfizer's strategy to begin selling its medicines to clinics serving the poor included hiring residents of the poorest areas and training them to call on doctors' offices. While it might seem easier to hire college or university graduates, Pfizer decided that training street-savvy local residents in biology would be more effective than training people to navigate the neighbourhoods safely without losing samples to theft.[4] Companies face a different challenge with regard to management talent: the fastest economic growth has been occurring in Asia where people with knowledge of business management have been scare. North American companies have filled positions with home-country and third-country nationals, but companies and governments in these countries have been ramping up their development of local management talent. To learn about a company that is developing employees in host countries, see the "HR Best Practices" box.

HR BEST PRACTICES

Innovation Is a Global Affair at Cisco

Cisco Systems, which develops and sells technology for computer networking, doesn't just hire people around the world. It also is committed to getting them fully engaged in the company's performance. As Cisco's CEO John Chambers sees it, high-tech companies can survive only as long as they keep ahead of developments in their industry. That means everyone has to be learning and creating new ideas.

Fundamentally, Cisco meets that goal with an organization that fosters collaboration, not control through some vast hierarchy. The company established an information-sharing tool it calls Ciscopedia, where employees are encouraged to share ideas with one another online.

Linking employees online is logical for a company with Internet-related products and customers spread around the globe. To connect with those customers, Cisco thinks beyond the conventional approach of staffing local offices with host-country nationals. The company serves clients in developing economies through a

"second headquarters," established in Bangalore, India, the home of many engineers from India and other developing nations. With that talent pool to draw from, Cisco hires employees and assembles teams that travel to client sites in nations as far-flung as Russia and Chile. When the teams return, the company assigns them to expand what they learned into a client solution that could help other customers worldwide.

Cisco also has established training aimed at developing its multinational workforce. To develop managers, Cisco recruits employees with experience on at least two continents plus the ability to speak at least two languages and places them in its Global Talent Acquisition Program. These young managers and engineers undergo six months of training in sales and finance, coupled with mentoring. Cisco also provides resources to support local training programs in the areas where its customers operate. Cisco's commitment to local communities doesn't stop with training. The company has also set up a program called "Cisco's Ready," which partners with 20 Red

Cross chapters to train thousands of Cisco employees in emergency response skills.

This commitment to develop employees and communities must be serving Cisco well. Even at a time when other companies have been struggling, Cisco recently announced plans to hire 10,000 people and to maintain growth plans calling for another 10,000 new employees in India.

SOURCES: Michael Useem, "Whether Up or Down, Always Innovating: John Chambers, CEO," *U.S. News & World Report*, November 1, 2009, Business & Company Resource Centre, http://galenet.galegroup.com; Peter Burrows, "Cisco Builds a Local Workforce in Emerging Markets," *Businessweek*, March 12, 2009, www.businessweek.com; "Just in Time for National Volunteer Weeks, Collaboration Creates Largest Corporate Disaster Response Volunteer Program in Red Cross History," News Release, April 20, 2010, http://newsroom.cisco.com; John Murawksi, "Cisco Hopes to Employ 10,000," *News and Observer* (Raleigh, N.C.), March 5, 2010, Business & Company Resource Center, http://galenet.galegroup.com; and "Cisco's India Hiring Plan on Track: CEO," *Asia Pulse News*, March 15, 2010, Business & Company Resource Center, http://galenet.galegroup.com.

EMPLOYERS IN THE GLOBAL MARKETPLACE

Just as there are different ways for employees to participate in international business—as home-country, host-country, or third-county nationals—so there are different ways for employers to do business globally, ranging from simply shipping products to customers in other countries to transforming the organization into a truly global one, with operations, employees, and customers in many countries. Figure 10.1 shows the major levels of global participation.

Most organizations begin by serving customers and clients within a domestic marketplace. Typically, a company's founder has an idea for serving a local, regional, or national market. The business must recruit, hire, train, and compensate employees to produce the product, and these people usually come from the business owner's local labour market. Selection and training focus on employees' technical abilities and, to some extent, on interpersonal skills. Pay levels reflect local labour conditions. If the product succeeds, the company might expand operations to other domestic locations, and HRM decisions become more complex as the organization draws from a larger labour market and needs systems for training and engaging employees in several locations. As the employer's workforce grows, it is also likely to become more diverse. Even in small domestic organizations, a significant share of workers may be immigrants. In this way, even domestic companies are affected by issues related to the global economy.

As organizations grow, they often begin to meet demand from customers in other countries. The usual way that a company begins to enter foreign markets is by *exporting*, or shipping domestically produced items to other countries to be sold there. For example, Loewen, the Steinbach, Manitoba-based manufacturer of premium wood doors and windows, produces all of its products in its 587,000 square-foot plant in Steinbach but sells products to countries including the United States, Japan, and Mexico.[5] Eventually, it may become economically desirable to set up operations in one or more foreign countries. An organization that does so becomes an **international organization**. The decision to participate in international activities raises a host of HR issues, including the basic question of whether a particular location provides an environment where the organization can successfully acquire and manage human resources.

While international companies build one or a few facilities in another country, **multinational companies** expand on a broader scale. They build facilities in a number of different countries as a way to keep production and distribution costs to a minimum. In general, when organizations become multinationals, they move production facilities from relatively high-cost locations to lower-cost locations. The lower-cost locations may have lower average wage rates, or they may reduce distribution costs by being nearer to customers. The HRM challenges faced by a multinational company are similar but larger than those of an international organization, because more countries are involved. More than ever, the organization needs to hire

> **international organization**
>
> An organization that sets up one or a few facilities in one or a few foreign countries.
>
> **multinational company**
>
> An organization that builds facilities in a number of different countries in an effort to minimize production and distribution costs.

E-HRM	

The Internet brings together P&G employees.

FIGURE 10.1

Levels of Global Participation

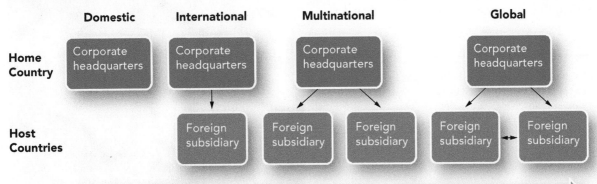

people who can function in a variety of settings, give them necessary training, and provide flexible compensation systems that take into account the different pay rates, tax systems, and costs of living from one country to another.

At the highest level of involvement in the global marketplace are **global organizations**. These flexible organizations compete by offering top products tailored to segments of the market while keeping costs as low as possible. A global organization locates each facility on the basis of the ability to effectively, efficiently, and flexibly produce a product or service, using cultural differences as an advantage. Rather than treating differences in other countries as a challenge to overcome, a global organization treats different cultures as a source of competitive advantage. It may have multiple headquarters spread across the globe, so decisions are more decentralized. This type of organization needs HRM practices that encourage flexibility and are based on an in-depth knowledge of differences among countries. Global organizations must be able to recruit, develop, retain, and fully utilize employees who can get results across national boundaries.

A global organization needs a **transnational HRM system**[6] that features decision making from a global perspective, managers from many countries, and ideas contributed by people from a variety of cultures. Decisions that are the outcome of a transnational HRM system balance uniformity (for fairness) with flexibility (to account for cultural and legal differences). This balance and the variety of perspectives should work together to improve the quality of decision making. The participants from various countries and cultures contribute ideas from a position of equality, rather than the home country's culture dominating.

global organization

An organization that chooses to locate a facility based on the ability to effectively, efficiently, and flexibly produce a product or service, using cultural differences as an advantage.

transnational HRM system

Type of HRM system that makes decisions from a global perspective, includes managers from many countries, and is based on ideas contributed by people representing a variety of cultures.

What Factors Affect HRM in International Markets?

Whatever their level of global participation, organizations that operate in more than one country must recognize that the countries are not identical and differ in terms of many factors (see Figure 10.2):

- culture
- education
- economic systems
- political-legal systems

L02 ▸ Identify the factors that most strongly influence HRM in international markets.

CULTURE

By far the most important influence on international HRM is the culture of the country in which a facility is located. *Culture* is a community's set of shared assumptions about how the world works and what ideals are worth striving for.[7] Cultural influences may be expressed through customs, languages, religions, and so on.

Culture is important to HRM for two reasons. First, it often determines the other three international influences. Culture can greatly affect a country's laws, because laws often are based on the culture's definitions of right and wrong. Culture also influences what people value, so it affects people's economic systems and efforts to invest in education.

Even more important for understanding human resource management, culture often determines the effectiveness of various HRM practices. Practices that are effective in Canada, for example, may fail or even backfire in a country with different beliefs and values.[8] Consider the five dimensions of culture

In Taiwan, a country that is high in collectivism, co-workers consider themselves more as group members instead of individuals.

FIGURE 10.2

Factors Affecting Human Resource Management in International Markets

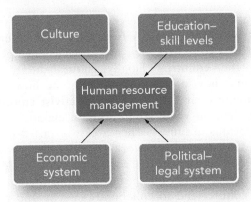

that Geert Hofstede identified in his classic study of culture:[9]

1. *Individualism/collectivism* describes the strength of the relation between an individual and other individuals in the society. In cultures that are high in individualism, such as Canada, Great Britain, and the Netherlands, people tend to think and act as individuals rather than as members of a group. People in these countries are expected to stand on their own two feet, rather than be protected by the group. In cultures that are high in collectivism, such as Colombia, Pakistan, and Taiwan, people think of themselves mainly as group members. They are expected to devote themselves to the interests of the community, and the community is expected to protect them when they are in trouble.

2. *Power distance* concerns the way the culture deals with unequal distribution of power and defines the amount of inequality that is normal. In countries with large power distances, including India and the Philippines, the culture defines it as normal to maintain large differences in power. In countries with small power distances, such as Denmark and Israel, people try to eliminate inequalities. One way to see differences in power distance is in the way people talk to one another. In the high power distance countries of Mexico and Japan, people address one another with titles (Señor Smith, Smith-san). At the other extreme, in Canada, in most situations people use one another's first names—behaviour that would be disrespectful in some other cultures.

3. *Uncertainty avoidance* describes how cultures handle the fact that the future is unpredictable. High uncertainty avoidance refers to a strong cultural preference for structured situations. In countries such as Greece and Portugal, people tend to rely heavily on religion, law, and technology to give them a degree of security and clear rules about how to behave. In countries with low uncertainty avoidance, including Singapore and Jamaica, people seem to take each day as it comes.

4. *Masculinity/femininity* is the emphasis a culture places on practices or qualities that have traditionally been considered masculine or feminine. A "masculine" culture is a culture that values achievement, money making, assertiveness, and competition. A "feminine" culture is one that places a high value on relationships, service, care for the weak, and preserving the environment. In this model, Germany and Japan are examples of masculine cultures, and Sweden and Norway are examples of feminine cultures.

5. *Long-term/short-term orientation* suggests whether the focus of cultural values is on the future (long term) or the past and present (short term). Cultures with a long-term orientation value saving and persistence, which tend to pay off in the future. Many Asian countries, including Japan and China, have a long-term orientation. Short-term orientations, as in the cultures of Canada, the United States, Russia, and West Africa, promote respect for past tradition, and for fulfilling social obligations in the present.

Such cultural characteristics as these influence the ways members of an organization behave toward one another, as well as their attitudes toward various HRM practices. For instance, cultures differ strongly in their opinions about how managers should lead, how decisions should be handled, and what motivates employees. In Germany, managers achieve their status by demonstrating technical skills, and employees look to managers to assign tasks and resolve technical problems. In the Netherlands, managers focus on seeking agreement, exchanging views, and balancing the interests of the people affected by a decision.[10] Clearly, differences like these would affect how an organization selects and trains its managers and measures their performance.

Cultures strongly influence the appropriateness of HRM practices. For example, the extent to which a culture is individualistic or collectivist will affect the success of a compensation program. Compensation tied to individual performance may be seen as fairer and more motivating by members of an individualistic culture; a culture favouring individualism will be more accepting of great differences in pay between the organization's highest- and lowest-paid employees. Collectivist cultures tend to have much flatter pay structures.

Job design aimed at employee involvement can be problematic in cultures with high power distance. In a Mexican slipper-manufacturing plant, an effort to expand the decision making authority of production workers stumbled when the workers balked at doing what they saw as the supervisor's proper responsibility.[11] Realizing they had moved too quickly, the plant's managers narrowed the scope of the workers' decision making authority so they could adapt to the role. On the other hand, a factor in favour of involvement at that plant was the Mexican culture's high collectivism. The workers liked discussing team-related information and using the information to benefit the entire team. As in this example, a culture does not necessarily rule out a particular HRM practice, such as employee involvement, but it should be a consideration in deciding how to carry out the practice. Imran Qureshi, international practice leader at Watson Wyatt Worldwide agrees one of the biggest challenges and payoffs for Canadian companies doing business globally is "understanding and tailoring strategies based on cultural differences." He cautions that companies should not be afraid of imposing certain standards or ways of business that define their own business culture, perspective, ethics or business processes. "You do need to be sensitive to environment but you also have to say what's important to [you] as a company. There may be a certain internal business cultural consideration that you really need to export."[12]

Despite cultural differences, the factors that engage workers are relatively similar across cultures. Table 10.1 provides a look at what engages employees in four countries. Finally, cultural differences can affect how people communicate and how they coordinate their activities. In collectivist cultures, people tend to value group decision making, as in the previous example. When a person raised in an individualistic culture works closely with people from a collectivist culture, communication problems and conflicts often occur. People from the collectivist culture tend to collaborate heavily and may evaluate the individualistic person as unwilling to cooperate and share information with them. Cultural differences in communication affected the way an agricultural company embarked on employee involvement at its facilities in North America and Brazil.[13] Employee involvement requires information sharing, but in Brazil, high power distance leads employees to expect managers to make decisions, so they do not desire information that is appropriately held by managers. Involving the Brazilian employees required engaging managers directly in giving and sharing information to show that this practice was in keeping with the traditional chain of command.

TABLE 10.1   What Keeps Foreign Workers Engaged

UNITED STATES	CHINA
• Confidence they can achieve career objectives	• Sense of personal accomplishment
• Sense of personal accomplishment	• Fair pay, given performance
• Confidence organization will be successful	• Comparable benefits to industry
• Quality is a high priority	• Confidence in senior management
• Opportunity for growth and development	• IT systems support business needs
• Information and assistance to manage career	• Opportunities for training

UNITED KINGDOM	BRAZIL
• Sense of personal accomplishment	• Sense of personal accomplishment
• Confidence in senior management	• Confidence in senior management
• Opportunities for training	• Opportunities for training
• Fair pay, given performance	• Fair pay, given performance
• Good reputation for customer service	• Good reputation for customer service
• Regular feedback on performance	• Comparable benefits to industry

SOURCE: Mercer HR Consulting, *Engaging Employees to Drive Global Business Success: Insight from Mercer's What's Working Research*, www.mercer.com/referencecontent.htm?idContent=1288115, retrieved September 14, 2008, quoted in Lesley Young, "Attracting, Keeping Employees Overseas," *Canadian HR Reporter*, April 7, 2008, www.hrreporter.com, retrieved May 26, 2008.

Also, because uncertainty avoidance is another aspect of Brazilian culture, managers explained that greater information sharing would reduce uncertainty about their work. At the same time, greater collectivism in Brazil made employees comfortable with the day-to-day communication of teamwork. The individualistic North American employees needed to be sold more on this aspect of employee involvement. The "HR Oops!" box describes another example of miscommunication resulting from cultural differences.

Because of these challenges, organizations must prepare both managers and employees to recognize and handle cultural differences. They may recruit managers with knowledge of other cultures or provide training, as described later in the chapter. For expatriate assignments, organizations may need to conduct an extensive selection process to identify individuals who can adapt to new environments. At the same time, it is important to be wary of stereotypes and avoid exaggerating the importance of cultural differences. Recent research that examined Hofstede's model of cultural differences found that differences among organizations within a particular culture were sometimes larger than differences from country to country.[14] This finding suggests that it is important for an organization to match its HR practices to its values; individuals who share those values are likely to be interested in working for the organization.

EDUCATION AND SKILL LEVELS

Countries also differ in the degree to which their labour markets include people with education and skills of value to employers. As discussed in Chapter 1, Canada suffers from a shortage of skilled workers in many occupations, and the problem is expected to increase. On the other hand, the labour markets in many countries are very attractive because they offer high skills and low wages.

Educational opportunities also vary from one country to another. In general, spending on education is greater per student in high-income countries than in poorer countries.[15] Poverty, diseases such as AIDS, and political turmoil keep children away from school in some areas. A concerted international effort to provide universal access to primary education has dramatically reduced the number and proportion of children without access to schooling. However, the problem persists in sub-Saharan Africa and is significant but declining in South Asia.[16]

Companies with foreign operations locate in countries where they can find suitable employees. The education and skill levels of a country's labour force affect how and the extent to which companies want to operate there. In countries with a poorly educated population, companies will limit their activities to low-skill, low-wage jobs. In contrast, India's large pool of well-trained technical workers

HR Oops! { Sometimes No One Reads Between The Lines

Employees in the British division of an oil and gas company were frustrated. They carefully researched ideas for where to conduct exploration in the Persian Gulf. They wrote reports presenting their recommendations and sent them to the company's headquarters in Texas. But no matter what they recommended, the British division's ideas were turned down.

As it turned out, the British employees had a cultural problem. They were using the careful, understated language of their business culture. They started off each report by identifying the risks of the proposal. Next, they laid out historical background. Finally, at the end of the report, the writers presented the possible opportunities.

Back in Texas, management had the optimistic, can-do spirit typical of U.S. business culture. They were looking for the positives and expected proposal writers to actively sell them on exploration ideas. Without that message, the managers at headquarters concluded that the proposals must not be very attractive. When the British team learned to reorganize and rephrase their reports for an American audience, they started winning approvals.

SOURCE: Based on Jill Rose, "Global Mindset," *American Executive*, January 2010, pp. 7–9.

QUESTIONS

1. In this example, who made a mistake—the writers of the proposal or the readers of the proposal? Why?

2. Imagine you are involved in recruiting a manager for a British facility of your company. Based on the example given here, what cultural differences in communication might you expect, and how might they affect your search for qualified candidates in Britain?

is one reason the country has become a popular location for outsourcing computer programming jobs.

ECONOMIC SYSTEM

A country's economic system whether capitalist or socialist, as well as the government's involvement in the economy through taxes or compensation, price controls, and other activities, influences human resource management practices in a number of ways.

As with all aspects of a region's or country's life, the economic system and culture are likely to be closely tied, providing many of the incentives or disincentives for developing the value of the labour force. Socialist economic systems provide ample opportunities for educational development because the education system is free to students. At the same time, socialism may not provide economic rewards (higher pay) for increasing one's education. In capitalist systems, students bear more of the cost of their education, but employers reward those who invest in education.

The health of an economic system affects human resource management. In developed countries with great wealth, labour costs are relatively high. Such differences show up in compensation systems and in recruiting and selection decisions.

In general, socialist systems take a higher percentage of each worker's income as the worker's income increases. Capitalist systems tend to let workers keep more of their earnings. In this way, socialism redistributes wealth from high earners to the poor, while capitalism apparently rewards individual accomplishments. In any case, since the amount of take-home pay a worker receives after taxes may thus differ from country to country, in an organization that pays two employees in two countries $100,000

each, the employee in one country might take home more than the employee in the other country. Such differences make pay structures more complicated when they cross national boundaries, and they can affect recruiting of candidates from more than one country.

POLITICAL-LEGAL SYSTEM

A country's political-legal system—its government, laws, and regulations—strongly impinges on human resource management. The country's laws often dictate the requirements for certain HRM practices, such as training, compensation, selection, and labour relations. As we noted in the discussion of culture, the political-legal system arises to a large degree from the culture in which it exists, so laws and regulations reflect cultural values.

For example, Canada has been a leader in eliminating discrimination in the workplace. Because the value of diversity is important in Canadian culture, legal safeguards such as human rights laws discussed in Chapter 2 exist, which affect hiring and other HRM decisions. As a society, Canada also has strong beliefs regarding the fairness of pay systems. Thus, pay equity legislation (discussed in Chapter 2), provides for equal pay for work of equal value. Other laws and regulations dictate much of the process of negotiation between unions and management. All these are examples of laws and regulations that affect the practice of HRM in Canada. When Canadian companies employ workers in other countries, the workers are usually covered by the employment

Students at the University of Warsaw in Poland are provided with a government-supported education. In general, former Soviet bloc countries tend to be generous in funding education, so they tend to have highly educated and skilled labour forces. Countries such as Canada and the United States generally leave higher education up to individual students to pay for, but the labour market rewards students who earn a college diploma or university degree.

laws in their own countries. Employment laws in many countries offer workers less protection than Canadian legislation provides.

Similarly, laws and regulations in other countries reflect the norms of their cultures. In Germany employees have a legal right to *codetermination* at the level of the company, facility, and individual. At the company level, an organization's employees have direct influence on the important decisions that affect them, such as large investments or new strategies. This influence comes from employee representatives on each company's supervisory council. At the level of each facility, codetermination exists through work councils. The councils have no rights in the economic management of the company, but they can influence HRM policies on issues such as working hours, payment methods, hirings, and transfers. Finally, at the individual level, employees have contractual rights, such as the right to read their employee files and the right to be informed about how their pay is calculated.[17]

An organization that expands internationally must gain expertise in the host country's legal requirements and ways of dealing with its legal system, often leading organizations to engage an international relocation consulting firm or hire one or more host-country nationals to help in the process. Some countries have laws requiring that a certain percentage of the employees of any foreign-owned subsidiary be host-country nationals, and in the context of our discussion here, this legal challenge to an organization's HRM may hold an advantage if handled creatively.

Workforce Planning in a Global Economy

As economic and technological change creates a global environment for organizations, workforce planning is involved in decisions about participating as an exporter or as an international, multinational, or global company. Even purely domestic companies may draw talent from the international labour market. For example, officials from Saskatchewan's five health regions and the provincial health recruitment agency have been actively hiring hundreds of registered nurses from the Philippines to help cope with identified shortages of nurses in the province.[18] As organizations consider decisions

L03 Discuss how differences among countries affect workforce planning at organizations with international operations.

about their level of international activity, HR professionals should provide information about the relevant human resource issues, such as local market pay rates and labour laws. When organizations decide to operate internationally or globally, workforce planning involves decisions about where and how many employees are needed for each international facility.

Decisions about where to locate include HR considerations such as the cost and availability of qualified workers. In addition, HR specialists need to work with other members of the organization to weigh these considerations against financial and operational requirements. Other location decisions involve outsourcing, described in Chapter 1. Many—but not all—of these arrangements involve workers outside North America in lower-wage countries.

In Chapter 3, we saw that workforce planning includes decisions to hire and lay off workers to prepare for the organization's expected needs. Compared with other countries, Canada allows employers wide latitude in reducing their workforce, giving Canadian employers the option of hiring for peak needs, then laying off employees if needs decline. Other governments put more emphasis on protecting workers' jobs. European countries, and France in particular, tend to be very strict in this regard.

Selecting Employees in a Global Labour Market

Many companies such as Fairmont have headquarters in Canada plus operations around the world. To be effective, employees in Fairmont's Mexico operations need to understand that region's business and social culture. Organizations often meet this need by hiring host-country nationals to fill most of their foreign positions. A key reason is that a host-country national can more easily understand the values and customs of the local workforce than someone from another part of the world can. Also, training for and transporting families to foreign assignments is more expensive than hiring people in the foreign country. Employees may be reluctant to take a foreign assignment because of the difficulty of relocating internationally. Sometimes the move requires the employee's partner to quit a job, and some countries will not allow the employee's partner to seek work, even if jobs might be available.

Even so, organizations fill many key foreign positions with home-country or third-country nationals.

L04 Describe how companies select and train human resources in a global labour market.

Qualities associated with success in foreign assignments are the ability to communicate in the foreign country, flexibility, enjoying a challenging situation, and support from family members. What would persuade you to take an international assignment?

Sometimes a person's technical and human relations skills outweigh the advantages of hiring locally. In other situations, such as the shortage of North American knowledge workers, the local labour market simply does not offer enough qualified people. At organizations located where needed skills are in short supply, hiring immigrant employees may be part of an effective recruitment and selection strategy.[19]

Whether the organization is hiring immigrants or selecting home-country or third-country nationals for international assignments, some basic principles of selection apply. Selection of employees for international assignments should reflect criteria that have been associated with success:

- Competency in the employee's area of expertise.
- Ability to communicate verbally and nonverbally in the foreign country.
- Flexibility, tolerance of ambiguity, and sensitivity to cultural differences.
- Motivation to succeed and enjoyment of challenges.
- Willingness to learn about the foreign country's culture, language, and customs.
- Support from family members.[20]

In research conducted a number of years ago, the factor most strongly influencing whether an employee completed a foreign assignment was the comfort of the employee's spouse and family.[21] Providing "trailing partner" career transition services may make the difference whether or not an international assignment will be accepted. Personality may also be important. Research has found successful completion of international assignments to be most likely among employees who are extroverted (outgoing), agreeable (cooperative and tolerant), and conscientious (dependable and achievement-oriented).[22]

Qualities of flexibility, motivation, agreeableness, and conscientiousness are so important because of the challenges involved in entering another culture.

culture shock
Disillusionment and discomfort that occur during the process of adjusting to a new culture.

virtual expatriates
Employees who manage an operation abroad without permanently locating in the country.

The emotions that accompany an international assignment tend to follow a cycle like that in Figure 10.3.[23] For a month or so after arriving, the foreign worker enjoys a "honeymoon" of fascination and euphoria as the employee enjoys the novelty of the new culture and compares its interesting similarities to or differences from the employee's own culture. Before long, the employee's mood declines as he or she notices more unpleasant differences and experiences feelings of isolation, criticism, stereotyping, and even hostility. As the mood reaches bottom, the employee is experiencing **culture shock**, the disillusionment and discomfort that occur during the process of adjusting to a new culture and its norms, values, and perspectives. Eventually, if employees persist and continue learning about their host country's culture, they develop a greater understanding and a support network. As the employee's language skills and comfort increase, the employee's mood should improve as well. Eventually, the employee reaches a stage of adjustment in which he or she accepts and enjoys the host country's culture.

Even if the organization determines that the best candidate for a position is someone from another country, employers often have difficulty persuading candidates to accept foreign assignments. Not only do the employee and employee's family have to contend with culture shock, but the employee's partner commonly loses a job when an employee makes an international move. Some organizations solve this problem with a compromise: the use of **virtual expatriates**, or employees who manage an operation abroad without

FIGURE 10.3

Emotional Stages Associated with a Foreign Assignment

SOURCE: Adapted from Delia Flanja, "Culture Shock in Intercultural Communication," *Studia Europaea* (October 2009), Business & Company Resource Center, http://galenet.galegroup.com.

locating permanently in that country.[24] They take frequent trips to the foreign country, and when they are home, they use technologies such as videoconferencing and electronic collaboration tools to stay in touch. An assignment as a virtual expatriate may be less inconvenient to family members and less costly to the employer. The arrangement, sometimes referred to as a "commuter assignment" does have disadvantages. Most notably, by limiting personal contact to sporadic trips, the virtual expatriate will likely have a harder time building relationships. Short-term assignments are also growing in popularity. According to a study involving more than 200 multinational organizations, 100 percent of these North American companies reported using short-term assignments.[25] The assignments generally last six to 12 months, avoiding the move of the whole family. Short-term and commuter assignments are gaining increasing acceptance by employees and decrease the risk of assignment failure, which provides a win-win for both the employee and the employer.[26]

Training and Developing a Global Workforce

In an organization whose employees come from more than one country, some special challenges arise with regard to training and development:

1. Training and development programs should be effective for all participating employees, regardless of their background.
2. When organizations hire employees to work in a foreign country or transfer them to another country, the employer needs to provide training in how to handle the challenges of working there.

TRAINING PROGRAMS FOR AN INTERNATIONAL WORKFORCE

Developers of effective training programs for an international workforce must ask certain questions.[27] The first is to establish the objectives for the training and its content. Decisions about the training should support those objectives. The developers should next ask what training techniques, strategies, and media to use. Some will be more effective than others, depending on the learners' language and culture, as well as the content of the training. For example, in preparation for training, Canadian employees might expect to discuss and ask questions about the training content, whereas employees from other cultures might consider this level of participation to be disrespectful, so for them some additional support might be called for. Language differences will require translations and perhaps an interpreter at training activities. Next, the developers should identify any other interventions and conditions that must be in place for the training to meet its objectives. For example, training is more likely to meet its objectives if it is linked to performance management and has the full support of management. Finally, the developers of a training program should identify who in the organization should be involved in reviewing and approving the training program.

The plan for the training program must consider international differences among trainees. For example, economic and educational differences might influence employees' access to and ability to use Web-based training. Cultural differences may influence whether they will consider it appropriate to ask questions and whether they expect the trainer to spend time becoming acquainted with employees or to get down to business immediately. Table 10.2 provides examples of how cultural characteristics can affect training design. For additional suggestions on providing effective training programs to an international workforce, see the nearby "HR How-To" box.

When working internationally, there may also be times when an employee requires immediate training or coaching to perform the job in a remote location. Schlumberger, one of the world's largest oilfield services providers, employs approximately 80,000 people in 80 countries, representing 140 nationalities. Schlumberger recently introduced technology that provides field engineers with immediate access to training needed to perform their jobs. For example, a field engineer working on a drilling project in a far-flung corner of Asia, notices an unexpected response and is uncertain what is causing the problem or how to proceed. The engineer receives on-the-spot

TABLE 10.2 Effects of Culture on Training Design

CULTURAL DIMENSION	IMPACT ON TRAINING
Individualism	Culture high in individualism expects participation in exercises and questioning to be determined by status in the company or culture.
Uncertainty avoidance	Culture high in uncertainty avoidance expects formal instructional environments. Less tolerance for impromptu style.
Masculinity	Culture low in masculinity values relationships with fellow trainees. Female trainers less likely to be resisted in low-masculinity cultures.
Power distance	Culture high in power distance expects trainer to be expert. Trainers expected to be authoritarian and controlling of session.
Time orientation	Culture with a long-term orientation will have trainees who are likely to accept development plans and assignments.

SOURCE: Based on B. Filipczak, "Think Locally, Act Globally," *Training*, January 1997, pp. 41–48.

training and expert advice by putting on headphones and a specially designed pair of glasses, fitted with a webcam, a small screen, and a two-way microphone. Using a wireless laptop, the engineer walks around the site demonstrating where the problem lies, and gets immediate on-the-job training from an expert (who may be based several thousand kilometres away) on how to diagnose and deal with the situation.[28]

cross-cultural preparation
Training to prepare employees and their family members for an assignment in a foreign country.

CROSS-CULTURAL PREPARATION

When an organization selects an employee for a position in a foreign country, it must prepare the employee for the foreign assignment. This kind of training is called **cross-cultural preparation**, preparing employees to work across national and cultural boundaries, and it often includes family members who will accompany the employee on the assignment. The training is necessary for all three phases of an international assignment:

1. Preparation for *departure*—language instruction and an orientation to the foreign country's culture.
2. The *assignment* itself—some combination of a formal program and mentoring relationship to provide ongoing further information about the foreign country's culture.
3. Preparation for the *return* home—providing information about the employee's community and home-country workplace (from company newsletters, local newspapers, and so on).

Methods for providing this training may range from lectures for employees and their families to visits to culturally diverse communities.[29] Employees and their families may also spend time visiting a local

family from the country where they will be working. In many organizations, cross-cultural training is mandatory. In the later section on managing expatriates, we provide more detail about such preparation. Canadian-based companies sometimes need to be reminded that foreign-born employees who come to Canada—*inpatriates*—need cross-cultural preparation as much as Canadian employees sent on foreign assignments.[30]

In spite of the many benefits of living in Canada, relocation can be challenging for inpatriates. As with expatriates, organizations can prepare inpatriate employees by providing information about getting the resources they need to live and work safely and comfortably in their new surroundings.

GLOBAL EMPLOYEE DEVELOPMENT

At global organizations, international assignments are a part of many career paths. The organization benefits most if it applies the principles of employee development in deciding which employees should be offered jobs in other countries. Career development helps expatriate and inpatriate employees make the transitions to and from their assignments and helps the organization apply the knowledge the employees obtain from these assignments.

Performance Management Across National Boundaries

The general principles of performance management may apply in most countries, but the specific methods that work in one country may not work well in

HR HOW-TO

Training Programs in Other Countries

Training professionals offer the following ideas for preparing and delivering training programs to employees in other countries.

- To get training sessions off to a positive start, learn the other culture's customs for greeting people and making eye contact. Know how to treat others with respect, and know how to interpret reactions to the presentation. In some cultures, speaking up is a sign of interest; in other cultures, listening quietly is preferred, because it signals that the participants are thinking about what they are learning.
- Learn about the other culture's values related to humour. A hilarious joke in Canada might be

puzzling or completely inappropriate somewhere else.
- Be aware that employees from different countries may be used to different learning methods. Trainees in Canada might expect to get involved in a group to practise concepts, whereas trainees in Africa or Asia might assume that good teaching involves a lecture from a person with authority. A mixture of learning activities can engage many kinds of learners.
- If the trainees are a multicultural group and are expected to engage in teamwork, don't leave them alone to flounder with cultural differences. The trainer should assign trainees to groups, rather than leaving them to divide

up on their own, and the trainee should monitor group activities, watching for individuals who seem not to be participating and asking questions that bring them into the activity.
- Devise training exercises that are relevant to all the participants. The exercises should not favour one cultural group of participants over another—for example, by investigating an issue that will be familiar only to part of the group.

SOURCES: Aliah D. Wright, "Respect Cultural Differences When Training, Experts Say," *HR Magazine,* December 2009 (HR Trendbook sup.) pp. 19–20; and Wei-Wen Chang, "Is the Group Activity Food or Poison in a Multicultural Classroom?" *T+D,* April 2010, Business & Company Resource Center, http://galenet.galegroup.com.

---

another. Therefore, organizations have to consider legal requirements, local business practices, and national cultures when they establish performance management methods in other countries. Differences may include which behaviours are rated, how and the extent to which performance is measured, who performs the rating, and how feedback is provided.[31]

For example, National Rental Car uses a behaviourally based rating scale for customer service representatives. To measure the extent to which customer service representatives' behaviours contribute to the company's goal of improving customer service, the scale measures behaviours such as smiling, making eye contact, greeting customers, and solving customer problems. Depending on the country, different behaviours may be appropriate. In Japan, culturally defined standards for polite behaviour include the angle of bowing as well as proper back alignment and eye contact. In Ghana and many other African nations, appropriate measures would include behaviours that reflect loyalty and repaying

of obligations as well as behaviours related to following regulations and procedures.

The extent to which managers measure performance may also vary from one country to another. In rapidly changing regions, such as Southeast Asia, the organization may have to update its performance plans more often than once a year.

Feedback is another area in which differences can occur. Employees around the world appreciate positive feedback, but Canadian employees are much more used to receiving direct feedback than are employees in other countries. In Mexico, managers are expected to provide positive feedback before focusing the discussion on behaviours the employee needs to improve.[32] At the Thai office of Singapore Airlines, managers resisted giving negative feedback to employees because they feared this would cause them to have bad karma, contributing to their reincarnation at a lower level in their next life.[33] The airlines therefore allowed the managers to adapt their feedback process to fit local cultures.

Compensating and Rewarding an International Workforce

Chapter 8 explained that *total rewards* includes decisions about pay structure, incentive pay, employee benefits and services and even development and career opportunities and other characteristics of the work environment such as work/life balance. All these decisions become more complex when an organization has an international workforce. In a recent survey of employers with international operations, 85 percent said they have a global compensation strategy to guide compensation decisions for employees at all levels and in all countries where they operate.[34] Still, HR specialists may need to make extra efforts to administer these systems effectively. In half of the companies surveyed, the person in charge of HRM in one country reports to the head of that company's operations, rather than to the leader of HRM at the company's headquarters.

L05 Discuss challenges related to compensating and rewarding employees globally.

PAY STRUCTURE

As Figure 10.4 shows, market pay structures can differ substantially across countries in terms of both pay level and the relative worth of jobs. For example, compared with the labour market in Germany, the market in Mexico provides much lower pay levels overall. In Germany, bus drivers average higher pay than kindergarten teachers, while the relative pay of teachers is greater in Mexico and South Korea. For all the types of jobs shown, the pay difference between jobs are much less dramatic in Germany than in the other two countries. One reason for such differences is the supply of qualified labour. In Nigeria and China, for example, the supply of management talent has not caught up to the demand, so in those countries there is a large gap between the pay for management jobs and the pay for clerical workers.[35]

Differences such as these create a dilemma for global companies: Should pay levels and differences reflect what workers are used to in their own countries? Or should they reflect the earnings of colleagues in the country of the facility, or earnings at

FIGURE 10.4

Earnings in Selected Occupations in Three Countries

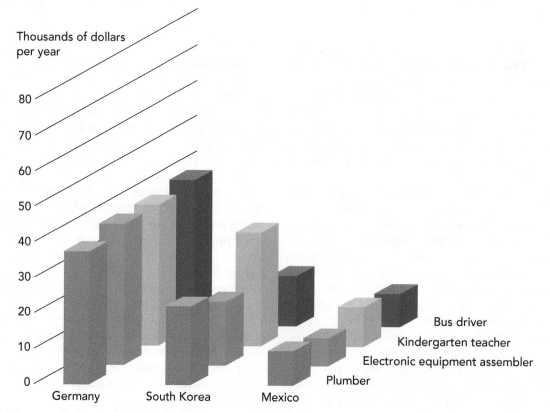

NOTE: Earnings are adjusted to reflect purchasing power.

SOURCE: Wage and hour data from International Labour Organization, LABORSTA Internet, http://laborsta.ilo.org, accessed May 7, 2010.

the company headquarters? For example, should a German engineer posted to Mumbai be paid according to the standard in Germany or the standard in Mumbai? If the standard is Germany, the engineers in Mumbai will likely see the German engineer's pay as unfair. If the standard is Mumbai, the company will likely find it impossible to persuade a German engineer to take an assignment in Mumbai. Dilemmas such as these make a global compensation strategy important as a way to show employees that the pay structure is designed to be fair and related to the value that employees bring to the organization.

These decisions affect a company's costs and ability to compete. The average hourly labour rates in industrialized countries such as Canada, the United States, Germany, and Japan are far higher than in newly industrialized countries such as Mexico, Hong Kong, and Brazil.[36] As a result, we often hear that Canadian labour costs are too high to allow Canadian companies to compete effectively unless the companies shift operations to low-cost foreign subsidiaries. That conclusion oversimplifies the situation for many companies. Merely comparing wages ignores differences in education, skills, and productivity.[37] If an organization gets more or higher-quality output from a higher-wage workforce, the higher wages may be worth the cost. Besides this, if the organization has many positions requiring highly skilled workers, it may need to operate in (or hire immigrants from) a country with a strong educational system, regardless of labour costs. Finally, labour costs may be outweighed by other factors, such as transportation costs or access to resources or customers. When a production process is highly automated, differences in labour costs may not be significant.

Cultural differences also play a role in pay structure. This became evident in the recent recession, when companies in many parts of the world, were slashing payrolls. Even fast-growing India experienced some downsizing, but many of the cuts came

from North American-based companies. India's business culture tends to be more "paternalistic," with managers feeling responsible for employees' well-being. So when business slowed, Indian companies were more likely to restructure, hold back on salary increases, and institute hiring freezes than to take actions like laying off employees or even reducing their hours.[38]

INCENTIVE PAY

Besides setting a pay structure, the organization must make decisions with regard to incentive pay, such as bonuses and stock options. International labour laws vary. For example, in Mexico, profit sharing is mandatory. Employers are required by law to distribute 10 percent of pre-tax earnings among employees other than senior managers.[39] Although stock options became a common form of incentive pay in North America during the 1990s, European businesses did not begin to embrace this type of compensation until the end of that decade. European companies usually link the options to specific performance goals, such as the increase in a company's share price compared with that of its competitors.

Employers are adding incentives to compensate employees working in high-risk parts of the world such as the Middle East. The list of dangerous hot spots in the world is long—"Iraq, Somalia, Afghanistan, Sudan, Chad, and Lebanon are just a few of the countries where employees can encounter a myriad of problems including disease, a higher incidence of crime, civil unrest, and war."[40] A study conducted by Watson Wyatt, found that many companies are offering added incentives to reward staff for working in high-risk areas.[41] For example, a "major U.S. engineering and construction company with federal contracts to rebuild Iraq compensates for the hazardous duty by offering each typical $130,000-a-year expatriate an extra $75,000 tax-free a year in foreign service, hardship and danger allowance."[42] Oil and gas companies, have adopted a "total security"

A large number of journalists found shelter in the old building of the French nongovernmental organization in Afghanistan. Taking an overseas assignment, especially in a harsh or potentially dangerous climate, requires the challenge of adjusting to life in a new country, so many companies pay employees higher salaries to compensate for this hardship.

approach to keep employees safe from harm that includes keeping employees "informed and isolated from the general population and surrounding them with security when they venture beyond their secure, well-protected enclaves. This approach is effective—and expensive."[43]

EMPLOYEE BENEFITS AND SERVICES

As in Canada, compensation packages in other countries include benefits and services. Decisions about benefits and services must take into account the laws of each country involved, as well as employees' expectations and values in those countries. Some countries require paid parental leave, and some countries, in addition to Canada, have nationalized health care systems, which would affect the value of private health insurance in a reward package. Availability of partner relocation assistance is a differentiator for many organizations in attracting employees to global assignments. For example, some organizations provide the "trailing partner" with educational and career assistance. Pension plans are more widespread in parts of Western Europe than in Canada, the United States, or Japan. Over 90 percent of workers in Switzerland have pension plans, as do all workers in France. Among workers with

pension plans, Canadian workers are significantly less likely to have defined benefit plans than workers in Japan or Germany.

Paid vacation, also discussed in Chapter 8, tends to be more generous in Western Europe than in North America. Figure 10.5 compares the number of hours the average employee works in various countries. Of these countries, only in South Korea, Japan, and the United States do workers put in more hours than Canadian workers. In the other countries, the norm is to work fewer hours than a Canadian worker over the course of a year.

International Labour Relations

In some industries, unions are seeking to form global labour alliances. For example, the United Steelworkers of America and Mexico's Miners and Metalworkers Union (250,000 members) want to create a coalition of metals and mining industry unions throughout the Western Hemisphere.[44]

Companies that operate across national boundaries will increasingly need to work with unions in more than one country. Organizations establish policies and goals for labour relations, overseeing labour

FIGURE 10.5

Normal Annual Hours Worked in Selected Countries

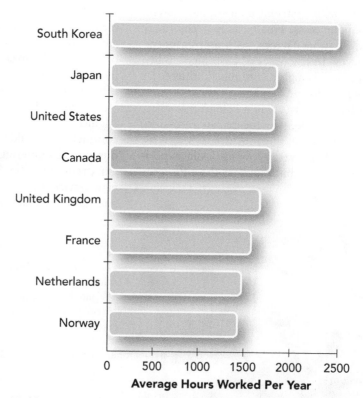

SOURCE: Data from Susan E. Fleck, "International Comparisons of Hours Worked: An Assessment of the Statistics," *Monthly Labour Review*, May 2009, pp. 3–31.

agreements, and monitoring labour performance (e.g., output and productivity).[45] The day-to-day decisions about labour relations are usually handled by each foreign subsidiary. The reason is that labour relations on an international scale involve differences in laws, attitudes, and economic systems, as well as differences in negotiation styles.

At least in comparison with European organizations, North American organizations exert more centralized control over labour relations in the various countries where they operate. Management therefore must recognize differences in how various countries understand and regulate labour relations. For example, in Canada, collective bargaining usually involves negotiations between a union local and an organization's management, but in Sweden and Germany, collective bargaining generally involves negotiations between an employer's organization and a union representing an entire industry's employees.[46] Legal differences range from who may form a union to how much latitude an organization is allowed in laying off workers. In China, for example, the government recently passed a law requiring employers to give new employees shorter probationary periods, consider workers' dependants in making layoff decisions, pay severance to fired workers, and give the Communist Party-run union more power in negotiating contracts and work rules.[47] In Germany, because labour representatives participate on companies' boards of directors, the way management handles labour relations can affect a broad range of decisions.[48] Management therefore has an incentive to build cooperative relationships.

International labour relations must also take into account that negotiations between labour and management take place in a different social context, not just different economic and legal contexts. Cultural differences that affect other interactions come into play in labour negotiations as well. Negotiators will approach the process differently depending on whether the culture views the process as primarily cooperative or competitive and whether it is local practice to negotiate a deal by starting with the specifics or agreeing on overall principles.[49] Working with host-country nationals can help organizations navigate such differences in negotiation style.

MANAGING EXPATRIATES

At some point, most international and global organizations assign employees to foreign posts. According to Statistics Canada, there are "about 68,000 Canadians working abroad at any given time and, with more companies active in the global marketplace, this number is expected to increase."[50] In addition, "North American companies are relying on more women to pursue international business opportunities—about four times as many as in 2001."[51] These assignments give rise to significant human resource challenges, from selecting employees for these assignments to preparing them, compensating them, helping them adjust, remain safe, providing support, and preparing for return home. The same kinds of HRM principles that apply to domestic positions can help organizations avoid mistakes in managing expatriates: planning and goal setting, selection aimed at achieving the HR goals, and performance management that includes evaluation of whether the overseas assignment delivered value relative to the costs involved.[52]

SELECTING EXPATRIATES

The challenge of managing expatriates begins with determining which individuals in the organization are most capable of handling an assignment in another country. Expatriates need technical competence in the area

3

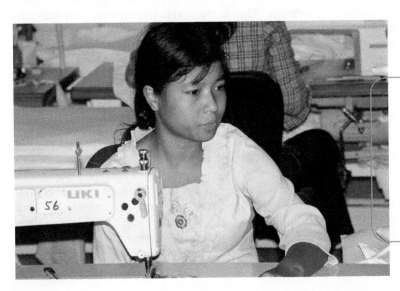

Due to the Multi Fibre Agreement which governs trade in the textile and clothing industry, the once prosperous clothing industry in Cambodia is failing to competitors in countries such as China. Many fear employees being laid off will be pushed to prostitution or become victims of human trafficking.

of operations, in part to help them earn the respect of employees. Of course, many other skills are also necessary for success in any new job, especially one that involves working overseas. Depending on the nature of the assignment and the culture where it is located, the organization should consider each candidate's skills, learning style, and approach to problem solving. Each of these should be related to achievement of the organization's goals, such as solving a particular problem, transferring knowledge to host-country employees, or developing future leaders for the organization.[53]

A successful expatriate must have a high level of *cross-cultural competence*—be sensitive to the host country's cultural norms, flexible enough to adapt to those norms, and strong enough to survive the culture shock of living in another culture. In addition, if the expatriate has a family, the family members must be able to adapt to a new culture. Adaptation requires three kinds of skills:[54]

1. Ability to maintain a positive self-image and feeling of well-being.
2. Ability to foster relationships with the host-country nationals.
3. Ability to perceive and evaluate the host country's environment accurately.

In a study that drew on the experience of people holding international assignments, expatriates told researchers that the most important qualities for an expatriate are, in order of importance, family situation, flexibility and adaptability, job knowledge and motivation, relational skills, and openness to other cultures.[55] To assess candidates' ability to adapt to a new environment, interviews should address topics such as the ones listed in Table 10.3. The interviewer should be certain to give candidates a clear and complete preview of the assignment and the host-country culture. This helps the candidate evaluate the assignment and consider it in terms of his or her family situation, so the employer does not violate the employee's privacy.[56]

Preparing Expatriates

Once the organization has selected an employee for an overseas assignment, it is necessary to prepare that person through training and development. Because expatriate success depends so much on the entire family's adjustment, the employee's partner should be included in the preparation activities. Employees selected for expatriate assignments already have job-related skills, so preparation for expatriate

assignments often focuses on cross-cultural training—that is, training in what to expect from the host country's culture. The general purpose of cross-cultural training is to create an appreciation of the host country's culture so expatriates can behave appropriately.[57] Paradoxically, this requires developing a greater awareness of one's own culture, so that the expatriate can recognize differences and similarities between the cultures and, perhaps, home-culture biases.

L06 Explain how employers prepare employees for international assignments and for their return home.

On a more specific level, cross-cultural training for foreign assignments includes the details of how to behave in business settings in another country—the ways people behave in meetings, how employees expect managers to treat them, and so on. As an example, Germans value promptness for meetings to a much greater extent than do Latin Americans—and so on. How should one behave when first meeting one's business counterparts in another culture? The "outgoing" personality style so valued in North America may seem quite rude in other parts of the world.[58]

Employees preparing for a foreign assignment also need information about such practical matters as housing, schools, recreation, shopping, and health care facilities in the country where they will be living. This is a crucial part of the preparation.

Communication in another country often requires a determined attempt to learn a new language. Some employers try to select employees who speak the language of the host country, and a few provide language training. Most companies assume that employees in the host country will be able to speak the host country's language. Even if this is true, host country nationals are not necessarily fluent in the home country's language, so language barriers often remain. This is true even when employees move to a country that nominally speaks the same language. For example, a Canadian employee working in England might be surprised to discover that when a project suddenly goes awry, it has "hit the buffers," while if it is proceeding smoothly, it is "on cam." And a client who says, "Give me a bell," isn't requesting an unusual sort of gift, but rather a phone call.[59]

Along with cross-cultural training, preparation of the expatriate should include career development activities. Before leaving for a foreign assignment, expatriates should discuss with their managers how the foreign assignment fits into their career plans and what types of positions they can expect upon their return. This prepares the expatriate to develop valuable skills during the overseas assignment and eases the return home when the assignment is complete.

TABLE 10.3   Topics for Assessing Candidates for Global Assignments

Motivation
- Investigate reasons and degree of interest in wanting to be considered.
- Determine desire to work abroad, verified by previous concerns such as personal travel, language training, reading, and association with foreign employees or students.
- Determine whether the candidate has a realistic understanding of what working and living abroad requires.
- Determine the basic attitudes of the spouse/partner toward an overseas assignment.

Health
- Determine whether any medical problems of the candidate might be critical to the success of the assignment.
- Determine whether the candidate is in good physical and mental health.

Language Ability
- Determine potential for learning a new language.
- Determine any previous language(s) studied or oral ability (judge against language needed on the overseas assignment).

Resourcefulness and Initiative
- Can the candidate make and stand by decisions and judgments?
- Does the candidate have the intellectual capacity to deal with several dimensions simultaneously?
- Is the candidate able to reach objectives and produce results with whatever people and facilities are available, regardless of the limitations and barriers that might arise?
- Is the candidate able to operate without a clear definition of responsibility and authority on a foreign assignment?
- Will the candidate be able to explain the aims and company philosophy to the local managers and workers?
- Does the candidate possess sufficient self-discipline and self-confidence to overcome difficulties or handle complex problems?
- Can the candidate work without supervision?
- Can the candidate operate effectively in a foreign environment without normal communications and supporting services?

Adaptability
- Is the candidate sensitive to others, open to the opinions of others, cooperative, and able to compromise?
- What are the candidate's reactions to new situations, and efforts to understand and appreciate differences?
- Is the candidate culturally sensitive, aware, and able to relate across the culture?
- Does the candidate understand his or her own culturally derived values?
- How does the candidate react to criticism?
- What is the candidate's understanding of the government system?
- Will the candidate be able to make and develop contacts with peers in the foreign country?
- Does the candidate have patience when dealing with problems?
- Is the candidate resilient; can he or she bounce back after setbacks?

Career Planning
- Does the candidate consider the assignment more than a temporary overseas trip?
- Is the move consistent with the candidate's career goals and aspirations?
- Is the employee's career planning realistic?
- What is the candidate's basic attitude toward the company?
- Is there any history or indication of interpersonal problems with this employee?

Financial
- Are there any current financial and/or legal considerations that might affect the assignment?
- Are financial considerations negative factors? Will undue pressures be brought to bear on the employee as a result of the assignment?

SOURCE: Excerpted with permission pages 55–57, *"Multinational People Management: A Guide for Organizations and Employees,"* by David M. Noer. Copyright © 1975 by the Bureau of National Affairs, Inc., Washington, DC, 20037. Published by the Bureau of National Affairs, Inc. Washington, DC 20037. For copies of BNA Books publications call toll free 1-800-960-1220.

When the employee leaves for the assignment, the preparation process should continue.[60] Employees need a chance to discuss their experiences with other expatriates, so they can learn from their failures and successes. The organization may provide a host-country mentor or executive coach with experience in the country to help expatriates understand their experiences. Successful expatriates tend to develop a bicultural or multicultural point of view, so as they spend more time in the host country, the value of their connections to other expatriates may actually increase.

MANAGING EXPATRIATES' PERFORMANCE

Performance management of expatriates requires clear goals for the international assignment and frequent evaluation of whether the expatriate employee is on track to meet those goals. Communication technology including e-mail, teleconferencing, and video conferencing provide a variety of ways for expats' managers to keep in touch with these employees to discuss and diagnose issues before they can interfere with performance. In addition, before employees leave for a global assignment, HR should work with managers to develop criteria for measuring the success of the assignment.[61] Measures such as productivity should take into account any local factors that could make expected performance different in the host country than in the company's home

country. For example, a country's labour laws or the reliability of the electrical supply could affect the facility's output and efficiency.

COMPENSATING AND REWARDING EXPATRIATES

One of the greatest challenges of managing expatriates is determining the compensation package. Most organizations use a *balance sheet approach* to determine the total amount of the package. This approach adjusts the employee's compensation so that it gives the employee the same standard of living as in the home country plus extra pay for any hardships of locating globally. As is shown in Figure 10.6, the balance sheet approach begins by determining the purchasing power of compensation for the same type of job in the employee's own country—that is, how much a person can buy, after taxes, in terms of housing, goods and services, and a reserve for savings. Next, this amount is compared with the cost (in dollars, for a Canadian company) of these same expenses in the foreign country. In Figure 10.6, the greater size of the second column means the costs for a similar standard of living in the foreign country are much higher in every category except the reserve amount. This situation would be likely in two of the countries identified in the "Did You Know?" box. For the expatriate

FIGURE 10.6

The Balance Sheet for Determining Expatriate Compensation

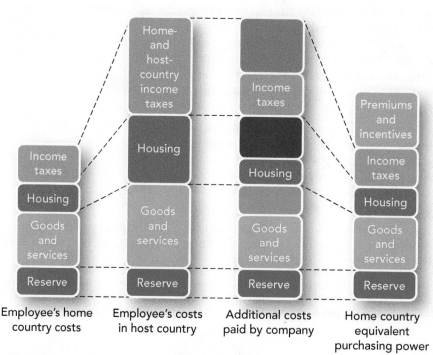

SOURCE: C. Reynolds, "Compensation of Overseas Personnel," in J. J. Famularo, ed., *Handbook of Human Resource Administration*, 2nd ed. (New York: McGraw-Hill, 1986), p. 51. Reprinted with permission. Copyright © 1986 by The McGraw-Hill Companies.

DID YOU KNOW?

Japan Tops Priciest Countries

According to report results from KMPG, Japan tops the list as the country with the highest business costs.

SOURCE: "KPMG's Guide to International Location Costs 2012 Edition," Exhibit 2.1, p. 7.

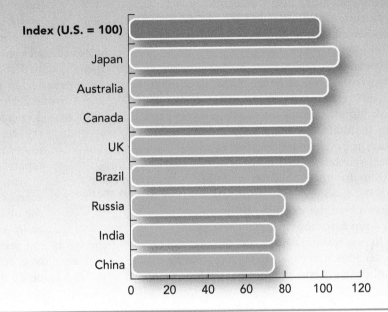

Index (U.S. = 100)

Japan · Australia · Canada · UK · Brazil · Russia · India · China

0   20   40   60   80   100   120

---

in this situation, the employer would pay the additional costs, as shown by the third column. Finally, the expatriate receives additional purchasing power from premiums and incentives. Because of these added incentives, the expatriate's purchasing power is more than what the employee could buy at home with the salary for an equivalent job. (Compare the fourth column with the first.) In practice, the total cost of an international assignment is roughly four times the employee's salary in the host country.[62] To restrain spending, some organizations are sending expatriates on shorter assignments. For instance, on an assignment of less than a year, an expatriate generally would not move his or her family, substantially reducing the cost of relocation and eliminating the need to cover children's education expenses.

After setting the total pay, the organization divides this amount into the four components of a total compensation package:

1. *Base* salary—determining the base salary is complex because different countries use different currencies (dollars, yen, euros, and so on). The exchange rate—the rate at which one currency may be exchanged for another—constantly shifts in response to a host of economic forces, so the real value of a salary in terms of dollars is constantly changing. Also, as discussed earlier,

the base salary may be comparable to the pay of other employees in the home country or comparable to other employees at the foreign subsidiary. Because many organizations pay a salary premium as an incentive to accept an overseas assignment, expatriates' salaries are often higher than pay for staying in the home country.

2. *Tax equalization allowance*—"Tax equalization holds that the worker neither gains nor loses with regards to tax liability as a result of an international assignment."[63] Countries have different systems for taxing income, and in some countries, tax rates are higher than in Canada. Usually, the employer of an expatriate withholds the amount of tax to be paid in the home country, then pays all of the taxes due in the country where the expatriate is working.

3. *Benefits and services*—Most of these issues have to do with whether an employee can use the same benefits in the foreign country. For example, if an expatriate has been contributing to a pension plan in Canada, does this person have a new pension plan in the foreign country? Or can the expatriate continue to contribute to the Canadian pension plan? Similarly, health benefits may involve receiving care at certain health facilities. While the person is abroad, does the same health plan cover services received in the

foreign country? In one case, flying an employee back to Canada for certain procedures actually would have cost less than having the procedures done in the country where the person was working. But the company's health plans did not permit this alternative. An employer may offer expatriates additional benefits to address the problem of uprooting a partner when assigning an employee overseas.

4. *Allowance to make a foreign assignment more attractive*—Cost of living allowances make up the differences in expenses for day-to-day needs. Housing allowances ensure that the expatriate can maintain the same standard of living as in Canada. Education allowances reimburse expatriates who pay tuition for their children to attend private schools. Relocation allowances cover the expenses of making the move to the foreign country, including transportation, shipping or storage of possessions, and expenses for temporary housing until the employee can rent or purchase a home.

repatriation
The process of preparing expatriates to return home from a foreign assignment.

HELPING EXPATRIATES RETURN AND MINIMIZING TURNOVER

As the expatriate's assignment nears its end, the human resource department faces a final challenge: helping the expatriate make the transition back to his or her home country. The process of preparing expatriates to return home from a foreign assignment is called **repatriation**. According to a study by a partnership between PricewaterhouseCoopers and Cranfield University School of Management, more than 25 percent of repatriated employees leave the company within one year after an international assignment ends.[64] Often, repatriation issues are discussed, at least informally, even before the candidate accepts an international assignment. The use of a well-written *international assignment letter* is a helpful means to clarify the rights and responsibilities of both the employer and employee for a relocation and subsequent return. Table 10.4 describes what to include in an

TABLE 10.4	What to Include in an International Assignment Letter
Assignment	• Location • Duration of assignment
Remuneration	• Base salary • Incentives and benefits • Pension plans • Currency of payment
Tax Issues	• Tax equalization • Tax advice • Tax reporting
Host Country	• Housing
Relocation Program	• Home and automobile sale • Family allowances (if family doesn't relocate) • House hunting • Moving • Schooling • Elder care • Language training • Cultural acclimatization programs
Vacation and Home Leave	• Number of trips • Emergency and compassionate travel provisions
Repatriation	• Timing (e.g., to coincide with family needs such as school terms) • Employment opportunities upon the employee's return • Assignment debriefing • Financial counselling • Dealing with dismissal or resignation

SOURCES: Joyce Head, "How Paper Can Protect International Relocations," *Canadian HR Reporter*, March 13, 2006, p. 14; and Margaret Sim and Liam Dixon, "Unraveling Comp, Benefits for Expatriates," *Canadian HR Reporter*, December 3, 2007, p. 23.

THINKING ETHICALLY

A Sustainable Advantage

Most growing companies have to contend with stiff industry competition, cash-flow troubles, and difficulties opening new sales channels. Not many have to dodge landmines, operate in isolated Third World locations, and train foreign workers who seriously distrust outsiders—all while introducing untested technology to industry skeptics.

Welcome to Frederick Davidson's everyday reality. The president and CEO of Vancouver-based contract mineral drilling company Energold Drilling Corp. has overcome all of these hurdles, to operate in 22 countries (most of them developing nations chosen for their high mineral-drilling potential and scarcity of direct competition) with a contingent of about 1,100 employees.

As Davidson explains, Energold's success came when it found a solution to a common drilling industry problem—the massive environmental damage left behind by rigs and crews. In 2011, five years after the company's launch, it shifted its focus from mineral exploration to contract drilling. While less risky, contract drilling remains highly competitive. Demand shifts constantly, rigs are difficult to relocate, and firms essentially rely on their own research to predict the next big market opportunity. To succeed, Energold would have to stand out. How? As is so often the case, inspiration came from an unexpected place: a remote mining site in the Dominican Republic.

To reach a proposed drilling location situated across a small town on the Caribbean island, Energold would have to drag a 10-ton drill across a river and farmers' fields, destroying the landscape in the process. Typical industry practice was for drilling companies simply to compensate farmers for the damaged land. Davidson felt there had to be a better way.

"I thought, 'Exploration is a high-risk business and the likelihood of finding something is very nominal, so why desecrate the landscape?'" he recalls. Besides, sustainability was becoming a key plan in corporate social responsibility mandates being adopted by most major mining companies.

Davidson and his team started researching options for less cumbersome drilling technologies and processes that would do less damage to surrounding ecosystems. That's when one of Energold's geologists came forward and explained that he'd once used a smaller, lighter underground drilling rig that could be disassembled and carried to a drilling site on foot. Intrigued, Davidson investigated and learned that no other firms in his field were using the equipment to green their drilling practices. He approached the manufacturer of the component drills, Delta, B.C.-based Hydracore Drills Ltd., and in short order was able to strike a supply deal, albeit a nonexclusive one.

With that, Energold had a clear competitive advantage. By incorporating component drilling rigs into its business model, the firm could move into frontier locations that its rivals had long ignored to drill for minerals—safely, cheaply, and without damaging the often fragile social and environmental fabrics. And by training locals and paying them competitively, Energold provided income to poor communities. All this gave its customers, including mining giant Rio Tinto PLC, a valuable chance to twin the public relations battle on the corporate social responsibility front.

Energolds's focus on frontier markets has meant contending with many challenges, one of the largest being oppressive or corrupt regulatory regimes in Third World nations. Never once, Davidson stresses, has Energold bribed an official to circumvent often obtuse local rules. "We don't pay people off," he says. "We've had occasion in which we've shipped a rig in and it has sat in customs for a year until [bribe-seeking officials] finally gave up and released it." Energold typically budgets about $200,000 per year to cover delays or equipment losses, yet Davidson is quick to point out that his firm has yet to lose a rig on-site or in transit. Energold also enlists on-the-ground expertise. In Mexico, for instance, the firm recruited skilled, multilingual locals to its on-site management teams to help overcome regulatory hurdles. Davidson says Energold's ethical stance appeals to sophisticated customers, even when they are very anxious to start drilling.

SOURCE: Chris Atchison, "A Sustainable Advantage," *Canadian Business*, June 1, 2011, www.canadianbusiness.com/article/47511--a-sustainable-advantage, retrieved May 28, 2012. Chris Atchison is the founder of Shockwave Strategic Communications, a Toronto-based marketing–communications agency.

QUESTIONS

1. Can a company remain profitable over the long term when it adopts a higher ethical standard than exists in the countries in which it operates?

2. Suppose you work in the HR department of Energold. How can your department support the principles behind these ethics-based decisions?

3. How is HRM affected when a company such as Energold takes an ethics-based position to refuse to offer bribes despite this practice being accepted as standard business practice in some countries? Will it be easier or harder to find and keep talented people? Why?

international assignment letter. Reentry is not as simple as it might sound. Culture shock takes place in reverse. The experience has changed the expatriate, and the company's and expatriate's home culture may have changed as well. Also, because of differences in economies and compensation levels, a returning expatriate may experience a decline in living standards. The standard of living for an expatriate in many countries includes household help, a car and driver, private schools, and club memberships.

Companies are increasingly making efforts to help expatriates through this transition and take steps to ensure expatriates stay with the company after their return. Expatriates are more likely to stay with a company that provides them opportunities to use their international experience.[65] Two activities help the process along: *communication* and *validation*.[66] Communication refers to the expatriate receiving information and recognizing changes while abroad. The more the organization keeps in contact with the expatriate, the more effective and satisfied the person

is likely to be upon return. The expatriate plays a role in this process as well. Expatriates should work at maintaining important contacts in the company and industry. Communication related to performance and career development before and during the international assignment also should help the employee return to a choice of positions that are challenging and interesting. Validation means giving the expatriate recognition for the international service when this person returns home. Expatriates who receive family repatriation support and recognition from colleagues and top managers for their international service and future contribution have fewer troubles with reentry than those whose contributions are disregarded. Validation should also include planning for how the returning employee will contribute to the organization. What skills will this person bring back? What position will he or she fill? The new skills may be much more than knowledge of a particular culture. For example, the person may have learned how to lead or negotiate with a diverse group of people.[67]

SUMMARY

L01 Summarize how the growth in international business activity affects human resource management.

- More and more companies are entering international markets by exporting and operating foreign facilities. To do this, organizations may hire a combination of home-country, host-country, and third-country nationals.

- They may operate on the scale of an exporter or an international, global, or multinational organization.

- A global organization needs a transnational HRM system, which makes decisions from a global perspective, includes employees from many countries, and is based on ideas contributed by people representing a variety of cultures.

L02 Identify the factors that most strongly influence HRM in international markets.

- By far the most important influence is the culture of each market—its set of shared assumptions about how the world works and what ideals are worth striving for.

- Countries also differ in the degree to which their labour markets include people with education and skills of value to employers. Another influence on international HRM is the foreign country's political-legal system—its government, laws, and regulations.

- Finally, a country's economic system, capitalist or socialist, as well as the government's involvement in the country's economy, such as through taxes and price controls, is a strong factor determining HRM practices.

L03 Discuss how differences among countries affect workforce planning at organizations with international operations.

- As organizations consider decisions about their level of international activity, HR professionals should provide information about the relevant human resource issues.

- When organizations decide to operate internationally or globally, workforce planning involves decisions about where and how many employees are needed for each international facility. Some countries allow employers more flexibility in meeting human resource needs. HRM professionals need to be conversant with such differences.

L04 Describe how companies select and train human resources in a global labour market.

- Many organizations with international operations fill most positions with host-country nationals. These employees can more easily understand the values and customs of the local workforce, and hiring locally tends to be less expensive than moving employees to new locations.

- Organizations also fill foreign positions with home-country and third-country nationals who have human relations skills associated with success in international assignments. They also may use "virtual expatriates," who do not go abroad for an extended period.
- When sending employees on international assignments, organizations prepare the employees (and often their families) through cross-cultural training.

L05 Discuss challenges related to compensating and rewarding employees globally.

- Pay structures can differ substantially among countries in terms of pay level and the relative worth of jobs. Organizations have to decide whether to set pay levels and differences in terms of what workers are used to in their own countries or in terms of what employees' colleagues earn at headquarters.
- These decisions affect the organization's costs and ability to compete, so organizations consider local labour costs in their location decisions. Along with the basic pay structure, organizations must make decisions regarding incentive pay, such as bonuses and stock options.

- Laws may dictate differences in benefit packages, and the value of benefits will differ if a country requires them or makes them a government service.

L06 Explain how employers prepare employees for international assignments and for their return home.

- When an organization has selected an employee for an international assignment, it must prepare the person for the experience. In cross-cultural training, the soon-to-be-expatriate learns about the foreign culture he or she is heading to, and studies her or his own home-country culture as well for insight.
- Preparation of the expatriate should also include career development activities to help the individual acquire valuable career skills during the international assignment and at the end of the assignment to handle repatriation successfully.
- Communication of changes at home and validation of a job well done abroad help the expatriate through the repatriation process.

Critical Thinking Questions

1. Identify the home country, host country(ies), and third country(ies) in the following example: A global soft-drink company called Cold Cola has headquarters in Halifax, Nova Scotia. It operates production facilities in the United States, and in Jakarta, Indonesia. The company has assigned a manager from Moncton to head the U.S. facility and a manager from Hong Kong to manage the Jakarta facility.
2. What are some HRM challenges that arise when a Canadian company expands from domestic markets by exporting? When it changes from simply exporting to operating as an international company? When an international company becomes a global company?
3. In recent years, many North American companies have invested in Russia and sent Canadian managers there in an attempt to transplant North American-style management. According to Hofstede, Canadian culture has low power distance and uncertainty avoidance, long-term orientation, and high individuality and masculinity. Russia's culture has high power distance and uncertainty avoidance, low masculinity and long-term orientation, and moderate individuality. In light of what you know about cultural differences, how well do you think Canadian managers can succeed in each of the following North American-style HRM practices? (Explain your reasons.)
   a. Selection decisions based on extensive assessment of individual abilities
   b. Appraisals based on individual performance
   c. Systems for gathering suggestions from workers
   d. Self-managing work teams
4. Besides cultural differences, what other factors affect human resource management in an organization with international operations?
5. Suppose you work in the HR department of a company that is expanding into a country where the law and culture make it difficult to lay off employees. How should your knowledge of that difficulty affect workforce planning for the overseas operations?
6. Why do multinational organizations hire host-country nationals to fill most of their foreign positions, rather than sending expatriates for most jobs?
7. Suppose an organization decides to improve collaboration and knowledge sharing by developing an intranet to link its global workforce. It needs to train employees in several different countries to use this system. List the possible cultural issues you can think of that the training program should take into account.
8. For an organization with operations in three different countries, what are some advantages and disadvantages of setting compensation according to the labour markets in the countries where the employees live and work? What are some advantages and disadvantages of setting compensation according to the labour market in the company's headquarters? Would the best arrangement be different for the

company's top executives and its production workers? Explain.

9. What abilities make a candidate more likely to succeed in an assignment as an expatriate? Which of these abilities do you have? How might a person acquire these abilities?

10. In the past, a large share of expatriate managers from Canada have returned home before successfully completing their international assignments. Suggest some possible reasons for the high failure rate. What can HR departments do to increase the success of expatriates?

What's Your HR IQ?

Connect offers more ways to check what you've learned so far. Find experiential exercises, Test Your Knowledge quizzes, videos, and many other resources to gauge your HR IQ.

CASE STUDY 10.1:   "Designed by Apple in California—Assembled in China"

Although Apple built computers in the U.S. for most of its corporate history it has joined other electronics companies in moving its assembly lines to China to achieve the cost advantages of less expensive labour. In recent years, working conditions at these factories have come under intense scrutiny, particularly after at least ten workers committed suicide at factories owned by Foxconn, the Taiwanese electronics manufacturer. Foxconn manufactures more than 40 percent of the world's electronics—the sheer scale and volume of its operations make it China's single biggest exporter. In addition to assembling iPhones, iPads, and other devices for Apple, Foxconn also manufactures products for many other companies including Dell, Hewlett-Packard, and Intel.

In January 2012, Apple became the first technology company to join the Fair Labor Association (FLA), a non-profit global monitoring group. Timothy Cook, Apple's chief executive invited the FLA to conduct inspections of its suppliers' factories in China and elsewhere. Cook also personally visited one of the factories where Apple products are made. "Our team has been working for years to educate workers, improve conditions and make Apple's supply chain a model for the industry, which is why we asked the FLA to conduct these audits."

The Fair Labor Association conducted an audit of three large Chinese factories owned by Foxconn: Guanlan (assembles iPhones and iPods); Longhua (assembles iPads, and Macs), and Chengdu (assembles iPads and components). The resulting audit criticized the long hours and dangerous working conditions—inspectors found at least 50 breaches of Chinese regulations as well as the code of conduct Apple signed when it joined the Fair Labor Association in January 2012. Assessors found cases of employees working longer hours and more consecutive days than allowed by FLA standards and Chinese law. For example, FLA's audit found that the average weekly working hours were 56.1 hours per week (49.1 hours permitted by Chinese law); average

maximum weekly hours was 61.1 hours, and longest consecutive period without a rest break was 11.6 days. The FLA auditors found no issues related to child or forced labour, according to the report—the average age of workers was 23 years. And it was reported that Foxconn employees received higher wages than required under Chinese law—starting at 1,800 yuan ($285) a month with the average pay reported as 2,687 yuan in one plant, 2,872 in another (the minimum set by government in China is 1,500 yuan). The FLA also interviewed more than 35,000 Foxconn employees—48 percent responded that how much they worked was "reasonable," 18 percent said "too long," and 34 percent "want to work more to earn more money." Although there was some variation among factories, 43 percent of workers overall said they had seen or experienced an accident at work and 65 percent said they felt pain after a full day of work.

Foxconn has agreed to bring hours in line with legal limits by July 2013 and compensate its more than 1.2 million employees for overtime lost due to the shorter workweek. "We are committed to work with Apple to carry out the remediation program, developed by both our companies," Foxconn said in an emailed statement. "Our success will be judged by future FLA audits and the monitoring of the implementation of the remediation program, by reviews carried out by Apple and other customers and by future employee surveys." Foxconn has also pledged that workers will not see a pay decline because of corresponding wage increases. "The eyes of the world are on them and there's just no way they can't deliver," FLA president Auret van Heerden says. "It's a real showstopper."

On May 21, 2012 it was reported that Apple plans to expand its manufacturing facilities in China—its contract manufacturer, Foxconn announced plans to invest $210 million to build an Apple production line in October 2012 in east China's Jiangsu province.

Questions

1. What effect do you think Apple's efforts to improve pay and working conditions for employees will have on other organizations that manufacture or assemble products in China?

2. What advice would you offer Apple's CEO and senior HR managers regarding their role in Foxconn's HR practices at its factories?

3. Would you be willing to pay more for Apple products assembled in factories with improved pay, safety, and working conditions for workers?

SOURCES: "Foxconn Technology," *The New York Times*, May 28, 2012, retrieved May 28, 2012; "Foxconn to Set Up $210 Million Apple production Line in China," *The Economic Times*, May 21, 2012, retrieved May 28, 2012; Nick Wingfield, "Fixing Apple's Supply Lines," *The New York Times*, April 2, 2012; Stanley James, "Foxconn Auditor Finds 'Serious' Violations of Chinese Law," *BusinessWeek*, March 30, 2012; and "A List of Labor Concerns at Foxconn," *The New York Times*, March 29, 2012.

CASE STUDY 10.2: Foreign Assignments Increasing, Along with Employee Resistance

Canadians are working outside the country in increasing numbers. Data from Statistics Canada show that about 68,000 Canadians had a place of work outside the country. In addition, as Canada continues to play a growing role in an expanding global marketplace, there is every expectation the need for Canadian talent to work abroad will grow.

In the Canadian Employee Relocation Council's recent Survey of Corporate Relocation Policies, more than two-thirds of the 88 firms surveyed had transferred staff overseas. In the same survey, family issues ranked as the number one challenge for an overseas assignment.

While working in foreign lands may hold appeal, it is clearly not for everybody. There are many barriers to overcome for both the organization and its employees when it comes to a foreign posting. Partly in response to the personal realities that individuals are coping with as well as to rapidly changing business opportunities, shorter-term assignments, lasting from six months to three years, are becoming more common.

Whether it's a short- or long-term assignment, many of the challenges remain the same: getting the right people in the right job, at the right place, and at the right time.

Today, most Canadian families have both partners working, so when it comes to taking on a foreign assignment, it's no surprise that family issues are top of mind. Statistics Canada also reports a 40-percent increase in the number of female managers since 1990. Today, dual careers are an even more important consideration than perhaps was the case ten or so years ago. The bottom line: moving is a far more complex undertaking than ever before.

"Moving people is a very expensive undertaking for the company," says Sue Irwin, responsible for international HR and relocations with ConocoPhillips Canada in Calgary. "It can cost three times as much to move somebody from say Houston than it does to hire a local person in Calgary and so it has to be the right fit."

Irwin manages a portfolio of both inpatriates (people coming to work in Canada) as well as expatriates. "While shorter-term assignments meet business needs, they also provide the much-needed career development and experience to the best talent in the organization," she says. "And it's not just about getting the right technical talent. Equally important is the ability to work with people with varied skill sets and from different backgrounds." All are critical skills on the global stage.

Terri Lynn Oliver, international HR advisor with Siemens Canada, notes that at Siemens, "the selection of high potentials [for international assignment] is part of the overall corporate approach for succession planning and career development."

With a global workforce of 420,000, of which 6,600 are in Canada, there is no shortage of foreign opportunities. At Siemens the process for selection is structured and the company maintains a pool of potential talent to draw from as opportunities arise. The challenge from a corporate perspective, says Oliver, is managing the expectation and linking the move to a strategic objective. "People want to know, 'What position will I come back to?' In most situations it's impossible to give a guarantee about opportunities on the completion of the assignment. And so people will often opt for the domestic promotion."

When it comes to individuals accepting an assignment, family and career issues dominate. "The spouse's career is a major consideration particularly on a longer assignment," says Oliver. "Schooling is also a challenge and Siemens tries to be innovative for both its inpatriates and expatriates in finding workable solutions within budget."

Schooling issues are echoed by Irwin who adds, "There are many students in gifted and extracurricular programs, people just don't want to uproot their families."

Thomas Vulpe, with the Canadian Foreign Service Institute, an agency within the Department of Foreign Affairs and International Trade, says family issues can predict the successful completion of an international assignment.

"Various studies have shown family issues to be the single most important issue in early repatriation," he says. These subtleties may not be readily apparent before the move, but culture shock and the inability to work in a foreign location can often be too much for the trailing spouse, leading to an early return.

"Companies are becoming more concerned about these soft issues," says Mike Watters, vice-president of sales with moving firm Allied International. These are not just Canadian problems, he adds. He tells the story of the wife of a French company executive who was "abandoned" in the Toronto-area, without access to any support. "She couldn't speak a word of English and left saying it was the worst two years of her life."

While family issues are the main barriers to individuals taking on a foreign assignment, safety is an escalating concern. Canada is a safe country to live and raise a family in. Many of the countries where Canadians are working are becoming more dangerous it seems with each passing day.

"One of the key parts of safety training for foreign-aid workers in hot spots like Columbia, Bolivia, and Afghanistan, includes looking under their vehicles with a mirror to check for bombs," Vulpe says. Not a pleasant routine, as you're also trying to comfort children who are used to walking to school. These issues are compounded by the fact the "megalopolises where people are being posted are becoming more polluted, and access to quality health care is a concern. Ten years ago it wasn't such a big issue, but today it's a big decision," he adds.

Perhaps that's why Terri Lynn Oliver says, "flexibility to shorten an assignment and planning for the worst," are a key part in the development of any foreign assignment.

Questions

1. What are some of the human resource challenges associated with relocating employees to jobs and work assignments outside Canada?
2. Would you be interested in working outside Canada? Why or why not? If you would consider working outside Canada at some point in your career, at what life/career stage would a global assignment be most appealing?

SOURCE: Stephen Cryne, "Foreign Assignments Increasing, Along with Employee Resistance," *Canadian HR Reporter*, September 27, 2004, www.hrreporter.com, retrieved April 15, 2005. © *Canadian HR Reporter*, September 27, 2004, by permission of Carswell, Toronto, Ontario, 1-800-387-5164, www.hrreporter.com.

 **Practise and learn online with Connect.**

Chapter 11

CREATING AND SUSTAINING
High-Performance Organizations

What Do I Need to Know?

After reading this chapter, you should be able to:

L01 Define high-performance work systems and identify the elements, outcomes, and conditions associated with such a system.

L02 Describe how organizations assess employee satisfaction and engagement.

L03 Explain how human resource management can contribute to high performance.

L04 Discuss the role of HRM technology in high-performance work systems.

L05 Summarize ways to measure the effectiveness of human resource management.

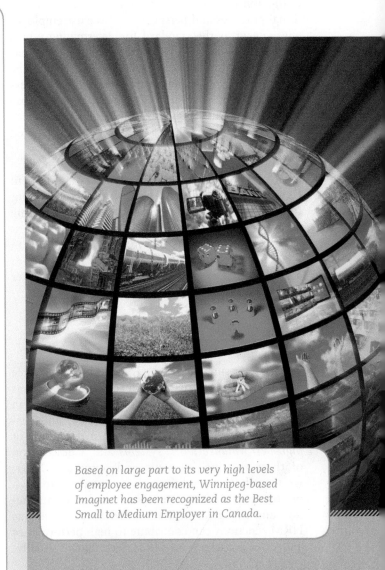

Based on large part to its very high levels of employee engagement, Winnipeg-based Imaginet has been recognized as the Best Small to Medium Employer in Canada.

Imaginet Ranks #1 in Queen's School of Business Study

"It's a tremendous honour to be named the Best Small to Medium Employer in Canada," says Rod Giesbrecht, CEO and co-founder of Winnipeg-based software application firm, Imaginet. "Our dynamic culture defines Imaginet and is demonstrated by the team's commitment to providing unsurpassed value to our customers." "We have some of the best people in the world working in Imaginet. They are positive, hard working and results oriented," adds co-founder Joel Semeniuk. "Building a strong company with a great culture is a lot of fun when you have like-minded people who are determined to succeed."

The process to become a "Top Best Small to Medium Employer" is a detailed and competitive process. Rankings are primarily based upon the analyzed results of 21 key engagement drivers detailed in employee opinion surveys, however, the evaluation process also includes assessing organizational practices and perspectives. "We use employee engagement as the standard for determining which organizations are the 'best' employers," said Einar Westerlund, director of project development at the Queen's School of Business Centre for Business Venturing. "In this study, feedback directly from employees about their workplace and their work experience enables us to measure how engaged they are."

Founded in 1997, Imaginet now has offices in the United States and South Africa, in addition to Canada. "As a small-business owner, it's important to build a strong community of high-performing employees who share your passion for the business and its goals," explains Giesbrecht. "We continue to attract new recruits at the top of their game, and as a result, Imaginet enjoyed a 250 percent growth over the past year."[1]

Introduction

This chapter summarizes the role of human resource management in creating an organization that achieves a high level of performance, measured in such terms as long-term profits, quality, and customer satisfaction. We begin with a definition of *high-performance work systems* and a description of these systems' elements and outcomes. Next, we identify the conditions that contribute to high performance and how to assess employee satisfaction and engagement. We explain how the various HRM functions can contribute to high performance and discuss the role of HRM technology. Finally, we introduce ways to measure the effectiveness of human resource management.

What Is a High-Performance Work System?

1,2

The challenge facing managers today is how to make their organizations into high-performance work systems with the right combination of people, technology, and organizational structure to make full use of resources and opportunities in achieving their organizations' goals. To function as a high-performance work system, each of these elements must fit well with the others in a smoothly functioning whole. Many manufacturers use the latest in processes including flexible manufacturing technology and just-in-time inventory control (meaning parts and supplies are automatically restocked as needed), but, of course, these processes do not work on their own; they must be run by qualified people. Organizations have to determine what kinds of people fit their needs, and then locate, train, and motivate those special people.[2] According to research, organizations that introduce integrated high-performance work practices usually experience increases in productivity and long-term financial performance.[3]

> **LO1** Define high-performance work systems and identify the elements, outcomes, and conditions associated with such a system.

Creating a high-performance work system contrasts with traditional management practices. In the past, decisions about technology, organizational structure, and human resources were treated as if they were unrelated. An organization might acquire a new information system, restructure jobs, or add an office in another country without considering the impact on its people.[4] More recently, managers have realized that success depends on how well all the elements work together. For instance, as health care providers feel increasing pressure to rein in costs, some are finding solutions in combinations of information technology, improved staffing, and the redesign of work processes.

ELEMENTS OF A HIGH-PERFORMANCE WORK SYSTEM

As shown in Figure 11.1, in a high-performance work system, the elements that must work together include organizational structure, task design, people (the selection, training, and development of employees), reward systems, and information systems, and

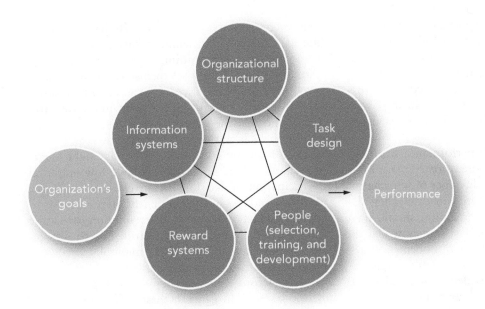

FIGURE 11.1

Elements of a High-Performance Work System

human resource management plays an important role in establishing all these.

Organizational structure is the way the organization groups its people into useful divisions, departments, and reporting relationships. The organization's top management makes most decisions about structure, for instance, how many employees report to each supervisor, and whether employees are grouped according to the functions they carry out or the customers they serve. Such decisions affect how well employees coordinate their activities and respond to change. In a high-performance work system, organizational structure promotes cooperation, learning, and continuous improvement.

Task design determines how the details of the organization's necessary activities will be grouped, whether into jobs or team responsibilities. In a high-performance work system, task design makes jobs efficient while encouraging high-quality results. In Chapter 3, we discussed how to carry out this HRM function through job analysis and job design.

The right *people* are a key element of high-performance work systems. HRM has a significant role in providing people who are well suited and well prepared for their jobs. Human resource professionals help the organization recruit and select people with the needed qualifications. Training, development, and career management ensure that these people are able to perform their current and future jobs and fit with the culture of the organization.

Reward systems contribute to high performance by encouraging people to

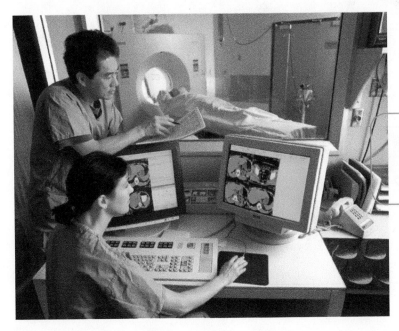

In a high-performance work system, all the elements—people, technology, and organizational structure—work together for success.

strive for objectives that support the organization's overall goals. Reward systems include the performance measures by which employees are assessed, the methods of measuring performance, and the incentive pay and other rewards linked to success. Human resource management plays an important role in developing and administering reward systems, as we saw in Chapter 8.

The final element of high-performance work systems is the organization's *information systems*. Managers make decisions about the types of information to gather and the sources of information. They also must decide who in the organization should have access to the information and how they will make the information available. Modern information systems, including the Internet, have enabled organizations to share information widely. HR departments take advantage of this technology to give employees access to information about benefits, training opportunities, job openings, and more, as we will describe later in this chapter.

OUTCOMES OF A HIGH-PERFORMANCE WORK SYSTEM

Consider the practices of steel minimills (which produce steel to make a limited quantity of products for the construction industry). Some minimills have strategies based on keeping their costs below competitors' costs; low costs let them operate at a profit while winning customers with low prices. Other steel minimills focus on "differentiation," meaning they set themselves apart in some way other than low price—for example, by offering higher quality or unusual product lines. Research has found that the minimills with cost-related goals tend to have highly centralized structures, so managers can focus on controlling through a tight line of command. These organizations have low employee participation in decisions, relatively low wages and benefits, and pay highly contingent on performance.[5] At minimills that focus on differentiation, structures are more complex and decentralized, so authority is more spread out. These minimills encourage employee participation and have higher wages and more generous benefits. They are high-performance work systems. In general, these differentiator mills enjoy higher productivity, lower scrap rates, and lower employee turnover than the mills that focus on low costs.

Outcomes of a high-performance work system thus include higher productivity and efficiency. These outcomes contribute to higher profits. A high-performance work system may have other outcomes, including high product quality, great customer satisfaction, and low employee turnover. Some of these outcomes meet intermediate goals that lead to higher profits (see Figure 11.2). For example, high quality contributes to customer satisfaction, and customer

FIGURE 11.2

Outcomes of a High-Performance Work System

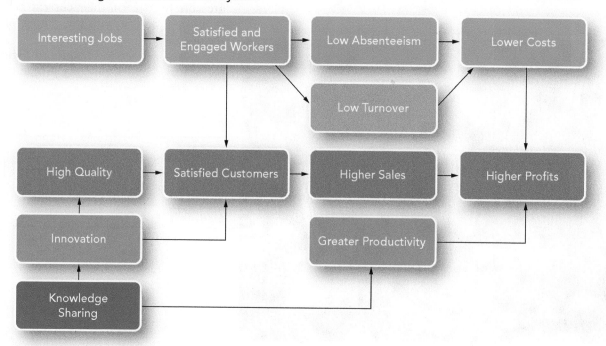

satisfaction contributes to growth of the business. Likewise, improving productivity lets the organization do more with less, which satisfies price-conscious customers and may help the organization win over customers from its competitors. Other ways to lower cost and improve quality are to reduce absenteeism and turnover, providing the organization with a steady supply of experienced workers. In the previous example of minimills, some employers keep turnover and scrap rates low. Meeting those goals helps the minimills improve productivity, which helps them earn more profits.

In a high-performance work system, the outcomes of each employee and work group contribute to the system's overall high performance. The organization's individuals and groups work efficiently, provide high-quality goods and services, and so on, and in this way, they contribute to meeting the organization's goals. When the organization adds or changes goals, people are flexible and make changes as needed to meet the new goals.

Conditions that Contribute to High Performance

Certain conditions underlie the formation of a high-performance work system:[6]

- Teams perform work.
- Employees participate in selection.
- Employees receive formal performance feedback and are actively involved in the performance improvement process.
- Ongoing training is emphasized and rewarded.
- Employees' rewards and compensation relate to the company's financial performance.

- Equipment and work processes are structured and technology is used to encourage maximum flexibility and interaction among employees.
- Employees participate in planning changes in equipment, layout, and work methods.
- Work design allows employees to use a variety of skills.
- Employees understand how their jobs contribute to the finished product or service.
- Ethical behaviour is encouraged.

Practices involving rewards, employee empowerment, and jobs with variety, contribute to high performance by giving employees skills, incentives, knowledge, autonomy—as well as satisfaction and engagement—conditions associated with high performance. Ethical behaviour is a necessary condition of high performance because it contributes to good long-term relationships with employees, customers, and the public.

TEAMWORK AND EMPOWERMENT

Today's organizations empower employees. **Employee empowerment** means giving employees responsibility and authority to make decisions regarding all aspects of product development or customer service.[7] They expect employees to make more decisions about how they perform their jobs. One of the most popular ways to empower employees is to design work so that it is performed by teams. On a work team, employees bring together various skills and experiences to produce goods or provide services. The organization may charge the team with making decisions traditionally made by managers, such as hiring team members and planning work schedules. Teamwork and empowerment contribute to high performance when they improve employee

> **employee empowerment**
> Giving employees responsibility and authority to make decisions regarding all aspects of product development or customer service.

It's important for companies to capture and share the knowledge of workers who have had years to learn their specialty.

satisfaction and engagement and give the organization fuller use of employees' ideas and expertise.

At Cognos Inc., an Ottawa-based software company, managers worldwide are required to attend workshops on how to recognize individual achievements and keep employees challenged and motivated to stay. According to Beverly Kaye, a California-based author and consultant whose theories form the basis of the Cognos program, the most consistent reason that people left their previous job was "my boss was a jerk." When asked, "What do you mean by jerk?" most of the responses came down to "lack of appreciation, or their manager's desire to always be in control."[8]

For empowerment to succeed, managers must serve in linking and coordinating roles[9] and providing the team with the resources it needs to carry out its work. The manager should help the team and its members interact with employees from other departments or teams and should make sure communication flows in both directions—the manager keeps the team updated on important issues and ensures that the team shares information and resources with others who need them. Along with these efforts at coordination, the team's manager should help team members resolve problems as needed. To provide such help, the manager may have to refer team members to resources outside the team or organization.

> **learning organization**
> An organization that supports lifelong learning by enabling all employees to acquire and share knowledge.

> **continuous learning**
> Each employee's and each group's ongoing efforts to gather information and apply the information to their decisions in a learning organization.

KNOWLEDGE SHARING

For more than a decade, managers have been interested in creating a **learning organization**, that is, an organization in which the culture values and supports lifelong learning by enabling all employees to continually acquire and share knowledge. The people in a learning organization have resources for training and development, and they are encouraged to share their knowledge with colleagues. Managers take an active role in identifying training needs and encouraging the sharing of ideas.[10] An organization's information systems, discussed later in this chapter, have an important role in making this learning activity possible. Information systems capture knowledge and make it available even after individual employees who provided the knowledge have left the organization. Ultimately, people are the essential ingredients in a learning organization. They

must be committed to learning and willing to share what they have learned. A learning organization has several key features:[11]

- It engages in **continuous learning**, each employee's and each group's ongoing efforts to gather information and apply the information to their decisions. In many organizations, the process of continuous learning is aimed at improving quality. To engage in continuous learning, employees must understand the entire work system they participate in, the relationships among jobs, their work units, and the organization as a whole. Employees who continuously learn about their work system are adding to their ability to improve performance.

- Knowledge is *shared*. Therefore, to create a learning organization, one challenge is to shift the focus of training away from merely teaching skills and toward a broader focus on generating and sharing knowledge.[12] In this view, training is an investment in the organization's human resources; it increases employees' value to the organization. Also, training content should be related to the organization's goals. Human resource departments can support the creation of a learning organization by planning training programs that meet these criteria, and they can help to create both face-to-face and electronic systems for employee collaboration to create, capture, and share knowledge.

- *Critical, systemic thinking is widespread.* This occurs when organizations encourage employees to see relationships among ideas and to test assumptions and observe the results of their actions. Reward systems can be set up to encourage employees and teams to think in new ways.

- The organization has a *learning culture*—a culture in which learning is rewarded, promoted, and supported by managers and organizational objectives. This culture may be reflected in performance management systems and pay structures that reward employees for gathering and sharing more knowledge. A learning culture creates the conditions in which managers encourage *flexibility* and *experimentation*. The organization should encourage employees to take risks and innovate, which means it cannot be quick to punish ideas that do not work out as intended.

- *Employees are valued.* The organization recognizes that employees are the source of its knowledge. It therefore focuses on ensuring the development and well-being of each employee.

The experience at Lopez Foods shows that the qualities of a learning organization aren't limited just to high-tech industries. Lopez Foods, which makes beef and sausage patties, involved employees in making production more efficient. Working with consultants, Lopez managers and engineers diagrammed production processes on huge sheets of brown paper hung on the walls. They made sticky notes available so that any worker passing by could post notes correcting the information or making suggestions based on their day-to-day experience on the front lines. Not only did the practice improve the quality of information, but it also engaged workers in helping their company become more efficient. The company also improved the communication of performance feedback, now posting hourly performance indicators, and it pays production workers modest but regular bonuses for exceeding productivity targets.[13]

EMPLOYEE SATISFACTION

2,4

A condition underpinning any high-performance organization is that employees experience *job satisfaction*—they experience their jobs as fulfilling or allows them to fulfill one's important job values.[14] See the "HR Best Practices" box. Several aspects of job satisfaction are:

- Job satisfaction is related to a person's values, defined as "what a person consciously or unconsciously desires to obtain."
- Different employees have different views of which values are important, so the same circumstances can produce different levels of job satisfaction.
- Job satisfaction is based on perception, not always on an objective and complete measurement of the situation. Each person compares the job situation to his or her values, and people are likely to differ in what they perceive.

Research supports the idea that employees' job satisfaction and job performance are related.[15] Higher performance at the individual level should contribute to higher performance for the organization as a whole. In sum, values, perceptions, and ideas of what is important are the three components of job satisfaction. People will be satisfied with their jobs as long

HR BEST PRACTICES

Creating a Positive Work Environment

The relatively new fields of positive psychology and positive organizational behaviour have contributed to the idea that individuals and organizations not only can work on problems but also can take steps that favour the creation of a happy outlook and upbeat workplace. Critics suspect that these kinds of approaches merely sugarcoat miserable situations, but used appropriately, some techniques can make work a more satisfying place. Here are some approaches that HR professionals might want to consider:

- Bring in a "happiness coach." Trainers with expertise in positive psychology can teach methods such as meditation and the practice and expression of gratitude.
- When confronted with news, dilemmas, and changes, start

with the assumption that the situation is not necessarily bad (or good). Define setbacks as learning experiences. Keeping an open mind can help you and your team identify more alternatives and opportunities.
- Look for employee behaviours to praise, and coach managers to do the same. Use performance feedback to identify strengths employees can build on, not just weaknesses to correct.
- Use selection and development tools that match employees' talents to positions and career paths in the organization.
- Structure work so employees can see why it matters and so they have enough control over their time to engage in activities they care about. Define how the organization contributes to

society, and express that mission to employees.
- Ask for ideas from employees, and listen to their ideas.
- Model positive behaviour by demonstrating compassion, forgiveness, and gratitude.

SOURCES: Sue Shellenbarger, "Thinking Happy Thoughts at Work," *Wall Street Journal*, January 27, 2010, http// online.wsj.com; Chet Taranowski, "Advocating for a Positive Workplace," *Journal of Employee Assistance*, January 2009, Business & Company Resource Center, http://galenet.galegroup.com; Ann Pace, "Unleashing Positivity in the Workplace," *T+D*, January 2010, Business & Company Resource Center, http://galenet.galegroup.com; and Stacey Burling, "Psychologists Converge on Philadelphia to Study Happiness," *Philadelphia Inquirer*, June 21, 2009, Business & Company Resource Center, http://galenet.galegroup.com.

FIGURE 11.3

Increasing Job
Satisfaction

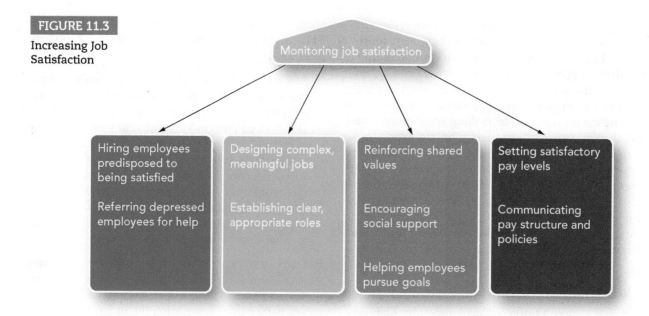

Monitoring job satisfaction

Hiring employees
predisposed to
being satisfied

Referring depressed
employees for help

Designing complex,
meaningful jobs

Establishing clear,
appropriate roles

Reinforcing shared
values

Encouraging
social support

Helping employees
pursue goals

Setting satisfactory
pay levels

Communicating
pay structure and
policies

as they perceive that their jobs meet their important values. As shown in Figure 11.3 organizations can contribute to job satisfaction in several ways.

EMPLOYEE ENGAGEMENT

As discussed in Chapter 1, some organizations are moving beyond a focus on employee job satisfaction and are striving to cultivate *employee engagement*—the extent that employees are satisfied, committed to, and prepared to support what is important to the organization. Engagement has both an emotional and cognitive component and is evidenced through employee behaviours. For example, employees are engaged when they:[16]

- Speak positively about the organization to co-workers, potential employees, and customers,
- Have an intense desire to be a member of the organization, and
- Exert extra effort and are dedicated to doing the very best job possible to contribute to the organization's business success.

Co-worker relationships can contribute to satisfaction and engagement, and organizations therefore try to provide opportunities to build positive relationships. Would a strong sense of teamwork and friendship help you enjoy your work more? Enhance your performance?

"An organization's capacity to manage employee engagement is closed related to its ability to achieve superior results." That's the conclusion of a compilation of data from Hewitt Associates that makes a clear connection between engaged employees and business results. An analysis of the Hewitt Associates Employee Engagement and Best Employer database of 1,500 companies over a four year period showed that companies with high engagement levels had markedly higher total shareholder returns (TSR) than those with low employee engagement results. Specifically, companies with 60–100 percent employee engagement scores achieved an average TSR of 24.2 percent. With engagement scores of 49–60 percent, TSR dropped off to 9.1 percent. Companies with engagement scores below 25 percent suffered negative TSR.[17]

The global HR consulting firm, Towers Perrin, surveyed nearly 90,000 workers from 18 countries and found that just 21 percent of employees reported "being engaged in their work and willing to go the extra mile to help their companies succeed."[18] This study also found that engaged employees are more likely to see a direct connection between what they do and company results. More than 80 percent of engaged employees believe they can and do contribute to the quality of products and services and to customer satisfaction, whereas only half as many of the disengaged share that view. In addition, engagement was found to have a direct impact on retaining employees. "Half of the engaged employees had no plans to leave their companies, compared with just 15 percent of the disengaged. Less than 5 percent of the engaged employees said they were actively looking for other jobs, compared with more than one-quarter of the disengaged employees."[19]

Organizations with high engagement strive to foster employees' *passion* for their work. Passionate people are fully engaged with something so that it becomes part of their sense of who they are. Feeling this way about one's work has been called *occupational intimacy*.[20] People experience occupational intimacy when they love their work, when they and their co-workers care about one another, and when they find their work meaningful. Human resource managers have a significant role in creating these conditions. For example, they can select people who care about their work and customers, provide methods for sharing knowledge, design work to make jobs interesting, and establish policies and programs that show concern for employees' needs. Such efforts may become more and more important as the competitive job market, baby boomer retirements,

and the multi-generational workforce all put more importance on engagement in the workplace.[21]

How Are Employee Satisfaction and Engagement Assessed?

The usual way to assess satisfaction and engagement is with some kind of survey. A systematic, ongoing program of employee surveys should be part of the organization's human resource strategy. This allows the organization to monitor trends. For example, if satisfaction with promotion opportunities has been falling over several years, the trend may signal a need for better career management (a topic of Chapter 6). An organizational change, such as a merger, also might have important consequences for employee satisfaction and engagement. In addition, ongoing surveys give the organization a way to measure whether policies adopted to enhance employee satisfaction and engagement are working. Organizations can also compare results from different departments to identify groups with successful practices that may apply elsewhere in the organization. Another benefit is that some scales provide data that organizations can use to compare themselves to others in the same industry. This information will be valuable for creating and reviewing human resource policies that enable organizations to attract and retain employees in a competitive job market. See Figure 11.4.

To obtain a survey instrument, an excellent place to begin is with one of the many established scales.

> **L02** Describe how organizations assess employee satisfaction and engagement.

Instructions: Think of your present work. What is it like most of time? In the blank beside each word given below, write

____Y____ for "Yes" if it describes your work

____N____ for "No" if it does NOT describe your work

____?____ if you cannot decide

Work Itself	**Pay**	**Promotion Opportunities**
_____ Routine	_____ Less than I deserve	_____ Dead-end job
_____ Satisfying	_____ Highly paid	_____ Unfair policies
_____ Good	_____ Insecure	_____ Based on ability
Supervision	**Co-workers**	
_____ Impolite	_____ Intelligent	
_____ Praises good work	_____ Responsible	
_____ Doesn't supervise enough	_____ Boring	

FIGURE 11.4

Example of a Job Descriptive Index (JDI)

SOURCE: W. K. Balzar, D. C. Smith, D. E. Kravitz, S. E. Lovell, K. B. Paul, B. A. Reilly, and C. E. Reilly, *User's Manual for the Job Descriptive Index (JDI)* (Bowling Green, OH: Bowling Green State University, 1990).

DID YOU KNOW?

Employee Engagement in Selected Countries

Employee engagement varies significantly among employees around the world. The following graph shows employee engagement ratings in Canada as well as several other countries by way of comparison. Of the 25 countries reported upon, Mexico had the highest levels of employee engagement, while Japan had the lowest.

SOURCE: "Are You Missing Something? Employee Engagement Values Around the World," Hay Group, May 3, 2010. Reprinted with the permission of Hay Group.

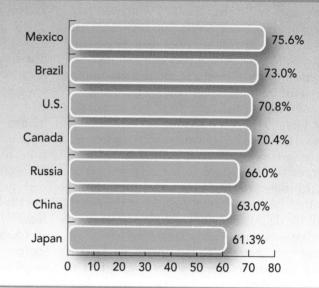

Country	Engagement
Mexico	75.6%
Brazil	73.0%
U.S.	70.8%
Canada	70.4%
Russia	66.0%
China	63.0%
Japan	61.3%

For example, the validity and reliability of many satisfaction scales have been tested, so it is possible to compare the instruments. The main reason for an organization to create its own scale would be that it wants to measure aspects of work specific to the organization (such as satisfaction with a specific training initiative).

A widely used measure of job satisfaction is the Job Descriptive Index (JDI). The JDI emphasizes specific aspects of satisfaction—pay, the work itself, supervision, co-workers and promotions. Figure 11.4 shows several items from the JDI scale. Other scales measure general satisfaction using broad questions such as "All in all, how satisfied are you with your job?"[22] Some scales avoid language altogether, relying on pictures. The faces scale in Figure 11.5 is an example of this type of measure. Other scales exist for measuring more specific aspects of satisfaction.

For example, the Pay Satisfaction Questionnaire (PSQ) measures satisfaction with specific aspects of pay, such as pay levels, structure, and raises.[23]

However, critics describe the traditional employee satisfaction feedback process as: "The individual has his or her moment of self-expression, a fleeting participation in the great collective search for truth, then silence, nada, frustration as the status quo prevails."[24] With this in mind, the Gallup Organization set about to create a better employee feedback process that linked the elements of employee engagement to improved business outcomes, for example, sales growth, productivity, customer loyalty, and the generation of value.[25] The HR How-To box identifies Gallup's questions for measuring employee engagement.

Conducting surveys is not something an organization should take lightly. Especially when the program is new, they often raise employees' expectations. The

FIGURE 11.5	**Job Satisfaction from the Faces Scale**
Job Satisfaction from the Faces Scale	Consider all aspects of your job. Circle the face that best describes your feelings about your job in general.

SOURCE: R. B. Dunham and J. B. Herman and published in the *Journal of Applied Psychology* (1975), pp. 629–31. © 1975 by the American Psychological Association. Adapted with permission.

HR HOW-TO

Measuring Employee Engagement

To identify the elements of worker engagement, Gallup conducted hundreds of focus groups and many thousands of worker interviews in all kinds of organizations, and at all levels, in most industries, and in many countries. The result was 12 key employee expectations that, when satisfied, form the foundation of strong feelings of engagement.

These are Gallup's 12 questions:

- Do you know what is expected of you at work?
- Do you have the materials and equipment you need to do your work right?
- At work, do you have the opportunity to do what you do best every day?
- In the last seven days, have you received recognition or praise for doing good work?

- Does your supervisor, or someone at work, seem to care about you as a person?
- Is there someone at work who encourages your development?
- At work, do your opinions seem to count?
- Does the mission/purpose of your company make you feel your job is important?
- Are your associates (fellow employees) committed to doing quality work?
- Do you have a best friend at work?
- In the last six months, has someone at work talked to you about your progress?
- In the last year, have you had opportunities at work to learn and grow?

The 12 engagement questions are answered by employees on a scale of one to five, according to their weak or strong agreement. The process also involves a feedback methodology for improving engagement by creating a factual base for discussion and debate of the causes behind the numbers. In this way, it yields actionable input from staff and managers for changes in behaviour, attitudes, policies, and processes. Follow-up surveys are conducted to track long-term progress—or backsliding—on the 12 questions.

SOURCE: John Thackray "Feedback for Real" March 15, 2001, http://gmj.gallup.com/content/default. asp?ci=811, retrieved November 28, 2004.

---

organization should be ready to act on the results. At the Canadian division of the Swiss pharmaceutical company, Hoffman-La Roche Ltd., comments from employee surveys are quickly acted on. For example, on the basis of the surveys, a holiday-hours program was set up, giving full-time employees an extra day off on long weekends.[26]

In spite of surveys and other efforts to retain employees, some employees inevitably will leave the organization. This presents another opportunity to gather information for retaining employees: the exit interview—a meeting of the departing employee with the employee's supervisor and/or a human resource specialist to discuss the employee's reasons for leaving. A well-conducted exit interview can uncover reasons why employees leave and perhaps set the stage for some of them to return. HR professionals can help make exit interviews more successful by arranging for the employee to talk to someone from the HR department (rather than the departing

exit interview
A meeting of a departing employee with the employee's supervisor and/or human resource specialist to discuss the employee's reasons for leaving.

stay interview
A meeting with an employee to explore his or her thoughts and feelings about the job and to uncover issues in the effort to prevent that employee from becoming disgruntled.

employee's supervisor) in a neutral location or over the phone.[27] Questions should start out open-ended and general, to give the employee a chance to name the source of the dissatisfaction or explain why leaving is attractive.

A recruiter armed with information about what caused a specific person to leave may be able to negotiate a return when the situation changes. And when several exiting employees give similar reasons for leaving, management should consider whether this indicates a need for change. Ultimately in the war for talent, the best way to manage retention is to engage in a battle for every valued employee, even when it looks as if the battle has been lost. A recent twist on the exit interview is a stay interview—a meeting with an employee to explore his or her thoughts and feelings about the job and to uncover issues in the effort to prevent that employee from becoming disgruntled.[28]

In the long run, a high-performance organization fosters the kind of work culture that encourages high levels of motivation, satisfaction, commitment, and engagement. The newer generations in the workforce are much more likely to speak up, saying: "I'm not a happy camper and you need to do more to keep me here, or I am going to pick up my skill set and go somewhere else."[29]

HRM's Contribution to High Performance

1,2

Management of human resources plays a critical role in determining companies' success in meeting the challenges of a rapidly changing, highly competitive environment.[30] Total rewards, staffing, training and development, performance management, and other HRM practices are investments that directly affect employees' motivation and ability to provide products and services that are valued by customers. Table 11.1 lists examples of HRM practices that contribute to high performance.

> **L03** Explain how human resource management can contribute to high performance.

Research suggests that it is more effective to improve HRM practices as a whole than to focus on one or two isolated practices, such as the organization's pay structure or selection system.[31] Also, to have the intended influence on performance, the HRM practices must fit well with one another and the organization as a whole.[32]

JOB DESIGN

3

For the organization to benefit from teamwork and employee empowerment, jobs must be designed appropriately. Often, a high-performance work system places employees in work teams where employees collaborate to make decisions and solve problems. Individual employees also may be empowered to serve on teams that design jobs and work processes.

RECRUITMENT AND SELECTION

At a high-performance organization, recruitment and selection aim at obtaining the kinds of employees who can thrive in this type of setting. These employees are enthusiastic about and able to contribute to teamwork, empowerment, and knowledge sharing. Qualities such as creativity and ability to cooperate as part of a team may play a large role in selection decisions. High-performance organizations need selection methods that identify more than technical skills like ability to perform accounting and engineering tasks. Employers may use group interviews, open-ended questions, and psychological tests to find employees who innovate, share ideas, and take initiative. For example, at Imaginet, the Winnipeg-based software application firm discussed at the beginning of the chapter, employees actively contribute to the hiring process to attract like-minded top talent.[33]

TRAINING AND DEVELOPMENT

4,6

When organizations base hiring decisions on qualities like decision making and teamwork skills, training may be required to help employees learn the specific skills they need to perform the duties of their job. Extensive training and development also are part of a learning organization, described earlier in this chapter. And when organizations delegate many decisions to work teams, the members of those teams likely will benefit from participating in team development activities that prepare them for their roles as team members.

TABLE 11.1   HRM Practices that Can Help Organizations Achieve High Performance

• HRM practices match organization's goals.	• Performance management system measures customer satisfaction and quality.
• Individuals and groups share knowledge.	• Organization monitors employees' satisfaction and engagement.
• Work is performed by teams.	• Discipline system is progressive.
• Organization encourages continuous learning.	• Pay systems reward skills and accomplishments.
• Work design permits flexibility in where and when tasks are performed.	• Skills and values of a diverse workforce are valued and used.
• Selection system is job-related and legal.	• Technology reduces time and costs of tasks while preserving quality.

Business Development Bank of Canada (BDC) demonstrates its commitment to training and development by annually investing approximately 5 percent of payroll in learning. The federal crown corporation, offers financing, business loans, consulting, and venture capital to businesses and is participating in a project sponsored by the federal government to substantiate the return on investment of training. "We know there's a declining investment in training overall in Canada. And we know that has a big impact on growth productivity, so it's sort of a win-win type of project to learn ourselves what a return-on-investment (ROI) project is all about," said Jacinthe Higgs, director of learning strategies at BDC.[34]

PERFORMANCE MANAGEMENT

In a high-performance organization, employees know the organization's goals and what they must do to help achieve those goals. HR departments can contribute to this ideal through the design of the organization's performance management system. As we discussed in Chapter 7, performance management should be related to the organization's goals.

To set up a performance management system that supports the organization's goals, managers need to understand the process of employee performance. As is shown in Figure 11.6, individual employees bring a set of skills and abilities to the job, and by applying a set of behaviours, they use those skills to achieve certain results. But success is more than the product of individual efforts. The organization's goals should influence each step of the process. The organization's culture and other factors influence the employees' abilities, behaviours, and results. It mustn't be forgotten that sometimes uncontrollable forces such as the current economic conditions enter the picture—for example, a salesperson can probably sell more during an economic expansion than during an economic slowdown.

This model suggests some guidelines for performance management. First, every aspect of performance management should be related to the organization's goals. Business goals should influence the kinds of employees selected and their training, the requirements of each job, and the measures used for evaluating results. Generally, this means the organization identifies what each department needs to do to achieve the desired results, then defines how individual employees should contribute to their department's goals. More specifically, the following guidelines describe how to make the performance management system support organizational goals:[35]

- *Define and measure performance in precise terms*—Focus on outcomes that can be defined in terms of how frequently certain behaviours occur. Include criteria that describe ways employees can add value to a product or service (such as through quantity, quality, or timeliness). Include behaviours that go beyond the minimum required to perform a job (such as helping co-workers).
- *Link performance measures to meeting customer needs*—"Customers" may be the organization's external customers, or they may be internal customers (employees receiving services from a co-worker). Service goals for internal customers should be related to satisfying external customers.
- *Measure and correct for the effect of situational constraints*—Monitor economic conditions, the organization's culture, and other influences on performance. Measures of employees' performance should take these influences into account.

FIGURE 11.6

Employee Performance as a Process

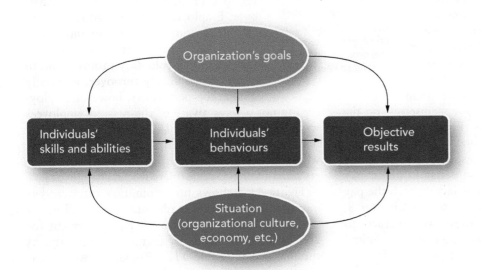

To develop future leaders, new IBM managers participate in IBM's Basic Blue program, an intensive nine-month training program. IBM is considered one of the best companies in the development of future leaders.

This approach gives employees the information they need to behave in ways that contribute to high performance. In addition, organizations should help employees identify and obtain the abilities they need to meet their performance goals.

COMPENSATION AND REWARDS

Organizations can reinforce the impact of this kind of performance management by linking employee rewards in part to performance measures. Chapter 8 described a number of methods for doing this, including merit pay, gainsharing, and profit sharing. Compensation systems also can help to create the conditions that contribute to high performance, including teamwork, involvement, and employee satisfaction and engagement. For example, compensation can be linked to achievement of team objectives.

Organizations can increase employee empowerment, satisfaction, and engagement by including employees in decisions about compensation and by communicating the basis for decisions about pay. When the organization designs a pay structure, it can set up a task force that includes employees with direct experience in various types of jobs. Some organizations share financial information with their employees and invite them to recommend pay increases for themselves, on the basis of their contributions. Employees may also participate in setting individual or group goals for which they can receive bonuses. Research has found that employee participation in decisions about pay policies is linked to greater satisfaction with the pay and the job.[36] And as we discussed in Chapter 8, when organizations explain their pay structures to employees, the communication can enhance employees' satisfaction and belief that the system is fair.

MANAGING VOLUNTARY AND INVOLUNTARY TURNOVER

Organizations must try to ensure that good performers want to stay with the organization and that employees whose performance is chronically low are encouraged—or forced—to leave. Both of these challenges involve *employee turnover*, that is, employees leaving the organization. When the organization initiates the turnover (often with employees who would prefer to stay), the result is **involuntary turnover**. Examples include terminating an employee for under-performance or laying off employees during a downturn. Most organizations use the word *termination* to refer only to a discharge related to a discipline problem, but some organizations call any involuntary turnover a termination. When the employees initiate the turnover (often when the organization would prefer to keep them), it is **voluntary turnover**. Employees may leave to retire or to take a job with a different organization.

In general, organizations try to avoid the need for involuntary turnover and to minimize voluntary turnover, especially among top performers, however employers are not always aware of the reasons employees would change jobs. Table 11.2 identifies the five key reasons top performers in Canadian organizations would change jobs and the five key reasons employers *think* their top performers would change jobs.

Figure 11.7 shows how voluntary turnover has increased recently in Canada, but is still well below the rate for some past years (e.g., 9.7 percent for 2007–08). Both kinds of turnover are costly, as summarized in Table 11.3. Replacing workers is

involuntary turnover
Turnover initiated by an employer (often with employees who would prefer to stay).

voluntary turnover
Turnover initiated by employees (often when the organization would prefer to keep them).

TABLE 11.2   Employers Are Not Always Aware of the Reasons Top Performers Would Change Jobs

	WHY WOULD TOP PERFORMERS LEAVE?	
RANK	**EMPLOYERS**	**EMPLOYEES**
1	Career development opportunities	Work-related stress
2	Promotion opportunities	Promotion opportunities
3	Relationship with supervisor	Base pay
4	Base pay	Trust/confidence in management
5	Work-related stress	Job security

Note: Rank represents the frequency the item was selected as one of the most important reasons (from a list of 23 items) top performers would leave an organization; Top performers are those whose performance was rated "far exceeds expectations" (i.e., in the top 10 percent) by their supervisors in their most recent performance review.

SOURCE: "Leading Through Uncertain Times, The 2011/2012 Talent Management and Rewards Study: North America," Towers Watson, p. 8, www.towerswatson.com. Reprinted with the permission of Towers Watson.

expensive, and new employees need time to learn their jobs. Although estimates of the cost of turnover fluctuate widely, Hay Group vice-president, David Sissons, cites the cost of turnover as 1.5 times the annual salary for a manager or professional, 0.5 times the annual salary for an hourly worker, and as much as 2.0 times annual salary for a top sales or senior-level person.[37] In addition, people today are more likely to take legal action against a former employer if they feel they were unfairly dismissed. The prospect of workplace violence also raises the risk associated with discharging employees. Effective human resource management can help the organization minimize both kinds of turnover, as well as carry it out effectively when necessary. Despite

a company's best efforts at selection, training, and compensation, some employees will fail to meet expectations, be uncoachable, or will violate company policies. When this happens, organizations need to apply a discipline program that might ultimately lead to discharging the individual.

For a number of reasons, discharging employees can be a very difficult but potentially important way to maintain a high-performance and engaging work culture. The decision also has legal aspects that can affect the organization. Historically, if the organization and employee do not have a specific employment contract, the employer or employee may end the employment relationship at any time. This is the *employment-at-will doctrine*. This doctrine has

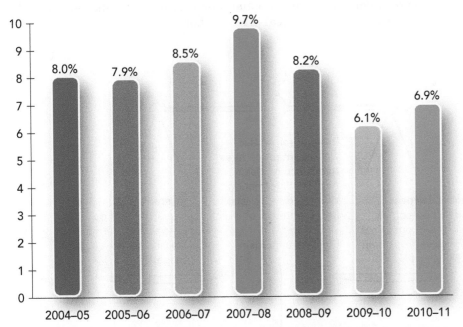

FIGURE 11.7

Voluntary Turnover Rates (average percentage of employees)

NOTE: Voluntary turnover applies to regular employees only, and does not include early retirements or severances.

SOURCE: Nicole Stewart, "Compensation Planning Outlook 2012," *The Conference Board of Canada*, October 2011, p. 15.

TABLE 11.3   Costs Associated with Turnover

INVOLUNTARY TURNOVER	VOLUNTARY TURNOVER
Recruiting, selecting, and training replacements	Recruiting, selecting, and training replacements
Lost productivity	Lost productivity
Lawsuits	Loss of talented employees
Workplace violence	

eroded significantly, however. Employees who have been terminated sometimes sue their employers for wrongful dismissal, and in such cases the courts may award employees significant financial settlements. Publicity associated with the proceedings may also be embarrassing or harmful to the employer's reputation. Along with the financial risks of dismissing an employee, there are issues of personal safety. Distressing as it is that some former employees go to the courts, far worse are the employees who react to a termination decision with violence. Although any number of organizational actions or decisions may incite violence among employees, the "nothing else to lose" aspect of an employee's dismissal makes the situation dangerous, especially when the nature of the work adds other risk factors.[38]

Employment/labour standards laws in each of the federal, provincial, and territorial jurisdictions set out the minimum requirements employers must follow when terminating or laying off employees. For example, no notice or compensation is legally needed if the employee quit or retired, the employee had been employed for less than the required minimum (usually three months), the employee was employed

on an "on-call" basis, or the employee was terminated for *just cause*. Examples of "just cause" for dismissal that are considered serious violations of the employment relationship are dishonesty; willful disobedience to a supervisor; and failure to comply with known policies or procedures or meet performance requirements.[39]

Because of the critical financial and personal risks associated with employee dismissal, it is easy to see why organizations must develop a standardized, systematic approach to discipline and discharge. These decisions should not be left solely to the discretion of individual managers or supervisors. The precedent-setting Supreme Court case of *Wallace v. United Grain Growers* (1997) sent a clear message that employers must act fairly and respectfully when handling an employee termination. The *Wallace* case gave judges a legal precedent to award employees additional notice or damages if the employer treats an employee callously or unfairly during termination. In summary, policies that can lead to employee separation should be based on not only the legal requirements but also on principles of justice to ensure the system is seen as fair. Figure 11.8 summarizes these

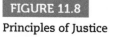

FIGURE 11.8

Principles of Justice

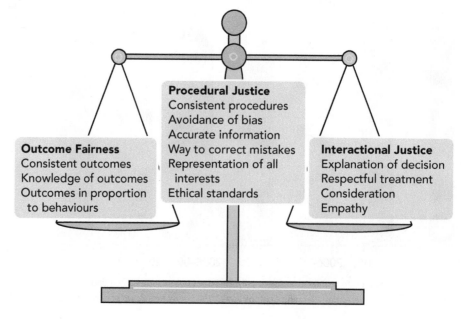

principles of justice. For example, in support of these principles, many organizations provide **outplacement counselling,** which tries to help dismissed employees manage the transition from one job to another. Some organizations have their own staff for conducting outplacement counselling. Other organizations have contracts with outside providers to help with individual cases. Either way, the goals for outplacement programs are to help the former employee address the psychological issues associated with losing a job—grief, depression, and fear in a respectful manner—while at the same time helping the person find a new job.

HANDLING EMPLOYEE DISCIPLINE APPROPRIATELY

In order to maintain a positive, motivating, and high-performance work environment for all employees, organizations look for methods of handling problem behaviour that are fair, legal, and effective.

The principles of justice suggest that the organization prepare for problems by establishing a formal discipline process in which the consequences become more serious if the employee repeats the offence. Such a system is called **progressive discipline.** A typical progressive discipline system identifies and communicates inappropriate behaviours and responds to a series of offences with the actions shown in Figure 11.9—spoken and then written warnings, temporary suspension, and finally, termination. This process fulfills the purpose of discipline by teaching employees what is expected of them and creating a situation in which employees must try to do what is expected. It seeks to prevent inappropriate behaviour (by publishing rules) and to correct, rather than merely punish, inappropriate behaviour.

Such procedures may seem exasperatingly slow, especially when the employee's misdeeds hurt the team's performance. In the end, however, if an employee must be discharged, careful use of the

outplacement counselling
A service in which professionals try to help dismissed employees manage the transition from one job to another.

progressive discipline
A formal discipline process in which the consequences become more serious if the employee repeats the offence.

procedure increases other employees' belief that the organization is fair and reduces the likelihood that the employee will take legal action (or at least that the employee will win in court). For situations in which inappropriate behaviour is dangerous, the organization may establish a stricter policy, even terminating an employee for the first offence. In that case, it is especially important to communicate the procedure—not only to ensure fairness, but also to prevent the dangerous inappropriate behaviour.

Creating a formal discipline process is a primary responsibility of the human resource department. The HR professional should consult with supervisors and managers to identify inappropriate behaviours and establish rules and consequences for violating the rules. The rules should cover disciplinary problems such as the following behaviours encountered in many organizations:

- Absenteeism
- Lateness
- Unsafe work practices
- Poor quantity or quality of work
- Harassment of co-workers or customers
- Theft or misuse of company property
- Cyberslacking (conducting personal business online during work hours)

For each infraction, the HR professional would identify a series of responses, such as those in Figure 11.9. In addition, the organization must communicate these rules and consequences to every employee. Ways of publishing rules include presenting them in an employee handbook, posting them on the company's intranet, and displaying them on a bulletin board. Supervisors should be familiar with the rules, so that they can discuss them with employees and apply them consistently.

Along with rules and a progression of consequences for violating the rules, a progressive discipline system should have requirements for documenting the

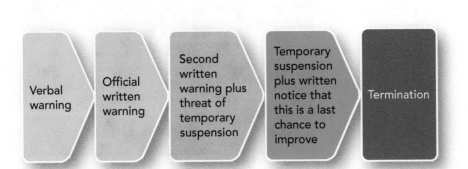

FIGURE 11.9

Progressive Discipline Responses

rules, offences, and responses. To ensure fairness, the discipline system should provide an opportunity to hear every point of view and to correct errors. Before discussing and filing records of misbehaviour, it is important for the supervisor to investigate the incident. The employee should be made aware of what he or she is said to have done wrong and should have an opportunity to present his or her version of events. A method of gathering objective performance data should be used to support the fairness and objectivity of the discipline system.

Besides developing these policies, HR professionals have a role in carrying out progressive discipline.[40] In meetings to communicate disciplinary actions, it is wise to have an HR representative there to support the employee's supervisor. When an employee is suspended or terminated, the organization should designate a person to escort the employee from the building to protect the organization's people and property.

Finally, the issue of off-the-job behaviour is also of concern to employers. Employers are frequently concerned if an employee's off-the-job behaviour, including social media activity, might affect the organization's business or reputation in some way.

Corporate Social Responsibility

Corporate social responsibility (CSR) is an evolving concept integrating social, environmental, and economic concerns into an organization's values, culture, decision making, strategy, and operations in a way that creates wealth and improves society.[41] CSR may also be referred to as *corporate responsibility*, *corporate citizenship*, *responsible business*, or *triple bottom line* (social, environmental, and economic performance) just to name a few frequently

used alternative terms. Canada is recognized as a leader in social responsibility and "CSR remains a concept that is openly embraced by a strong majority of Canadians."[42] For example, research firm GlobeScan found that 92 percent of Canadians said that "the more socially and environmentally responsible a company is, the more likely they are to purchase its products or services." Additionally, "91 percent of Canadians surveyed prefer to work for a company that is socially and environmentally responsible." The more socially and environmentally responsible a company is, the more attractive it becomes as an employer.[43]

Demonstrating corporate social responsibility such as sustainability, promoting volunteerism, providing meaningful work, and having high ethical standards are important factors to retain and engage employees. These factors may be particularly important among young employees.

SUSTAINABILITY—GOING GREEN

There is a growing trend among young, intelligent employees leaving lucrative private sector jobs to integrate their personal values with their professional goals. Monica Da Ponte, manager of marketing alliances for World Wildlife Fund (WWF)—Canada, spent seven years with a leading consumer packaged-goods company after finishing her undergraduate degree. "After some travelling and a better understanding of what was happening globally, I realized

Vancity, Canada's largest Credit Union, built its head office on Vancouver's SkyTrain line to encourage employees to commute to work.

I was doing all this great work for something I did not believe in. That's when I started volunteering at WWF—Canada and pursuing my MBA with a focus on sustainability and nonprofit management," says Da Ponte. Now Da Ponte has struck a balance where she gets to 'walk her talk' with respect to her values, while fully utilizing her business knowledge and skills.[44] According to Ron Dembo, CEO of Zerofootprint, a Toronto-based consultancy focusing on sustainable commerce: "Two years ago, if you went to a company's corporate responsibility person, you would have found that environmental issues did not rank high." The cultural change has been so sudden that a lot of corporations haven't caught up to the fact that this issue can have an impact on employee morale, loyalty, and engagement, he said.[45] For example, a recent poll on green employment by MonsterTRAK.com, a job website for students and entry-level hires, found that "92 percent would be more inclined to work for an environmentally friendly company and 80 percent of young professionals are interested in securing a job that has a positive impact on the environment."[46]

In 2007, Vancity became the first carbon neutral financial institution in North America. Vancity met this goal two years ahead of schedule with the help of experts including the University of British Columbia, Ecotrust Canada, and the David Suzuki Foundation.[47] Vancity has been committed to the environment since the early 1990s. The company makes it easier for employees to commute to work—back in the mid-1990s Vancity built its corporate head office on the SkyTrain line and encourages alternative transportation. For example, Vancity has a pool of Smart Cars and cruiser bikes at its Vancouver head office for employees to use to get to meetings and appointments (so they can leave their cars at home). Vancity appears to be attracting and retaining employees with similar values—63 percent of Vancity employees commute to work using alternative transportation compared to 33 percent in metro Vancouver overall.[48]

VOLUNTEERISM

Charitable initiatives—whether ongoing fundraisers or annual events—foster a sense of community within an organization, thereby increasing employees' satisfaction, engagement, and retention. For example, one of Deloitte's company values is "commitment to each other." Deloitte "believes that supporting the communities in which we do business makes good business sense and is an important part of our corporate responsibility." In one year, Deloitte staff raised $2 million for United Way across Canada, and it sponsors a nationwide Impact Day on which employees are encouraged to spend one paid workday together involved in local community projects. Beth Tyndall, senior manager of human resources at Deloitte, says, "By supporting people through their community activities, Deloitte generates employee engagement and commitment. Local charities benefit as well."[49]

A similar sense of volunteerism is fostered at TD Bank Financial Group, where employees are provided time off to work as volunteers for a charitable organization of their choice. If they put in more than 40 hours of volunteering, they can even apply for a $500 grant that goes directly to their charity. Says Teri Currie, a member of the senior executive team, "Pride in an organization is best described as what employees are doing when no one is looking: Are they engaged with customers? With fellow employees? With the larger community?"[50]

MEANINGFUL WORK

Another way organizations foster engagement is to match employees with on-the-job roles and projects that are connected to their values and create a sense of meaning and purpose for the employee. For example, when John Hancock joined Microsoft Canada in Toronto as a consultant, he went to work on an 18-month project with law enforcement agencies to develop a Child Exploitation Tracking System (CETS) to battle online sexual abuse. Five years later, Microsoft assigned him to be in charge of helping police forces around the world get CETS up and running. He says he's proud that the resources of Microsoft could be put toward developing such an important social tool. "Knowing that Microsoft Canada was the driving force behind the initiative is part of the attraction of coming into work every day."[51] Fostering pride and engagement through the opportunity to make a difference is also being promoted by governments across the country. For example the Nova Scotia government promotes pride in the public sector through the slogan "Make a Difference" as part of its strategy to attract, engage, and retain employees.[52]

ETHICS

In the long-run, a high-performance organization meets high ethical standards. Ethics, defined in Chapter 1, establishes fundamental principles for behaviour, such as honesty and fairness. Organizations and their employees must meet these standards if they are to maintain positive long-term relationships with their employees, customers, and community.

For example, Gerlinde Herrmann, president of The Herrmann Group, an HR management consulting firm in Ontario, cautions employers not to make empty promises about being an eco-friendly organization to attract candidates—a practice experts call *greenwashing*. Herrmann, who serves on SHRM's Corporate Social Responsibility and Sustainability Special Expertise Panel, notes that potential employees check organizations' backgrounds and talk with employees to find out whether organizations deliver.[53]

Ethical behaviour is most likely to result from values held by the organization's leaders combined with systems that promote ethical behaviour. A number of organizational systems can promote ethical behaviour.[54] These include a written code of ethics that the organization distributes to employees and requires them to use in decision making. Publishing a list of ethical standards is not enough, however. The organization should reinforce ethical behaviour. For example, performance measures should include ethical standards. The organization should provide channels employees can use to ask questions about ethical behaviour or to seek help if they are expected to do something they believe is wrong. Organizations also can provide training in ethical decision making, including training for supervisors in how to handle employees' concerns about ethical matters.

As these examples suggest, ethical behaviour is a human resource management concern. The systems that promote ethical behaviour include such HRM functions as training, performance management, and discipline policies. In today's business climate, ethical behaviour can also help a company attract workers—and customers—who share those high standards.

Taking a Key Role in Mergers and Acquisitions

Mergers and acquisitions dominate the business landscape. But the risks are high. It is estimated that 80 percent of mergers and acquisitions actually reduce shareholder value due to a combination of business and people issues. Reasons for these failures include:

- Combining strategic weaknesses rather than strategic strengths
- Top management conflict
- Failure to win employee support
- Loss of competitive position due to extended time to complete the deal.[55]

"In the past, HR issues might have been an afterthought in mergers and acquisitions (M&As), with the HR department only stepping in and playing a role once the deal was done. But there is growing recognition HR can and should contribute right from the start."[56] According to a survey conducted by Towers Perrin, a global consulting organization, and the Society for Human Resource Management Foundation, "there is a direct correlation between involvement by human resources and successful mergers and acquisitions."[57]

Josee Dykun, vice-president of HR at Montreal-headquartered Yellow Pages Group, says that she gets involved "right at the start of the process, when the company decides to purchase another business." At this early stage, often referred to as *due diligence*, her work involves "identifying potential risks and liabilities and any potential integration issues in terms of alignment of things like working conditions, benefits, and pensions."[58] Sandra Munteanu, TELUS's director of mergers and acquisitions describes the importance of HR work during this due diligence phase. "We have a very comprehensive list of questions. We assess market culture, management team skills, key employees and potential cultural gaps. We collect data on everything," said Munteanu.[59]

The change and upheaval that accompanies a merger or acquisition is a key opportunity for HR to demonstrate its expertise to executives and serve as a trusted advisor. The key areas of HR due diligence are outlined in Table 11.4.

What Is the Role of HRM Technology?

Human resource departments can improve their own and their organization's performance by appropriately using new technology. New technology usually involves *automation*—that is, using equipment and information processing to perform activities that had been performed by people. Over the last few decades, automation has improved HRM efficiency by reducing the number of people needed to perform routine tasks. Using automation can free HRM experts to concentrate on ways to determine how human resource management can help the organization meet its goals, so technology also can make this function more valuable.[60] For example, information technology provides ways to

LO4 Discuss the role of HRM technology in high-performance work systems.

TABLE 11.4 Key Areas of HR Due Diligence in Mergers and Acquisitions

KEY M&A CONSIDERATIONS	HR'S ROLE
Culture	• Assess the similarities and differences between the two companies with respect to issues such as where authority lies and how decisions are made. • Assess the emotional element of how employees feel about the company, leaders, and their openness to the change. • Map out differences between the acquiring company and the target company including how to bridge the gaps. • Create and execute a comprehensive communication plan to share a vision of the future and engage employees.
Analysis and retention of talent	• Ensure leadership talent is in place to lead and implement the transition. • Assess each key individual relative to competencies aligned to the needs of the new group. • Identify key people and take steps to retain them. • Put people in the right roles during the merger/acquisition. • Discuss individual job and career options.
Rewards structure	• Examine rewards and work environment factors.
Legal issues, e.g., outstanding human rights challenges	• Assess all outstanding legal issues including timetable for resolution and stakeholders involved.
Union issues, e.g., collective agreements	• Identify key stakeholders including history of relationship, and develop an integration timetable.

SOURCES: Adapted from Ruth N. Bramson, "HR's Role in Mergers and Acquisitions—Human Resource Management," http://findarticles.com, retrieved June 10, 2008; and Uyen Vu, "HR's Role in Mergers, Acquisitions," *Canadian HR Reporter*, December 4, 2006, pp. 17, 21.

build and improve systems for knowledge generation and sharing, as part of a learning organization. Among the applications are databases or networking sites where employees can store and share their knowledge, online directories of employee skills and experiences, and online libraries of learning resources, such as technical manuals and employees' reports from seminars and training programs.

HRM APPLICATIONS

New technologies continue to be introduced. In fact, so many HRM applications are developed that publications serving the profession (such as *HR Magazine* and *Workforce*) devote annual issues to reviewing this topic. Some of the technologies that have been widely adopted are transaction processing, decision support systems, and expert systems.[61]

Transaction processing refers to computations and calculations involved in reviewing and documenting HRM decisions and practices. It includes documenting decisions and actions associated with employee relocation, training expenses, and enrolments in courses and benefit plans. Transaction processing also includes

the activities required to meet government reporting requirements, such as filling out employment equity reports on which employers report information about employment equity group participation rates. Computers enable companies to perform these tasks more efficiently. Employers can fill out computerized forms and store HRM information in databases, so that it is easier to find, sort, and report.

Decision support systems are computer software systems designed to help managers solve problems. They usually include a "what if?" feature that managers can use to enter different assumptions or data and see how the likely outcomes will change. This type of system can help managers make decisions for workforce planning. The manager can, for example, try out different assumptions about turnover rates to see how those assumptions affect the number of new employees needed. Or the manager can test a range of assumptions about the availability of a certain skill in the labour market, looking at the impact of the assumptions on the success of different recruiting plans. Possible applications for a decision support system include forecasting (discussed in Chapter 3) and succession planning (discussed in Chapter 4).

transaction processing
Computations and calculations involved in reviewing and documenting HRM decisions and practices.

decision support systems
Computer software systems designed to help managers solve problems by showing how results vary when the manager alters assumptions or data.

Expert systems are computer systems that incorporate the decision rules used by people who are considered to have expertise in a certain area. The systems help users make decisions by recommending actions based on the decision rules and the information provided by the users. An expert system is designed to recommend the same actions that a human expert would in a similar situation. For example, an expert system could guide an interviewer during the selection process. Some organizations use expert systems to help employees decide how to allocate their money for benefits (as in a flexible plan) and help managers schedule the labour needed to complete projects. Expert systems can deliver both high quality and lower costs. By using the decision processes of experts, an expert system helps many people to arrive at decisions that reflect the expert's knowledge. It helps avoid the errors that can result from fatigue and decision-making biases, such as biases in appraising employee performance, described in Chapter 7; and it can increase efficiency by enabling fewer or less-skilled employees to do work that otherwise would require many highly skilled employees.

In proactive HR departments, transaction processing, decision support systems, and expert systems are often part of a human resource information system. Also, these technologies may be linked to employees through a network such as an intranet. Information systems and networks have been evolving rapidly; the following descriptions provide a basic introduction.

> **expert systems**
> Computer systems that support decision making by incorporating the decision rules used by people who are considered to have expertise in a certain area.

HUMAN RESOURCE INFORMATION SYSTEMS

A standard feature of a modern HRIS is the use of *relational databases*, which store data in separate files that can be linked by common elements. These common elements are fields identifying the type of data. Commonly used fields for an HR database include name, social insurance number, job status (full- or part-time), hiring date, position, title, rate of pay, job history, job location, mailing address, birth date, and emergency contacts. A relational database lets a user sort the data by any of the fields. For example, depending on how the database is set up, the user might be able to look up tables listing employees by location, rate of pay for various jobs, or training courses employees have completed. This system is far more sophisticated than the old-fashioned method of filing employee data by name, with one file per employee.

The ability to locate and combine many categories of data has a multitude of uses in human resource management. Databases have been developed to track employee benefit costs, training courses, and compensation. The system can meet the needs of managers as well as the HR department. On an oil rig, for example, management might look up data listing employee names along with safety equipment issued and appropriate skill certification. HR managers at headquarters might look up data on the same employees to gather information about wage rates or training programs needed. Another popular use of an HRIS is applicant tracking, or maintaining and retrieving records of job applicants. This is much faster and easier than trying to sort through stacks of résumés. With relational databases, HR staff can retrieve information about specific applicants or obtain lists of applicants with specific skills, career goals, work history, and employment background. Such information is useful for workforce planning, recruitment, succession planning, and career development. Taking the process a step further, the system could store information related to hiring and terminations. By analyzing such data, the HR department could measure the long-term success of its recruiting and selection processes.

E-HRM

Learn about Web 2.0 for human resource management.

HUMAN RESOURCE MANAGEMENT ONLINE: E-HRM

As we discussed in Chapter 1, more and more organizations are engaging in e-HRM—processing and accessing digitized HR information using an intranet or Web portal. As Internet use has increasingly taken the form of so-called Web 2.0 applications, e-HRM has moved in this direction as well. Generally speaking, Web 2.0 refers to tools that bring networks of people together to collaborate on projects, solve problems, or socialize. For instance, IBM applied social networking tools to its mentoring program. Any IBM employee interested in offering advice or getting help can participate by filling out an online profile in a directory called BluePages. Then when they want a mentor, they use a search engine to find the person with the necessary expertise. The program brings together employees from around the world and gives them personal control over the mentoring process.[62]

As discussed in Chapter 1, organizations are enhancing their HR technology to provide for *self-service,* which allows an employee to handle many job-related tasks (such as applications for reimbursement, updates to personal information, and access to company information) that otherwise would have fallen to HR, management, or administrative staff. A self-service application may be made available over the company's intranet or portal, or through specialized kiosks, and may be confined to a company's private network or may be part of a Web self-service solution for customers, employees, and managers.[63] With self-service, employees are responsible for keeping their personal information up to date, thus freeing up the time of HR and increasing the accuracy of employee data. Nine-eight percent of organizations responding to a recent survey of HR service delivery trends indicate they offer online benefit enrolment. Thomas Keebler, leader of Towers Perrin's global HR technology practice that conducted the surveys, says, "The benefits of [self-serve] are widespread and include a more empowered workforce that is more apt to take responsibility for its own HR and benefits decisions, greater accuracy of employee data and faster HR processes." Adds Keebler, [self-service] is an area that has truly lived up to the hype of relieving HR from administrative work to focus on more strategic issues.[64]

Most administrative and information-gathering activities in human resource management can be part of e-HRM. For example, online recruiting has become a significant part of the total recruiting effort, as candidates submit résumés online. Employers go online to retrieve suitable résumés from job search sites or retrieve information from forms they post at their own websites. For selection decisions, the organization may have candidates use one of the online testing services available; these services conduct the tests, process the results, and submit reports to employers. Online appraisal systems can help managers make pay decisions consistent with company policies and employee performance. Employees and managers can update performance goals and update results. Employees can view training histories and many types of training can be conducted online, as we discussed in Chapter 6. Online surveys of employee satisfaction or engagement can be quick and easy to fill out. Besides providing a way to administer the survey, an intranet is an effective vehicle for communicating the results of the survey and management's planned response.

Not only does e-HRM provide efficient ways to carry out human resource functions, it also poses new challenges to employees and new issues for HR managers to address. The Internet's ability to link people anytime, anywhere has accelerated such trends as globalization, the importance of knowledge sharing within organizations, and the need for flexibility. These trends, in turn, change the work environment for employees. For example, employees are increasingly expected to be highly committed but flexible, able to move from job to job. Employees also may be connected to the organization 24/7. In the car, on vacation, in airports, and even in the washroom, employees with smart phones and tablets can be accessible to deal with work demands. Organizations depend on their human resource departments to help prepare employees for this changing work world through such activities as training, career development, performance management, and benefits packages that meet the need for flexibility and help employees manage stress.

Effectiveness of Human Resource Management

In recent years, human resource management at many organizations has been taking a customer-oriented approach. For an organization's human resource division, "customers" are the organization as a whole and its other divisions. They are customers of HRM because they depend on HRM to provide a variety of services that result in a supply of talented, motivated employees. Taking this customer-oriented approach, human resource management defines its customer groups, customer needs, and the activities required to meet those needs, as shown in Table 11.5. These definitions give an organization a basis for defining goals and measures of success.

L05 Summarize ways to measure the effectiveness of human resource management.

Depending on the situation, a number of techniques are available for measuring HRM's effectiveness in meeting its customers' needs. These techniques include reviewing a set of key indicators, measuring the outcomes of specific HRM activity, and measuring the economic value or ROI (return on investment) of HRM programs.

HUMAN RESOURCE MANAGEMENT AUDITS

An **HRM audit** is a formal review of the outcomes of HRM functions. To conduct the audit, the HR

HRM audit
A formal review of the outcomes of HRM functions, based on identifying key HRM functions and measures of organizational performance.

TABLE 11.5   Customer-Oriented Perspective of Human Resource Management

WHO ARE OUR CUSTOMERS?	WHAT DO OUR CUSTOMERS NEED?	HOW DO WE MEET CUSTOMER NEEDS?
• Managers and supervisors	• Committed employees	• Qualified staffing
• Strategic planners	• Competent employees	• Performance management
• Employees		• Rewards
		• Training and development

department identifies key functions and the key measures of organizational performance and customer satisfaction that would indicate each function is succeeding. Table 11.6 lists examples of these measures for a variety of HRM functions: staffing, compensation, benefits, training, appraisal and development, and overall effectiveness. The audit may also look at any other measure associated with successful management of human resources—for instance, compliance with employment-related legislation, succession planning, maintaining a safe workplace, and positive labour relations. An HRM audit using customer satisfaction measures supports the customer-oriented approach to human resource management. When HR functions are outsourced, these audits need to look at both HR functions performed internally and those that are outsourced.

After identifying performance measures for the HRM audit, the staff carries out the audit by gathering information. The information for the key business indicators is usually available in the organization's documents. Sometimes the HR department has to create new documents for gathering specific types of data. The usual way to measure customer satisfaction is to conduct surveys. Employee surveys provide information about the satisfaction of these internal customers. Many organizations conduct surveys of top executives to get a better view of how HRM practices affect the organization's business success. Of course, the benefits of the audit are only as great as the company's response to what it learns and applies to enhance existing processes and tools.

ANALYZING THE EFFECT OF HRM PROGRAMS

Another way to measure HRM effectiveness is to analyze specific programs or activities. The analysis can measure a program's success in terms of whether it achieved its objectives and whether it delivered value in an economic sense. Increasingly HR is being called on to measure its impact. The Conference Board of Canada identifies "measurement" as an important HR issue and indicates that HR measures

must be meaningful due to the importance of HR's role in building organizational capabilities.[65]

Senior management and other organizational stakeholders are asking for metrics or measures that relate to the value of the firm's human capital and the return on investment in that human capital. A report from CFO Research Services and Mercer Human Resource Consulting revealed that chief financial officers' opinions of HR are improving—most of the 180 CFOs surveyed see human capital as a value driver rather than a cost. However, the survey also showed that just 16 percent of CFOs said they knew to a "considerable" or "great" extent the return on investments in human capital.[66]

"Traditional financial numbers are an indicator of past performance, but reliable measures of human capital are much better indicators of future performance, and therefore growth, and therefore shareholder value," says Curt Coffman of the Gallup Organization.[67] The European Union is currently looking at *human capital reporting* measures. For example, Denmark requires publicly traded companies to report on the "human dimension" of their business to provide investors a background of the value of human capital and it is expected some type of reporting requirement will also be required in North America.[68]

However, caution about calculating the value of human capital is needed. "Accounting deals principally with fixed assets. Once you buy them all they do is depreciate over time," says Jac Fitz-enz, the founder of Human Capital Source. "But humans are just the opposite: they appreciate over time as they grow and develop."[69] Furthermore, the return on investment of specific, isolated HR initiatives is needed. When individual HR initiatives are evaluated in isolation on strictly quantitative terms, there may be a tendency to focus on cost containment only with a failure to consider qualitative considerations and indirect benefits. For example, if an investment in human capital, such as a training program, yields tangible results, such as an increase in product quality and a decrease in product returns, this only quantifies part of the return on investment. The

TABLE 11.6 Key Measures of Success for an HRM Audit

BUSINESS INDICATORS	CUSTOMER SATISFACTION MEASURES
Staffing Average days taken to fill open requisitions Ratio of acceptances to offers made Ratio of employment equity target group applicant representation in local labour market Per capita requirement costs Average years of experience/education of hires	Anticipation of human resource needs Timeliness of referring qualified workers to line supervisors Treatment of applicants Skill in handling terminations Adaptability to changing labour market conditions
Compensation Per capita (average) merit increases Ratio of recommendations for reclassification to number of employees Percentage of overtime hours to regular time Ratio of average salary offers to average salary in community	Fairness of existing job evaluation system Competitiveness in local labour market Relationship between pay and performance Employee satisfaction with pay
Benefits Average workers' compensation payments Benefit cost per payroll dollar Percentage of sick leave to total pay	Promptness in handling claims Fairness and consistency in the application of benefit policies Communication of benefits to employees Assistance provided to managers in reducing potential for unnecessary claims
Training Percentage of employees participating in training programs Percentage of employees receiving tuition reimbursement Training dollars/days per employee	Extent to which training programs meet the needs of employees and the company Communication to employees about available training opportunities Quality of orientation/onboarding programs
Employee Appraisal and Development Distribution of performance appraisal ratings Appropriate psychometric properties of appraisal forms	Assistance in identifying management potential Organizational development activities provided by HRM department
Overall Effectiveness Ratio of human resource staff to employee population Turnover rate Absenteeism rate Ratio of per capita revenues to per capita cost Net income per employee	Accuracy and clarity of information provided to managers and employees Competence and expertise of staff Working relationship between organizations and HRM department

SOURCE: Reprinted with permission, excerpts from Chapter 1.5, "Evaluating Human Resource Effectiveness," pp. 187–227, by Anne S. Tsui and Luis R. Gomez-Mejia, from *Human Resource Management: Evolving Roles and Responsibilities*, ed. Lee Dyer. © 1988 by The Bureau of National Affairs, Inc., Washington, DC 20037.

ROI calculation may not fully capture the improved employee and/or customer satisfaction achieved as a result of the training. Figure 11.10 provides the math for calculating the return on investment of an investment in human capital including both direct and indirect costs and benefits.

In general, HR departments should be able to improve their performance through some combination of greater efficiency and greater effectiveness. Greater efficiency means the HR department uses fewer and less-costly resources to perform its functions. Greater effectiveness means that what the HR

$$ROI\ \% = \frac{Realized\ direct/indirect\ benefits - Total\ direct/indirect\ costs \times 100}{Total\ direct/indirect\ costs}$$

FIGURE 11.10

ROI Math

SOURCE: Adapted from "ROI Math," *Canadian HR Reporter*, February 28, 2005, p. 15.

THINKING ETHICALLY

Can HRM Make Organizations More Ethical?

Ed Gubman, executive editor of *People & Strategy*, once received a proposed article from writers describing how their company had improved performance and leadership by using social networking applications. It was an inspiring story, except that it came from one of the financial institutions blamed for questionable practices leading to the recent near-meltdown of the financial services industry. Gubman was left to ponder what kind of "leadership" had resulted from the HR effort. Did the HR staff think it was fine to enable the company to become proficient at unethical conduct, or did they not understand what major parts of their company were doing?

The answers to these questions relate to the extent of HR professionals' knowledge and influence. The tools are available to provide an unprecedented level of guidance in how the company's HR practices affect business outcomes. If HRM is to promote ethical conduct, its practitioners must understand what their organization does, be committed to using goals and policies that reinforce ethical conduct, and be able to advocate for this effort. In practice—perhaps because of the *human* focus of human resource management—top executives seem happy to leave decisions about ethics up to this department. The obvious risk is that if the HR director is the only executive thinking about ethics, then ethics is unlikely to be a true strategic priority.

SOURCES: Ed Gubman, "Where is HR?" *People and Strategy*, September 2009, p. 3; and Stefan Stern, "Resources Are Limited and HR Must Raise Its Game," *Financial Times*, February 17, 2009, Business & Company Resource Center, http://gale net.galegroup.com.

QUESTIONS

1. If HR managers are the only managers charged with ensuring ethical conduct, then how much impact can they have on their organization's ethical behaviour? Who else in an organization might an HR executive persuade to be an ally in advocating for ethics to be on the agenda?

2. Suppose you are an HR executive meeting with the company's board of directors. You have been asked to draft a code of ethics for the company. Make a business case for why other leaders should join you in this effort.

---

department does—for example, selecting employees or setting up a performance management system—has a more beneficial effect on employees' and the organization's performance. Employee turnover is a measure that can relate to both efficiency and effectiveness if an organization is spending money on recruiting, selection, and training because it loses people with valuable experience. Home Depot tracks a variety of measures to see whether it is effective at meeting goals for attracting, motivating, and keeping skilled employees. The company uses a database that includes data on job applications, career, paths, performance ratings, employee satisfaction, and attrition (employees leaving the company). Managers can analyze the data by region, district, and store, as well as compare numbers over time.[70]

HRM's potential to affect employees' well-being and the organization's performance makes human resource management an exciting and rewarding field. As we have shown throughout the book, every HRM function calls for decisions that have the potential to help individuals and organizations achieve their goals. For HR professionals to fulfill that potential, they must ensure that their decisions are well grounded. The field of human resource management provides tremendous opportunity to future researchers and managers who want to make a difference in many people's lives and contribute to the success of organizations.

SUMMARY

L01 Define high-performance work systems and identify the elements, outcomes, and conditions associated with such a system.

- A high-performance work system is the right combination of people, technology, and organizational structure that makes full use of the organization's resources and opportunities in achieving its goals.
- The elements of a high-performance work system are organizational structure, task design, people, reward systems, and information systems. These elements must work together in a smoothly functioning whole.
- A high-performance work system achieves the organization's goals, typically including growth, productivity, and high profits.
- On the way to achieving these overall goals, the high-performance work system meets such intermediate goals as high quality, innovation, customer satisfaction, job satisfaction, and reduced absenteeism and turnover.
- Many conditions contribute to high-performance work systems by providing employees with skills, incentives, knowledge, and autonomy.

L02 Describe how organizations assess employee satisfaction and engagement.

- Employee satisfaction and employee engagement is usually assessed with a survey. Having a systematic ongoing program of surveys allows the organization to monitor trends and should be part of the HR strategy.
- Conducting surveys should be taken seriously because they raise employee expectations.
- Exit interviews may be used to uncover reasons employees leave. Stay interviews may uncover issues that if addressed effectively, support employee retention.

L03 Explain how human resource management can contribute to high performance.

- Jobs should be designed to foster teamwork and employee empowerment. Recruitment and selection should focus on obtaining employees who have the qualities necessary for teamwork and knowledge sharing. Training also is important, because of its role in creating a learning organization.

- The performance management system should be related to the organization's goals, with a focus on meeting internal and external customers' needs. Total compensation and rewards should include links to performance, and employees should be included in decisions about compensation.
- Generally, organizations try to avoid the need for involuntary turnover and minimize voluntary turnover. Organizations also need to handle employee discipline effectively in order to foster fairness and meet legal requirements.
- Although HR has historically been excluded from playing an early and strategic role in a merger or acquisition, there is growing evidence that when HR is involved early, the merger or acquisition is more likely to be successful.

L04 Discuss the role of HRM technology in high-performance work systems.

- Technology can improve the efficiency of the human resource management functions and support knowledge sharing.
- HRM applications involve transaction processing, decision support systems, and expert systems, often as part of a human resource information system using relational databases, which can improve the efficiency of routine tasks and the quality of decisions.
- With Internet technology, organizations can use e-HRM to let all the organization's employees help themselves to the HR information they need whenever they need it.

L05 Summarize ways to measure the effectiveness of human resource management.

- Taking a customer-oriented approach, HRM can improve quality by defining the internal customers who use its services and determining whether it is meeting those customers' needs.
- An HRM audit is a formal review of the outcomes of HRM functions.
- Another way to measure HRM effectiveness is to analyze specific programs or activities. The analysis can measure success in terms of whether a program met its objectives, and whether it delivered value in an economic sense, such as by leading to productivity improvements and generating a return on investment.

Critical Thinking Questions

1. What is a high-performance work system? What are its elements? Which of these elements involve human resource management?

2. How does your workplace compare to the conditions for high performance identified near the beginning of this chapter? Discuss.

3. As it has become clear that HRM can help create and maintain high-performance work systems, it appears that organizations will need two kinds of human resource professionals: one focuses on identifying how HRM can contribute to high performance; the other develops expertise in particular HRM functions, such as how to administer a benefits program that complies with legal requirements. Which is more interesting to you? Why?

4. Consider your current job or a job you recently held. Overall, were you satisfied or dissatisfied? How would you describe your level of engagement? How did your level of satisfaction and engagement affect your behaviour and performance on the job?

5. Why are exit interviews important? Should an organization care about the opinions of people who are leaving? How are those opinions relevant to employee retention?

6. How can an organization promote ethical behaviour among its employees?

7. Summarize how each of the following HR functions can contribute to high performance.
   a. Job design
   b. Recruitment and selection
   c. Training and development
   d. Performance management
   e. Compensation and rewards

8. What steps would you take to protect yourself from being "greenwashed" by a potential employer? Would you be prepared to earn less/work more to be employed by an organization with an outstanding corporate social responsibility track record?

9. Why do you think that a merger or acquisition is more likely to be successful when HR is involved from the start of the process?

10. How can HRM technology make a human resource department more productive? How can technology improve the quality of HRM decisions?

11. Why should human resource departments measure their effectiveness? What are some ways they can go about measuring effectiveness?

What's Your HR IQ?

 Connect offers more ways to check what you've learned so far. Find experiential exercises, Test Your Knowledge quizzes, videos, and many other resources to gauge your HR IQ.

CASE STUDY 11.1: Fairmont Hotels & Resorts: Growing Environmental Stewardship

While the health of the world's ecosystem is a hot topic, it has been a priority at Fairmont Hotels & Resorts, one of "Canada's Greenest Employers" since 1990. With the debut of its "Green Partnership Program," the Toronto-based company initiated a chain-wide environmental program, and literally wrote the book in its industry on how to build a greener business—entitled the "Green Partnership Guide," now in its third edition. The program has expanded to 50 locations around the world, garnered several international awards, and been an inspiration for others in the hospitality industry and beyond. The move to greener pastures was prompted by the company's locations (then known as Canadian Pacific Hotels) in sensitive environments, such as national parks, biosphere reserves, and coastal zones or wetlands. "We realized we had to mitigate our operation impacts on the environment, because if you take care of the environment, you take care of the very resource that brings your guests to explore in the first place," said Michelle White, director of environmental affairs at Fairmont.

Looking to have a gentler environmental footprint, the company first focused on waste management (recycling, organics diversion, and food and goods redistribution), energy conservation (lighting retrofits, HVAC upgrades, alternative technology, and sustainability), and water conservation (tap aerators, low-flow shower heads, low-flush toilets, and wastewater recycling).

The rise of responsible tourism has also meant Fairmont is sharing the benefits of business with the community, particularly in emerging markets where economic development is a challenge. A Fairmont property in

Mexico is selling local tours, and giving part of the proceeds back to the community and the rest to a conservation fund for the biosphere. "Over time, we realized you couldn't be a really green hotel and good corporate citizen unless you also look at your community involvement," said White.

Beyond helping the environment, Fairmont has seen gains in areas such as guest loyalty, brand identity, and media interest, while developing a reputation as an environmental leader and demonstrating corporate social responsibility. There have also been cost efficiencies, such as lighting or retrofits that reduce utilities consumption, though White admits costs can vary, depending on the supporting infrastructure.

Fairmont has garnered award-praise for its efforts. For example Fairmont received the global tourism business award for the best corporate social responsibility program at MKG's Worldwide Hospitality Awards, the global tourism business award from the World Travel and Tourism Council, and is recognized as one of Canada's Greenest Employers. But behind it all is the commitment and enthusiasm of its 26,000 employees around the world, including 10,500 in Canada. "Before implementing a program of this scale, you want to make sure you have a lot of employee buy-in," she said. "If they care about those things at home, they like to see that brought over to their workplace as well."

"The biggest challenge in any environmental program is making sure your employees are engaged, and that often comes with making sure employees are informed," White adds. For every new hotel or new market, the green program has been heartily embraced, said Mike Taylor, manager of media relations for Fairmont. "It's definitely something new employees latch on to and feel passionate about and are very connected to from day one," said Taylor. "At every single hotel, that's the predominant program that really resonates with employees." For example, Toronto's Royal York has an organic rooftop garden and Vancouver's Fairmont Pacific Rim established a partnership with the Stanley Park Ecology

Society in support of their efforts as stewards of the city's landmark park.

While the program is administered corporately, volunteer "green teams" at each property meet monthly to discuss and review ways to improve the operational performance in various departments. Fairmont also runs an environmental incentive program that recognizes the green team that has performed the best on a quarterly basis, and rewards two hotels that have had the best overall environmental performance each year. The green focus is definitely used as a retention tool and makes employees feel empowered. "They have an ownership or a management group that supports that approach to sustainable tourism," said Taylor. "And at the end of the day, it's the right thing to do and it's the right thing for the planet."

Michael Adams, president of The Environics Group of research and communications consulting companies in Toronto, says he sees people increasingly concerned about whether they work for environmentally responsible companies. "They don't want to go home and have to apologize to their children about where they work and what they do. They want to feel proud of what they do," said Adams.

Questions

1. On the basis of the information provided in the case, what costs and benefits has Fairmont experienced by implementing its Green Partnership program?
2. Would you be more likely to be satisfied, engaged, and/or loyal, and/or remain with a company that shows evidence of corporate social responsibility such as being committed to the environment? Explain your response.

SOURCES: "Employer Review: Fairmont Hotels & Resorts (2012)," www.eluta.ca/green-at-fairmont, retrieved June 14, 2012; "Green Partnership Program," www.fairmont.com/EN_FA/AboutFairmont/environment/GreenPartnershipProgram/, retrieved June 14, 2012; Sarah Dobson, "Fairmont Finds It's Easy Being Green," *Canadian HR Reporter*, March 26, 2007, p. 14; Uyen Vu, "Climate Change Sparks Attitude Shift," *Canadian HR Reporter*, March 26, 2007, p. 11; and Adine Mees and Jamie Bonham, "Corporate Social Responsibility Belongs with HR," *Canadian HR Reporter*, April 4, 2004.

CASE STUDY 11.2: Gold Standard—The Merger of Two Rival Mines

A successful merger of two organizations is many things, but how often does it involve building bridges among neighbourhoods and sports teams? Such was the challenge faced recently by Canadian gold producer Goldcorp Inc. after it took over operations of its rival Campbell Mine in Red Lake, a remote northwestern Ontario town.

Since 1949, the mine site—Canada's largest gold mine, at 700,000 ounces per year—was home to two rival and neighbouring mines: Placer Dome's Campbell Mine and Goldcorp's Red Lake Mine. The 5,000 residents of the mining town owed their livelihoods—and

allegiances—to one of the operations, and it was rare when the two sides mixed.

"There was a lot of history between the two mines and there was quite a rivalry—to the extent there were separate sports teams and social events," says Goldcorp human resources VP Gerry Atkinson. People even lived in different locations depending on where they were working. The decision to merge the two mines came after Barrick bought Placer's Campbell site and then sold its entire Canadian operations to Goldcorp. Since Goldcorp already had the neighbouring Red Lake mine, "We felt there were good synergies there to bring the two mines together under one jurisdiction, physically linking them via an underground shaft," says Atkinson.

Challenges

If there were engineering challenges in linking the two mines below ground, there were also big HR challenges in merging the two workforces—and communities—above ground.

"The biggest merger challenges have definitely been on the people side," says mine general manager Dan Gagnon. "You're basically putting together two very different cultures. One mine [Red Lake] has a 50-year history with full-time employees, and the other [Campbell] was mostly contract employees. Everything was different, including wages and benefits. We had to review every HR policy with the eventual goal of creating one team and absorbing most workers as full-time employees."

In terms of organizational structure, Campbell had a large corporate structure, with local managers used to direction from head office. The Red Lake mine was more independent, with local managers entrusted with day-to-day decision making. "Today we're a little bit in between, although we still lean toward decentralization. We want the mine management to be actively involved with decisions, with some guidance from corporate—but we don't intervene on a daily basis." Unfortunately for Gagnon, choosing a management group from the two organizations was one of his harder tasks because both teams were strong. But it was this handpicked management team from both organizations that led the way in selling the merger to Red Lake's "two solitudes."

"In terms of linking the community, there was a new corporate identity in town and we picked the management structure to make it work within the community," says Atkinson. "From the beginning, we brought in a mine general manager from one of our other Canadian mine sites because one of his particular strengths is building teams and getting them involved in the community."

Key to Success

Critical to building bridges within the community were spokespeople, chosen from both organizations to act as liaisons between management, workers, and the greater community. The spokespeople were articulate staffers with long-term links to the mines who could act as advocates and speak positively of the move. Part of their role was to meet with employees and the community and be supportive of the whole amalgamation process—answering questions and dispelling rumours.

"A big part of the merger's success was these spokespeople," says Atkinson. "They were heavily involved with communication in terms of what was happening." "The worst thing that anyone can do during periods of massive change is tell people that nothing's going to change," says Gagnon. "You have to communicate that things will change, but we're going to try to make it as painless as possible and we'll work it through with you. And the changes are positive changes for the company, the operation and the community."

Questions

1. What were some of the HR issues that needed to be addressed for the merger to proceed?
2. Were the "due diligence" aspects of the merger handled effectively from an HR perspective? Refer to Table 11.4 in making your assessment.
3. Do you have any additional advice or recommendations to this newly merged organization to ensure outcomes of a high-performance organization are sustained over time?

SOURCE: Duff McCutcheon, "Gold Standard," *HR Professional*, June/July 2008, pp. 45–47. This article originally appeared in the June/July 2008 issue of *HR Professional Magazine*, published for the Human Resources Professional Association by Naylor (Canada) Inc.

Video Cases

PART 1: The Human Resource Environment

What CEOs Want From HR Professionals

President and CEO of Ricoh Canada, Glen Laverty suggests that HR has tended to be positioned functionally rather than strategically in most organizations. Although HR has many regulatory and administrative responsibilities, he wants to see HR thinking outside the box and taking the role of strategic partner to the business. Establishing that role at the executive level provides HR the opportunity to establish credibility and create ability to execute for each and every department.

Laverty suggests that HR needs the CEO's assistance to break through the mindset that still exists in some organizations that HR is just a function and work to open up a true partnership relationship for HR with other departments. He says that should begin with HR being present at strategic planning sessions where HR can put forward their strategies and be highly involved in understanding how they can help leaders in the organization accomplish their strategies. This means that HR needs to be at the executive level, at the strategic planning sessions, and recognize what it takes to partner with the organization to achieve the firm's goals.

Questions

1. What competencies do you think HR professionals need to fulfill the expectations this CEO has for HR?
2. Does this role for HR sound like the kind of career you would like to have? Why or why not?

SOURCE: Based on "What CEOs Want from HR Professionals," *Canadian HR Reporter TV*, November 23, 2011.

PART 2: Preparing For and Acquiring Human Resources

Hiring for Culture Fit at Lululemon

Director of People Potential at Lululemon Athletica, Jaci Edgeworth describes how Lululemon hires for culture fit. Jaci describes Lululemon's hiring process as being a very slow process that typically starts with inviting five to seven people who have come into the store and expressed interest, or have applied online to come in for an informal group interview. These prospective employees are observed to see how they interact with each other. Candidates determined to be a potential fit might be invited to go to a yoga class in the community or some other event to see how they interact in another atmosphere. Individual interviews are the next step, typically with the store manager, assistant store manager and/or key leader, and an educator in the store. Lululemon is looking for people that are fun, engaging, and inspiring—that others would want to be around or perhaps spend time with outside of work.

Lululemon has a well-defined onboarding process for store employees that teaches about the store, the guest experience, and the products. New hires in other parts of the company, such as Finance and IT also start by spending time in a store. Throughout their careers, all employees at Lululemon do a shift in the stores each month to stay connected with guests, products, and the store experience.

Questions

1. What advice would you offer Lululemon about their selection process—are these the right steps in the right order?
2. All Lululemon employees are required to do a shift in the stores each month. Do you think this requirement makes Lululemon more or less attractive to potential employees? Explain your answer.

SOURCE: Based on "Hiring for Fit at Lululemon Athletica," *Canadian HR Reporter TV*, October 11, 2011.

PART 3: Managing Talent

Moving Entry-Level Employees through the Ranks

Vice-president of People at Softchoice, Maria Odoardi talks about how her company provides opportunities for employees who start in entry-level positions at its call centre. Maria describes how the call centre at Softchoice is more than a place where customers are served—it's a place where talent is incubated not just for the call centre but for the rest of the company. Thirty-three percent of the employee population works in the call centre and like other companies, Softchoice has been challenged by the perception that in call centres employees are low-paid, people come to start a career but never to grow a career, and the work is monotonous. Softchoice set out to re-imagine what a sales (call) centre could be and focus on development so employees can find career opportunities elsewhere in the company.

At Softchoice, the traditional career path was for people from the call centre to move into outbound sales jobs. However, as other areas of the business grew, demand for resources and skills began to grow and ambitious people were able to find interest to expand their careers. Currently, people are promoted not only into outbound sales roles but also into business development, corporate marketing, and more recently, into technical roles. Softchoice has found that an employee who gets promoted into an outbound sales job is significantly more effective than an outside hire. Last year, approximately 25 percent of call centre employees were promoted and 20 percent of the senior management team—directors and vice-presidents started their careers in Softchoice's call centre.

Questions

1. What evidence does the video provide that Softchoice is committed to valuing and developing its talent (people)?
2. Does Softchoice sound like a good place to build a career? Why or why not?

SOURCE: Based on "Moving Entry-level Employees through the Ranks," *Canadian HR Reporter TV*, May 28, 2012.

PART 4: Compensating and Rewarding Human Resources

Changing Employee Benefits at Longos

Liz Volk, vice-president of Human Resources at grocery chain Longos, discusses how changes were made to their employee benefits plan, including adding flex benefits and how they communicated with employees. The organization had doubled its size in the last 3½ years and it was recognized that the traditional benefits plan in place for the previous 25 years needed to change to be sustainable as well as current and relevant for employees. With all different stages of generations and needs within the business it was viewed to be critical to provide a flex benefits plan.

Challenges encountered included the diverse employee population; working different hours; being able to bring all team members together; and dealing with language issues. It was also recognized that employees had a limited knowledge of their current benefits. During the design stage HR went out and did "sneak peaks" with employees at the stores. Explanation of current benefits was provided and employees were able to provide input that led to plan design changes.

Face-to-face enrolment sessions were conducted a few months later. The new employee benefits program was branded, "Fresh Journey to A Whole New You." To help ensure employees know what they have, a variety of communication methods are being used—communication boards on total rewards, newsletters, huddles for messages around wellness, and "lunch-and-learns" with benefits vendors.

Questions

1. How is Longos' redesigned approach to employee benefits rewarding to employees? To the organization overall?
2. Compare and contrast Longos' approach to communication with the recommendations provided in Chapter 8 for communicating total rewards to employees. Is there anything else that Longos should do to ensure that employees receive and fully understand their benefits?

SOURCE: Based on "Changing Employee Benefits at Longos," *Canadian HR Reporter TV*, October 25, 2011.

PART 5: Meeting Other HR Goals

Fostering Employee Engagement

Senior vice-president of Strategy and Stakeholder Relations at the Healthcare of Ontario Pension Plan (HOOPP), Victoria Hubbell discusses how the organization significantly enhanced its employee engagement scores—from 52 percent to 91 percent. Hubbell describes how the organization, in a very methodical way, started focusing on employees and their needs. Overall, HOOPP's approach to enhancing employee engagement was to identify the business practices; incorporate better development, training, and learning opportunities; foster increased empowerment; and create decision making where it should be.

Four specific elements identified as the biggest drivers of engagement at HOOPP are:

1. *Culture*—Hubbell describes HOOPP as having a culture of profound respect and collaboration and that people look forward to coming to work.

2. *Work/life balance*—Although it's not always the perfect balance, work is regarded in a healthy way in order to avoid a toxic, frenzied approach.

3. *Resilience training*—To help people focus, make better decisions, and improve clarity and creativity during times of change, a corporate-wide program was launched starting with the CEO and his team.

4. *Opportunities for interesting work*—HOOPP recognizes the importance of having work that is valued and that taps into employees' intellect and creativity.

Questions

1. What elements of a high-performance work system are discussed in the video?

2. What effect will this high level of employee engagement likely have on HOOPP employees' behaviour and performance on the job?

SOURCE: "Fostering Employee Engagement," *Canadian HR Reporter TV*, October 11, 2011.

Notes

CHAPTER 1

1. www.canada stop100.com; www.google.com/ support/jobs; *Fortune*'s "100 Best Companies to Work For"; http://money.cnn.com/magazines/fortune/ best-companies/2012/full_list/index.html, retrieved January 19, 2012.

2. Janice Cooney and Allison Cowan, "Training and Development Outlook 2003: Canadian Organizations Continue to Under-Invest" (Ottawa: Conference Board of Canada, 2003), p. 1.

3. Ruth Wright, "The Strategic Value of People: Human Resource Trends and Metrics" (Ottawa: Conference Board of Canada, July 2006), p. i.

4. A. S. Tsui and L. R. Gomez-Mejia, "Evaluating Human Resource Effectiveness," in *Human Resource Management: Evolving Rules and Responsibilities*, ed. L. Dyer (Washington, DC: BNA Books, 1988), pp. 1187–227; M. A. Hitt, B. W. Keats, and S. M. DeMarie, "Navigating in the New Competitive Landscape: Building Strategic Flexibility and Competitive Advantage in the 21st Century," *Academy of Management Executive* 12, no. 4 (1998), pp. 22–42; J. T. Delaney and M. A. Huselid, "The Impact of Human Resource Management Practices on Perceptions of Organizational Performance," *Academy of Management Journal* 39 (1996), pp. 949–69.

5. Owen Parker, "It's the Journey That Matters: 2005 Strategic HR Transformation Study Tour Report 2006" (Ottawa: Conference Board of Canada, 2006), p. 1.

6. Ibid.

7. S. A. Snell and J. W. Dean, "Integrated Manufacturing and Human Resource Management: A Human Capital Perspective," *Academy of Management Journal* 35 (1992), pp. 467–504; M. A. Youndt, S. Snell, J. W. Dean Jr., and D. P. Lepak, "Human Resource Management, Manufacturing Strategy, and Firm Performance," *Academy of Management Journal* 39 (1996), pp. 836–66.

8. Charles Greer, *Strategic Human Resource Management*, 2nd ed. (New Jersey: Prentice-Hall, 2001), p. 1.

9. D. Hansen, "2006 Data Bank Annual," *Workforce Management*, December 11, 2006, p. 48.

10. E.E. Lawler, "From Human Resource Management to Organizational Effectiveness," *Human Resource Management*, 44 (2005), pp. 165–169.

11. D. Ulrich, *Human Resource Champions* (Boston: Harvard Business School Press, 1998).

12. A. Halcrow, "Survey Shows HRM in Transition," *Workforce*, June 1998, pp. 73–80; J. Laabs, "Why HR Can Win Today," *Workforce*, May 1998, pp. 62–74; C. Cole, "Kodak Snapshots," *Workforce*, June 2000, pp. 65–72; Towers Perrin, *Priorities for Competitive Advantage: An IBM Study Conducted by Towers Perrin*, 1992.

13. David Brown, "HR Pulled in Two Directions at Once," *Canadian HR Reporter*, February 23, 2004, p. 1.

14. A. Arcand and M. Lefebvre, "Canada's Lagging Productivity: What If We Had Matched the U.S. Performance?" (Ottawa: Conference Board of Canada, November 2011), p. 1.

15. J. Kahn, "The World's Most Admired Companies," *Fortune*, October 26, 1998, pp. 206–26; A. Fisher, "The World's Most Admired Companies," *Fortune*, October 27, 1997, p. 232.

16. "2006 Census: Immigration, Citizenship, Mobility, & Immigration," *The Daily*, December 4, 2007, www.statcan.ca/Daily/English/071204/d0712049. htm, retrieved December 22, 2007.

17. www.statcan.ca/english/Pgdb/dem046a.htm, retrieved April 3, 2004.

18. www.statcan.gc.ca/daily-quotidien/100309/ dq100309a-eng.htm, retrieved March 2, 2012.

19. "Saskatchewan Jobs Mission: Premier Brad Wall to Ireland Amid Skilled Labour Shortage," www .huggingtonpost.ca, retrieved March 2, 2012.

20. Jeff Hale, "Ask What Another Country Can Do for You," *The Globe and Mail*, February 22, 2007, p. B11.

21. Jean-Francois Potvin, "HR Outsourcing is Gaining Ground," *Benefits Canada*, November 23, 2012, www.benefitscanada.com/news/hr-outsourcing-is-gaining-ground-570, retrieved January 21, 2012.

22. Ibid.

23. P. McDougal, "IBM Lands $80 Million Air Canada HR Deal," *Information Week*, October 7, 2011, www.informationweek.com/news/services/ business/231900305, retrieved January 18, 2012.

24. Lydia Saad, "Nurses Shine, Bankers Slump in Ethics Ratings," Gallup Poll report, November 24, 2008, www.gallup.com; Angela Monaghan, "Survey Highlights 'Crisis of Ethics," *Daily Telegraph*, January 19, 2010, Business & Company Resource Center, http:// galenet.galegroup.com.

25. G.F. Cavanaugh, D. Moberg, and M. Velasquez, "The Ethics of Organizational Politics," *Academy of Management Review*, pp. 363–374.

26. Uyen Vu, "Climate Change Sparks Attitude Shift," *Canadian HR Reporter*, March 26, 2007, p. 11.

27. J. Wiscombe, "Your Wonderful, Terrible HR Life," *Workforce,* June 2001, pp. 32–38.

28. www.chrp.ca/become-a-chrp/get-started/, retrieved March 2, 2012; "Become a CHRP," www.chrp.ca/become-a-chrp/get-started/, retrieved July 11, 2012.

29. www.cchra.ca/about-us, retrieved January 24, 2012.

30. N. Lockwood, *The Aging Workforce,* Alexandria, VA: Society for Human Resource Management, 2003.

31. Marian Scott, "Study Shows High Workplace Diversity Encourages Tolerance," *Leader-Post,* January 21, 2012, p. B5.

32. Piali Roy, "Steam Whistle's Commitment to Hiring New Immigrants," *YongeStreet,* September 1, 2010, www.yongestreetmedia.ca/features/steamwhistle0901.aspx, retrieved January 24, 2012.

33. Andrew Wahl, "Opening Doors," *Canadian Business,* March 29–April 4, 2004, www.canadianbusiness.com/article.jsp?content=20040329_59084_58084, retrieved October 20, 2008.

34. "Aboriginal Identity Population by Age Groups, Median Age and Sex, 2006 Counts, for Canada, Provinces and Territories—20% Sample Data (Table)" (Ottawa: Statistics Canada, 2008); "Aboriginal Peoples Highlight Tables, 2006 Census," Catalogue No. 97-558-XWE2006002, January 15, 2008 (Ottawa: Statistics Canada, 2008), www12.statcan.ca/english/census06/data/highlights/aboriginal/index.cfm?Lang=E, retrieved April 24, 2008.

35. www.chrc-ccdp.ca/discrimination/barrier_freeen.asp, retrieved April 3, 2004.

36. "How Canada Performs: A Report Card on Canada," (Ottawa: Conference Board of Canada, June 2007), p. 82.

37. "Industry Report 2000," *Training,* October 2000, p. 48.

38. J.A. Neal and C.L. Tromley, "From Incremental Change to Retrofit: Creating High-Performance Work Systems," *Academy of Management Executive* 9 (1995), pp. 42–54.

39. A. Carnevale and D. Desrochers, "Training in the Dilbert Economy," *Training & Development,* December 1999, pp. 32–36.

40. "Population 15 years and Over by Highest Degree, Certificate or Diploma (1986–2006 Census)," www40.statcan.gc.ca/l01/cst01/educ42-eng.htm, retrieved March 2, 2012.

41. Ray Turchansky, "Proof Education Is Smart Investment," *Financial Post,* March 22, 2004, p. FP13.

42. M. J. Kavanaugh, H. G. Guetal, and S. I. Tannenbaum, *Human Resource Information Systems: Development and Application* (Boston: PWS-Kent, 1990).

43. N. Lockwood, *Maximizing Human Capital: Demonstrating HR Value with Key Performance Indicators* (Alexandria, VA: SHRM Research Quarterly, 2006).

44. This section is based on L. Grensing-Pophal, "Are You Suited for a Dot-Com?," *HR Magazine,* November 2000, pp. 75–80; and Leslie A. Weatherly, "HR Technology: Leveraging the Shift to Self-Service," *HR Magazine,* March 2005, http://web7.infotrac.galegroup.com; and Bill Roberts, "Empowerment or Imposition?," *HR Magazine,* June 2004, http://web7.infotrac.galegroup.com.

45. See Weatherly, "HR Technology."

46. J. O'Toole and E. Lawler III, *The New American Workplace* (New York: Palgrave Macmillan, 2006).

47. D. M. Rousseau, "Psychological and Implied Contracts in Organizations," *Employee Rights and Responsibilities Journal* 2 (1989), pp. 121–29.

48. D. Rousseau, "Changing the Deal While Keeping the People," *Academy of Management Executive* 11 (1996), pp. 50–61; M. A. Cavanaugh and R. Noe, "Antecedents and Consequences of the New Psychological Contract," *Journal of Organizational Behavior* 20 (1999), pp. 323–40.

49. P. Kiger, "Flexibility to the Fullest," *Workforce Management,* September 25, 2006, pp. 1, 16–23.

CHAPTER 2

1. www.thestevenfletcherstory.ca/about_steven.php, retrieved March 23, 2012; Paul Samyn, "Tearing Down Barriers Big Job," *Winnipeg Free Press,* July 16, 2004, p. A3; Paul Egan, "He's Breaking Barriers," *Winnipeg Free Press,* July 4, 2004, pp. A1, A2; Parliament of Canada website, www2.parl.gc.ca, retrieved April 13, 2008.

2. "Canada's Best Diversity Employers," www.canadastop100.com/diversity, retrieved March 23, 2012.

3. Shannon Klie, "Lots of Talk, Not Much Action on Diversity," *Canadian HR Reporter,* January 15, 2008, p. 1.

4. "2003 Employment Equity Annual Report," p. 24, www.hrsdc.gc.ca/en, retrieved July 13, 2004.

5. "HR Leaders Talk," *Canadian HR Reporter,* January 28, 2008, pp. 11-12.

6. "Business Results Through Health and Safety," Ontario Workplace Safety and Insurance Board website, www.wsib.on.ca/wsib/website.nsf, retrieved April 19, 2004.

7. www.ccohs.ca/oshanswers/legisl/ire.htm, retrieved February 25, 2004.

8. "Anti-Discriminatory Casebook," www.chrcccdp.ca/Legis&Poli/AntiDiscriminationCasebook_Recueil Decisions, retrieved February 18, 2004.

9. Ran LeClair, "The Evolution of Accommodation," *Canadian HR Reporter,* February 24, 2003, p. 7.

10. "Bona Fide Occupational Requirements and Bona Fide Justifications Under the Canadian Human Rights Act," pp. 4, 5, www.chrc-ccdp.ca/publications/BFOR, retrieved February 18, 2004.

11. "Mandatory Retirement in Canada," www.hrsdc.gc.ca/en/lp/spila/clli/eslc/19Mandatory_Retirement.shtml, retrieved October 20, 2008; "Retiring Mandatory Retirement," February 21, 2008, www.cbc.ca/news/background/retirement/mandatory_retirement.html, retrieved October 20, 2008.

12. www.chrc-ccdp.ca/discrimination/apfa_uppt/page 4-eng.aspx, retrieved March 23, 2012

13. Canadian Human Rights Commission, "Fact Sheet: Duty to Accommodate," January 2006, p. 2.

14. "Anti-Harassment Policies for the Workplace: An Employer's Guide," p. 4, www.chrc-ccdp.ca/ publications, retrieved February 26, 2004.

15. www.senecac.on.ca/policies/srr.html, retrieved March 26, 2012.

16. "Anti-Harassment Policies for the Workplace: An Employer's Guide."

17. Bernard Warner, "European Law Puts Employees on Hook for E-Mail Porn," *Financial Post*, April 28, 2004, p. FP14.

18. B. Carton, "At Jenny Craig, Men Are Ones Who Claim Sex Discrimination," *The Wall Street Journal*, November 29, 1995, p. A1; "Male-on-Male Harassment Suit Won," *Houston Chronicle*, August 12, 1995, p. 21A.

19. Gerry Bellet, "Harassed Woman Awarded $950,000," *Leader-Post*, January 24, 2006, p. A3.

20. Patrick White, "Bullying a Serious Job Hazard," *The Globe and Mail*, March 10, 2008, www.theglobe andmail.com/servlet/story/RTGAM.20080310. wlbullying10/BNStory/lifeWork/home?cid=al_gam_ mostview, retrieved October 20, 2008.

21. Virginia Galt, "Cracking Down on Workplace Harassment," *The Globe and Mail*, October 5, 2007, www.theglobeandmail.com/servlet/Page/document/ v5/content/subscribe?user_URL=http://www.the globeandmail.com%2Fservlet%2Fstory%2FLAC .20071006.RCOACH06%2FTPStory%2FBusine ss&ord=22120745&brand=theglobeandmail&fo rce_login=true, retrieved October 20, 2008.

22. www.chrc-ccdp.ca/employment_equity/visible minorities-en.asp, retrieved April 3, 2004.

23. www.chrc-ccdp.ca/employment_equity/aboriginal- en.asp, retrieved April 3, 2004.

24. www.chrc-ccdp.ca/employment_equity/disabilities- en.asp, retrieved April 3, 2004.

25. Human Resources and Social Development Canada, "Employment Equity Act: Annual Report 2006," p. 31.

26. Ibid., p. 35.

27. www.priv.gc.ca/fs-fi/02_05_d_15_e.cfm#contenttop, retrieved March 23, 2012.

28. "A Guide for Canadians: What Is the Personal Information Protection and Electronic Documents Act?," www.privcom.gc.ca/information.

29. Jacquie McNish and Tara Perkins, CIBC overtime lawsuit dismissed, *The Globe and Mail*, June 19, 2009, www.theglobeandmail.com/report-on-business/ cibc-overtime-lawsuit-dismissed/article1188529/, retrieved March 24, 2012; "CN Faces $250M Class Action Lawsuit," www.cbc.ca/money/ story/2008/03/25/en.html, retrieved April 14, 2008; "CN Hit with Class-Action Lawsuit on Unpaid Overtime," *Canadian HR Reporter*, website posting, www.hrreporter.com, March 25, 2008; Gary Norris, "KPMG Faces Employee Class Action Lawsuit in Ontario for Overtime Pay," www.cbc.ca/cp/business/ 070904/b0904111A.html, retrieved October 4, 2007; Virginia Galt and Janet McFarland, "CIBC Faces Massive Overtime Lawsuit," *The Globe and Mail*, June 5, 2007, www.theglobeandmail.com, retrieved March 18, 2008; "CIBC Faces $600-Million Suit over Unpaid Overtime," *CanWest News Service*, June 5, 2007, www.canada.com/components, retrieved March 18, 2008.

30. www.labour.gov.on.ca/english/es/pubs/guide/organ donor.php, retrieved March 23, 2012; Lesley Young, "Job-Protected Leave for Organ Donations Possible," *Canadian HR Reporter*, October 8, 2007, p. 1.

31. www.chrc-ccdp.ca/publications/employee_rights_ en.asp, retrieved July 23, 2004.

32. Matthew McClearn, "Mind the Gap," *Canadian Business*, November 5, 2007, pp. 21–22.

33. Sarah Schmidt, "Report Says Male Profs Paid More Than Females," *Winnipeg Free Press*, July 17, 2004, p. A11.

34. Ibid.

35. David Brown, "New Rules Proposed for Pay Equity," *Canadian HR Reporter*, May 31, 2004, p. 1, 3.

36. Canadian Human Rights Commission, "2007 Annual Report," p. 6, www.chrc-ccdp.ca/publication/ ar_2007_ra/page6-en.asp#41, retrieved April 14, 2008.

37. "Privacy Commissioner of Canada: A Guide for Canadians," www.privcom.gc.ca/information, retrieved March 21, 2004.

38. www.labour.gov.on.ca/english/hs/, retrieved March 23, 2012.

39. www.ccohs.ca/oshanswers/legisl/ire.htm, retrieved February 25, 2004.

40. "Information on Occupational Health and Safety," Government of Canada website, http://info.load-otea .hrdc-drhc.gc.ca/publications/ohs/committees.pdf, retrieved February 25, 2004.

41. Mark Rogers, "Supporting Our Supervisors," p. 4, www.hrpao.org/Knowledge_Centre/kc_s04120403 .asp, retrieved April 12, 2004.

42. Russel Zinn, "Driving Under Influence—of a Cell-phone," *Canadian HR Reporter*, February 25, 2008, p. 5.

43. "Initiative Puts Driver Safety First," *Canadian Occupational Health and Safety News*, August 2, 2004, www.ohscanada.com/article.asp?id=33374& issue=08032004, retrieved August 3, 2004.

44. "Nova Scotia Gives Occupational Health and Safety Officers New Enforcement Tool," *Canadian HR Reporter*, February 2, 2004, www.hrreporter.com, retrieved February 5, 2004.

45. Ann Perry, "Workplace Safety Gets a Boost," *Toronto Star*, March 27, 2004, p. D10.

46. "Occupational Health and Safety: Labour Operations," http://info.load-otea.hrdc-drhc.gc.ca/~oshweb/ homeen.shtml, retrieved February 26, 2004.

47. Uyen Vu, "Right to Refuse Dangerous Work Expands," *Canadian HR Reporter*, August 9, 2004, pp. 1, 2.

48. Andy Shaw, "Slow Evolution from WHMIS to GHS," *Canadian HR Reporter*, March 10, 2008, p. 11.

49. Ibid.

50. "The Globally Harmonized System of Classification and Labelling of Chemicals (GHS)," *Health Canada,* www.hc-sc.gc.ca/ahc-asc/intactiv/ghs-sgh/index_e.html, retrieved May 29, 2008.

51. Association of Workers' Compensation Boards of Canada, "Number of Fatalities, by Jurisdiction, 1993–2010," Table 22, www.awcbc.org, retrieved March 23, 2012.

52. J. Roughton, "Managing a Safety Program Through Job Hazard Analysis," *Professional Safety* 37 (1992), pp. 28–31.

53. M. A. Verespec, "OSHA Reform Fails Again," *Industry Week,* November 2, 1992, p. 36.

54. Roughton, ibid.

55. R. G. Hallock and D. A. Weaver, "Controlling Losses and Enhancing Management Systems with TOR Analysis," *Professional Safety* 35 (1990), pp. 24–26.

56. H. Herbstman, "Controlling Losses the Burger King Way," *Risk Management* 37 (1990), pp. 22–30.

57. "Young Worker Awareness Program," www.youngworker.ca/English/index.htm, retrieved August 18, 2004.

58. Amanda Silliker, "Shift Workers' Poor Diet a Health Hazard," *Canadian HR Reporter,* February 13, 2012, p. 1, 12.

59. T. Markus, "How to Set Up a Safety Awareness Program," *Supervision* 51 (1990), pp. 14–16.

60. J. Agnew and A. J. Saruda, "Age and Fatal Work-Related Falls," *Human Factors* 35, no. 4 (1994), pp. 731–736.

61. R. King, "Active Safety Programs, Education Can Help Prevent Back Injuries," *Occupational Health and Safety* 60 (1991), pp. 49–52

62. T. W. Turriff, "NSPB Suggests 10-Step Program to Prevent Eye Injury," *Occupational Health and Safety* 60 (1991), pp. 62–66.

63. "BC Firm Receives Safety Award," *Canadian Health and Safety News,* www.ohscanada.com/article.asp, retrieved August 13, 2004.

64. Shannon Klie, "Do Incentives Help Change Behaviour?," *Canadian HR Reporter,* April 21, 2008, www.hrreporter.com, retrieved May 7, 2008.

65. Nikki Pavlov, "A Healthy Workplace Means Recognizing Stress Is the Enemy," *Canadian HR Reporter,* April 9, 2001, www.hrreporter.com, retrieved September 29, 2004.

66. J. C. Erfurt, A. Foote, and M. A. Heirich, "The Cost-Effectiveness of Work Site Wellness Programs for Hypertension Control, Weight Loss, Smoking Cessation and Exercise," *Personnel Psychology* 45 (1992), pp. 5–27.

67. Amanda Silliker, "Shift Workers' Poor Diet a Health Hazard," *Canadian HR Reporter,* February 13, 2012, p. 1, 12.

68. Brian Lindenberg, "Choosing the Right EAP," *Canadian HR Reporter,* March 24, 2008, pp. 22, 27.

69. Amanda Silliker, "Employers in Best Position to Fight Depression," *Canadian HR Reporter,* January 30, 2012, p. 3, 8.

70. M. Janssens, J. M. Brett, and E J. Smith, "Confirmatory Cross-Cultural Research: Testing the Viability of a Corporation-wide Safety Policy," *Academy of Management Journal* 38 (1995), pp. 364–82.

CHAPTER 3

1. "A Day in the Life," Careers in Oil + Gas website, http://careersinoilandgas.com/working-in-oil-gas-/a-day-in-the-life-.aspx, retrieved July 26, 2012.

2. D. Little, "Even the Supervisor Is Expendable: The Internet Allows Factories to Be Managed from Anywhere," *Business Week,* July 23, 2001, p. 78.

3. J. R. Hollenbeck, H. Moon, A. Ellis, et al., "Structural Contingency Theory and Individual Differences: Examination of External and Internal Person-Team Fit," *Journal of Applied Psychology* 87 (2002), pp. 599–606.

4. W. Cascio, *Applied Psychology in Personnel Management,* 4th ed. (Englewood Cliffs, NJ: Prentice Hall, 1991).

5. P. Wright and K. Wexley, "How to Choose the Kind of Job Analysis You Really Need," *Personnel,* May 1985, pp. 51–55.

6. C. Joinson, "Refocusing Job Descriptions," *HR Magazine,* January 2001, Findarticles.com.

7. "Middle Management Competency Profile," www.canadascapital.gc.ca/sites/default/files/pubs/ncc_middle_management_competency_profile_0.pdf, retrieved March 10, 2012.

8. G. Koretz, "Perils of the Graveyard Shift: Poor Health and Low Productivity," *Business Week,* March 10, 1997, p. 22; C. R. Maiwald, J. L. Pierce, and J. W. Newstrom, "Workin' 8 P.M. to 8 A.M. and Lovin' Every Minute of It," *Workforce,* July 1997, pp. 30–36.

9. A. O'Reilly, "Skill Requirements: Supervisor–Subordinate Conflict," *Personnel Psychology* 26 (1973), pp. 75–80; J. Hazel, J. Madden, and R. Christal, "Agreement between Worker–Supervisor Descriptions of the Worker's Job," *Journal of Industrial Psychology* 2 (1964), pp. 71–79.

10. *PAQ Newsletter,* August 1989.

11. E. Fleishman and M. Reilly, *Handbook of Human Abilities* (Palo Alto, CA: Consulting Psychologists Press, 1992); E. Fleishman and M. Mumford, "The Ability Requirements Scales," in *The Job Analysis Handbook for Business, Industry, and Government,* ed. S. Gael (New York: Wiley), pp. 917–35.

12. Canadian Human Rights Commission website, www.ccrc-ccdp.ca/discrimination/barrier_free-en.asp, retrieved April 3, 2004.

13. M. K. Lindell, C. S. Clause, C. J. Brandt, and R. S. Landis, "Relationship between Organizational Context and Job Analysis Ratings," *Journal of Applied Psychology* 83 (1998), pp. 769–76.

14. D. S. DeRue, J. R. Hollenbeck, M. D. Johnson, D. R. Ilgen, and D. K. Jundt, "How Different Team

Downsizing Approaches Influence Team-Level Adaptation and Performance," *Academy of Management Journal* 51 (2008), pp. 182–196; F. Hanson, "A Leg Up in Down Times," *Workforce Management,* January 19, 2009, p. 14.

15. R. Hackman and G. Oldham, *Work Redesign* (Boston: Addison-Wesley, 1980).

16. W. E. Byrnes, "Making the Job Meaningful All the Way Down the Line," *Business Week,* May 1, 2006, p. 60.

17. F. W. Bond, P. E. Flaxman, and D. Bunce, "The Influence of Psychological Flexibility on Work Redesign: Mediated Moderation of a Work Reorganization Intervention," *Journal of Applied Psychology* 93 (2008), pp. 645–654.

18. M. A. Campion, G. J. Medsker, and A. C. Higgs, "Relations Between Work Group Characteristics and Effectiveness: Implications for Designing Effective Work Groups," *Personnel Psychology* 46 (1993), pp. 823–50.

19. "A Few Facts About Distributed Work," *Canadian HR Reporter,* August 14, 2006, p. 21.

20. Uyen Vu, "A Variety of Options Gives Boost to Remote Work," *Canadian HR Reporter,* August 14, 2006, p. 15.

21. Ernest B. Akyeampong, "Working at Home: An Update," *Perspectives,* June 2007, p. 16 (Statistics Canada, Catalogue No. 75-001-XIE).

22. "Evolution of the Workplace: The Growing Demand for Distributed Work," *Suite Works,* www.suiteworks .ca/pdfs/Revolution@Work%20SuiteWorks.pdf, retrieved March 23, 2008.

23. See, for example, S. Sonnentag and F. R. H. Zijistra, "Job Characteristics and Off-the-Job Activities as Predictors of Need for Recovery, Well-Being, and Fatigue," *Journal of Applied Psychology* 91 (2006), pp. 330–350.

24. D. May and C. Schwoerer, "Employee Health by Design: Using Employee Involvement Teams in Ergonomic Job Redesign," *Personnel Psychology* 47 (1994), pp. 861–86.

25. S. F. Brown, "International's Better Way to Build Trucks," *Fortune,* February 19, 2001, pp. 210k–210v.

26. Canadian Centre for Occupational Health and Safety website, www.ccohs.ca/oshanswers/ergonommics, retrieved April 28, 2004.

27. Peter Budnick and Rachel Michael, "What Is Cognitive Ergonomics?," *Ergonomics Today,* www.ergoweb.com/news/detail.cfm?id=352, retrieved March 25, 2008.

28. N. W. Van Yperen and M. Hagerdoom, "Do High Job Demands Increase Intrinsic Motivation or Fatigue or Both? The Role of Job Support and Social Control," *Academy of Management Journal* 46 (2003), pp. 339-348; and N. W. Van Yperen and O Janseen, "Fatigued and Dissatisfied or Fatigued but Satisfied? Goal Orientations and Responses to High Job Demands," *Academy of Management Journal* 45 (2002) pp. 1161–1171.

29. Steve Ranger, "Email: The Root of Your Work Stress?" Silicon.com, August 13, 2007, http:// hardware.silicon.com/desktops/.

30. "Email Marketing: Despite Significant Increases in Email Spam, Canadian's Willingness to Subscribe to Permission Based Email Continues," June 26, 2007, www.ipsos.com, retrieved March 21, 2008.

31. "The Office of the Future Isn't Paperless. It's Wireless. And It's Wherever You Are," December 19, 2006, www.ipsos.com, retrieved March 21, 2008.

CHAPTER 4

1. Joe Castaldo, "Who the Hell is Responsible for This Anyway?" *Canadian Business,* February 20, 2012, pp. 46–52; Iain Marlow, "Restarting Research In Motion," *The Globe and Mail Report on Business,* January 28, 2012, pp. B1, B6; Matt Hartley, "RIM's Damaged Brand," *National Post,* September 22, 2011, p. FP 10.

2. I. Brat, "Where Have All the Welders Gone, as Manufacturing and Repair Boom?" *Wall Street Journal,* August 15, 2006, pp. B2–B3.

3. Matt Hartley, "Other Shoe Drops for RIM Staff; 2000 Announced Layoffs by Research In Motion," *National Post,* July 26, 2011, p. FP1.

4. J. P. Guthrie, "Dumb and Dumber: The Impact of Downsizing on Firm Performance as Moderated by Industry Conditions," *Organization Science* 19 (2008), pp. 108–123; and J. McGregor, A. McConnon, and D. Kiley, "Customer Service in a Shrinking Economy," *Business Week,* February 19, 2009, pp. 34–35.

5. C. D. Zatzick and R. D. Iverson, "High-Involvement Management and Workforce Reduction: Competitive Advantage or Disadvantage?" *Academy of Management Journal* 49 (2006), pp. 101-112.

6. P. P. Shaw, "Network Destruction: The Structural Implications of Downsizing," *Academy of Management Journal* 43 (2000), pp. 101–12.

7. W. E Cascio, "Downsizing: What Do We Know? What Have We Learned?," *Academy of Management Executive* 7 (1993), pp. 95–104.

8. Justin Lahart, "Even in a Recovery, Some Jobs Won't Return," *Wall Street Journal,* January 12, 2010, http://onlinewsj.com; and Sarah E. Needleman, "Entrepreneurs Prefer to Keep Staffs Lean," *Wall Street Journal,* March 2, 2010, http://online.wsj.com.

9. P. Coy, "Golden Paychecks," *Business Week,* July 2, 2007, p. 13; and J. Weber, "This Time Old Hands Keep Their Jobs," *Business Week,* February 9, 2009, p. 50.

10. Olga Kharif, "The Rise of the Four-Day Work Week?" *Business Week,* December 18, 2008, www.businessweek.com.

11. R. Stodghill, "The Coming Job Bottleneck," *Business Week,* March 24, 1997, pp. 184–85.

12. S. Kim and D. Feldman, "Healthy, Wealthy, or Wise: Predicting Actual Acceptances of Early Retirement

Incentives at Three Points in Time," *Personnel Psychology* 51 (1998), pp. 623–42.

13. D. Fandray, "Gray Matters," *Workforce,* July 2000, pp. 27–32.

14. P. Engardio, "Let's Offshore the Lawyers," *Business-Week,* September 18, 2006, pp. 42–43.

15. Steve Minter, "Moving Sourcing Closer to Home," *Industry Week,* September 2009, Business & Company Resource Center, http://galenet.galegroup.com; and Josh Hyatt, "The New Calculus of Offshoring," *CFO,* October 2009, pp. 58–62.

16. A. Tiwana, Does Firm Modularity Complement Ignorance? A Field Study of Software Outsourcing Alliances," *Strategic Management Journal* 29 (2008), pp. 1241–1252.

17. Minter, "Moving Sourcing Closer"; and Hyatt, "The New Calculus of Osffshoring."

18. P. Engardio, "The Future of Outsourcing," *Business-Week,* January 30, 2006, pp. 50–58.

19. "Employment Equity in the Public Service of Canada 2005–2006: Annual Report to Parliament," *Canada Public Service Agency,* www.psagency-agencefp.gc.ca, retrieved March 18, 2008.

20. W. J Rothwell, *Effective Succession Planning,* 2nd ed. (New York: AMACOM, 2001).

21. B. E. Dowell, "Succession Planning," in *Implementing Organizational Interventions,* ed. J. Hedge and E. D. Pulakos (San Francisco: Jossey-Bass, 2002), pp. 78–109.

22. A. E. Barber, *Recruiting Employees* (Thousand Oaks, CA: Sage, 1998).

23. J. D. Olian and S. L. Rynes, "Organizational Staffing: Integrating Practice with Strategy," *Industrial Relations* 23 (1984), pp. 170–83.

24. "Employers Take Recruiting Seriously," http://globeandmail.workopolis.com, retrieved March 16, 2004.

25. G. T. Milkovich and J. M. Newman, *Compensation* (Homewood, IL: Richard D. Irwin, 1990).

26. Kim Peters, "Employment Branding Best Way to Reach Untapped Talent," *HR Voice,* November 1, 2007, www.hrvoice.org/story, retrieved March 18, 2008.

27. Kim Peters, "Passive Jobseekers Solution to Labour Woes," *Canadian HR Reporter,* July 16, 2007, p. 18.

28. Carolyn Brandon, "Truth in Recruitment Branding," *HR Magazine* 50, no. 11 (November 2005), pp. 89–96.

29. Patrick J. Kiger, "Burnishing Your Employment Brand," *Workforce Management,* October 22, 2007, http://web.eboscost.com, retrieved March 18, 2008.

30. Judith MacBride-King, "Governments, Start Your Recruitment Campaigns," *Canadian HR Reporter,* October 8, 2007, p. 18.

31. M. A. Conrad and S. D. Ashworth, "Recruiting Source Effectiveness: A Meta-Analysis and Reexamination of Two Rival Hypotheses," paper presented at annual meeting of Society of Industrial/Organizational Psychology, Chicago, 1986.

32. Breaugh, *Recruitment.*

33. Susan Singh, "Looking Inside for Leaders at CCL, Alliance Atlantis," *Canadian HR Reporter,* January 12, 2004, www.hrreporter.com, retrieved February 17, 2004.

34. Breaugh, *Recruitment,* pp. 113–114.

35. R. S. Schuler and S. E. Jackson, "Linking Competitive Strategies with Human Resource Management Practices," *Academy of Management Executive* 1 (1987), pp. 207–19.

36. G. Colvin, "How to Manage Your Business in a Recession," *Fortune,* January 19, 2009, pp. 88–93; M. Orey, "Hang the Recession, Let's Bulk Up," *BusinessWeek,* February 2, 2009, pp. 80–81; and J. Collin, "How Great Companies Turn Chris into Opportunity," *Fortune,* February 2, 2009, p. 49.

37. Gerry Crispin and Mark Mehler, "Career Xroads 9th Annual Source of Hire Study," February 2010, www.careerxroads.com.

38. S. Gegley, "Behind 'Shortage' of Engineers Employers Grow More Choosey," *Wall Street Journal,* November 16, 2005, pp. A1, A12.

39. Eric Beneroff, "Microsoft Takes on CareerBuilder Stake," *Chicago Tribune,* May 10, 2007, sec. 3, pp. 1, 6.

40. Amanda Silliker, "*Recruiters connect via LinkedIn,*" Canadian HR Reporter, September 26, 2011, p. 2.

41. B. Dineen and R. A. Noe, "Effects of Customization on Applicant Decisions and Applicant Pool Characteristics in a Web-Based Recruiting Context," *Journal of Applied Psychology* 94 (2009), pp. 224-234.

42. Antonio Da Luz, "Video Enhances Online Job Ads," *Canadian HR Reporter,* February 11, 2008, p. 16.

43. P. Smith, "Sources Used by Employers When Hiring College Grads," *Personnel Journal,* February 1995, p. 25.

44. J. W. Boudreau and S. L. Rynes, "Role of Recruitment in Staffing Utility Analysis," *Journal of Applied Psychology* 70 (1985), pp. 354–66.

45. R. Hawk, *The Recruitment Function* (New York: American Management Association, 1967).

46. C. K. Stevens, "Effects of Preinterview Beliefs on Applicants' Reactions to Campus Interviews," *Academy of Management Journal* 40 (1997), pp. 947–66.

47. C. Collins, "The Interactive Effects of Recruitment Practices and Product Awareness on Job Seekers' Employer Knowledge and Application Behaviors," *Journal of Applied Psychology* 92 (2007), pp. 180–190.

48. M. S. Taylor and T. J. Bergman, "Organizational Recruitment Activities and Applicants' Reactions at Different Stages of the Recruitment Process," *Personnel Psychology* 40 (1984), pp. 261–285; and C. D. Fisher, D. R. Ilgen, and W. D. Hoyer, "Source Credibility, Information Favorability, and Job Offer Acceptance," *Academy of Management Journal* 22 (1979), pp. 94–103.

49. L. M. Graves and G. N. Powell, "The Effect of Sex Similarity on Recruiters' Evaluation of Actual Applicants: A Test of the Similarity-Attraction Paradigm," *Personnel Psychology* 48 (1995), pp. 85–98.

50. R. D. Tretz and T. A. Judge, "Realistic Job Previews: A Test of the Adverse Self-Selection Hypothesis," *Journal of Applied Psychology* 83 (1998), pp. 330–337.

51. P. Hom, R. W. Griffeth, L. E. Palich, and J. S. Bracker, "An Exploratory Investigation into Theoretical Mechanisms Underlying Realistic Job Previews," *Personnel Psychology* 51 (1998), pp. 421–451.

52. G. M. McEvoy and W. F. Cascio, "Strategies for Reducing Employee Turnover: A Meta-Analysis," *Journal of Applied Psychology* 70 (1985), pp. 342–353; and S. L. Premack and J P. Wanous, "A Meta-Analysis of Realistic Job Preview Experiments," *Journal of Applied Psychology* 70 (1985), pp. 706–719.

53. P. G. Irving and J. P. Meyer, "Reexamination of the Met-Expectations Hypothesis: A Longitudinal Analysis," *Journal of Applied Psychology* 79 (1995), pp. 937–949.

54. R. W. Walters, "It's Time We Become Pros," *Journal of College Placement* 12 (1985), pp. 30–33.

55. S. L. Rynes, R. D. Bretz, and B. Gerhart, "The Importance of Recruitment in Job Choice: A Different Way of Looking," *Personnel Psychology* 44 (1991), pp. 487–522.

CHAPTER 5

1. "Be careful Who You Google," *Investment Executive,* March 1, 2012; "Pitfalls of Social Media in Background Checks," *24 Hours Toronto,* March 19, 2012; Amanda Silliker, "Tread Carefully with Social Media Checks," *Canadian HR Reporter,* January 30, 2012, p. 1, 11.

2. www.intelligencematters.ca/en/jobs/intelligence-officer, retrieved April 1, 2012; "Intelligence Officers" and "Stages in the 10 Recruitment Process," www.csis-scrs.gc.ca, retrieved June 23, 2004.

3. J. C. Nunnally, *Psychometric Theory* (New York: McGraw-Hill, 1978).

4. N. Schmitt, R. Z. Gooding, R. A. Noe, and M. Kirsch, "Meta-Analysis of Validity Studies Published Between 1964 and 1982 and the Investigation of Study Characteristics," *Personnel Psychology* 37 (1984), pp. 407–22.

5. C. H. Lawshe, "Inferences from Personnel Tests and Their Validity," *Journal of Applied Psychology* 70 (1985), pp. 237–38.

6. D. D. Robinson, "Content-Oriented Personnel Selection in a Small Business Setting," *Personnel Psychology* 34 (1981), pp. 77–87.

7. M. V. Rafter, "Assessment Providers Scoring Well," *Workforce Management,* January 19, 2009, pp. 24–25.

8. F. L. Schmidt and J. E. Hunter, "The Future of Criterion-Related Validity," *Personnel Psychology* 33 (1980), pp. 41–60; F. L. Schmidt, J. E. Hunter, and K. Pearlman, "Task Differences as Moderators of Aptitude Test Validity: A Red Herring," *Journal*

of *Applied Psychology* 66 (1982), pp. 166–85; R. L. Gutenberg, R. D. Arvey, H. G. Osburn, and R. P. Jeanneret, "Moderating Effects of Decision-Making/Information Processing Dimensions on Test Validities," *Journal of Applied Psychology* 68 (1983), pp. 600–08.

9. www.chrc-ccdp.ca/publications/screening_employment-eng.aspx, retrieved April 1, 2012.

10. T. W Dougherty, D. B. Turban, and J. C. Callender, "Confirming First Impressions in the Employment Interview: A Field Study of Interviewer Behavior," *Journal of Applied Psychology* 79 (1994), pp. 659–65.

11. Alice Snell, "Using Technology in Sourcing Talent," *Canadian HR Reporter,* January 20, 2007, www.hrreporter.com, retrieved April 6, 2008.

12. Judy Greenwald, "Layoffs May Spark Defamation Suits," *Business Insurance,* June 1, 2009, Business & Company Resource Center, http://galenet.galegroup.com.

13. "Guide to Screening and Selection in Employment," May 2007, www.chrc-ccdp.ca/publications/screening_employment-eng.aspx, retrieved April 1, 2012.

14. A. Ryan and M. Lasek, "Negligent Hiring and Defamation: Areas of Liability Related to Preemployment Inquiries," *Personnel Psychology* 44 (1991), pp. 293–319.

15. A. Long, "Addressing the Cloud over Employee References: A Survey of Recently Enacted State Legislation," *William and Mary Law Review* 39 (October 1997), pp. 177–228.

16. Lynne Van Buskirk "Can I Get a Reference?," *Canadian HR Reporter,* March 10, 2008, www.hrreporter.com, retrieved April 3, 2008.

17. Ann Zimmerman, "Wal-Mart to Probe Job Applicants," *The Wall Street Journal,* August 12, 2004, pp. A3, A6.

18. "Corporate Testimonials," http://backcheck.net/testimonials.htm#scotiabank, retrieved April 1, 2012; http://backcheck.net/background-check-solutions-and-services.htm, retrieved April 1, 2012.

19. Jim Middlemiss, "Didn't You Check?" *National Post,* January 31, 2007, p. WK3.

20. Shannon Klie, "Weeding Out the Fakes," *Canadian HR Reporter,* May 7, 2007, www.hrreporter.com, retrieved April 6, 2008.

21. Public Service Commission of Canada, "Office Skills Test," July 7, 2007, www.psc-cfp.gc.ca/ppc/assessment_pg2_ba_e.htm, retrieved April 6, 2008.

22. L. C. Buffardi, E. A. Fleishman, R. A. Morath, and P. M. McCarthy, "Relationships Between Ability Requirements and Human Errors in Job Tasks," *Journal of Applied Psychology* 85 (2000), pp. 551–64; J. Hogan, "Structure of Physical Performance in Occupational Tasks," *Journal of Applied Psychology* 76 (1991), pp. 495–507.

23. "RCMP Fact Sheets—Recruitment," www.rcmp-grc.gc.ca/factsheets/fact_recruit_e.htm, retrieved April 6, 2008.

24. www.psc-cfp.gc.ca/ppc/assessment, retrieved February 13, 2004.

25. M. J. Ree, J. A. Earles, and M. S. Teachout, "Predicting Job Performance: Not Much More Than *g*," *Journal of Applied Psychology* 79 (1994), pp. 518–24; L. S. Gottfredson, "The *g* Factor in Employment," *Journal of Vocational Behavior* 29 (1986), pp. 293–96; J. E. Hunter and R. H. Hunter, "Validity and Utility of Alternative Predictors of Job Performance," *Psychological Bulletin* 96 (1984), pp. 72–98; Gutenberg et al., "Moderating Effects"; F. L. Schmidt, J. G. Berner, and J. E. Hunter, "Racial Differences in Validity of Employment Tests: Reality or Illusion," *Journal of Applied Psychology* 58 (1974), pp. 5–6; J. A. LePine, J. A. Colquitt, and A. Erez, "Adaptability to Changing Task Contexts: Effects of General Cognitive Ability, Conscientiousness, and Openness to Experience," *Personnel Psychology* 53 (2000), pp. 563–93.

26. See, for example, C. Winkler, "Job Tryouts Go Virtual," *HRMagazine,* September 2006, pp. 10–15.

27. "Human Resources Consultant Simulation Exercise," www.psc-cfp.gc.ca/ppc-cpp/psc-tests-cfp/sim-410-eng.htm, retrieved April 4, 2012.

28. D. J Schleiger, V. Venkataramani, F. P. Morgeson, and M. A. Campion, "So You Didn't Get the Job…Now What Do You Think? Examining Opportunity to Perform Fairness Perceptions," *Personnel Psychology* 59 (2006), pp. 559–90.

29. F. L. Schmidt and J. E. Hunter, "The Validity and Utility of Selection Methods in Personnel Psychology: Practical and Theoretical Implications of 85 Years of Research Findings," *Psychological Bulletin* 124 (1998), pp. 262–74.

30. W. Arthur, E. A. Day, T. L. McNelly, and P. S. Edens, "Meta-Analysis of the Criterion-Related Validity of Assessment Center Dimensions," *Personnel Psychology* 56 (2003), pp. 125–54; C. E. Lance, T. A. Lambert, A. G. Gewin, F. Lievens, and J. M. Conway, "Revised Estimates of Dimension and Exercise Variance Components in Assessment Center Postexercise Dimension Ratings," *Journal of Applied Psychology* 89 (2004), pp. 377–85.

31. N. M. Dudley, K. A. Orvis, J. E. Lebieki, and J. M. Cortina, "A Meta-analytic Investigation of Conscientiousness in the Prediction of Job Performance: Examining the Intercorrelation and the Incremental Validity of Narrow Traits," *Journal of Applied Psychology* 91 (2006), pp. 40–57; W. S. Dunn, M. K. Mount, M. R. Barrick, and D. S. Ones, "Relative Importance of Personality and General Mental Ability on Managers' Judgments of Applicant Qualifications," *Journal of Applied Psychology* 79 (1995), pp. 500–509; P. M. Wright, K. M. Kacmar, G. C. McMahan, and K. Deleeuw, "P=f(M × A): Cognitive Ability as a Moderator of the Relationship between Personality and Job Performance," *Journal of Management* 21 (1995), pp. 1129–1139.

32. M. Mount, M. R. Barrick, and J. P. Strauss, "Validity of Observer Ratings of the Big Five Personality Factors," *Journal of Applied Psychology* 79 (1994), pp. 272–280.

33. L. A. Witt and G. R. Ferris, "Social Skill as Moderator of the Conscientiousness-Performance Relationship: Convergent Results across Four Studies," *Journal of Applied Psychology* 88 (2003), pp. 809-820.

34. N. Schmitt and F. L. Oswald, "The Impact of Corrections for Faking on the Validity of Non-cognitive Measures in Selection Contexts," *Journal of Applied Psychology* (2006), pp. 613–621.

35. S. A. Birkland, T. M. Manson, J. L. Kisamore, M. T. Brannick, and M. A. Smith, "Faking on Personality Measures," *International Journal of Selection and Assessment* 14 (December 2006), pp. 317–335.

36. C. H. Van Iddekinge, P. H. Raymark, and P. L Rother, "Assessing Personality with a Structured Employment Interview: Construct-Related Validity and Susceptibility to Response Inflation," *Journal of Applied Psychology* 90 (2005), pp. 536–552; R. Mueller-Hanson, E. D. Heggestad, and G. C. Thornton, "Faking and Selection: Considering the Use of Personality from Select-In and Select-Out Perspectives," *Journal of Applied Psychology* 88 (2003), pp. 348–355; and N. L. Vasilopoulos, J. M. Cucina, and J.M. McElreath, "Do Warnings of Response Verification Moderate the Relationship between Personality and Cognitive Ability?" *Journal of Applied Psychology* 90 (2005), pp. 306–322.

37. E. Freudenheim, "Personality Testing Controversial, but Poised to Take Off," *Workforce Management,* August 14, 2006, p. 38.

38. V. Knight, "Personality Tests as Hiring Tools," *Wall Street Journal*, March 15, 2006, p. B1; G. L. Stewards, I. S. Fulmer, and M. R. Barrick, "An Exploration of Member Roles as a Multilevel Linking Mechanism for Individual Traits and Team Outcomes," *Personnel Psychology* 58 (2005), pp. 343–365; and M. Mount, R. Ilies, and E. Johnson, "Relationship of Personality Traits and Counterproductive Work Behaviors: The Mediation Effects of Job Satisfaction," *Personnel Psychology* 59 (2006), pp. 591–622.

39. A. Hedger, "Employee Screening: Common Challenges, Smart Solutions," *Workforce Management,* March 17, 2008, pp. 39–46; and J. Welch and S. Welch, "Team Building: Right and Wrong," *BusinessWeek,* November 24, 2008, p. 130.

40. D. S. One, C. Viswesvaran, and E. L. Schmidt, "Comprehensive Meta-Analysis of Integrity Test Validities: Findings and Implications for Personnel Selection and Theories of Job Performance," *Journal of Applied Psychology* 78 (1993), pp. 679–703; H. J. Bernardin and D. K. Cooke, "Validity of an Honesty Test in Predicting Theft Among Convenience Store Employees," *Academy of Management Journal* 36 (1993), pp. 1079–1106.

41. www.chrc-ccdp.ca/legislation, retrieved May 31, 2004.

42. "Canadian Human Rights Commission Policy on Alcohol and Drug Testing," www.chrc-ccdp.ca/pdf/poldrgalceng.pdf, retrieved April 2, 2012.

43. Duncan, Marsden, "Drug and Alcohol Testing: A Divided Nation?" *Canadian HR Reporter*, October 5, 2009, pp. 5-6; Todd Humber, "Pre-employment Drug Tests Dealt Blow," *Canadian HR Reporter*, July 17, 2006, www.hrreporter.com, retrieved April 8, 2008.

44. M. A. McDaniel, E. P. Morgeson, E. G. Finnegan, M. A. Campion, and E. P. Braverman, "Use of Situational Judgment Tests to Predict Job Performance: A Clarification of the Literature," *Journal of Applied Psychology* 86 (2001), pp. 730–740; J. Clavenger, G. M. Perreira, D. Weichmann, N. Schmitt, and V. S. Harvey, "Incremental Validity of Situational Judgment Tests," *Journal of Applied Psychology* 86 (2001), pp. 410–417.

45. M. A. Campion, J. E. Campion, and J. P. Hudson, "Structured Interviewing: A Note of Incremental Validity and Alternative Question Types," *Journal of Applied Psychology* 79 (1994), pp. 998–1002; E. D. Pulakos and N. Schmitt, "Experience-Based and Situational Interview Questions: Studies of Validity," *Personnel Psychology* 48 (1995), pp. 289–308; and A. P. J. Wllis, B. J. West, A. M. Ryan, and R. P DeShon, "The Use of Impression Management Tactics in Structured Interviews: A Function of Question Type?" *Journal of Applied Psychology* 87 (2002), pp. 1200-1208.

46. Todd Humber, "How BMO Financial Selects Employees," *Canadian HR Reporter*, December 6, 2004, p. G2.

47. N. Schmitt, F. L. Oswald, B. H. Kim, M. A. Gillespie, L. J. Ramsey, and T. Y Yoo, "The Impact of Elaboration on Socially Desirable Responding and the Validity of Biodata Measures," *Journal of Applied Psychology* 88 (2003), pp. 979–88; N. Schmitt and C. Kunce, "The Effects of Required Elaboration of Answers to Biodata Questions," *Personnel Psychology* 55 (2002), pp. 569–87.

48. Hunter and Hunter, "Validity and Utility of Alternative Predictors of Job Performance."

49. R. Pingitore, B. L. Dugoni, R. S. Tindale, and B. Spring, "Bias Against Overweight Job Applicants in a Simulated Interview," *Journal of Applied Psychology* 79 (1994), pp. 184–190.

50. M. A. McDaniel, D. L. Whetzel, F. L. Schmidt, and S. D. Maurer, "The Validity of Employment Interviews: A Comprehensive Review and Meta-Analysis," *Journal of Applied Psychology* 79 (1994), pp. 599–616; A. I. Huffcutt and W. A. Arthur, "Hunter and Hunter (1984) Revisited: Interview Validity for Entry-Level Jobs," *Journal of Applied Psychology* 79 (1994), pp. 184–190.

51. Y. Ganzach, A. N. Kluger, and N. Klayman, "Making Decisions from an Interview: Expert Measurement and Mechanical Combination," *Personnel Psychology* 53(2000), pp. 1–21; G. Stasser and W. Titus, "Effects of Information Load and Percentage of Shared Information on the Dissemination of Unshared Information During Group Discussion," *Journal of Personality and Social Psychology* 53 (1987), pp. 81–93.

CHAPTER 6

1. "Learning 2.0: Creating a Collaborative, Connected Continuous Learning Culture," Webinar—*The Conference Board of Canada*, February 2012, www.conferenceboard.ca/e-Library/abstract.aspx?did=4648, retrieved April 9, 2012; "New Grads: Flexible Rotation Programs," http://about.telus.com/community/english/careers/working_at_telus/students_and_new_grads/new_grads, retrieved April 6, 2012; "For You: What's In It for You?" http://about.telus.com/community/english/careers/working_at_telus/students_and_new_grads/for_you retrieved April 6, 2012.

2. "Developing Skills in the Canadian Workplace," *Canadian Workplace Gazette* 2, no. 1, p. 98, http://labour-travail.hrdc-drhc.gc.ca.

3. Jon Younger, Norm Smallwood, and Dave Ulrich, "Developing Your Organization's Brand as a Talent Developer," *HR: Human Resource Planning* 30, no. 2 (2007), p. 21.

4. Carrie Lavis, "Learning and Development Outlook 2011" (Ottawa: The Conference Board of Canada, October 2011), p. 14. Based on data from International Institute for Management Development, *World Competitiveness Yearbook, 2010* (Lausanne, Switzerland: 2011), pp. 8–9.

5. Ibid., p. 19.

6. R. Noe, *Employee Training and Development*, 4th ed. (New York: Irwin/McGraw-Hill, 2008).

7. Ryann K. Ellis, *A Field Guide to Learning Management Systems*, Learning Circuits (American Society for Training & Development, 2009), accessed at www.astd.org.

8. I. L. Goldstein, E. P. Braverman, and H. Goldstein, "Needs Assessment," in *Developing Human Resources*, ed. K. N. Wexley (Washington, DC: Bureau of National Affairs, 1991), pp. 5–35–5–75.

9. J. Z. Rouillier and I. L. Goldstein, "Determinants of the Climate for Transfer of Training" (presented at Society of Industrial/Organizational Psychology meetings, St. Louis, MO, 1991); J. S. Russell, J. R. Terborg, and M. L. Powers, "Organizational Performance and Organizational Level Training and Support," *Personnel Psychology* 38 (1985), pp. 849–63; H. Baumgartel, G. J. Sullivan, and L. E. Dunn, "How Organizational Climate and Personality Affect the Payoff from Advanced Management Training Sessions," *Kansas Business Review* 5 (1978), pp. 1–10.

10. Jull Casner-Lotto et al., *Are They Really Ready to Work?* (New York: Conference Board; Washington, DC: Corporate Voices for Working Families; Tucson, AZ: Partnership for 21st Century Skills; Alexandria, VA: Society for Human Resource Management,

(2006), available at www.infoedge.com; R. Davenport, "Eliminate the Skills Gap," *T&D*, February 2006, pp. 26–34; and M. Schoeff, "Amid Calls to Bolster U.S. Innovation, Experts Lament Paucity of Basic Math Skills," *Workforce Management*, March 2006, pp. 46–49.

11. R. A. Noe, "Trainees' Attributes and Attitudes: Neglected Influences on Training Effectiveness," *Academy of Management Review* 11 (1986), pp. 736–49; T. T. Baldwin, R. T. Magjuka, and B. T. Loher, "The Perils of Participation: Effects of Choice on Trainee Motivation and Learning," *Personnel Psychology* 44 (1991), pp. 51–66; S. L Tannenbaum, J. E. Mathieu, E. Salas, and J. A. Cannon-Bowers, "Meeting Trainees' Expectations: The Influence of Training Fulfillment on the Development of Commitment, Self-Efficacy, and Motivation," *Journal of Applied Psychology* 76 (1991), pp. 759–69.

12. L. H. Peters, E. J. O'Connor, and J. R. Eulberg, "Situational Constraints: Sources, Consequences, and Future Considerations," in *Research in Personnel and Human Resource Management,* ed. K. M. Rowland and G. R. Ferris (Greenwich, CT: JAI Press, 1985), vol. 3, pp. 79–114; E. J. O'Connor, L. H. Peters, A. Pooyan, J. Weekley, B. Frank, and B. Erenkranz, "Situational Constraints' Effects on Performance, Affective Reactions, and Turnover: A Field Replication and Extension," *Journal of Applied Psychology* 69 (1984), pp. 663–72; D. J. Cohen, "What Motivates Trainees?," *Training and Development Journal,* November 1990, pp. 91–93; Russell, Terborg, and Powers, "Organizational Performance."

13. S. Allen, "Water Cooler Wisdom," *Training,* August 2005, pp. 30–34.

14. B. Mager, *Preparing Instructional Objectives,* 2nd ed. (Belmont, CA: Lake Publishing, 1984); B. J. Smith and B. L. Delahaye, *How to Be an Effective Trainer,* 2nd ed. (New York: Wiley, 1987).

15. Carrie Lavis, "Learning and Development Outlook 2011" (Ottawa: The Conference Board of Canada, October 2011), p. 14. Based on data from International Institute for Management Development, *World Competitiveness Yearbook, 2010* (Lausanne, Switzerland: 2011), p. 22.

16. E. Wagner and P. Wilson, "Disconnected," *T&D,* December 2005, pp. 40–43.

17. Gail Dutton, "Training TechCheck," *Training,* January 12, 2009, Business & Company Resource Centre, http://galenet.galegroup.com.

18. American Society for Training and Development, *Learning Circuits: Glossary,* www.astd.org/LC/glossary.htm, accessed March 26, 2010.

19. Red Seal Program, Human Resources Development Canada, www.red-seal.ca/English/redseal_e.shtml, retrieved March 21, 2004.

20. Ibid.

21. "MBA Internships/Industry Related Partnerships," www.sauder.ubc.ca/Programs/MBA/MBA_Full_Time/Career_Services/Internships_and_Industry_Projects, retrieved April 7, 2012.

22. www.uregina.ca/coop/students/current/handbook .shtml, retrieved March 11, 2004.

23. W. J. Rothwell and H. C. Kanzanas, "Planned OJT Is Productive OJT," *Training and Development Journal,* October 1990, pp. 53–56.

24. CATSA News, April 2007, p. 6, www.catsa-acsta .gc.ca/english/media/bulletin/2007-04.pdf, retrieved May 23, 2008.

25. Pat Galagan, "Second That," *T+D,* February 2008, pp. 4, 34–37.

26. Ryan Ori, "OSF, Medical College Receive $25 Million Donation," *Journal Star (Peoria, Ill.),* February 28, 2010, Business & Company Resource Center, http://galenet.galegroup.com; and "Welding Simulation Software Enhances Training Efforts," *Product News Network,* November 23, 2009, Business & Company Resource Center," http://galenet.gale group.com.

27. www.stratxsimulations.com/markstrat_online_ home.aspx, retrieved May 23, 2008.

28. G. P. Latham and L. M. Saari, "Application of Social Learning Theory to Training Supervisors Through Behavior Modeling," *Journal of Applied Psychology* 64 (1979), pp. 239–46.

29. D. Brown and D. Harvey, *An Experiential Approach to Organizational Development* (Englewood Cliffs, NJ: Prentice Hall, 2000); and Larissa Jogi, review of *The Handbook of Experiential Learning and Management Educatios,* eds. Michael Reynolds and Russ Vince, *Studies in the Education of Adults* 40 no. 2 (Autumn 2008): pp. 232–234, accessed at OCLC FirstSearch, http://newfirstsearch .oclc.org.

30. C. Clements, R. J. Wagner, C. C. Roland, "The Ins and Outs of Experiential Training," *Training and Development,* February 1995, pp. 52–56.

31. Lesley Young, "All in the Family at Toronto Hydro," *Canadian HR Reporter,* March 24, 2008, p. 16.

32. P. Froiland, "Action Learning," *Training,* January 1994, pp. 27–34.

33. C. E. Schneier, "Training and Development Programs: What Learning Theory and Research Have to Offer," *Personnel Journal,* April 1974, pp. 288–93; M. Knowles, "Adult Learning," in *Training and Development Handbook,* 3rd ed., ed. R. L. Craig (New York: McGraw-Hill, 1987), pp. 168–79; B. J. Smith and B. L. Delahaye, *How to Be an Effective Trainer,* 2nd ed. (New York: Wiley, 1987); and Traci Sitzmann, "Self-Regulating Online Course Engagement," *T&D,* March 2010, Business & Company Resource Center, http://galenet.galegroup.com.

34. K. A. Smith-Jentsch, F. G. Jentsch, S. C. Payne, and E. Salas, "Can Pretraining Experiences Explain Individual Differences in Learning?," *Journal of Applied Psychology* 81 (1996), pp. 110–16.

35. W. McGehee and P. W. Thayer, *Training in Business and Industry* (New York: Wiley, 1961).

36. R. M. Gagne and K. L. Medsker, *The Condition of Learning* (Fort Worth, TX: Harcourt-Brace, 1996).

37. J. C. Naylor and G. D. Briggs, "The Effects of Task Complexity and Task Organization on the Relative Efficiency of Part and Whole Training Methods," *Journal of Experimental Psychology* 65 (1963), pp. 217–24.

38. Levels of training evaluation by Janice Cooney and Allison Cowan, "The Conference Board of Canada: Training and Development Outlook 2003: Canadian Organizations Continue to Under-Invest," May 2003, pp. 15, 16, 0070979863 0-88763-584-9.

39. Ibid.

40. K. Mantyla, *Blended E-Learning* (Alexandria, VA: ASTD, 2001).

41. Adapted from "Measurement Standards: Training Evaluation and Effectiveness Reporting," copyright 2003 TD Bank Financial Group Learning and Development Measurement 2003, www.cstd.ca/nettworks/Eva/sampleTD.doc, retrieved March 10, 2004.

42. M. R. Louis, "Surprise and Sense Making: What Newcomers Experience in Entering Unfamiliar Organizational Settings," *Administrative Science Quarterly* 25 (1980), pp. 226–51.

43. Kira Vermond, "Rolling Out the Welcome Mat," *The Globe and Mail,* April 26, 2008, www.theglobeandmail.com, retrieved April 28, 2008.

44. Ibid.

45. Ibid.; and "Bringing New Hires Up to Speed: How Structured Onboarding Can Help," *The Conference Board of Canada,* August 2011, p. 6.

46. Danielle Harder, "Diversity Takes Flight at Air Canada," *Canadian HR Reporter,* May 5, 2008, www.hrreporter .com, retrieved May 23, 2008.

47. S. Rynes and B. Rosen, "What Makes Diversity Programs Work?," *HR Magazine,* October 1994, pp. 67–73; Rynes and Rosen, A Field Survey of Factors Affecting the Adoption and Perceived Success of Diversity Training," *Personnel Psychology* 48, no. 2 (1995), pp. 247–271; J. Gordon, "Different from What? Diversity as a Performance Issue," *Training,* May 1995, pp. 25–33.

48. Tavia Grant, "Diversity: Easier Said Than Done, but with Tenacity, It Can Be Done," *The Globe and Mail,* April 25, 2008, www.theglobeandmail.com, retrieved April 28, 2008.

49. M. London, *Managing the Training Enterprise* (San Francisco: Jossey-Bass, 1989) and D. Day, *Developing Leadership Talent* (Alexandria, VA: SHRM Foundation, 2007).

50. R. W. Pace, P. C. Smith, and G. E. Mills, *Human Resource Development* (Englewood Cliffs, NJ: Prentice Hall, 1991); W. Fitzgerald, "Training versus Development," *Training and Development Journal,* May 1992, pp. 81–84; R. A. Noe, S. L. Wilk, E. J. Mullen, and J. E. Wanek, "Employee Development: Issues in Construct Definition and Investigation of Antecedents," in *Improving Training Effectiveness in Work Organizations,* ed. J. K. Ford (Mahwah, NJ: Lawrence Erlbaum, 1997), pp. 153–189.

51. J. H. Greenhaus and G. A. Callanan, *Career Management,* 2nd ed. (Fort Worth, TX: Dryden Press, 1994); and D. Hall, *Careers in and out of Organizations* (Thousand Oaks, CA: Sage, 2002).

52. R. Noe, *Employee Training and Development,* 5th ed. (New York: McGraw-Hill Irwin, 2010).

53. A. Howard and D. W. Bray, *Managerial Lives in Transition: Advancing Age and Changing Times* (New York: Guilford, 1988); J. Bolt, *Executive Development* (New York: Harper Business, 1989); J. R. Hintichs and G. P. Hollenbeck, "Leadership Development," in *Developing Human Resources,* ed. K. N. Wexley 237; and Day, *Developing Leadership Talent.*

54. Joyce Rowlands, "Soft Skills Give Hard Edge," *The Globe and Mail,* June 9, 2004, p. C8.

55. Ibid.

56. C. D. McCauley, M. M. Lombardo, "Benchmarks: An Instrument for Diagnosing Managerial Strengths and Weaknesses," in *Measures of Leadership,* pp. 535–545; and Center for Creative Leadership, "Benchmarks–Overview," www.ccl.org, accessed March 28, 2006.

57. S. B. Silverman, "Individual Development through Performance Appraisal," in *Developing Human Resources,* pp. 5–120–5–151.

58. J. F. Brett and L. E. Atwater, "360-Degree Feedback: Accuracy, Reactions, and Perceptions of Usefulness," *Journal of Applied Psychology* 86 (2001), pp. 930–42; Marshall Goldsmith, "How to Increase Your Leadership Effectiveness," *Business Week,* November 20, 2009, www.businessweek.com; and Brenda Bence, "Would You Want to Work for You?" *Supervision,* February 2010, Business & Company Resource Center, http://galenet.galegroup.com.

59. L. Atwater, P. Roush, and A. Fischthal, "The Influence of Upward Feedback on Self- and Follower Ratings of Leadership," *Personnel Psychology* 48 (1995), pp. 35–59; J. F. Hazucha, S. A. Hezlett, and R. J. Schneider, "The Impact of 360-Degree Feedback on Management Skill Development," *Human Resource Management* 32 (1193), pp. 325–351; J. W. Smither, M. London, N. Vasilopoulos, R. R. Reilly, R. E. Millsap, and N. Salvemini, "An Examination of the Effects of an Upward Feedback Program over Time," *Personnel Psychology* 48 (1995), pp. 1–34; J. Smither and A. Walker, "Are the Improvements in Multirater Feedback Ratings Over Time?" *Journal of Applied Psychology* 89 (2004), pp. 575–581; and J. Smither, M. London, and R. Reilly, "Does Performance Improve Following Multisource Feedback? A Theoretical Model, Meta-analysis, and Review of Empirical Findings," *Personnel Psychology* 58 (2005), pp. 33–66.

60. M. W. McCall Jr., *High Flyers* (Boston: Harvard Business School Press, 1998).

61. R. S. Snell, "Congenial Ways of Learning: So Near yet So Far," *Journal of Management Development* 9 (1990), pp. 17–23.

62. C. D. McCauley, M. N. Ruderman, P. J. Ohlott, and J. E. Morrow, "Assessing the Developmental Components of Managerial Jobs," *Journal of Applied Psychology* 79 (1994), pp. 544–60.

63. Andrew Wahl, "Leaders Wanted," *Canadian Business,* March 1–14, 2004, pp. 33, 34.

64. M. London, *Developing Managers* (San Francisco: Jossey-Bass, 1985); M. A. Camion, L. Cheraskin, and M. J. Stevens, "Career-Related Antecedents and Outcomes of Job Rotation," *Academy of Management Journal* 37 (1994), pp. 1518–42; London, *Managing the Training Enterprise.*

65. Margaret Fiester, "Job Rotation, Total Rewards, Measuring Value," *HR Magazine,* August 2008, Business & Company Resource Centre, http://galenet.galegroup.com; and "Energize and Enhance Employee Value with Job Rotation," *HR Focus,* January 2008, OCLC FirstSearch, http://newfirst search.oclc.org.

66. R. A. Noe, B. D. Steffy, and A. E. Barber, "An Investigation of the Factors Influencing Employees' Willingness to Accept Mobility Opportunities," *Personnel Psychology* 41 (1988), pp. 559–80; S. Gould and L. E. Penley, "A Study of the Correlates of Willingness to Relocate," *Academy of Management Journal* 28 (1984), pp. 472–78; J. Landau and T. H. Hammer, "Clerical Employees' Perceptions of Intraorganizational Career Opportunities," *Academy of Management Journal* 29 (1986), pp. 385–405; J. M. Brett and A. H. Reilly, "On the Road Again: Predicting the Job Transfer Decision," *Journal of Applied Psychology* 73 (1988), pp. 614–20.

67. D. B. Turban and T. W. Dougherty, "Role of Protégé Personality in Receipt of Mentoring and Career Success," *Academy of Management Journal* 37 (1994), pp. 688–702; E. A. Fagenson, "Mentoring: Who Needs It? A Comparison of Protégés' and Non-Protégés' Needs for Power, Achievement, Affiliation, and Autonomy," *Journal of Vocational Behavior* 41 (1992), pp. 48–60.

68. A. H. Geiger, "Measures for Mentors," *Training and Development Journal,* February 1992, pp. 65-67; Beth N. Carvin, "The Great Mentor Match," *T + D,* January 2009, OCLC FirstSearch, http://newfirst search.oclc.org; and Pamela Craig, "Looking for Help at Work? Get a Mentor," *BusinessWeek,* March 2, 2010, www.businessweek.com.

69. K. E. Kram, *Mentoring at Work: Developmental Relationships in Organizational Life* (Glenview, IL: Scott, Foresman, 1985); L. L. Phillips-Jones, "Establishing a Formalized Mentoring Program," *Training and Development Journal* 2 (1983), pp. 38–42; K. Kram, "Phases of the Mentoring Relationship," *Academy of Management Journal* 26 (1983), pp. 608–25; G. T. Chao, P. M. Walz, and P. D. Gardner, "Formal and Informal Mentorships: A Comparison of Mentoring Functions and Contrasts with Non-mentored Counterparts," *Personnel Psychology* 45 (1992), pp. 619–36; and C. Wanberg, E. Welsh, and S. Hezlett, "Mentoring Research: A Review and Dynamic Process Model," in *Research in Personnel and Human Resources Management,* eds. J. Martocchio and G. Ferris (New York: Elsevier Science, 2003), pp. 39-124.

70. L. Eby, M. Butts, A. Lockwood, and A Simon, "Protégés Negative Mentoring Experiences Construct Development and Nomological Validation," *Personnel Psychology* 57 (2004), pp. 411–447; and M. Boyle "Most Mentoring Programs Stink—but Yours Doesn't Have To," *Training,* August 2005, pp. 12–15.

71. Keynote presented by Nancy Nazer, Consultant Bell Canada-Mentoring Connections National Conference, www.mentorcanada/ca/en/en_keynote/nnazer .ppt, retrieved March 29, 2004.

72. R. A. Noe, D. Greenberger, and S. Wang, "Mentoring: What We Know and Where We Might Go," in *Research in Personnel and Human Resources Management,* vol. 21, ed. G. R. Ferris and J. J. Martocchio (Oxford: Elsevier Science, 2002), vol. 21, pp. 129–174; and T. D. Allen, L. T. Eby, M. L. Poteet, E. Lentz, and L. Lima, "Career Benefits Associated with Mentoring for Proteges: A Meta-Analysis," *Journal of Applied Psychology* 89 (2004), pp. 127–136.

73. D. B. Peterson and M. D. Hicks, *Leader as Coach* (Minneapolis: Personnel Decisions, 1996).

74. David Brown, "Mentoring Boosts Retention, T&D. But It's a Long-Term Game," *Canadian HR Reporter,* July 12, 2004, p. 7.

75. J. Smither, M. London, R. Flautt, Y. Vargas, and L. Kucine, "Can Working with an Executive Coach Improve Multisource Ratings over Time? A Quasi-experimental Field Study," *Personnel Psychology,* 56 (2003), pp. 23–44.

76. J. Toto, "Untapped World of Peer Coaching," *T + D,* April 2006, pp. 69–71.

77. Rajiv L. Gupta and Karol M. Wasylyshyn, "Developing World Class Leaders: The Rohm and Haas Story," *People & Strategy,* December 2009, pp. 36–41; and Kathleen Koster, "This Too Shall Pass," *Employee Benefit News,* July 1, 2009, Business & Company Resource Center, http://galenet.galegroup.com.

78. Claudine Kapel and Catherine Shepherd, "Career Ladders Create Common Language for Defining Jobs," *Canadian HR Reporter,* June 14, 2004, p. 15.

79. Mary Teresa Bitti, "Online Career Branding," *The National Post,* November 21, 2007, http://digital .nationalpost.com, retrieved November 21, 2007.

80. Liz Mulligan-Ferry, Morgan Friedrich, and Sabra Nathanson, "2011 Catalyst Census: Financial Post 500 Board Directors," www.catalyst.org/ publication/525/2011-catalyst-census-financial-post-500-women-board-directors, retrieved April 8, 2012.

81. P. J. Ohlott, M. N. Ruderman, and C. D. McCauley, "Gender Differences in Managers' Developmental Job Experiences," *Academy of Management Journal,* 37 (1994), pp. 46–67; L. A. Mainiero, "Getting Anointed for Advancement: The Case of Executive Women," *Academy of Management Executive* 8 (1994), pp. 53–67; and P. Tharenov, S. Latimer, and D. Conroy, "How Do You Make It to the Top? An examination of Influences on Women's and Men's Managerial Advancements," *Academy of Management Journal* 37 (1994), pp. 899–931.

82. U.S. Department of Labor, *A Report on the Glass Ceiling Initiative* (Washington, DC: Labor Department, 1991); R. A. Noe, "Women and Mentoring: A Review and Research Agenda," *Academy of Management Review* 13 (1988), pp. 65–78; B. R. Ragins and J. L. Cotton, "Easier Said Than Done: Gender Differences in Perceived Barriers to Gaining a Mentor," *Academy of Management Journal* 34 (1991), pp. 939–51; and Jesse Washington, "Study: Networking Hinders Black Women Execs," *Yahoo News,* January 7, 2009, http://news.yahoo.com.

83. Alice H. Eagly and Linda L. Carli, "Women and the Labyrinth of Leadership," *Harvard Business Review,* September 2007, pp. 63–71.

84. C. B. Derr, C Jones, and E. L. Toomey, "Managing High-Potential Employees: Current Practices in Thirty-Three U.S. Corporation," *Human Resource Management,* 27 (1988), pp. 273–290; K. M. Nowack, "The Secrets of Succession," *Training and Development* 48 (1994), pp. 49–54; and "2009 Trends in Review: What Do You Know?" *T + D,* December 2009, pp. 33–39.

85. L. W. Hellervik, J. F. Hazucha, and R. J. Schneider, "Behavior Change: Models, Methods, and a Review of Evidence," in *Handbook of Industrial and Organizational Psychology,* 2nd ed., eds. M. D. Dunnette and L. M. Hough (Palo Alto, CA: Consulting Psychologists Press, 1992), vol. 3, pp. 823–899.

86. D. B. Peterson, "Measuring and Evaluating Change in Executive and Managerial Development," paper presented at the annual conference of the Society for Industrial and Organizational Psychology, Miami, 1990.

CHAPTER 7

1. M. Parker, "Culture Clash: Performance-managing Culture," *Financial Post,* February 20, 2012, retrieved May 4, 2012 http://business.financialpost.com/2012/02/20/culture-clash-performance-managing-culture/; "Investment in Feedback Pays Off," *National Post,* May 14, 2008, FP14; M. Parker, "It's How You Do Things, Not What You Do: Results From the 2010, Canadian Corporate Culture Study," *The Waterline,* Issue 7, July 13, 2010, retrieved May 2, 2012 www.waterstoneehc.com/news-events/newsletters/issue-7.

2. Carolyn Heinze, "Fair Appraisals," *Systems Contractor News,* July 2009, Business & Company Resource Center, http://galenet.galegroup.com.

3. "Measuring People Power," *Fortune,* October 2, 2000.

4. Wallace Immen, "Handling the First 100 Days on the Job," *The Globe and Mail,* March 14, 2008, p. C2.

5. Nicole Stewart, "Compensation Planning Outlook 2012" (Ottawa: Conference Board of Canada, October 2007), p. 17.

6. "Ceridian Canada and Harris Decima Survey Reveals Surprising Employee Attitudes Towards Performance Reviews and Corporate Training," October 24, 2011, www.ceridian.ca/en/news/2011/1024-pulse-of-talent.html.

7. M. Sallie-Dosunmu, "Born to Grow," *T+D,* May 2006, pp. 33–37.

8. S. Scullen, P. Bergey, and L. Aiman-Smith, "Forced Choice Distribution Systems and the Improvement of Workforce Potential: A Baseline Simulation," *Personnel Psychology* 47 (1963), pp. 149–155.

9. Nicole Stewart, "Compensation Planning Outlook 2012" (Ottawa: Conference Board of Canada, October 2007), p. 19.

10. P. Smith and L. Kendall, "Retranslation of Expectations: An Approach to the Construction of Unambiguous Anchors for Rating Scales," *Journal of Applied Psychology* 47 (1963), pp. 149–55.

11. K. Murphy and J. Constans, "Behavioral Anchors as a Source of Bias in Rating," *Journal of Applied Psychology* 72 (1987), pp. 573–77; M. Piotrowski, J. Bames-Farrel, and F. Estig, "Behaviorally Anchored Bias: A Replication and Extension of Murphy and Constans," *Journal of Applied Psychology* 74 (1989), pp. 823–26.

12. G. Latham and K. Wexley, *Increasing Productivity Through Performance Appraisal* (Boston: Addison-Wesley, 1981).

13. U. Wiersma and G. Latham, "The Practicality of Behavioral Observation Scales, Behavioral Expectation Scales, and Trait Scales," *Personnel Psychology* 39 (1986), pp. 619–28.

14. D. C. Anderson, C. Crowell, J. Sucec, K. Gilligan, and M. Wikoff, "Behavior Management of Client Contacts in a Real Estate Brokerage: Getting Agents to Sell More," *Journal of Organizational Behavior Management* 4 (2001), pp. 580–90; F. Luthans and R. Kreitner, *Organizational Behavior Modification and Beyond* (Glenview, IL: Scott, Foresman, 1975).

15. K. L. Langeland, C. M. Jones, and T. C. Mawhinney, "Improving Staff Performance in a Community Mental Health Setting: Job Analysis, Training, Goal Setting, Feedback, and Years of Data," *Journal of Organizational Behavior Management* 18 (1998), pp. 21–43.

16. J. Komaki, R. Collins, and P. Penn, "The Role of Performance Antecedents and Consequences in Work Motivation," *Journal of Applied Psychology* 67 (1982), pp. 334–40.

17. S. Snell, "Control Theory in Strategic Human Resource Management: The Mediating Effect of Administrative Information," *Academy of Management Journal* 35 (1992), pp. 292–327.

18. R. Pritchard, S. Jones, P. Roth, K. Stuebing, and S. Ekeberg, "The Evaluation of an Integrated Approach to Measuring Organizational Productivity," *Personnel Psychology* 42 (1989), pp. 69–115.

19. G. Odiorne, *MBO II: A System of Managerial Leadership for the 80's* (Belmont, CA: Pitman Publishers, 1986).

20. R. Rodgers and J. Hunter, "Impact of Management by Objectives on Organizational Productivity,"

Journal of Applied Psychology 76 (1991), pp. 322–26.

21. P. Wright, J. George, S. Farnsworth, and G. McMahan, "Productivity and Extra-Role Behavior: The Effects of Goals and Incentives on Spontaneous Helping," *Journal of Applied Psychology* 78, no. 3 (1993), pp. 374–81.

22. "What Is a Balanced Scorecard?," www.2gc.co/UK/pdf/2GC-FAQ1.pdf, retrieved July 14, 2004.

23. Cam Scholey, "Alignment—Has Your Organization Got It?," *CMA Management* 81, no. 6, pp. 16–18.

24. Mehrdad Derayeh and Stephane Brutus, "Learning from Others' 360-Degree Experiences," *Canadian HR Reporter,* February 10, 2003, www.hrreporter.com, retrieved February 15, 2005.

25. R. Heneman, K. Wexley, and M. Moore, "Performance Rating Accuracy: A Critical Review," *Journal of Business Research* 15 (1987), pp. 431–48.

26. T. Becker and R. Klimoski, "A Field Study of the Relationship Between the Organizational Feedback Environment and Performance," *Personnel Psychology* 42 (1989), pp. 343–58; H. M. Findley, W. F. Giles, K. W. Mossholder, "Performance Appraisal and Systems Facets: Relationships with Contextual Performance," *Journal of Applied Psychology* 85 (2000), pp. 634–40.

27. K. Wexley and R. Klimoski, "Performance Appraisal: An Update," in *Research in Personnel and Human Resource Management,* vol. 2, ed. K. Rowland and G. Ferris (Greenwich, CT: JAI Press, 1984).

28. F. Landy and J. Farr, *The Measurement of Work Performance: Methods, Theory, and Applications* (New York: Academic Press, 1983).

29. G. McEvoy and P. Buller, "User Acceptance of Peer Appraisals in an Industrial Setting," *Personnel Psychology* 40 (1987), pp. 785–97.

30. A. Pomeroy, "Agent of Change," *HR Magazine,* May 2005, pp. 52–56.

31. D. Antonioni, "The Effects of Feedback Accountability on Upward Appraisal Ratings," *Personnel Psychology* 47 (1994), pp. 349–56.

32. John Kiska, "Do an Employee Self-Assessment," *HR Professional Magazine,* February/March 2004, www.hrpao.org/knowledge_Centre/HR_Professional/2003_issues, retrieved May 28, 2004.

33. H. Heidemeier and K. Moser, "Self-Other Agreement in Job Performance Rating: A Meta-Analytic Test of a Process Model," *Journal of Applied Psychology* 94 (2008), pp. 353–70.

34. J. Bernardin, C. Hagan, J. Kane, and P. Villanova, "Effective Performance Management: A Focus on Precision, Customers, and Situational Constraints," in *Performance Appraisal: State of the Art in Practice,* pp. 3–48.

35. K. Wexley and W. Nemeroff, "Effects of Racial Prejudice, Race of Applicant, and Biographical Similarity on Interviewer Evaluations of Job Applicants," *Journal of Social and Behavioral Sciences* 20 (1974), pp. 66–78.

36. Phillip L. Hunsaker and Dale Dilamarter, *Training in Management Skills,* Cdn. ed. (Toronto: Pearson Education Canada Inc., 2004), p. 330.

37. Ibid.

38. D. Smith, "Training Programs for Performance Appraisal: A Review," *Academy of Management Review* 11 (1986), pp. 22-40; and G. Latham, K. Wexley, and E. Pursell, "Training Managers to Minimize Rating Errors in the Observation of Behavior," *Journal of Applied Psychology* 60 (1975), pp. 550–55.

39. E. Pulakos, "A Comparison of Rater Training Programs: Error Training and Accuracy Training," *Journal of Applied Psychology* 69 (1984), pp. 581–88.

40. "Most Large Companies Calibrate Performance Poll Finds," *HR Magazine,* February, 2012, p. 87.

41. J. Sammer, "Calibrating Consistency," *HR Magazine,* January 2008, pp. 73-75; and Fox, "Curing What Ails Performance Reviews," pp. 55–56.

42. S. W. J. Kozlowski, G. T. Chao, and R. F. Morrison, "Games Raters Play: Politics, Strategies, and Impression Management in Performance Appraisal," in *Performance Appraisal: State of the Art in Practice,* pp. 163–205; and C. Rosen, P. Levy, and R. Hall, "Placing Perceptions of Politics in the Context of the Feedback Environment Employee Attitudes, and Job Performance," *Journal of Applied Psychology* 91 (2006), pp. 211–20.

43. Deborah Busser, "Delivering Effective Performance Feedback, *T+D,* April 2012, pp. 323.

44. Malcolm Gabriel and Pierre Robitaille, "Sustaining High Performance with Generation-Y Employees," *Canadian HR Reporter,* January 14, 2008, p. 13.

45. Ann Pace, "Cultivating a Coaching Culture," *T+D,* February 2012, p. 16; Ann Pace, "A New Era of Performance Management," *T+D,* October 2011, p. 12.

46. K. Wexley, V. Singh, and G. Yukl, "Subordinate Participation in Three Types of Appraisal Interviews," *Journal of Applied Psychology* 58 (1973), pp. 54–57; K. Wexley, "Appraisal Interview," in *Performance Assessment,* ed. R. A. Berk (Baltimore: Johns Hopkins University Press, 1986), pp. 167–85; B.D Cawley, L.m. Keeping, and P.E. Levy, "Participaion in the Performance Appraisal Process and Employee Reactions: A Meta-analytic Review and Field Investigations," *Journal of Applied Psychology* 83, no. 3 (1998), pp. 615–63; H. Aguinis, *Performance Management* (Upper Saddle River, NJ: Pearson Prentice-Hall, 2007); and C. Lee, "Feedback, Not Appraisal," *HR Magazine,* November 2006, pp. 111–14.

47. D. Cederblom, "The Performance Appraisal Interview: A Review, Implications, and Suggestions," *Academy of Management Review* 7 (1982), pp. 219–27; B. D. Cawley, L. M. Keeping, and P. E. Levy, "Participation in the Performance Appraisal Process and Employee Reactions: A Meta-analytic Review of Field Investigations," *Journal of Applied Psychology*

83, no. 3 (1998), pp. 615–63; W. Giles and K. Mossholder, "Employee Reactions to Contextual and Session Components of Performance Appraisal," *Journal of Applied Psychology* 75 (1990), pp. 371–77.

48. James Heeney, "Personal Harassment Liability Always a Danger for Employers," *Canadian HR Reporter,* October 22, 2007, p. B15; Stuart Rudner, "Psychological Harassment Hurts Employees' Productivity," *Canadian HR Reporter,* October 22, 2007, p. 31; Christopher M. Andree Crawford, "Poor Treatment Is Constructive Dismissal," *Canadian Bar Association,* www.cba.org/CBA/newsletters/lab-2003/18.aspx, retrieved April 27, 2008; "Bullying at Work: Another Form of Workplace Violence," www.emond-harnden.com/publications/feb03/bullies.shtml, retrieved April 27, 2008.

49. James Heeney, "Personal Harassment Liability Always a Danger for Employers," *Canadian HR Reporter,* October 22, 2007, p. B15.

50. Kristina Dell, "A Spy in Every Pocket," *Time,* March 27, 2006, p. 31; http://trackingthe world.com/gps-asset-tracking html, retrieved April 24, 2008.

51. Uyen Vu, "Privacy Law Working Well: Commissioner," *Canadian HR Reporter,* December 18, 2006, p. 1, 13.

CHAPTER 8

1. "Trillium Health Centre," *The Globe and Mail,* June 17, 2011, p. B4; Sarah Dobson, "Hospital Focuses on Value of People to Boost Employee Engagement, Retention," *Canadian HR Reporter,* May 3, 2010, pp. 19-20; and "Trillium's 4 Quadrants of Total Rewards," *Canadian HR Reporter,* May 3, 2010, p. 20.

2. "WorldatWork Total Rewards Model," www.world atwork.org/waw/aboutus/html/aboutus-whatis.html#model, retrieved October 22, 2008.

3. "Strategic Rewards in Canada: Building the Optimal Reward Plan—Watson Wyatt's 2004 Survey of Canadian Strategic Rewards and Pay Practices," in "Why Firms Develop a Total Rewards Strategy," *Canadian HR Reporter,* February 14, 2005, p. R5.

4. Nicole Stewart, "Compensation Planning Outlook 2012" (Ottawa: Conference Board of Canada, October 2007), p. 12.

5. "What Is Total Rewards?," www.worldatwork.org/waw/aboutus/html/aboutus-whatis.html, retrieved October 22, 2008.

6. B. Gerhart and G. T. Milkovich, "Organizational Differences in Managerial Compensation and Financial Performance," *Academy of Management Journal* 33 (1990), pp. 663–91; E. L. Groshen, "Why Do Wages Vary among Employers?," *Economic Review* 24 (1988), pp. 19–38.

7. J. S. Adams, "Inequity in Social Exchange," in *Advances in Experimental Social Psychology,* ed. L. Berkowitz (New York: Academic Press, 1965); P.

8. S. Goodman, "An Examination of Referents Used in the Evaluation of Pay," *Organizational Behavior and Human Performance* 12 (1974), pp. 170–95; J. B. Miner," *Theories of Organizational Behavior* (Hinsdale, IL: Dryden Press, 1980).

8. J. P. Pfeffer and A. Davis-Blake, "Understanding Organizational Wage Structures: A Resource Dependence Approach," *Academy of Management Journal* 30 (1987), pp. 437–55.

9. This section draws freely on B. Gerhart and R. D. Bretz, "Employee Compensation," in *Organization and Management of Advanced Manufacturing,* ed. W. Karwowski and G. Salvendy (New York: Wiley, 1994), pp. 81–101.

10. E. E. Lawler III, *Strategic Pay* (San Francisco: Jossey-Bass, 1990); G. Ledford, "3 Cases on Skill-Based Pay: An Overview," *Compensation and Benefits Review,* March/April 1991, pp. 11–23; G. E. Ledford, "Paying for the Skills, Knowledge, Competencies of Knowledge Workers," *Compensation and Benefits Review,* July/August 1995, p. 55.

11. B. C. Murray and B. Gerhart, "An Empirical Analysis of a Skill-Based Pay Program and Plant Performance Outcomes," *Academy of Management Journal* 41, no. 1 (1998), pp. 68–78; N. Gupta, D. Jenkins, and W. Curington, "Paying for Knowledge: Myths and Realities," *National Productivity Review,* Spring 1986, pp. 107–23.

12. B. Gerhart and G. T. Milkovich, "Organizational Differences in Managerial Compensation and Financial Performance," *Academy of Management Journal* 33 (1990), pp. 663–91.

13. Nicole Stewart, "Compensation Planning Outlook 2012" (Ottawa: Conference Board of Canada, October 2007), p. 18.

14. G. T. Milkovich and A. K. Wigdor, *Pay for Performance* (Washington, DC: National Academy Press, 1991); Gerhart and Bretz, "Employee Compensation"; C. Trevor, B. Gerhart, and J. W. Boudreau, "Voluntary Turnover and Job Performance: Curvilinearity and the Moderating Influences of Salary Growth and Promotions," *Journal of Applied Psychology* 82 (1997), pp. 44–61.

15. Shannon Klie, "New Challenges in Pay for Performance," *Canadian HR Reporter,* April 23, 2007, p. 9.

16. R. D. Bretz, R. A. Ash, and G. F. Dreher, "Do People Make the Place? An Examination of the Attraction-Selection-Attrition Hypothesis," *Personnel Psychology* 42 (1989), pp. 561–81; T. A. Judge and R. D. Bretz, "Effect of Values on Job Choice Decisions," *Journal of Applied Psychology* 77 (1992), pp. 261–71; D. M. Cable and T. A. Judge, "Pay Performance and Job Search Decisions: A Person–Organization Fit Perspective," *Personnel Psychology* 47 (1994), pp. 317–48.

17. R. D. Bretz, G. T. Milkovich, and W. Read, "The Current State of Performance Appraisal Research and Practice," *Journal of Management* 18 (1992), pp. 321–52; R. L. Heneman, "Merit Pay Research," *Research in Personnel and Human Resource*

Management 8 (1990), pp. 203–63; Milkovich and Wigdor, *Pay for Performance.*

18. Bretz et al., "The Current State of Performance Appraisal Research and Practice."

19. T. L. Ross and R. A. Ross, "Gainsharing: Sharing Improved Performance," in *The Compensation Handbook,* 3rd ed., ed. M. L. Rock and L. A. Berger (New York: McGraw-Hill, 1991).

20. T. M. Welbourne and L. R. Gomez-Mejia, "Team Incentives in the Workplace," in Rock and Berger.

21. L. R. Gomez-Mejia and D. B. Balkin, *Compensation, Organizational Strategy, and Firm Performance* (Cincinnati: South-Western, 1992).

22. This idea has been referred to as the "share economy." See M. L. Weitzman, "The Simple Macroeconomics of Profit Sharing," *American Economic Review* 75 (1985), pp. 937–53. For supportive research, see the following studies: J. Chelius and R. S. Smith, "Profit Sharing and Employment Stability," *Industrial and Labor Relations Review* 43 (1990), pp. 256S–73S; B. Gerhart and L. O. Trevor, "Employment Stability Under Different Managerial Compensation Systems," working paper, Cornell University Center for Advanced Human Resource Studies, 1995; D. L. Kruse, "Profit Sharing and Employment Variability: Microeconomic Evidence on the Weitzman Theory," *Industrial and Labor Relations Review* 44 (1991), pp. 437–53.

23. James Thomson, "Rich Pickings: Four Challenges for Facebook's New Millionaires," *Business Spectator,* May 18, 2012, www.businessspectator.com.au/bs.nsf/Article/facebook-ipo-zuckerberg-millionires-billionaires-i-pd20120518-UE5TK?OpenDocument&src=sph&src=rot, retrieved May 18, 2012.

24. Gerhart and Milkovich, "Organizational Differences in Managerial Compensation."

25. http://c3dsp.westjet.com/intemet/sky/jobs/whywestjetTemplate.jsp, retrieved February 28, 2005.

26. M. A. Conte and J. Svejnar, "The Performance Effects of Employee Ownership Plans," in *Paying for Productivity,* pp. 245–94.

27. B. Gerhart and G. T. Milkovich, "Employee Compensation: Research and Practice," in *Handbook of Industrial and Organizational Psychology,* vol. 3, 2nd ed., eds. M. D. Dunnette and L. M. Hough (Palo Alto, CA: Consulting Psychologists Press, 1992), vol. 3; and J. Swist, "Benefits Communications: Measuring Impact and Values," *Employee Benefit Plan Review,* September 2002, pp. 24–26.

28. "Canadian Employers Rate Health Plans over Cash," *The Globe and Mail,* May 12, 2004, p. C2.

29. Bureau of Labor Statistics, "Employer Costs for Employee Compensation," http://data.bls.gov, accessed April 28, 2010.

30. Sarah Beech, "Lifestyle Choices," *Benefits Canada,* March 2008, p. 45.

31. Mary Teresa Bitti, "Alternative Health Plan Benefits Small Firms," *National Post,* March 8, 2004, pp. FE1, FE4.

32. Tammy Burn, "Employers promoting healthier workforce," *Benefits Canada,* May 9, 2012, www.benefitscanada.com/benefits/health-wellness/employers-promoting-healthier-workforce-28660, retrieved May 16, 2012.

33. Shannon Klie, "Do Incentives Help Change Behaviour?," *Canadian HR Reporter,* April 21, 2008, www.hrreporter.com, retrieved May 7, 2008.

34. Brian Lindenberg, "Choosing the right EAP," *Canadian HR Reporter,* March 24, 2008, pp. 22, 27.

35. Statistics Canada, "Pension Plans in Canada," *The Daily,* May 9, 2011, www.statcan.gc.ca/daily-quotidien/110509/dq110509a-eng.htm, retrieved May 17, 2012.

36. "Phased Retirement: Aligning Employer Programs with Worker Preferences—2004 Survey Report," www.watsonwyatt.com/research/resrender.asp, retrieved April 21, 2004.

37. Deborah McMillan, "Redefining Retirement," *Benefits Canada,* August 2007, pp. 13, 15, 17.

38. Statistics Canada, "Pension Plans in Canada," *The Daily,* May 9, 2011, www.statcan.gc.ca/daily-quotidien/110509/dq110509a-eng.htm, retrieved May 17, 2012.

39. Tara Perkins, "RBC to stop offering defined benefit plan," *Globe and Mail Update,* September 23, 2011, www.theglobeandmail.com/globe-investor/investment-ideas/streetwise/rbc-to-stop-offering-defined-benefit-plan/article2176656/, retrieved May 17, 2012.

40. Richard Yerema and Kristina Leung, "Canada's Top Family-Friendly Employers 2012: Ontario Public Service, www.eluta.ca/top-employer-ontario-public-service, and Georgian College, www.eluta.ca/top-employer-georgian-college, retrieved May 18, 2012.

41. Marlene Habib, "'Sandwich Generation' has Smorgasbord of Options," *Globe and Mail Update,* November 20, 2011, www.theglobeandmail.com/globe-investor/personal-finance/financial-road-map/sandwich-generation-has-a-smorgasbord-of-options/article2255328/, retrieved May 18, 2012 and Statistics Canada, "Study: The Sandwich Generation," *The Daily,* September 28, 2004, www.statcan.ca/Daily/English/040928/d040928b.htm, retrieved October 22, 2008.

42. Government of Canada, "Part-Time Work and Family-Friendly Practices in Canadian Workplaces—June 2003," p. 1, www.hrsdc.gc.ca/en/cs/sp/sdc/pkrf/publications/research/2003-000183/page00.shtml, retrieved October 22, 2008.

43. R. Broderick and B. Gerhart, "Nonwage Compensation," in *The Human Resource Management Handbook,* ed. D. Lewin, D.J.B. Mitchell, and M. A. Zadi (San Francisco: JAI Press, 1996).

44. Michael Fradkin, "An Ounce of Prevention Also Can Cut Disability Costs," *National Underwriter Life & Health,* April 21, 2008, Business & Company Resource Center, http://galenet.gale group.com.

45. Sarah Coles, "Package: Scratch Head at Start," *Employee Benefits,* January 14, 2008, Business & Company Reosurce Center, http://galenet.gale group.com.

46. B. T. Beam Jr. and J. J. McFadden, *Employee Benefits,* 6th ed. (Chicago: Real Estate Education Co., 2001).

47. Cathy O'Bright, "Flex Benefits Drive Culture Change, Contain Costs at Superior Propane," *Canadian HR Reporter,* September 8, 2003, www.hrreporter.com, retrieved March 21, 2004.

48. David Johnston, "Poorly Communicated Plans Worse Than None at All," *Canadian HR Reporter,* February 14, 2005, p. R7.

49. M. Wilson, G. B. Northcraft, and M. A. Neale, "The Perceived Value of Fringe Benefits," *Personnel Psychology* 38 (1985), pp. 309–20; H. W. Hennessey, P. L. Perrewe, and W. A. Hochwarter, "Impact of Benefit Awareness on Employee and Organizational Outcomes: A Longitudinal Field Experiment," *Benefits Quarterly* 8, no. 2 (1992), pp. 90–96.

50. Todd Humber, "The Power to Change," Supplement to *Canadian HR Reporter,* May 31, 2004, pp. G1, G10.

51. Leigh Doyle, "The Growing Role of Social Media," *Benefits Canada,* April 17, 2012, www.benefits canada.com/pensions/cap/the-growing-role-of-social-media-27688, retrieved May 16, 2012.

52. "Total Rewards Statements Help to Engage Employees," *Benefits Canada,* November 17, 2011, www.benefitscanada.com/benefits/health-benefits/total-rewards-statements-help-to-engage-employees-22892, retrieved May 16, 2012

53. Hugh Mackenzie, "Canada's CEO Elite 100," *Canadian Centre for Policy Alternatives,* January 2012, p. 17, www.policyalternatives.ca/sites/default/files/uploads/publications/National%20Office/2012/01/Canadas%20CEO%20Elite%20100FINAL.pdf, retrieved May 20, 2012.

54. Ibid.

55. Stephen O'Byrne, "Assessing Pay for Performance," *The Conference Board,* October 2011, p. 3, www.conferenceboard.org, retrieved May 16, 2012.

56. Andy Holloway, "Change is Good," *Financial Post Magazine,* November 1, 2011, retrieved May 16, 2012, and "CEO Scorecard 2011," www.financial post.com/executive/ceo/scorecard/index.html, retrieved May 20, 2012.

57. Hugh Mackenzie, "Canada's CEO Elite 100," *Canadian Centre for Policy Alternatives,* January 2012, p. 4. www.policyalternatives.ca/sites/default/files/uploads/publications/National%20Office/2012/01/Canadas%20CEO%20Elite%20100FINAL.pdf, retrieved May 20, 2012.

CHAPTER 9

1. "Air Canada Pilots Turn to Arbitration," *The Canadian Press,* May 19, 2012, www.cbc.ca/news/canada/story/2012/05/19/air-canada-pilots-arbitration.html, retrieved May 20, 2012; Scott Deveau, "Air Canada Union Fight Threat of Sick-out; Rogue Pilots," *National Post,* April 13, 2012, p. FP 1; "Air Canada Pilots' Job Action Declared Illegal," *CTV News,* April 13, 2012, www.ctv.ca/CTVNews/TopStories/20120413/air-canada-pilots-120413/, retrieved May 18, 2012; and Brent Jang, "Air Canada Duels with Pilots," *The Globe and Mail,* March 19, 2012, p. A3.

2. J.T. Dunlop, *Industrial Relations Systems* (New York: Holt, 1958); and C. Kerr, "Industrial Conflict and Its Mediation," *American Journal of Sociology* 60 (1954), pp. 230–245.

3. T. A. Kochan, *Collective Bargaining and Industrial Relations* (Homewood, IL: Richard D. Irwin, 1980), p. 25; and H. C. Katz and T. A. Kochan, *An Introduction to Collective Bargaining and Industrial Relations,* 3rd ed. (New York: McGraw-Hill, 2004).

4. "About the CLC," www.canadianlabour.ca/about-clc, retrieved May 21, 2012.

5. Whether the time the union steward spends on union business is paid for by the employer, the union, or a combination is a matter of negotiation between the employer and the union.

6. "History of Unions in Canada," www.mapleleaf web.com/old/education/spotlight/issue_51/history .html?q=education/spotlight/issue_51/history.html, retrieved October 22, 2008.

7. Suzanne Payette, "Yesterday and Today: Union Membership," excerpt from the *Workplace Gazette* 5, no. 3 (Fall 2002), www.rhdcc.gc.ca, retrieved November 5, 2004.

8. "Union Coverage in Canada: Unionization Rate Stable Over Past Four Years," *Human Resources and Skills Development Canada,* www.hrsdc.gc.ca/eng/labour/labour_relations/info_analysis/overview/2010/section_6.shtml, retrieved May 16, 2012.

9. Sharanjit Uppal, "Unionization 2011: Component of Statistics Canada Catalogue no. 75-001-X Perspectives on Labour and Income," Table 1, October 26, 2011, p. 6.

10. Katz and Kochan, *An Introduction to Collective Bargaining,* building on J. Fiorito and C. L. Maranto, "The Contemporary Decline of Union Strength," *Contemporary Policy Issues* 3 (1987), pp. 12–27; G. N. Chaison and J. Rose, "The Macrodeterminants of Union Growth and Decline," in *The State of the Unions,* ed. G. Strauss et al. (Madison, WI: Industrial Relations Research Association, 1991).

11. T. A. Kochan, R. B. McKersie, and J. Chalykoff, "The Effects of Corporate Strategy and Workplace Innovations in Union Representation," *Industrial and Labor Relations Review* 39 (1986), pp. 487–501; Chaison and Rose, "The Macrodeterminants of Union Growth and Decline"; J. Barbash, *Practice of Unionism* (New York: Harper, 1956), p. 210; W. N.Cooke and D. G. Meyer, "Structural and Market Predictors of Corporate Labor Relations Strategies," *Industrial and Labor Relations Review* 43 (1990), pp. 280–93; and T. A. Kochan and P. Capelli, "The Transformation of the Industrial

Relations and Personnel Function," in *Internal Labor Markets,* ed. P. Osterman (Cambridge, MA: MIT Press, 1984).

12. Sharanjit Uppal, "Unionization 2011: Component of Statistics Canada Catalogue no. 75-001-X Perspectives on Labour and Income," Table 1, October 26, 2011, p. 6.

13. "Study: The Union Movement in Transition," *The Daily,* August 31, 2004, www.statcan.ca/Daily/ English/040831/d040831b.htm, retrieved November 6, 2004.

14. Sharanjit Uppal, "Unionization 2011: Component of Statistics Canada Catalogue no. 75-001-X Perspectives on Labour and Income," Table 1, October 26, 2011, p. 6.

15. Christopher Hallamore, "Industrial Relations Outlook 2008" (Ottawa: Conference Board of Canada, January 2008), p. 20.

16. Ibid., p. 21.

17. www.cupe.ca/environment/enviroguide, retrieved May 14, 2008; "News Briefs," *Canadian HR Reporter,* December 3, 2007, www.hrreporter.com.

18. C. Brewster, "Levels of Analysis in Strategic HRM: Questions Raised by Comparative Research," Conference on Research and Theory in HRM, Cornell University, October 1997.

19. J. T. Addison and B. T. Hirsch, "Union Effects on Productivity, Profits, and Growth: Has the Long Run Arrived?," *Journal of Labor Economics* 7 (1989), pp. 72–105; and R. B. Freeman and J. L. Medoff, "The Two Faces of Unionism," *Public Interest* 57 (Fall 1979), pp. 69–93.

20. L. Mishel and P. Voos, *Unions and Economic Competitiveness* (Armonk, NY: M. E. Sharpe, 1991); Freeman and Medoff, "Two Faces"; and S. Slichter, J. Healy, and E. R. Livernash, *The Impact of Collective Bargaining on Management* (Washington, DC: Brookings Institution, 1960).

21. A. O. Hirschman, *Exit, Voice, and Loyalty* (Cambridge, MA: Harvard University Press, 1970); and R. Batt, A. J. S. Colvin, and J. Keefe, "Employee Voice, Human Resource Practices, and Quit Rates: Evidence from the Telecommunications Industry," *Industrial and Labor Relations Review* 55 (1970), pp. 573–94.

22. R. B. Freeman and J. L. Medoff, *What Do Unions Do?* (New York: Basic Books, 1984); E. E. Herman, J. L. Schwartz, and A. Kuhn, *Collective Bargaining and Labor Relations* (Englewood Cliffs, NJ: Prentice Hall, 1992); Addison and Hirsch, "Union Effects on Productivity"; Katz and Kochan, *An Introduction to Collective Bargaining;* and P. D. Lineman, M. L. Wachter, and W. H. Carter, "Evaluating the Evidence on Union Employment and Wages," *Industrial and Labor Relations Review* 44 (1990), pp. 34–53.

23. B. E. Becker and C. A. Olson, "Unions and Firm Profits," *Industrial Relations* 31, no. 3 (1992), pp. 395–415; and B. T. Hirsch and B. A. Morgan, "Shareholder Risks and Returns in Union and Nonunion Firms," *Industrial and Labor Relations Review* 47, no. 2 (1994), pp. 302–18.

24. Sharanjit Uppal, "Unionization 2011: Component of Statistics Canada Catalogue no. 75-001-X Perspectives on Labour and Income," October 26, 2011, p. 10.

25. "Campaigns and Issues," *CAW website,* www.caw.ca/ en/campaigns-issues.htmwww.caw.ca, retrieved May 22, 2012.

26. "History and Development of Unions in Canada: The Rand Formula," www.law-faqs.org/nat/un-ran.htm, retrieved October 22, 2008.

27. S. Webb and B. Webb, *Industrial Democracy* (London: Longmans, Green, 1987); J. R. Commons, *Institutional Economics* (New York: Macmillan, 1934).

28. Laura Payton, "Canadian Pacific Railway Strike Leads to 2,000 Layoffs, *CBC News,* May 23, 2012, www.cbc.ca/news/business/story/2012/05/23/ canadian-pacific-strike.html, retrieved May 23, 2012; David K. Shepherdson, "Industrial Relations Outlook 2012 Going Sideways, With a Twist," November 2011, *The Conference Board of Canada,* p. 4; Scott Deveau, "Ottawa Ready to Act as CP Rail Strike Shuts Down Freight Service," *Ottawa Citizen,* May 23, 2012, www.ottawacitizen.com/ business/fp/Ottawa+read+Rail+strike+shuts+down +frieght+service/6664795/storyhtml, retrieved May 23, 2012; "Air Canada legislation OK'd by Ottawa," *CBC News,* March 13, 2012, www.cbc.ca/news/ business/story/2012/03/13/air-canada-union.html, retrieved May 23, 2012; and "Postal Back-to-work Bill becomes Law," *The Globe and Mail,* June 25, 2011, www.theglobeandmail.com/news/politics/ postal-back-to-work-bill-becomes-law-mail-could- resume-tuesday/article2075879/, retrieved May 23, 2012.

29. Adapted from "Publication: Information Circulars No. 5," Canada Industrial Relations Board website, www.cirb-ccri.gc.ca/publications/info/05_eng.asp, retrieved May 23, 2012.

30. "Trade Union Application for Certification," www.sdc.gc.ca, retrieved November 1, 2004.

31. Kris Maher and Janet Adamy, "Do Hot Coffee and 'Wobblies' Go Together?," *The Wall Street Journal,* www.starbucksunion.org/node/756, retrieved May 8, 2008.

32. R. B. Freeman and M. M. Kleiner, "Employer Behavior in the Face of Union Organizing Drives," *Industrial and Labor Relations Review* 43, no. 4 (April 1990), pp. 351–65.

33. Freeman and Medoff, *What Do Unions Do?* National Labor Relations Board annual reports for 1980s and 1990s.

34. J. A. Fossum, *Labor Relations,* 5th ed. (Homewood, IL: Richard D. Irwin, 1992), p. 149.

35. Department of Justice Canada website, http://laws .justice.gc.ca/en/L-2/16931.html, retrieved November 6, 2004.

36. Labour Relations Board British Columbia website, www.lrb.bc.ca/mediation/new_cert.htm, retrieved November 8, 2004.

37. Fossum, *Labor Relations,* p. 262.

38. R. E. Walton and R. B. McKersie, *A Behavioral Theory of Negotiations* (New York: McGraw-Hill, 1965).

39. C. M. Steven, *Strategy and Collective Bargaining Negotiations* (New York: McGraw-Hill, 1963); and Katz and Kochan, *An Introduction to Collective Bargaining.*

40. Sharanjit Uppal, "Unionization 2011: Component of Statistics Canada Catalogue no. 75-001-X Perspectives on Labour and Income," Table 4, October 26, 2011, p. 11.

41. Kochan, *Collective Bargaining and Industrial Relations,* p. 272.

42. Katz and Kochan, *An Introduction to Collective Bargaining.*

43. Kochan, *Collective Bargaining and Industrial Relations,* p. 386; and John W. Budd and Alexander J.S. Colvin, "Improved Metrics for Workplace Dispute Resolution Procedures: Efficiency, Equity, and Voice," *Industrial Relations* 47, no. 3 (July 2008), p. 460.

44. T. A. Kochan, H. C. Katz, and R. B. McKersie, *The Transformation of American Industrial Relations* (New York: Basic Books, 1986), chap. 6; E. Appelbaum, T. Bailey, and P. Berg, *Manufacturing Advantage: Why High-Performance Work Systems Pay Off* (Ithaca, NY: Cornell University Press, 2000).

45. L. W. Hunter, J. P. MacDuffie, and L. Doucet, "What Makes Teams Take? Employee Reactions to Work Reforms," *Industrial and Labor Relations Review* 55 (2002), pp. 448–472.

46. J. B. Arthur, "The Link Between Business Strategy and Industrial Relations Systems in American Steel Minimills," *Industrial and Labor Relations Review* 45 (1992), pp. 488–506; M. Schuster, "Union Management Cooperation," in *Employee and Labor Relations,* ed. J. A. Fossum (Washington, DC: Bureau of National Affairs, 1990); E. Cohen-Rosenthal and C. Burton, *Mutual Gains: A Guide to Union–Management Cooperation,* 2nd ed. (Ithaca, NY: ILR Press, 1993); T. A. Kochan and P. Osterman, *The Mutual Gains Enterprise* (Boston: Harvard Business School Press, 1994); and E. Applebaum and R. Batt, *The New American Workplace* (Ithaca, NY: ILR Press, 1994).

47. A. E. Eaton, "Factors Contributing to the Survival of Employee Participation Programs in Unionized Settings," *Industrial and Labor Relations Review* 47, no. 3 (1994), pp. 371–89.

48. "Preventive Mediation: Nova Scotia Industrial Relations Conciliation Services," www.gov.ns.ca/enla/conciliation/prevbro.htm, retrieved March 5, 2005.

49. Judith Lendvay-Zwicki, "The Canadian Industrial Relations System: Current Challenges and Future Options" (Ottawa: Conference Board of Canada, April 2004), www.conferenceboard.ca, retrieved April 19, 2004.

CHAPTER 10

1. Hollie Shaw, "Lululemon Beats Expectations, but Trims Outlook," *Financial Post,* March 22, 2012, http://business.financialpost.com/2012/03/22/lululemon-shares-down-on-revised-outlook/, retrieved May 28, 2012; Michael Babad, "Bums v. Thumbs: Lululemon Now Worth More than Rim," *The Globe and Mail,* January 12, 2012, www.theglobeandmail.com/report-on-business/top-business-stories/bums-v-thumbs-lululemon-now-worth-more-than-rim/article2299304/, retrieved May 28, 2012; and Sunny Freeman, "Lululemon Founder Chip Wilso Steps Down from Management, Will Stay on Board," *Toronto Star,* January 6, 2012, www.thestar.com/business/article/1111891--lululemon-founder-chip-wilson-steps-down-from-management-will-stay-on-board, retrieved May 28, 2012.

2. Vladimir Pucik, "Human Resources in the Future: An Obstacle or a Champion of Globalization," *Tomorrow's HR Management,* ed. Dave Ulrich, Michael R. Losey, and Gerry Lake (John Wiley & Sons, Inc. New York, 1997), pp. 326–327.

3. "The Developer Matrix," *Financial Express,* April 12, 2010, Business & Company Resource Center, http://galenet.galegroup.com; and Steve Lohr, "Global Strategy Stabilized I.B. During Downturn," *New York Times,* April 20, 2010, Business & Company Resource Center, http://galenet.galegroup.com.

4. Avery Johnson, "Drug Firms See Poorer Nations as Sales Cure," *Wall Street Journal,* July 7, 2009, http://online.wsj.com.

5. Loewen website, www.loewen.com/whyLoewen/aboutUs/companyProfile.html, retrieved May 27, 2012.

6. N. Adler and S. Bartholomew, "Managing Globally Competent People," *The Executive* 6 (1992), pp. 52–65.

7. V. Sathe, *Culture and Related Corporate Realities* (Homewood, IL: Richard D. Irwin, 1985); and M. Rokeach, *Beliefs, Attitudes, and Values* (San Francisco: Jossey-Bass, 1968).

8. N. Adler, *International Dimensions of Organizational Behavior,* 2nd ed. (Boston: PWS-Kent, 1991).

9. G. Hofstede, "Dimensions of National Cultures in Fifty Countries and Three Regions," in *Expectations in Cross-Cultural Psychology,* ed. J. Deregowski, S. Dziurawiec, and R. C. Annis (Lisse, Netherlands: Swets and Zeitlinger, 1983); G. Hofstede, "Cultural Constraints in Management Theories," *Academy of Management Executive* 7 (1993), pp. 81–90.

10. Hofstede, "Cultural Constraints in Management Theories."

11. W. A. Randolph and M. Sashkin, "Can Organizational Empowerment Work in Multinational Settings?" *Academy of Management Executive* 16, no. 1 (2002), pp. 102–115.

12. Lesley Young, "Attracting, Keeping Employees Overseas," *Canadian HR Reporter,* April 7, 2008, www.hrreporter.com, retrieved May 26, 2008.

13. Randolph and Sashkin, pp. 102–115.

14. B. Gerhart and M. Fang, "National Culture and Human Resource Management: Assumptions and Evidence," *International Journal of Human Resource Management* 16, no. 6 (June 2005); pp. 971–986.

15. National Center for Education Statistics (NCES), "International Comparisons of Education," *Digest of Education Statistics, 2000,* chap. 6, NCES website, http://nces.ed.gov, retrieved September 23, 2002.

16. Organization for Economic Cooperation and Development, *EdStats,* www.worldbank.org, accessed March 20, 2008.

17. P. Conrad and R. Peiper, "Human Resource Management in the Federal Republic of Germany," in *Human Resource Management: An International Comparison,* ed. R. Peiper (Berlin: Walter de Gruyter, 1990).

18. "Saskatchewan Looking to Lure Nurses from Philippines," February 21, 2008, www.cbc.ca/canada/saskatchewan/story/2008/02/21/nurses-philippines.html, retrieved June 7, 2008.

19. Lawrence A. West Jr. and Walter A. Bogumil Jr., "Foreign Knowledge Workers as a Strategic Staffing Option," *The Academy of Management Executive,* November 2000.

20. W. A. Arthur Jr. and W. Bennett Jr., "The International Assignee: The Relative Importance of Factors Perceived to Contribute to Success," *Personnel Psychology* 48 (1995), pp. 99–114; and G. M. Spreitzer, M. W. McCall Jr., and J. D. Mahoney, "Early Identification of International Executive Potential," *Journal of Applied Psychology* 82 (1997), pp. 6–29.

21. J. S. Black and J. K. Stephens, "The Influence of the Spouse on American Expatriate Adjustment and Intent to Stay in Pacific Rim Overseas Assignments," *Journal of Management* 15 (1989), pp. 529–44.

22. P. Caligiuri, "The Big Five Personality Characteristics as Predictors of Expatriates' Desire to Terminate the Assignment and Supervisor-Rated Performance," *Personnel Psychology* 53 (2000), pp. 67–88.

23. Delia Flanja, "Culture Shock in Intercultural Communication," *Studia Europaea* (October 2009), Business & Company Resource Center, http://galenet.galegroup.com.

24. J. Flynn, "E-mail, Cell Phones, and Frequent-Flier Miles Let 'Virtual' Expats Work Abroad but Live at Home," *The Wall Street Journal,* October 25, 1999, p. A26.

25. Liam Dixon and Margaret Sim, "Short-Term Assignments Growing in Popularity," *Canadian HR Reporter,* March 10, 2008, p. 17.

26. Ibid.

27. D. M. Gayeski, C. Sanchirico, and J. Anderson, "Designing Training for Global Environments: Knowing What Questions to Ask," *Performance Improvement Quarterly* 15, no. 2 (2002), pp. 15–31.

28. "Explore," *The Schlumberger Campus Magazine,* November 2006, p. 7, www.slb.com, retrieved June 10, 2008.

29. J. S. Black and M. Mendenhall, "A Practical but Theory-Based Framework for Selecting Cross-Cultural Training Methods," in *Readings and Cases in International Human Resource Management,* ed. M. Mendenhall and G. Oddou (Boston: PWS-Kent, 1991), pp. 177–204.

30. C. Lachnit, "Low-Cost Tips for Successful Inpatriation," *Workforce,* August 2001, pp. 42–44, 46–47.

31. D. D. Davis, "International Performance Measurement and Management," in *Performance Appraisal: State of the Art in Practice,* ed. J. W. Smither (San Francisco: Jossey-Bass, 1998), pp. 95–131.

32. M. Gowan, S. Ibarreche, and C. Lackey, "Doing the Right Things in Mexico," *Academy of Management Executive* 10 (1996), pp. 74–81.

33. L. S. Chee, "Singapore Airlines: Strategic Human Resource Initiatives," in *International Human Resource Management: Think Globally, Act Locally,* ed. D. Torrington (Upper Saddle River, NJ: Prentice Hall, 1994), pp. 143–59.

34. D. D. Davis, "International Performance Measurement and Management," in *Performance Appraisal: State of the Art in Practice,* ed. J. W. Smither (San Francisco: Jossey-Bass, 1998), pp. 95–131.

35. Hay Group, "Hay Group Report Reveals Global Managers Spending Power and Pay Gaps, news release, December 8, 2009, www.haygroup.com.

36. Bureau of Labor Statistics, "International Comparisons of Hourly Compensation Costs in Manufacturing, 2007," news release, March 26, 2009, www.bls.gov.

37. See, for example, A. E. Cobet, and G. A. Wilson, "Comparing 50 Years of Labor Productivity in U.S. and Foreign Manufacturing," *Monthly Labor Review,* June 2002, pp. 51–63; and Bureau of Labor Statistics, "International Comparisons of Manufacturing Productivity and About Cost Trends, 2008," news release, October 22, 2009, www.bls.gov.

38. "Job Cuts vs. Pay Cuts: In a Slowing Economy, What's Better for India?" *India Knowledge @ Wharton,* November 13, 2008, http://knowledge, wharton.upenn.edu/india/.

39. "Mexican Labour Relationship," www.solutions-abroad .com/d_mexicanlaborlaws.asp.

40. Ann Macaulay, "Scouting the Danger Online," *Canadian HR Reporter,* September 24, 2007, p. 13.

41. "Employers Compensating Employees in High-Risk Areas," August 5, 2003, www.hrreporter.com, retrieved January 23, 2004.

42. Macaulay, ibid.

43. Craig Malcolm, "Protecting Employees in Danger Zones," *Canadian HR Reporter,* September 24, 2007, p. 9.

44. Paul Glader and Kris Maher, "Unions Look for Cross-Border Allies," *The Globe and Mail,* March 15, 2005, p. B17.

45. P. J. Dowling, D. E. Welch, and R. S. Schuler, *International Human Resource Management,* 3rd ed. (Cincinnati: South-Western, 1999), pp. 235–36.

46. Ibid.; J. La Palombara and S. Blank, *Multinational Corporations and National Elites: A Study of Tensions* (New York: Conference Board, 1976); A. B. Sim, "Decentralized Management of Subsidiaries and Their Performance: A Comparative Study of American, British and Japanese Subsidiaries in Malaysia," *Management International Review* 17, no. 2 (1977), pp. 45–51; Y. K. Shetty, "Managing the Multinational Corporation: European and American Styles," *Management International Review* 19, no. 3 (1979), pp. 39–48; and J. Hamill, "Labor Relations Decision-Making Within Multinational Corporations," *Industrial Relations Journal* 15, no. 2 (1984), pp. 30–34.

47. J. K. Sebenius, "The Hidden Challenge of Cross-Border Negotiations," *Harvard Business Review,* March 2002, pp. 76-85.

48. Ibid.

49. E. Krall, "Evaluating Returns on Expatriates, *HRMagazine,* March 2005, downloaded from Infotract at http://web5.infotrac.galegroup.com.

50. Stephen Cryne, "Avoiding the Perils of Foreign Assignments," *Canadian HR Reporter,* March 12, 2007, p. 14.

51. Margaret Sim and Liam Dixon, "Number of Women Expats Increasing," *Canadian HR Reporter,* May 21, 2007, p. 14.

52. E. Krell, "Evaluating Returns on Expatriates," *HR Magazine,* March 2005, http://web5.infotrac.galegroup.com.

53. Ibid.; M. Harvey and M. M. Novicevic, "Selecting Expatriates for Increasingly Complex Global Assignments," *Career Development International* 6, no. 2 (2001), pp. 69–86.

54. M. Mendenhall and G. Oddou, "The Dimensions of Expatriate Acculturation," *Academy of Management Review* 10 (1985), pp. 39–47.

55. Arthur and Bennett, "The International Assignee."

56. J. I. Sanchez, P. E. Spector, and C. L. Cooper, "Adapting to a Boundaryless World: A Developmental Expatriate Model," *Academy of Management Executive* 14, no. 2 (2000), pp. 96–106.

57. P. Dowling and R. Schuler, *International Dimensions of Human Resource Management* (Boston: PWS-Kent, 1990).

58. Sanchez, Spector, and Cooper, "Adapting to a Boundaryless World."

59. Catherine Aman, "Horses for Courses," *Corporate Counsel,* December 15, 2008, Business & Company Resource Center, http://galenet.galegroup.com.

60. Javier Espinoza, "Location, Location, Location," *Wall Street Journal,* February 5, 2010, http://online.wsj.com; and David Everhart, "Preparing Execs for Asia Assignments," *Business Week,* April 1, 2008, www.businessweek.com.

61. "How Can a Company Manage an Expatriate Employee's Performance?" *SHRM India,* www.shrmindia.org, accessed May 6, 2010.

62. Siobhan Cummisand and Ed P. Hannibal, "Should Your Business Axe Overseas Assignments?" *Business-Week,* April 26, 2010, www.businessweek.com.

63. Lynne Molmar, "Addressing Expatriate Tax Issues," *Canadian HR Reporter,* March 13, 2006, p. 15.

64. Amy Maingault, Lesa Albright, and Vicki Neal, "Policy Tips, Repatriation, Safe Harbor Rules," *HR Magazine,* March 2008, p. 34.

65. "Minimizing Expatriate Turnover," *Workforce Management Online,* August 2004, www.workforce.com/section/09/article/23/81/28.html, retrieved March 22, 2005.

66. Adler, *International Dimensions of Organizational Behavior.*

67. L. G. Klaff, "The Right Way to Bring Expats Home," *Workforce,* July 2002, pp. 40–44.

CHAPTER 11

1. Mia Pearson, "Top-Gun Talent Make Ideal Recruiters," *The Globe and Mail,* July 21, 2011, www.theglobeandmail.com/report-on-business/small-business/sb-tools/sb-columnists/top-gun-talent-make-ideal-recruiters/article2103859/, retrieved June 11, 2012; "Best Employers Focus on Engagement," *Benefits Canada,* February 13, 2012, www.benefitscanada.com/news/best-employers-focus-on-engagement-25489, retrieved June 10, 2012; "Imaginet is the Best Small and Medium Employer in Canada," *PRWeb,* February 9, 2012, www.prweb.com/printer/91788875.htm, retrieved June 11, 2012; and www.imaginet.com.

2. S. Snell and J. Dean, "Integrated Manufacturing and Human Resource Management: A Human Capital Perspective," *Academy of Management Journal* 35 (1992), pp. 467–504.

3. M. A. Huselid, "The Impact of Human Resource Management Practices on Turnover, Productivity, and Corporate Financial Performance," *Academy of Management Journal* 38 (1995), pp. 635–72; U.S. Department of Labor, *High-Performance Work Practices and Firm Performance* (Washington, DC: U.S. Government Printing Office, 1993); and J. Combs, Y. Liu, A. Hall, and D. Ketchen, "How Much Do High-Performance Work Practices Matter? A Meta-Analysis of Their Effects on Organizational Performance," *Personnel Psychology* 59 (2006), p. 501–528.

4. R. N. Ashkenas, "Beyond the Fads: How Leaders Drive Change with Results," *Human Resource Planning* 17 (1994), pp. 25–44; Ronald M. Katz, "OPTimize Your Workforce," *HRMagazine,* October 2009, p. 85; and Jim Catalino, "Software Solutions Can Trim Rising Costs," *Health Management Technology,* March 2010, pp. 10–11.

5. J. Arthur, "The Link Between Business Strategy and Industrial Relations Systems in American Steel Mini-Mills," *Industrial and Labor Relations Review* 45 (1992), pp. 488–506.

6. J. A. Neal and C. L. Tromley, "From Incremental Change to Retrofit: Creating High-Performance Work Systems," *Academy of Management Executive* 9 (1995), pp. 42–54; and M. A. Huselid, "The Impact of Human Resource Management Practices on Turnover, Productivity, and Corporate Financial Performance," *Academy of Management Journal* 38 (1995), pp. 635–72.

7. T.J. Atchison, "The Employment Relationship: Untied or Re-Tied," *Academy of Management Executive* 5 (1991), pp. 52–62.

8. Wallace Immen, "Managers Hold Key to Keep Staff Happy," *The Globe and Mail,* June 16, 2004, p. C3.

9. D. McCann and C. Margerison, "Managing High-Performance Teams," *Training and Development Journal,* November 1989, pp. 52–60.

10. D. Senge, "The Learning Organization Made Plain and Simple," *Training and Development Journal,* October 1991, pp. 37–44.

11. M. A. Gephart, V. J. Marsick, M. E. Van Buren, and M. S. Spiro, "Learning Organizations Come Alive," *Training and Development* 50 (1996), pp. 34–45.

12. T. T. Baldwin, C. Danielson, and W. Wiggenhorn, "The Evolution of Learning Strategies in Organizations: From Employee Development to Business Redefinition," *Academy of Management Executive* 11 (1997), pp. 47–58; J. J. Martocchio and T. T. Baldwin, "The Evolution of Strategic Organizational Training," in *Research in Personnel and Human Resource Management* 15, ed. G. R. Ferris (Greenwich, CT: JAI Press, 1997), pp. 1–46; and "Leveraging HR and Knowledge Management in a Challenging Economy," *HR Magazine,* June 2009, pp. 81–89.

13. A. Hanacek, "Star Power," *National Provisioner,* February 2008, downloaded from General Reference Center Gold, http://find.galegroup.com.

14. E. A. Locke, "The Nature and Causes of Job Dissatisfaction," in *The Handbook of Industrial & Organizitonal Psychology,* ed. M. D. Dunnette (Chicago: Rand McNally, 1976), pp. 901–961

15. T. A. Judge, C. J. Thoresen, J. E. Bono, and G. K. Patton, "The Job Satisfaction-Job Performance Relationship: A Qualitative and Quantitative Review," *Psychological Bulletin* 127 (2001), pp. 376–407; and R. A. Katzell, D. E. Thompson, and R. A. Guzzo, "How Job Satisfaction and Job Performance Are and Are Not Linked," *Job Satisfaction,* ed. C. J. Cranny, P. C. Smith, and E. F. Stone (New York: Lexington Books, 1992), pp. 195–217.

16. "Best Employer Studies Canada: What is Employee Engagement," Aon Hewitt website, https://ceplb03.hewitt.com/bestemployers/canada/pages/driving_engagement.htm, retrieved June 11, 2012.

17. Hewitt Associates, "The Link Between Employee Engagement and Business Results," http://was4.hewitt.com/hewitt/resource/rptspubs/hewitcmagazine/vo16, retrieved November 29, 2004.

18. Theresa Minton Eversole, "Less Engagement, Less Profit, Research Finds," *HR Magazine,* December 2007, p. 20.

19. Ibid.

20. P.E. Boverie and M. Kroth, *Transforming Work: The Five Keys to Achieving Trust, Commitment, and Passion in the Workplace* (Cambridge, MA: Perseus, 2001), pp. 71–72, 79.

21. R. P. Gephart Jr., "Introduction to the Brave New Workplace: Organizational Behavior in the Electronic Age," *Journal of Organizational Behavior* 23 (2002), pp. 327–44.

22. R. P. Quinn and G. L. Staines, *The 1977 Quality of Employment Survey* (Ann Arbor, MI: Survey Research Center, Institute for Social Research, University of Michigan, 1979).

23. T. Judge and T. Welbourne, "A Confirmatory Investigation of the Dimensionality of the Pay Satisfaction Questionnaire," *Journal of Applied Psychology* 79 (1994), pp. 461–66.

24. John Thackray, "Feedback for Real," March 15, 2001, http://gmj.gallup.com/conent/default.asp?ci=811, retrieved November 28, 2004.

25. Ibid.

26. Suzanne Wintrob, "Reward a Job Well Done, *Financial Post,* May 10, 2004, p. FP7.

27. Terence F. Shea, "Getting the Last Word," *HR Magazine,* January 2010, Business & Company Resource Center, http://galenet.galegroup.com; and L. M. Sixel, "Keeping Top Talent Has Employers Worried," *Houston Chronicle,* March 14, 2010, Business & Company Resource Center, http://galenet.galegroup.com.

28. "Stay Interviews," www.bcjobs.ca/re/hr-centre/interview-techniques/human-resource-advice/stay-interviews, retrieved June 11, 2012.

29. Kettler, ibid.

30. M. Lewis Jr., "The Heat is On," *Inside Business,* October 2007, downloaded from General Reference Center Gold, http://find.galegroup.com.

31. B. Becker and M. A. Huselid, "High-Performance Work Systems and Firm Performance: A Synthesis of Research and Managerial Implications," in *Research in Personnel and Human Resource Management* 16, ed. G. R. Ferris (Stamford, CT: JAI Press, 1998), pp. 53–101.

32. B. Becker and B. Gerhart, "The Impact of Human Resource Management on Organizational Performance: Progress and Prospects," *Academy of Management Journal* 39 (1996), pp. 779–801.

33. Pearson, ibid.

34. Sarah Dobson, "Project Connects Dots Between T&D, Profit," *Canadian HR Reporter,* April 21, 2008, p. 3.

35. H. J. Bernardin, C. M. Hagan, J. S. Kane, and P. Villanova, "Effective Performance Management: A Focus on Precision, Customers, and Situational

Constraints," in *Performance Appraisal: State of the Art in Practice,* ed. J. W. Smither (San Francisco: Jossey-Bass, 1998), p. 56.

36. L. R. Gomez-Mejia and D. B. Balkin, *Compensation, Organizational Strategy, and Firm Performance* (Cincinnati: South-Western, 1992); and G. D. Jenkins and E. E. Lawler III, "Impact of Employee Participation in Pay Plan Development," *Organizational Behavior and Human Performance* 28 (1981), pp. 111–28.

37. Uyen Vu, "What's the Real Cost of Turnover?" *Canadian HR Reporter,* July 14, 2008, www.hrreporter.com, retrieved July 14, 2008.

38. M. M. Le Blanc and K. Kelloway, "Predictors and Outcomes of Workplace Violence and Aggression," *Journal of Applied Psychology,* 87, 2002, pp. 444–53.

39. "Wrongful Dismissal Law in Canada," Duhaime's Employment and Labour Law Centre, www.duhaime.orgfEmployment/ca-wd.aspx, retrieved March 28, 2005.

40. K. Karl and C. Sutton, "A Review of Expert Advice on Employment Termination Practices: The Experts Don't Always Agree," in *Dysfunctional Behavior in Organizations,* eds. R. Griffin, A. O'Leary-Kelly, and J. Collins (Stanford, CT: JA1 Press, 1998).

41. Government of Canada, "Corporate Social Responsibility: An Implementation Guide for Canadian Business," 2006, p. 5, www.commdev.org/content/document/detail/1468.

42. Paul Tsaparis, "Social Responsibility Gives Canadian Firms an Edge," *Canadian HR Reporter,* May 23, 2005, p. 18.

43. Ibid.

44. Anthony Watanabe, "From Brown to Green," *HR Professional,* February/March 2008, p. 49.

45. Uyen Vu, "Climate Change Sparks Attitude Shift," *Canadian HR Reporter,* March 26, 2007, p. 11.

46. Adrienne Fox, "Get in the Business of Being Green," *HR Magazine,* June 2008, p. 45.

47. Vancity website, https://www.vancity.com/AboutUs/OurValues/VancityIsCarbonNeutral/, retrieved June 12, 2012; and Shannon Klie, "Credit Union Aims to Be CO_2-Neutral by 2010," *Canadian HR Reporter,* March 26, 2007, p. 12; www.vancity.com, retrieved June 3, 2008.

48. Vancity website, www.vancity.com/AboutUs/OurValues/VancityIsCarbonNeutral/TheJourneyToZero/Transportation/, retrieved June 12, 2012.

49. Beth Tyndall, "Charitable Giving ROI," *HR Professional,* April/May 2007, p. 34.

50. Andrew Wahl et al., "The Best Work Places in Canada 2007," *Canadian Business,* April 23, 2007.

51. Ibid.

52. Nova Scotia Public Service Commission website, www.gov.ns.ca/psc/jobCentre/, retrieved June 12, 2012.

53. Fox, ibid.

54. Wayne F. Cascio and Peter Cappelli, "Lessons from the Financial Services Crisis," *HR Magazine,* Jauary 2009, Business & Company Resource Center, http://galenet.galegroup.com; Chris Petersen, "Thou Shalt Not…," *Construction Today,* September 2009, p. 13; and Carolyn Hirschman, "Giving Voice to Employee Concerns," *HR Magazine,* August 2008, pp. 51–53.

55. Gwyn Morgan, "'Merger of Equals' Pitch Created EnCana, but It Would Flop Today," *The Globe and Mail,* April 30, 2007, p. B2.

56. Uyen Vu, "HR's Role in Mergers, Acquisitions," *Canadian HR Reporter,* December 4, 2006, p. 17, 21.

57. "Involve HR Early in M&As for Success, Survey Shows," *The Globe and Mail,* December 17, 2004, p. C3.

58. Uyen Vu, ibid.

59. Ibid.

60. S. Shrivastava and J. Shaw, "Liberating HR Through Technology," *Human Resource Management* 42, no. 3 (2003), pp. 201–17.

61. R. Broderick and J. W. Boudreau, "Human Resource Management, Information Technology, and the Competitive Edge," *Academy of Management Executive* 6 (1992), pp. 7–17.

62. Steve Hamm, "IBM Reinvents Mentoring, via the Web," *Business Week,* March 12, 2009, www.businessweek.com.

63. L. Baird and I. Meshoulam, "Managing Two Fits of Strategic Human Resource Management," *Academy of Management Review* 13, no. 1 (1988), pp. 116–128.

64. "Towers Perrin Survey Shows Companies Making Major Strides in Implementing and Streamlining HR Technology Systems," August 29, 2007, www.towersperrin.com, retrieved June 10, 2008.

65. "Hot HR Issues for the Next Two Years," (Ottawa: Conference Board of Canada), September 2004.

66. "CFOs Showing More Interest in HR," *Canadian HR Reporter,* October 25, 2004, p. 4.

67. David Brown, "Measuring Human Capital Crucial, ROI Isn't, Says New Think-Tank Paper," *Canadian HR Reporter,* October 25, 2004, p. 4.

68. Ibid.

69. Jeff Sanford, "Value for the Money," *Canadian Business,* February 18, 2008, pp. 31–32.

70. R. F. Stolz, "CEOs Who 'Get It," *Human Resource Executive,* March 16, 2005, pp. 1, 18–25.

achievement tests Tests that measure a person's existing knowledge and skills.

action learning Training in which teams get an actual problem, work on solving it, commit to an action plan, and are accountable for carrying it out.

ADR See *alternative dispute resolution.*

adventure learning A teamwork and leadership training program based on the use of challenging, structured outdoor activities.

alternative work arrangements Methods of staffing other than the traditional hiring of full-time employees (e.g., use of independent contractors, on-call workers, temporary workers, and contract company workers).

applicant tracking system (ATS) A software application that streamlines the flow of information between job seekers, HR staff, and hiring managers.

apprenticeship A work-study training method that teaches job skills through a combination of on-the-job training and technical training.

aptitude tests Tests that assess how well a person can learn or acquire skills and abilities.

arbitration Conflict resolution procedure in which an arbitrator or arbitration board determines a binding settlement.

assessment Collecting information and providing feedback to employees about their behaviour, communication style, or skills.

assessment centre A wide variety of specific selection programs that use multiple selection methods to rate applicants or job incumbents on their management potential.

ATS See *Applicant tracking system.*

avatars Computer depictions of trainees, which the trainees manipulate in an online role-play.

balanced scorecard An organizational approach to performance management that integrates strategic perspectives including financial, customer, internal business processes, and learning and growth.

BARS See *behaviourally anchored rating scale.*

behavioural interview A structured interview in which the interviewer asks the candidate to describe how he or she handled a type of situation in the past.

behavioural observation scale (BOS) A variation of BARS, which uses all behaviours necessary for effective performance to rate performance at a task.

behaviourally anchored rating scale (BARS) Method of performance measurement that rates behaviour in terms of a scale showing specific statements of behaviour that describe different levels of performance.

benchmarking A procedure in which an organization compares its own practices against those of successful competitors.

benchmarks A measurement tool that gathers ratings of a manager's use of skills associated with success in managing.

BFOR See *bona fide occupational requirement.*

Bill C-45 (Westray Bill) Amendment to the Criminal Code making organizations and anyone who directs the work of others criminally liable for safety offences.

bona fide occupational requirement (BFOR) A necessary (not merely preferred) requirement for performing a job.

BOS See *behavioural observation scale.*

broadbanding Reducing the number of pay ranges in the organization's pay structure.

calibration session Meeting at which managers discuss employee performance ratings and provide evidence supporting their ratings with the goal of eliminating the influence of rating errors.

Canada Pension Plan (CPP)/Quebec Pension Plan (QPP) A contributory, mandatory plan that provides retirement pensions, disability benefits, and survivor benefits.

Canadian Labour Congress (CLC) A union federation that serves as an umbrella organization for dozens of affiliated Canadian and international unions, as well as provincial federations of labour and regional labour councils.

career paths The identified pattern or progression of jobs or roles within an organization.

central tendency Incorrectly rating all employees at or near the middle of a rating scale.

checkoff provision A requirement that the employer, on behalf of the union, automatically deducts union dues from employees' paycheques.

CLC See *Canadian Labour Congress.*

closed shop A union security arrangement under which a person must be a union member before being hired.

coach A peer or manager who works with an employee to provide a source of motivation, help him or her develop skills, and provide reinforcement and feedback.

cognitive ability tests Tests designed to measure such mental abilities as verbal skills, quantitative skills, and reasoning ability.

collective bargaining Negotiation between union representatives and management representatives to arrive at an agreement defining conditions of employment for the term of the agreement and to administer that agreement.

commissions Incentive pay calculated as a percentage of sales.

compensatory model Process of arriving at a selection decision in which a very high score on one type of assessment can make up for a low score on another.

competencies Knowledge, skills, abilities, and other characteristics associated with effective job performance.

competency framework Competencies the entire organization requires to be successful.

competency-based pay systems Pay structures that set pay according to the employees' levels of skill or knowledge and what they are capable of doing.

conciliation Conflict resolution procedure in which a third party to collective bargaining reports the reasons for a dispute, the views and arguments of both sides, and possibly a recommended settlement, which the parties may decline.

concurrent validation Research that consists of administering a test to people who currently hold a job, then comparing their scores to existing measures of job performance.

construct validity Consistency between a high score on a test and a high level of a construct such as intelligence or leadership ability, a s well as between mastery of this construct and successful performance on the job.

constructive dismissal Occurs when the employer makes a significant change to a worker's condition of employment.

content validity Consistency between the test items or problems and the kinds of situations or problems that occur on the job.

continuous learning Each employee's and each group's ongoing efforts to gather information and apply the information to their decisions in a learning organization.

contrast error Rating error caused by comparing employee's performance to co-workers rather than to an objective standard.

contributory plan All costs of the plan are funded by employees, employers, and the plan's own investments.

cooperative education A plan of higher education that incorporates paid work experience as an integral part of academic studies.

coordination training Team training that teaches the team how to share information and make decisions to obtain the best team performance.

corporate social responsibility (CSR) An organization's commitment to meeting the needs of its stakeholders.

CPP See *Canada Pension Plan.*

craft union Labour union whose members all have a particular skill or occupation.

criterion-related validity A measure of validity based on showing a substantial correlation between test scores and job performance scores.

critical-incident method Method of performance measurement based on managers' records of specific examples of the employee behaving in ways that are either effective or ineffective.

cross-cultural preparation Training to prepare employees and their family members for an assignment in a foreign country.

cross-training Team training in which team members understand and practise each other's skills so that they are prepared to step in and take another member's place.

CSR See *corporate social responsibility.*

culture shock Disillusionment and discomfort that occur during the process of adjusting to a new culture.

decision support systems Computer software systems designed to help managers solve problems by showing how results vary when the manager alters assumptions or data.

defined benefit plan A pension plan that guarantees a specified level of retirement income.

defined contribution plan A retirement plan in which the employer sets up an individual account for each employee and specifies the size of the investment into that account.

development The acquisition of knowledge, skills, and behaviours that improve an employee's ability to meet the challenges of a variety of new or existing jobs.

differential treatment Differing treatment of individuals where the differences are based on a prohibited ground.

direct applicants People who apply for a vacancy without prompting from the organization.

direct compensation Financial rewards employees receive in exchange for their work.

direct discrimination Policies or practices that clearly make a distinction on the basis of a prohibited ground.

discrimination Treating someone differently, negatively, or adversely because of their race, age, religion, sex, or other prohibited ground.

distributed work A combination of work options, including work from the corporate office, work from home, work from a satellite office, or work from another remote location.

diversity training Training designed to change employee attitudes about diversity and/or develop skills needed to work with a diverse workforce.

downsizing The planned elimination of large numbers of employees with the goal of enhancing the organization's competitiveness.

downward move Assignment of an employee to a position with less responsibility and authority.

duty to accommodate An employer's duty to consider how an employee's characteristic such as disability, religion, or sex can be accommodated and to take action so the employee can perform the job.

EAP See *employee assistance program.*

e-HRM See *electronic human resource management.*

EI See *Employment Insurance.*

e-learning Receiving training via the Internet or the organization's intranet.

electronic human resource management (e-HRM) The processing and transmission of digitized HR information, especially using computer networking and the Internet.

employee assistance program (EAP) Referral service that employees can use to seek professional treatment for emotional issues or substance abuse.

employee benefits Compensation in forms other than cash.

employee development The combination of formal education, job experiences, relationships, and assessment of personality and abilities to help employees prepare for the future of their careers.

employee empowerment Giving employees responsibility and authority to make decisions regarding all aspects of product development or customer service.

employee engagement The extent that employees are satisfied, committed to, and prepared to support what is important to the organization.

employee stock ownership plan (ESOP) An arrangement in which the organization distributes shares of stock to all its employees by placing it in a trust.

employee wellness program A set of communications, activities, and facilities designed to change health-related behaviours in ways that reduce health risks.

employer branding A strategic approach of attaching a visual, emotional, or cultural brand to an organization.

Employment Insurance (EI) A federally mandated program to provide temporary financial assistance to unemployed workers.

ergonomics The study of the interface between individuals' physiology and the characteristics of the physical work environment.

ESOP See *employee stock ownership plan.*

ethics The fundamental principles of right and wrong.

evidence-based HR Collecting and using data to show that human resource practices have a positive influence on the company's bottom line or key stakeholders.

exit interview A meeting of a departing employee with the employee's supervisor and/or human resource specialist to discuss the employee's reasons for leaving.

expatriates Employees who take assignments in other countries.

experiential programs Training programs in which participants learn concepts and apply them by simulating behaviours involved and analyzing the activity, connecting it with real-life situations.

expert systems Computer systems that support decision making by incorporating the decision rules used by people who are considered to have expertise in a certain area.

external labour market Individuals who are actively seeking employment.

externship Employee development through a full-time temporary position at another organization.

feedback Information employers give employees about their skills and knowledge and where these assets fit into the organization's plans.

Fleishman Job Analysis System Job analysis technique that asks subject-matter experts to evaluate a job in terms of the abilities required to perform the job.

flexible benefits plan A benefits plan that offers employees a set of alternatives from which they can choose the types and amounts of benefits they want.

flextime A scheduling policy in which full-time employees may choose starting and ending times within guidelines specified by the organization.

focus on activities Rating error when employees are assessed on how busy they appear rather than how effective they are in achieving results.

forced-distribution method Method of performance measurement that assigns a certain percentage of employees to each category in a set of categories.

forecasting The attempts to determine the supply of and demand for various types of human resources to predict areas within the organization where there will be labour shortages or surpluses.

gainsharing Team incentive program that measures improvements in productivity and effectiveness and distributes a portion of each gain to employees.

generalizable Valid in other contexts beyond the context in which the selection method was developed.

glass ceiling Circumstances resembling an invisible barrier that keep most women and other members of the employment equity groups from attaining the top jobs in organizations.

global organization An organization that chooses to locate a facility based on the ability to effectively, efficiently, and flexibly produce a product or service, using cultural differences as an advantage.

graphic rating scale Method of performance measurement that lists attributes and provides a rating scale for each attribute; the employer uses the scale to indicate the extent to which an employee displays each attribute.

grievance procedure The process for resolving union–management conflicts over interpretation or violation of a collective agreement.

halo error Rating error that occurs when the rater reacts to one positive performance aspect by rating the employee positively in all areas of performance.

harassment Any behaviour that demeans, humiliates, or embarrasses a person, and that a reasonable person should have known would be unwelcome.

health spending account A specific amount of money set aside per employee by the employer to cover health-related costs.

high-performance work system An organization in which technology, organizational structure, people, and processes all work together to give an organization an advantage in the competitive environment.

home country The country in which an organization's headquarters is located.

horns error Rating error that occurs when the rater responds to one negative aspect by rating an employee low in other aspects.

host country A country (other than the home country) in which an organization operates a facility.

hourly wage Rate of pay for each hour worked.

HR dashboard A display of a series of HR measures, showing human resource goals and objectives and progress toward meeting them.

HRIS See *human resource information system.*

HRM See *human resource management.*

HRM audit A formal review of the outcomes of HRM functions, based on identifying key HRM functions and measures of organizational performance.

human capital An organization's employees, described in terms of their training, experience, judgment, intelligence, relationships, and insight.

human resource information system (HRIS) A computer system used to acquire, store, manipulate, analyze, retrieve, and distribute information related to an organization's human resources.

human resource management (HRM) The practices, policies, and systems that influence employees' behaviour, attitudes, and performance.

incentive pay Forms of pay linked to an employee's performance as an individual, group member, or organization member.

indirect compensation The benefits and services employees receive in exchange for their work.

indirect discrimination Policies or practices that appear to be neutral but have an adverse effect on the basis of a prohibited ground.

industrial engineering The study of jobs to find the simplest way to structure work in order to maximize efficiency.

industrial union A labour union whose members are linked by their work in a particular industry.

instructional design A process of systematically developing training to meet specified needs.

internal labour force An organization's workers (its employees and the people who work at the organization).

internal responsibility system Philosophy of occupational health and safety whereby employers and employees share responsibility for creating and maintaining safe and healthy work environments.

international organization An organization that sets up one or a few facilities in one or a few foreign countries.

internship On-the-job learning sponsored by an educational institution as a component of an academic program.

involuntary turnover Turnover initiated by an employer (often with employees who would prefer to stay).

job A set of related duties.

job analysis The process of getting detailed information about jobs.

job description A list of the tasks, duties, and responsibilities (TDRs) that a particular job entails.

job design The process of defining the way work will be performed and the tasks that a given job requires.

job enlargement Broadening the types of tasks performed in a job.

job enrichment Engaging workers by adding more decision-making authority to jobs.

job evaluation An administrative procedure for measuring the relative internal worth of the organization's jobs.

job experiences The combination of relationships, problems, demands, tasks, and other features of an employee's job.

job extension Enlarging jobs by combining several relatively simple jobs to form a job with a wider range of tasks.

job hazard analysis technique Safety promotion technique that involves breaking down a job into basic elements, then rating each element for its potential for harm or injury.

job posting The process of communicating information about a job vacancy on company bulletin boards, in employee publications, on corporate intranets, and anywhere else the organization communicates with employees.

job rotation Enlarging jobs by moving employees among several different jobs.

job sharing A work option in which two part-time employees carry out the tasks associated with a single job.

job specification A list of the competencies an individual must have to perform a particular job.

job structure The relative pay for different jobs within the organization.

knowledge workers Employees whose main contribution to the organization is specialized knowledge, such as knowledge of customers, a process, or a profession.

labour relations A field that emphasizes skills managers and union leaders can use to minimize costly forms of conflict (such as strikes) and seek win-win solutions to disagreements.

Labour Relations Board (LRB) A specialized tribunal with authority to interpret and enforce the labour laws in their jurisdiction.

leading indicators Objective measures that accurately predict future labour demand.

learning management system (LMS) A computer application that automates the administration, development, and delivery of training and development programs.

learning organization An organization that supports life-long learning by enabling all employees to acquire and share knowledge.

leniency error Rating error of assigning inaccurately high ratings to all employees.

lockout A closure of a place of employment or refusal of the employer to provide work as a way to compel employees to agree to certain demands or conditions.

long-term disability insurance Insurance that pays a percentage of a disabled employee's salary after an initial period and potentially for the rest of the employee's life.

LRB See *Labour Relations Board.*

management by objectives (MBO) A system in which people at each level of the organization set goals in a process that flows from top to bottom, so employees at all levels are contributing to the organization's overall goals; these goals become the standards for evaluating each employee's performance.

material safety data sheets (MSDSs) Detailed hazard information concerning a controlled (hazardous) product.

MBO See *management by objectives.*

mediation Conflict resolution procedure in which a mediator hears the views of both sides and facilitates the negotiation process but has no formal authority to dictate a resolution.

mentor An experienced, productive senior employee who helps develop a less experienced employee (a protégé or mentee).

merit pay A system of linking pay increases to ratings on performance appraisals.

mixed-standard scales Method of performance measurement that uses several statements describing each attribute to produce a final score for that attribute.

MSDSs See *material safety data sheets.*

multinational company An organization that builds facilities in a number of different countries in an effort to minimize production and distribution costs.

multiple-hurdle model Process of arriving at a selection decision by eliminating some candidates at each stage of the selection process.

National Occupational Classification (NOC) Tool created by the federal government to provide a standardized source of information about jobs in Canada's labour market.

needs assessment The process of evaluating the organization, individual employees, and employees' tasks to determine what kinds of training, if any, are necessary.

negligent hiring A situation where an employer may be found liable for harm an employee causes to others if references and background checks were not performed adequately at the time of hiring.

nepotism The practice of hiring relatives.

NOC See *National Occupational Classification.*

nondirective interview A selection interview in which the interviewer has great discretion in choosing questions to ask each candidate.

OBM See *organizational behaviour modification.*

offshoring Setting up a business enterprise in another country (e.g., building a factory in China).

OJT See *on-the-job training.*

on-the-job training (OJT) Training methods in which a person with job experience and skill guides trainees in practising job skills at the workplace.

organization analysis A process for determining the appropriateness of training by evaluating the characteristics of the organization.

organizational behaviour modification (OBM) A plan for managing the behaviour of employees through a formal system of feedback and reinforcement.

orientation Training designed to prepare employees to perform their jobs effectively, learn about their organization, and establish work relationships.

outplacement counselling A service in which professionals try to help dismissed employees manage the transition from one job to another.

outsourcing The practice of having another company (a vendor, third-party provider, or consultant) provide services.

paired-comparison method Method of performance measurement that compares each employee with each other employee to establish rankings.

panel interview Selection interview in which several members of the organization meet to interview each candidate.

PAQ See *Position Analysis Questionnaire.*

passive job seekers Individuals who are not actively seeking a job.

pay equity Equal pay for work of equal value.

pay grades Sets of jobs having similar worth or content, grouped together to establish rates of pay.

pay level The average amount (including wages, salaries, and bonuses) the organization pays for a particular job.

pay policy line A graphed line showing the mathematical relationship between job evaluation points and pay rate.

pay ranges A set of possible pay rates defined by a minimum, maximum, and midpoint of pay for employees holding a particular job or a job within a particular pay grade or band.

pay structure The pay policy resulting from job structure and pay-level decisions.

performance improvement plan Summary of performance gaps and includes an action plan mutually agreed to by the employee and supervisor with specific dates to review progress.

performance management The process of ensuring that employees' activities and outputs match the organization's goals.

person analysis A process for determining individuals' needs and readiness for training.

Personal Information Protection and Electronic Documents Act (PIPEDA) Federal law that sets out ground rules for how private sector organizations may collect, use, or disclose personal information.

phased retirement A gradual transition into full retirement by reducing hours or job responsibility.

piecework rate Rate of pay for each unit produced.

PIPEDA See *Personal Information Protection and Electronic Documents Act.*

Position Analysis Questionnaire (PAQ) A standardized job analysis questionnaire containing 194 questions about work behaviours, work conditions, and job characteristics that apply to a wide variety of jobs.

position The set of duties (job) performed by a particular person.

predictive validation Research that uses the test scores of all applicants and looks for a relationship between the scores and future performance of the applicants who were hired.

productivity The relationship between an organization's outputs (products, information or services) and its inputs (e.g., people, facilities, equipment, data, and materials).

profit sharing Incentive pay in which payments are a percentage of the organization's profits and do not become part of the employees' base salary.

progressive discipline A formal discipline process in which the consequences become more serious if the employee repeats the offence.

promotion Assignment of an employee to a position with greater challenges, more responsibility, and more authority than in the previous job, usually accompanied by a pay increase.

protean career A career that frequently changes based on changes in the person's interests, abilities, and values and in the work environment.

psychological contract A description of what an employee expects to contribute in an employment relationship and what the employer will provide the employee in exchange for those contributions.

QPP See *Quebec Pension Plan.*

Quebec Pension Plan (QPP) A contributory, mandatory plan that provides retirement pensions, disability benefits, and survivor benefits.

Rand Formula A union security provision that makes payment of labour union dues mandatory even if the worker is not a member of the union.

readability The difficulty level of written materials.

readiness for training A combination of employee characteristics and positive work environment that permit training.

realistic job preview Background information about a job's positive and negative qualities.

recency emphasis Rating error that occurs when an annual rating is based only on most recent work performed.

recruiting Any activity carried on by the organization with the primary purpose of identifying and attracting potential employees.

recruitment The process through which the organization seeks applicants for potential employment.

referrals People who apply for a vacancy because someone in the organization prompted them to do so.

reliability The extent to which a measurement generates consistent results, i.e., is free from random error.

repatriation The process of preparing expatriates to return home from a foreign assignment.

sabbatical A leave of absence from an organization to renew or develop skills.

salary Rate of pay for each week, month or year worked.

selection The process by which the organization attempts to identify applicants with the necessary knowledge, skills, abilities, and other characteristics that will help the organization achieve its goals.

self-assessment The use of information by employees to determine their career interests, values, aptitudes, behavioural tendencies, and development needs.

self-service System in which employees have online access to information about HR issues and go online to enrol themselves in programs and provide feedback through surveys.

sexual harassment Unwelcome behaviour that is of a sexual nature or is related to a person's sex.

short-term disability insurance Insurance that pays a percentage of a disabled employee's salary as benefits to the employee for six months or less.

similar-to-me error Rating error of giving a higher evaluation to people who seem similar to oneself.

simple ranking Method of performance measurement that requires managers to rank employees in their group from the highest to the lowest performer.

simulation A training method that represents a real-life situation, with trainees making decisions resulting in outcomes that mirror what would happen on the job.

situational interviews A structured interview in which the interviewer describes a situation likely to arise on the job, then asks the candidate what he or she would do in that situation.

social unionism A type of unionism that attempts to influence social and economic policies of government.

stakeholders The parties with an interest in the company's success (typically, shareholders, the community, customers, and employees).

standard hour plan An incentive plan that pays workers extra for work done in less than a preset "standard time."

stay interview A meeting with an employee to explore his or her thoughts and feelings about the job and to uncover issues in the effort to prevent that employee from becoming disgruntled.

stock options Rights to buy a certain number of shares of stock at a specified price.

strictness error Rating error of giving low ratings to all employees, holding them to unreasonably high standards.

strike A collective decision by union members not to work or to slow down until certain demands or conditions are met.

structured interview A selection interview that consists of a predetermined set of questions for the interviewer to ask.

succession planning The process of identifying and tracking high-potential employees who will be able to fill top management positions or other key positions when they become vacant.

task analysis The process of identifying the tasks and competencies that training should emphasize.

teamwork The assignment of work to groups of employees with various skills who interact to assemble a product or provide a service.

technic of operations review (TOR) Method of promoting safety by determining which specific element of a job led to a past accident.

360-degree performance appraisal Performance measurement that combines information from the employee's managers, peers, direct reports, self, and customers.

third country A country that is neither the home country nor the host country of an employer.

TOR See *technic of operations review.*

total compensation All types of financial rewards and tangible benefits and services employees receive as part of their employment.

total rewards A comprehensive approach to -compensating and rewarding employees.

training A planned effort to enable employees to learn job-related knowledge, skills, and behavior.

transaction processing Computations and calculations involved in reviewing and documenting HRM decisions and practices.

transfer Assignment of an employee to a position in a different area of the company, usually in a lateral move.

transfer of training On-the-job use of knowledge, skills, and behaviours learned in training.

transitional matrix A chart that lists job categories held in one period and shows the proportion of employees in each of those job categories in a future period.

transnational HRM system Type of HRM system that makes decisions from a global perspective, includes managers from many countries, and is based on ideas contributed by people representing a variety of cultures.

trend analysis Constructing and applying statistical models that predict labour demand for the next year, given relatively objective statistics from the previous year.

unfair labour practice A prohibited conduct of an employer, union, or individual under the relevant labour legislation.

union shop A union security arrangement that requires employees to join the union within a certain amount of time after beginning employment.

union steward An employee elected by union members to represent them in ensuring that the terms of the collective agreement are enforced.

unions Organizations formed for the purpose of representing their members' interests in dealing with employers.

utility The extent to which the selection method provides economic value greater than its cost.

validity The extent to which performance on a measure (such as a test score) is related to what the measure is designed to assess (such as job performance).

variable pay See *incentive pay.*

virtual expatriates Employees who manage an operation abroad without permanently locating in the country.

virtual reality A computer-based technology that provides an interactive, three-dimensional learning experience.

voluntary turnover Turnover initiated by employees (often when the organization would prefer to keep them).

Westray Bill See *Bill C-45.*

work flow design The process of analyzing the tasks necessary for the production of a product or service.

Workers' Compensation Acts Provincial programs that provide benefits to workers who suffer work-related injuries or illnesses.

workforce planning Identifying the numbers and types of employees the organization will require to meet its objectives.

workforce utilization review A comparison of the proportion of employees in protected groups with the proportion that each group represents in the relevant labour market.

workplace health and safety committee A committee jointly appointed by the employer and employees at large (or union) to address health and safety issues in a workplace.

yield ratio A ratio that expresses the percentage of applicants who successfully move from one stage of the recruitment and selection process to the next.

Photo Credits

Name and Company Index

Subject Index